# Cultural Anthropology: TRIBES, STATES, AND THE GLOBAL SYSTEM

# Cultural Anthropology

## TRIBES, STATES, AND THE GLOBAL SYSTEM

John H. Bodley
Washington State University

Mayfield Publishing Company
Mountain View, California
London • Toronto

Library of Congress Cataloging-in-Publication Data

Bodley, John H.
    Cultural anthropology: tribes, states, and the global
system / John H. Bodley.
        p.   cm.
    Includes bibliographical references and index.
    ISBN 1–55934–017–7
    1. Ethnology. I. Title.
GN316.B63 1994
    306—dc20                                    93–13999
                                                CIP


Manufactured in the United States of America
10 9 8 7 6 5 4 3

Mayfield Publishing Company
1280 Villa Street
Mountain View, California 94041

Sponsoring editor, Janet M. Beatty; production editor,
Sharon Montooth; manuscript editor, Betty Duncan; art editor, Jean Mailander; text and cover designer, Joan Greenfield;
cover photo, © Robert Holmes; illustrators, Judith Ogus and
Joan Carol; photo researcher, Melissa Kreischer; manufacturing manager, Martha Branch. The text was set in 9/11
Aster by Graphic Composition, Inc. and printed on 50# Butte
des Morts by Banta Company.

Credits appear on page 478 as a continuation of the copyright page.

 This book is printed on recycled paper.

# PREFACE

Given the interconnections among cultural groups on the current world stage (and the rapidity with which those dynamics change), it is imperative that we learn as much as we can about world culture, history, and geography in order to lead informed, productive lives in our global village. What better way to start than by applying the traditional methods of anthropology to a modern view of the world? With this as my underlying goal, I've presented the basic concepts of cultural anthropology in this introductory text by comparing cultures of increasing scale and focusing on specific universal issues. The end result, I hope, is a stimulating, culturally integrated alternative to topically arranged and encyclopedic texts.

To demonstrate the vitality of fieldwork and to generate enthusiasm for the discipline, Chapter One begins with a personal account of my fieldwork with the Ashaninka of Amazonia. Not only does it explain why I was inspired to approach anthropology from a humanistic, culture-scale perspective, but it also introduces the field methods employed by cultural anthropologists. Ensuing chapters examine a representative sample of cultures in sufficient depth to maintain cultural context and to provide students with a sound understanding of the world's major cultural areas and dominant civilizations.

The book is designed to provide balanced coverage of three dramatically different cultural types. After Part One's introduction to fieldwork, Part Two examines small-scale, autonomous tribal cultures. Part Three presents large-scale, class-based civilizations and ancient empires, and Part Four surveys global, industrial, market-based civilization. Scale is used as an organizing principle in order to provide a basis for comparison; I've avoided, however, the implicit value judgments that are part of the popular ideas of evolutionary progress. Universal issues about the human condition are explored from a comparative, anthropological perspective to determine how the difference in scale influences such basic matters as quality of life, domestic organization, intergroup relations, and relationship to the environment. The text devotes special attention to how anthropological explanations themselves have developed and where controversies have arisen over interpretation. The causes and consequences of changes in cultural scale are central themes.

Ethnographic case studies are used to describe the functional interconnections between the material bases and the social and ideological systems of representative cultures at each scale. The cultures selected as case studies are those which are best described in ethnographic films and monographs, and they are the subject of abundant analytical materials. Australian Aborigines, Amazon villagers, and East African pastoralists represent small-scale cultures and are treated in separate chapters. Large-scale cultures are represented by Pacific Island chiefdoms and the ancient and modern great civilizations of Mesopotamia, the Inca, China, Islam, and Hindu India. The United States, the British Empire, contemporary indigenous peoples, and the rural peasantry are examined as part of the global system. The text shows cultures in depth, as adapting, integrated systems, and as part of regional, continental, and global systems, as appropriate.

Throughout the text, I've challenged students to consider the "big" questions about the nature of cultural systems: How are cultures structured to satisfy basic human needs? What is it to be human under different cultural conditions? Are race, language, and environment determinants of culture? Are materialist explanations more useful than ideological ones? What are the major turning points in human history?

The culture scale perspective highlights the unique problems of the present world system. Roughly one-third of the text is devoted to issues of current concern, especially the problem of inequality and how to make our world sustainable. A wide range of global humanitarian issues such as ethnocide, genocide, and ecocide are also considered, along with a variety of more narrow theoretical and methodological issues. My hope is that understanding how tribes, states, and global systems work and how they differ might help policy makers design a more secure and equitable world.

The history of thought on theoretical issues is presented throughout the text *as needed* to illustrate the development of anthropological arguments and issues at hand. The text shows that "scientific" theories have been shaped by the historical context in which they were framed, and they have often had direct implications for public policy. For those students who want further background, the text concludes with a chapter on the history of an-thropological theory and important figures in the discipline.

To further strengthen the thought-provoking nature of this text, I've included a number of critical thinking and learning aids. End-of-chapter study questions highlight and reinforce important issues and arguments. Timelines of the prehistory and early history of the major sociocultural systems are included. Key terms appear in bold type and are defined at the foot of the page where they first appear. Suggested readings at the ends of chapters, coupled with an extensive bibliography, encourage students to pursue specific case materials and issues in greater depth. A topical glossary at the end of the book groups key terms and their definitions into eight major topics.

Because many anthropology courses are organized by standard topics such as subsistence, social organization, and religion, the Instructor's Manual provides an alternative course outline that breaks up the integrated cultures covered in the text and sorts their components into their respective topical categories. A topical classroom presentation can enhance cross-cultural comparisons and draw attention to cultural institutions, while the organization of the book will ensure that the fundamental integration of individual cultures and the significance of differences in culture scale will not be overlooked.

## ACKNOWLEDGMENTS

This book began as a one-page outline in spring 1981, and over the years it has benefitted greatly from discussions with my colleagues and suggestions from numerous readers. I'm very grateful to all who offered me advice and support.

I'd like to thank especially Jan Beatty, Gerald Berreman, Geoffrey Gamble, and Thomas Headland who wrote in support of my sabbatical leave from Washington State University in 1990, which enabled me to complete much of the primary research and writing in one concentrated effort. In July 1991, I made the first public presentation of the culture scale approach in a paper entitled "Indigenous Peoples vs. the State: A Culture Scale Approach," which I gave at a conference called "Indigenous People in Remote Regions: A Global

Perspective," organized by historian Ken Coates at the University of Victoria, British Columbia.

My students and colleagues at Washington State who listened to my ideas and offered suggestions and materials were particularly helpful; I'd like to thank Robert Ackerman, Diana Ames-Marshall, Michael Blair, Mark Fleisher, Fekri Hassan, Barry Hewlett, Tim Kohler, Lee Freese, Barry Hicks, Grover Krantz, William Lipe, Robert Littlewood, Nancy McKee, Peter J. Mehringer, Jr., Frank Myka, Margaret Reed, Allan Smith, and Linda Stone.

At the risk of omitting someone, I also want to thank those who provided me with materials that found their way into the book: Clifford Behrens, Diane Bell, Gerald D. Berreman, Jean-Pierre Bocquet-Appel, Cecil H. Brown, Stephen B. Brush, John W. Burton, Shelton H. Davis, Gudren Dahl, Nancy M. Flowers, Richard A. Gould, Brian Hayden, Thomas Headland, Howard M. Hecker, L. R. Hiatt, Arthur Hippler, Betty Meehan, Peter G. Roe, Nicholas Thomas, Norman B. Tindale, and Gerald Weiss.

I'm grateful to the following reviewers for their many incisive comments and helpful suggestions: Gerald D. Berreman (University of California, Berkeley), Peter J. Bertocci (Oakland University), Daniel L. Boxberger (Western Washington University), Jill Brody (Louisiana State University), Thomas E. Durbin (California State University, Stanislaus), James F. Eder (Arizona State University), James F. Garber (Southwest Texas State University), James W. Hamilton (University of Missouri, Columbia), Patricia Lyons Johnson (Pennsylvania State University), Arthur C. Lehmann (California State University, Chico), Fran Markowitz (DePaul University), David McCurdy (Macalester College), Michael D. Olien (University of Georgia), Mary Kay Gilliland Olsen (Pima Community College and University of Arizona), Aaron Podolefsky (University of Northern Iowa), Scott Rushforth (New Mexico State University), and Daniel J. Yakes (Muskegon Community College).

Many people at Mayfield worked very hard on this project. I'd particularly like to thank Jan Beatty for providing editorial guidance and Sharon Montooth and Jean Mailander for shepherding the project through production. Copyeditor Betty Duncan gave the entire manuscript a careful reading.

Finally, I'd especially like to thank Kathi, Brett, and Antonie for their encouragement and patience.

# CONTENTS

# 3 NATIVE AMAZONIANS: VILLAGERS OF THE RAIN FOREST

# 4 AFRICAN CATTLE PEOPLES: TRIBAL PASTORALISTS

# 5 BODY, MIND, AND SOUL: THE QUALITY OF TRIBAL LIFE

# PART 3
# Large-Scale Cultures: The End Of Equality

# 6 PACIFIC ISLANDERS: THE RANKED CHIEFDOMS    129

# 7 EARLY STATES: THE NEAR EAST AND THE ANDES    159

# 1

# UNDERSTANDING OTHER CULTURES

The long-term survival of the human species depends on our ability to understand and manage the complex, often conflicting, cultural systems that have come to dominate the globe. The threats of military conflict, poverty, famine, and environmental deterioration cannot be treated only as specialized technological issues—they are sociocultural problems. Cultural anthropology can help us think about these problems in new and creative ways because it offers a view of many alternative ways of living. We need to understand and respect the diverse cultures that operate at local, regional, and global levels so that different peoples can coexist while safeguarding the vulnerable biosphere that we all depend on and share. Familiarity with only a single national tradition leaves one ill equipped to cope with perplexing issues arising even within multiethnic states. Internationally, efforts to solve global problems may require broad theoretical understanding of cultural systems, as well as detailed understanding of major regional civilizations and specific local cultures.

This book deals with understanding cultures in several respects. The primary concern is with understanding the significance of cultures for the security and well-being of humanity. To provide a

technical understanding of how specific cultures work, we will examine many details of various representative culture types. This kind of understanding will convey a rationale of cultural practices that might otherwise appear irrational to an outsider. Understanding also refers to the cultural meanings as experienced by the members of specific cultures and as interpreted by researchers.

Any understanding of cross-cultural function and meaning requires a basic understanding of the theories, methods, and concepts of cultural anthropology, which will be introduced in this and the following chapters. The final objective is to convey a sense of tolerance and respect for the world's cultures, which can only be gained through understanding in its broadest meaning.

The first part of this chapter draws on my field experiences in South America to show what it is like to actually do anthropology and to explain why I chose to organize this book around the theme of culture scale. The second part introduces some of the technical vocabulary and key concepts that will be used throughout the book, emphasizing the concepts of culture, culture scale, and the problem of ethnocentrism. It also demonstrates that anthropology has enormous practical signifi-

1

cance and is directly concerned with the great public issues of our time.

## DOING ANTHROPOLOGY

### Adventures in the Field

Doing cultural anthropology is a continuous adventure. It means exploring the unknown to gain a better understanding of other peoples and cultures. Such understanding can be gained indirectly from books and in the classroom, but it is most exciting and vivid when it comes directly from real-life experiences, sometimes in unexpected ways. For example, my richest understanding of native Amazonian political leadership was gained during a 2-day encounter with Chonkiri, a proud and independent Ashaninka **bigman**, who lived with his small band in the rugged foothills of the Andes along the headwaters of the Peruvian Amazon. Bigman leadership is based entirely on force of personality, and Chonkiri displayed these qualities admirably.

In 1969 my wife Kathleen and I were exploring the remote interior of the Ashaninka homeland in order to assess the living conditions of those Ashaninka who still maintained a self-sufficient way of life. A bush pilot flew us to Obenteni, a tiny frontier outpost in the Gran Pajonal—an unmapped maze of savanna-covered ridges and deep forested canyons. It seemed to be a vast untouched wilderness, and it contained the most isolated, still fiercely independent Ashaninka.

After a hard day's walk from Obenteni, we spotted four Ashaninka men on the skyline of an intersecting ridge. They were carrying bows and arrows and shotguns and presented an awe-inspiring sight in their long brown cotton robes (*cushmas*) and bright red face paint. They approached briskly and then halted astride the trail a few paces in front of us. There was fear and uncertainty on both sides because potentially hostile strangers were meeting, but the Ashaninka were armed and on their home ground. They controlled the situation. Their leader Chonkiri, obviously a traditional bigman, stepped forward, struck a defiant pose and shouted a tirade of angry questions at me. The same scene might have greeted the first European explorers to enter Ashaninka territory in 1673.

Chonkiri demanded to know where we were going, why we had come, and whether or not we were bringing sickness. These were legitimate questions, and I knew that his hostile manner was a formal ritual, but I was still uneasy because the Pajonal Ashaninka had every reason to resent outsiders. Recent measles epidemics had killed many Ashaninka, and colonists and missionaries were appearing in ever greater numbers. In isolated areas such as this, Ashaninka often fled at the approach of strangers. Chonkiri, however, betrayed no fear; he was playing the role of a powerful and supremely self-confident bigman leader.

Satisfied with my answers, Chonkiri became a generous host. He led us to his house and offered his hospitality—cooked manioc and taro tubers along with handfuls of live ants, which he and his sons had just collected. (Insects are an important food throughout the Pajonal because game is scarce, but I was amazed to see children sorting through neatly tended heaps of corn husks and extracting fat, inch-long white grubs, and popping them, still wiggling, into their mouths.) I declined to sample this delicacy, although I enjoyed the roast manioc from Chonkiri's cooking fire.

After dinner, Chonkiri and his well-armed men followed us back to our camp. They were eager to see what we had brought, and Chonkiri insisted that we unload our backpacks for his inspection (Figure 1.1). Smiling broadly, he immediately took possession of the box of shotgun shells that were to be used for trading purposes. "These are mine!" he announced, handing the shells out one at a time to his men. I nodded my approval, hoping that he would be satisfied with such a lavish gift but feeling more and more uneasy at his brashness.

The next morning, Chonkiri returned with a gift basket of corn and bananas. His gesture was a textbook example of **generalized reciprocity** in a **nonmarket economy**. This was simple sharing—giving and receiving—with no monetary score keeping. However, my instinctive distrust of Chonkiri's real motives were immediately justified. With no further preliminaries, he began to sort through our possessions on his own, taking whatever he wanted—clothing, trade goods, medical supplies, food, and utensils (Figure 1.2). In my culture, this was armed robbery, and we were outnumbered, unarmed, and virtually defenseless. An

FIGURE 1.2  *Chonkiri's sons are eagerly snatching up all of my trade goods.*

FIGURE 1.1  *Chonkiri, the Ashaninka bigman, seated, investigating the contents of my backpack. The ears of corn on the left foreground are his reciprocal gift. The boy in shirt and pants is the son of one of my Ashaninka field assistants.*

earlier warning that some Pajonal bigmen were killers suddenly flashed to mind, and I graciously allowed Chonkiri's followers to share all my trade goods even though this would leave me in an awkward position.

Chonkiri betrayed his own nervousness when he ripped open a box of unexposed film and started to unreel it, but dropped it with a start when my wife Kathleen involuntarily yelled at him to stop. He quickly regained his composure, and his boisterous demands soon became so totally outrageous that we were forced to call his bluff. He was turning our encounter into a test of will. First, he demanded the hunting knife that Kath-

leen wore in a sheath on her belt. She refused, insisting that it belonged to her father. Becoming frustrated, Chonkiri picked up my *cushma*, which I used as my only blanket, announcing loudly that it was newer than his and he intended to take it. I said "No!" and he flung it to the ground, angrily stomping his feet in a display of temper, which was appropriate for a true bigman. I cautiously assumed that this outburst was for show and would not escalate to violence.

I had a general understanding of the rules. Normally, one was expected to show generosity by giving away anything that was asked for, but Chonkiri was clearly asking for too much. He was showing his bigman status by pushing the limits. I was obliged to refuse his request with no show of fear,

**bigman**  A self-made leader in a small-scale culture. His position is temporary, depending on personal ability and consent of his followers.

**generalized reciprocity**  Distribution of goods and services by direct sharing. It is assumed that in the long run giving and receiving balances out, but no accounts are maintained.

**nonmarket economy**  Goods and services distributed by direct exchange or reciprocity in the absence of markets and money.

although I had no idea how the game would end. The final test came when Chonkiri appropriated the fat roll of cash (50 Sole bills worth approximately $2 each) hidden in my pack. He triumphantly peeled off the bills and handed them out to his men. Using unmistakable gestures, I responded with my most emphatic "No!" If I had not shown personal strength at that moment, it would have been a humiliating, perhaps even dangerous, defeat. To my considerable relief, he promptly collected the money and restored it to my pack. Chonkiri and I had reached an understanding based on mutual respect. In this situation, familiarity with the culture was as important as courage.

After our standoff, Chonkiri became the generous host again. He gave us a grand tour of his house and garden and provided one of his sons to serve as a trail guide. However, he continued to emphasize his dominance by firmly kicking aside Kathleen when she sat on the overturned beer trough that he wanted to occupy. I chose not to consider that gesture a personal affront, but it helped me decide that we would cut short our visit. We parted on friendly terms.

This episode was a brief glimpse of daily politics in an autonomous *small-scale culture* beyond the reach of government control. However, the apparent isolation was illusory, for Chonkiri and his band were part of the *global system*, even though its direct influence was slight. Several of Chonkiri's men were wearing factory-made pants under their *cushmas*. There were steel axes and metal pots lying about. Obenteni had been a Franciscan mission since the 1930s, and the entire region had been briefly missionized in the eighteenth century. Chonkiri's house was located near an abandoned cattle ranch that 3 years earlier had served as a temporary base for Marxist guerrillas. Nevertheless, the vitality and autonomy of Ashaninka culture after three centuries of European pressure was inspiring to witness.

## Anthropological Research in Amazonia

Doing cultural anthropology means asking questions and collecting and interpreting data to gain new understandings about culture and people. The goal is usually to produce an *ethnography*, an in-

terpretive description of some aspect of a culture or of a culture as an integrated whole. Often it is written as a description of the culture at a particular time period called the *ethnographic present*. This is an analytic device that temporarily suspends the dynamics of culture change in order to more effectively demonstrate the relationships between interconnected components of the culture such as food production, household organization, and religious rituals. A well-done ethnography can be a guidebook to culturally appropriate behavior in an unfamiliar culture. It might also be used to see one's own culture in a new light, and it might lead to further questions. In this section, we will discuss how anthropological research is carried out in the field, with an emphasis on question asking, data collection, and interpretation.

During my first visit to the Peruvian Amazon in 1964, my experience with the Ashaninka led me to question many fundamental assumptions about the place of small-scale cultures in the contemporary world. I developed a profound respect for the Ashaninka and their ability to live so well and so self-sufficiently in their rain forest environment. I also recognized that, even though the Ashaninka were one of the largest indigenous groups in the entire Amazonian basin, their independence and their culture were being threatened by outsiders seeking to exploit Ashaninka resources. I learned that whereas some Ashaninka were avoiding all contacts with the colonists who were invading their territory, others were attempting to adjust to their changing circumstances by establishing economic relationships with the intruders.

According to conventional anthropological theory, the Ashaninka were undergoing rapid *acculturation*, and their culture would soon disappear as Ashaninka *society* became absorbed into the dominant Peruvian national society. I was disturbed by the obviously negative aspects of this process and wanted to learn in detail how the Ashaninka and Ashaninka culture were being affected by their increasing involvement with the global system. My knowledge of the long history of Ashaninka resistance to foreign intrusion convinced me that there was nothing inevitable about acculturation. Furthermore, the neutral term *acculturation* seemed to disguise the harsh fact that the Ashaninka were being forcibly conquered and dispossessed. This did not seem to be a "natural" process and was perhaps neither fair nor wholly beneficial. No one, however, had gone to the trouble of asking the questions that would illuminate the process. I hoped that my research findings would contribute to new government policies that would allow the Ashaninka and similar peoples to maintain their independent lifestyle.

Altogether I spent some 15 months working on this problem on three separate visits to Peru over a 5-year period. I wanted to understand how specific changes in Ashaninka economic adaptation were reflected in changes in their society. I collected most of my data by directly observing and participating in the daily life of Ashaninka settlements. This basic anthropological field method is known as *participant observation*. It involves total immersion in the alien culture and a suspension of one's own cultural judgments about appropriate behavior. However, the participant observer never loses his or her own cultural identity and can never become a full member of the other culture. I never pretended to be an Ashaninka, although I lived in their houses, studied their language, ate their food, accompanied them to their gardens and on foraging expeditions, and listened to their nightly stories and songs. This allowed me to *see* Ashaninka economy and society in ways that would never have been possible if I had remained a complete outsider. Participant observation also generates empathy and respect for the other culture, especially when it is used as a method of learning, rather than as a means to induce others to change their way of life.

Effective participant observation is combined with the *ethnographic method*, which means that the anthropologist observes everyday activities and asks informal questions, often working closely with a few *key informants*, rather than relying entirely on formal interviews or impersonal survey questionnaires. The key informant may be one's host in the community or a hired guide, translator, or teacher. Because cultures are integrated in complex, often unexpected ways, at first I could not be sure what Ashaninka activities had economic or social implications. Thus, it was critical to keep an open mind and record as much as possible. I kept a daily journal in which I recorded all my observations and interviews with informants. Even the

most obscure observations might have eventually proven useful. For example, it turned out that knowing the native names of the palm trees used for roof thatch became a clue to the intensity with which forest resources were being used in any given area.

Anthropologists often work intensively in a single village, and with one or two key informants, but my research required a broader approach. Relying on photos shot from aircraft to locate isolated settlements, I worked in four different regions, collecting detailed census data on more than 400 Ashaninka households living in some forty local groups and speaking four dialects. Altogether, six men, one twelve-year-old boy, and one woman were my primary Ashaninka assistants.

The key to much of my work was the use of the *genealogical method*. This meant sitting down with the senior man in a group or household and asking him to name his wife or wives and all his children by relative age. I would ask where everyone was born and determine where they were liv-

---

*small-scale culture*   Self-sufficient, egalitarian way of life shared by members of small societies of approximately 500 to 1000 people.

*global system*   An international, hierarchically organized cultural system based on industrial manufacturing and a market economy, spanning the globe.

*ethnography*   An interpretive description of some aspect of a culture in a form such as a monograph or film.

*ethnographic present*   An arbitrary time period when the process of culture change is ignored in order to describe a given culture as if it were a stable system.

*acculturation*   Culture change brought about by contact between peoples with different cultures. Usually refers to the loss of traditional culture when the members of small-scale cultures adopt elements of global-scale cultures.

*society*   An interacting group of people who share a common culture.

*participant observation*   Field method in which the observer shares in community activities.

*ethnographic method*   Reliance on direct participant observation, key informants, and informal interviews as a data-collecting technique.

*key informant*   A member of the host culture who helps the anthropologist learn about the culture.

*genealogical method*   Tracing the marriage and family relationships between people as a basis for identifying cultural patterns in a community.

ing or where and how they had died. If possible I would compile similar information on more distant kin. Then I drew a sketch map of the village, numbering each house, and identifying the occupants by name (Figure 1.3). I also worked intensively with many individuals to outline their life histories in greater detail. All this material allowed me to begin recognizing culturally meaningful social patterns. Without knowing people by name, where they lived, and who their relatives were, I would have remained an outsider. This information allowed me to analyze settlement and household structure, migration, marriage, kinship terms, fertility, and mortality and proved indispensable for understanding the impact of changing economic patterns.

What emerged from these data was a shocking pattern of depopulation and exploitation suffered by the Ashaninka. For example, I found that epidemic disease spread by uncontrolled contact with colonists had dramatically elevated Ashaninka mortality. In some areas, the Ashaninka were indeed disappearing. Many had also died violently or were taken captive to work for colonists. Local groups and families were fragmented and scattered, and subsistence activities suffered as people were drawn into virtual debt slavery. Opportunities for individual Ashaninka to participate successfully in the market economy were extremely limited. Many joined mission communities in hopes of escaping exploitation, but living conditions at the missions were often poor because the

FIGURE 1.3    *A page from my field notebook showing an Ashaninka local group and genealogical relationships.*

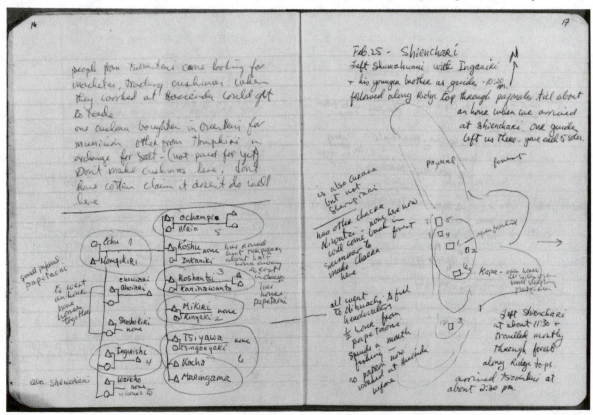

concentrated population quickly depleted local resources. Furthermore, the missionaries disapproved of many Ashaninka cultural practices. It was a discouraging picture; however, Ashaninka culture was extremely resilient, and vast areas of their traditional lands remained undisturbed. I was certain that both people and culture could survive if given the chance.

Eventually, I presented my findings in a doctoral dissertation (Bodley 1970) and in a series of published papers (Bodley 1972a, 1972b, 1973, 1981a). Some of my Ashaninka ethnographic material illustrates important aspects of independent small-scale cultures as they existed in the ethnographic present before they were seriously disrupted by intruders from global-scale, market-based, politically organized cultures (see Chapters 3 and 5). Of course, anthropology involves much more than ethnographic description. It can also provide insights on critical issues of national and international policy. For example, my research led me to recommend that the Peruvian government legally recognize and respect the political and economic autonomy of the Ashaninka on the lands that they traditionally occupied (see Chapter 14).

My research with the Ashaninka also forced me to ask questions about my own culture. I was impressed by the contrast between the precariousness and inequality of our market-based, industrial way of life and the ability of the Ashaninka to provide all of their material needs—food, clothing, and shelter—while maintaining a high-quality environment and high levels of social equality. In this respect, their culture seems to be more effective than our own, and its integrity deserves to be safeguarded from uninvited intrusion. This realization launched me into a much larger research project to systematically compare small-scale tribal cultures, like the Ashaninka, with larger-scale cultures in politically organized states and modern, industrial cultures whose influences span the globe. Understanding how tribes, states, and global systems work and how they differ might help policymakers design a more secure and equitable world. This book is a product of this ongoing investigation.

Before further exploring the global implications of cultural understanding, it will be necessary to introduce several basic anthropological concepts.

# ANTHROPOLOGICAL CONCEPTS: CULTURE, CULTURE SCALE, AND ETHNOCENTRISM

## Culture: The Key Concept

*Culture, or civilization, . . . is that complex whole which includes knowledge, belief, art, law, morals, custom, and any other capabilities and habits acquired by man as a member of society.* (Tylor 1871)

Culture is such an important concept in cultural anthropology that it deserves extended discussion. In this book, I will use the term *culture* to refer collectively to a society and its way of life or in reference to human culture as a whole. I will also refer to similar cultures in particular regions, such as the Melanesian **culture area**, and to **culture types**, such as small-scale cultures, that are similar in important respects even though they may exist in geographically separate regions.

The modern technical definition of **culture**, as socially patterned human thought and behavior, was originally proposed by the nineteenth-century British anthropologist, Edward Tylor. This definition is an open-ended list, which has been extended considerably since Tylor first proposed it. Some researchers have attempted to create exhaustive universal lists of the content of culture, usually as guides for further research. Others have listed and mapped all the **culture traits** of particular geographic areas.

The first inventory of cultural categories was undertaken in 1872 by a committee of the British Association for the Advancement of Science, which was assisted by Tylor. The committee prepared an anthropological field manual that listed seventy-six culture topics, in no particular order, including such diverse items as cannibalism and language. The most exhaustive such list is the "Outline of Cultural Materials," first published in

---

**culture area**  A geographically discrete region containing several cultures that share specified traits.
**culture type**  Cultures grouped on the basis of some common feature such as scale or technology.
**culture**  The patterned and learned ways of life and thought shared by a human society.
**culture trait**  A specific cultural item, material artifact, behavior, belief, or symbol.

1938 and still used as a guide for cataloging great masses of worldwide cultural data for cross-cultural surveys (Murdock et al. 1982). Like the table of contents of a giant encyclopedia, the outline lists 79 major divisions and 637 subdivisions. For example, "Food Quest" is a major division with such subdivisions as collecting, hunting, and fishing. Many introductory textbooks continue this tradition and are arranged by cultural topics. In contrast, this book is organized by *culture scale* and highlights the functional integration of the different aspects of culture by examining specific cultures within their cultural, environmental, and historic context.

There has been considerable theoretical debate by anthropologists since Tylor over the most useful attributes that a technical concept of culture should stress. For example, in 1952 Alfred Kroeber and Clyde Kluckhohn, American anthropologists, published a list of 160 different definitions of culture. Although simplified in the accompanying box, their list indicates the diversity of the anthropological concept of culture. The specific culture concept that particular anthropologists work with is an important matter because it may influence the research problems they investigate, their methods and interpretations, and the positions they take on public policy issues.

Culture involves at least three components: what people think, what they do, and the material products they produce. Thus, mental processes, beliefs, knowledge, and values are parts of culture. Some anthropologists would define culture entirely as mental rules guiding behavior, although often wide divergence exists between the acknowledged rules for correct behavior and what people actually do. Consequently, some researchers pay most attention to human behavior and its material products. Culture also has several properties: It is shared, learned, symbolic, transmitted cross-generationally, adaptive, and integrated.

The shared aspect of culture means that it is a social phenomenon; idiosyncratic behavior is not cultural. Culture is learned, not biologically inherited, and involves arbitrarily assigned, symbolic meanings. For example, Americans are not born knowing that the color white means purity, and indeed this is not a universal cultural *symbol*. The human ability to assign arbitrary meaning to any

object, behavior, or condition makes people enormously creative and readily distinguishes culture from animal behavior. People can teach animals to respond to cultural symbols, but animals do not create their own symbols. Furthermore, animals have the capability of limited tool manufacture and use, but human tool use is extensive enough to rank as qualitatively different and human tools often carry heavy symbolic meanings. The symbolic element of human language, especially speech, is again a vast qualitative expansion over animal communication systems. Speech is infinitely more productive and allows people to communicate about things that are remote in time and space.

The cross-generational aspect of culture has led some anthropologists, especially Kroeber (1917) and Leslie White (1949), to treat culture as a *superorganic* entity, existing beyond its individual human carriers. Individuals are born into and are shaped by a preexisting culture that continues to exist after they die. Kroeber and White argued that the influence that specific individuals might have over culture would itself be largely determined by culture. Thus, in a sense, culture exists as a different order of phenomena that can best be explained in terms of itself.

Some researchers believe that such an extreme superorganic interpretation of culture is a dehumanizing denial of "free will," the human ability to create and change culture. They would argue that culture is merely an abstraction, not a real entity. This is a serious issue because treating culture as an abstraction may lead one to deny the basic human rights of small-scale societies and ethnic minorities to maintain their cultural heritage in the face of threats from dominant societies. In this book, culture will be treated as an objective reality. I depart from the superorganic approach in that I insist that culture includes its human carriers. At the same time, people can be deprived of their culture against their will. Many humanistic anthropologists would agree that culture is an observable phenomenon and a people's unique possession. For example, Gerald Weiss (1988) bases his spirited condemnation of *ethnocide*, the destruction of a particular culture, on his earlier theoretical argument that culture is a "matter of fact reality" (1973).

# Diverse Definitions of Culture

**Topical**   Culture consists of everything on a list of topics, or categories, such as social organization, religion, or economy.

**Historical**   Culture is social heritage, or tradition, that is passed on to future generations.

**Behavioral**   Culture is shared, learned human behavior, a way of life.

**Normative**   Culture is ideals, values, or rules for living.

**Functional**   Culture is the way humans solve problems of adapting to the environment or living together.

**Mental**   Culture is a complex of ideas, or learned habits, that inhibit impulses and distinguish people from animals.

**Structural**   Culture consists of patterned and interrelated ideas, symbols, or behaviors.

**Symbolic**   Culture is based on arbitrarily assigned meanings that are shared by a society.

SOURCE: Modified from Kroeber and Kluckhohn (1952).

---

*Cultural systems* as adaptive systems will be a prominent theme of this book because, whether culture is thought of as an entity or as an abstraction, it is clearly the key to human survival and well-being. Effective adaptation to the natural environment means more than mere survival; it also involves establishing a sustainable balance between resources and consumption while maintaining a satisfying and secure society. One of the major issues we will explore is the degree to which particular cultures at different levels of complexity have achieved such adaptation and how sustainability might be assessed.

## Viewing Other Cultures: The Problem of Observer Bias

Given that culture is the central anthropological *concept*, how one thinks about another culture is the central *issue*. This is because it is impossible to really know any culture except from the inside as a native member. Even the most skilled anthropologist will always be an outsider when viewing a different culture. The problem for anthropologists is how to overcome or at least become aware of their own cultural biases while attempting to understand other cultures from the inside. Translation of cultural symbols from one culture into categories that will be meaningful to outsiders will always be imprecise. The problem is compounded because cultural insiders may be unconscious of the underlying meanings of their own cultural categories.

Anthropologists use the terms *emic/etic* to refer to the inside/outside perspective on a culture (Headland, Pike, and Harris 1990). This distinction between emic and etic is based on the use of

---

*culture scale*   Level of organizational complexity based on size of population, economy, and political structure.
*symbol*   Anything with a culturally defined meaning.
*superorganic*   Culture viewed as an entity apart from its human carriers.
*ethnocide*   The destruction of a society's patterned, learned, and shared ways of life and thought.
*cultural system*   A functionally complete culture, including interconnected technological, social, and ideological subsystems.
*emic*   Cultural meanings derived from inside a given culture and presumed to be unique to that culture.
*etic*   Cultural meanings as translated for cross-cultural comparison.

these terms in linguistics to refer to phon*emic* and phon*etic* transcription, following Kenneth Pike (1954). **Phonemes** are the unique sounds recognized as significant by speakers of a given language. For example, the words *pray* and *play* are distinguished by speakers of English because *r* and *l* are different phonemes and are thus heard as different sounds. Speakers of a language that did not recognize a phonemic difference between *r* and *l* would have difficulty differentiating between the words *pray* and *play* when learning English. A linguist might even need to invent a unique graphic symbol to make a written transcription of an unfamiliar phoneme in a previously unwritten language. A phonetic transcription records the sounds as heard by a nonspeaker of the language who does not know which sound distinctions are meaningful. Phonetic transcriptions may some-

times be only clumsy approximations of the "real" sounds of a language. Linguistic categories often do not have precise parallels in different languages. Similarly, the meanings of unique symbols, rituals, and institutions may be difficult to translate cross-culturally. Even a trained observer can only watch what people do and record native explanations. Observations must be selectively screened through the observer's own cultural categories, then an interpretation of the culture must in effect be created.

One of anthropology's most important contributions toward the understanding of other cultures is its recognition of the problem of **ethnocentrism**—the tendency to evaluate other cultures in reference to one's own presumably superior culture (Figure 1.4). Ethnocentrism contributes to internal social solidarity, but as observer bias it can seriously distort one's perception of others and hinders cross-cultural understanding. Learning to recognize one's own ethnocentrism and consciously striving to suspend it when attempting to understand other cultures is a constant preoccupation for anthropologists. As an alternative to ethnocentrism, anthropologists often advocate **cultural relativism**, or the position that other cultures have intrinsic worth and can only be evaluated, or understood, in their own terms.

Ethnocentrism can influence both what an observer "sees" and how observations are interpreted. Ethnocentrism can also influence a researcher's choice of research problem and the mode of explanation adopted. The problem of ethnocentrism is now a standard part of modern anthropological training, but at the height of colonial expansion in the nineteenth century, European anthropologists were convinced of their own cultural superiority and were blissfully unaware of the concept of ethnocentrism, as the following section demonstrates.

## An Ethnocentric Look at Australian Aborigines

Ethnocentric distortion is well illustrated by an outrageous paper on Australian aborigines read before the Anthropological Institute in London in 1871 by the institute's director Charles Staniland Wake (1872). I pick this example because it shows

FIGURE 1.4 *A sixteenth-century interpretation of Columbus's landings in the New World. This event symbolizes the ethnocentrism of the beginning of European colonialism and the early development of global-scale culture.*

*El Almirante Christoval Colon Descubre la Isla Española, i haze poner una Cruz, etc.*

how theories of cultural development can be biased by ethnocentrism and because Chapter 2, which is entirely devoted to Australian aboriginal culture, will emphatically demonstrate how misleading Wake's views were. The language of Wake's paper is so offensive that it is difficult to imagine that it was presented as objective science. Wake's ethnocentrism is readily betrayed by his derogatory references to "moral defects" and the "barbarity" and "absurdity" of aboriginal customs, which he claims were founded on "unmitigated selfishness."

In Wake's view, aborigines, with their simple material culture, were living examples of the earliest stage of human evolution. He sought to describe their mental characteristics but felt it was inaccurate to speak of their "intellectual" abilities because aborigines operated almost by instinct, barely above the animal level. They had ". . . no aim in life but the continuance of their existence and the gratifications of their passions, with the least possible trouble to themselves."

Their technological achievements, such as the boomerang, were derided as accidental discoveries, whereas their art was likened to "the productions of children." Even aboriginal languages and complex marriage systems were treated as mere unconscious developments, reflecting no particular intellectual ability.

Morally, aborigines were described as children, who enjoyed song and dance and became "extremely indolent" when food was abundant. The aboriginal mind was "saturated with superstition," but they had no religion. In Wake's view, they also had no abstract concept of morality, could not form any idea of death, and routinely mistreated women, the young, and the weak. They cannibalized their children and beat, speared, and enslaved their wives. Wake even had doubts about whether aboriginal mothers had "natural affection" for their children although he also accused them of being overindulgent parents.

In regard to their relations with Europeans, Wake found the aborigines to be haughty, insolent, cunning, and treacherous, thieves and liars, who unpredictably killed strangers. He made no connection between these negative personality traits and the obvious facts of colonial invasion, yet he did attribute their treachery to suspicion. Wake's

interpretation of aboriginal culture did not go beyond his original assumption that aborigines represented the very "childhood of humanity." They were moral and intellectual children, not degenerates from a higher state. Given Wake's assumptions that European culture was the most highly evolved and that Europeans would inevitably dominate the world, his ethnocentrism is hardly surprising. Wake never actually saw an aborigine, and his knowledge of the culture apparently did not go beyond the superficial stereotypes of unsympathetic European explorers and settlers.

Not even modern anthropologists have been immune from this kind of ethnocentrism. In 1978 American anthropologist Arthur Hippler published a remarkably similar characterization of the Australian aboriginal personality. Hippler deprecated aboriginal personality and worldview as "infantile." Aborigines were "superstitious" and had difficulty separating reality from fantasy. They routinely mistreated women. Aboriginal parents were thoughtless, selfish, inconsistent, harsh, and lacking in empathy toward their children.

Hippler's work is not typical of contemporary anthropology and was promptly condemned by outraged aboriginal specialists, but it illustrates how easily the ethnocentrism of an earlier century can be repeated. Hippler only briefly visited the aboriginal community he described and relied heavily on other sources. His research was based on his prior theory that the child-rearing practices of tribal cultures are inferior and thus produce inferior adults. Hippler (1979) deliberately rejected the anthropological standard of cultural relativism, that one at least attempt to view other cultures in their own terms. Furthermore, he began with the openly ethnocentric assumption that ". . . there is not much question that Euro-American culture is vastly superior in its flexibility, tolerance for variety, scientific thought, and interest in emergent

---

*phoneme* Minimal unit of sound that carries meaning and is recognized as distinctive by the speakers of a given language.

*ethnocentrism* Evaluating other cultures from the perspective of one's own presumably superior culture.

*cultural relativism* Understanding other cultures by their own categories, which are assumed to be valid and worthy of respect.

possibilities to *any* primitive society extant" (1981:395).

We will challenge this assertion in the following chapters. Small-scale cultures are a highly flexible and very effective way of life. They encourage cultural creativity and promote cultural and biological diversity. They develop and store an impressive wealth of technical knowledge. Furthermore, the relative social equality of small-scale cultures means that more people can enjoy their "emergent possibilities."

Understanding other cultures requires a significant degree of cultural relativism. One need not approve of every aspect of another culture, but its internal logic should be accurately understood. In practice, anthropologists reduce observer bias by conscious objectivity, empathy, and extensive fieldwork. The best ethnography is based on knowledge of the language and lengthy participation in community life, but ethnocentric bias may still be a problem. Bronislaw Malinowski, the premier anthropological fieldworker, spent over two years living with the Trobriand Islanders of New Guinea before writing his classic ethnographies, but even so his personal diary (Malinowski 1967) reveals a remarkable level of ethnocentrism behind his exemplary research.

## An Overview of World Culture History

Understanding other cultures is especially difficult for members of an urban industrial culture because they are convinced that their own culture is the superior end product of inevitable and progressive evolutionary changes. This assumption guided earlier generations of social scientists and continues to underlie much of the economic development and humanitarian aid work that is currently spreading the global culture throughout the world. However, without denying the obvious material benefits of industrialization and market economies, a less ethnocentric view of world culture history forces one to question the universal superiority of any specific culture. Figure 1.5 shows the major culture areas of the world in 1500 AD and highlights the areas discussed in detail in the following chapters.

Historically, population density has increased, societies have become larger, food production has intensified, and "control over nature" has increased, but social equality and overall security have also declined, as has cultural and biological diversity. These changes are "evolutionary," but it is misleading to call them "progressive" because the benefits may outweigh the costs. Furthermore, because many peoples have been forced against their will to share in these changes, it is unreasonable to call them "inevitable."

In the 50,000 years since the emergence of fully human culture, people have occupied the entire world and diversified into at least 5000 known ethnolinguistic groups. During the first 35,000 years of human existence, people lived exclusively in small-scale, self-sufficient societies based on mobile foraging. Sedentary village life, which began a mere 15,000 BP (before the present), when the world population stood at less than 8 million, was rapidly followed by the **domestication** of plants and animals. By about 5000 BP, large-scale, stratified societies living in cities became organized into political **states**. The number of independent political units and the degree of social equality has steadily declined as the scale of society has expanded. During the past 200 years, an interdependent global market system has emerged, based on industrial technology driven by fossil fuels. By the late twentieth century, the world's 5 billion people are organized into some 180 politically sovereign states and are threatened by enormous wealth inequalities, dangerous armaments, and major disruptions of the global ecosystem.

The main events of world culture history are the framework for the more detailed presentation in later chapters. These events—**sedentization**, domestication, state formation, urbanization, and industrialization—steadily increased the scale and complexity of cultures, changed the quality of life, and altered the relationships between cultures and between cultures and ecosystems. Figures 1.6 and 1.7 show how some of these changes occurred throughout the world.

Figure 1.6 shows the primary areas in which plants and animals were first domesticated and settled village life began. This domestication occurred in part as a response to the dramatic environmental changes that occurred with the end of

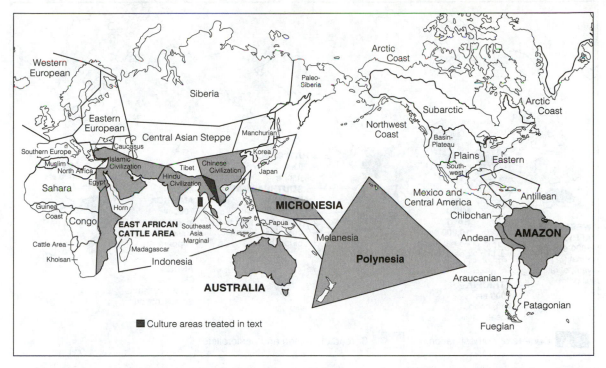

FIGURE 1.5 *Major culture areas of the world in* AD *1500. The following culture areas are treated extensively in the text: Australia, Amazonia, and the East African cattle area (small-scale cultures); Micronesia, Polynesia, Islamic civilization, Hindu civilization, Chinese civilization, and the Andean area (large-scale cultures).* (SOURCE: *Adapted from Spencer and Johnson 1960.*)

the Ice Age. For many thousands of years, the world was dominated by small-scale cultures; even after many people became sedentary, at least half of the world was still controlled by mobile foragers.

The initial appearance and early spread of large-scale cultures is represented in Figure 1.7. This figure illustrates the six relatively independent centers of state formation and the surrounding areas that were brought under varying degrees of state domination by 1500 BP. The shallow time depth and the relative instability of these "civilizations" are striking when they are compared to the great depth and apparent security of the small-scale cultures with which they shared the world.

## The Scale of World Cultures: Small, Large, and Global

To simplify the diversity of the world's cultures, while avoiding assumptions of cultural superiority, Chapters 2–15 group cultures by scale of organizational complexity into three broad categories: small, large, and global. Significant differences in

**domestication** The process by which the reproduction of a wild plant or animal species is brought under human control in order to increase the supply (see Chapter 7).
**state** A politically centralized society with at least two levels of authority above the local community.
**sedentization** The process by which people began to live for a year or more in a fixed settlement.

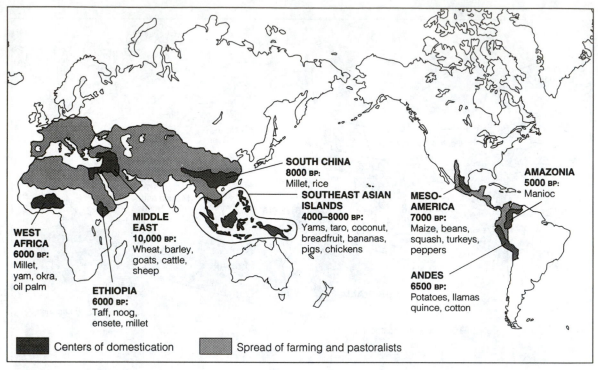

**FIGURE 1.6** *The world of tribal villagers (small-scale cultures), showing independent centers of plant and animal domestication and the areas where farming or pastoralism had spread by approximately 5000 BP.*

economy, society, and ideology characterize cultures at each scale and provide a useful basis for comparison and analysis (Table 1.1). The following chapters use detailed case studies to examine the basic way of life in diverse cultures representing each of the three scales. In Chapters 2–10, small- and large-scale cultures are described in an ethnographic present in which they are assumed to be undisturbed by the global-scale culture. The objective is to explore anthropological understandings of how all these cultures developed; to understand how their principal features fit together, or function, in a culturally meaningful way; and to objectively evaluate the quality of life in each.

The basic assumption is that these three culture scales reflect great divides in human history and fundamentally different conditions of existence. Each culture scale displays a unique constellation of demographic, technological, economic, social, political, and ideological features that set it apart. However, the culture scale concept is an artificial analytic tool, and specific cultures cannot always be so neatly categorized. Larger-scale cultures, because they are more powerful, regularly dominate and incorporate smaller-scale cultures, modifying them in the process but not completely eliminating their preexisting patterns. Cultures of different scale coexist and interact, and individuals may move between cultures of different scale.

Each culture scale was historically produced and continues to be shaped by a dominant cultural process, as shown in Table 1.2. Small-scale cultures were the outcome of **sapienization**, a complex cultural and biological process that produced fully modern *Homo sapiens* some 50,000 BP or, as some suggest, perhaps as long ago as 100,000 BP.

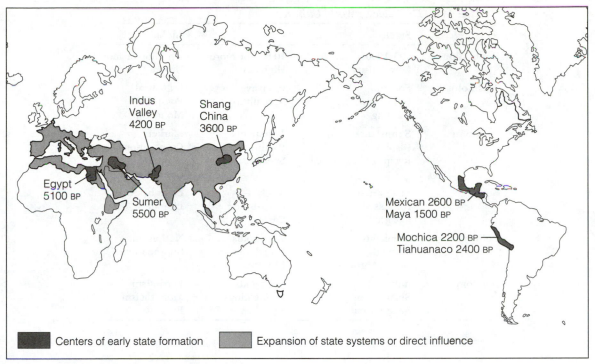

Egypt
5100 BP

Sumer
5500 BP

Indus
Valley
4200 BP

Shang
China
3600 BP

Mexican 2600 BP
Maya 1500 BP

Mochica 2200 BP
Tiahuanaco 2400 BP

■ Centers of early state formation    ■ Expansion of state systems or direct influence

**FIGURE 1.7**  *Six early centers of state formation (large-scale cultures) from 1500 to 5500* BP *and the regions that they influenced.*

This does not mean that people who live in small-scale cultures today are "stone age" in an archaeological sense because, as larger-scale cultures appeared, smaller-scale cultures have had to accommodate to their new cultural neighbors. The physical and cultural environment of the world changed with the emergence of a culture scale hierarchy. However, as a product of sapienization, small-scale culture coevolved with humans and is therefore highly adapted to specific natural environments, coexistence with other small-scale cultures, and the satisfaction of basic human needs.

*Large-scale cultures*, whether chiefdoms, states, or empires, were created by *politicization* under circumscribed conditions that prevented independent villages from escaping political domination. Small-scale cultures normally survived by constantly limiting the political power and wealth of ambitious individuals. When this proved impos-

sible, however, hierarchy and inequality emerged. War, as an instrument of political conquest, must have been a primary path to large-scale culture. Many small-scale cultures were forced to transform themselves into large-scale cultures in self-defense.

*sapienization*  The coevolution of human culture, language, and the human physical type that produced modern *Homo sapiens*, by at least 50,000 BP.

*large-scale culture*  A society that is organized politically as a chiefdom, state, or empire, but in which no developed market economy and little or no industrial production occur.

*politicization*  The process of maintaining and expanding the power of central political authority, which becomes the dominant cultural process.

*chiefdom*  A politically organized society with a permanent head, usually with one layer of control over more than one local community (see Chapter 6).

TABLE 1.1    *The Scale of World Cultures*

|  | Small | Large | Global |
|---|---|---|---|
| **Population** | 500–1000<br>Low-density | 10,000 or more<br>High-density | 1 million or more<br>Urban |
| **Technology** | Foraging<br>Gardening<br>Herding | Intensive<br>Agriculture | Industrial<br>Fossil fuel<br>Monocrop |
| **Economy** | Subsistence<br>Display<br>Reciprocal exchange | Tribute tax<br>Wealth<br>Specialists | Markets<br>Corporations<br>Capitalist<br>Consumer |
| **Society** | Egalitarian<br>Kin-based<br>Age grades | Ranked<br>Class-based<br>Castes | Class-based<br>Literate |
| **Polity** | Acephalus<br>Bigman<br>Descent groups | Chiefdoms<br>Kingdoms<br>Empires | Nation states<br>Supranational |
| **Ideology** | Animism<br>Shamanism<br>Ancestor cults | High gods<br>Divine kings | Patriotism<br>Monotheism<br>Progress |

TABLE 1.2    *Culture Scale and Culture Process*

| Culture<br>Scale | Culture<br>Process | Food<br>Objective | Cost/<br>Benefit |
|---|---|---|---|
| Small | Sapienization | Nutrition | Stability<br>Equality |
| Large | Politicization | Taxable<br>Surplus | Instability<br>Inequality |
| Global | Commercial-<br>ization | Profit making<br>Commodity | Inequality<br>Instability<br>Poverty |

**Chiefdoms** were historically the first multicommunity political units and were thus the first large-scale cultures. This occurred only within the past 7500 years. The term *chiefdom* refers to a hierarchy of villages and districts under a paramount chief. Many theorists emphasize that chiefs were redistributors of economic surplus, but the essential feature of chiefdoms was their political organization. Small-scale cultures were characterized by political autonomous villages or mobile bands. The societies of small-scale cultures are often referred to as *tribes*, especially when they retain their political and economic autonomy. Independent tribal societies, however, lack permanent political leadership and rarely act as units. The great divide was the surrender of tribal village autonomy in order to create a second level of political authority. Adding a third administrative level to form a state, and a fourth to form an empire, would then follow logically as the politicization process proceeded to concentrate more power in fewer hands.

The primary economic function of large-scale cultures is the extraction of a food surplus by political elites in the form of tribute and taxes used to maintain nonfood-producing specialist classes. This politically motivated economic objective of food production is a powerful force that takes precedence over the domestic function of food production in small-scale cultures. The costs and benefits of intensified food production under large-scale cultures are necessarily unequally distributed. Furthermore, production intensification and political and economic inequality introduce significant degrees of instability, causing chief-doms, states, and empires to rise and fall.

The world today is dominated by a relative handful of powerful industrial nations interconnected by a complex web of market exchanges and political alliances. A relatively new scale of organization, this global culture has emerged within only the past 200 years. Its consequences have been enormous and complex. This global system has systematically absorbed large- and small-scale cultures and is itself so homogeneous that it could be treated as a single culture. *Industrialization* has enriched, impoverished, and destabilized the world. The global system was created by a *commercialization* process that reversed the relationship between political and economic organization. Political organization is now in the service of ever-more powerful economic interests. The global economy is primarily dedicated to the production of profit for the stockholders of corporations. When the costs and benefits of global-scale culture are considered, poverty must be added to inequality and instability because the global system contains economically stratified nations, which are themselves highly stratified internally. It is the dominance of the commercial market economy that best distinguishes global culture. The unique features of this system represent a total contrast to the subsistence-based, reciprocal production and exchange system that operates in small-scale cultures. Understanding the global system in relation to the whole span of human cultural development is perhaps anthropology's greatest challenge.

## SUMMARY

Culture, the most important concept of cultural anthropology, refers to the learned ways of life shared by a human society. The goal of cultural anthropology is to increase cultural understanding. Cultural anthropology's most important research technique, the ethnographic method, relies on participant observation and key informants and strives to achieve a sympathetic nonethnocentric view of other cultures from an inside, or emic, perspective. The concept of culture scale is used as a convenient way to compare cultures in order to make broad patterns and trends more understand-able. As cultural scale increases, societies become larger and more complex, and political and economic processes become more and more important.

## STUDY QUESTIONS

1. Discuss the "great divides" of cultural development in relation to culture scale. Refer to sapienization, politicization, commercialization, sedentization, domestication, state formation, and industrialization and to small-, large-, and global-culture.

2. What are the principal components and aspects of culture as traditionally viewed by anthropologists?

3. Use the encounter with Chonkiri to illustrate emic and etic interpretations, ethnocentrism, and cultural relativity.

4. In what nonethnocentric respect might it be argued that small-scale tribal cultures were more or less successful as cultural systems than large-scale chiefdoms and states?

5. In what way would modern anthropological research methods have changed Wake's interpretation of ab-original culture? Why did Hippler seem to agree with Wake?

## SUGGESTED READING

DeVita, Philip R. 1990. *The Humbled Anthropologist: Tales from the Pacific.* Belmont, Calif.: Wadsworth. A collection of personal accounts of fieldwork experiences in the Pacific written by 20 anthropologists.

Fagan, Brian. 1992. *People of the Earth.* New York: HarperCollins. An overview of world prehistory.

Gamst, Frederick C., and Edward Norbeck. 1976. *Ideas of Culture: Sources and Uses.* New York: Holt, Rinehart & Winston. An extensive examination of the culture concept.

---

*tribe, tribal*   A small-scale society or culture with no central political authority.

*industrialization*   Mechanized mass production using assembly-line techniques for commercial purposes.

*commercialization*   The process in which profit making in the market economy becomes a dominant cultural process, as under capitalism (see Chapter 11).

# 2

# AUSTRALIAN ABORIGINES: MOBILE FORAGERS FOR 50,000 YEARS

Australia, the only continent in the modern world to be occupied exclusively by tribal foragers, has always been central to anthropological theories about small-scale cultures. The 40,000–50,000 year prehistory of aboriginal culture raises major questions about cultural stability and change, carrying capacity and population regulation, quality of life, and the inevitability of cultural evolution. Furthermore, Australian aborigines are justly famous for their elegant kinship systems and elaborate ritual life, supported by one of the world's simplest known material technologies. The Australian aboriginal culture also raises important questions about the function of initiation rituals and the meaning of equality in a tribal society where, according to the standard view, the old men appear to control much of the ideological system. The extent to which such cultures can be considered affluent, egalitarian, and "in balance with nature" will also be issues for debate.

The discovery and successful colonization of the Australian continent by foraging peoples and its continuous occupation for 50,000 years is surely one of the most remarkable events in human history. It clearly demonstrates the tremendous potential of mobile foraging technology and egalitarian social systems, which adapted to a wide range of diverse often unpredictable environments and long-term climatic change. The foraging way of life is certainly one of the most successful human adaptations ever developed and persists in scattered locations throughout the world.

It is estimated that at European contact (1788) Australia was occupied by at least 300,000 people, perhaps 1 million or more, representing some 600 culturally distinct groups, or "tribes," and speaking some 200 languages (Tindale 1974). Throughout the millennia, the aborigines intensified their subsistence techniques and managed and shaped their natural resources, but never resorted to farming or sedentary village life. Australia was, in fact, the largest world area to avoid domestication and social stratification. The all-pervasive and authoritarian religious system seems to be the central integrative key to the entire culture.

## AUSTRALIAN ENVIRONMENT AND PREHISTORY

The suitability of Australia for occupation by foraging peoples (Figure 2.1) is determined by the availability of plants and animals, which in turn

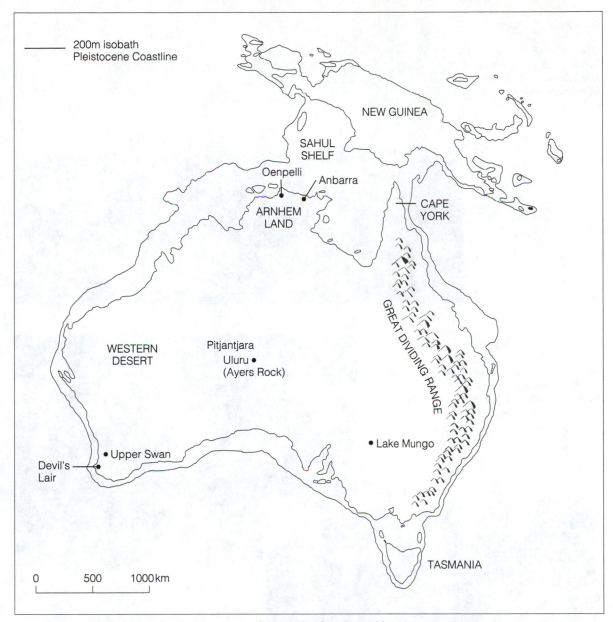

FIGURE 2.1  *Map of Australia showing principal geographic features and locations of groups and sites.* (SOURCE: *Adapted from Lourandos 1987, Figure 2.)*

is shaped by the complex interaction of geologic history and geography. It is remarkable that the Australian continent, which is the same land area as the lower forty-eight United States, is almost totally lacking in major rivers and mountains and has been called the driest continent in the world. Australia is situated in the dry latitudes astride the temperate and tropical zones, and rainfall is low and extremely variable. Aridity is the principal factor limiting the density and diversity of organisms,

FIGURE 2.2   *Desert landscape in the Olga National Park, Australian Northern Territory. The luxuriant vegetation followed an unusually wet year.*

FIGURE 2.3   *Australia's unique animals are a result of its biological isolation from the world's other major faunal areas: (a) gray kangaroos, one of Australia's largest marsupials; (b) the duck-billed platypus, an egg-laying mammal.*

(a)

(b)

TABLE 2.1  *Australian Prehistory*

| AD 1500–1788 | 1788 | European colonization |
|---|---|---|
| | 1500 | Indonesian fishermen visit |
| 5000–6000 BP | 5000 | Small Tool Tradition; spear points, backed-blade microliths; spear-thrower, dingo; subsistence intensification |
| | 6000 | Sea level stabilizes |
| 8000–15,000 BP | 8000 | Cape York separated from New Guinea |
| | 10,000 | Earliest dated wooden implements: spear, digging stick, firestick, boomerang; Kangaroo Island isolated; desert interior fully occupied |
| | 12,000 | Tasmania cut off from mainland; bead ornaments (Devil's Lair) |
| | 15,000 | Sea levels begin to rise |
| 20,000–60,000 BP | 20,000 | Widespread occupation, rock art; heavy "horse hoof" core tools; choppers, ground-stone axes, ochre; low sea levels |
| | 26,000 | Cremation (Lake Mungo) |
| | 30,000 | Earliest human remains (Lake Mungo) |
| | 38,000 | Earliest dated cultural remains (Upper Swan site) |
| | 12,000–50,000 | Pleistocene extinctions of megafauna |
| | 40,000–60,000 | Initial settlement |

SOURCES: Flood (1983), Lourandos (1987), and White and O'Connell (1982).

including foraging humans, throughout the continent (Figure 2.2).

Biologically, Australia is famous for its unique flora and fauna, which developed in relative isolation. The zoological uniqueness of Australia is recognized by its designation, together with New Guinea, as the Australian Region, one of the world's six major faunal regions or zoogeographical realms, distinguished by its egg-laying mammals, numerous *marsupials*, and unique birds (Figure 2.3).

## The Earliest Australians

The first major event in Australian prehistory was the original settlement of the continent (Table 2.1). The ancestors of Australian aborigines must have come from southeast Asia, but it will never be known precisely how they crossed the 44-mile (70-kilometer [km]) stretch of open water that separated the closest Asian islands from Australia. Because this must have occurred some 40,000–60,000 BP (before the present) when Australia and New Guinea were connected by the **Sahul shelf**,

any evidence of these earliest pioneers would have been obliterated by rising sea levels. Historically, aborigines have used several varieties of watercraft including rafts and bark canoes. Because they seldom ventured across more than 6 miles (10 km) of open ocean, however, most authorities assume that the earliest settlement of Australia must have been accidental.

At present, the oldest, securely dated cultural remains are thought to be some 38,000 years old, and the oldest human remains involve a red ochre–coated burial estimated at 30,000 BP. An Australian cremation burial dated at some 26,000 years is the oldest known ritual cremation in the world (Flood 1983).

Given the vast time period that people have lived in Australia and the relatively low total popu-

**marsupial** Mammals, such as kangaroos and opossums, of the order Marsupialia whose young complete their development in an external pouch.
**Sahul shelf** The continental shelf that formerly connected Australia and New Guinea but that is now under the Arafura Sea and the Gulf of Carpentaria.

lation when Europeans arrived, many anthropologists have wondered whether aborigines achieved a balance between population and resources. Joseph Birdsell (1957) believed that aborigines rapidly reached the maximum potential population that could be supported by their foraging technology throughout Australia and then maintained a constant balance between population and resources. Others suggest that aborigines steadily but very gradually expanded their population and elaborated their technology over many thousands of years (Bowdler 1977, Lourandos 1985, 1987). In either case, the aboriginal achievement is impressive.

S. Bowdler (1977) believes that the first aboriginal colonists simply filled up the food-rich coastal areas and the few major river valleys first and only much later moved into the interior. The great interior deserts may not have been fully occupied until 10,000 BP and the highest mountain areas only during the last 4000 years. Harry Lourandos (1985) finds archaeological evidence for widespread but low population densities during the earlier periods and infers that, at first, food-gathering techniques were relatively simple and extensive.

### Pleistocene Extinctions and Rising Sea Levels

During the **Pleistocene** geological epoch, which ended some 10,000 BP, Australia contained many giant animals, or **megafauna**, including giant flightless birds, kangaroos 10 ft (3 m) tall, and other large marsupials, which disappeared by 12,000 BP. This coincides with the disappearance of the mammoths, mastodons, and other megafauna in Eurasia and the Americas and was originally attributed to **overkill** by human hunters (Martin 1967, Merrilees 1968).

Australian aborigines did coexist with these giant animals, but there is little evidence for overkill in this case. Not all of the Australian megafauna disappeared, and several very large kangaroos survived; it has been suggested that many large species persisted as dwarfed forms. There are few indisputable examples of human exploitation of the megafauna and no evidence of a specialized big-game hunting adaptation in Australia. Modifica-

tion of the vegetation by deliberately lit fires might have caused problems for some of the megafauna, but not enough is known about their ecological requirements to be certain. It has also been argued that the megafauna, because of its large size, was especially vulnerable to drought and may have been more stressed than smaller species by changes in vegetation. The precise causes of the extinctions must have been varied and may never be known in detail.

Global sea levels dropped to lows of 328–492 ft (100–150 m) below present levels about 20,000 BP during the Ice Age. As the ice retreated at the end of the Pleistocene, sea levels began to rise until stabilizing some 6000 BP. The Sahul shelf was rapidly inundated during this time. New Guinea and Tasmania were both cut off from the mainland. It is estimated that the sea might have advanced across the Sahul by as much as 3 miles (5 km) in a single year, 62 miles (100 km) in a generation (Flood 1983). These events have been enshrined in aboriginal myths. It is a tribute to the success of aboriginal foraging technology that they were able to adjust to this enormous reduction in resources without adopting farming and settled village life.

### MAKING A LIVING WITH FORAGING TECHNOLOGY

*Foraging* technology is a brilliant human achievement based on mobility and the productivity of natural *ecosystems*. Foraging allows an appropriately organized, culturally outfitted, regional population of a mere 500 people to maintain itself indefinitely in virtually any environment with no outside assistance. Human survival under such conditions is an impressive challenge. It is unlikely that a contemporary urban population of 500 people, including families with dependent children and elderly, could make it successfully through a single year if placed empty-handed in a wilderness. Foraging requires a vast store of knowledge about plants and animals, specialized manufacturing and food-processing techniques, and hunting-and-gathering skills, as well as assorted material implements and facilities.

*Biological productivity*, as reflected by the density and diversity of plants and animals, is the best overall predictor of *subsistence* potential for foragers. In Australia, human population densities varied directly with rainfall and were greatest in the biologically richest coastal regions, especially in the tropical north and east. Population densities remained extremely low in the arid interior.

Foragers are ultimately constrained by the level of food resources produced by the natural ecosystems they occupy, but many options exist for adjusting subsistence output to meet basic human needs, including the tools used, the species eaten, and the organization of labor. Most important is the ability to move as resources decline.

For optimum efficiency and sociability, foragers in temperate and tropical areas typically organize themselves into camps of twenty-five to fifty people, based on a flexible *sexual division of labor*; women collect plant food and small animals within a 3-mile (5-km) radius of camp, and men hunt within a 6-mile (10-km) range. These distances are generalized averages that assume people will be able to return easily to camp within the day. Except as compensation for severe seasonal shortages, food storage is rare, and camps are moved as soon as food yields decline. The degree of mobility is directly related to the size of camps and resource availability. As long as the human population density remains low, there is little danger of serious resource depletion.

## Lizards and Grass Seeds: Aboriginal Food Resources

Virtually every edible plant and animal in Australia has been part of the aboriginal diet. The list would include insects, lizards, whales, birds, mammals, turtles, fish, and shellfish and nuts, fruits, greens, and grass seeds. Named aboriginal categories commonly distinguish between plant and animal foods, and the latter is usually ranked more highly. Animal fat, rather than meat as such, is often the food most desired by foragers.

Although animal food might be preferred, there is great variation throughout Australia in the actual consumption patterns that have been recorded (Figure 2.4). The Anbarra and Oenpelli aborigines live in the tropical monsoon north and have enjoyed the greatest abundance of animals, especially when they have had access to marine

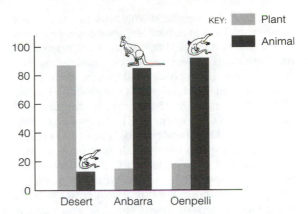

FIGURE 2.4  *Food-consumption patterns, in percentage by weight, of plants and animals by three aboriginal groups: Western desert (Gould 1980), Anbarra (Meehan 1982), and Oenpelli (McArthur 1960).*

ecosystems (Figure 2.5). Foragers have considerable difficulty maintaining a high intake of meat in the desert where species diversity and abundance is low, and they rely heavily on lizards as a staple, supplemented with insects.

The importance of lizard meat in the western desert is striking (Figure 2.6). Lizards made up

*Pleistocene*  Geological epoch beginning approximately 2 million BP and ending about 10,000 BP.

*megafauna*  Giant animals, such as mammoths and mastodons, most of which became extinct near the end of the last Ice Age.

*overkill*  The theory that overhunting by human hunters contributed to the extinction of the Pleistocene megafauna.

*foraging*  Subsistence based on harvesting naturally occurring plants and animals by hunting, gathering, and/or fishing.

*ecosystem*  A community of plants and animals interconnected to one another and the physical environment by a flow of energy and materials.

*biological productivity*  Food energy stored by green plants in organic compounds; expressed as the weight of organic material (biomass) or in kilocalories.

*subsistence*  The production of basic survival resources such as food and shelter.

*sexual division of labor*  The performance of separate economic activities based on gender; for example, customarily, women gather plant food and men hunt. May also be referred to as gender division of labor.

nearly half, by weight, of the total meat animals brought in by a group of ten aborigines observed in the 1960s (Gould 1980). Lizards are one of the most efficient desert resources, considering the time and energy to collect and process them in relation to their food value (O'Connell and Hawkes 1981). It takes only 15 minutes to capture and cook 2.2 lb (1 kilogram [kg]) of lizards yielding more than 1000 kilocalories (kcal) of food energy. Kangaroos, though highly desired, are not so easy to secure and contributed only 16 percent to the total meat supply. The famous Witchetty grub, actually a wood-boring moth larva extracted from the roots of certain desert trees, is also energy-efficient. The grubs may weigh a little over 1 oz (30 g) each and are almost pure fat and protein. When encountered, 1 kg of grubs can be extracted in one-half hour (O'Connell and Hawkes 1981, Tindale 1981).

In the arid center of Australia, water is certainly the most critical factor shaping the availability of both plant and animal foods and determining human population movements and density. Conditions are most extreme in the western desert where there is no real seasonality or predictability in rainfall, and drought conditions may continue for years. In the open country, distant rainstorms can be observed for up to 50 miles (80 km), and people watch the clouds and rely on their detailed knowledge of the locations of specific rock holes and soaks to plan their nomadism. Population densi-

ties there were among the lowest for foragers in the world, averaging less than .01 person per square kilometer (Gould 1980).

Desert aborigines have relatively few plant foods available to them, but they use them intensively. In the central desert, more than one hundred plant species were eaten, especially grasses and seeds, which are among the most costly food resources. Seed collecting and grinding require up to 6 hours of work per kilogram produced (O'Connell and Hawkes 1981:123). Their use is a testimony to the skill and resourcefulness of the desert foragers.

Throughout Australia the primary concern was to maintain long-term food security because unpredictable fluctuation and shortages of key staples could occur even in the richest areas. Techniques of food storage were known, but they were used only for short-term emergencies or to sustain temporary aggregations of people. Rather than stockpiling food, the basic strategy was to maintain access to resources over a wide area through kinship ties and social networks. In the desert, a combination of rain and an unusual abundance of kangaroos might provide the occasion for a joint encampment of 100 or more people for feasting, performing rituals, and arranging marriages. The most remarkable food bonuses were the great masses of moths that congregated in the summer on the rock walls of the Great Dividing Range (Flood 1980, 1983; Gould 1980). They were a rich

FIGURE 2.5  *Meat-consumption pattern, in percentage by weight, of shellfish, fish, reptiles, mammals, and birds by Anbarra (coastal) aborigines.* (SOURCE: *Meehan 1982.*)

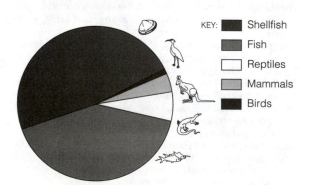

KEY:
- Shellfish
- Fish
- Reptiles
- Mammals
- Birds

FIGURE 2.6  *Meat-consumption pattern, in percentage by weight, of lizards, small game, kangaroos, and birds by desert aborigines.* (SOURCE: *Gould 1980.*)

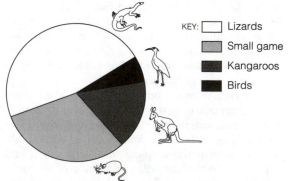

KEY:
- Lizards
- Small game
- Kangaroos
- Birds

source of fat and could be eaten immediately or ground to a paste and shaped into cakes. The moth feast supported aggregations of up to 700 aborigines at specific campgrounds.

## Aboriginal Tools: Digging Stick, Firestick, and Spear

The diverse foraging activities of the aborigines were supported for 50,000 years by a remarkably sparse toolkit of simple stone, bone, and wood implements, which underwent significant expansion only 4000–5000 BP. The oldest and most universal food-getting tools in Australia are the *digging sticks* used by women to collect roots and small animals, the man's wooden hunting spear, and the firestick.

The tools themselves are simple, but they can only be successfully manufactured, maintained, and used in combination with a vast store of specialized environmental knowledge. Aborigines on the move always carry glowing firesticks. Students schooled in the dangers of forest fire and the value of systematic fire suppression are usually shocked to see the seemingly casual manner in which aborigines in ethnographic films light brush fires and leave them burning. Such practices, however, are neither reckless nor destructive. Besides its obvious use for cooking and warmth, fire is also a vital resource-management tool used extensively to drive game, to keep the country open for easy travel, and to favor the growth of valuable food plants. Signal fires also help widely scattered groups keep track of one another. Many plants will not reproduce without periodic burning, and frequent burning prevents the accumulation of plant litter that might fuel destructive fires.

Some 5000 BP, a technological change known as the Small Tool Tradition spread throughout Australia. It was distinguished by the mounting of small stone flakes on spear shafts, use of the spear-thrower, and the appearance of the dingo, a semi-domesticated dog. These new developments may have increased hunting efficiency and made possible increased ritual activities and the expansion of social networks.

The *woomera*, or *spear-thrower*, increases the power and accuracy of the spear. It is a long, thin, curved piece of wood with a hook on one end and

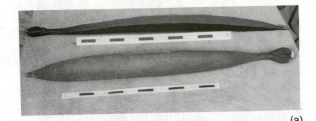

(a)

(b)

FIGURE 2.7  *The spear-thrower, or* woomera, *has been in use in Australia for at least 5000 years. (a) Side and top views—note gum-mounted chipped-stone blade and wooden hook on ends; (b) aboriginal man launching spear using spear-thrower.*

**digging stick**  A sharpened stick, sometimes fire-hardened, used by women to collect plant food.
**spear-thrower**  A device that extends the length of the arm and allows a spear to be thrown with greater force.

a chipped-stone blade, or adze, mounted on the other end (Figure 2.7). This is a multipurpose tool that can be used as a shovel, fire starter or percussion musical instrument (Gould 1970).

In much of Australia, very simple stone-flaked tools satisfied all aboriginal cutting needs. However, where boomerangs and throwing clubs were frequently used, as Brian Hayden (1977a) notes, it made sense to use edge-ground rather than chipped-stone tools. Grinding an edge is more work than chipping, but a ground tool can be resharpened many times. Furthermore, because they are so durable, ground-stone tools can be mounted on handles to make a stone ax with twice the striking force of a hand-held tool (Dickson 1981). The edge must be carefully aligned and painstakingly ground on sandstone with water. Crafting the head shape is not easy, and the hafting technique requires much skill. The haft must be rigid enough to keep the head in place while maintaining enough flexibility to cushion the shock of chopping blows. The head was usually grooved to receive a wraparound, heat-treated, wooden handle, which was glued with vegetable gum and tied in place. Stone axes can be very sharp and efficient tools, but they take longer for a given cutting task than steel axes because the stone blade is thicker and more wood must be removed to cut to a given depth (Dickson 1981).

## The Original Affluent Society?

Perhaps the most important questions about aboriginal foraging are, How effective was it? How hard did people work? Unfortunately, anthropologists have disagreed on these issues, and concrete data have been scarce and difficult to evaluate. At first, the general assumption was that all foragers lived a precarious existence. Without farming and storage, they were thought to have little control over their resources. This view began to change when detailed studies of modern foragers began to appear in the 1960s. Marshall Sahlins (1968) drew on a 1948 study of Arnhem Land aborigines (McCarthy and McArthur 1960) to conclude that foragers were, in fact, "the original affluent society" because men and women worked no more than 4–5 hours a day to collect and process enough food to keep themselves well nourished and

healthy (Figure 2.8). They appeared to have plenty of leisure time and were in that sense more highly "evolved" than agricultural peoples. Sahlins pointed to the absence of food storage and the apparent underutilization of resources as further indication of the "affluence" of aboriginal foragers.

Other researchers found conditions only slightly less affluent in the desert interior. Richard Gould (1969, 1980), who studied self-sufficient Pitjantjatjara foragers in the western desert in 1966–1970 during a period of moderate drought, found that women were putting in 5–7 hours a day collecting and processing food. They relaxed 5 hours a day during the heat of the afternoon and were still able to provide 80 percent of the household diet.

This affluence and leisure view has been challenged by more recent studies rating women's foraging as significantly less productive than previous estimates (Hawkes and O'Connell 1981, O'Connell and Hawkes 1981). These new findings, however, are not convincing refutations of forager affluence. The aboriginal groups involved in these studies had largely replaced the bush food collected by women with store-bought food, and they were not fully nomadic and thus probably not as skilled as full-time foragers.

Other critics of forager affluence pointed out that most modern aborigines permanently abandoned the desert interior during episodes of severe drought. However, drought is nothing new in Australia. In earlier times, people likely abandoned certain areas temporarily when the environment became uninhabitable, relied on their social support network in more favorable areas, and then returned to their homelands when conditions improved. The European invasion disrupted this support system.

Perhaps the strongest evidence for the affluence view is the fact that aborigines did not become farmers. Earlier anthropologists attributed the absence of farming in aboriginal Australia to isolation and extreme conservatism, if not ignorance and backwardness. These explanations can be easily rejected. Aboriginal technology was sophisticated and required high-level skill and knowledge. Aborigines certainly understood how plants grew and, in some cases, deliberately left cuttings to regrow. Some technological items, such as ground-stone axes and boomerangs, appeared earlier in Australia than anywhere else in the world. The spear-thrower was apparently independently invented in Australia. Many cultural traits were borrowed from New Guinea, but not New Guinea farming, domesticated pigs, pottery, or the bow and arrow. It can be inferred that aborigines simply did not consider these technologies to be an improvement.

## Aborigines as "Stone Age" Peoples

Australian aborigines were often considered to be "Stone Age" or "Paleolithic" peoples by earlier anthropologists who followed an evolutionary stage approach. Aborigines did not use metal, but the concept of Stone Age as an inferior evolutionary stage contributes little understanding and implies that aboriginal culture must be obsolete.

Aside from the political implications of labeling any contemporary people Paleolithic, there are many logical difficulties with stage categories based on tool types. Tools are poor indicators of economic productivity because even very simple tools, as the Australian case shows, can be very productive and efficient. Furthermore, tool types that are supposed to be diagnostic for Paleolithic, Mesolithic, and Neolithic stages often overlap in unexpected ways. For example, aborigines who seemed to lack Upper Paleolithic stone blades were assigned to the Middle Paleolithic, along with Neanderthals, whereas aborigines who used Neolithic ground-stone axes were considered Paleolithic because they did not farm. The notions of inevitability and directionality in tool types are also problematic, especially given the vast time periods that the use of certain tool types has lasted. Rather than reflecting differences in mental ability or ingenuity, it is more likely that the tools used by a particular people reflect their culturally defined needs.

FIGURE 2.8  *Aboriginal men spear fishing in the coastal waters of the tropical north. They have speared a stingray.*

## ABORIGINAL RELIGION AND SOCIETY

*The Australians have been the historical, evolutionary and sociological prototype for the study of hunter-gatherers and for the relations between man and nature. From the onset of modern anthropology they have inspired, challenged or provided the limiting case for nearly every view of man's behavior. . . .* (Peterson 1986:v)

Australian aboriginal society had its roots in the most remote antiquity and was sustained by an extremely simple material technology, but the society was a fully developed and dynamic system. Treating it as either a fragile fossil left over from the Paleolithic or as a temporary step on the way to statehood would be a serious distortion. The basic challenge for aborigines was the circular problem of maintaining a small-scale cultural system that would perpetuate their population and, in turn, reproduce the culture. Understanding how aborigines actually solved this problem has preoccupied anthropologists for more than a century and has generated a continuing debate.

Anthropological interpretations of aboriginal culture have shifted dramatically through time as theoretical perspectives have changed and as new data have become available. This debate has helped establish many of the most basic concepts of cultural anthropology while gradually revealing the genius of aboriginal culture. The broadest theoretical issues concern how the culture actually worked: the role of the belief system and how the culture related to environmental and demographic factors. Important humanistic issues concern the degree of social equality and whether women and young men were being exploited by old men.

The foraging technological subsystem provided the energy, nutrients, and raw materials needed by the population, but the technology depended on a much more complex social and ideological system.

Misunderstanding of aboriginal culture began with the British colonization of Australia in 1788. Because they saw no aboriginal farms or permanent houses, British authorities reached the outrageously mistaken conclusion that the aborigines had no fixed relationship to the land. Australia was declared *terra nullius*, an empty wasteland, free for the taking, and aboriginal land was appropriated without the signing of treaties. Only over the past

100 years have anthropologists begun to appreciate the subtle complexities of the enduring aboriginal ties to their land. Nineteenth-century evolutionary anthropologists did little to help the situation. Lewis Henry Morgan (1877) considered aborigines to be living representatives of middle savagery, elevated one step above the subhumans of lower savagery (see Chapter 16).

### The Band–Horde Controversy

Australian aboriginal society appears to be based on multifamily foraging groups, or bands, and a ritual estate, or religious property, which is tied to the land. *Band* and *estate* are functionally interconnected in the *range*, which is the territory defined by religious landmarks and occupied by the band. This band–estate system serves a resource-management function and helps space out and define the optimum limits for local populations, thus contributing directly to long-term stability.

Anthropological understanding of the band got off to a bad start with the first definitions by A. R. Radcliffe-Brown (1913, 1918), who described a formal, highly structured system based on *patrilineal descent*. Radcliffe-Brown saw the band, or "horde" as he called it, as a rigid landowning organization with membership recruited patrilineally, by inheritance through males. The horde practiced *exogamy*, or out marrying, with women joining their husband's horde, while the male permanent horde members foraged exclusively on their own horde land. The assumption of most early ethnographers was that men controlled all foraging activities and needed to stay on familiar ground where their detailed local knowledge of resources would be most useful. Couples practiced *patrilocal residence,* which created localized *patrilineages*. Radcliffe-Brown made the role of patrilineal descent even more emphatic, by calling the horde a "clan-horde." The term *clan* is usually applied to named exogamous groups composed of related *lineages*.

Calling Australian bands "clans" confused the band—actually a land-using group containing members recruited through a variety of means—with the clan, a descent-based group, that at best could only be a landowning unit.

Radcliffe-Brown's clan-horde was reinterpreted

FIGURE 2.9
*An aboriginal camp. Several families that camp and forage together make up the band.*

as the ***patrilocal band*** by cultural ecologist Julian Steward (1936) and for decades served as the anthropological model of the social organization of foraging peoples worldwide. Steward called the patrilocal (sometimes patrilineal) band a cultural type that was the product of foraging in particular environments. He believed that the formation of the band, which averaged fifty persons in size, was produced by the relative scarcity of wild-food resources, which kept the human population at very low levels (one person per square mile or less) and prevented larger permanent social groups from forming. At the same time, it was advantageous for related men to use and defend a common territory. Exogamy resulted from the universal ***incest taboo***, which prohibited the intermarriage of close kin.

More recent field research on aboriginal societies has raised many questions about earlier theories of band society (Lee and DeVore 1968). The most surprising discovery was that real bands were much more flexible than originally thought. Men actually spent much of their time living away from their clan land. Furthermore, bands were not defended by armed force, but resource use was regulated by a policy of open admission to social groups. Even the notion that hunting required patrilocality has been questioned because foraging by women also requires detailed local knowledge.

Careful new research in Australia reveals that emic aboriginal concepts do correspond in general to the anthropological categories of band and range but not to the patrilineal band of anthropological theory (Hiatt 1984a, Peterson 1986). For aborigines, band refers to the families that camp and forage together (Figure 2.9). Different native terms may distinguish the camp, the residents of the camp, and the ***country*** they occupy, but these

---

***band*** A group of twenty-five to fifty people that camp and forage together.

***estate*** Property held in common by a descent group and might include territory, sacred sites, and ceremonies.

***range*** The territory occupied by an Australian aboriginal band.

***patrilineal descent*** Descent traced through a line of men to a male ancestor.

***exogamy*** Marriage outside a culturally defined group.

***patrilocal residence*** A cultural preference for a newly married couple to live near the husband's parents or patrilineal relatives.

***patrilineage*** A lineage based on descent traced through a line of men to a common male ancestor and sharing a joint estate.

***clan*** A named group claiming descent from a common but often remote ancestor and sharing a joint estate.

***lineage*** A descent group based on specific, known links to a common ancestor and sharing a joint estate; sometimes a subdivision of a clan.

***patrilocal band*** A theoretical form of band organization based on exogamy and patrilocal residence.

***incest taboo*** A prohibition on marriage or sexual relations between culturally specified categories of kin.

***country*** English term used by aborigines to refer to their estate territories.

terms have multiple meanings. For example, depending on the context, country may refer to land as a religious estate or as a foraging territory. Band members may be referred to as "people of" a particular place, whereas individuals may claim affiliation with several countries. The band is not exclusively patrilocal and may change composition frequently as individual families visit relatives in other areas; nevertheless, it is an important social group, and individual bands retain their unity during temporary multiband encampments.

The range over which the band forages is a discrete territory containing the critical resources that sustain the band during normal years. Band territorial boundaries are recognized but not directly defended. Visitors must observe special entry rites upon arrival at a camp. They also must ask permission before they can forage within band territory. Under this system, the "owners" of the country operate as resource managers. Permission to forage would rarely be denied, but knowing who is foraging where makes resource exploitation much more efficient and minimizes potential conflicts.

The role of patrilineal descent in band organization is nowhere as simple and direct as anthropologists once thought. Wide regional variation exists in the composition of the "clan," and it may be completely absent in some areas. Rigid adherence to the patrilineal band model would be an unreliable organizational strategy for foragers in an unpredictable desert environment.

It is important to distinguish between *use rights* to band territory as a range and *ownership rights* to the land as a religious estate. All band members and those asking permission can use range resources, but only those qualified to be estate owners can give permission and act as managers. Many sorts of overlapping claims are recognized, both to the right to ask to use a range and to the right to estate ownership. Patrilineal descent invariably provides the strongest claim, but a person also has special claims on mother's estate and use rights in spouse's country. Extended residence can also provide a claim, as can one's place of conception and birth and the burial place of kin.

As Steward (1936) pointed out, the size and density of the band is, in part, determined by environmental, demographic, and cultural factors.

Worldwide, band population seems to average around twenty-five to fifty people. Because food, especially game, is pooled between families within the band, the minimum average of twenty-five people is probably determined by the number required to maintain foraging security by ensuring that enough adult food producers are available. There are strong reasons for people to hold down the upper limits of band size. Given fixed territories, increased numbers above minimum levels would soon result in a reduction in leisure and more frequent moves as resources became depleted.

The minimum size of bands may also be shaped by the need to maintain marriage alliances that would reduce the likelihood of interband conflict. Bands tend to space themselves uniformly across the landscape in roughly hexagonal territories, such that each band is surrounded by five to six neighboring bands. The cultural requirement of band exogamy, which Steward (1936) attributed to an innate incest taboo, is a good excuse for marrying otherwise potentially hostile neighbors.

While the band is a clearly defined unit in aboriginal society, the existence of the tribe is not so obvious, even though the term *tribe* was used as a descriptive label by generations of anthropologists. Many authorities now question the utility of tribe as an analytic concept, and in Australia the term has almost vanished from contemporary anthropological writing. The problem is that small-scale societies do not typically have tribal political units and no permanent leadership above the band or village, although "tribes" have been artificially created by colonial governments for administrative purposes. Nevertheless, politically independent bands and villages do share a common culture with their neighbors, and this connection is recognized by the people themselves. For Australia, Birdsell (1973) called this common culture the *dialect tribe*. He described it as a minimal breeding population, a collection of adjacent bands who interact frequently enough through marriage alliances, joint ceremonies, and visiting that they maintain a common language and culture. Birdsell suggested that such tribes fluctuate in size around 500 people. In theory when dialect tribes fall below 200 people, members will have difficulty finding mates and will be absorbed by larger neighbors, whereas tribes growing to 1000 or more people will be expected to split as interaction between bands become diffused.

Tribal territories, like bands, tend to be hexagonally shaped and seem to vary in size according to the productivity of the environment, while the total number of people in the tribe remains relatively constant. Birdsell (1973) found a predictable inverse relationship between rainfall, as a measure of biological productivity, and population density, such that in areas with higher rainfall tribal territories became smaller.

The problem with the dialect tribe is that language boundaries are not always as distinct as the maps imply. Aboriginals are multilingual, and intermarriage and joint ceremonies between language groups are common. Language groups are often associated with territories, but such territories are probably defacto artifacts of the aggregated territorial estates when viewed from the outside. There are few, if any, occasions when the members of a dialect tribe would act as a unit, and joint defense of tribal territory must have been a rare event. However, there is often a strong sense of "tribal" identity reflecting shared language, territory, and culture.

## Population Stability and Balance with Nature?

Australian aboriginal society offers an interesting test case of the proposition that foraging peoples were more "in balance" with the environment than were village farmers or large-scale societies. The archaeological record shows that the foraging way of life has existed vastly longer than any other, and there is no evidence that foraging peoples experienced periodic population crashes or depleted their resources (except in the most extreme cases as in the Arctic). The implication is that *stationary populations* must have been the norm. Some culturally regulated population controls must have operated because even the smallest deviation from balanced fertility and mortality rates operating over thousands of years would have lead either to extinction, overpopulation, and hardship or to drastic cultural change. The Australian band did have an optimum size, but how population was actually regulated remains a problem.

Birdsell (1973) estimated that tribal territories were optimally populated at 60 percent of their *carrying capacity* to allow for random fluctuation in resources. He assumed that intentional infanticide of up to 50 percent of births was the primary mechanism limiting population. It is known that babies were sometimes killed at birth, but there is little direct evidence for the actual rate. Infanticide was most likely carried out by women who were motivated by their desire to either eliminate deformed children or to space out their families in order to have only one child under 3 or 4 years of age to carry and nurse at a time. This kind of family planning increased the likelihood that a given child could be raised to maturity. Given the relatively high "natural" infant mortality rates and overall low life expectancy, which probably characterized tribal demography, spacing births every 4 years could produce a stationary population.

Infanticide was related to foraging conditions because mobility and the burden of carrying children increase when resources are scarce. Similarly, given existing food sources and preparation techniques, there was no baby food other than mother's milk, thus nursing would be prolonged, often for 4 years or more. The balance between population and resources was also under unconscious biological control because extended lactation and nutritional deficiency can lower fertility by causing hormonal changes in a woman's reproductive cycle.

Infanticide was an indication of the autonomy that women maintained in reproductive decision making, and it gave them some covert political leverage in a society that was publicly dominated by men. Gillian Cowlishaw (1978) has argued that some women expressed their resentment over ar-

---

*use rights*   The right to use property, such as territory or ceremonies, owned by others.

*ownership rights*   Among foragers, the right to grant to others permission to use certain property.

*dialect tribe*   An intermarrying group of bands sharing a common language and culture and occupying a common territory.

*stationary population*   A population in which births exactly replace deaths and total numbers remain constant over time.

*carrying capacity*   The number of people who could, in theory, be supported indefinitely in a given environment with a given technology and culture.

ranged marriages by killing their firstborn, although this type of infanticide would not be a response to resource depletion.

It has sometimes been suggested, on the basis of census data showing sex ratios skewed in favor of boys, that girls were more likely to be killed than boys, thereby making infanticide a more powerful means of population control. However, the census data are suspect because girls may have been hidden from census takers and in Australia a careful review of completed families shows no evidence that girls were selectively killed (Yengoyan 1981). Computer-simulation studies also suggest that, if systematically applied, even very low rates of selective female infanticide would lead to population extinction. The concept of selective female infanticide is related to theories about a widespread male supremacy cult in small-scale societies and will be discussed further in Chapter 3.

## The Dreaming and the Structure of Aboriginal Society

The key element of aboriginal culture is the complex, multidimensional concept aborigines call the **Dreaming**, which recognizes the interdependence and vitality of all parts of the cosmos. Humans are actors in a balanced living system along with other

FIGURE 2.10   *A functional model of aboriginal culture.*

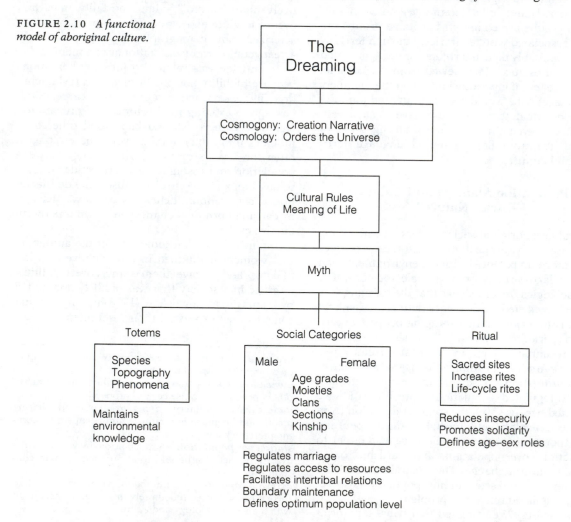

species, whose goal is the continuity of life and the maintenance of the cosmos itself. Regardless of what anthropologists decide about the balance and stability of aboriginal culture, aborigines themselves believe their culture to be fundamentally changeless and in balance with nature.

The emic term *Dreaming* refers variously to creation, the moral order, an ancestral being, people, a spirit, the origin point of a spirit, a specific topographic feature, and a *totem* species, object, or phenomenon. Furthermore, all of these can be thought of as the same, whereas in European thought they would be sharply distinguished. Outsiders have treated the Dreaming as aboriginal religion, but it is a profound concept that permeates all aspects of the culture and evades easy categorization. Aborigines identify themselves completely with their culture and their land through the Dreaming in a way that nonaborigines have had great difficulty comprehending. For an aborigine to say "I am a kangaroo" might sound like nonsense, but within the Dreaming context such a statement carries special significance.

As a philosophy of life, the Dreaming provides both a *cosmogony* to account for the origin of everything and a *cosmology* to explain the fundamental order of the universe. The Dreaming thus answers the basic meaning-of-life questions, offers a detailed charter for the cultural rules for day-to-day living, including basic social categories and ritual activities, and ascribes cultural meanings to the natural environment (Figure 2.10).

When regarded as a mythic cosmogony, the Dreaming is sometimes imprecisely called the Dreamtime, referring to the creation time when a series of heroic ancestor beings crisscrossed the landscape and transformed specific topographic features as a permanent record of their activities. The problem with referring to creation as the Dreamtime is that aborigines are not really concerned with origins as historical events; instead, origin myths are timeless explanations. Time, culture, and nature are viewed as cyclical and changeless. The *Dreamtime ancestors* followed the same cultural rules that are practiced today, and their influence is still so vital that it is more reasonable to refer to the Dreaming as the Everywhen, or the Eternal Dreaming, rather than placing it in the Dreamtime past.

When the Dreaming is referred to as the moral authority for behavior, it may be called simply the Law or the Dreaming Law, and in this respect it is beyond question. Stability is thus a fundamental feature of the culture.

The aboriginal cosmos differs in striking ways from the religions of larger-scale cultures. There is no all-powerful god and no rank order in the Dreaming. Similarly, there is no heaven or hell, and the distinctions between sacred and profane, natural and supernatural, are blurred. Aborigines experience the mystical as a perpetual unity with the cosmos as they follow the Dreaming Law in their daily life. For example, a seemingly mundane activity, such as seasonally burning grass, can be considered a religious act because it perpetuates life and the cosmic balance between sun and rain, people and game.

## Sacred Sites and Dreamtime Pathways at Uluru

The Dreamtime ancestors, or totemic beings, make a direct link between people and their land by means of the *sacred sites*, which are the physical remains of the ancestors or their activities. The role of these beings is dramatically illustrated at Uluru, or Ayers Rock, a giant monolith near the center of Australia (Figure 2.11). Uluru is a weath-

---

*Dreaming*  An aboriginal English term referring to the mythic time and related objects and rituals that are the continuing bases of aboriginal culture, cosmogony, and cosmology.

*totem*  In Australia, specific animals, plants, natural phenomena, or other objects that originate in the Dreaming and are the spiritual progenitors of aboriginal descent groups. Elsewhere refers to any cultural association between specific natural objects and human social groups.

*cosmogony*  An ideological system that seeks to explain the origin of everything: people, nature, and the universe.

*cosmology*  An ideological system that explains the order and meaning of the universe and people's places within it.

*Dreamtime ancestors*  Spiritual mythic beings who established aboriginal culture and founded specific descent groups.

*sacred sites*  Specific locations and topographic features associated with important Dreaming events. May be centers for ritual activities.

FIGURE 2.11   *Uluru, or Ayers Rock, in the desert center of Australia, contains many important Dreamtime sacred sites.*

ered dome, some 5 miles (8 km) around and rising more than 1100 ft (335 m) from the desert plain. As the largest such monolith in the world, it was designated as a national park and biosphere reserve in 1985 and is administered jointly by the aboriginal owners and the Australian National Park and Wildlife Service. More importantly for aborigines, Uluru is a perpetual Dreamtime monument crammed with cultural meaning.

The north side of the rock belongs to the clan of hare wallabies, rabbit-sized kangaroos, whereas the south side belongs to the carpet boa clan. A series of stories recount the activities of ten totemic beings and their relatives, including various snakes, reptiles, birds, and mammals, who created the existing landscape and established the clan boundaries. Charles Mountford (1965), who recorded some of these myths from the Pitjandjara people between 1935 and 1960, published some 200 photographs detailing specific rock outcrops, stains, caves, and pockmarks that represent the bodies, camps, and physical signs of these totemic beings.

The same totemic beings that created sites at Uluru traveled widely across the country, leaving permanent ***Dreaming paths***. During their travels, they interacted with other beings and created simi-lar sites elsewhere. Specific Dreaming paths can stretch for hundreds of miles, crossing the territory of different clans and tribes.

Dreaming locations, or sacred sites, such as those at Uluru, are centers for ritual activity and help define territorial boundaries and regulate use of resources. Some sites contain the spirit essence of their creators and are the places where special "increase ceremonies" are performed to perpetuate particular species. For example, control of a kangaroo increase site means ritual control over the supply of kangaroos. Entry to or even knowledge of such sites is often restricted, and unauthorized intrusion may be severely punished. Other sites contain especially dangerous substances and must be avoided by everyone. To avoid the risks of trespassing, people must seek permission before entering unfamiliar areas. Since 1976 many of these sacred sites have been officially protected by federal legislation, and fines can be levied for trespass.

The spirit essence localized at certain sites also completes the direct link between people and their individual Dreamings, because this animating power is believed to be an essential but not an exclusive element in human conception and reproduction. Pregnancy is identified with the totemic

FIGURE 2.12  *A Dreamtime kangaroo in a rock painting from the Northern Territory.*

"soul stuff" emanating from a specific Dreaming site, and this soul stuff returns to the site at death. Thus, in a real sense, an individual is a physical part of the Dreaming, and this spiritual connection is a more important cultural fact than biological paternity.

An added value of the Dreaming paths is that they serve as mnemonic devices to help fix in memory the location of permanent waterholes, which are critically important. The Dreaming myths and related rituals are dramatic reminders of specific geographic details and preserve them in people's minds as accurately as would any large-scale printed map. The Dreaming also takes on visible form in body paint, sand drawings, rock art, and paintings or carvings on ritual objects, all of which may incorporate an elaborate iconography (Munn 1973) (Figure 2.12).

## Functionalism, Structuralism, and the Illusion of Totemism

The special association between aborigines and their Dreamings was called *totemism* by anthropologists and became the subject of widespread theoretical speculation. The Dreaming species were called *totems* and were equated with other cases around the world wherever natural species were associated with individuals or social groups, especially exogamous clans. Those practicing totemism were even called *totemites*, and totemism was considered to be the earliest stage in the evolution of religion. How totemism originated and how it became associated with out-marrying, or exogamous, social groups, however, remained a contentious issue for decades. By 1920 one researcher distinguished some forty-one different theories of totemism (Van Gennep 1920), but real understanding seemed as illusive as ever.

Sir James Frazer (1910), who devoted some 2200 pages to the subject in his four-volume *Totemism and Exogamy*, attributed the origin of Australian totemism to the supposed aboriginal ignorance of the physiological basis of conception. According to Frazer (1905), in their "astounding ignorance," aborigines attributed pregnancy to the magical influences of spirits. Frazer then inferred that exogamy was instituted as a social reform designed to avoid incest. Totems then became convenient labels for the social groups. Psychiatrist

**Dreaming paths**  Routes followed by Dreamtime ancestors during their mythic travels.

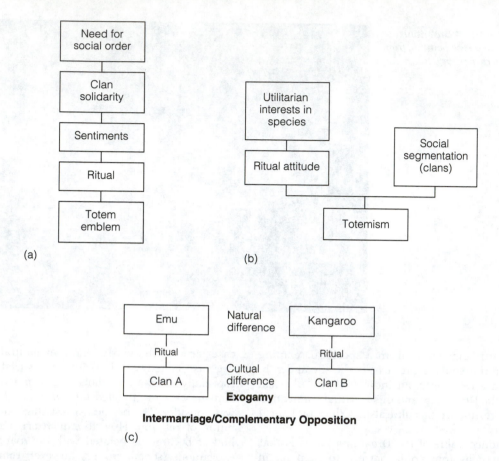

FIGURE 2.13  *Theories of functionalism and structuralism: (a) French functionalism, Durkheim; (b) British functionalism, Radcliffe-Brown; (c) French structuralism, Lévi-Strauss.*

Sigmund Freud (1913) conjectured that both totemism and exogamy resulted from the guilt caused by a primal act of patricide and cannibalism.

Functionalist interpretations, first proposed by French sociologist Émile Durkheim (1912), founded totemism in the need for social order (Figure 2.13). According to this explanation, clan solidarity was maintained by sentiments acted out in rituals, which in turn required totems as visible symbols or emblems. In worshiping totems, aborigines were in effect worshiping the mystical power of their own society, which could only be visualized in the objective form of the totem species. Inspired by Durkheim, the British functional-ist A. R. Radcliffe-Brown (1929) argued that totemism arose because people were naturally interested in the species they relied on as resources. Aborigines first adopted a ritual attitude toward species that were "good to eat," and then these species became group emblems or totems. The functionalist line of argument proved inconclusive because not all valuable species were totems, whereas some highly nonutilitarian species, such as mosquitoes and diseases, were often considered totems.

French structuralist anthropologist Claude Lévi-Strauss (1963) contends that totemism is an illusion as an anthropological category because it merges too many diverse phenomena that cannot be explained as a unity. Elaborating on one of Radcliffe-Brown's (1951) ideas, Lévi-Strauss (1963, 1966) observes that totemism can profitably be considered an example of **complementary opposition**, the tendency for people to create mental sets of paired opposites such as day and night, male and female, nature and culture. Natural species represent social units "not because they are 'good to eat' but because they are 'good to think'" (Lévi-Strauss 1963:89). This is a structuralist argument because cultural meaning is derived from the way different elements, species, and clans can form a logical structure. A single totem has no meaning by itself.

The advantage of this mental classification process is that opposition can create social integration. Clan A differs from clan B in the same way that a kangaroo differs from an emu. There are two homologous systems of differences, one operating in nature and the other in culture. Species are "naturally" different, whereas totemic clans are distinguished by the "cultural illusion" of the ritual functions thought to perpetuate the totemic species. Exogamy means that women who are "naturally" similar because of their sex are culturally differentiated into marriageable and nonmarriageable categories. The result is that totemic social groups can be integrated by intermarriage. The social groups opposed by totemic classification are made complementary because one clan can not reproduce without the other. In the end, it seems that both Durkheim and Lévi-Strauss would agree that totemism is simply a way in which people conceptualize society in order to create solidarity.

## The Basics of Kinship and Marriage

Aboriginal society is highly decentralized and egalitarian, with people in overlapping and interdependent roles that minimize the possibility that divisive interest groups will come into serious conflict. The social system allows an individual to sort the 500 or so people that one might potentially encounter into a workable number of social categories that specify appropriate interpersonal behavior, especially in the critical areas of marriage and access to spiritual property. The totemic estate groups are among the most important social categories. In a given aboriginal society, there might be dozens of totemic estate groups, or clans, who organize rights in spiritual property and indirectly provide access to natural resources. Who one marries is partly determined in reference to the totemic groups of one's parents, and marriage establishes access to territory associated with additional totemic estates.

All social interaction takes place between people who can place themselves in specific kinship categories. Kinship terms define an individual's personal network of culturally significant categories that are conceptually based on the relationships arising from the **nuclear family** of mother, father, and children. Aboriginal **kinship terminology** systems typically distinguish some fifteen to twenty relationship pairs such as father/daughter, brother/sister, and so on. Kin terms may distinguish sex and relative age or generation and whether one is a **consanguine**—that is, related by a common ancestor—or an **affine**—that is, related by marriage. Aboriginal kin terms also indicate marriageability and relative totemic estate group affiliation. Because everyone must be fitted into a "kinship" category, most people are not necessarily what nonaboriginals would consider "real" consanguines and affines; the terms, however, reflect shared understandings of social status, and they become basic guides for expected behavior.

Kinship in aboriginal society is not strictly a system of consanguinity and affinity as early anthropologists believed. Kinship terms represent cultural categories, and their specific application varies considerably cross-culturally. For example, in a given system, someone might refer to several women using the same term applied to mother.

---

**complementary opposition** A structural principle in which pairs of opposites, such as male and female, form a logical larger whole.

**nuclear family** The primary family unit of mother, father, and their dependent children.

**kinship terminology** An ego-centered system of terms that specify genealogical relationships of consanguinity and affinity in reference to a specific individual.

**consanguine** A relative by culturally recognized descent from a common ancestor; sometimes called a "blood" relative.

**affine** A relative by marriage.

The term *mother* might then mean "woman of mother's generation who belongs to mother's totemic estate group" (clan). The biological facts of motherhood might be irrelevant in this context. When the biological relationship needs to be designated, a modifier such as *true* or *real* might be attached to the term. Similarly, a man might refer to several women as "wife's mother," yet not be married to any of their daughters. From an aboriginal viewpoint, what is most important is potential marriageability and relationship to totemic estate groups.

The complexity inherent in kinship terminologies and estate groups is reduced by another system of categories in aboriginal society known as moieties and section systems. **Moieties** sort people into two sides by estate groups, or they may divide the entire society into "own group" and "other group" from the viewpoint of a specific individual. In some aboriginal societies, all people, totems, and natural phenomena are assigned to a specific moiety. For example, one-half of a society might be associated with the color black, kangaroos, acacia trees, and goanna lizard Dreaming sites, whereas the other half is white, emus, gum trees, and rainbow serpent Dreaming sites. Membership may be assigned through mother (matrimoiety) or father (patrimoiety) or by generation level.

Moiety groupings help organize ritual activities and can be used to specify roles in initiation ceremonies, marriages, and funerals. For example, one moiety may "own" a particular ritual, while the other moiety actually carries out the ritual. This is a form of complementary opposition because the ceremony could not be performed without the cooperation of both groups.

The **section system** simply extends the number of summary social categories from two moieties to four sections and sometimes eight subsections. Because a given society may be crosscut by overlapping moiety systems, sections can significantly simplify social status and help determine who people can marry.

Aboriginal marriage practices provide an important key to understanding many aspects of the social system. Marriages, normally arranged by the elders, fit within precisely defined cultural categories, which vary in detail from group to group. Frequently, the ideal mate for a man (ego in Figure

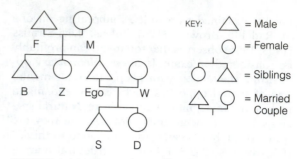

FIGURE 2.14  *Conventions of kinship diagramming.*

2.14) would be the daughter of someone he would refer to as wife's mother (WM).* In many systems, wife's mother might also be a woman of father's totemic clan and in the father's sister (FZ) category. Wife's mother might be married to a man ego would place in the mother's brother (MB) category. Mother's brother could be any man who was a member of the same totemic clan to which ego's actual mother belonged; of course, several men could be in this category, and they would not need to be the actual brother of ego's actual mother. Also, an appropriate spouse will often be someone in the kinship category of **cross-cousin** (MBD, FZD) because these women could not belong to ego's descent group.

A person would be expected to marry within a certain range of ego-based kin and in reference to specific clan, moiety, and section categories. One would always marry outside of one's own clan and might even refer to one's own generation fellow clan members as brother and sister, emphasizing the incestuous nature of clan **endogamy**. Where

---

*Anthropologists find it useful to describe all kinship terms using combinations of standard abbreviations based on the following eight primary relationship categories: F = father, M = mother, S = son, D = daughter, B = brother, Z = sister, H = husband, and W = wife. Thus, FB = father's brother, MB = mother's brother, FF = father's father, FBD = father's brother's daughter, MBD = mother's brother's daughter, etc. Ego, always the reference point in any kinship diagram, is the person who applies the terms shown. These designations are culturally specific social categories, they need not represent actual biological relationships. Even primary terms such as *mother* can be applied to several people who are not one's biological mother.

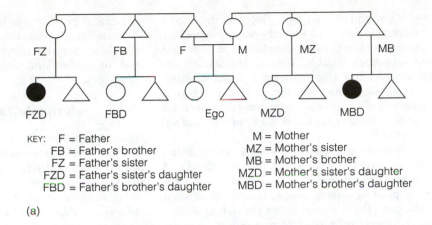

FIGURE 2.15
*Australian aborigine marriage systems:*
*(a) Cross-cousins;*
*(b) a simple two-section moiety system;*
*(c) a four-section system, alternate generations.*

KEY:   F = Father
FB = Father's brother
FZ = Father's sister
FZD = Father's sister's daughter
FBD = Father's brother's daughter

M = Mother
MZ = Mother's sister
MB = Mother's brother
MZD = Mother's sister's daughter
MBD = Mother's brother's daughter

(a)

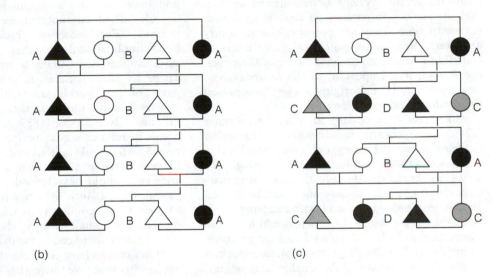

(b)                                          (c)

societywide moieties exist, spouses would be drawn from opposite moieties, and the moiety groups could be called exogamous.

Appropriate marriages can also be described in relation to the section system. With a four-section system, there are four named sections, and an individual can marry into only one specific section (Figure 2.15). Siblings always belong to the same section but belong to different sections from their parents, reflecting the fact that marriage within parent–child and sibling categories would be incestuous. Sections only indirectly regulate marriage because not all women in the appropriate section will be in the marriageable MBD category.

Knowing someone's section identity simply narrows the search. Because sections are not ego-based categories, people belong to the same cate-

*moiety*   One part of a two-part social division.
*section system*   a social division into four (sections) or eight (subsections) intermarrying, named groups, which summarize social relationships. Members of each group must marry only members of one other specific group.
*cross-cousin*   The son or daughter of mother's brother or father's sister and often considered to be in a marriageable category.
*endogamy*   Marriage within a culturally defined group; the opposite of exogamy.

gory in relation to everyone. Sections thus serve as convenient labels to identify people, especially because aborigines often consider it rude to use personal names in public. Knowing someone's section would allow one to make reasonable inferences about more specific social categories. Furthermore, because sections are recognized intertribally, strangers can quickly fit into a local social network.

Early anthropologists mistakenly assumed that sections existed simply to regulate marriage and arose as a reform from an earlier stage of completely promiscuous matings. Evolutionists such as Morgan (1877) thought that aboriginal society was the most "primitive" of any existing people, citing the section system as evidence of an even earlier stage of group marriage. Aborigines are *not* earlier in time. They are not our "contemporary ancestors," and such hypothetical reconstructions contribute little to an understanding of their society. Rather, it is important for us to understand how these details of aboriginal society have helped their culture endure so long.

More recent theorists, such as Lévi-Strauss (1949), have constructed ingenious strucuralist models that assume aboriginal society consisted of a series of groups tied together by marriage alliances based on a specific rule of cross-cousin marriage. In this system, the society would be seen as divided into wife-giving and wife-receiving localized descent groups, and women would move between them as "gifts." Such a scheme does provide an intellectually satisfying outside picture that can "explain" many details of the kinship terminology, but it is a distinctly male-centered view and appears to be far removed from the realities of the system as either experienced or imagined by aborigines. Women do not simply move as objects between groups at the whim of men. Also, aboriginal society is much more flexible than **alliance theory** suggests. The members of the totemic estates act as a group only on ritual occasions; even then, not all members may be present, and nonmembers would also play important roles. Marriages do create "alliances," but these are expressed through overlapping ego-based networks.

Moieties, sections, totems, and kinship terms all work together in a neatly integrated system to guide people in their daily interaction with one an-

other and in their relationships to their countries and spiritual properties. It is a remarkably successful system that significantly reduces the potential for conflict and makes authoritarian rule unnecessary.

## Mother-in-Law Avoidance

One very striking form of kinship behavior is the extreme avoidance operating between a man and any woman that he calls wife's mother (WM). In some aboriginal groups, a man cannot look at, remain near, or speak directly to his wife's mother. She is considered to be a source of "shame"; he must avoid any sexual references in her presence and may even use a special form of avoidance speech full of circumlocutions to avoid embarrassment. Early observers thought such customs were simply absurd, but when understood in cultural context, they make a great deal of sense. There are close parallels to this custom in many parts of the world, and anthropologists have proposed many interpretations. For example, evolutionist Edward Tylor (1889) argued that mother-in-law avoidance was a survival from a prior universal matrilineal stage in which a man would be likely to move in with his wife's family. The avoidance rule would have helped reduce conflict. Although there is little evidence for a universal matrilineal stage, conflict reduction is a useful idea especially in small groups where a man might come into frequent contact with his mother-in-law.

Other researchers point out that a man may often live in close proximity with WM and may provide her with meat as a form of bride-service, even before marrying his WMD (Hiatt 1984b). Given the often great age differential at marriage, a man may be nearly the same age as his WM and could find her attractive, while WM might find a young daughter's husband more attractive than the old man who would be her husband. Meat giving also has sexual implications and takes place between husband and wife. Under these circumstances, extreme avoidance would certainly reduce or eliminate the possibility of conflict between a man and WF. Avoidance would also prevent the possibility of father–daughter incest because, if a man did have an affair with his WM, he could be his own WF.

## Polygyny, Gerontocracy, and Social Equality

Many aspects of aboriginal society are related to the widespread practice of *polygyny* (plural wives). Polygyny automatically creates a scarcity of potential wives, which is partially alleviated by the large age difference between men and women at marriage. Girls may be promised in marriage long before they are born, and men might be well beyond 30 years of age before their first marriage, perhaps to a much older widow, while a 12-year-old girl might marry a 50-year-old man. If one assumes an even sex ratio, then the only way in which some men could have more than one wife would be for women to marry at a younger age than men. The wider the age differential at marriage, the more polygynous marriages can take place. A recent study in Arnhem Land found that nearly one-half of the men over 40 years of age had more than one wife, and one-third had three or more (Shapiro 1981). More than one-third of the men age 20 to 40 years were still unmarried.

Although the marriage age differential facilitates polygyny, the existence of polygyny itself remains to be explained. It may appear to be the direct result of manipulation by self-interested and influential older men, but this is a narrow view. Polygyny also creates stress for individuals, but it offers important benefits for the entire society. Polygynous households may provide childbearing women with greater security. An older man is more likely than a younger man to have a thorough knowledge of the territory and a wider network of kinship connections, which will benefit his entire household, especially in times of resource shortage. Similarly, delayed marriages provide the young men with the opportunity to learn the intricacies of the totemic landscape and the locations of critical waterholes, while they remain free of domestic responsibilities.

The way in which aboriginal marriage customs are discussed by anthropologists, as with the terms *wife givers* and *wife-receivers*, often implies male domination where it is not present. The terms *wife bestowal* and even *mother-in-law bestowal* are sometimes applied to the spouse-selection process. Mother-in-law bestowal refers to a ceremony in which a young girl is publicly designated as wife's mother to a young man. The term *bestowal*, rather than the more neutral term *betrothal*, may suggest that a father is "giving away" a daughter, when in fact the girl's mother or mother's brother is more likely to make the arrangements, and the marriage might never take place. Given a man's age at marriage, he might not even be around when his daughter actually marries, although he might have had some involvement in her prenatal betrothal.

Many anthropologists have called aboriginal society a polygynous *gerontocracy* (Bern 1979, Godelier 1975, Meillassoux 1981). They argue that the old men occupy the upper "class" and use polygyny and Dreamtime ideology to control women and the labor supply. In this view, women as a class are mystified and subordinated by the secret ritual life of men, and they are oppressed by arranged marriages and polygyny. The young men are deprived of wives and kept subservient by the male initiation system. Such an interpretation makes aboriginal society resemble the rank-and-class systems of larger-scale societies and may reflect the perceptions of some of the old men, particularly when they are describing the system to male anthropologists, but it is an inadequate and misleading generalization. Emphasis on male gerontocracy ignores the important role of women both in the ritual system and domestic life and obscures the essentially egalitarian nature of aboriginal society.

The place of women in aboriginal culture has been interpreted in many different ways. Ethnocentric European travelers mistakenly described women as degraded and passive servants of the men. The sharp sexual divisions in the activity spheres of aboriginal culture made it difficult for anthropologists to obtain a balanced picture. Early anthropologists were mostly men who necessarily observed male culture and talked to male informants. These male anthropologists were also quite comfortable with the male superiority view be-

---

*alliance theory*    Assumes, from a male perspective, that particular marriage systems create interdependence between social groups that give and receive wives.

*polygyny*    A form of marriage in which a man may have more than one wife.

*gerontocracy*    An age hierarchy that is controlled or dominated by the oldest age groups.

cause it corresponded closely to their own Victorian biases. Victorian anthropologists considered women in general to be spiritually inferior and even described them as "profane," whereas men were seen as "sacred." More recent fieldwork by female anthropologists working with aboriginal women has broadened the picture by showing that women have a very active secret ritual life and exercise considerable autonomy in domestic affairs.

Australian anthropologist Diane Bell (1987) spent many months living in aboriginal communities in northern Australia. As a divorced woman with children, she was treated as an adult widow, given a kinship status, and included in public ceremonies. When her female hosts were satisfied that she would respect their secrecy, she was allowed to participate in women's secret rituals. From this perspective, she discovered that aboriginal women share joint and complementary responsibility with men for maintaining their spiritual heritage. Whereas men's rituals emphasize creative power, women's rituals focus on the nurturing role of women, health, social harmony, and connections with the land.

Women also play a major role in subsistence, may arrange marriages, control family size by means of infanticide, and can influence the choice of conception totems. Some anthropologists still consider aboriginal men "superior" but would grant women the status of "junior partners." However, the notion of rank by gender is probably not a culturally significant issue for aborigines. Throughout the world, foraging peoples who are characterized by high mobility and low population density are the most egalitarian societies known. Equality is reflected in the conspicuous absence of differences in material wealth between individuals and in the absence of permanent political leaders with coercive power over others. Such equality is apparent in the fact that each household has available to it the resources needed to secure its existence. However, social equality does not mean that everyone is totally alike. Obvious differences exist between men and women, between young and old, and between individuals with different personalities and physical characteristics.

Foragers, like the aborigines, who operate with *immediate-return systems* provide little basis for people or corporate groups to maintain coercive power over others (Lee 1981, Woodburn 1982). With immediate-return systems, there is no investment of labor in fixed structures, gardens, or herds that will produce a *delayed-return system* and that might require long-term storage. Thus, there is no particular advantage in long-term control of a labor force. When basic production is left to nature and food is harvested and consumed on a daily basis, population densities must remain low, and social groups remain highly flexible and mobile in order to respond to natural fluctuation in supply. Reciprocity, especially pooling and sharing of food, levels out individual variation in production and operates between all households in a camp. In immediate-return systems, every household has freely available the productive tools and natural resources that it requires. Mobility reduces the potential for social domination and exploitation by discouraging wealth accumulation and making it easy for people to walk away from aversive interpersonal situations.

Social equality is also closely related to the "openness" of aboriginal society. Open societies derive their special characteristics from their mobility and the absence of permanent houses, tombs, temples, and institutionalized leadership. Domestic life takes place in the open, where people can pay close attention to one another (Wilson 1988). Under these conditions, there are few secrets and few sources of conflict. Furthermore, with weapons always at hand, the use of force is open to everyone and is unlikely to become a basis for domination.

Outsiders may be struck by the apparent frequency of conflict in aboriginal society, the violence of domestic quarrels, charges of infidelity, or failure to share. Conflicts of this sort are apparently more common under the crowded conditions of modern settlements. Furthermore, any conflict will be a public event in an open society and cannot be hidden behind walls as they may be in other societies. The religious life in open societies is primarily concerned with healing, love magic, and natural fertility rather than with witchcraft. Individual souls are recycled and may exist briefly as ghosts, but they are not permanently commemorated in ancestor cults. Groups, even those based on kinship, are not rigidly bounded corporate entities. Both individual friendships and kinship categories define social relationships, and they are not exclusively determined by genealogical criteria.

Paradoxically, aboriginal society is at the same time intensely egalitarian and religiously authoritarian (Hiatt 1987). Although aboriginal society is sometimes described as a society without politics because of the absence of formal chiefs, elders do have moral authority over their juniors, and this authority is based in the Dreaming. This would apply to both men and women. Relationships between individuals at different generation levels are hierarchical. This may be expressed as a kinship responsibility to "hold" or "look after" or "raise" the junior (Myers 1980). This is nurturing and guiding and is not considered domination or exploitation. In aboriginal English, one's elder may be referred to as a "boss" who has control over one's marriage and ritual advancement. Such an elder–junior system extends throughout the society so that everyone but the youngest child would be responsible for a junior, but the context is always specific. No one has generalized power over all others.

An *age hierarchy* is different from a government bureaucracy because, in the age system, status is always relative, everyone at a given level is equivalent, and everyone moves up. No one is permanently excluded from access to basic resources or political power by membership in a lower social class. As they mature, everyone, men and women alike, move to positions of greater decision-making ability in society.

For aborigines, the ideological foundation of their society is the Dreaming, which defines and is perpetuated by the generational hierarchy. Knowledge of the Dreaming is concentrated in the elders who are obligated to transmit it to the juniors. Holding and transmitting such knowledge can be considered an exercise of political power, but it is a very special kind of power that cannot be directly compared with political power in large-scale, non-egalitarian societies.

There often are aboriginal "bigmen" or "men of high renown" who stand out because of their vast ritual knowledge or oratorical skills, but their range of action is limited. They may have considerable influence in the ceremonial life and may be able to manipulate certain social relationships to their advantage with threats of supernatural punishment; in the larger society, however, even such powerful individuals can take little political action without broad popular consensus.

## Male Initiation: The Terrible Rite

*It is the price that must be paid for tribal membership, and all must pay. . . . That the price is high puts an enhanced value on these bonds of tribal union.* (Porteus 1931:280–281)

The physical ordeals of scarification, nose piercing, bloodletting, tooth evulsion, genital mutilation, and fingernail extraction associated with aboriginal male initiation rituals have been a continuing source of amazement for outsiders and have generated countless speculation to explain their origin and persistence. These rites occur throughout Australia, but not all groups share the same specific forms. They mark different age grades in the social maturity of a young man and his acquisition of ritual knowledge. Women and girls pass through similar maturation grades but with few physical ordeals.

The obvious functionalist interpretation of these rituals is that they are *rites of passage* publicly marking an individual's change of status. For example, a boy must be circumcised before he can marry. The pain makes the new status more valuable and increases one's pride of membership, thus contributing to social solidarity. The value of body mutilation, especially where little clothing is worn, is that the change in status is permanently visible and unlikely to be faked; genital mutilation is also gender-specific. These rituals are part of the formal instruction in ritual lore and make the ritual more valuable and more memorable. The initiates must accept the discipline of the older men, and they owe respect and gifts of meat to their tutors.

---

**immediate-return system**  A subsistence system that does not normally require storage because production occurs daily without special advance labor inputs.
**delayed-return system**  A subsistence system requiring food storage because production must be preceded by a significant investment of labor, such as with farming.
**age hierarchy**  A social system in which people are ranked by age.
**rite of passage**  A ritual marking a culturally significant changes in individual's life cycle, such as birth, puberty, marriage, old age, and death.

The most dramatic male ordeal is subincision, which follows circumcision and involves slitting the underside of the penis lengthwise to open the urethra. The operation is performed by the initiate's MB or WF who uses a very sharp stone knife. The initiate must remain passive and show no pain. After healing, the incision remains open, but infection or reproductive impairment does not normally occur.

Subincision appears to have been a recent invention and was actively spreading from tribe to tribe when Europeans arrived. Young men willingly submit to the ordeal because it admits them to the privileges of manhood in a society where other tests of strength and courage such as warfare are of little importance. From the aboriginal viewpoint, subincision requires no special explanation beyond the fact that it originated in the Dreaming, and they may point to the physical resemblance between the subincised penis and the genitals of kangaroos and emus as confirmation of the Dreaming connection (Cawte 1974).

Psychoanalysts have suggested that subincision is a subconscious way for aboriginal men to deal with oedipal fears, castration anxiety, or their supposed envy of female reproductive powers. In opposition to the aboriginal interpretation, the subincision would represent a woman's vagina, not a totemic kangaroo penis. The best support for the psychoanalytic view is that the initiates are symbolically killed in the ritual and reborn as men, but because men already have a culturally acknowledged role in fertility through totemic increase ceremonies, vagina envy seems unnecessary. A conflicting psychological argument is that boys who grow up too closely associated with their mothers need a painful initiation to affirm their identity as males.

It can never be known how rituals such as subincision originated in the first place, but they play an important role in the culture and are best understood as expressions of the overwhelming importance of the Dreaming.

## SUMMARY

Australian aborigines demonstrate that a small-scale culture can remain egalitarian and in balance with its resource base indefinitely as long as it is not invaded by larger-scale neighbors. For over 50,000 years, gradual adjustments in aboriginal technology occurred as environmental conditions changed, and the ritual system and social organization underwent continuous elaboration; aboriginal culture, however, retained its fundamental character as a small-scale system. This was clearly a dynamic, responsive, and highly creative system, but it appears to have changed in such a way that the most fundamental cultural elements remained in place. The Dreaming itself, and all its associated features, seems to be the key element in understanding this remarkable cultural stability.

## STUDY QUESTIONS

1. In what sense could the aboriginal subsistence system be considered a luxury or an affluent economy?

2. Discuss the role of women in aboriginal society. Are they really oppressed and exploited by the old men as some suggest?

3. Demonstrate the connections between religion and society *or* between religion and adaptation to the natural environment in aboriginal Australia.

4. Discuss explanations for the remarkable initiation practices of the aboriginals, distinguishing between emic and etic views.

5. Describe the marriage practices of aborigines.

6. In what sense can aboriginal society be considered egalitarian? What cultural mechanisms contribute to equality?

7. What is the evidence for or against long-term stability in aboriginal culture?

## SUGGESTED READING

FLOOD, JOSEPHINE. 1983. *Archaeology of the Dreamtime*. Honolulu: University of Hawaii Press. A comprehensive overview of the prehistory of Australia.

GOULD, RICHARD A. 1980. *Living Archaeology*. Cambridge, Eng.: Cambridge University Press. Gould is an archeologist who studied contemporary aborigines in the Western Desert to help understand the prehistoric remains.

SAHLINS, MARSHALL. 1968. "Notes on the Original Affluent Society." In *Man the Hunter*, edited by Richard B. Lee and Irven DeVore, pp. 85–89. Chicago: Aldine. This short section draws a comparison between foraging and market economies.

TONKINSON, ROBERT. 1991. *The Mardudjara Aborigines: Living the Dream in Australia's Desert*, 2nd ed. New York: Holt, Rinehart & Winston. A well-rounded ethnography of aboriginal culture in the Western Desert.

# 3

# NATIVE AMAZONIANS: VILLAGERS OF THE RAIN FOREST

Since early in the sixteenth century, European accounts of the native inhabitants of Amazonia fueled the myth of the "noble savage." The earliest European explorers correctly described the relative social and political equality and the communalism of the rain forest villagers, but they mistakenly equated the prevailing nudity of the natives with the innocence and perfection of the biblical Eden. Native Amazonians were not perfect peoples, but their cultures still fascinate outsiders because they continue to offer a dramatic contrast to life in large-scale states and global cultures organized by the commercial economy. Amazonia is the last large area of the world where autonomous tribal cultures continued to function within regional intertribal worlds well into the twentieth century. Amazonia is also home to the world's largest tropical rain forest, which is now receiving international attention from environmentalists and humanitarians because of the global implications of deforestation and the related issue of the destruction of traditional cultures. Furthermore, an important and still independent Amazonian people, the Yanomamo, are the subject of one of the most widely used ethnographic monographs and are vividly portrayed in several ethnographic films. As sedentary villagers, the native peoples of Amazonia offer a striking contrast with Australian aborigines and raise further questions about social equality, political power, balance with resources, and the role of ideological systems in small-scale cultures. In this chapter, we focus on an ethnographic present that assumes political and economic independence of tribal Amazonia.

## AMAZONIAN ENVIRONMENT AND PREHISTORY

### The Fragile Abundance of the Rain Forest

Amazonia contains one of the world's great ecosystems, combining the largest continuous stand of tropical rain forest with the greatest river system in the world (Figure 3.1). The Amazon River drains an area of 2.25 million square miles (mi²) (5.87 million square kilometers [km²]) and discharges four times the volume of water carried by the Congo, the next largest river in the world. The rain forest stretches for some 2000 miles (3218 km) east to west across the center of South America. This warm, wet region is an ideal climate for plant growth and serves as a veritable treasury of biological diversity.

FIGURE 3.1 *Map of the Amazonian culture area showing the culture groups discussed. Note that the Amazon basin proper covers only part of the culture area.*

Amazonia is a land without winter, where the coolest month does not drop below 64.4°F (18°C), and no month receives less than 2.4 inches (6 centimeters [cm]) of rain. It is entirely in the tropics, mostly within 10 degrees of the equator, where daylight is always 12 hours long and the sun's rays strike the earth with maximum intensity. Rainfall is abundant throughout the region, usually averaging over 80 inches (203 cm) a year. Daytime high temperatures reach 90°F (32°C) and nighttime lows about 70°F (21°C). This daily range is greater than the seasonal variation in temperature.

The basic biological productivity of tropical rainforest is three to five times that of most temperate forests, and the total biomass is among the highest of any terrestrial ecosystem. The forest is composed predominately of woody plants, and small, familiar temperate plants such as violets and grass are represented here as trees. Rain forest trees are usually straight and tall, their interlocking limbs forming a closed canopy laced with woody vines (Figure 3.2).

The vast number of plant and animal species in Amazonia is remarkable. It is not unusual to find twenty to eighty or more species of trees per acre, whereas temperate forests might have only four tree species per acre (Richards 1973). A study from central Amazonia reported some 500 plant species over 4 ft (1.2 m) high in a plot of less than half an acre (Fittkau and Klinge 1973). Amazonian rivers may contain as many as 3000 fish species (Goulding 1980), whereas only 60 species occur in western Europe and only 250 species occur in the Mississippi system. There are probably more species of birds in Amazonia than in any area of similar size in the world. More than 500 species were found in one 2-mi² (5-km²) area in the Peruvian Amazon, whereas only 440 species are known in the entire eastern half of North America.

The biological wealth of the rain forest hides some curious paradoxes. High productivity does not mean high human-carrying capacity because much energy goes to the production of inedible forest litter. Marketable timber seems to be produced at about the same rate as in temperate forests, but there is a heavy output of small branches and leaves. Soil fertility is often very low and quickly depleted. There are little easily harvested carbohydrates in the woody vegetation, and 90 percent of the animal biomass is composed of ants, termites, and other small invertebrates that can eat leaves and wood. Large vertebrates are relatively scarce, and animal protein is difficult for hunters to secure because game is often nocturnal or hides in the forest canopy. Natural food resources for people are so scarce that some authorities argue that no full-time foraging peoples have been able to live in the rain forest unless they have access to aquatic resources or can obtain garden produce from village farmers (Bailey et al. 1989).

The infertility of Amazonian soils is due to the combination of heavy humidity and warm temperature, which fosters both luxuriant growth and the rapid breakdown of forest litter. The top humus layer of the soil is actually very shallow, and most tree roots are near the surface where they can quickly take in the nutrients liberated by decomposition. Trees recycle litter so efficiently that more nutrients are held in the forest itself than in the soil. The forest also regulates the water cycle, contributing directly to the daily thundershowers through transpiration and moderating the potential for erosion by cushioning and dispersing the heavy downpours. The forest also sustains the Am-

FIGURE 3.2    *The Amazon rain forest is one of the world's most biologically diverse regions. High waterfalls are found in the Guiana highlands and along the Andean foothills.*

azon's wealth of fish because many species are specialized to feed on fruit on the floor of seasonally flooded forests (Goulding 1980). The extreme complexity of the Amazonian ecosystem is still very poorly understood by the scientific community, but it is apparent that successful long-term human utilization of this region requires maintaining the forest.

## The Prehistory of Amazonia

Amazonia presents special problems for archaeologists because preservation of perishable remains is poor in the wet tropics, recoverable stone artifacts are rare, and meandering rivers steadily destroy existing sites. Furthermore, relatively little fieldwork has been carried out in this vast region. Given this situation, the precise origins of Amazonian village life will probably never be known with certainty.

The physical evidence of teeth, bones, and blood indicates that people reached the New World from Asia by at least 12,000 BP (Table 3.1). Periods of a lowered sea level during the Ice Age created a land connection between Asia and

TABLE 3.1   *Prehistory of Amazonia*

| | |
|---|---|
| **Floodplain Chiefdoms and Autonomous Forest Villagers (AD 1542–2000 BP)** | |
| 1542 AD | Orellana expedition—European invasion |
| 1150 BP | Incised pottery in central Amazonia |
| 1400 | Incised pottery on Orinoco |
| 1800 | Polychrome pottery in central Amazonia |
| 2000 | Varzea chiefdoms |
| **Spread of Tropical Forest Culture (2000–5000 BP)** | |
| 2800 | Maize on Orinoco |
| 3500 | Maize in coastal Brazil |
| 3000–5000 | Zoned hachure pottery style, earliest ceramics in South America |
| 4000 | Manioc griddles, manioc beer vessels |
| **Sedentism and Domestication (5000–9000 BP)** | |
| 5000–7000 | Domestication of manioc inferred |
| 7000 | Maize domesticated in Central America |
| **Foragers and First Settlers (12,000–32,000 BP)** | |
| 12,000 | Earliest widely accepted entry into the New World |
| 17,000 | Rock paintings, northeast Brazil |
| 32,000 | Rock shelter hearths, northeast Brazil |

America known as Beringia, which would have facilitated the first settlement of the New World. There are reports that rock shelters were occupied in the dry zone of northeast Brazil by 32,000 BP and that rock paintings were being made by 17,000 BP, but such early dates are not yet widely accepted. Certainly by 11,000 BP, foraging peoples had reached Patagonia at the southern tip of South America.

There is no archaeological record of the occupation of the Amazonian rain forest by mobile foragers, but people may have still lived in that region for many thousands of years, without leaving a trace, before becoming settled village farmers. Even if the rain forest itself was not easily exploited by foragers, they might have remained near the rivers. It is also likely that the rain forest was not always as extensive and continuous as historically observed. Studies of soils, fossil pollen, and the distribution of plants and animals suggest that during the Ice Age the climate of Amazonia fluctuated between wetter and drier periods. The forest perhaps retreated during the coldest, driest periods, to be temporarily replaced by scrub forest or savanna that would have been provided more food resources for foraging peoples. We can only speculate about the living patterns of these early groups, but they must have remained in very small and highly mobile bands, except where abundant coastal or riverine resources permitted larger, more permanent settlement.

## The Origins of Amazonian Village Life

During the period between 5000 and 9000 BP, a steady intensification of subsistence activities must have occurred in Amazonia, paralleling similar events that occurred in the *Archaic* of North America, the Old World Mesolithic, and the Australian Small Tool Tradition at about the same time. These events mark the end of the Ice Age and must have been related to global changes in climate, vegetation, and fauna. Rising sea levels reduced productive coastal zones, and many biggame animals disappeared at this time. People had to work harder to make a living and expanded their food base to include not only the smaller, more numerous species, such as fish and shellfish, but also a broad range of plant species. These changes meant more careful scheduling of seasonal activities and more work in food acquisition and processing, but it resulted in greater food production per unit of territory and more permanent settlement at greater densities. This process has been called **subsistence intensification**.

In many parts of the world, including Amazonia, subsistence intensification marked the transition from mobile foraging to settled village life and plant domestication. However, it is important to recall, as noted in Chapter 2, that Australian aborigines apparently managed to remain in balance with their resources during this time without turning to domestication. Use of fully domesticated plants defines the Old World Neolithic, and European scholars at first considered domestication to be a remarkable invention or discovery that occurred in very few places. It is now known that there were many centers of domestication and that domestication was a gradual process rather than an instant discovery (see Figure 1.6). It must have been compelled by intractable imbalances between population and resources. Paradoxically, domestication was a response to the need to increase food production, but it promoted further population growth by reducing the incentives for family planning encouraged by mobile foraging and by making further increases in food production readily achievable. Thus, village farmers were more likely to experience gradual population growth and had to work harder to maintain balances than did mobile foragers. They were also prone to expand as pioneer settlers into territories formerly occupied exclusively by foragers.

Domestication really implies drastic changes in human activities because, as plants become dependent on people for their care and reproduction, people become increasingly specialized and dependent on the plants. People must have made major sacrifices in personal freedom to till their new gardens. In its earliest stages, domestication was not distinguishable from the careful management of wild resources or the simple transplanting of wild plants to more convenient locations. The transition from dependence on wild to genetically altered, domestic plants, and from mobile foraging to relatively permanent villages, must have occurred over several thousand years. This transition did not occur everywhere, and some village farm-

ers, such as those in Amazonia, never became dependent on domesticated animals.

Archaeologist Donald Lathrap (1977) has speculated that early plant domestication in Amazonia may have resulted from efforts to intensify fishing production by people living along the rivers, in response to the decline of game as the forest expanded. He observed that increased use of nets and fish poisons would have encouraged people to selectively cultivate cotton (for nets and lines), bottle gourds (for floats), and poisonous plants in easily tended **house gardens** near their settlements. Cultivation would have been an advantage because in the tropical forest most plant species are widely dispersed and might be unavailable in the quantity needed.

The domestication of **manioc** (genus *Manihot*), the most important food plant in Amazonia, probably took place along with the intensification of fishing technology, but there is no direct evidence of its presence prior to 4000 BP when ceramic cooking griddles and beer vessels are associated with its use. Manioc is a woody shrub that grows readily from cuttings, and the tuber can be stored in the ground until needed. Although protein-deficient, manioc is very rich in carbohydrates, is highly productive even on poor soils, and is an ideal complement to the fish and game of Amazonia. It can also be fermented to produce a nutritious, mildly alcoholic drink, which may have been an important incentive for its domestication. It is likely that manioc was domesticated in Amazonia and did not spread there from elsewhere. As a **root crop**, it represents a distinctive cultivation system

---

**archaic** Archaeologically recognized period of initial sedentism and subsistence intensification preceding domestication in North America.

**subsistence intensification** Technological innovations that produce more food from the same land area but often require increased effort.

**house garden** An assortment of useful plants, often including semidomesticates, that are cultivated around the house.

**manioc** The most important cultivated food plant in Amazonia, grown for its starchy edible tuber. Also known as yuca and cassava, genus *Manihot*.

**root crop** Domesticated plants that reproduce from cuttings such as manioc or from root bundles such as bananas, often cultivated with hoes or digging sticks.

from maize, the major New World **seed crop**, which originated in **Mesoamerica** and spread to Amazonia.

During the period from approximately 2000 to 5000 BP, population increased, and the basic tropical forest cultural pattern of small autonomous tribal villages, based on shifting cultivation, hunting, and fishing, became firmly established throughout Amazonia. With average population densities of perhaps .4 person/square mile, the total population may have exceeded 1 million people. At least five major protolanguages—Tupi, Carib, Arawak, Panoan, and Ge—diversified into some 200 languages (Migliazza 1982). Everywhere people lived in small, widely separated villages of up to 500 people, sometimes in large communal houses (**malocas**). The bow and arrow was the most common weapon. Dugout canoes provided river transportation and an impressive array of wood, stone, basketry, and pottery implements was used in food processing. Cotton was used to make hammocks and clothing, while colorful plumes were made into elaborate headdresses and other ornaments. An impressive diversity of regional culture patterns, or culture areas, can be distinguished based on variations in material culture and details of social organization and religion, but the broad pattern is the same.

Within the past 2000 years, large-scale cultures developed along the Amazon and Orinoco rivers and the Bolivian lowlands. These groups were politically organized chiefdoms, distinguished archaeologically by distinctive pottery styles, and had dense populations presumably based on maize cultivation in alluvial soils and on fishing. They were quickly destroyed by invading Europeans after the first Spanish expedition descended on the Amazon in 1542 under the direction of Francisco de Orellana and will not be examined in this chapter. Small-scale cultures continued to occupy most of the rain forest and Amazon tributaries.

## SUBSISTENCE IN THE RAIN FOREST

### Rain Forest Gardening and Manioc Processing

Manioc production, the key to successful human occupation of Amazonia, depends on a specialized system of shifting cultivation that minimally disrupts the forest ecosystem. It is the forest that ultimately maintains soil quality, regulates local climate, recycles nutrients and water, and sustains fish and game resources. With shifting cultivation, as still practiced by native peoples throughout Amazonia, food is harvested from small, temporary forest clearings, containing mixed gardens at different successional stages in the regrowth of the forest.

In comparison with the large monocrop farms and plantations that have recently been introduced in Amazonia for commercial purposes, native gardens, or **swiddens**, rely on a diverse mix of crops. The vertical overlapping layers of different plant species minimize erosion and losses to insects and disease, while making efficient use of the space. Sweet potato vines and beans quickly cover the ground, then are shaded by maize and manioc, which in turn are shaded by bananas and various fruit trees.

This gardening system is sometimes called **slash and burn** because it is based on an apparently simple technology of cutting the forest and then burning the dry slash (Figure 3.3). The burn is usually incomplete, and many trees survive and quickly regrow. Some plants may even be deliberately protected. The burning concentrates nutrients in the ash, thus eliminating the need for additional fertilizer. Unburned logs provide an easy source of wood for cooking fires.

Shifting cultivation requires a great deal of specialized knowledge, which has an elaborate vocabulary. Native Amazonians distinguish several different types of soil and forest, and they take into account the special characteristics of each when selecting a garden site. Because many varieties of manioc require more than 6 months to produce large tubers, manioc must be grown on land that is not seasonally flooded; thus, manioc gardens cannot take advantage of the annually renewed alluvial soils along the major rivers. Gardens are usually about an acre in size and are seldom carefully tended for more than 1 year but may yield manioc for up to 3 years. New gardens might be made each year, so that at a given time every household has gardens at different stages of production. This is a **forest fallow system**, and usually a plot would not be replanted for a minimum

FIGURE 3.3  *Shifting cultivation is the primary source of carbohydrates in Amazonia. An Ashaninka mother and child rest in the shade in a newly cleared swidden (left); an Ashaninka man plants manioc cuttings (above).*

of 25 years to allow ample time for forest regrowth. Actually, full forest regrowth might require 50–100 years or more, but as long as gardens remain small and widely scattered, a 25-year cycle can adequately protect the forest.

Native people prefer the forest fallow system to more intensive cultivation for several reasons. Gardens are abandoned in part because rapid forest regrowth quickly makes weeding a burden. In most forest soils, continuous replanting would soon lead to a decline in fertility and yield. Re-clearing of old garden sites is avoided because, during the early stages of forest succession, the vegetation is very dense and difficult to clear with hand tools. Village sites themselves may be shifted every few years to reduce conflict or to find better hunting ground.

The productivity of manioc is truly impressive and readily explains its importance in the subsistence system. I estimate that a single garden belonging to an Ashaninka family in the Peruvian Amazon could potentially produce some 30,000 pounds of manioc in a year. This is more than double the household's consumption requirements and disregards replanting. Such apparent overproduction provides an important security margin. Other researchers found that the nearby Machi-

---

**seed crop**  Domesticated plants such as beans and maize that reproduce from seeds; sometimes cultivated by plow.

**Mesoamerica**  Cultural area extending from central Mexico through Central America to Panama, especially the area occupied by the Aztec and Maya civilizations and their archaeological antecedents.

**maloca**  Brazilian term for a communal house containing several families.

**swidden**  A garden cultivated by the slash-and-burn technique.

**slash and burn**  A farming technique in which forest is cleared and burned to enrich the soil for planting; a forest fallow system depending on forest regrowth.

**forest fallow system**  A system of cultivation in which soil nutrients are restored by allowing the forest to regrow.

TABLE 3.2    *Machiguenga Subsistence per Household per Year*

|  | Production (kg) | (%) | Energy Cost (kcal/kg) | Subsistence Effort (%) |
|---|---|---|---|---|
| Gardening* | 6755 | 93 | 80 | 55 |
| Fishing | 298 | 4 | 740 | 22 |
| Hunting/ Gathering | 194 | 3 | 1151 | 22 |
| *Total* | 7247 | 100 |  | 99 |

SOURCE: Johnson and Behrens (1982).
*Manioc alone = 4887 kg, or 67 percent of total production weight.

guenga Indians obtained more than two-thirds of their food by weight from manioc, which was produced at roughly 10 percent of the labor cost by weight of food produced by hunting, foraging, and fishing (Table 3.2). The recent use of metal axes has no doubt increased the relative advantage of manioc by making tree felling easier, but even with stone tools, manioc cultivation would have been very attractive. The Machiguenga allocated just over half of their total subsistence effort to gardening, which in total produced over 90 percent of their food by weight (Johnson and Behrens 1982). Manioc alone does not provide an adequate diet, and the Machiguenga raise a dozen other important crops and cultivate some eighty named plant varieties for various purposes (A. Johnson 1983).

Most tribal peoples may grow a dozen or more varieties of manioc, carefully distinguishing between them based on characteristics of tuber and leaf. The Kuikuru on the upper Xingu River in Brazil can name 46 manioc varieties, and the Aguaruna and Huambisa of Peru recognize more than 100 varieties (Boster 1983, Carneiro 1983). Such diversity indicates that long-term selective breeding is taking place.

All manioc tubers contain potentially toxic substances. In "sweet" varieties, they can be eliminated by merely peeling and simple cooking, whereas the "bitter" varieties require more elaborate processing and are especially suitable for flour. The Waiwai of Guyana have developed at least fourteen types of bread and thirteen beverages based on bitter manioc and its by-products (Yde 1965). (See Figure 3.4 for an example of manioc preparation.)

Manioc can be stored in the ground until it is used, or it can be stored as processed flour or bread as long as it can be kept dry. Potentially, it could provide an important **surplus** that could help support a large-scale society, but as will be shown, a variety of other factors—both cultural and ecological—keep this surplus only potential.

## Village Limits: Gardens, Fish, or Game?

It is a striking fact that rain forest villages usually remain small, averaging less than 100 people and seldom exceeding 300 people. These villages are relatively impermanent and move every few years. Cultural ecologists have often assumed that environmental factors in Amazonia must set upper limits on village size. Unfortunately, posing the problem in such terms may imply that large-scale cultures are somehow more "natural" and desirable than small-scale cultures and that the environment is the only limit. A closer look at Amazonia suggests that the rewards of life in small-scale society may encourage people to resist pressures for increasing village size and permanence.

The most obvious possible limiting factors in Amazonia are poor soils and the scarcity of animal protein. At first, theorists viewed Amazonia as a uniform environment that could not support large-scale cultures because it was assumed that infertile forest soils could not support the intensive agricultural systems needed to maintain higher population densities (Meggers 1954). Robert Carneiro (1960) was quick to demonstrate that manioc gardening could produce enough calories to support permanent villages of 500 people, as long

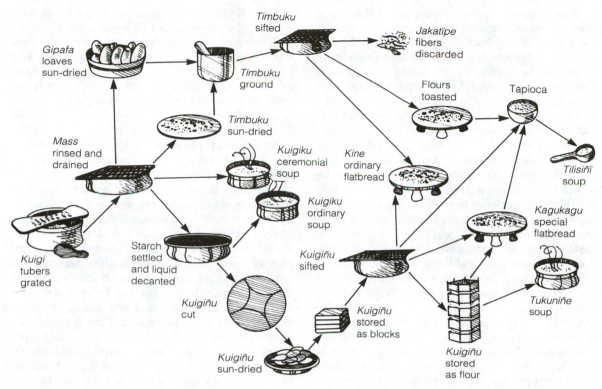

**FIGURE 3.4** *Steps in the preparation of manioc among the Kuikuru. (SOURCE: Adapted from Dole 1978.)*

as they could get enough animal protein from fish and game.

Carneiro's (1960) basic formula specified the critical variables that determine how large a village could remain in one location if it were limited only by manioc production (Figure 3.5). The amount of arable land is primarily limited by the maximum distance women prefer to carry produce from the garden—usually about 3 miles (5 km), yielding a maximum of about 18,000 acres (7290 hectares). Assuming Carneiro's modest figure of 13,500 acres (5468 hectares) of arable land, gardens cultivated 3 years, and a 25-year fallow, a village of 2043 people could in theory meet its manioc needs without ever moving. This is more than six times the usual upper limit for Amazonian villages. Extending the fallow to 100 years would reduce the potential size of the village to 561, still a figure seldom reached in Amazonia.

---

Basic Formula:

$$P = \frac{[T/(R+Y)]Y}{A}$$

Where $P$ = village population, $T$ = arable land, $R$ = years in forest fallow, $Y$ = years garden cultivated, and $A$ = garden area per person.

If $T$ = 13,350 acres, $R$ = 25 yr, $Y$ = 3 yr, and $A$ = .7 acres, then $P$ = 2043 people.

If $R$ = 100 yr, then $P$ = 561 people.

---

**FIGURE 3.5** *Environmental gardening limits on Amazonian villagers. (SOURCE: Carneiro 1960.)*

---

**surplus** Subsistence production that exceeds the needs of the producer households and that is extracted by political leaders to support nonfood-producing specialists.

If garden production does not set the upper limit of village size, then perhaps animal protein is the critical factor. Further research led to the distinction between the **riverine environments**—known as the Varzea, or the flood forest zone, in Brazil—and the **interfluvial environments**, the terra firma zone (Lathrap 1970, Meggers 1971). The riverine areas generally have larger, more permanent villages whose occupants exploit the abundant supplies of fish and other aquatic animals such as manatees, turtles, and caiman. Furthermore, fast-growing crops such as maize can be grown on the seasonally exposed alluvial soils and are significantly richer in protein than manioc. Villages in the terra firma zone must rely more on hunting for their protein, and generally villages are smaller and densities lower. Protein availability does seem to be a critical limiting factor, but many purely cultural factors must also be considered.

Protein is a basic human nutritional requirement; people need an average of about 2 oz (50 grams [g]) of protein daily with a correct balance of amino acids. In both the riverine and interfluvial forests of Amazonia, however, this figure is usually exceeded by a healthy margin, especially when plant protein is included (Gross 1975). It appears that throughout Amazonia, villages could be larger if people were willing to either hunt and fish more intensively, maintain domestic animals, or accept a nutritionally lower standard of living and/or the higher levels of political authority that such changes might require. Cultural factors connected with the advantages of small-scale society must encourage people to halt gardening, hunting, and fishing production at levels well below what would be theoretically sustainable. Maximum leisure and household-level autonomy seem to be more important objectives than supporting the largest possible villages.

Deriving protein entirely from plant sources is possible, but the cultural preference in Amazonia is for animal protein from fish and game. Dennis Werner (1983) suggests that villagers seek optimal diets while holding their work loads at moderate levels. This means that they must vary their village size or mobility to balance these goals as resource availability varies. It is remarkable that average daily intake of animal protein per person invariably remains within nutritionally acceptable ranges, whether based on fish or game, while total work load averages about 50 hours a week.

Fishing can be a very productive source of protein, but only in very specific environments. For example, the Cocamilla Indians of eastern Peru can supply a village of 300 people with a daily average of 1.5 oz (44 g) of protein per person from a single oxbow lake of .7 mi² (1.82 km²) (Stocks 1983). This represents an incredible 386 lb (175 kilograms [kg]) of fish per 2.5 acres (1 hectare) of lake annually. Other major floodplain rivers in Amazonia are apparently capable of producing 110 lb (50 kg) of fish per 2.5 acres (1 hectare) annually (Goulding 1981). There are problems with fish as a protein source because yields decline on smaller rivers and may be lower in nutrient-poor "blackwater" rivers. More importantly, many fish are migratory, and catches usually decline during flood seasons, so there may be considerable fluctuation in availability, which is masked by seasonal averages. Very large catches may be made on irregular occasions using fish poisons, but much fishing depends on routine use of nets, weirs, harpoons, arrows, and hook and line. Storage is usually for a short period and depends on smoking and salting. However, very large villages could certainly be supported in these environments, given the appropriate political changes.

The potential productivity of hunting in the rain forest is more difficult to estimate than gar-

FIGURE 3.6 *A formula for estimating the number of people who could be supported by hunting within a 10-km (6-mile) radius of a rain forest village.*

Basic Formula:

$$P = \frac{BHSCN}{R}$$

Where $P$ = people/km², $B$ = mammal biomass, $H$ = mammals hunted, $S$ = sustainable harvest, $C$ = carcass weight, $N$ = protein content, $R$ = protein required per person per year.

If $B$ = 5300 kg/km², $H$ = .43, $S$ = .10, $C$ = .50, $N$ = .16, and $R$ = 50 g × 365 days = 18 kg, then $P$ = 1 person/km².

Therefore, a 10-km hunting radius covering an area of 314 km² supports 314 people.

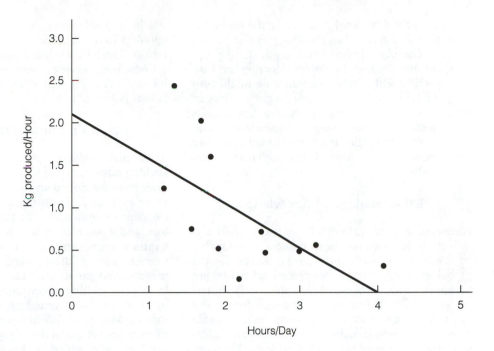

FIGURE 3.7
*Hunting-and-fishing time and efficiency for twelve Amazonian societies. (SOURCE: Hames 1987.)*

den productivity because game populations are diverse and poorly known. Figure 3.6 lists some of the variables that must be taken into account, along with a formula for calculating the number of people that could theoretically obtain 2 oz (50 g) of protein from game per year per .4 mi² (1 km²) on a sustained basis. The most critical value is the biomass of the game, and this can only roughly be estimated based on zoological surveys of rain forest mammals giving a range of 6623–11,700 lb/.4 mi² (3000—5300 kg/km²) (Eisenburg and Thorington 1973, Walsh and Gannon 1967). This base value must be further reduced to reflect cultural definitions of edibility and the proportion that can feasibly be hunted given existing technology and the requirement of sustainability. These calculations predict a potential village size remarkably close to that seen ethnographically. The low biomass figure suggests that 150 people could supply all of their protein needs within a 6-mile (10-km) hunting radius of a permanent village, while the highest biomass values would support 314 people.

Field data show that hunting efficiency within the daily hunting radius declines as villages re-

main in place or increase in size. The simplest ways for villagers to respond to declining hunting yields include intensifying their hunting effort, going on extended treks, relocating villages to new territory, or village fissioning. Kenneth Good (1987) observes that villages may split and move apart when conflicts arise over meat sharing. The hunting efficiency of different groups can vary considerably, as shown in Figure 3.7, but total hunting effort is unlikely to exceed an average of about 4 hours a day.

Although the availability of animal protein might be a valid limiting factor on village size, production might be increased by changing the cultural definition of edibility and the specific technology in use. The formula in Figure 3.6 includes both large and small species, but hunters might intensify production by trapping rodents. Most

---

*riverine environment*    A large river that is rich in fish, turtles, and other aquatic life; includes seasonally flooded lowlands with rich alluvial soils.

*interfluvial environment*    A forest on high ground (terra firma) between major rivers, where fishing is poor and animal protein is relatively scarce.

hunting is done by single men using the multipurpose bow and arrow, but the blowgun and poison darts can harvest birds very efficiently. Taking reptiles and insects could also considerably increase the protein yield. Economies of scale might also be gained if large groups organized game drives or used nets. More importantly, Native Amazonians never took the obvious step of domesticating animals, even though they made pets of wild pigs and large rodents such as agoutis and pacas, which enjoy manioc.

## Ethnoecological Knowledge

Native environmental knowledge is especially significant today because the rain forest is rapidly being cleared to provide short-term resources for the global economy. Many concerned scientists are seeking ways to safeguard the still poorly understood biological diversity of the rain forest and are attempting to identify economically valuable plants and animals before they disappear. Extensive ethnozoological research among the Jivaroan-speaking Aguaruna and Huambisa in the Peruvian Amazon provides an indication of the depth of knowledge of forest animals that Amazonians have accumulated (Berlin and Berlin 1983). Brent and Elois Ann Berlin found that the Aguaruna and Huambisa had names for nearly 90 mammals, some 300 birds, 85 reptiles and amphibians, 150 fish, and more than 250 invertebrates. The native categories correspond closely to the formal taxonomies recognized by professional zoologists and are based on natural species groupings. Such detailed knowledge of wildlife is typical of that found among many small-scale societies and represents more than simple concern with food. With the Aguaruna and Huambisa, barely 67 percent of their named species were edible, and just 10 percent supplied most of the game actually eaten.

Knowledge of animals is matched by knowledge of forest plants. Carneiro (1978) elicited 187 tree identifications from the Kuikuru and obtained 45 named trees in a .17-acre (.07-hectare) tract and 43 plants from a 10-ft$^2$ (.9-m$^2$) tract. He even found that the Kuikuru could identify 45 plant varieties based on the decomposing leaves collected from 1-ft$^2$ (.09 m$^2$) of forest floor. They also had an intimate understanding of the relationships between specific animals and specific plants. Successful adaptation to the rain forest certainly requires accurate ecological knowledge based on careful observations, but precise taxonomies also satisfy a basic human need for order, as Claude Lévi-Strauss (1966) points out.

## Rain Forest Affluence

Amazonian villagers clearly demonstrate some striking advantages of life in small-scale societies. They have developed an equitably balanced subsistence system. Men do the heavy work of garden clearing in seasonally concentrated bursts of effort, and women carry out the bulk of routine cultivation, harvesting, and food processing. Men, women, and children forage for wild plant food, insects, and small animals. Everyone may join large-scale fishing expeditions, but men provide most of the daily animal protein by hunting and fishing. Meat and fish are pooled and distributed to each household in the village to smooth out the variation in productivity between households. All these activities are individually directed, and everyone controls the necessary tools. There are no inequalities here.

This production system guarantees that each household can meet its nutritional needs with relatively moderate work loads, while maintaining a reasonable labor balance between the sexes. It also provides strong incentives for maintaining low population densities because, as densities increase, work loads quickly accelerate due to game depletion and the increasing distances that women must walk to their gardens. Work loads would also be increased dramatically if people needed to produce food to support the nonfood-producing specialists, which inevitably accompany increases in societal scale. Thus, an incentive to maintain the social equality is also the foundation of small-scale societies.

Several recent extensive investigations show that subsistence work loads in Amazonia are not significantly different from those reported earlier for Australian aborigines. In both cases, there is abundant leisure time. The figures presented in Table 3.3 indicate that on the average all food production needs can be met with just 2–3 hours of work a day. Men average about 3 hours and

TABLE 3.3   *Workloads in Amazonia, Daily Averages (in hours) for Men and Women*

| | Food Production* | | Other Work† | | Total Work | |
|---|---|---|---|---|---|---|
| | *Men* | *Women* | *Men* | *Women* | *Men* | *Women* |
| Machiguenga | 5.9 | 2.2 | 1.6 | 4.4 | 7.5 | 7.8 |
| Yanomamo | 2.8 | 2.4 | — | — | — | — |
| Mekranoti | 2.5 | 2.7 | 3.2 | 4.2‡ | 5.7 | 6.9 |
| Shipibo | 1.6 | 0.3 | 0.8 | 3.9 | 2.4 | 4.2 |
| Xavante | 3.9 | 3.2 | 1.1 | 5.2‡ | 5.0 | 8.4 |
| *Average* | 3.3 | 2.2 | 1.7 | 4.4 | 5.2 | 6.8 |

SOURCES: Machiguenga (Johnson 1975); Yamomamo (Lizot 1977); Mekranoti (Werner 1983); Shipibo (Bergman 1974); Xavante (Flowers 1983).
*Includes gardening, forest clearing, hunting, fishing, and gathering.
†Includes food preparation, miscellaneous household maintenance, and manufacturing.
‡Includes child care.

women about 2 hours. Total work loads, including everything that must be done around the house, require only 5–7 hours daily and would be unlikely to exceed 8 hours. This means that if the workday begins at 6 AM, with the equatorial sunrise, one can possibly spend the whole afternoon lounging in the hammock.

These data must be used with caution because they were collected by different researchers who did not always classify activities in the same way. Some researchers did not count child care as work. There is also the basic problem of the cross-cultural validity of the concept of "work." For example, should hunting, which is often an exciting and enjoyable activity, be considered work? Researchers also used different techniques for recording time expenditures. Roland Bergman (1974), for example, relied on self-reporting by the Shipibo, whereas Allen Johnson (1975) used a system of randomly scheduled spot checks of activities. All these studies were continued for several months and thus minimized seasonally induced biases. When taken together, they do show a consistent tendency, which is difficult to refute, to limit work loads to immediate household needs.

Johnson (1985) made a useful comparison of the work load of the Machiguenga, which is heavy by Amazonian standards, with how the modern urban French spend their time (considering women working both in and outside the home). He shows that, although both the Machiguenga and

the French get about 8 hours of sleep a night, the Machiguenga work about 2 hours less a day than the French, to satisfy their basic needs. The Machiguenga have fewer other demands on their time than the French and enjoy 5 hours more of free time a day, which they spend resting and visiting. Data such as these tend to confirm the idea of affluence in small-scale societies, and it lends credibility to the early reports from frustrated colonial plantation owners that Native Amazonians were "lazy" and hated to work. In fact they do work, but only until their basic needs are satisfied, and their society is structured so that no one works for an overlord.

It would be a mistake to view these systems as underdeveloped technological stages that will inevitably evolve into something better. These are already highly developed systems, which elegantly solve the problems posed for them. They would be difficult to improve upon, given their culturally defined objective of equitably meeting the physical needs of small communities.

## AMAZONIAN SOCIETY AND POLITICS

### Residence and Descent in Amazonia

Local settlements in Amazonia resemble the bands of Australian aborigines in that both are usually exogamous groups. Amazonian villages, however, average much larger populations than Australian

TABLE 3.4    *Residence and Descent in Amazonia*

| | | Descent | | |
|---|---|---|---|---|
| *Residence* | *Patrilineal* | *Matrilineal* | *Bilateral* | *Total* |
| Patrilocality | 6 | 0 | 10 | 16 |
| Matrilocality | 2 | 2 | 13 | 17 |
| Bilocality/Neolocality | 0 | 0 | 4 | 4 |
| *Total* | 8 | 2 | 27 | 37 |

SOURCE: Murdock (1981).

bands, and the villages are much more sedentary. There is also little tendency for even nominal **descent groups** to form in Amazonia, as George Murdock (1981) shows in a sample of thirty-seven Amazonian groups (Table 3.4). Using cross-cultural survey data of this sort is inherently difficult because they likely reflect the categories of different anthropologists and their particular theoretical perspectives, rather than the culturally significant emic categories of the native societies themselves. Nevertheless, such surveys provide a useful starting point for assessing broad patterns. Nearly three-fourths of these societies are listed as **bilateral**, indicating the absence of **unilineal descent groups**. This may be a reflection of the relative mobility of villages dependent on shifting cultivation and hunting, which means that individual landholdings are not inherited. Gardens are ordinarily only owned by those who clear and cultivate them until they are abandoned to forest. There are also no Australian-like sacred sites, and although clan groupings may have ritual functions, clans are very uncommon. Genealogical reckoning is shallow and even discouraged by frequent taboos on using the names of dead ancestors. The result is a social system that is highly egalitarian and encourages easy access to natural resources. Larger social groups are often named after rivers, but territories often overlap and generally seem much more flexible than in Australia. This flexibility is reflected in the dispersed locations of related languages and the recent prehistory of expansions and migrations.

Some anthropologists (especially Murdock 1949) argue that descent organization is determined by the residence pattern followed by newly married couples. This is because residential groupings create alignments of people who may share enough common interests to become cross-generational groups based on descent. Figure 3.8 illustrates the domestic groupings that are created by patrilocality and **matrilocality**; these two patterns create de facto patrilineages and **matrilineages**, respectively. However, if these alignments are not culturally named or otherwise operationally significant, then the society would best be described as bilateral, or non-unilineal. This is clearly the predominant situation in Amazonia.

Global cross-cultural surveys have shown statistical associations between residence and descent organization, indicating that patrilocality may lead to patrilineality and is compatible with bilaterality, or the absence of formal descent organization. Matrilocality may lead to matrilineality and is also compatible with bilaterality. **Bilocality** and **neolocality** are associated with bilaterality. Statistical association does not prove causality, however, and some argue that descent organization might precede residence patterns.

In Amazonia the emphasis on manioc gardening seems to encourage matrilocal residence patterns, in which a husband lives with or near his wife's family. This may be because mothers, daughters, and sisters often form cooperative work groups when gardening, processing manioc, or making ceramics. More than 80 percent (31) of a sample of thirty-seven Amazonian societies are either matrilocal (17) or show matrilocality as a temporary or alternative pattern (14). With temporary matrilocality, a newly married couple will remain near her mother until after their first child is born so that the new mother has help from her mother. Given the prevalence of matrilocality, it is interesting that matrilineality is rare in Amazonia. In part, this must be due to the relative infrequency of descent organization. The high fre-

FIGURE 3.8  *Residence patterns.*

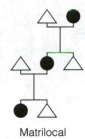

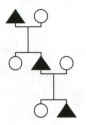

Matrilocal                    Patrilocal

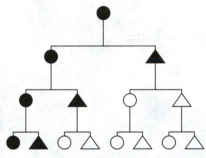

Matrilineal descent groups

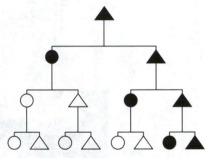

Patrilineal descent groups

quency of patrilocality may be related to the common pattern of revenge raiding in Amazonia, which makes it advantageous for closely related men to remain close together.

At least three major settlement types can be distinguished in Amazonia: (1) dispersed homesteads and isolated communal houses, (2) compact villages, and (3) linear villages. The dispersed homesteads and isolated communal houses, or *malocas*, would normally have from fifteen to sixty people living at a single site, whereas compact villages might contain several communal houses arranged in a circle, with more than one hundred people. Houses in linear villages are lined up facing a river and often contain over one hundred people. A major advantage of the communal *maloca*, or compact village, is that it facilitates the sharing of game between households because it is impossible to hide the results of a successful hunt.

The Ashaninka of the interfluvial forests in the Peruvian Amazon illustrate the dispersed homestead pattern. Ashaninka homesteads consist of a few individual houses (Figure 3.9), often only two and usually located in the same ridgetop clearing, each occupied by closely related, individual nu-

clear families (husband, wife, and children). A homestead, or household group, is either an *extended family* or the households are connected by sibling ties (Figure 3.10). Extended families are formed when married children reside near their parents, either matrilocally or patrilocally. Each

*descent group*  A social group based on genealogical connections to a common ancestor.
*bilateral*  Groups either formed by tracing any line to a common ancestor or no descent groups present.
*unilineal descent group*  Membership based on descent traced through a line of ancestors of one gender to a common ancestor.
*matrilocality*  Residence near the wife's kin, normally near her parents.
*matrilineage*  A lineage based on descent traced through a line of women to a common female ancestor and sharing a joint estate.
*bilocality*  Residence near either husband's or wife's kin, with no clear preference for either alternative; sometimes also called ambilocality.
*neolocality*  Residence established independently of the kin of either husband or wife.
*extended family*  A joint household based on a parent family and one or more families of its married children.

FIGURE 3.9 *Each Ashaninka household usually occupies a single palm leaf–thatched house constructed of posts and beams, with slats peeled from palm trunks as flooring: (a) construction details, and (b) a photograph of the house in the diagram.*

(a)

(b)

**household** is an independent domestic unit with its own kitchen and garden, but there is daily economic cooperation between the households, and fish and game would be pooled. Household groups might be an hour's walk from any neighboring groups, but such groups might periodically combine to socialize over manioc beer and to sing and dance. They might also combine to form raiding parties.

Because Native Amazonians typically spend most of the year at a permanent residence, they could be considered "domesticated" societies, as opposed to "Paleolithic" mobile foragers, according to the evolutionary theories proposed by

Peter Wilson (1989). Life in houses has the potential to change the relationship between people and between people and place. Mobile foragers are likely to be socially more open and less territorial than sedentary villagers, where the privacy of houses creates a potentially closed society where witchcraft and suspicion can thrive and social hierarchy can arise. The house itself can be treated metaphorically in the cosmology as the foundation for ancestor cults, tombs, and hierarchical descent groups. However, except for the chiefdoms along the Amazon itself, most Native Amazonians have not taken this route. The communal *maloca* certainly minimizes household privacy, and the re-

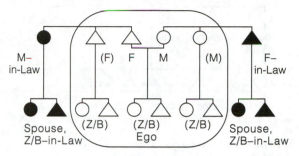

FIGURE 3.11  *Iroquois kinship terminology.*

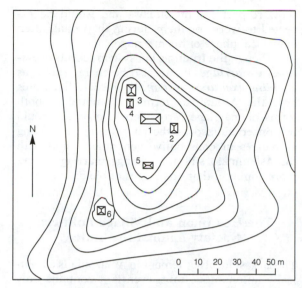

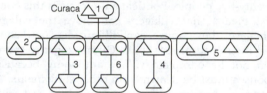

FIGURE 3.10  *Ground plan of Ashaninka extended family household group situated on a ridgetop clearing. Curaca is the Quechua (Inca) term for headman. House numbers correspond to the circled household members in the genealogical diagram.*

quirements of rain forest hunting and shifting horticulture make hierarchical organization distinctly unattractive. Native Amazonians clearly prefer low-density, small-scale societies and minimize the disadvantages of domesticated society.

## The Basics of Ashaninka–Iroquois Kinship

In small-scale societies, social interaction is shaped primarily by kinship categories. The Ashaninka basically recognize three categories of people: kin, formal trading partners, and strangers who are potential enemies. If friendly interaction is to take place, strangers are immediately placed in a kinship category and treated appropriately.

For example, men who wanted to request a favor from me would address me as "brother." When they wanted to show deference, they called me "father-in-law."

The Ashaninka kinship terminological system is of the **Iroquois** type, which is the most common system throughout Amazonia (Figure 3.11).* The distinctive feature of all Iroquois systems is that one's immediate kin are sorted into just two groups: (1) parents and siblings, or near parents and siblings, who are close family and thus not marriageable and (2) those who are potential in-laws and spouses. As is common in Australian aboriginal society, one marries someone who can be called a **cross-cousin**, and the parents of cross-cousins are called in-laws. **Parallel cousins**, the children of father's brother and mother's sister, are often treated as siblings, and their parents are treated like one's own parents.

*This system is called Iroquois because it was first described by Lewis Henry Morgan (1851) for the Iroquois tribe in New York State.

---

**household**  A social unit that shares domestic activities such as food production, cooking, eating, and sleeping, often under one roof, and usually based on the nuclear or extended family.

**Iroquois kinship**  A system of kinship terminology in which cross-cousins are distinguished from parallel cousins, who are sometimes called the same as siblings; often occurs together with cross-cousin marriage.

**cross-cousin**  A son or daughter of someone who is ego's mother's brother or father's sister.

**parallel cousins**  A son or daughter of someone who is ego's mother's sister or father's brother.

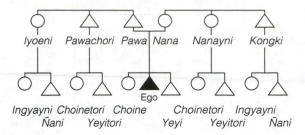

**FIGURE 3.12**  *Ashaninka kinship.*

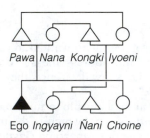

**FIGURE 3.13**  *Sibling-exchange marriages and cross-cousin marriages as reflected in Ashaninka kinship terminology.*

Figure 3.12 illustrates some of the actual terms that are used in one Ashaninka language. Father is called *Pawa*, and father's brother is called *Pawachori*, which might be translated as "step," or "potential," father. *Pawachori* might in fact marry one's mother if one's father died (a practice known as the ***levirate***), and his spouse would be called *Nanayni*, or mother's sister. Mother is *Nana*; brother and sister are *Yeyi* and *Choine*, respectively. Parallel cousins are *Yeyitori* and *Choinetori;* they resemble siblings and cannot be married.

When an Ashaninka man seeks a spouse, he must find someone whom he can call *Ingyayni*, or cross-cousin. The terms need not refer to actual biological relationships. Any unrelated woman might be placed in that category if everyone agrees, but this is an important decision because it has obvious sexual implications. A man's lover will almost certainly be called *Ingyayni*. The parents of someone called *Ingyayni* would be called *Kongki* and *Iyoeni* (in-laws). A husband would

show respect for his in-laws and would be expected to work for them during the initial, often matrilocal phase of his marriage.

Although the Iroquois kin system reflects ***cross-cousin marriage***, it can also be characterized as a ***sibling-exchange system***. Figure 3.13 illustrates how the Ashaninka terms accommodate both forms of marriage. Cross-cousin marriage could be conceptualized as the continuation of sibling exchanges in consecutive generations, and with the Ashaninka, sibling-exchange marriages were more common than marriages of biological cross-cousins.

## The Headman and Village Politics: Society Against the State

The largest local settlement in Amazonia is a politically autonomous unit, even if it contains only twenty-five people. Political autonomy in this context means that villagers can move the village whenever they choose, can kill intruders, and control their natural resources. Given exogamy, there can not be complete village autonomy because spouses must be drawn from other settlements. A leader, or ***headman***, is often recognized and may even be called a "chief" by outsiders, but his authority is extremely limited. A headman's responsibilities would increase with the size of the village, but he would normally be only a powerless coordinator who would formally announce what everyone had already decided to do, such as clean the village plaza or begin a group fishing expedition. Such a headman cannot force anyone to do anything against his or her will.

As the French ethnologist Pierre Clastres (1977) observed, an Amazon village is essentially a "society against the state" in that it is designed to prevent the concentration of political power that would allow anyone to gain control of the economy for his own benefit. In some respects, the headman is held hostage by the community. He is given a certain degree of privileged status, often indicated by polygyny, which is more likely to be practiced by a headman, but he often works harder than everyone else and is denied real power. Polygyny is not an exclusive prerogative of headmen and should not be construed as payment for the headman's leadership services; rather, it is man's oratorial skills further shows that he cannot use coercive violence. He must be verbally persuasive at setting intravillage conflicts; but if he fails as a peacemaker, the village simply splits. Society's refusal to grant political power to the headman may be the most critical limit on the size of villages in Amazonia. As we noted in the discussion of game depletion, disputes over meat distribution increase as villages become larger. When a headman's powers are limited to verbal persuasion, he may be unable to keep the peace in a community larger than 200 to 300 people.

Denying real political power to the headman could also indirectly contribute to keeping pressure on game resources below critical levels, because intravillage conflicts, whether due to meat-distribution inequities or sexual competition, can be related to the balance between game supply and village size. Janet Siskind (1973) argues that the underlying source of village conflict is competition between village men for access to women, which in the absence of a powerful headman can lead to village fragmentation. Sexual competition is intensified by the relative "scarcity" of women created by exogamy and by even a limited practice of polygyny. Throughout Amazonia, hunting success is equated with virility, and the successful hunter can support wives and lovers through gifts of meat. Successful hunters are also left with free time to engage in infidelities while less skilled hunters are in the forest. This leads to conflict, and villages split before potentially irreversible game depletion sets in (Figure 3.14). When game is really abundant, Siskind argues, individual differences in hunting abilities are less prominent, and men may turn to raiding other villages to capture women. Successful raiding would increase village size, raising hunting pressure, and result in village fragmentation, through the previous mechanism.

FIGURE 3.14  *A group of Yanomamo men armed with bows and arrows embarking on a peccary hunt. White-lipped peccary occur in large herds, and hunters can sometimes kill many at one time.*

a requirement of the job because extra wives are needed to help brew the extra manioc beer expected from a generous headman. Society is not paying for his services, but he can hold his position only as long as he serves the community. As Lévi-Strauss (1944) has argued, leadership in this system is its own reward, and only a few would take on the responsibility.

A good headman must be a good public speaker and especially generous, giving things away on request, but he is not distinguished by special dress or insignias of office. The importance of the head-

*levirate*  A cultural pattern in which a woman marries a brother of her deceased husband.
*cross-cousin marriage*  A culturally defined preference for marriage with someone who is called cross-cousin.
*sibling-exchange marriage*  A cultural pattern in which a brother and sister marry another brother and sister.
*headman*  A political leader who coordinates group activities and is a village spokesman but serves only with the consent of the community and has no coercive power.

## Yanomamo Warfare:
## Sociobiology Versus History

Just as the tranquillity of village life can be disturbed by internal conflict, small-scale society is characterized by chronic intervillage conflict because there is no overall political authority to enforce a peace. Such conflict is sometimes called "warfare," but this is a misleading label because intervillage conflicts are qualitatively different from the wars waged by states for political conquest and control of economic resources. In Amazonia, intervillage conflict is carried out for personal reasons—to capture wives, to gain individual prestige, or to avenge previous wrongs. The objective is not to conquer territory or to gain economic advantage, and such conflict is better characterized as raiding and/or *feuding*.

In the absence of any legal authority such as a police force, people must resort to self-help in the event of serious trouble. A single homicide can set off a chain of revenge killings, which can go on for years because there are few mechanisms for making peace. This is a situation of political *anarchy* in the sense of an absence of formal government, but it does not mean that total chaos reigns. There is great variability in the frequency and intensity of such conflict, but normally the loss of life is not great. Exogamy works to reduce the potential for conflict by creating in-law/kinship relationships between people in different villages. Formal trading partnerships and feasting can prepare the way for marriage ties. Everyday objects such as arrows may be traded on the basis of *deferred exchanges* in which the initial gift will not be reciprocated for several months or even years. In this way, a continuing relationship is maintained, and there is always an excuse for further visits.

Whatever its extent, even the possibility that such conflict might occur has consequences for the pattern of life in Amazonia. For example, villages may be located on easily defended ridgetops, or they may have stout log palisades built around them. There may also be pressures to maintain larger villages for defense. Where raiding is especially common, extensive "no-man's lands" may develop between hostile groups and can serve as de facto game reserves to replenish adjacent hunting territories.

The actual causes of intervillage conflict are just as complex as the multiple factors causing intravillage conflict and will probably never be fully understood. However, Amazonia has proven a fertile area for anthropological theorists interested in tribal "warfare." Because extensive tribal areas have remained beyond effective government control until very recently and various native groups have maintained their political autonomy long enough, anthropologists have been able to collect fresh material on conflict. Unfortunately, the attention this material has received has supported popular stereotypes of Native Amazonians as exotic subjects and as bloodthirsty, almost inhuman killers. It also raises questions about the "reality" of cultural facts and the social responsibility of anthropologists.

The Yanomamo Indians (also called Yanomami and Yanoama) of the Orinoco headwaters along the Brazil–Venezuela frontier were the largest Amazonian group to come under Euro-American influence in the last half of the twentieth century. With their vigorous culture and an estimated 21,000 people living in more than one hundred autonomous villages, they became a major focus for anthropological research beginning with the work of Napoleon Chagnon in 1964. They have been the subject of several books, films, and theoretical debates. For two decades, the Yanomamo have provided students with textbook examples of endemic tribal warfare, explained as either a response to environmental constraints by the cultural materialist perspective (Harris 1974, 1979) or in sociobiology terms, as an aspect of tribal politics that enhances the reproductive success of individual warriors (Chagnon 1979, 1983, 1988) (Figure 3.15).

Chagnon called early editions of his text *Yanomamo: The Fierce People*, declaring in his first edition "that is the most accurate single phrase that describes them" (1968a:1). He suggested that the entire culture fosters violent behavior, and he found that the recent history of the villages he studied were a succession of raids and counterraids. According to Chagnon, the ideal Yanomamo man is "sly, aggressive, and intimidating" (1968a:9). Up to 30 percent of adult men die violently (1988). Wife beating is common, and men goad one another into contests marked by escalat-

**FIGURE 3.15**
*Interpretations of Yanomamo feuding: (a) Yanomamo feuding as an adaptation to cultural environment (Chagnon 1968b); (b) Yanomamo feuding as an improved inclusive fitness (Chagnon 1979, 1988); (c) cultural materialist explanation of Yanomamo feuding (Harris 1984).*

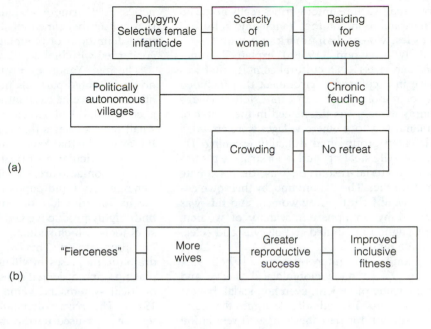

(a)

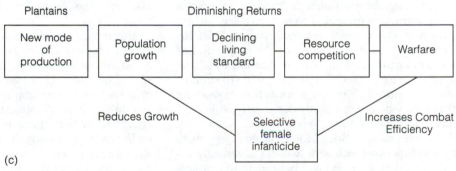

(b)

(c)

ing levels of violence from chest pounding, to side slapping, to club or machete fights. Women, who expect to be mistreated and are constantly in fear of abduction, are miserable and vindictive pawns of the men (1983). The general editors of the series in which the first edition appeared noted in their foreword that the Yanomamo reversed the conventional meanings of "good" and "desirable" by condoning "brutal, cruel, and treacherous behavior."

This is certainly not a flattering picture in our view, and it has been severely criticized, but Chagnon has defended his basic characterization of Yanomamo culture and the scientific merit of his emphasis on Yanomamo violence. In later editions

of his text (1977, 1983), he has attempted to "balance the image of fierceness" by stressing the basic humanity of the Yanomamo, and in 1992 he abandoned the subtitle *The Fierce People*. Chagnon also

*feud*  Chronic intergroup conflict that exists between communities in the absence of centralized political authority. May involve a cycle of revenge raids and killing that is difficult to break.
*anarchy*  The absence of centralized political authority and formal government institutions.
*deferred exchange*  A form of trade in which a gift is reciprocated with a return gift at a later time, thus providing an excuse for maintaining contacts and establishing alliances between potentially hostile groups.

observes that warfare among tribes really needs no special explanation and that Yanomamo culture is perhaps less violent than American culture.

Initially, Chagnon (1968b) explained Yanomamo "fierceness" as a cultural complex that was adaptive in a cultural environment that included hostile neighbors. It was an expression of village autonomy, which was intensified in the center of Yanomamo territory where villages were crowded and defeated groups had difficulty escaping. He found that wife stealing, and not a struggle for territory or material resources, was the proximate cause of conflict. The Yanomamo, by their own admission, were fighting over women, and this was aggravated by an apparent scarcity of women, which Chagnon attributed to polygyny and selective female infanticide.

Chagnon's later interpretations (1979, 1983, 1988) are based on sociobiological theory and stress the value of violent, even homicidal, behavior to Yanomamo individuals. He argues that gaining a reputation for fierceness by swift retaliation against aggressors makes a Yanomamo man a more attractive mate and makes it easier for him to prevent others from stealing his wives. Thus, his individual *inclusive fitness*, or the proportion of his genetic material that will be contributed to succeeding generations, will be increased. To support this contention, Chagnon presents figures showing that men who are culturally designated as "killers" have statistically more wives and children than those who do not. Sociobiological theory predicts that competitive behavior will be genetically selected for when the genetic benefits to individuals are greater than the costs. Therefore, Yanomamo men are simply following the genetically favored goals of their culture, although they may not be consciously attempting to improve their inclusive fitness.

Critics of Chagnon's interpretations have attacked the applicability of sociobiology to culture and have presented alternative historical and ecological explanations for Yanomamo violence. The weakest link in the sociobiological interpretation is that it is difficult to demonstrate any specific genetic basis for any complex cultural behavior such as revenge killing. Genes only determine the broadest parameters of human behavior. Culture can vary and change independently of human genetics. Furthermore, abundant evidence indicates that culturally defined kinship categories and cultural definitions of parentage are only marginally concerned with biology (Sahlins 1976).

The high Yanomamo rate of violent death has no documented parallels in Amazonia and stands out as an extreme case; although as shown earlier, a certain level of violence is to be expected in small-scale societies that reject political authority. It may well be that Yanomamo violence was amplified by particular historical factors. For example, some Yanomamo areas appear to have been experiencing very rapid population growth due to the recent introduction of bananas and plantains, both highly productive Old World food crops, and steel tools, which suddenly elevated their gardening productivity. This might have resulted in dramatic increases in village size and sedentism, placing unprecedented stresses on both the sociopolitical system and game resources (Colchester 1984). The recent depopulation of surrounding territories caused by the intrusion of Europeans also gave the Yanomamo empty land to quickly fill up.

Europeans began to have a more direct impact in Yanomamo territory after about 1950, and this could also have elevated Yanomamo violence. The spread of epidemic diseases such as influenza and measles into Yanomamo territory has caused devastating mortality rates. Chagnon's (1974) own figures show that approximately 60 percent of all male deaths, including those attributed to sorcery, were due to illness. Because the Yanomamo attribute all deaths to malevolent human intention and are obligated to seek revenge, any increase in mortality would be likely to escalate revenge killings. The simultaneous introduction of axes, machetes, and shotguns has also made all conflicts more violent and provided further motives for raiding. Clearly, there are important historical explanations of violence in Amazonian societies that cannot be ignored (Davis 1976, Ross 1984).

## Yanomamo Warfare: The Cultural Materialist Perspective

The most vocal foe of Chagnon's genetic interpretations of Yanomamo warfare has been cultural materialist Marvin Harris (1971b), who considers war in small-scale societies to be a cultural adaptation that functions to balance population and resources. Harris's basic argument is that the high standard of living of small-scale societies depends on female infanticide, warfare, and a **male supremacy complex**. As he originally formulated his theory of tribal warfare in 1971, Harris followed the earlier lead of cultural ecologist A. P. Vayda (1968) that warfare in small-scale societies regulated population directly through war deaths and because dispersal of defeated groups lowered densities. In 1974 Harris incorporated the suggestions of William Divale that warfare encouraged people to selectively raise boys to become warriors, while systematically neglecting and even killing girls. This increased hostilities by imbalancing the sex ratio and making wives scarce, but it had the adaptive advantage of limiting population growth more directly than by killing boys. Drawing on cross-cultural survey data showing unbalanced sex ratios correlated with warfare, broadly defined as intergroup homicide, Divale and Harris (1976) argued that **selective female infanticide** and war were related to a series of "male supremacy" traits in small-scale societies, including patrilocality, polygyny, inequitable sexual division of labor, and male domination of headmanship, shamanism, and ritual subordination of women. However, the presumed male centeredness of some of these traits may be a product of male-centered ethnography as discussed in Chapter 2.

Referring specifically to the Yanomamo, Harris unfortunately suggested that they had already exceeded the carrying capacity of the forest and were suffering from protein deficiencies. He thought that women would recognize that it would be in their best interests to kill their newborn daughters because boys would grow up to be hunters, and they would ultimately have more meat to eat. As further data on actual rates of protein consumption began to confirm that deficiencies were, in fact, rare among any Amazonian groups, including the Yanomamo (Gross 1975, Lizot 1977), Harris revised his theory. He replaced the carrying-capacity argument with the view that **diminishing returns** in protein production was the critical mechanism to call up female infanticide and warfare (Harris 1984). He also endorsed the possibility that the Yanomamo were undergoing rapid population growth because of the recent adoption of plantains.

Harris's theory suffers from the deficiencies of most functionalist arguments. That is, the functions identified for warfare may be perfectly reasonable, but it is difficult to prove that they actually work in the way proposed. It also does not explain why warfare was selected for when other traits might "function" equally well, and it does not explain the widespread variation in homicide rates, even in Amazonia. The Yanomamo do appear to be an extreme case. It is also important to note that diminishing returns, conflict, and village fissioning do not necessarily mean violence and warfare. Villages can split with hard feelings but no loss of life.

One can accept Harris's general argument, acknowledging many of the potential functions of hostilities, while questioning the specifics. For example, selective female infanticide may not be the principal means of population regulation, and warfare may not always occur at high rates. What is significant is that the threat of conflict always exists, and the threat itself, rather than its realization, can contribute to the environmental regulating functions attributed to warfare. This argument closely parallels Harris's own argument that actual protein deficiency need not occur, as long as there are diminishing returns to hunting efforts and the implied threat of a shortfall.

Regardless of which theoretical perspective regarding Yanomamo conflict one chooses to en-

---

*inclusive fitness*  A sociobiology concept referring to the degree to which individuals are successful in passing on a higher proportion of their genes to succeeding generations.

*male supremacy complex*  A functionally interrelated series of presumably male-centered traits, including patrilocality, polygyny, inequitable sexual division of labor, male domination of headmanship and shamanism, and the ritual subordination of women.

*selective female infanticide*  According to cultural materialist theory, a cultural pattern in which infant girls are selectively killed or neglected in favor of boys who will become hunters and warriors.

*diminishing returns*  A decline in output for each increase in effort that accompanies an attempt to increase total production beyond a certain point. Overhunting often produces diminishing returns.

(a)                                                                          (b)

FIGURE 3.16   *Although the Yanomamo do engage in raiding, much of their daily life is leisured: (a) people resting inside the communal* shabono; *and (b) women grooming.*

dorse, "fierceness" is only one aspect of Yanomamo culture (Figure 3.16). Other observers have presented ethnographic portrayals of the Yanomamo that are so strikingly different that they are powerful reminders that anthropological writing is not pure observation or pure science (Ramos 1987). For example, Jacques Lizot (1985) focuses on the romantic adventures that fill the daily life of the Yanomamo, and Bruce Albert (1985) explores their intellectual life, symbolic systems, and related beliefs about illness.

## AMAZONIAN COSMOLOGY

The Amazonian equivalent of the Australian Dreamtime is found in a rich body of myth, beliefs,

and ritual practices concerned with the meaning of life issues subsumed under the anthropological concept of cosmology. The issues dealt with are the universal human problems of creation, life and death, male and female, and the relationship between nature and culture.

## The World of Spirits

In small-scale societies, there are no priests, no full-time professionals to formalize the belief system, and nothing codified in writing. There is considerable fluidity in individual beliefs, but there are underlying uniformities. Certainly there is religion, with the unifying theme that nineteenth-century British anthropologist, Edward Tylor (1871) called **animism**, a belief in spirits. The spirit world is animated with human, animal, and plant souls and a wide variety of anthropomorphic beings with superhuman characteristics. These beings can intrude directly on humans, bring misfortune, and control natural resources. **Shamans** are the religious specialists, who by training and self-selection, are particularly adept at communicating with the spirit world.

Although outsiders might consider the religious beliefs of Native Amazonians to be an irrational and irrelevant concern with the supernatural, closer analysis shows that these beliefs are part of a highly elaborated, logical, and consistent philosophy of life, which is much more real than our split between natural and supernatural implies. An understanding of some of the details of these beliefs helps make sense of many aspects of daily life in Amazonia. Spirit beings are normally invisible, but they can assume visible form and freely transform from human to animal form and back again. In Ashaninka thought, any unusual animal or otherwise unexplained event may be attributed to a spirit (Weiss 1975). The Ashaninka recognize and name scores of specific spiritual entities; some include the souls of their own ancestors, which are ordinarily considered harmless. Malevolent spirit beings may appear as blue butterflies, tapirs, jaguars, hairy red humanoid dwarfs, or hoof-footed human impersonators. They are found in the deep forest, and they frequent whirlpools and rocky cliffs. Human contact with or even sight of malevolent spirit beings may cause illness or death.

### Mythic Jaguars and Anacondas: A Structuralist View

Peter Roe (1982) sifted through some 800 **myths** and bits of ethnographic detail, drawn from 105 cultures, to construct a simplified descriptive model, a "metacosmology," as a common framework for understanding the diverse beliefs of different cultural groups throughout Amazonia (Figure 3.17). His model is abstract and not necessarily applicable to any particular group. It codifies what is otherwise an inherently dynamic and fluid system, and many of the relationships shown would not be consciously recognized by individual believers.

Roe (1982) builds on the earlier insights of Lévi-Strauss (1955), who has written several books in which he demonstrates that many South American myths are concerned with the opposition between nature and culture (1969, 1973, 1978). Lévi-Strauss assumes that myths function to help people deal with life's basic contradictions by restating them in different ways. He derives the meaning of myth from the structural relationships between major elements of the myth, as illustrated in his famous reduction of the Oedipus myth to an algebraic formula (see Figure 3.18). He views the Oedipus myth as an encoded restatement of the logical dilemma in the fact that the first people must have had a single origin, implying original incest that is universally tabooed. The contradiction is resolved through the story because it is shown to be part of a larger whole, the opposed parts belong to each other.

Roe (1982) uses a biogenetic structuralism; this departs from Lévi-Strauss's conventional structuralism that derives meanings from the relationship between symbols, while the symbols themselves are virtually meaningless. Roe finds universal meanings in the **natural symbols**, which are the key actors in the Amazonian myths that he analyzes. Roe employs the logical structures (Table 3.5) and the algebraic formulas of Lévi-Strauss (Table 3.6), but he assumes that people pick particular natural symbols, such as the jaguar and the sun, as characters in their myths because they are drawing analogies between them and particular human concerns. Particular features of natural symbols make them obvious signs or metaphors

---

**animism**  A belief in spirits, which occupy plants, animals, and people. Spirits are supernatural and normally invisible but may transform into different forms. Considered by cultural evolutionists to be the simplist and earliest form of religion.

**shaman**  A part-time religious specialist with special skills for dealing with the spirit world. May help his community by healing, by divination, and by directing supernatural powers against enemies.

**myth**  A narrative that recounts the activities of supernatural beings. Myths are often acted out in ritual and encapsulate a culture's cosmology and cosmogony and provide justification for culturally prescribed behavior.

**natural symbols**  Inherent qualities of specific plants and animals used as signs or metaphors for issues that concern people.

FIGURE 3.17 *Schematic rendering of the Roe (1982) model.*

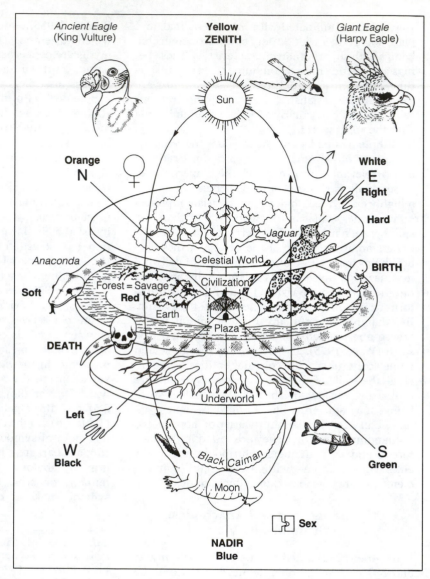

FIGURE 3.18
*Lévi-Strauss's structural interpretation of myth.*

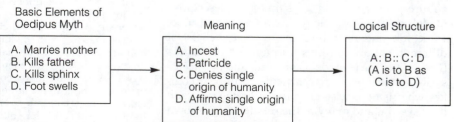

Incest is to patricide as denying the single origin of humanity
is to affirming it; they are both logical opposites.

TABLE 3.5  *Male–Female Oppositions in Amazonian Cosmology*

| Male | Female |
| --- | --- |
| Hard | Soft |
| Virtue | Corruption |
| Order | Chaos |
| Aggressiveness | Passivity |
| Life | Death |
| Marriage rules | Incest, promiscuity |
| Culture | Nature |
| Right hand | Left hand |
| Red, yellow | Blue, green |
| White | Black |
| Sun | Moon |
| Closed | Open |
| Land | Water |
| Dry | Wet |

SOURCES: Riviere (1969) and Roe (1982).

for something else. For example, a great snake, the phallic anaconda, may represent a male figure, whereas a hollow gourd may represent a womb.

Amazonian myths consistently focus on the cosmic issues of reproduction and fertility, the relationship between the sexes, the origin of culture, illness, and death. The dominant characters are drawn from especially powerful natural symbols found in the rain forest, such as the anaconda, jaguar, tapir, caiman, and harpy eagle (see the box "An Anaconda Myth"). To introduce novelty, Amazonian storytellers can explore the classic themes using a complex series of character transformations based on logical chains of association that may depend on specific knowledge of the animal in question. For example, the anaconda, caiman, tapir, king vulture, and frog may all be associated as feminine symbols. Hollow bee hives may replace gourds as a feminine symbol, while the giant anteater may replace the anaconda as a masculine symbol because he introduces a long, phallic tongue into the hive.

Roe's (1982) basic model (see Figure 3.17) depicts a three-tiered cosmos of earth, celestial world, and underworld, centered on the communal house and joined together by a world tree rooted in the underworld. Some Amazonian groups recognize more than three layers to the cosmos, but three is the minimum needed to explain the daily cycle of sun and moon. The house is surrounded by a cleared plaza that represents culture in opposition to the surrounding forest that is savage nature inhabited by demons. The underworld is a source of death and disease and has many feminine associations, whereas the celestial world is dominated by male symbols. The underworld is represented in the night sky as the Milky Way, which is also associated with the rainbow, and the multicolored anaconda.

The dominant symbol in the cosmology is the world tree represented by the kapok or silk cotton tree and its relatives. This tree has predominately feminine associations because it is soft and hollow and filled with water. It is considered to be a source of life and culture and may appear in myths in varied form, sometimes as a dragon tree, a fish woman, a tree with fish and frogs inside, and so on.

TABLE 3.6  *Structural Equations and Associations in Amazonian Cosmology*

| Chains of Association | Structural Equations |
| --- | --- |
| Sun = bird = jaguar | Sun : moon :: life : death |
| Moon = fish = caiman (dragon) | Up : good things :: down : bad things |
| Yellow jaguar = master of animals | Wasps : dragon :: birds : yellow jaguar |
| Black jaguar = master of fish | |
| Master of fish = dolphin = Forest ogre = dragon | |
| World tree = dragon tree = fish woman | |
| Rainbow = Milky Way = anaconda | |
| Woman = poison = death | |
| Menstrual blood = fish poison = death = night | |

SOURCE: Roe (1982).

## An Anaconda Myth

The following myth was recounted to archaeologist Peter Roe by my Shipibo assistant Manuel Rengifo in 1971. It shows that the anaconda can be a source of noxious pests and illustrates how spirit beings take on human form and can influence hunter success (from Roe 1982:52).

One day a man who was a very bad hunter set out once more to pursue the game of the forest with his blowgun. He had had no luck, as usual, until he approached the shores of a lake. There he noticed a man wearing a decorated *cushma* [woven cotton robe]. The man greeted him and asked him if he would like to accompany him so that the strange man could show the hunter his "real *cushma*." The hunter agreed, and they set off, only to finally encounter a huge coiled "Mother of All Boas," the anaconda. This, the man informed the hunter, was his real *cushma*. The hunter was very frightened, but the man reassured him and said that he would show him how to be a good hunter. The anaconda man first blew through his blowgun but out came only a horde of stinging, poisonous animals like mosquitos, black biting flies, stingrays, scorpions, and spiders. When the stranger blew again, hosts of deadly vipers as well as all the other evil snakes of the jungle poured forth from the tip of his blowgun. He then handed his blowgun to the hunter, whom he instructed to do as he had done. The hunter blew through the instrument and immediately killed a monkey. From that day on the hunter, thanks to his friendship with the anaconda man, always enjoyed success as a great hunter.

Two primary opposing associations center on the dragon versus the jaguar. The dragon, usually represented by the caiman, is a sinister underworld being. The jaguar has both male and female associations and is an ambiguous figure, mediating between oppositions. The most striking natural features of real jaguars is that they are active day and night; they are at home in the water and on land, in trees and on the ground; and they are dangerous to people. It is not surprising that powerful shamans may transform into jaguars.

A central feature in Amazonian cosmology is the theme that women in animal form were originally the possessors of culture, which was wrested from them by men who humanized them and took control of culture in the form of fire and cultivated plants. Sometimes this mythic event is celebrated in rituals involving sacred flutes, which are assumed to have once belonged to women but are now kept hidden from them by men. Sexual antagonism permeates the entire cosmology, which seems to be primarily a male construction and seems to relegate women to a negative role, as in their association with sickness and death. The principal actors in the myths and their spirit representatives in the forest and rivers are invariably oversexed demons seeking to seduce people, especially vulnerable women.

Roe (1982) suggests that much of this sexual antagonism in the cosmology can be attributed to the sharply drawn division of labor in Amazonian society, which often keeps men and women apart. This division is so pervasive in daily life that some speak of a dual organization into male and female societies. Men and women often eat apart, and there may be men's houses for sleeping or craft work, yet each "society" is completely dependent on the other. The vivid sexual imagery in the myth can also be attributed to the fact that sex is one of the only activities that men and women engage in together and is a major preoccupation. Men also seem to be jealous of women's role in reproduction, and in the myths masculine characters sometimes assume important creative roles. This jealousy has its counterpart in the special vulnerability of women to assaults by demons when their biological role is especially evident at puberty, menstruation, and pregnancy. During these times, women may be secluded and may observe specific food taboos.

Gerardo Reichel-Dolmatoff (1971, 1976), who analyzed the cosmology of the Tukano of the Colombian Amazon, has called attention to the similarity between Tukano cosmology and basic ecological principles. He notes that the Tukano believe in a circuit of solar sexual energy that fertilizes the earth and flows through both people and animals. They assume that a balance must be maintained between a finite supply of fish and game and the human population that depends on them. People threaten that balance through overhunting and uncontrolled sexual behavior that leads to overpopulation. Sexual repression through observing the rules of exogamy and basic restraint helps maintain the energy cycle. The game animals are protected by a spirit-being, the **Keeper of the Game**, who is identified with the jaguar in Roe's model but can exist in many forms. The Keeper of the Game regulates the supply of animals and may release them to be hunted at the request of the shaman who communicates with him while in hallucinogenic drug-induced trance or with the aid of tobacco smoke. This explains the obsessive concern of the Keeper of the Game with the sex life of humans. He may withhold game or send sickness if he feels that people are being irresponsible. Hunting itself is replete with sexual imagery. Hunting is literally seen as making love to the animals and in preparation requires sexual abstinence and observance of other specific requirements.

There is no doubt a connection between the belief systems of Native Amazonians, as seen in their cosmologies, and sexual behavior, food taboos,

### TABLE 3.7 *Food Taboos and Animal Size\**

| Taboos | Animal Size | | Total |
| --- | --- | --- | --- |
| | Large† | Small | |
| Strong‡ | 20 | 13 | 33 |
| Weak | 10 | 26 | 36 |
| *Total* | 30 | 39 | 69 |

SOURCE: McDonald (1977).
\*Food taboos practiced by eleven Amazonian groups, representing sixty-nine different cases in which a specific cultural group restricted their food use of a particular game animal. Each case is sorted by size of animal and strength of restriction (or taboo).
†Large animals = 35 lb (16 kg) and over.
‡Strong taboos = 10 percent or greater reduction in potential demand based on length of the restriction and segment of the population to which it applies.

and hunting patterns—all of which can have important adaptive significance. Examining the distribution of dietary restrictions in sixty-nine Amazonian societies, David McDonald (1977) has shown, for example, that there is a tendency for the strongest food taboos to be applied to larger animals, which would be more vulnerable to overhunting (see Table 3.7). Evidence such as this and Reichel-Dolmatoff's ecological argument show the mutual compatibility of structuralist and materialist interpretations. Both interpretations lend meaning and understanding to the otherwise bewildering complexity of religious belief and practice in small-scale societies, but neither interpretation is completely satisfactory in itself.

## SUMMARY

Amazonia provides a background for discussing a variety of theories on the causes and consequences of sedentary village life based on domesticated plants. Sedentary living, certainly a great divide, undermines many of the mechanisms that promote social equality and stability among mobile foragers. Major issues for villagers are conflict resolution, limiting individual acquisition of political

---

**keeper of the game**    A spirit personality believed to control the supply of game animals and who punishes human behavior that shows disrespect for animals or threatens their viability.

power, and maintaining access to resources as density increases. Ecological factors, in combination with cultural preferences for wild game and a desire to keep work loads low, help keep villages small and population densities low.

We also examined several important cultural ecological issues in Amazonia, such as the contrasts between the river and the forest environments, the success of shifting cultivation, and the controversy over the cultural importance of animal protein. We also discussed the conflicting sociobiology and cultural materialist interpretations of infanticide and raiding in Amazonia. The social functions of village headman and shaman was presented as a basis for later comparison with the chief and priest in large-scale cultures.

The Ashaninka–Iroquois kinship system was examined in some detail to show how kin terms are used to define social relationships and are related to marriage and family patterns.

The structuralist interpretations pioneered by Claude Lévi-Strauss were presented using examples of Amazonian myth and symbolism and related ritual practices, which express an underlying pan-Amazonian cosmology. This cosmology illustrates symbolic patterns that are virtually universal, but it also distinctly reflects tribal culture in the rain forest environment and provides an important point of comparison and contrast with the cosmology underlying the Inca empire to be described in Chapter 7. In functional terms, Amazonian cosmology works to resolve important logical contradictions while contributing to the basic adaptation of the culture.

## STUDY QUESTIONS

1. Why might protein be considered a population-control factor in Amazonia? What other factors also influence village size?

2. How is shifting cultivation adapted to the special conditions of the tropical rain forest environment?

3. Describe the kinship terminology system of the Ashaninka and show how it is related to marriage practices.

4. Discuss the sociobiological, historical, and materialist interpretations of Yanomamo conflict.

5. In what ways do the religious beliefs and practices of Native Amazonians relate to social and ecological conditions?

## SUGGESTED READING

CHAGNON, NAPOLEON. 1992. *The Yanomamo*, 4th ed. New York: Holt, Rinehart & Winston. Well-rounded ethnography, but focused on the issue of conflict.

HAMES, RAYMOND B., AND WILLIAM T. VICKERS (eds.). 1983. *Adaptive Responses of Native Amazonians*. New York: Academic Press. A collection of detailed cultural ecological studies of different Amazonian groups.

REICHEL-DOLMATOFF, GERARDO. 1971. *Amazonian Cosmos: The Sexual and Religious Symbolism of the Tukano Indians*. Chicago: University of Chicago Press. Very detailed analysis of an Amazonian belief system covering ritual and myth and relating it to rain forest adaptation.

# 4

# AFRICAN CATTLE PEOPLES: TRIBAL PASTORALISTS

The Nuer, Karimojong, Maasai, and other Nilotic-speaking peoples in East Africa have fascinated casual European observers and anthropologists for more than a century. The pride and arrogant self-confidence of these peoples were so striking, and their warriors were so brave and numerous, that they commanded the immediate respect of the first European colonialists. The Maasai were viewed with special awe because their warriors made a contest out of killing lions with spears and wore their manes as a badge of courage. Even more impressive was the fact that all these peoples could support themselves almost entirely from their cattle in an environment that Europeans considered virtually useless. Furthermore, cattle dominated all aspects of their culture, to a degree that outsiders thought irrationally obsessive. However, these East Africans, who may respectfully be called "cattle peoples," have maintained themselves up to the present day through many cycles of drought and epidemics, and they have retained much of their autonomy despite many government-imposed changes.

Since the end of the Ice Age, animals were domesticated in many parts of the world. This opened up new possibilities for people while creating many new problems. In the absence of animal domesticates, the density of farming peoples was limited by the availability of fish and game, as was discussed in Chapter 3. Animals such as cattle are a valuable source of protein and can serve as a mobile food surplus and a reproducible source of wealth. Cattle can also be readily stolen and must be defended. They can make social equality more difficult to maintain, and they may be handled in ways that alter the relations between men and women and the structure of domestic groups.

Ethnographic material illustrates how African herders manage their animals for subsistence needs in an unpredictable environment. Cattle are so important in these Cattle Complex cultures that they provide ideal case material to illustrate functionalist interconnections and for making comparisons between the explanatory power of idealist, values interpretations of cultural patterns and materialist, cultural ecological interpretations. Cattle cultures are also useful for introducing such important anthropological concepts as segmentary lineage systems, bride-price, age–class warrior systems, animal sacrifice, and acephalous politics. In societies such as these, where status is so closely tied to ownership of animals and success in raiding, the potential for both social inequality and environmental deterioration through overgrazing is significant. A major issue we will explore is the extent to which poverty and desertification, which

FIGURE 4.1 *Map of savanna regions of Africa showing Nilotic-speaking East African cattle cultures discussed in the text.*

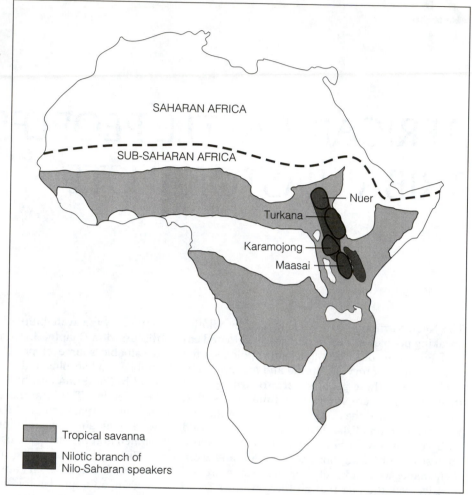

FIGURE 4.1 *Map of savanna regions of Africa showing Nilotic-speaking East African cattle cultures discussed in the text.*

are certainly problems in contemporary East Africa, are intrinsic features of traditional pastoral cultures. Arguments on both sides of this issue will be presented.

## EAST AFRICAN ENVIRONMENT AND PREHISTORY

### The Tropical Savanna Ecosystem

Anthropologists often group the "cattle peoples" of East Africa into a single culture area stretching from the Sudan to South Africa, but they are a diverse group of cultures organized at different scales of social complexity and are united only by their common interest in cattle. Speakers of three major language phyla may be included: Afro-Asiatic, Niger-Kordofanian, and Nilo-Saharan (Ruhlen 1987). Afro-Asiatic speakers include the Cushitic languages of Ethiopia, Somalia, and northeast Kenya, which are related to Semitic languages such as ancient Egyptian, Hebrew, and Arabic. As pastoralists, Cushitic peoples often occupy the drier regions of East Africa and may depend more on camels than cattle. Niger-Kordofanian languages include the Bantu speakers, who cover much of sub-Saharan Africa. Cattle are often important for Bantu peoples, but many

**FIGURE 4.2**   *The East African savanna ecosystem is a complex product of the interaction of human activity and natural conditions.*

are also village farmers. The **Nilo-Saharan** speakers occupy a wide area of north central Africa in the upper Nile region and in the Sahara. The most famous cattle cultures, such as the Nuer, Dinka, Karamojong, Turkana, and Maasai, all belong to the **Nilotic** branch of Nilo-Saharan. These peoples occupy the swampy plains along the White Nile in southern Sudan, the high savannas of the Rift Valley system, and the south and east of Lake Victoria to the Serengeti plains of Tanzania. The Nilotic peoples will be the primary focus of this chapter.

East Africa, in general, is part of the tropical *savanna* ecosystem, but it is topographically a highly diverse region (Figure 4.1). Much of the area occupied by the Nilotic pastoralists in Kenya and Tanzania straddles the equator along a zone lying 3000–7000 ft (914–2134 meters [m]) in elevation and consisting of arid plains and wetter, grassy uplands. Today this region includes some of the most famous game parks in the world, such as the Amboseli and Serengeti National parks in

Kenya and Tanzania, respectively. It is also home to many small-scale cultural groups involved in a wide range of subsistence economies.

The tropical savanna ecosystem is a grassland zone, which may have a few trees and shrubs, separating tropical rain forest zones from arid deserts (Figure 4.2). Fire and grazing play an important role in maintaining and extending savannas, but they result primarily from climate, soil, and topographic conditions, especially a pronounced wet

---

*Nilo-Saharan language*   A very large phylum of related African-language families, whose speakers are spread throughout North and East Africa.

*Nilotic language*   A group of related Nilo-Saharan languages, whose speakers live in East Africa. Sometimes Nilotic refers to the very tall physical type of Nilotic speakers.

*savanna*   An ecosystem dominated by grasses, often with scattered trees or shrubs, and maintained by frequent fires, sparse rainfall, and poor soils.

and dry season. In striking contrast to the diversity and stability of tropical rain forests, savannas are dominated by very few species, and they exist in an unstable, dynamic equilibrium. Drought cycles or changes in grazing pressure caused by disease can rapidly change the inventory of plant species and shift the balance between trees and grasses. Biological productivity is high in relation to biomass, but plants are short-lived in comparison with rain forest species. Nutrients are turned over, or cycled, much more rapidly in the savanna. There are proportionately more leaves and grass and less wood in the savanna, and the foliage is more palatable because it contains fewer resins and other chemical defenses. The advantage for consumer species is that there is more food available than in the forest. Extreme seasonal variations in rainfall create periodic pulses of primary production resulting in brief food surpluses that are best exploited by nomadic grazers (Bourliere and Hadley 1983).

## The Prehistoric Origins of African Pastoralism

East Africa is well known for the earliest hominid *australopithecine* remains, which were found in Olduvai Gorge, along Lake Turkana, and in the Omo region of Ethiopia, all dating roughly in the period 1.5–5 million years ago (mya) (Table 4.1). The Lower Paleolithic, known in Africa as the Early Stone Age, began some 2 mya and is identified with heavy Acheulean stone chopping tools used by early hominids. The Middle Paleolithic, or Middle Stone Age, began approximately 200,000 BP (before the present) and is recognized by finer, more controlled, stone toolmaking techniques and more tool types, including points, adzes, and blades, presumably made by *archaic Homo sapiens*. Some of these tools may have been hafted, and a limited working of wood and skin probably occurred. Fire was presumably used, pigments were collected, and intentional burials may have

TABLE 4.1   *Prehistory of East Africa*

| 1000–2000 BP | Expansion of Bantu-speaking, iron-using village farmers |
|---|---|
| **Pastoral Neolithic in Kenya (2500–5200 BP)** | |
| 2500 | Southern Nilotic speakers from southern Sudan enter highlands as mixed farmer/pastoralists with livestock, millet, and sorghum |
| 3300 | Modern climate and vegetation established |
| | Savanna pastoral Neolithic in highlands |
| 4500 | Domestic camel reaches Horn of Africa from southern Arabia |
| 3000–5600 | Climate drying after wet phase; tsetse bush in highlands inhibits pastorists |
| | Scattered foragers in highlands |
| 5200 | Savanna pastoral Neolithic introduced in lowlands by Cushitic speakers bringing domestic livestock and ceramics |
| **Saharan Pastoralism (4000–8000 BP)** | |
| 4000–5400 | Domestic livestock and ceramics in central Sudan |
| 7000–8000 | Local domestication of cattle in Sahara |
| | Domestic sheep and goats reach North Africa from Near East |
| ***Homo Sapiens* Foragers (40,000–200,000 BP)** | |
| 40,000 | Late Stone Age cultures; microlith tools, personal adornments |
| 200,000 | Middle Stone Age; core tools, flake points, scrapers |
| **Protohumans (200,000 BP–2 mya)** | |
| 2 mya | *Homo erectus;* Acheulean stone tools |
| **Early Hominids (1.5–5 mya)** | |
| 2–3 mya | Earliest stone toolmaking, Oldowan |
| 4.5 mya | Australopithecines |

SOURCES: Ambrose (1984), Clark (1984), Phillipson (1985), Smith (1984), and Wendorf and Schild (1984).

occurred, but there is no real indication that symbols were in use; thus, these people must have been *precultural*.

While there have been many attempts to draw parallels between modern African foragers and Early and Middle Stone Age peoples, Lewis Binford (1981, 1984) has persuasively argued that there is no evidence for the use of base camps, food sharing, and the hunting of medium and large game prior to the Late Stone Age, which began a mere 40,000 BP. Fully human culture in southern Africa was signaled by the widespread appearance during the Late Stone Age of personal adornments, rock art, and burials, together with the supporting technology that was distinguished by glue-hafted microlithic tools made from thin, stone-blade fragments. Regular hunting of larger game and plant collecting are clearly in evidence during this time as well (Deacon 1984). Rock art is securely dated from 26,000 BP in southern Africa. These findings make foraging lifestyles seem more human, while still granting them a very respectable antiquity.

African food-producing systems based on *pastoralism* and farming probably arose some 7000–8000 BP. Developments in Africa roughly paralleled with the Middle Eastern Neolithic; in both areas, developments were due to a combination of still poorly understood factors involving both resource constraints and new opportunities. In European archaeological tradition, the term *Neolithic* has been applied to peoples using domesticated plants and animals, pottery, and polished stone tools. In Africa the term *Neolithic* refers only to food production because other Neolithic elements are not always combined in the same way. For example, pottery may have been independently developed in North Africa as settlement became more sedentary some 2000 years before domestication.

Domestication of animals involves a process of mutual changes in the behavior of both people and animals, which offers certain benefits to both. It should not be thought of as a remarkable discovery or invention because the young of wild animals can be easily tamed and kept under human control as adults. The question is, Why did people decide to raise animals, and which animals did they choose? Cattle, sheep, and goats are ideally suited for domestication for two reasons: First, as herd

animals they can be easily controlled. Second, because these ruminants have multichambered stomachs, they can digest cellulose, which humans cannot, that converts to animal protein, which humans can digest. Animal domestication may have been undertaken as a gradual process of increasing control over game animals to make up for the shortfall in animal protein that occurred under increasing human pressure as the balance between population and resources intensified after the Ice Age.

As cultural control, animal domestication involves any systematic human intervention that makes the animals more available for human exploitation. The process can move from seasonal culling of wild herds to increase their growth rates, to corralling and maintaining herds year round, to selective breeding (Hecker 1982). Such activities were probably underway with sheep, goats, and cattle in the Middle East by 9000 BP and quickly resulted in physical changes in the animals that could be recognized as domesticates. Archaeological evidence of domestication includes such things as reduction in size of the animal; specific changes in morphology, such as horn shape in goats; and an increase in the skeletal remains of young animals slaughtered as a result of selective culling (Stein 1986).

Pastoralism, as a full-time specialization in domestic animals, has probably been practiced in Africa as long as anywhere in the world (Figure 4.3). Sheep and goats were probably brought into North Africa from the Middle East, whereas wild cattle may have been locally domesticated by 7000 BP or earlier (Smith 1984). The Zebu, or hump-backed cattle, apparently reached Africa from India about 4000 BP. Because there are no wild ancestors of cattle, sheep, or goats known from sub-Saharan Africa, it is assumed that they were introduced to East Africa from elsewhere as domesticates.

The spread of pastoralism depended on envi-

---

***australopithecine*** A bipedal, humanlike (hominid) ape, some of which made simple stone tools and were presumably human ancestors.

***archaic homo sapiens*** The earliest, physically modern human, appearing perhaps 50,000–200,000 BP and showing little evidence of language and culture.

***pastoralism*** A way of life based on raising livestock.

FIGURE 4.3 *Hump-backed Zebu cattle may have been in Africa for 4000 years. Samburu Maasai warriors preparing to slaughter a Zebu ox at a wedding.*

ronmental conditions. Over the past 10,000 years, small changes in rainfall have made the Sahara environment fluctuate abruptly between conditions favoring or discouraging pastoralism. The first favorable period began about 7000 BP and presented an open niche for pastoralist expansion. After pastoralism became established as a basic way of life in the Sahara, people apparently carried it south into appropriate environments in sub-Saharan Africa as they became available. The primary barrier to the spread of pastoralism in sub-Saharan Africa was the **tsetse fly** (*Glossina* sp.), which transmits **trypanosomiasis**, a form of sleeping sickness often fatal to cattle. The tsetse fly flourishes in forested and brushy vegetation and effectively precludes cattle from large areas of Africa.

Pastoralism first became established in East Africa in the central Sudan by 5400 BP and then in the arid zone of northeast Kenya by 5200 BP where it was presumably introduced by early Cushitic-speaking peoples from Ethiopia. The higher savannas of East Africa were apparently not occupied by pastoralists, because of tsetse flies, until changes in climate and vegetation made conditions more favorable by 3300 BP. Shortly thereafter, by 2500 BP Nilotic-speaking ancestors of the modern Maasai and Turkana peoples arrived (Ambrose 1984). African pastoralism is a very long established human adaptation and can reasonably be considered a basic component of the savanna ecosystem.

## MAKING A LIVING WITH CATTLE

### Pastoral Subsistence: Meat, Blood, and Milk

Pastoralism in East Africa, like the savanna itself, exists along a rainfall continuum from wet to dry, showing greater dependence on animals and greater nomadism as rainfall declines. In areas where the average annual rainfall exceeds approximately 25 inches (650 millimeters [mm]) per year, people are likely to be village farmers, with livestock raising carried on as a minor subsistence activity. Where rainfall drops lower than 25 inches, pastoralism becomes increasingly attractive, nomadism increases, and people become more and more dependent on their animals, while farming becomes supplemental. In extreme cases, as with some Maasai groups, people may subsist virtually entirely on animal products, whereas others may exchange animal products for grains from their settled neighbors.

The great advantage of domestic livestock is that they convert otherwise inedible plant material into meat, blood, and milk for human consumption, in areas where farming would at best be a marginal activity. The use of domestic animals also permits dramatic increases in human population density over that supported in the same environment by foraging. East Africa is world famous for

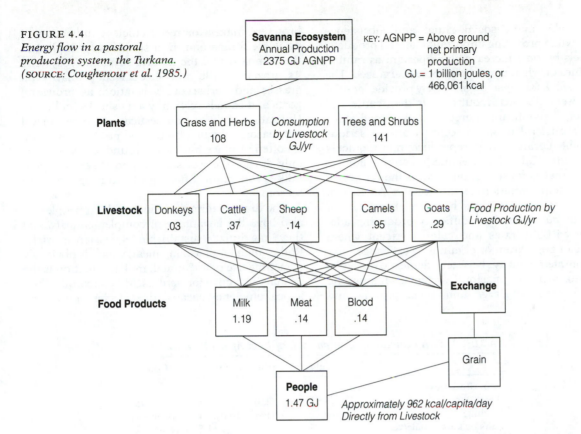

**FIGURE 4.4**
*Energy flow in a pastoral production system, the Turkana. (SOURCE: Coughenour et al. 1985.)*

Savanna Ecosystem
Annual Production
2375 GJ AGNPP

KEY: AGNPP = Above ground net primary production
GJ = 1 billion joules, or 466,061 kcal

**Plants**

Grass and Herbs 108

*Consumption by Livestock GJ/yr*

Trees and Shrubs 141

**Livestock**

Donkeys .03

Cattle .37

Sheep .14

Camels .95

Goats .29

*Food Production by Livestock GJ/yr*

**Food Products**

Milk 1.19

Meat .14

Blood .14

**Exchange**

Grain

**People** 1.47 GJ

*Approximately 962 kcal/capita/day Directly from Livestock*

its game parks and can support up to 10,000 kilograms (kg) (22,076 lb) of wildlife biomass per square kilometer (km²) with some fifty species of large grazing mammals. The Hadza of Tanzania, who forage in this hunter's paradise, take only a small fraction of the game and maintain themselves at typically low population densities of just .4 person/km². Their Maasai pastoral neighbors support 2 to 6 people/km². Pastoralism permits precise control over reproduction and harvesting of the animals and leads to large increases in food production per unit of land. However, successful pastoralism is a complex and delicately balanced system, which poses many difficult problems and requires major adjustments in the organization of society and labor.

Among the important problems that a herder must solve are which animals to use, what food products to produce, how many animals are needed, what age and sex categories to maintain in the herds, when to slaughter, when to time breeding, feeding and watering the herds, and protection of the herds from disease and predators. Hunters let nature take care of most of these matters, but herders find that their lives must be constantly modified to take care of their animals.

Most East African pastoralists are considered, and consider themselves, to be cattle peoples because of the dominant cultural role that cattle are assigned, but they actually depend on several functionally distinct domesticates including cattle, camels, sheep, goats, and donkeys (see Figure 4.4).

*tsetse fly* A blood-sucking African fly that lives in brushy areas. Its bite can spread trypanosomiasis.
*trypanosomiasis* Sleeping sickness, a disease caused by a parasitic protozoan in blood and spread by biting flies. Can be fatal to both humans and livestock.

Cattle play major social, ritual, and subsistence roles while providing important material products. Camels become increasingly important as rainfall declines or when pastures become overgrazed. The small stock (sheep and goats) may provide more of a household's meat requirements than cattle and can be a significant source of milk. Small stock also are useful to speed recovery after a serious drought because they reproduce more quickly than cattle (Table 4.2). Reliance on animal domesticates makes for a situation that is the reverse of the protein-limitation factor seen in Amazonia. East African pastoralists have an abundance of protein but have some difficulty producing adequate carbohydrates and calories except where they can grow grain or obtain it by exchange.

Complementarity between domesticates is a striking aspect of pastoral systems. Maintaining mixed herds of large and small grazers and browsers makes for more efficient utilization of available forage and, in a simple way, duplicates the complexity of the natural savanna ecosystem. As grazers, cattle and sheep feed primarily on grasses and herbaceous vegetation; as browsers, goats and camels rely on woody shrubs and trees. Utilization of diverse domesticates also helps level out seasonal fluctuation in food production. Camels often produce milk year-around, cows produce only during the wet season, and sheep and goat milk production often peaks during the dry season.

The diverse animal products, which people eat, also have the advantage of complementarity, and they maximize sustainable subsistence yield. Rather than emphasizing meat, which is obviously a onetime use of an animal, milk production is the primary objective for herders. Milk maximizes biological efficiency because the calories in milk can

TABLE 4.2    *A Functional Comparison of East Africa Livestock\**

|  | Camels | Cattle | Sheep | Goats |
|---|---|---|---|---|
| **Vital Statistics** | | | | |
| Weight/kg | 453 | 250 | 45 | 45 |
| Feeding | Browser | Grazer | Grazer | Browser |
| Calfs or kids/female/year | .5 | .7 | 1.5 | 2 |
| Herd growth, %/year | 1.5 | 3.4 | 18 | 33 |
| **Subsistence Production/Animal** | | | | |
| Milk   (kg/day) | 4 | 2 | .01 | .03 |
| Blood   (Ls/year) | 60 | 6 | — | — |
| Carcass/(kg) | 226 | 125 | 10–25 | 10–25 |
| **Production/Herd of 100 Animals/Year** | | | | |
| Milk | | | | |
|    kcal† | 17,374 | 5497 | 2340 | 1847 |
|    Protein (kg) | 918 | 245 | 131 | 91 |
| Blood | | | | |
|    kcal† | 163 | 108 | — | — |
|    Protein (kg) | 38 | 27 | — | — |
| Meat | | | | |
|    kcal† | 664 | 4536 | 2017 | 608 |
|    Protein (kg) | 142 | 278 | 50 | 65 |
| Fat (camel hump) | | | | |
|    kcal† | 527 | — | — | — |

SOURCE: Dahl and Hjort (1976).
*These figures are estimates; actual figures can vary widely. Annual production for herd reflects average age and sex distributions and natural mortality as well as intentional slaughtering. Milk production represents the human share after the needs of calfs and kids are satisfied.
†In thousands.

be produced four times more efficiently in energy cost than the calories in meat. Blood and milk can be produced without harm to the animal and complement each other in that blood is a major source of iron and can be drawn from animals that are not producing milk. This is especially important when cow milk production drops during the dry season. Cattle are not as efficient as goats at meat production, so cattle are rarely slaughtered except ritually, although they will be eaten when they die naturally. Subsistence pastoralists extract the maximum food value from their animals for direct consumption; in this way, their herd-management strategy differs radically from that of market-oriented ranchers (Dyson-Hudson and Dyson-Hudson 1969).

## Irrational Overgrazers or Sustainable Adaptation?

East African pastoralists have been seriously misunderstood by both development planners and conservationists who widely accuse pastoralists of irrationality. They think that pastoralists raise far more poor-quality animals than they need for mere subsistence because of culturally determined motives of prestige and social value that are thought to overemphasize numbers. Pastoralists are accused of overstocking their ranges and degrading their environments, thus contributing to *desertification*. This is sometimes seen as a classic *tragedy of the commons* situation, because grazing lands are communal property and an individual herder would have no incentive to hold down the size of his herd. Planners often recommend that it would be better for pastoralists to raise beef for the market as private ranchers. Actually, little firm evidence supports the view that traditional pastoralism is inherently prone to overstocking, whereas abundant evidence indicates that outside development pressures do contribute to overgrazing (Homewood and Rodgers 1984).

Whether or not African pastoralists are self-conscious conservationists, their traditional subsistence practices contain important limiting factors that reduce the likelihood of overgrazing. First, the subsistence needs of a household determines herd size (Tables 4.3 and 4.4), and the labor supply and the declining feeding efficiencies that arise as herds grow set its upper limits. Second, in the absence of trucks, pumps, and deep wells, the frequency that animals must be watered and the distance they can travel between grazing areas and water severely limit grazing during the dry season.

African cattle under traditional nomadic pastoralism do appear to be of lower quality when compared with U.S. beef and dairy cattle (Table 4.5). African animals convert less of their forage into meat for human consumption and produce less body weight because the frequent droughts cause animals to channel more of their energy into biological maintenance than into meat production. They must adjust their metabolisms to cycles of periodic thirst and starvation followed by recovery (Coughenour et al. 1985, Western and Finch 1986). Low production is thus a long-range adaptation to severe environmental constraints. U.S. cattle achieve their high biological efficiencies thanks to a significant fossil fuel–energy subsidy, which is not counted in these calculations but which is required to produce and distribute tractors, farm chemicals, feed, and agricultural research.

Comparative analysis of subsistence herders requires several types of data and concepts, which are outlined in Figures 4.4 and 4.5. Calculating the carrying capacity for herd animals and the number of people that could be supported by pastoralism is a deceptively simple theoretical problem. One need only know the amount of plant biomass that animals can consume in a given area each year on a sustained basis and the amount of human food that the herds can produce. Range-management specialists usually assume that 50 percent of the annual new plant growth (AGNPP) can safely be consumed by herbivores without degrading the grazing resources. Carrying capacity is rated in TLUs (tropical livestock units of 250 kg [552 lb] of biomass)/km² year and varies according to the AGNPP, which in turn depends on rainfall. It is assumed that each TLU will consume approximately 3105 kg (6854 lb) of dry forage annually.

---

**desertification**   The process by which a savanna is converted into arid desert by overgrazing and/or climate change.
**tragedy of the commons**   Destruction of a communally held resource, such as grazing lands, by unchecked individuals seeking their own self-interest.

In practice, none of these figures can be precise, and the formula is not so easily applied. This explains why there is so much professional disagreement over whether pastoralists are managing their herds rationally and maintaining the quality of their pastures. The primary problem is that AGNPP, the most critical value, varies dramatically in time and space in the pastoral zones. Successful pastoralists must plan for long-term, minimum carrying-capacity values, taking into account the frequency of droughts. The actual productivity of human food will depend on the particular mix of animals in use and the specific pattern of herd management.

Traditional herding is a labor-intensive activity.

Individual herds may be subdivided to better reflect the abilities and requirements of animals according to condition. Herds are moved seasonally to take advantage of the best pasture, and in some areas, a regular altitudinal *transhumance* may be practiced. Pastoralists manage their herds to maximize the number of female animals to keep milk yields and growth potential high. Given the natural mortality rates of cattle and their reproductive biology, a herd is unlikely to contain more than about 30 percent fertile cows, and only half of these will be producing milk.

The actual number of animals needed to satisfy household nutritional requirements can be estimated in theory, based on calculations of the annual production of a standard herd; however, there are many variables, and published estimates range from thirty to ninety or more head of cattle per household. Different researchers may use different estimates of household size and daily per-capita minimum caloric requirements. The widely accepted 2300 minimum daily kilocalorie (kcal) figure is probably too high because it is based on Euro-American standards. East African cattle herders are smaller people and should have correspondingly lower energy needs. Use of the high-calorie figure must inflate minimum herd requirements. Although the production of milk per ani-

**TABLE 4.3**  *Minimum Estimated Herd Size to Support One Household**

|  | Camels | Cattle | Sheep | Goats |
|---|---|---|---|---|
| kcal | 28 | 64 | 116 | 205 |
| Protein | 11 | 28 | 64 | 74 |

SOURCE: Dahl and Hjort (1976).

*Reference household assumes six people, including husband and wife, boy age 18 years, girl age 15 years, and two small children ages 3 and 8 years. Total daily nutritional needs of 318 g of protein and 13,800 kcal.

**TABLE 4.4**  *Average Reported Household Herd Size and Composition**

|  | Camels | Cattle | Sheep | Goats | Totals |
|---|---|---|---|---|---|
| **Rendille** | | | | | |
| TLU/household† | 12 | 11 | 40 | 61 | 31 |
| kcal (%) | 19 | 16 | 11 | 15 | 61 |
| Protein (%) | 50 | 33 | 23 | 32 | 138 |
| **Karimojong** | | | | | |
| TLU/household | — | 33 | — | — | 16 |
| kcal (%) | — | 34 | — | — | 34 |
| Protein (%) | — | — | — | — | |
| **Turkana** | | | | | |
| TLU/household | — | — | — | — | 30 |
| kcal (%) | 43 | 14 | 17 | | 74 |
| Protein (%) | — | — | — | — | |

SOURCES: Rendille (Field 1985); Karimojong (Little and Morren 1976); Turkana (Coughenour et al. 1985).

*All based on average family of 8 people, counted as 6.5 adult equivalents.

†TLU = tropical livestock unit.

**TABLE 4.5** *Biological Efficiency of African Nomadic Subsistence Cattle in Comparison with U.S. Cattle\**

|  | Ecological Efficiency | Production/ Biomass |
|---|---|---|
| African Nomadic | .9 | .2 |
| U.S. Beef | 5.5 | .78–1.1 |
| U.S. Dairy | 17.0 | .8–2.6 |

SOURCE: Coughenour et al. (1985).

\*Ecological efficiency = production/energy consumed by animal. U.S. dairy production refers only to milk.

Basic Formulas:

$$CC = (AGNP/.5)/C$$
$$P = CC/R$$

Carrying-Capacity Variables:

Where $CC$ = Carrying capacity, the number of animals in TLU that can be supported/km²/year on a sustained basis

$AGNPP$ = Above-ground net primary productivity in kilograms of DM (dry plant matter)/ km²/year (new plant biomass produced each year)

$DM$ = 19 mJ/kg, or 4500 kcal/kg

$TLU$ = Tropical livestock units, 250 kg of animal biomass

$C$ = kg of DM consumed/TLU/year

$R$ = TLU required for human subsistence/ person/year

$P$ = Number of people supported/km²/year

**FIGURE 4.5** *Environmental limits on African pastoralists.*

mal under pastoral nomadism is lower than on European dairy farms, pastoral milk is more concentrated and its nutritional value is 30 percent higher than European milk. Given the archaeological record of pastoralism in East Africa and the incredible resilience of the system under the impact of colonial invasion and recent forces for change, it seems that traditional herders are operating rationally. Their herding strategies contribute to the long-range survival of their families in a very difficult environment.

## The Cattle Complex

American anthropologist Melville Herskovits (1926) was apparently the first to refer to the East African cattle area and to describe the **Cattle Complex** as an irrational culture value on cattle for nonutilitarian purposes. According to Herskovits, Cattle Complex peoples used cattle more for social and ritual purposes than for subsistence. They were treated as wealth objects and sources of prestige. People rarely ate cattle, instead they exchanged cattle at marriage, used them to settle disputes, and sacrificed them on ritual occasions. Besides these noneconomical uses, people seemed to have an exaggerated and emotional personal attachment to their animals. When range-management professionals later found that pastoral cattle were underweight and less productive than their counterparts in the American West, it is not surprising that the pastoralists were accused of overgrazing and blamed for desertification.

British anthropologist E. E. Evans-Pritchard conducted one of the first and most detailed studies of a cattle culture among the Nuer of the Sudan between 1930 and 1936. This study (Evans-Pritchard 1940), which became a classic in ethnographic literature, showed the social, ritual, and emotional value of cattle but also demonstrated their utilitarian function.

Evans-Pritchard (1940) called the Nuer "preeminently pastoral." He reported that they considered themselves herdsmen above all else and only grudgingly resorted to farming because they didn't have enough animals. They looked contemptuously at people without cattle, as he found on his arrival in Nuerland, when the Nuer refused to carry his baggage. He found that they had "the herdsman's outlook on the world" and considered cattle "their dearest possessions." Cattle were or-

**transhumance** Seasonal movement of livestock herds to maintain optimum grazing conditions; often involves altitudinal shifts.
**Cattle Complex** A cultural system in which cattle are important in subsistence, social and political organization, and religion. Sometimes described as an irrational cultural emphasis on nonutilitarian values.

namented and named and their genealogies remembered. Boys received an "ox-name" at birth. Men were addressed using names that referred to their favorite oxen, and women were named after the cows they milked. They raided their neighbors for cows. They always talked about their animals:

*I used sometimes to despair that I never discussed anything with the young men but livestock and girls, and even the subject of girls led inevitably to that of cattle. Start on whatever subject I would, and approach it from whatever angle, we would soon be speaking of cows and oxen, heifers and steers. . . .* (Evans-Pritchard 1940:18–19)

For Evans-Pritchard, this "pastoral mentality" took on the appearance of an "over-emphasis," a "hypertrophy of a single interest." As further indication of Nuer obsession with cattle, he pointed to the "linguistic profusion" of cattle terminology. He found 10 terms for describing cows of one solid color and hundreds of possible permutations of terms based on combinations of white with various patterns and associations with natural objects. Further, Nuer terminological distinctions are based on horn shape, ear cropping, and age and sex categories. In all, the Nuer had thousands of ways of describing cattle and composed poetry and songs using their names. A. B. C. Ocholla-Ayayo (1979) has listed 125 terms applied by the Luo, Nilotic neighbors of the Nuer, to cattle internal and external anatomy, covering bones and internal organs in great detail (Figure 4.6).

Evans-Pritchard (1940) recognized that this extreme interest in cattle had a utilitarian basis. He noted that the Nuers' flat, clay-soiled, seasonally flooded environment was deficient in such basic raw materials as stone and wood and was a difficult area to grow crops, but it provided excellent pasturage. The Nuer therefore lavished seemingly extravagant care on their animals, such that the cattle enjoyed a "gentle, indolent, sluggish life" (1940:36). He described the virtually symbiotic relationship between the Nuer and their cattle, in which each depended on the other. The Nuer extract an impressive array of material resources from cattle. Milk is the primary product, and it may be consumed fresh, sour, or processed as cheese. Blood is drawn from veins in the neck and is boiled or allowed to coagulate and roasted in a block. An animal would ordinarily only be slaughtered for ritual purposes, but then it would be butchered and the parts immediately distributed. Dung is a critical fuel for cooking, and dung fires help drive off biting insects. Dung is also used as a construction plaster, and it finds medical and cosmetic uses. Cattle urine is used in cheese making and tanning, whereas skin and bones find many uses in the manufacture of various artifacts such as containers and ornaments. Without cattle and their products, life would be very difficult in Nuerland.

## EAST AFRICAN SOCIAL ORGANIZATION AND IDEOLOGY

### Nuer Society: Bride-Wealth and Ghost Marriage

Apart from their obvious utilitarian value, the Nuer told Evans-Pritchard (1951) that the "supreme value" of cattle came from their use as **bride-wealth**, which was the basic requirement for establishing a fully legitimate household. I avoid the use of the term *legal* to refer to marriage or household in this concept because legal implies formal law, supported by courts and jails that did not exist in Nuer society. Nuer marriage involves rights over cattle and women and is basically an agreement between the families of the bride and groom. It requires a lengthy series of negotiations, public and private ceremonies, and transactions, which are not complete until children are born to the couple. Because Nuer marriage is so complex and involves so many different rights, it is an ideal case from which to examine the meaning of marriage, family, and household as cross-cultural concepts.

The process of Nuer marriage is initiated by preliminary talks between the two families in order to specify the animals that can be transferred. The bride's family can demand cattle for six levels of claimants by order or precedence: the bride's grandparents or their ghosts, the bride's parents, her uncles, her aunts, the spirits of her father and mother, and her brothers and half-brothers, as shown in Figure 4.7. Ideally, some forty head of cattle can ultimately be transferred to the bride's father, and he is then obligated to distribute them to each of the claimants on his side of the family

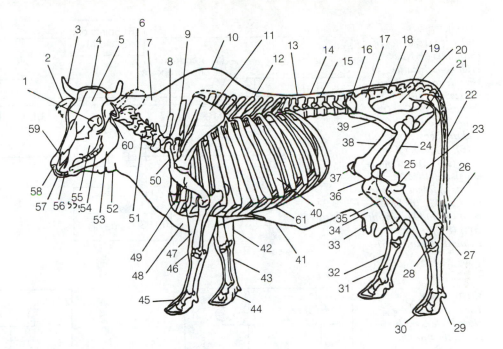

FIGURE 4.6
*Anatomical terms applied to cattle by the Nilotic-speaking Luo (Ocholla-Ayayo 1979).*

1. Chokndorro
2. It
3. Tuṅg
4. Tatwich
5. Sihanga or patwich
6. It (omwot it)
7. Ṅgut
8. Chok ṅgutmachiek
9. Chok ṅgutmabor
10. Kuom
11. Opal
12. Ariedi lihumblu
13. Giko nyakmeru
14. Dierṅgech
15. Giko nyakmeru
16. Wichok oguro
17. Chokoguro
18. Choktie ip
19. Oguch dhiang
20. Ringsarara
21. Dhokisonga

22. Ip
23. Ring em maoko
24. Odiere machien
25. Fuond odire gi ogwala
26. Orengo
27. Fuond ogwala
28. Nyapoṅg tielo
29. Odofuny tielo
30. Okak tielo
31. Chok oluko
32. Ogwala
33. Thuno
34. Dagthuno
35. Chok em
36. Fundodiere
37. Nyapoṅg odiere
38. Odiere
39. Chokbam
40. Ṅgede
41. Pinyich
42. Bat korachich

43. Ogwala
44. Ofunjtielo or ṅguttielo
45. Witielo
46. Choṅg
47. Bat korjachien
48. Agoko
49. Chokbat mar oriere
50. Chokrangach (collar bone)
51. Choke ṅgudi
52. Jund dhiaṅg
53. Choklem mapiny
54. Nyiponge
55. Choklem mamalo
56. Lep
57. Leke mamon
58. Um
59. Chok um
60. Tiend it
61. Chokagoko

and to the bride's mother's family. In a typical distribution, twenty animals go to the bride's immediate family, with her father getting the largest share, and ten animals go to each set of uncles and aunts (Figure 4.8). Each category of claimant receives a specific number and type of animal. For example, the bride's full brother can receive three cows, two oxen, and a cow with its calf, seven animals in all.

In the negotiations, animals are promised by name to specific people.

The preliminary negotiations are formalized in

**bride-wealth** Goods, often livestock, that are transferred from the family of the groom to the family of the bride in order to legitimize the marriage and the children of the couple.

**FIGURE 4.7**
*Order of precedence of claimants on Nuer bride-wealth cattle: (1) Grandparents or their ghosts; (2) father (F) and mother (M); (3) father's brother(s) (FB) and mother's brother(s) (MB); (4) father's sister(s) (FZ) and mother's sister(s) (MZ); (5) spirits of father (F) and mother (M); (6) brother(s) (B) and half-brother(s) (FS). (SOURCE: Evans-Pritchard 1951.)*

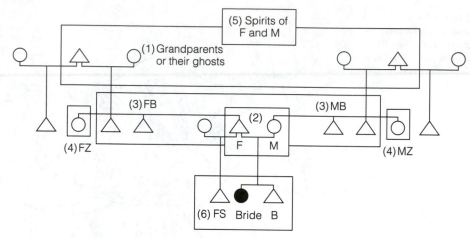

**FIGURE 4.8**
*The distribution of Nuer bride-wealth cattle; the numbers in parentheses indicate the number of cattle received. (SOURCE: Evans-Pritchard 1951.)*

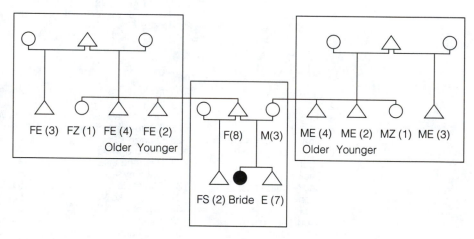

the betrothal ceremony, which is the first public marriage ritual. Betrothal is marked by the sacrifice and distribution of an ox by the bride's father to the groom's family. The first installment of bride-wealth cattle is also transferred to the bride's father. Several weeks later at the wedding ceremony, negotiations are finalized, and more cattle transferred, but the transfer and the marriage are not considered official until a later consummation ceremony with its series of rituals. After this, the groom's family can demand compensation in the event of his wife's infidelity, but the couple does not establish a joint homestead until after their first child is weaned. Until then, the wife remains

in her parent's homestead, and her husband is a visitor who must maintain a ritual distance from his in-laws.

Once completed, the "ordinary" Nuer marriage creates a simple nuclear family household based on husband, wife, and child (Figure 4.9). Such a household is headed by a man, as husband, and draws its subsistence from his herd and from the wife's garden. The homestead contains a byre (a cattle barn) and its kraal (corral), cooking hearth, and a small sleeping house for the wife. In a polygynous marriage, each wife would have her own house. Several such homesteads belonging to a group of brothers or a father and his sons might

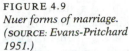

FIGURE 4.9
*Nuer forms of marriage.*
(SOURCE: *Evans-Pritchard 1951.*)

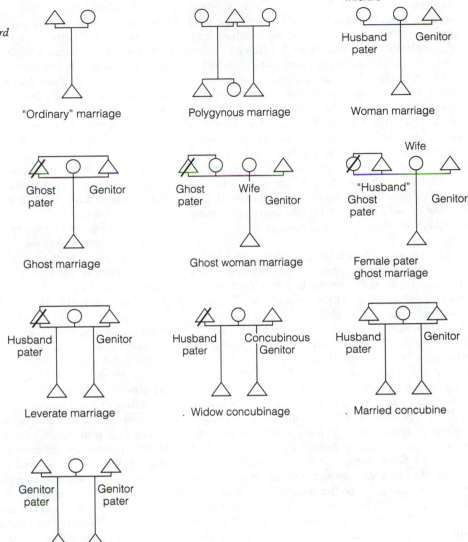

cluster together around a common kraal as a composite homestead.

Many other domestic arrangements are possible (see Figure 4.9). For example, a woman, especially if she is infertile, might become a "husband" and have children by marrying another woman who then takes a male lover who becomes the biological father, or **genitor**, of the female husband's children. In this case, the female husband is the legitimate father, or **pater**, of the children, as well as the husband, and her family transfers cattle as

*genitor*  The biological father of a child.
*pater*  The culturally legitimate, or sociological, father of a child.

bride-wealth to the family of her wife. In a "ghost marriage," someone marries in the name of a dead sibling or other relative who had died without having completed a marriage and who thus left no descendents. In all such cases, cattle are transferred to the bride's family, while the deceased, male or female, becomes the pater; the stand-in relative lives with the wife as "husband" and genitor but has no rights over the children. Levirate marriage, when a man marries his deceased brother's wife, resembles ghost marriage, except that the dead husband was already married and the bride-wealth had been transferred. The original, now dead, husband is still considered the husband, and the brother who stands in his place has less control over his wife than the "husband" of a ghost marriage.

Women have considerable freedom in Nuer domestic arrangements, even though all marriages are officially arranged by the families involved. Instead of remarrying, widows sometimes live with lovers, who may father children by them. However, the original, legitimate family, established by bride-wealth, remains intact, and her children will all belong to her original husband, who is always their pater. Evans-Pritchard (1951) called such arrangements "widow concubinage." In some cases, a woman may move in with a lover while she is still married. She will be a "married concubine," and again her children will all belong to her husband because of the bride-wealth.

For the Nuer, the concept of paternity, or "belonging to," is a far more important matter than biological parentage or the details of domestic arrangements. Paternity is established by bride-wealth cattle, thereby providing one with claims to cattle that may, in turn, be used for bride-wealth. Marriage also links one to a set of ancestor ghosts and spirits that must be ritually acknowledged. Maintaining such claims for individuals is more important than whether a "father" is living or dead, male or female, or with whom your mother cohabits.

The use of bride-wealth, such as cattle, to formalize a marriage has so many ramifications throughout the culture that some anthropologists recognize societies based on bride-wealth and those based on **bride-service** as distinctive societal types (Collier 1988). These two marriage systems create different culturally defined systems of domestic relations organizing the inequalities of age and sex in different ways. Young men in bride-service societies, such as in aboriginal Australia and Amazonia, do not incur long-term debt obligations when they marry and need only hunt or provide other services to their in-laws during the early stages in their marriage. In bride-wealth societies, the exchange of bride-wealth valuables between male heads of families sharply defines the social statuses of husband, wife, parent, and child. The social importance of bride-wealth cattle gives a man more of a vested interest in the marriages of his brothers and sisters than he might have in a bride-service society.

Bride-wealth has sometimes been called bride-price by anthropologists who may even refer to wife markets, but these terms are better avoided because they imply purchase and incorrectly suggest that women are chattels in cattle societies. With the Nuer, this is certainly *not* the case because women have the final say over who they marry. It would be foolish for a father to force his daughter into a marriage against her wishes because bride-wealth cattle would have to be returned in the event of a divorce before children were born to the marriage. There are, however, inequalities of age and gender built into the system: The marriage transaction gives a man, or a woman acting as a man, the right to establish paternity, to claim cattle as an indemnity for adultery, and to claim cattle when his wife's daughters marry. Men in this system sometimes explicitly equate women with cattle because, when women are "given" in marriage, they bring cattle in exchange.

From a Marxist perspective, marriage in such systems is considered an instrument of political power that allows men to gain rights to exploit a woman's reproductive powers and the labor that it produces (Meillassoux 1981). This could be considered the case because, through marriage, a man gains the labor not only of his wife but also of his sons, who will work as herdsmen, and his daughters, who will be gardeners and milkmaids along with their mothers, until they move to their husband's households. Furthermore, young men are also being dominated because it is the male elders who ultimately control the cattle that young men need to marry, just as in aboriginal Australia where the old men controlled ritual knowledge and the initiation process that were the requirements for adulthood. There are explicit dependency relationships here between men and women and young and old. Equating this with the domination and exploitation that produces poverty in large-scale societies and divides households by social class is misleading because households in small-scale societies have relatively equal access to strategic resources such as food and shelter.

## Cattle and Kinship Terminology

The importance of bride-wealth exchanges is also seen in the kinship terminologies of cattle peoples. The Nuer and related northern Nilotic groups are noted for using highly *descriptive kinship* systems (sometimes called *Sudanese*) that place each of ego's cousins in a distinctive category based on terms that are combinations of terms applied to primary relatives, as in the English expression "father's sister's daughter." This makes sense given the different positions these kin take in respect to bride-wealth cattle and because none of them are marriageable. It is important for people to distinguish between kin on mother's side and father's side and between distinct groups of kin related through males, because that is the primary line through which cattle and rights in cattle are inherited. Cattle, as movable property with important social, ritual, and economic significance, make all the difference. The Iroquois kinship systems of Australian aborigines and Native Amazonians (see Chapters 2 and 3) need to make fewer distinctions and can merge kin on father and mother's side.

The Maasai kinship system represents another type commonly associated with groups that emphasize the rights of kin related through males and where complex property relations must also be distinguished. In this system, which is usually called *Omaha*, ego groups mother's *agnates*, kin-related through males, into a single category regardless of generation (Figure 4.10). A. R. Radcliffe-Brown (1941) originally interpreted this as the operation of the principle of the unity of the lineage group, inferring that males of mother's patrilineage were treated as a single group, which reflects the fact that ego did not actually belong to the group but was still connected to it in important

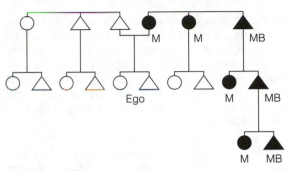

FIGURE 4.10 *Omaha kinship terminology system, which emphasizes mother's patrilineage.*

ways. Such an interpretation is not a fully adequate explanation for why the Maasai have Omaha terminology, but it does make the system understandable.

## Vanishing Segmentary Lineages

Evans-Pritchard (1940) devised a remarkably ingenious model to describe the political organization of Nuer society. The Nuer, with a population of some 300,000 in the 1930s, were said to be organized by clans, lineages, and territorial groups into an *acephalous*, or headless, political system, which operated in the absence of formal political offices. The clans and lineages were descent groups thought to be based on an *agnatic principle*, which meant that they recruited members exclusively through males by means of patrilineal de-

---

*bride-service* The cultural expectation that a newly married husband will perform certain tasks for his in-laws.
*descriptive kinship* Terms derived from combinations of the primary kin terms (F, M, B, Z, S, D). For example, an uncle might be called FB (father's brother).
*Sudanese* A highly "descriptive" kinship system, especially one that distinguishes four different types of cousins: FBS/D, FZS/D, MBS/D, MZS/D.
*omaha* A kinship terminological system in which the members of ego's mother's patrilineage are merged across generations and differentiated from the members of ego's father's patrilineage.
*agnate* Kin who are related through male links.
*acephalous* A political system without central authority or permanent leaders.

scent, or **filiation**. In Evans-Pritchard's scheme, the highest descent-based unit was the clan, which was composed of maximal, major, minor, and minimal lineages at the lowest level. These units corresponded to the territorial units with the tribe at the top and primary, secondary, and tertiary tribal sections down to the village community at the lowest territorial level.

This system could be represented in a tidy diagram (Figure 4.11a), but the Nuer themselves may well understand it differently, as Michel Verdon (1982) suggests. The Nuer apparently have no term in their own language for clan or lineage; when Evans-Pritchard pressed them for lineage affiliations, he found that it was most difficult to make them understand what he wanted to know. He was able to obtain names for lineage segments, but these were merely the names of particular ancestors. When he asked the Nuer to draw their lineages, they came up with lines radiating from a center (Figure 4.11b), not the branching trees and pyramids that he preferred. He also observed that "lineages" did not, in fact, form discrete localized groups. That is, the members of a lineage often did not live in the same village, nor were they strictly patrilineal. He found that lineages often incorporated children filiated through women or through adoption.

Despite the inconsistencies, Evans-Pritchard (1940) declared that clans and lineages appeared on ritual occasions when people made sacrifices to their ancestors or when groups mobilized to settle disputes or for raids and feuds. Such ephemeral

descent groups acquired their own reality in the anthropological literature, especially in the work of British functionalists in Africa where they became standard descriptive devices, and in major comparative studies. However, regardless of the emic reality of clans and lineages for the Nuer, they do divide their society into segments of increasing levels of inclusiveness based on their own assumptions about their relations to ancestors and territory. Perhaps most important, they do successfully organize large numbers of people without central political authority.

When it became obvious that the natives were not very concerned with the purity or even the existence of their descent groups, some argued that descent was simply "ideology." Marshall Sahlins (1965) observed that different ideological models of descent organization could be projected onto the same arrangement of people. A given group might, for example, consider themselves to be patrilineal, matrilineal, or even bilateral, without making any changes in personnel. Descent thus became a cultural fiction that people adopted for whatever purpose and then imposed on themselves.

As anthropological models, lineages and clans grew out of nineteenth-century evolutionary theories that viewed them as stages on the way to statehood, according to Adam Kuper (1982). A clan-based society was thought to represent an evolutionary advance over societies organized only by families, but because they were still based on kinship or the biology of descent, clan societies

FIGURE 4.11    *The segmentary lineage of Nuer society as devised by (a) Evans-Pritchard (1940) and (b) the Nuer themselves.*

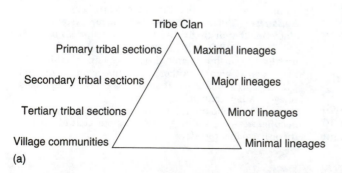

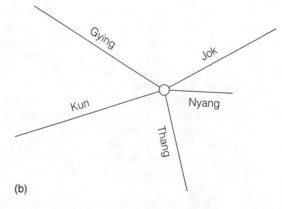

were considered to be more "primitive" than territorially organized states. Lineages and clans were thought to be equivalent to corporate legal entities that, like business corporations, existed in perpetuity apart from their individual members. However, in case after case, critical examination shows that clans and lineages do not form consistent, culturally recognized units. East African pastoralists do remember ancestors, and they marry outside of specific categories of kin; but like Australian aborigines, they seem not to organize themselves into corporate descent groups. Instead, their lives are organized around politically autonomous villages, households, and overlapping networks of kinship. The Nuer categories that Evans-Pritchard called patrilineages have also been described as interest groups concerned with claims in cattle (Verdon 1982). Ranked descent lines may be traced to elite persons in hierarchically organized societies; in such cases, "royal" or "noble" clans and lineages may be culturally significant, but such is not the case with the Nuer nor the other African pastoralists considered here.

## Leopard-Skin Chiefs and Politics in Headless Societies

Before his 1965 critique of descent theory, Sahlins (1961) suggested that the Nuer were a critical "type specimen" of the **segmentary lineage system** operating as a political mechanism for "predatory expansion" by tribal societies against other tribal societies contesting a common ecological niche. Thus, segmentary lineages made a sort of ordered anarchy possible in acephalous ("headless") societies lacking a permanent ranking system, formal political offices, or government institutions. In his early reading of Nuer ethnography, Sahlins ignored the repeated evidence that lineages were not culturally recognized and that local residential groups did not represent descent groups. He accepted Evans-Pritchard's contention that local villages were organized around lineages and lineage principles and argued that sociability increased with spatial and genealogical proximity. The lineage structure determined the severity of conflict and what groups would mobilize.

If the Nuer were not really organized around segmentary lineages, how did they handle conflict without resorting to political hierarchy? This is no small problem because we are talking about relatively large societies that make Australian and Amazonian societies seem insignificant in comparison. Government census figures for 1955–1956 list some 460,000 Nuer and 1.152 million Dinka, a closely related group (Southall 1976). Organizing this many people into a vast network of politically autonomous villages of no more than a few hundred people each must be recognized as a major achievement.

The key feature of the Nuer segmentary system was **complementary opposition**, or what Sahlins called the "massing effect," which means that political alliances form according to the affiliation of individual combatants. So, for example, if a conflict developed between two villages, members of other villages would not join in; but if someone stole a cow from another district, then neighboring villages might form a temporary alliance against the perceived common enemy. Similarly, all members of an ethnic group might move against a different ethnic group. All this was very similar to the type of conflict described for Amazonian groups but on a larger scale.

Evans-Pritchard (1940) described a political system with increasing levels of violence as social distance increased. Within a village, men might fight with clubs, but serious disputes would be settled quickly. Between villages men might fight with spears, and blood feuds were possible, but cattle could be accepted as compensation for homicide. Raiding for cattle routinely occurred between more distant groups of Nuer villages, which Evans-Pritchard designated as tribes but which were probably shifting alliances of adjacent villages. Women and children and granaries were spared in "intertribal" raiding, but they might not

---

**filiation** A parent–child relationship link used as a basis for descent-group membership.
**segmentary lineage system** A system in which complementary opposition and genealogical principles of unilineal descent are used by residential groups as a basis for political mobilization in the absence of centralized political leadership.
**complementary opposition** A situation in which people assume a group identity in political opposition to another group at the same level.

FIGURE 4.12 *The Nuer leopard-skin chiefs were mediators rather than political leaders.*

be spared in raids against non-Nuer groups such as the Dinka, who nevertheless developed from a common protoculture.

Conflicts seemed to arise primarily over cattle, either from cattle raiding or from disputes over unpaid bride-wealth transfers. Homicides could lead to feuds between kin groups, which could lead to further vengeance killings as in Amazonia, but among the Nuer there was a mechanism for mediation. Specific individuals, who Evans-Pritchard (1940) called **leopard-skin chiefs**, served as mediators and attempted to persuade the parties to a conflict to settle the dispute by means of compensation in the form of a transfer of cattle (Figure 4.12). Leopard-skin chiefs were respected as ritual practitioners and as mediators, but they were not chiefs with political authority. In his mediator role, the chief was expected to threaten to curse a reluctant party with supernatural sanc-

tions but, in fact, had no coercive power. Although cattle are a major cause of conflict, they are also an incentive for reducing conflict. Intervillage feuding would disrupt bride-wealth transfers because wide extension of incest restrictions, which reduces confusion in bride-wealth transfers, means that villages are usually exogamous. This divides the loyalties of people who might be obligated to support one another in blood feuds as co-villagers, as close kin, or as claimants to bride-wealth cattle. It is thus virtually in everyone's self-interest to reduce feuding to an absolute minimum. This sort of crosscutting memberships creates in small-scale societies what has been called the **peace in the feud** (Gluckman 1956). It appears that cattle both made possible increased population densities and their cultural use provided an incentive and a mechanism for limiting the feud.

Viewed in its own terms, Nuer politics makes perfectly good sense for a small-scale society of autonomous villages maximizing equality and economic self-sufficiency. The advantage of the segmentary system is that it comes into effect only when it is needed. It seems to have given the Nuer a decisive advantage in their raids for Dinka cattle and allowed them to steadily gain territory at the expense of the Dinka. Some observers have called Nuer expansion a "conquest" and "tribal imperialism" (Kelly 1985), but such terms are more applicable to war conducted by a central authority. It is important to distinguish between wars of conquest as state policy and raids and feuds between small-scale societies. Nuer expansion, a relatively gradual process over many decades, involved steady incorporation of the Dinka through intermarriage and adoption, with a relatively small loss of life, because the Dinka were consistently harassed by Nuer raiders. Because the Nuer and Dinka are such close cultural relatives, the issue of the Nuer conquest raises the question of ethnic identity in small-scale societies.

### Ethnic Identity: Who Are the Nuer? Or the Maasai?

The distribution map of Nilotic-speaking ethnic groups in the upper Nile does suggest that a rapid military conquest of the Dinka by the Nuer occurred along the "predatory expansion" lines suggested by Sahlins (1961) and Raymond Kelly (1985) (Figure 4.13), especially given the Nuer predilection for raiding Dinka cattle and their negative stereotype of the Dinka. Kelly even suggests that the Nuer motive for expansion was their higher bride-wealth rates. The conquest theory originated with the early British administrators and explorers who were themselves members of a conquest society, and it is hardly surprising that they were quick to see evidences of imperialism among peoples they were themselves conquering. Peter Newcomer (1972) challenged the conquest theory and initiated the debate over Nuer identity. He asserts that the Nuer were, in fact, originally a Dinka subgroup who were lucky enough to develop the segmentary system as a social mutation that gave them an advantage over other Dinka in competition for finite pastoral resources. In this view, the Nuer were simply Dinka who became more successful raiders.

Newcomer's argument, which was elaborated by Maurice Glickman (1972), is that the Nuer became more effective cattle raiders because herders from different Nuer villages were forced to interact amicably in dry-season cattle camps and found it easy to form intervillage raiding parties. In contrast, the Dinka occupied more favorable grazing lands, made less extensive seasonal moves, and consequently did not need to develop the elaborate social network that formed the basis of Nuer "segmentation." Thus, ecological factors related to cattle herding might account for the superior organizational ability of the Nuer (Glickman 1972).

This discussion still leaves unanswered the question of who the "Nuer" are. A careful reader of Evans-Pritchard's *The Nuer* (1940) might be surprised to learn that the Nuer do not call themselves "Nuer." They are "Nath" or "Naath." In a footnote, we find that "the word 'Nuer' is sanctioned by a century of usage" and is what the Naath are called by the Dinka and all other outsiders, we might add. The Dinka, in turn, call themselves "Jieng." In both cases, as so often occurs with ethnic self-appellations, the words *Naath* and *Jieng* mean "people" (Southall 1976). When both Nuer and Dinka speak of an individual person, they use the same term, *Raan*. Linguists refer to the "Nuer" and "Dinka" languages, but they are closely related and both are divided into many dialects such that the

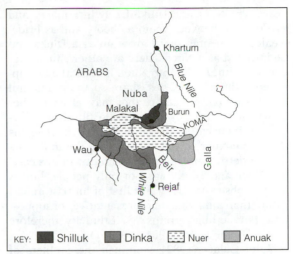

FIGURE 4.13    *The Nuer and neighboring peoples.*

differences between any two Dinka dialects might be greater than between two Nuer and Dinka dialects. Thus, even treating Nuer and Dinka as two distinct languages is somewhat of a "convenient fiction" to facilitate communication among linguists, missionaries, anthropologists, and government administrators (Southall 1976).

Calling the Nuer, Naath, only shifts the question to, Who are the Naath? The Nuer become as difficult to pin down as their phantom segmentary lineages. Because there is no permanent Nuer tribal entity, it follows that there is no Nuer "tribe." Indeed, anthropologist John Burton declares, "Such ethnic designation as 'Nuer' and 'Dinka' . . . are at best marginally indicative of observable interethnic relations and associations" (1981:157). The only consensus, apparently shared by the Nuer and the Dinka and their observers is that the Nuer raid cattle from the Dinka.

The absence of fixed boundaries between Nuer and Dinka frustrated British administrators for

**leopard-skin chief** A respected Nuer religious practitioner who served as a conflict mediator. He was not a political leader and could use only ritual sanctions.
**peace in the feud** The divided loyalties of individuals in small-scale societies caused by overlapping networks of kinship and marriage that provide important incentives for ending feuds.

years. The Nuer and Dinka freely intermarry, and cattle move between them as booty and as bridewealth. Someone might grow up as a Dinka and be initiated as a Nuer. There are other rituals that convert adult Dinka into Nuer. Indeed, the two apparent ethnic categories share so many cultural traits that in mixed camps they may tell each other apart most easily by referring to physical difference in their cattle. In the final analysis, it seems that "true Nuer" are those who are the most successful herders in a given community. In this case, the Nuer and Dinka are not only people, but as Burton observes, "They are first of all pastoralists rather than antagonistic representatives of supposedly pure ethnic groups. . . . Ethnicity therefore moves on the hoof" (1981:160, 161).

John Galaty (1982) examined the problem of ethnic identity from the viewpoint of another Nilotic people, the Maasai of Kenya and Tanzania. According to Maasai **ethnosociology**, the Maasai are speakers of the Maa language who belong to any of a number of named tribal sections of a single Maasai "nation," which has no formal political organization. The term *Maasai* literally means, "I will not beg" and is a frequently used polite expression associated with the dominant Maasai value of bravery and arrogance. In their self-designation, Maasai also call attention to the beads that are featured in their dress and, most prominently, to their association with cattle. In their own eyes, the Maasai are "people of cattle." However, as the term *Maasai* is used, it has multiple meanings that shift depending on context. Galaty has represented this as a series of three nested triangles of three sets of contrasting identities, based on distance from a central Maasai identity (Figure 4.14). In the widest context (triangle A in the diagram), Maasai speakers see themselves as pastoralists distinguished from other people who emphasize hunting or farming in their subsistence. Non-Maasai-speaking pastoral peoples such as the Somali may be considered "Maasai" in deference to their herd-

FIGURE 4.14
*The Maasai ethnosociological system.*

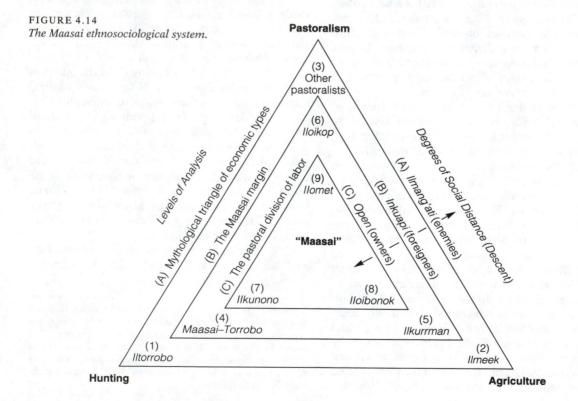

TABLE 4.6    *The Nuer Concept of Spirit (Kwoth)*

| Spirit Type | Location | Social Association | Manifestation | Genealogy | Rank |
|---|---|---|---|---|---|
| God | Sky | Humanity | Pure spirit | Father | Aristocratic |
| Air spirits | Air, clouds, breezes | Political movements, raiding | Prophets | Upper: God's children<br>Lower: God's grandchildren | |
| Totemic spirits | Earth | Kinship groups | Animals | Children of God's daughters | Dinka-like |
| Nature, spirits, fetishes | Earth, underworld | Individuals | Things | Children of daughters of air spirit | Foreigners |

SOURCE: Evans-Pritchard (1953).

ing and are treated with special respect. At a second level, encompassing all Maasai speakers, there are specific categories based on dominant economy, such that Maasai who hunt are called *Torrobo*, those who farm are *Ilkurrman*, and "other Maasai" herders are *Iloikop*. Thus, at this level, common descent from mythical Maasai ancestors is invoked to verify one's Maasai identity even when herding is not practiced. Closest to the center, Maasai blacksmiths are *Ilkunono*, diviners are *Iloibonok*, and ordinary herders are called *Ilomet* by Maasai blacksmiths and diviners. Because the specific meaning of Maasai and the nine related social categories are so dependent on the context in which the terms are used, the confusion experienced by colonial-era Europeans when they attempted to elicit East African "tribal" names is understandable. They were looking for discrete, territorially based, politically organized "tribes," led by "chiefs" with whom they could sign treaties, that they could "administer" as colonial dependencies. In reality things were not that simple.

## Nuer Spirits, Symbolism, and Sacrifice

The religious beliefs of African pastoralists such as the Nuer and Maasai are primarily expressed in life-cycle rituals or during other crisis events, such as drought and disease, and often feature the sacrifice of animals. The most basic distinctions in Nuer cosmology are made between Spirit and Creation, or between the immaterial and material

worlds, which exist in complementary opposition (Beidelman 1966, 1971). When people show proper respect (*thek*) for these distinctions, their lives can normally be expected to go smoothly; misfortune can occur, however, when these categories intrude on each other, either in natural events or due to immoral human actions involving natural categories or human society. Failure to observe incest restrictions, for example, can bring illness. Confusion of categories causes ***ritual pollution***, or contamination by "dirt," as "matter out of place" (Douglas 1966:35). Sacrifice and ritual can restore the previous order by mediating between the opposing principles of Spirit and Creation.

In his analysis of the Nuer concept of Spirit (his translation for the Nuer word *Kwoth*), Evans-Pritchard (1953) described a hierarchy of spirit manifestations ranked from high to low and with distinctions based on their location and social associations (Table 4.6). He thought that all these different spirits were simply different "refractions" of a single unitary Spirit concept. The highest level is called God and is considered to be a pure spirit who is located in the sky and is associated with humanity in general. Genealogically, he may be referred to as father, but his involvement with hu-

***ethnosociology***   A society's own concept of cultural identity.
***ritual pollution***   A dangerous spiritual condition caused by symbolically opposed categories becoming mixed or confused.

man affairs is indirect. The air spirits occur at a lower level, in the atmosphere, and are represented by charismatic religious specialists known as prophets who are thought to communicate directly with these spirits. They may help warriors prepare themselves spiritually for cattle raiding and may be instrumental in organizing relatively large-scale military expeditions. Lower-level spirits may be manifest in animals and objects and are associated with kin groups and individuals. There are many ritual specialists including earth priests, cattle priests, and grass priests, to name a few, and a wide range of curers and diviners, all of whom maintain special relationships with these spirits. According to T. O. Beidelman's (1966, 1971) analysis, Nuer religious specialists demonstrate their association with Spirit by assuming the ambiguous characteristics of confused categories. Prophets have long hair and beards, wear clothing, and appear unkempt, when ordinary Nuer would be unclothed, clean-shaven, and neat. They accomplish their role as mediators between Spirit and Creation because they partake of both categories and are thus in position to realign them. When anyone performs a ritual sacrifice, he in effect, helps restore the cosmic order.

The preferred sacrificial animal is an ox (a bull, castrated at maturity), and every sacrifice is called an ox even when a sheep or goat is used. Because cattle are only slaughtered on ritual occasions and because herds are managed for maximum growth potential and milk production, it is reasonable on strictly utilitarian grounds that male animals would be sacrificed. However, Beidelman (1966) argues that oxen are chosen for sacrifice because of their close symbolic association with men and because oxen are male animals but sterile, thus in an ambiguous category making them ideal mediators between Spirit and Creation. Nuer cows are equated with women. They are allocated cows from bride-wealth, and women may be named after the cows that they milk. Men have ox names and a favorite ox, which is "initiated" with cuts on its horns, which duplicate the deep incisions that are made on the foreheads of Nuer young men at their initiations. Young men marry after their initiation, but their oxen (technically bulls until that point) are then castrated. Beidelman (1966) stresses the parallels between marriage and restrained sexual morality for men and castration as moral domestication of the animal. Some men are called bulls, but, like real bulls, they are seen as aggressive and troublesome.

Even with the ethnographic reports of high gods, priests, and prophets for cattle pastoralists, these ideological systems are essentially egalitarian. There is no codified religious system and no fraternity of religious specialists. Spirit possession is available to anyone. Individuals retain a brief identity after death in relation to cattle and children, but there is no ancestor cult. Any man can perform sacrifices, and the political roles that prophets and leopard-skin chiefs play are strictly limited. These roles do not give them control over strategic resources or allow them to extract labor or tribute. At least one especially charismatic nineteenth-century Nuer prophet gained enough influence to convince people to erect a dirt-mound pyramid shrine, but he was unable to convert it into permanent political power or an enduring ancestor cult.

## The Maasai Age-Class System

The Maasai pastoral system has remained viable even after years of colonial rule, cycles of drought and disease, persistent penetration by the market economy, and political control by the modern independent states of Kenya and Tanzania. African pastoralism has proven to have remarkable resilience, to not only the natural environment but also the wider political economy surrounding it. The Maasai demonstrate that a small-scale culture based on subsistence herding organized at a family level can maintain a high degree of social equality and autonomy while coexisting with larger-scale social systems. Anthropologist Paul Spencer (1988) argues that perhaps the principal reason for the success of Maasai pastoralism is not the pervasiveness of "cattle complex values" but the personal rewards offered by the *age-class system* common to many East African cattle peoples.

Maasai pastoralism, in its ideal form, represents the extreme in subsistence dependence on herding by African cattle peoples. As described by Spencer (1988), the Maasai system depends on three critical social roles: the elders, who control normal herding activities; the wives, who do the milking and take care of the animals within the domestic compound; and the moran, unmarried warriors who until recently raided for cattle. The Maasai settlement pattern resembles the Nuer pattern described previously. Family herds are managed by the male heads of households, which are ideally polygynous. A man's married sons live in the same homestead compound (Figure 4.15), with their individual corrals grouped around a common corral. Control by the older men over the wives and children is a more overt cultural pattern with the Maasai than among the Nuer and is perhaps a reflection of the subsistence dominance of herding for the Maasai. Marriages are entirely arranged by a girl's father who selects a future husband for her from among her suitors. It is also assumed that men will make the important decisions concerning the cattle, and they may beat wives who flout their authority.

As is frequently the case with polygynous societies, women marry at a very young age, whereas men marry significantly later. This arrangement makes polygyny possible and makes it the prerogative of the older men, as in aboriginal Australia. With the Maasai surveyed by Spencer (1988), only 16 percent of the young men age 18–25 years were married, and none polygynously, whereas 60 percent of the men over 40 (ages 41–70 years) had more than one wife. Polygyny offers direct advantages to the herd manager because it increases his labor force and allows him to subdivide responsibility for his animals.

The age-class system with its associated ritual helps balance the social stresses created by polygyny and patriarchy. Life stages and generation levels are ritually marked by a series of rituals that occur throughout an individual's lifetime (Table 4.7). Step-by-step, prepubescent children are named, their heads are shaved, lower incisors removed, and ears pierced and stretched. Each ceremony indicates increasing maturity. Removal of the lower incisors, for example, means that a young boy is old enough to herd livestock near the homestead, but he does not go far afield with the animals until he is old enough to tolerate large incisions in his earlobes. A calf is ritually slaughtered at the first stage of adulthood, but this must occur after the father has been ritually inducted into his status as a full elder by having an ox ritu-

ally slaughtered and after the mother has ritually completed the process of her marriage. The spacing of these two ceremonies thus marks a generation. Ceremonies surrounding initiation make the initiation process a ritual rebirth, and the initiate symbolically becomes a dependent child. Initiation itself is marked by genital mutilation—clitoridectomy for girls and circumcision for boys. Shortly after the operation, girls are lead to their new husband's homesteads as brides, and boys move through other ceremonies that ritually separate them from their status as children and prepare them for moranhood. Only males participate in the age-class system. Age groupings are sometimes described using a variety of terms, but in this discussion, which follows the definitions employed by Bernardo Bernardi (1985), age class refers to the group of people who are promoted together through the same sequence of *age grades*, or culturally designated stages. The age class is here equivalent to the age set or age group of some authors. Males of roughly the same age move as a class sequentially through a series of subgrades from boyhood; to warriorhood, or the moran grade; to elderhood; and finally retirement. Age classes are named, and the members of each class carry a distinct style of a hand-forged iron spear and form a fraternity (Larick 1986).

Each tribal section independently operates its own age-class system. A new class is formed roughly every 15 years under the sponsorship of the elders who are two classes ahead of them, or approximately 30 years their senior, and who will serve as patrons of the new class. The recruitment period for each class is ritually closed by the elders in the class immediately senior to it. Each class is, in effect, forced up the age-grade ladder by the demands of the youths below who do not want to be the last to join a class that is about to advance. Late recruits experience a foreshortened time period in the favored warrior grade. The extended

---

*age-class system*    A system in which individuals of similar age are placed in a named group and moved as a unit through the culturally defined stages of life. Specific rituals mark each change in age status.

*age grade*    A culturally defined stage of an age-class system such as childhood, adolescence, parenthood, and old age.

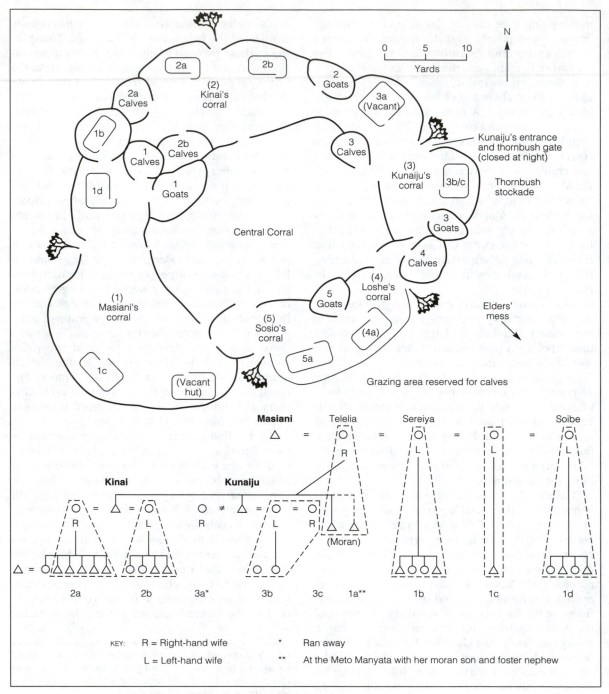

FIGURE 4.15  *Maasai homestead.* (SOURCE: *Spencer, 1988.*)

TABLE 4.7   *Maasai Age Grades*

| Grade | Age* | Feature |
|---|---|---|
| Senior elder | 50+ | Religious and ritual power, charisma of old age assumed |
| *Great Ox* Ceremony—Precedes Son's Initiation | | |
| Junior elders | 35–50 | Incest avoidance of daughters of the age class, not expected to fight, have power to curse, sponsor new age class |
| *Olngesher* Ceremony—Moran Become Elders Age Class United and Named | | |
| Senior moran | 20–35 | Preparation of elderhood, may marry, meat and milk avoidances lifted |
| *Eunoto* Ceremony | | |
| Junior moran | 15–20 | Wear red ochre, braid hair, dance with girls, have distinctive spears, perform ritual rebellion, form *manyata* warrior village, avoid meat and milk |
| Initiates | 12–15 | Age mates begin to associate distinctive regalia |
| *Circumcision* Ceremony | | |
| Boyhood | 10–12 | Earlobes cut and stretched, work as herdboys |
| Childhood | 0–10 | Naming, lower incisors removed |

SOURCE: Spencer (1965, 1988).
*Age intervals overlap because the actual age of specific individuals in a particular grade will vary widely.

time during which a given age class can recruit means that there will be a relatively wide spread of ages within a given class; some Maasai set up junior and senior subsets within a single class, granting each different privileges and moving each subset through their own ritual stages of maturation. When the youngest subset of a class enters the grade of elderhood, the entire class assumes a single name.

The highlight of the entire age sequence is the moran grade, which young men enter after going through ceremonies that ritually separate them from their natal families. As moran, they become the warrior protectors of their communities; at the same time, however, these young men form their own egalitarian community of age mates united by special bonds of loyalty and shared experience. Freed from domestic routines and still unmarried, the novice moran are expected to dress in special finery, wear their hair in braids, dance and display, and carry on with young girls. Traditionally, they conducted raids to capture cattle and defended the local herds against raiders and lions. The most important privilege of the moran is the few years they spend in segregated warrior villages, known as *manyat* (singular, *manyata*), which are set up to defend individual districts. The moran flaunt their independence and live the communalistic ideals of moran brotherhood in their *manyat*. The supreme ideal of the *manyata* is represented by individual warriors known as "diehards" who pledge themselves to die in combat rather than retreat (Figure 4.16).

To establish the *manyata*, the moran conduct raids on their parental homes and carry off their mothers and small herds of cattle, sometimes against the protests of their fathers. As Spencer (1988) points out, this is clearly a ritual rebellion against the father's patriarchal control and has obvious Freudian overtones. The *manyat* villages of the moran are organized around egalitarian and communalistic principles in direct opposition to the age hierarchy and individualism of the domestic homestead.

The midpoint of moranhood is ritually marked by an extended ceremony known as *eunoto*, which begins 5 years into the grade and initiates a 10-year series of steps leading to elderhood. After this ceremony, a moran may be expected to marry. In the *eunoto*, the *manyat* villages are disbanded, and the combined age class is formally launched. This ceremony involves a spectacular display of massed warriors, which even attracts fee-paying European tourists and film crews.

Although many ceremonial phases of the Maasai age-class system incorporate ritualized rebellions against parental authority, the excesses of the moran are held in check, and they are guided through the maturation process by their elder patrons who maintain ultimate control by their power to curse their charges. It could certainly be argued that the age-class system constructively channels the otherwise potentially disruptive energies of the young men who grow up as subservient herdboys and must wait at least 10 years before

## Maasai Women

In the film *Maasai Women*, anthropologist Melissa Llewelyn-Davies, who speaks the Maasai language and has some 10 years research experience with the Maasai, engages several Maasai women in a free-ranging discussion about their experiences as women. In their own words, these Maasai women define and accept as a given the gender roles of their culture. Women milk cows, bear children, and build their own houses. A woman "has nothing." They care for animals and have milking rights but no ownership rights over them. Men make the decisions about herds. Yet in this discussion with a sympathetic and knowledgeable nonnative woman, the Maasai women are quick to place their own cultural roles in a positive light. Clitoridectomy (female circumcision), which is strongly condemned by international feminists, is defended as something "we've always done." One woman explains, "It is something God began long ago. A girl wants to hurry up and be circumcised. It is a very good thing." When Llewelyn-Davies asks if the initiate is happy about the experience, she is told emphatically that she is "very happy" because the girl will then be thought of as a woman and will be able to marry soon.

A Maasai woman elaborates further on a woman's role: "It has always been since things first began that men marry women so that they will give birth to children. Then husbands won't die in poverty with no wife and no child. A man takes a wife and she conceives. She tends his cattle. She gives birth and her husband becomes a rich man."

In the film, the women tell Llewelyn-Davies that although they accept arranged marriages to old men, they are not always happy about it and may select young warriors as lovers even though their husbands would be angry if they found out. When Llewelyn-Davies raises the possibility of women being jealous over young co-wives in this polygynous society, a Maasai woman declares,

*We're not jealous like you Europeans. . . . To us a co-wife is something very good because there is much work to do. When it rains, the village gets mucky, and it's you who clears it out. It's you who looks after the cows. You do the milking, and your husband may have very many cows. That's a lot of work. You have to milk and smear the roof and see to the calves. . . . So when you give birth and it rains, who will smear the roof if you have no co-wife? No one. Who will clear the muck from the village? No one. So Maasai aren't jealous because of all this work.*

It is a hard life, but there are rewards. After a girl's initiation, a group of women in the film sing,

*Listen God to what suits women. It suits us to prepare charms for the initiates, to be busy with our children's circumcisions, to have celebrations, which are lavish in honey beer and milk and meat and butter. It suits us when our sons go out herding. It suits us to sit resting in the shade. It suits us when we suckle children. God, nursing mother, remember what suits us.*

FIGURE 4.16  *Maasai warriors.*

they can marry. Spencer (1988) suggests that the age system diverts the stresses that are inherent in the family system away from the senior male household heads to elders in general. In some respects, the *manyata* phase placed the moran in what Arnold Van Gennep (1909) would call a ***liminal phase***. It is a rite of transition in which the moran are ritually suspended in the space between being herdboys and elders.

The age-class system is functionally related to incest avoidance and marriage practices in a mutually reinforcing way. Spencer (1988) points out that Maasai incest restrictions are more elaborated toward daughters and mothers-in-law than for mothers and sisters. This is apparently because a system of age-class exogamy operates in which the men of one age class marry the daughters of the men in the class senior to them, rather than marrying the daughters of their own age mates. The age classes are thus linked by marriage alliances, such as might operate between exogamous clans. This reinforces the respect that must obtain between junior and senior classes if the age-class system is to survive as a whole because the junior class will find their fathers-in-law in the senior class. Age-class exogamy also means that men will tend to marry much younger women, thereby cre-

ating the age differential that makes frequent polygyny possible.

The persistence of the Maasai as a society up to the present day is evidence of the importance of their age-class system. It is significant that while the population of Kenya as a whole has recently experienced extremely high population-growth rates that threaten the economic viability of the entire country, settled farming groups are growing at twice the rate of the Maasai and other pastoralists (4 percent vs. 2.2 percent or less). Isaac Sindiga (1987) suggests that the traditional Maasai practices of polygyny, postpartum taboos on sexual intercourse, and prolonged lactation, which are all linked to patriarchy and the age-class system, were significant child-spacing and fertility-dampening factors.

Although the position of Maasai women is usually described by men as relatively inferior, this must be qualified (see the box "Maasai Women"). Within the age-class system, young men are also subject to the authority of the elders who control bride-wealth cattle and marriages. Women do not become elders, but they do clearly have a stake in

---

***liminal phase***  An ambiguous phase of ritual transition in which one is on the threshold between two states.

their society and work to maintain the system, especially as they grow older. Senior wives may welcome polygyny because it lightens their domestic routine. Women themselves perform the clitoridectomy of girls, and they accept it as a precondition of marriage. Divorce is an option, especially early in an unhappy marriage. After women have children, they gain more autonomy, and because they marry young, they will usually outlive their husbands. Abused wives may appeal to the elders for help; men who commit serious offenses against women may be perceived as a threat to all women, and they may be assaulted, beaten, and their cattle slaughtered by a large group of enraged women acting in a publicly sanctioned role as enforcers of community morality. Women also conduct their own rituals of rebellion against patriarchal authority.

In some respects, the age-class system can be considered a highly egalitarian form of political organization used by stateless societies to regulate rights, privileges, and responsibilities between men who might otherwise find themselves in frequent conflict (Bernardi 1985). The division of labor places women outside the public political arena as is often the case in small-scale societies. The underlying principle of male age classes is that every male enjoys the same potential to be a warrior, marry, raise a family, officiate at rituals, and so on, and these potentials are realized in orderly sequence by virtue of his membership in an age class where these rights are jointly shared. Conflicts do arise in the system, but they occur primarily over the timing of promotions. Political struggle takes place between groups and not individuals. Political power is thus widely distributed and strictly regulated. The system is not simply a gerontocracy with power concentrated at the top.

## SUMMARY

East African cattle peoples have certainly developed a highly successful system that makes effective use of a difficult environment. Age hierarchy and apparent male dominance in many spheres exist alongside basic equality between households. Individual households maintain considerable self-sufficiency. To be poor in such a system is to have too few animals for subsistence and bride-wealth,

but social support systems normally take care of both problems. There is little overt poverty in that cattle are widely loaned or shared between households according to need, regardless of their actual ownership. The effects of variation in herd composition are leveled out such that people are only likely to go hungry under the most severe drought conditions when people would be forced to draw on their small stock, but then everyone would go hungry. Sharing cattle between households also reduces the possibility that all of one's animals would be lost to raids or disease and makes the most efficient use of unpredictable and highly variable grazing and water resources. Raiding served to redistribute animals and allowed young men to build their herds rapidly. People who find themselves cattleless might opt out of the system by becoming foragers or sedentary farmers.

## STUDY QUESTIONS

1. Describe the subsistence uses East African pastoralists make of their cattle.

2. What are the most critical limiting factors that African pastoralists must adapt to?

3. Why is it difficult to determine how many cattle African pastoralists actually need and to establish the carrying capacity of the range?

4. Describe the marriage process for the Nuer, including the concepts of bride-wealth, household, husband, wife, pater, and genitor.

5. How does the Maasai age-class system relate to gerontocracy and patriarchy, and how does it contribute to the resilience of Maasai society?

6. Describe the social and ritual uses of cattle in East Africa.

## SUGGESTED READING

EVANS-PRITCHARD, E. E. 1940. *The Nuer: A Description of the Modes of Livelihood and Political Institutions of a Nilotic People.* New York and Oxford, Eng.: Oxford University Press. The most famous early ethnography of East African cattle people, this book vividly describes their dependence on cattle, emphasizing ecological relationships.

SPENCER, PAUL. 1988. *The Maasai of Matapato: A Study of Rituals of Rebellion.* Bloomington and Indianapolis: Indiana University Press. An excellent modern ethnography that focuses on social organization, life cycle, and ritual.

# 5

# BODY, MIND, AND SOUL: THE QUALITY OF TRIBAL LIFE

The thought, beliefs, and health practices of small-scale cultures raise many important, intriguing, and critical problems for cross-cultural understanding. The basic issue is how to evaluate the mental, emotional, and physical well-being of tribal peoples in order to assess the overall effectiveness of their cultures. This is an important problem because welfare-intervention programs undertaken on behalf of tribal peoples by missionaries, government educators, and health workers often assume that these people must be ignorant and backward. Members of wealthy industrial nations easily equate hospitals, schools, and sewage-treatment plants with health and intelligence and assume that anyone lacking these standards must be sick. Such ethnocentric views are reinforced by the seemingly bizarre and irrational elements in tribal shamanism, witchcraft, and magic. Whereas earlier chapters showed these aspects of religion and ideology within their cultural context, in this chapter we consider their significance for individuals.

We will review some of the classic interpretations of tribal religion and "primitive mentality" by such historically prominent anthropological theorists as Edward Tylor, Sir James Frazer, Franz Boas, Lucien Lévy-Bruhl, and Bronislaw Malinowski, along with the more recent views of Claude Lévi-Strauss and C. R. Hallpike. Linguistic and ethnoscience material on biological classification systems and color terminologies will be included, with ethnographic material from Australia.

A wide range of archaeological, nutritional, epidemiological, and demographic evidence will be examined on the health status of independent tribal peoples. Special emphasis will be placed on Australian and Amazonian examples because full cultural context has been established in previous chapters.

## THE MENTAL ABILITIES OF TRIBAL PEOPLES

### Lévy-Bruhl, Collective Representations, and Primitive Mentality

The rapid European colonial domination of Africa, which was in full swing by the late nineteenth century, made it imperative for the new European administrators and petty colonial officials to understand the peoples that they were attempting to control. Because it was so difficult for foreigners to predict the behavior of natives, it was widely believed that native thought processes were inferior to those of Europeans. Because explicitly racist evolutionary theories were used to justify colonialism, Europeans readily assumed that people living in small-scale societies must be physically and culturally underdeveloped and therefore childlike in their thinking.

American anthropologists under Franz Boas distanced themselves somewhat from such interpretations. Boas rated Euro-American civilization as the highest human cultural achievement, but he was firmly antiracist and believed that no significant differences existed in basic mental faculties separating "uncivilized primitives" from "civilized" peoples. In his book *The Mind of Primitive Man* (1911), he easily refuted a list of presumably inferior mental features that were widely attributed to tribal people, including their supposed inability to inhibit their emotions, their shortened attention spans, and their limited power of original thought. Boas found that natives were impulsive and improvident when it was culturally appropriate and showed remarkable restraint when necessary. He noted that the supposed inability of natives to focus their attention was most likely to be reported by frustrated ethnographers who found it difficult to get reluctant informants to answer a long series of irrelevant questions. Similarly, within their own cultural context, natives showed plenty of creativity. Boas certainly acknowledged differences in forms of thought between tribal and civilized peoples, but these he attributed to social, or cultural, differences, not racial factors. He concluded that tribal peoples simply classified experience differently and merged concepts in ways that appeared peculiar to us.

British anthropologist Edward Tylor (1871) argued that bizarre tribal religious beliefs and rituals developed of what he called **animistic thinking**, in which intellectually curious people attempted to explain dream experiences and death by attributing a detachable animating soul to people, animals, plants, and "inanimate" objects. Tylor believed that the soul concept was the basis of all religion, shamanism, and witchcraft and that tribal people arrived at it by logical mental processes, which were basically like our own. Sir

James Frazer elaborated this intellectualist approach in *The Golden Bough* ([1890] 1900) when he identified the laws that he thought underlay magical practices. His **law of sympathy** held that things such as hair, which were once part of someone, could still influence that person even after they were separated. Therefore, someone's hair clippings might be used by shamans to harm them. Like Tylor, Frazer argued that primitives were crude logicians, who thought like Englishmen, but simply made mistakes.

French positivist philosopher, Lucien Lévy-Bruhl (1857–1939), was one of the first to systematically examine the thought processes of tribal peoples with the practical purpose of showing how they differed from the thoughts of "civilized" peoples, applying the concept of **collective representations**, or group ideas, developed by French sociologist Émile Durkheim. His first major book on the subject appeared in French in 1910 under the title *The Mental Functions of Lower Societies* (*Les Fonctions Mentales dans les Societes Inferieures*). It appeared in English as *How Natives Think* (1926). By the time his second volume *Primitive Mentality* (French original 1922) appeared, his ideas were so widely acclaimed that this book was quickly translated into English (1923). Lévy-Bruhl was pleased to observe in the 1926 English edition of *How Natives Think* that many administrators and missionaries had already written to tell him how much his books had helped them understand the otherwise "unintelligible and ridiculous" thinking of the natives with whom they worked, thereby improving their relations with them.

According to Lévy-Bruhl, collective representations, like culture in general, are emotion-laden thoughts, or ideas, that are shared by the members of a specific society and transmitted across generations. These thoughts are collective, in that they are not the unique property of specific individuals, and they cannot therefore be understood according to the principles of individual psychology. He insisted throughout that primitive mentality was not inferior and natives were not childlike; their thinking was simply different. However, this point was easily overlooked when he referred to primitive mentality as "prelogical," not "illogical," and when he declared that the collective representations of "undeveloped peoples" could not be understood by studying the categories and logical principles used by "adult, civilized, white man" (1926:13). Lévy-Bruhl agreed with Boas that thought was culturally conditioned, but he emphatically departed from Boas, and from Tylor and Frazer, by declaring that the mental processes of "primitives" are distinctively different and can only be understood by their own "laws." He rejected animist, intellectualist explanations because they were based on individual, not collective, thought.

The most critical aspect of primitive thought, Lévy-Bruhl argued, was that it assumed a "mystic" reality—it was based on a socially conditioned belief in imperceptible forces. This was *prelogical thinking*, based on a *law of participation*, under which concerns for contradiction were ignored and something could be two things at once. Thus, primitives saw nothing contradictory in a shaman being a man and a tiger at the same time. Of course, all peoples have this ability. For example, Christians, who may be members of large-scale and global cultures, have no apparent difficulty considering Jesus Christ to be both a man and a god at the same time.

Lévy-Bruhl declared, "Primitives perceive nothing in the same way as we do" (1926:43), even though their brains and their senses are the same as ours. In primitive thought, according to Lévy-Bruhl, causation for natural events like disease and accident might be sought for in what we would call the supernatural. Physical cause was irrelevant in collective representations, even though individuals were certainly logical enough to know when to come in out of the rain and could successfully manage their daily affairs. Prelogical natives formed concrete impressions that they felt and lived emotionally, whereas civilized people worked with abstract, conceptual thought. In his own contradictory terms, Lévy-Bruhl suggested that primitive thought was thus "concrete," whereas civilized thinking was abstract and conceptual. This misleading distinction still plagues anthropological theorists.

Despite the difficulties Lévy-Bruhl experienced in grappling with cross-cultural understanding, he correctly observed that barriers to emic understanding were in a sense insurmountable. Translation problems are critical because categories are seldom precisely the same even when superficial resemblances exist. For example, traditional exchange objects, which are often called "money," are not actually money as it exists in a market economy. Although the differences in meaning may not be accurately characterized as that between concrete and abstract, Lévy-Bruhl was correct in calling for in-depth linguistic knowledge because it was perfectly possible to have a minimal speaking knowledge without really being able to think in another language.

Claude Lévi-Strauss (1966) begins his work on primitive thought by calling into question the entire distinction between abstract and concrete words by relating it to difference in level of attention and interest and not to differences in method of thought. Lévi-Strauss argues that primitive people, like civilized people, use many abstract words and pursue objective knowledge about the environment for its own sake. People name things, not just because they are objects of immediate utilitarian interest, but because people find it aesthetically pleasing to impose order on the world through careful observation and cataloging. Such attention to detail was well illustrated in our previous discussion of the ethnoecological knowledge of Native Amazonians and the Dreaming maps of Australian aborigines. According to Lévi-Strauss, it is this common drive for order that underlies

---

*animistic thinking*   The soul concept used by tribal individuals as an intellectural explanation of life, death, and dream experiences; part of Tylor's theory of animism as the origin of religion.

*law of sympathy*   Frazer's explanation for the logic underlying magic, sorcery, and shamanism. He thought that tribal peoples believed that anything ever connected with a person, such as hair or blood, could be manipulated to influence that person.

*collective representations*   Ideas, or thoughts, and emotions common to a society as a whole, especially in reference to the supernatural.

*prelogical thinking*   Lévy-Bruhl's characterization of the collective representations of tribal peoples, which he thought reflected concrete thought and a mystic reality unique to tribal cultures.

*law of participation*   The assumption that a thing can participate in or be part of two or more things at once. Identified by Lévy-Bruhl as the principle underlying his concept of prelogical thought.

all human thought and that makes unfamiliar thought patterns understandable.

The view that biological folk taxonomies, the way people classify plants and animals, may be an intellectual pursuit reflecting what is "good to think" as much as an interest in what is "good to eat" or useful has been challenged by Robert Randall and Eugene Hunn (1984, Hunn 1985). They argue that, in many cases, labeling is directly utilitarian. For example, some peoples carefully name caterpillars that are significant as food and pests, while paying little attention to otherwise conspicuous adult butterflies and moths.

Lévi-Strauss does not find it particularly mystical that people identify with totemic animals. Natives are not confused by a law of participation into thinking that they are their totems. There is

no contradiction in holding empirical and emotional knowledge about a single object. Instead of speaking of a prelogical mentality, Lévi-Strauss maintains that magical thought, or what he prefers to call **mythical thought**, differs from formal scientific thought in method and purpose, but not in logic. Mythical thought is scientific in that it produced the important technical developments of the Neolithic, such as domestication, pottery, and weaving, but the "Neolithic paradox" for Lévi-Strauss is the difficulty in explaining why technological development seemingly stabilized after the scientific achievements of the Neolithic until the establishment of formal science. To resolve the paradox, Lévi-Strauss argues that there are two distinct but opposite types of scientific thought, each equally valid and neither a stage in the devel-

FIGURE 5.1  *Ritual activities are rich in symbolic associations connecting mind, body, and soul. The Pokot, East African pastoralists, are dancing to celebrate a male initiation ceremony.*

TABLE 5.1  *Piaget's Stages of Mental Development*

| Stage | Description |
| --- | --- |
| Sensorimotor | Age 0–2 years: nonverbal, private learning from experience through concrete objects |
| Preoperational | Age 2–7 years: words represent objects |
| Concrete operations | Age 7–12 years: objects classified by similarities and differences; coordination of multiple dimensions of length, number, weight, area, volume |
| Formal (scientific) | Age 12–adult: formal logic; propositional, deductive reasoning |

opment of the other: the **science of the concrete**, based on perceptions and signs, and formal science, which works with concepts.

Mythical thought works with a culturally limited set of signs, including significant images and events, which it orders into structured relationships that provide aesthetic satisfaction while helping people understand reality (Figure 5.1). Lévi-Strauss is here referring to the structured sets of logical associations and complementary oppositions that are so characteristic of myths and the ritual beliefs and practices that are related to them. These were discussed in some detail in the Amazonian cosmology examined in Chapter 3. Formal scientific concepts remain as close to natural reality as possible. They are derived from structured theories and hypotheses and are used to expand the total cultural inventory and to make changes, or create events, in the external world.

## Hallpike's Primitive Mentality and the Problem of Cross-Cultural Intelligence Testing

Anthropologist C. R. Hallpike (1979), carries on Lévi-Bruhl's argument that "primitives" think differently than civilized peoples, by substituting the term *preoperatory* for *prelogical*. Hallpike's theories deserve attention because, even though they are not a major influence in anthropology, they could be uncritically used to support the view that tribal peoples are mentally inferior and thus in need of improvement by more enlightened outsiders.

Primitives, for Hallpike, are the rural illiterate and unschooled, as well as the members of the small-scale societies dealt with in Chapters 2–5 of

this book. Their thinking is not actually different from our own—it is just incomplete and less developed. Hallpike uses the stages devised by Swiss psychologist Jean Piaget (1896–1980) to describe the acquisition of cognitive abilities by children (Table 5.1) in order to catalog the cognitive abilities of tribal adults. The Piagetian sensorimotor, preoperational, concrete operation, and formal stages, are assumed to be biologically determined levels of intellectual development that individuals progress through as they mature. The stages were based on a variety of performance tests applied to European children. Preoperational children are assumed to be incapable of realizing that a liquid conserves its original quantity when poured into a taller glass. This implies that, although they may understand comparatives such as taller and shorter, preoperational children do not yet grasp the abstract concept of volume. They also show themselves cognitively inferior to the operational and formal thinking of older children in many other ways.

Hallpike finds resemblances between the collective representations of tribal peoples, such as the mystical thinking identified by Lévi-Bruhl, and thinking characteristics of children at the preoperational stage and infers that this means that the

---

**mythical thought**  Lévi-Strauss's term for the thinking underlying myth and magic; logically similar to scientific thought but based on the science of the concrete and used for aesthetic purposes and to solve existential problems.

**science of the concrete**  Thought based on perceptions and signs, images, and events, as opposed to formal science based on concepts.

majority of primitive adults are incapable of what Piaget defined as adult thought. They are mentally equivalent to 7-year-old European children, but because they are grown up, they are, in effect, retarded. Such retardation, Hallpike argues, is caused by the absence of schools and literacy. He softens this conclusion by noting that although primitives may be cognitive children, as adults they nevertheless have acquired enough knowledge and experience to make them smarter than children. However, such a distinction would probably be lost on anyone wishing to limit the political rights of tribal people by treating them as legal minors.

Hallpike (1979) cites a wide variety of psychological tests performed on "primitives" to support his conclusions. These tests seem to show that primitives cannot verbally sort objects into classes by obvious differences, cannot sort the events of a narrative into a logical sequence, cannot grasp the argument of simple syllogisms, and so on. Hallpike makes a careful point-by-point comparison of primitive thought with our presumably more developed formal thought and finds primitive thinking profoundly inadequate (see Table 5.2). However, both the validity and the reliability of the cross-cultural tests of cognition that Hallpike relies on are open to serious question. For example,

TABLE 5.2   *Primitive, Preoperational Thought Versus Operational Thought*

| Primitive | Operational |
| --- | --- |
| Contextual | Generalizable |
| Concrete | Abstract |
| Nonspecialized | Specialized |
| Ethnocentric | Objective |
| Dogmatic | Relativistic |
| Simple | Complex |
| Incomplete | Complete |
| Inexplicit | Explicit |
| Personal | Impersonal |
| Percept based | Concept based |
| Animistic | Causal |
| Purposeless | Utilitarian |
| Undifferentiated | Differentiated |
| Tacit | Reflective |

SOURCES: Hallpike (1979:126) and Shewder (1982:356).

Hallpike decided that a 37-year-old Russian peasant was cognitively preoperational because he refused to tell a psychological fieldworker that the bears in Novaya Zemlya must all be white when he was presented with a logical syllogism emphatically declaring that Novaya Zemlya was in the far north where it always snows and that in the far north where it always snows, all the bears are white. The subject might have been displaying rational cynicism of bureaucratic authority when he declared, "What I know, I say, and nothing beyond that." Hallpike interpreted this test as further demonstration that primitives lack the cognitive ability to handle the hypothetical in a logical problem.

As Richard Shweder observes (1982, 1985), Hallpike is vulnerable on a number of issues. In the first place, Piagetian stage theory has come under increasing attack by developmental psychologists who stress that the boundaries between the stages are not as sharp as once thought. Young children may be capable of operational and formal thinking at much earlier ages than previously believed; they may simply not often use these abilities and may have difficulty verbalizing about them. Furthermore, Hallpike (1979) infers too easily that collective representations result from the cognitive abilities of the majority of the individuals in a society, when collective representations, such as literacy, themselves may encourage certain types of thinking, as Hallpike acknowledges. Hallpike also infers that an apparent similarity in thinking between children and primitives must be due to the same cause, that is, a shared absence of certain cognitive skills.

Hallpike's developmentalist view is in opposition to both universalist and relativist approaches to thought. In Lévi-Strauss's view, the mental processes that people use to construct classification systems and that would, in Piagetian terms, be considered operational are a human universal shared by all peoples. The relativist position would emphasize the priority of language in the development of thought, suggesting that individuals do not invent their own mentalities but take on the mental processes that their language hands them. Such a view is not incompatible with a universalist interpretation to the extent that linguistic universals are recognized.

Failure to identify higher cognitive skills in children or "primitives" may tell us more about deficiencies in testing techniques and our concepts of cognition than about their thought processes. Many cross-cultural psychologists have questioned the validity of applying test procedures developed in one culture to people in an entirely different culture, especially where there is no practical context, content, or experience for the procedure or any familiarity with the concept of an intelligence test. Language is an obvious barrier in cross-cultural testing, and even when interpreters are used and in-depth interviews attempted, questioning will still be an impersonal, out-of-context ritual, which subjects will be likely to treat as irrelevant, if not as an unwelcome invasion of their privacy. Test subjects may also be justified in objecting to testing because it has often had harsh consequences for people and has seldom been carried out as "pure science." For example, early in the twentieth century, the Stanford–Binet IQ test was extensively used in the United States to identify the "feebleminded" and was used to influence policies concerning immigration, eugenics, education, institutionalization, and military service (Gould 1981).

The most significant differences in thought patterns between the members of small-scale societies and urban industrial peoples probably do relate to differences in the basic way of life, but there is no necessary implication that such differences reflect developmental stages or absolute superiority of one culture over the other. Perhaps the most serious problem with earlier attempts to assess the cognitive abilities of peoples living in small-scale societies is that they have focused on a rather narrow, culture-specific concept of "pure intelligence." Surely, intelligence must mean more than scores achieved on a test schedule that might relate to academic achievement or some other performance in large-scale urban societies. Cross-cultural psychologists J. W. Berry and S. H. Irvine (1986, Irvine and Berry 1988) stress that for test scores to be meaningful, they must be conducted within the cultural and ecological context of the people being assessed. They categorically reject the validity of tests that are applied outside the culture for which they were originally devised. Taking a firmly cultural relativist position on cognitive ability, Irvine and Berry have formulated a *law of cultural differentiation*, which states:

*Cultural factors prescribe what shall be learned and at what age; consequently different cultural environments lead to the development of different patterns of ability.* (1988:4)

They prefer to speak of cognitive abilities, rather than "intelligence" because there is no agreement on a global theory of human intelligence. Few researchers have even asked, What does intelligence mean to a particular people? What do they value? Too often, intelligence testing has shown what people do not do and has not examined the cognitive skills, or the "practical intelligence," that is required for the successful performances of everyday life. In the following section, we consider this kind of intelligence for Australian aborigines.

## The Cognitive Abilities of Australian Aborigines

The European invaders of Australia were convinced of the intellectual inferiority of aborigines from the very beginning. This ethnocentric assessment found frequent "scientific" support, as the selection from Staniland Wake (1872) in Chapter 1 demonstrated. The first formal test of the cognitive abilities of aborigines was conducted in 1915 using the Porteus Maze Solving Test, which could be taken by illiterates. S. D. Porteus (1917) first applied his maze test to a control group of forty-two delinquent and criminal white Australian boys to make sure the test would identify the lack of foresight, prudence, and general mental deficiency, which he assumed would accompany social deviancy. When he applied the test to twenty-eight aboriginal children at a mission, he discovered that they actually performed better than the white delinquents and criminals, but he attributed this to the assumed rapid physical maturation of aborigines. He argued that aboriginal mental development occurred rapidly and then stopped. Unshaken in his belief in the racial inferiority of aborigines, he concluded that by early adolescence

---

*law of cultural differentiation*    A statement of the cultural relativity of cognitive ability or basic intelligence. Assumes that no single, culture-bound test can adequately test cognitive ability because different cultures produce different cognitive abilities in individuals.

"the common racial characteristics of indolence, shiftlessness, and lack of foresight become apparent" (Porteus 1917:38).

Porteus recognized the difficulties of cross-cultural testing and granted that within their own culture aborigines exhibited considerable "social intelligence." He attempted to make his tests more culturally relevant by using photographs of footprints, for example, but he still considered aboriginal mentality to be relatively inferior, not just different.

Psychological testing in Australia, as elsewhere, is used by the state to diagnose mental health, educational problems, and vocational potential; thus, for aborigines, tests may have significant implications. During the period from 1960 to 1980, as the government became increasingly concerned with the social problems of aborigines, some 280 separate cognitive studies were conducted on aborigines (Klich 1988). This research often turned up contradictory results; considerable debate ensued over whether the diagnosed aboriginal "inferiority" was due to their culture or their genes, but the prevailing view that aborigines were somehow mentally inferior seemed unshaken. For example, Piagetian tests applied to aborigines showed performance levels consistently lower than the European standard, and because the aboriginal environment was assumed to be the problem, some researchers concluded that aboriginal children should be removed from their retarding environments so that they could develop "normally" (see reviews by Keats and Keats 1988 and Klich 1988).

A modern study of aboriginal mentality by psychoanalytic anthropologist Arthur Hippler (1978) takes a Freudian twist and ethnocentrically attributes assumed aboriginal mental deficiencies to their "inferior" child-rearing practices. Hippler rejects racist explanations but explicitly retains the biased evolutionist position that peoples can usefully be ranked by cognitive and emotional ability according to a Euro-American standard. As a self-styled "psychocultural evolutionist," Hippler believes that all people are born with equal mental potential, but primitive cultures stifle this potential by faulty child rearing. Following a modified Piagetian stage approach, he argues that primitives are retarded at the preoperational level and

thus as adults allow the magical fantasies of childhood to cloud their perception of the real world. This retardation occurs because primitives are frozen at a correspondingly low stage in the evolutionary development of child-rearing practices. According to Hippler (1977), primitives practice an "infanticidal and abandoning" evolutionary stage of child rearing, which is so cruel and inconsistent that children are unable to repress their sexual impulses and childish fantasies and are thus unable to reach their cognitive potentials.

Hippler paid a brief visit to aboriginal communities in Arnhem Land where he administered a few Rorschach inkblot tests and, as expected, concluded that the Yolngu people were "impulse-ridden, sexually anxious, jealous and fearful." They had difficulty separating fantasy from reality. They were unimaginative, impulsive yet rigid, and had cognitively "lesser" capacities than Western norms. He considered sacred sites to be a "cultural pathology" because they overvalued land forms. In remarkable detail, he pointed out the shortcomings of Yolngu child rearing, which he felt accounted for their cognitive problems. He found parents to be "infantile, thoughtless and selfish," and their child rearing was characterized by such "neglect and harshness," "anger and hostility," that the physical welfare of children was in constant peril and they were left with "emotional and cognitive scarring."

Australian anthropologists who were familiar with the Yolngu people were outraged by Hippler's assessment, both theoretically and substantively, and found it a totally unfounded distortion (Hamilton 1979, Reser 1981). They had no difficulty presenting respectable and convincing evidence based on in-depth field experience to refute Hippler's ethnocentric stereotypes. In response, rather than defending his specific interpretations, Hippler (1981) reiterated his view that traditional culture was "incredibly repressive" and argued for the complete abandonment of cultural relativism. Such a move would make serious cross-cultural understanding unlikely and would represent a return to the Eurocentrism of the nineteenth century. If Hippler's work had not appeared in a serious professional journal in the last quarter of the twentieth century, it might be shrugged off as representative of the lunatic fringe; as it is, however, it offers a textbook example of how theoretical preconceptions can influence one's "scientific" observation.

Belatedly, researchers began to examine the cognitive skills that aborigines actually used in their daily lives and found that they consistently rated higher than Europeans. For example, aborigines excelled on visual memory and spatial tests, which were skills that served them well in route finding, tracking, hunting, and gathering (Klich 1988). Earlier anthropological observers were also impressed by the superior visual acuity and observational abilities of aborigines; but in line with their racist and evolutionary biases, they devalued them as instinctive survival skills and "lower" mental functions. D. Lewis (1976) found that aborigines routinely kept detailed mental track of the topographical features that they passed when traveling across country that to him seemed virtually featureless. In random tests in which he used a compass, he found that aborigines could point with great precision in the direction of sacred sites that were 77 or more miles (200 kilometers [km]) away. Such accuracy required them to constantly update a mental map of their movements, and they were able to do this even in unfamiliar country. Such spatial abilities are well supported by the aboriginal language and the Dreamtime cosmology. A European would have rated as feeble-minded in such a test.

## LANGUAGE AND CULTURE

### Linguistic Relativity and the Sapir–Whorf Hypothesis

A major point of theoretical debate in anthropology is between the extreme relativists, who insist that each culture can only be understood in its own terms, versus those who are more interested in comparison and seek cultural universals or stages of development. This debate was introduced in Chapter 1 with the emic/etic distinction, and it appeared again in the previous section on cognitive ability. In this section, we view the issue from the perspective of language. The relativist view

of language, as it developed in American anthropology under Boas and his student Edward Sapir, was a direct response to the extreme Eurocentric evolutionary schemes that were developed by nineteenth-century linguists who maintained that Indo-European languages were the most highly evolved in the world. German linguist Max Müller (1823–1900) constructed a scale of linguistic evolutionary development based on an earlier grammatical classification of languages into isolating, agglutinating, and amalgamating types. The most primitive types were called isolating because they were thought to use words that were unaltered roots. Agglutinating languages made composite words from previously isolated roots, and amalgamating languages such as Indo-European changed the meaning of words by inflection. In Müller's scheme of evolutionary progress, the appearance of amalgamating languages corresponded to the rise of the Middle Eastern state and thus was identified with civilization and progress, whereas more primitive languages were associated with nomadism (Figure 5.2).

As non-Indo-European languages became better known, it quickly became apparent that Müller's evolutionary scheme had little empirical foundation. Using Native American languages, Boas argued that with language, as with mentality generally, there was no basis for ranking into higher and lower stages of evolutionary progress. Although Boas recognized many specific differences in languages, he believed that all were equally capable of expressing complex ideas and did so as the need arose. Boas also implied that linguistic categories were characterized by a certain arbitrariness. For example, he observed that while many hues of color could be distinguished, a given language might name only a few and in ways that were not readily translatable into the color terms of another language (Boas 1911). Ruth Benedict (1934) used this position when she argued that each culture was built from behaviors arbitrarily selected from the spectrum of possible behavior. Edward Sapir, a linguistic student of Boas, and Sapir's student Benjamin Whorf carried these ideas further and implied that linguistic categories defined the reality that the speakers of a given language perceived. In effect, the speakers of different languages live in different perceptual worlds. This general view that language somehow shapes perception became known as the **Sapir–Whorf hypothesis**, although Sapir and Whorf never formulated their views as a single testable hypothesis (Kay and Kempton 1984).

## Color Classifications and Folk Taxonomies

The most famous examination of the issues implied by the Sapir–Whorf hypothesis was the comparative analysis of color terms by Brent Berlin

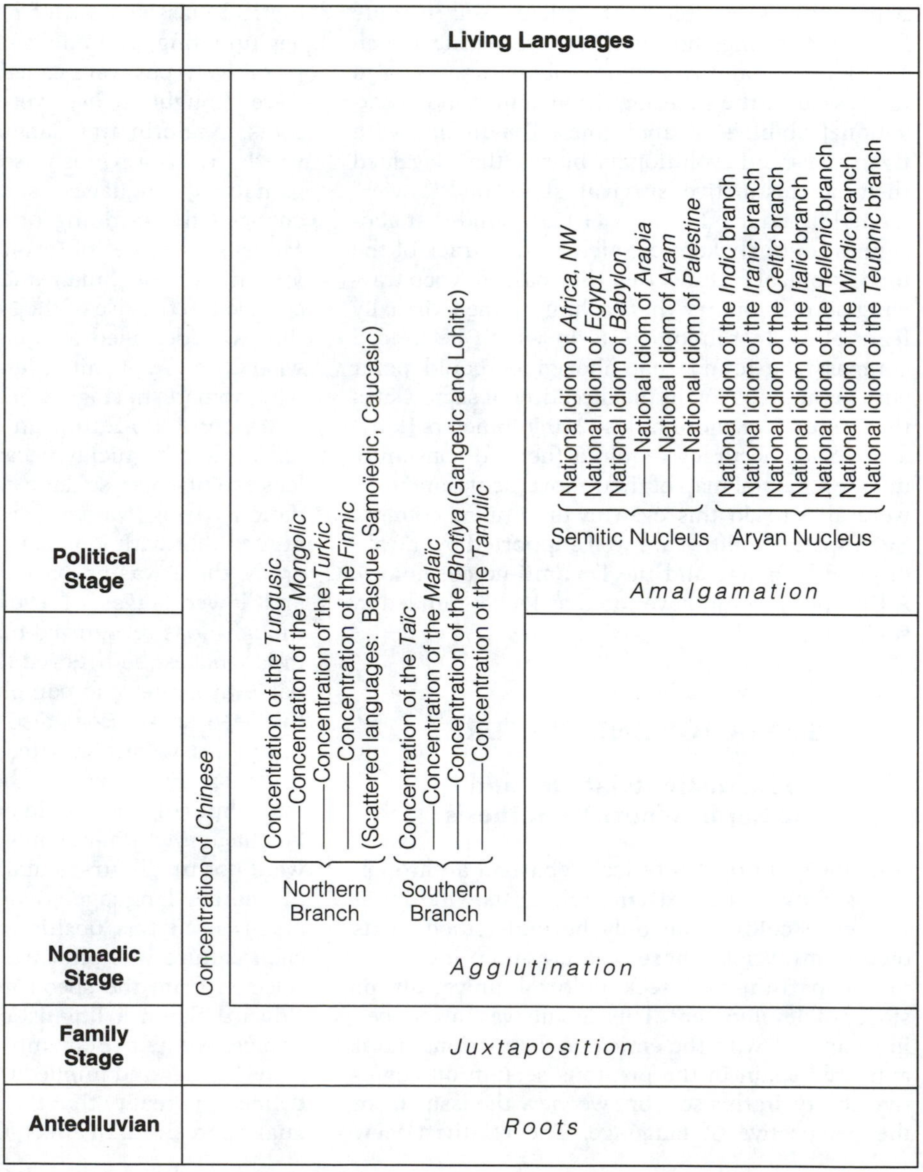

FIGURE 5.2
*Stages of evolutionary progress in the development of languages, according to Müller. (SOURCE: From Max Müller's contribution to C. C. J. Bunsen,* Outlines of the Philosophy of University History Applied to Language and Religion, *2 vols. London: Longman, 1854.)*

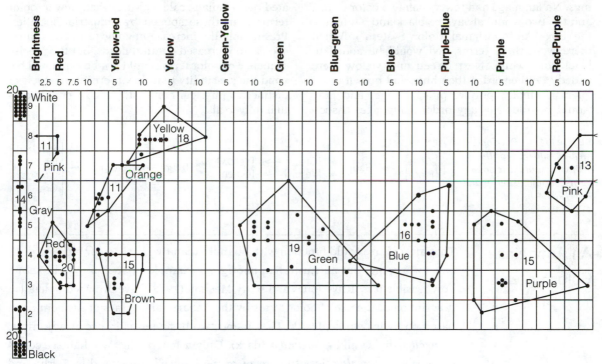

**FIGURE 5.3**  *Normalized foci of basic color terms in twenty languages. Numerals appearing along the borders of the chart refer to the Munsell system of color notation. Numerals appearing in the body of the chart refer to the number of languages in the sample of twenty that encode the corresponding color category. The smallest possible number of lines are used to enclose each color area.* (SOURCE: *Berlin and Kay 1969.*)

and Paul Kay (1969). These researchers collected color terms from speakers of twenty widely diverse languages by placing a transparent sheet over a chart of 329 color chips arranged by degree of hue and brightness. Native speakers were asked to mark with a grease pen the focal point of each color term or the chip that best represented it, as well as the total range of chips to which each term could refer. Basic color terms could not be composites or narrowly applied, so terms like blue-green, pinkish, or apple red were excluded.

It was found that among all the languages, only eleven basic color terms were recognized (white, black, red, green, yellow, blue, brown, purple, pink, orange, and gray) and there was remarkable agreement on the focal points of each term (Figure 5.3). This was a surprising blow to those who thought that color terms were not constrained by

nature, but even more surprising was the discovery that the set of terms used by any particular language was limited and to a certain extent predictable. Although, in theory, there were 2048 possible combinations of the eleven basic color terms, only 22 sets or combinations actually occurred. Furthermore, these combinations could be grouped into seven stages, which implied an evolutionary sequence because they appeared to correspond to levels of cultural complexity (Figure 5.4).

By searching the literature, Berlin and Kay (1969) expanded their sample to include ninety-eight languages and confirmed their original find-

---

***Sapir–Whorf hypothesis***  Suggests that one's view of the world is shaped by language, such that the speakers of different languages may live in different perceptual worlds.

ings. No language had fewer than two color terms, and the two would always be black and white (see the box "An Aboriginal Color System"). When there were three terms, red would be added to black and white. Next, green and yellow were added in either order, then blue, and brown in sequence. Finally, purple, pink, orange, and gray would be added in any order. Languages associated with small-scale cultures had fewer color terms than those spoken by industrial societies. Presumably the increase in color terms was in response to increased cultural needs, but the precise sequence of color terms could not be explained beyond the possibility that they represented levels of distinctive physical contrast, which were perceptual universals.

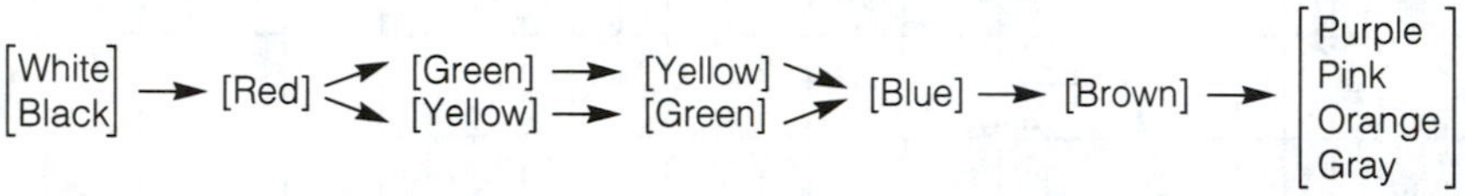

FIGURE 5.4 *Developmental sequence for the acquisition of basic color terms. (SOURCE: Berlin and Kay 1969:4.)*

$$\begin{bmatrix} White \\ Black \end{bmatrix} \rightarrow [Red] \begin{smallmatrix} \nearrow \\ \searrow \end{smallmatrix} \begin{matrix} [Green] \rightarrow [Yellow] \\ [Yellow] \rightarrow [Green] \end{matrix} \begin{smallmatrix} \searrow \\ \nearrow \end{smallmatrix} [Blue] \rightarrow [Brown] \rightarrow \begin{bmatrix} Purple \\ Pink \\ Orange \\ Gray \end{bmatrix}$$

## An Aboriginal Color System

That any culture could function with no more than two basic color terms is difficult to imagine, but an Australian aboriginal example of such a system shows how feasible it is. Rhys Jones and Betty Meehan (1978) have provided a detailed description of the use of color terms by the Anbarra aborigines of Arnhem Land based on their own fieldwork. They found two basic terms in use as adjectives: *-gungaltja* (light) and *-gungundja* (dark). Only a few of the very lightest colors were called *-gungaltja*, just 10 percent of the Munsell chips used by Berlin and Kay (1969), including bright red. All objects could be described using these two terms. For example, storm clouds, the sky, granite, and aborigines were "dark," whereas other clouds, the sea, sandstone, newborn babies, Europeans, and sunsets were "light." Four mineral pigments were used as paints and were distinctively named: white clay, black charcoal, red ochre, and yellow ochre. These pigments have great archaeological depth in Australia and have great symbolic significance. Objects painted with these pigments, or that resembled their color, could be described in reference to the pigment. Thus, a sunset might be described as "light, red ochre present within it," but such restricted use would seem to disqualify such pigment terms for recognition as basic color terms as defined by Berlin and Kay. A gray-green colored, waterborne algal scum was also treated as a paint pigment term. The restricted nature of pigment terms was also apparent from the fact that each belonged to a specific moiety, whereas the basic color terms, *light* and *dark*, had no moiety affiliation. Many plant dyes were in use, and dyed objects were described by reference to the specific plant used, but such terms were not generalized further. In recent years, the Anbarra have readily applied English color terms to the brightly colored European objects that have entered their region.

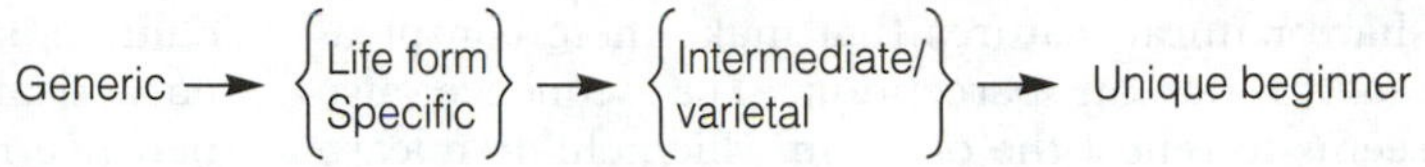

FIGURE 5.5  *Universal taxonomic categories of folk biological taxonomies.* (*SOURCE: Berlin 1972.*)

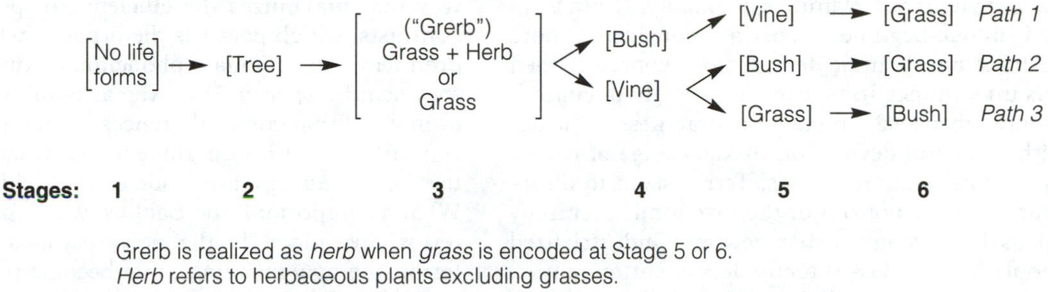

Generic ⟶ {Life form / Specific} ⟶ {Intermediate/ varietal} ⟶ Unique beginner

[No life forms] ⟶ [Tree] ⟶ [("Grerb") Grass + Herb or Grass] ⟨ [Bush] ⟨ [Vine] ⟶ [Grass] *Path 1* / [Bush] ⟶ [Grass] *Path 2* ⟩ [Vine] ⟨ [Grass] ⟶ [Bush] *Path 3* ⟩

Stages:   1        2            3            4         5          6

Grerb is realized as *herb* when *grass* is encoded at Stage 5 or 6.
Herb refers to herbaceous plants excluding grasses.

FIGURE 5.6   *Lexical-encoding sequence for folk botanical life forms (showing three possible paths for adding life-form terms). "Grerb" is realized as* herb *when* grass *is encoded at Stage 5 or 6.* Herb *refers to herbaceous plants excluding grasses. (SOURCE: Brown 1977.)*

The search for universals in linguistic classification and their possible evolutionary implications quickly expanded to other domains. Berlin and his associates turned their attention to ethnobiology and established a hierarchy of folk taxonomic terms that appeared to resemble the color-term sequence. They first inferred that languages could potentially recognize five taxonomic categories that they called generic, life form, specific, varietal/intermediate, and unique beginner (Berlin 1972; Berlin, Breedlove, and Raven 1973) (Figure 5.5).

In an inferred developmental sequence of plant taxonomies, a language first acquires generic terms, such as *oak* and *pine*, before differentiating between them with specific terms, such as *black oak*, or generalizing by adding a few life-form terms, such as *tree*. Varietal terms are most likely to be applied to cultivated plants. Most peoples find little need to recognize the unique beginner term *plant*.

Cecil Brown (1977) suggests that six globally distributed life-form terms for plants—*tree, grass, herb, "grerb"* (grass and herb), *bush*, and *vine*—were added to a language in a predictable sequence, like basic color terms (Figure 5.6). The six life-form terms could, in theory, occur in sixty-four different combinations; however, in a survey of

105 languages, Brown found that only eleven patterns actually occurred and these could be grouped into six stages. A language might have no life-form terms, or it might only recognize the *tree* life form. In Stage 3, a single life-form term was added, *grerb*, which might refer to either grass and herbs, or both. By Stage 6, all six life-form terms would be recognized. The first three stages of development thus used no more than two life-form terms and were thought to be associated with small-scale societies. Brown (1979a) also identifies five animal life-form terms: *fish, bird, snake, "wug"* (small insectlike creatures, bugs, and worms), and *mammal*, which follow similar sequential stages (Figure 5.7).

Brown (1979a) infers that the actual sequence of life-form terms reflects the universal tendency for classification to be based on simple binary oppositions and the fact that biological groupings

FIGURE 5.7   *Lexical-encoding sequence for folk zoological life forms.* (*SOURCE: Brown 1979a.*)

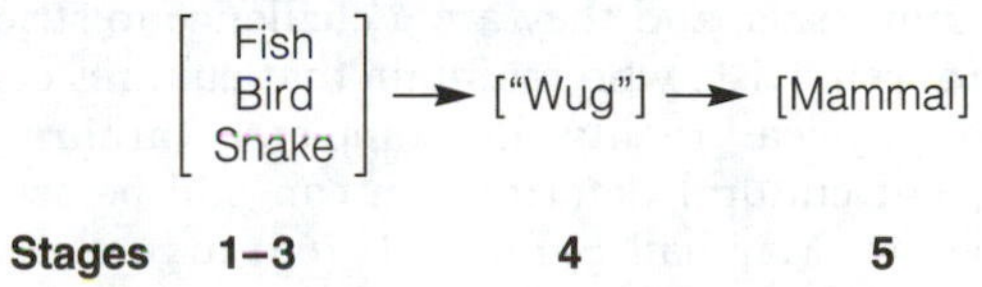

[Fish / Bird / Snake] ⟶ ["Wug"] ⟶ [Mammal]

Stages   1–3                 4              5

share natural features that make them conspicuous to human perception. The sequence also seems to reflect the order in which children learn to classify nature.

This analysis has interesting implications for the debate about primitive mentality. If life-form and unique-beginner terms are considered more abstract and generic terms more concrete, then this undermines some expectations about cultural progress because increased abstractness coincides with a general devolution in knowledge of nature as cultural scale increases. Terms seem to disappear from the bottom of the taxonomic hierarchy up as increasingly urbanized and industrialized people become less directly dependent on nature. It is common for individuals in small-scale societies to be able to name 500 to 1000 plants, whereas urban people may know barely 50 to 100 plants. Based on detailed linguistic reconstructions within specific language groups, Brown (1979b) infers that life-form terms have been added largely within the last 2000–4000 years in step with the rise of political complexity, while use of generic terms has sharply declined.

Randall and Hunn (1984, Hunn 1985) are critical of the life-form concept used by Brown, arguing that it is unjustified to define it by morphological criteria. They point out that some life-form terms such as *bird* are distinctive biological categories, whereas others such as *tree* are neither natural nor very distinctive as categories, although they be important for people to distinguish for utilitarian reasons. Randall and Hunn suggest that languages judged to be more "primitive" because they lack life-form terms may actually group generic taxa into many abstract utilitarian categories such as by edibility or method of extraction. There are also serious methodological issues in Brown's work, especially the possibility that folk taxonomies may be altered by schooling and translation problems. Biological categories are inherently more difficult to work with than color, which has relatively few dimensions to control.

Basic color terms do appear to be genuine cultural universals, and they are a challenge to strict cultural relativists who maintain that cultures can define physical reality in completely arbitrary ways, but cultural determinism can still be seen to operate. Marshall Sahlins (1976a) argues that cultures systematically make symbolic use of the natural distinctions that people can most readily perceive in color, just as natural sounds are used for linguistic purposes. Berlin and Kay (1969) point out that languages add new color terms in a way that maximizes the efficiency of perceptible contrasts, which parallels the order in which children learn to articulate phonemic distinctions as they acquire speech. However, as Sahlins stresses, even given that color differences are naturally perceptible, it is still important to ask what cultural uses, or meanings, are made of these differences. What is important for Sahlins when new color terms are added is the new relations between terms, the new meanings, that become possible.

Sahlins (1976a) observes that Stage 1 color terms, which distinguish only two colors, light and dark, are used for simple, dualistic, symbolic oppositions such as between life and death, male and female, sacred and profane. The addition of red creates a mediated opposition in which red can variously be opposed to either dark or light, like the ambiguous jaguar mediating between the complementary opposites of male and female in Chapter 3. The further addition of either green or yellow in Stage 3 creates a pair of analogous opposition as in the familiar $a : b :: c : d$ pattern. These perceptual structures can be created using jaguars, caimans, and anacondas, as well as with colors, and they can then be made to carry a variety of cultural meanings.

## MAGIC, BELIEF, AND THE SUPERNATURAL

### Shamanism and Psychopathology

**Shamans** are part-time religious specialists and healers who personify the most extreme elements of so-called primitive mentalities and magical thinking in small-scale societies. Early missionaries, who often called shamans, witch doctors, attributed their supernatural powers to the devil and confronted them as enemies of Christianity. Government authorities often disapproved of shamans because they sometimes used their powers within the community to organize resistance to government programs and because shamanistic curing practices were often considered to be contrary to modern medical science if not actually dangerous. Even anthropologists have had difficulty being objective about shamans. For example, Alfred Kroeber, a prominent Boas-trained anthropologist, suggests in the 1948 edition of *Anthropology*, long a standard textbook, that modern civilization's rejection of shamanism and related beliefs was a measure of scientific progress. He observed that people in our own society recognize as abnormal or insane anyone who talks to the dead or who thinks they can turn into a bear, whereas "backward people" consider such behavior socially acceptable and even admirable. Kroeber considered shamanism to be a psychopathology, and emphatically declared,

*When the sane and well in one culture believe what only the most ignorant, warped, and insane believe in another, there would seem to be some warrant for rating the first culture lower and the second higher. Or are our discards, insane, and hypersuggestibles perhaps right and the rest of us wrong?* (1948:298)

Shamanism does involve a striking collection of phenomena including various trance states, magical flight, and spirit possession (Peters and Price-Williams 1980), all of which may be very difficult to understand outside the cultural context in which they occur. Shamans induce trances using rhythmical chanting, dancing, deprivation, and the ingestion of psychoactive drugs. Anthropologist Michael Harner (1980), who conducts popular workshops and seminars on shamanism, has demonstrated that under the proper conditions virtually anyone can induce such trance states. Shamanism may well be tens of thousands of years old, judging from parallels between the distinctive lines and grid patterns scratched on cave walls during the Ice Age in Europe and similar designs characteristic of rock art associated with shamans in many parts of the world. Some researchers infer that these images are entoptic phenomena, images that tribal shamans see inside their eyes during trance states (J. D. Lewis-Williams and T. A. Dowson 1988). In ecstatic trance, shamans contact the otherwise invisible spirit world and perform amazing feats, including the magical killing of enemies and transformations into animals. Using their spirit helpers to cure, shamans massage their patients and dramatically suck out intrusive objects

thought to be the causes of illness, or they shoot invisible darts into the bodies of enemies to harm them. Australian aboriginal shamans have reportedly killed people by simply pointing a bone in their direction.

The cultural reality of Amazonian shamanism was impressed upon me while conducting a routine residence pattern survey in an Ashaninka village, when I was surprised to encounter a man who maintained a separate house from his wife. It is common for young unmarried Ashaninka men to build separate houses, but this case was unusual enough for me to question further. I discovered that this man was a powerful jaguar shaman who could cure people and transform himself into a jaguar to magically attack his enemies. He explained to me very matter of factly that it sometimes upset his wife when he became a jaguar at night, so he often slept in his own house.

Ashaninka shamans are called "tobacco-eaters," after the bamboo tubes they carry containing a thick, tarlike tobacco paste that is licked from a stick to help induce shamanic visions. Jaguar shamans are widely respected and feared by the Ashaninka, and their exploits are well known. I heard accounts of someone shooting an intruding jaguar at night and then discovering that they had killed a shaman. Another incident demonstrated the social context of shamanistic curing. My Shipibo field assistant developed a chronic leg infection that refused to heal. He consulted a shaman who attributed the problem to the otter spirit, which had been sent by another villager who was a bitter personal enemy of my assistant. The cure was effected when the two reached a reconciliation.

Many observers have questioned the authenticity of shamanic performances, pointing to incidences in which the shaman seems not be in a genuine trance or when a curer has hidden in his mouth the object that he intended to suck from his patient. Deliberately hidden objects of this sort simply add drama to the curing performance. It is possible that some shamans may pretend to be in trance, but most suspicions of fraud may be due to a misunderstanding of the nature of shamanism,

---

**shaman**  A part-time religious specialist who manipulates the spirit world for divination and curing.

FIGURE 5.8
*A Yanomamo shaman in a "lucid trance" during a feast.*

especially the fact that shamanic trance often differs from other forms of spirit possession. A shaman typically is in a "lucid trance" or a "waking dream" in which he communicates both with the spirits and with his audience, and he will usually be able to remember the events later (Figure 5.8). This is not the same as pathological hysteria, and it does not mean that the shaman becomes totally dissociated. The shamanic trance is a temporary reduction of normal reality testing in which dream images are treated as if real within a specific cultural context and are then used for social purposes (Peters and Price-Williams 1980).

The psychopathology view of shamanism by anthropologists was in favor for a long time. For example, Julian Silverman (1967) emphasized the parallels between acute schizophrenics who take on bizarre behavior and shamans who experience cognitive disturbances, or altered states of consciousness, as an apparent reaction to a major personal crisis involving guilt or failure. In Silverman's view, like Kroeber's, the most significant difference between schizophrenics in our society and shamans in small-scale societies is that schizophrenics find no social support for their behavior and it is consequently maladaptive, whereas shamans are culturally accepted. Thus, in this view, shamanism can be considered a therapeutic psychological adjustment to a psychopathology.

The connection between schizophrenia and shamanism is also implied in the authoritative *Diagnostic and Statistical Manual of Mental Disorders* (*DSM-III*), the basic guidebook published by the American Psychiatric Association (APA) in 1980, for use by clinicians. According to *DSM-III*, "magical thinking" is seen "in children, in people in primitive cultures, and in Schizotypal Personality Disorder, Schizophrenia, and Obsessive Compulsive Disorder" (APA 1980:363). The belief that the members of small-scale cultures are sick and childlike dies hard, even among scientists!

The clinical concept of schizophrenia has been refined considerably since Silverman's analysis was published, and even using the definition of schizophrenic disorders contained within *DSM-III*, it now seems clear that there are striking differences between schizophrenics and shamans. As Richard Noll (1984) points out, attributing shamanistic experiences to an altered state of consciousness implies out-of-control hallucinations and other paranoid delusions, which we tend to view negatively but which are not characteristic of shamanism. Noll speaks of the **shamanic state of** *consciousness (SSC)*, which he distinguishes from the altered state of consciousness (ASC) as it is usually recognized. The ASC of the schizophrenic is obviously maladaptive. It comes unbidden, and he hears uncontrollable mocking voices, whereas the shaman can enter the SSC virtually at will, remains aware of his state, sees visions, uses them for socially beneficial purposes, and then freely returns to his normal consciousness. A successful shaman achieves a balance between his spiritual experiences and the demands of everyday life, but there is no reason to view the SSC as a psychopathology.

## Aboriginal Voodoo Death and Culture-Bound Syndromes

Anthropologists and medical researchers have been fascinated by reports of mysterious deaths and illnesses in tribal societies that are culturally attributed to supernatural causes and that have not always been readily explainable in purely physical terms. A prime example from aboriginal Australia are cases of so-called voodoo death, such as bone pointing referred to previously, in which people are killed by sorcery. The long-established anthropological interpretations of such incidents was that the victim died from shock, caused by intense fear of death combined with an absolute belief in the reality of sorcery (Cannon 1942). More extensive observations in recent years by medically trained individuals have clarified both the physical and cultural basis of such deaths. Harry Eastwell (1982), who conducted periodic psychiatric clinics in aboriginal communities in Arnhem Land between 1969 and 1980, treated thirty-nine patients for a variety of physical and emotional symptoms, which he called "fear of sorcery syndrome." In nearly all cases, some specific event such as the death or illness of close kin, interpersonal conflicts, or a ritual violation led to suspicions of supernatural danger. Patients showed the typical symptoms of extreme fear: bulging eyes, dilated pupils, sweating, agitation, and sleeplessness. Two of the patients died, one with an abnormality of the adrenal glands, which may have made him more vulnerable to stress, and the other from kidney and heart failure.

Because so few deaths actually occurred in these cases, Eastwell began to suspect that more than just fear was involved in voodoo death. This was further supported when two patients thought to be dying from sorcery were found to be severely dehydrated and were saved by prompt medical intervention. Further analyses of the process of dying experienced by elderly aborigines revealed a regular cultural pattern in which both dying person and kin decide that death is imminent and mutually facilitate the process—the dying person refuses to drink, and the kin withhold water so that death occurs within 24–48 hours by dehydration.

The parallels between aboriginal patient-assisted euthanasia and voodoo death are striking. In both cases, the actual mechanism of death is probably dehydration, but it occurs because the patient and the community both agree that the patient is dying. Water is withheld at the same time as wailing and formal funeral rituals are begun. It is believed that only the totemic spirit animates the dying person and it does not need to drink. At death this spirit returns to the ancestral well.

Psychiatrist John Cawte (1976) describes another Australian culture-bound syndrome, *Malgri*, from the Wellesley Island aborigines in the Gulf of Carpentaria. In this case, the violation of ritual restrictions on keeping land foods and seafoods separate causes local totemic spirits to afflict a person with severe abdominal swelling and pain. The condition usually responds to specific ritual treatment and is apparently not fatal. To observers trained in psychoanalysis, *Malgri* suggested hysterical "displacement" of oedipal conflicts, but Cawte believes that it was more understandable as part of the totemically regulated system of territoriality based on the Dreaming. He noted that *Malgri* was most likely to affect people outside their own estate territories, and the most dangerous spirits were those controlling the richest resource zones where foraging pressure was the greatest. Furthermore, *Malgri* did not occur on the nearby main-

---

*shamanic state of consciousness (SSC)* An interpretation of the shamanic trance phenomenon that distinguishes it from the altered state of consciousness of schizophrenics. A shaman may enter and leave the SSC at will, remains aware of his surroundings, and uses the SSC for socially beneficial purposes.

land where population densities were lower and resources would be less critical.

## The Healing Power of Myth and Symbols

Medically trained observers broadly agree that shamanistic healers can successfully treat people suffering from a variety of psychiatric complaints such as *Malgri,* using ritual techniques. Native curers may also be adept at treating injuries and illnesses with herbal remedies that have empirically identifiable chemical properties. Researchers further concede that shamanic ritual may involve important psychotherapeutic techniques including the power of suggestion, the restructuring of social relations, catharsis, and the stimulation of neurochemicals (Dow 1986).

Whatever the specific healing mechanism might be, James Dow (1986) suggests that shamanistic ritual works because culturally defined symbols are manipulated in ways that influence the body–mind relationship by helping people to alter their self-perceptions. Symbols, whether they involve totemic spirits or psychoanalytic concepts such as guilt and repression, are drawn from cultural myths, which condense important truths about the human experience in society. For psychotherapy to succeed, the patient and practitioner must establish a working relationship, and the shaman may facilitate this through what Dow calls the "shamanic paradox." That is, the patient must suspend any disbelief about the validity of the empirically unbelievable supernatural powers claimed by the shaman—he must implicitly believe in the authenticity of the therapeutic process before it can be effective. When the patient fully participates in the curing process, through his belief, or the suspension of disbelief, he may be able to reevaluate his own experiences and gain control over his feelings. These therapeutic principles help explain the persistence and apparent success of many ritual symbols.

The effectiveness of symbols is illustrated by Australian material, again from Arnhem Land. In this area, the central Dreamtime myth, which is reenacted in a major series of rituals including circumcision ceremonies, concerns the Wawilak sisters, two Dreaming ancestors who created the local cultural landscape during their Dreamtime travels. The myth details the creative activities of the Wawilak sisters and recounts how they lose ritual power to men when they are swallowed by the Rainbow Serpent who is attracted when the sisters' menstrual blood contaminates the snakes' pool. The Wawilak sisters and women in general are associated with the fertile dry season. The Rainbow Serpent rising up to eat the Wawilak sisters has obvious male associations and creates the widespread flooding of the lowlands during the Arnhem Land wet season (Figure 5.9).

The Wawilak myth parallels the sacred flute myths found in Amazonia and deals with the same classic issues of life and death, reproduction, and male and female roles. Although the Wawilak ritual complex does not directly involve shamanic curing, according to the analysis of Nancy Munn (1969), participants in the rituals consciously identify with the characters in the myth, and as they enact it they convert their personal fears of death into more positive outcomes and satisfying images of health and community well-being. For example, circumcision of a boy is metaphorically compared to the swallowing of the sisters, only in this case he is ritually reborn. In other ceremonial reenactments, women happily avoid being eaten by the serpent. Blood letting conducted in connection with circumcision ceremonies is equated with the menstrual blood of the Wawilak sisters and is converted to ritual use as body paint, thus transferring symbolic strength and actual positive feelings to the participant. As one aboriginal man explained,

*It makes us feel easy and comfortable and it makes us strong. It makes us good. . . . We have that . . . strength from that blood. It goes inside when we put that blood on.* (Munn 1969:195, citing Warner 1958:195)

Interpreting the meaning of many other specific practices, which we identify as "magical" because we assume they have no empirical basis, is equally challenging. Michael Brown (1984) examined ritual songs that the Aguaruna of the Peruvian Amazon use to improve their hunting, especially when they go after spider monkeys with blowguns. The songs may be sung before a man goes hunting, or they are sung silently as the hunt is in progress, and they contain complex allusions to myths and images of hunting success. Brown argues that the Aguaruna consider these songs to be as instrumen-

FIGURE 5.9 *The rainbow serpent is an important mythic figure central to ritual performances that strengthen community well-being in many areas of northern Australia.*

tal for their hunting success as the technical quality of their blowguns and stalking skills. In his view, the Aguaruna are right because these "magical" songs help them focus their energy on the hunting task. They alter their internal mental states, giving them confidence, in the same way that ritual symbols can have a psychotherapeutic effect. This line of argument is similar to Bronislaw Malinowski's functionalist theory that magic helps people deal with the uncertainties that lie beyond the limits of their technical capabilities.

## HEALTH AND NUTRITION IN TRIBAL SOCIETIES

### Myth and Reality of the "Noble Savage"

Most early visitors to undisturbed tribal societies were impressed with the health and vigor of the peoples they saw. It is likely that these first impressions were basically accurate, but they were confused and embellished with unnecessary pronouncements about morality and human perfection that became the myth of the "noble savage." For example, some of the first Europeans to visit Brazil reported that the Indians "naturally follow goodness" and "live together in harmony, with no dissension" (Hemming 1978:15). From such glowing descriptions, it was easy to conclude that "savages" were superior human beings living idyllic lives in Eden-like innocence. The comfortable nudity of most Amazonian Indians, which astonished Europeans, certainly attributed to this noble savage image.

Most anthropologists have been careful to disassociate themselves from such noble savage romanticism. There can be no doubt that the members of small-scale cultures are no more superior or inferior as people than any other group of human beings. Tribal peoples can be selfish and cruel. They quarrel and kill each other just as people who live in cities. Tribal culture is also not perfect. It is not in perfect balance with nature. Tribal societies are not perfectly egalitarian. Individuals must pay personal costs for tribal membership, as people must to live in any human society. Nevertheless, generally good health and vigor seem to be two advantages of life in small-scale culture for those who reach adulthood.

Evidence for the overall high quality of life in relatively independent tribal societies appears in a report by geneticist James Neel (1970). He summarized the findings of 8 years of basic biochemical and health research among Native Amazonians, carried out by an interdisciplinary team of more than a dozen researchers using sophisticated techniques. Neel reported that, in general, they found the Xavante, Yanomamo, and Makiritare, who they examined in Brazil and Venezuela, to be in "excellent physical condition." (See also the box "Health Report on the Waorani.") Infant and childhood mortality rates were higher than in fully industrialized countries, but the general pattern of life expectancy was better than in colonial India at the end of the nineteenth century.

Neel (1970) concluded that these tribal peoples were well adjusted to the viruses, bacterial diseases, and internal parasites naturally occurring in their territory. The Yanomamo and Xavante were found to have levels of gamma globulin, the blood protein containing infection-fighting antibodies, that were twice the levels found in civilized populations. Yanomamo babies are born with a very high degree of passive immunity acquired from their mothers. These immunities are maintained by prolonged breast feeding. Yanomamo infants then quickly develop active immunities because they are continuously exposed to all the local pathogens. The most significant diseases, including malaria and measles, were assumed to be post-Columbian introductions to which people were not yet well adjusted.

Theoretically, there are many reasons why the quality of life should be high in small-scale societies—most importantly, the generally low population densities and relative social equality of small-scale societies would help ensure equal access to basic subsistence resources so that everyone would enjoy good nutrition. Furthermore, low population densities and frequent mobility would significantly reduce the occurrence of epidemic diseases, and natural selection—in the absence of the antibiotics, immunizations, surgery, and other forms of medical intervention—would develop high levels of disease resistance. Healthy people are those who survive. Tribal societies, in effect, maintain public health by emphasizing prevention of morbidity rather than treatment. The healthiest conditions would likely exist under mobile foraging and pastoralism, whereas there might be some health costs associated with the increased densities and reduced mobility of settled farming villages.

## Teeth and Tribal Diets

Health researchers have increasingly recognized that the typical diet found among small-scale subsistence foragers and farmers, which is low in fat, salt, and refined sugars and high in fiber and vitamin C, is actually the most ideal human diet. Significant epidemiological evidence suggests that many forms of cancer are associated with relatively recent dietary changes related to food marketing, processing and storage (such as salting, pickling, and refining), and dramatic increases in consumption of fat and simple carbohydrates, or refined sugars (Cohen 1987). Of course, foods eaten by self-supporting, subsistence peoples are

also free of the contaminants and additives that are introduced into industrially produced foods by the chemicals used in agriculture and in processing.

Perhaps the first scientific evidence that tribal peoples could be shown to be physically superior to "civilized" peoples appeared in an article published in 1894 in the *Journal of the Royal Anthropological Association* by Wilberforce Smith, who compared the teeth of Sioux Indians with typical Londoners. Smith became interested in this problem while conducting a survey of the teeth of his fellow Englishmen, which he found to be disastrously decayed. He knew that the skulls of prehistoric European "savages" invariably contained healthier teeth than contemporary peoples and decided to find out if modern "savages" also had healthy teeth. Taking advantage of the visit of Buffalo Bill's Wild West Show, which was then in London, he obtained permission to examine the teeth of ten Sioux men, ranging from 15 to about 50 years in age. He found that all had "massive admirably formed teeth, evenly ranged." They were well worn, but none were decayed and no molars were missing. He concluded, "Their teeth alone proved them to have led the life of genuine savages" (1894:110). In comparison, the younger portion of the 300 Londoners that he also examined had half as many usable pairs of opposed molars as the Sioux of the same age category, and Londoners ages 35–45 years had some 80 percent fewer paired molars than the older Sioux.

When Smith (1894) presented his findings in a lecture before the Royal Anthropological Institute, he displayed a dental cast made from a member of his own family, which showed the terrible condition of a typical Londoner's teeth, alongside the skull of an average "savage" showing beautifully preserved teeth. To test the possibility that the remarkable health of the Siouxs' teeth was because they were exceptionally robust and healthy people, Smith did a comparison check of the teeth of twelve men of the regiment of Horse Guards from the Royal Household Cavalry, who would have been in superb physical condition. He found that the cavalrymen unfortunately had teeth that were only a "trifling degree better preserved" than the average Londoner's.

## Health Report on the Waorani

A very detailed assessment of the health status of another Native Amazonian group, the Waorani of Ecuador, was conducted in the field by a seven-person medical team in 1976. At that time, the Waorani were living independently as manioc gardeners and hunters and maintained only limited contacts with outsiders. In all, 293 people received very thorough medical exams. On the positive side, more than 95 percent of the sample appeared to be "very robust" and in "excellent health" (Larrick et al. 1979). There was no malnutrition, no obesity, no high blood pressure, no cardiovascular disease. Everyone had excellent eyesight, with no color blindness. No one was deaf.

On the negative side: Many children had scalp infections, but these were attributed to contacts with outsiders; some two-thirds out of a sample of 63 people showed evidence of light intestinal parasite infestation; 2 old women had pneumonia; 3 people were blind in one eye due to accidents; and there were many scars from spears and jaguar and peccary bites, while nearly all of the men had survived snake bites. Six people were described by the Waorani themselves as mentally deficient, and most of these cases were readily attributed to head injuries, fevers, or genetic defects. Surprisingly, the Waorani of all ages had high rates of dental decay. Only 5 out of the 230 people checked by the dentist were found to be completely free of cavities. It was suggested that such exceptionally high cavity rates were due to the unusual fact that the Waorani, unlike most Amazonians, consumed their manioc drink unfermented, while it still had a high sugar content. Although no estimate of mortality rates was given, it appears that many adults died in violent conflicts. As in Neel's (1970) report, the Waorani study attributed much of the excellent health of the Indians to the high quality of their diet, low population density, and relative isolation from outside diseases.

---

Smith (1894) correctly concluded that the lack of dental decay and tooth loss observed in tribal peoples was due to increased tooth wear, which kept the teeth clean and polished. He attributed the increased wear to the consumption of less cooked and less refined food and the absence of knives and forks, which meant that more chewing was required, as well as the presence of grit, or "dirt," in the food. It was later learned that the absence of refined carbohydrates also contributed to healthy tribal teeth. The reduced tooth wear of contemporary peoples who eat industrially processed foods is also likely related to the common problem of impacted molars, as Grover Krantz (1978) has observed. People eating coarse foods wear down not only the grinding surfaces of their teeth but also the sides of their teeth, which create enough jaw space to accommodate the third molars when they erupt. When there is no significant wear, the "wisdom teeth" often must be extracted.

The association between traditional dietary patterns and healthy teeth was documented more systematically in a series of field studies conducted by American dentist Weston Price (1945), between

1931 and 1936. Price visited some of the most traditional peoples in Amazonia, East Africa, Australia, and throughout the Pacific and found that tooth decay and peridontal disease was virtually absent among self-sufficient peoples but steadily increased as they adopted the food patterns of industrial societies.

In 1956, shortly after Price's dental research, T. L. Cleave, a physician in the British Royal Navy, used medical data on tribal peoples to isolate a single feature in the diets of industrialized people that caused what he called the "saccharine disease," a wide-ranging complex of conditions including tooth decay, ulcers, appendicitis, obesity, diabetes, constipation, and varicose veins. Like both Smith and Price before him, Cleave (1974) was impressed by the fact that tribal peoples did not suffer from many of the common ailments of civilization, and he attempted to find the special conditions that made tribal peoples healthier. His primary finding was that the traditional foods of tribal groups were consistently much higher in dietary fiber than were the highly refined foods consumed by industrialized peoples. High-fiber diets speed the transit time of food through the digestive system, thereby reducing many common diseases of civilization. It took many years for his findings to be incorporated into popular nutritional wisdom in the industrial world, but now high fiber, along with low fat and low salt, is widely accepted as an important component of a healthy diet.

Clifford Behrens (1986) provides some insights on how traditional classification systems are related to the maintenance of a high level of nutrition in tribal diets. Behrens found that the Shipibo of the Peruvian Amazon grouped their most preferred foods into two main emic categories, which he called "not-wild and cooked" and "wild and cooked." The Shipibo placed garden products such as plantains, maize, and manioc, which were high in carbohydrates, into the first category and fish and game, which were high in protein and fat, into the second category. The Shipibo considered their diet adequate only when it contained a balance of foods drawn from both categories. They accurately identified garden foods as the source of the energy needed for daily activities, while they felt that fish and game were needed for long-term health and growth.

## Tribal Life Expectancy and Quality of Life

At a special symposium held at the CIBA Foundation in London in 1976 and attended by more than two dozen specialists on the health of tribal peoples, it was concluded that self-sufficient tribal groups were generally healthy, and it was recognized that intervention by outsiders, even when well intended, could seriously undermine existing balances (CIBA 1977). However, Betsy Lozoff and Gary Brittenham (1977) found that some important tribal health "paradoxes" remained unanswered:

1. How is population growth regulated?
2. If foragers were well nourished, why were they physically small?
3. If disease rates are low, why is tribal mortality high?

These apparent paradoxes are challenging questions that still cannot be fully answered. Population regulation is a critical issue because maintaining a stationary population seems to be a key to relative balance with resources and to a high quality of life. Population stability at constant, low-density levels also seems to be a general, but not invariable, characteristic of tribal groups. More recent interpretations suggest that fertility-limiting cultural mechanisms, such as prolonged lactation and postpartum sex taboos, referred to in previous chapters, were probably more important population regulators than raiding and infanticide, but the evidence is incomplete. High mortality due to raiding and infanticide would imply a reduced quality of life because it would lower average life expectancy; however, from a functionalist perspective, it might arguably increase life quality for the survivors by promoting stability between people and resources.

There are some troubling and probably unanswerable philosophical issues involved in the preceding paradoxes. Although tribal peoples in general are often smaller and lighter than Europeans and appear to have shorter life expectancies, how does one decide that a given stature or life expectancy should be an appropriate cross-cultural measure of well-being? There is some evidence to suggest that very low birth weights or relatively low infant-weight gain or growth rates may be associated with higher infant mortality rates. Some researchers also argue that small stature may indicate poor nutrition, especially in densely populated tribal areas (Dennett and Connell 1988). However, taller and longer may not always be better, especially if taller or longer-lived people experience a reduced quality of life within their particular cultural and environmental setting. Furthermore, many important data questions cannot be answered.

Estimating the life expectancy of tribal populations is an inherently difficult task because there are little reliable data that unambiguously represent fully independent populations. Many widely cited demographic profiles of tribal peoples are actually inferences based on paleodemographic techniques of questionable validity. Life tables, such as those used by insurance companies to show the probability of someone surviving to a given age, have been drawn up for various tribal and prehistoric populations and generally show a significantly lower life expectancy for tribal peoples than for contemporary industrial populations (Table 5.3). When using life tables, it is important to specify at what age life expectancy is based because life expectancy at birth may be skewed down by high infant mortality rates in tribal populations. The figures compiled by Fekri Hassan (1981) in Table 5.3 yield an estimated average life expectancy at age 15 years for seven ethnographically known foraging groups, including three from Australia, of just 26.4 years. By comparison, the figure for white Americans in 1986 was 61.3 years at age 15; however, 26.4 years was higher than the figures estimated for several archaeological populations and was higher than in fourteenth-century England.

Although tribal life expectancy is lower than that of modern industrial populations, this should not be surprising because, historically, life expectancy has made dramatic increases only within the past two centuries. Tribal peoples compare favorably with many preindustrial groups. However, all demographic estimates for tribal peoples must be used cautiously. Only figures based on reliable census records can be accepted at face value.

There are significant sources of bias and uncertainty in demographic research on tribal populations, as noted in our previous discussion of

**TABLE 5.3** *Estimated Life Expectancy of Prehistoric and Tribal Populations*

| Population | Life Expectancy at Age 15 |
| --- | --- |
| Upper Paleolithic | 16.9 |
| Catal Huyuk (Neolithic) | 17.0 |
| Neandertals | 17.5 |
| Natufians (Mesolithic) | 17.5 |
| Angamgssalik Eskimo* | 19.2 |
| Aborigines (Groote Eylandt)* | 23.3 |
| East Greenland Eskimo* | 23.5 |
| Birhor (foragers, India)* | 24.0 |
| England (fourteenth century) | 25.8 |
| Baker Lake Eskimo* | 27.7 |
| Aborigines (Tiwi)* | 33.1 |
| Aborigines (Northern Territory)* | 34.0 |
| White Americans (1986)† | 61.3 |

SOURCE: Hassan (1981:118).
*Ethnographically described foragers; average life expectancy = 26.4 years.
†Data from Wright (1990:225).

estimating infanticide rates from sex ratios. Hypothetical life expectancy tables for tribal populations are sometimes generated from fixed age-specific mortality rates, which must be specified ahead of time. An inherent circularity here makes it illegitimate to read mortality rates from life tables because the rates must be known before the table can be constructed. French researchers Jean-Pierre Bocquet-Appel and Claude Masset (1981) warn that attempts to reconstruct life tables based on estimated age of death in prehistoric skeletal populations can yield life expectancies that are systematically too low. Paleodemographic age estimates can only be valid if the burials are compared with a population that is already known to be identical in age structure. Furthermore, they caution that the common indicators of skeletal age, such as the age at which certain cranial sutures close, have changed over time.

## SUMMARY

This chapter demonstrates the difficulties of making meaningful cross-cultural quality-of-life comparisons of mental ability and health. It should make anyone cautious of simple stereotypes about tribal peoples as "underdeveloped." Although tribal individuals have the same basic intellectual and perceptual abilities as people in larger-scale cultures, their collective view of the world as reflected in myth, religion, and linguistic classification differs in significant ways that may be related to cultural scale and the absence of writing. However, when viewed from a relativistic and culturally sensitive position, tribal peoples are no more irrational, ignorant, nor childish than people anywhere.

Tribal peoples have tremendous stores of culturally transmitted knowledge about the world around them, and their religious beliefs are perpetuated because they work effectively and because their validity is reinforced by the experience of daily life. This position must be spelled out clearly because some anthropologists have suggested that, developmentally, tribal peoples are children who do not use adult logic and have difficulty separating fantasy from reality. Others have argued that tribal religious practices such as shamanism are the product of psychopathology.

Formal schooling and institutionalized medicine are clearly not the only routes to understanding and health. Not only are there inherent problems in data collection on these issues, but there are also dangers in generalizing from individuals to groups and major problems in deciding what standard of comparison can be used. The evidence suggests that, although infant mortality rates appear to be high and life expectancy is low relative to urban industrial populations, tribal peoples are generally free of infectious disease and nutritional deficiencies and avoid many of the dental problems and degenerative diseases that are so common in other populations. The most conservative conclusion is that tribal peoples show no basic differences in their mental abilities, even though they lack writing. The average tribal person would appear to enjoy a healthy vigorous life, relatively free of disease.

## STUDY QUESTIONS

1. Explain the views that each of the following took on the nature of "primitive" mentality: Boas, Tylor, Frazer, Lévy-Bruhl, Lévi-Strauss, and Hallpike.

2. Explain the cultural context of *Malgri*.

3. Use the Wawilak myth to illustrate the effectiveness of symbols.

4. Why are cross-cultural tests of cognitive ability difficult to apply and interpret?

5. Critique the psychopathology explanation of shamanism.

6. What conditions of small-scale cultures contribute to health?

## SUGGESTED READING

COHEN, MARK, AND GEORGE ARMELEGOS (eds.). 1984. *Paleopathology and the Origins of Agriculture*. Orlando, Fla.: Academic Press. Considers the health consequences of the transition to agriculture.

EATON, S. B. BOYD, MELVIN KONNER, AND MARJORIE SHOSTAK. 1988. *The Paleolithic Prescription*. New York: Harper & Row. Examines the health aspects of forager dietary patterns and applies them to contemporary society.

HARNER, M. J. 1980. *The Way of the Shaman*. New York: Harper & Row. A "how-to-do-it" manual that can be used by anyone interested in experimenting with the shamanic experience.

# 6

# PACIFIC ISLANDERS: THE RANKED CHIEFDOMS

The vast Pacific region, known as Oceania, was successfully explored and colonized by Austronesian-speaking voyagers, who spread out from their earlier footholds in the western Pacific, beginning some 3500 BP (before the present). By 1000 BP, virtually every habitable Pacific island supported thriving societies. When Europeans began to arrive in significant numbers in the nineteenth century, they found the Pacific islanders, except in New Guinea, organized into chiefdoms, or small kingdoms. Pacific cultures were perched on the "great divide" between tribes and states, displaying much of the social equality and equilibrium of small-scale cultures, yet maintaining a pervasive concern with rank. Remote from the centers of power in the industrializing world and offering relatively few resources to attract outsiders, many Pacific islands have still maintained much of their traditional cultural system. They also offer ideal material for examining the contrasts between tribes and states and for understanding the initial rise of large-scale cultures. Given the severe environmental constraints of small islands, Oceania also offers an important place to examine the relationships between population, culture, and resources.

## OCEANIA: ENVIRONMENT AND PREHISTORY

### The Island World

The Pacific Ocean covers roughly one-third of the earth's surface; yet focusing on the area from Hawaii south and excluding the Asian continental islands of Taiwan, Indonesia, the Philippines, and Australia, the remaining area, which is traditionally called *Oceania*, contains less than 500,000 square miles (mi²)(1.3 million kilometers [km²]) of land. If the islands of *Melanesia*, Hawaii, and New Zealand, which are mostly large, are also excluded, there remains a vast area of ocean containing some 10,000 islands comprising a mere 4500 mi² of land, an area less than half the size of Vermont, and an estimated population in 1970 of 570,000

---

*Oceania* The greater Pacific region as a culture area comprising Melanesia, Micronesia, Polynesia, and sometimes Australia.
*Melanesia* A culture area in the southwest Pacific containing the large islands of New Guinea, the Solomons, Vanuatu, and New Caledonia and inhabited by Papuan- and Austronesian-speaking peoples.

people. These islands are scattered over an immense distance. For example, it is some 8000 ocean miles (12,872 km) from Belau in western *Micronesia* to Easter Island at the extreme of eastern *Polynesia*. Micronesia includes 2000 islands, with just 715 mi² (1852 km²) of land and a native population of 180,000 people, scattered over an area of ocean the size of the contiguous forty-eight United States. Before the arrival of Europeans, the two largest cultural areas, Polynesia and Micronesia, which will be the focus of this chapter, together contained a population estimated at 700,000 people (Oliver 1989).

Following the original distinctions drawn in 1832 by French geographer Dumont d'Urville, it is customary to divide Oceania into three ethnogeographic regions: Melanesia, Polynesia, and Micronesia (Figure 6.1). These divisions make sense geographically but are anthropologically less precise. Melanesia (meaning "black islands") includes New Guinea, New Britain, Bougainville, the Solomons, Vanuatu, New Caledonia, and the Fijis. Melanesia was originally distinguished from Polynesia on ethnocentric and racist grounds. The early European explorers were more comfortable with the Polynesians because they were lighter skinned and more hierarchically organized than the Melanesians. Cannibalism and headhunting were reported for the relatively dark-skinned Melanesians, who were associated with Africans and were viewed as savage, tribal, and hostile, whereas the rank-and-status conscious Polynesians were seen as attractive, friendly, and almost civilized (Thomas 1989). In fact, the boundaries between Melanesia, Micronesia, and Polynesia were not that sharp, either biologically or culturally, as will be shown. Furthermore, the emphasis on Melanesian cannibalism is problematic, and even its very existence has been questioned because accusations of cannibalism are such a common negative stereotype (Arens 1979).

Melanesian islands are predominately large, mountainous islands formed on the Indian continental plate of granite, andesite, and folded and faulted metamorphic rocks. They derive their rich and varied terrestrial ecosystems from their close proximity to the Southeast Asian mainland and Australia. The true oceanic islands, which make up most of Polynesia and Micronesia, are formed

on the vast Pacific plate, a huge sheet of magma-fed basalt, which, according to plate tectonics theory, is floating slowly toward the northwest and sliding under the Philippine and Indian plates, creating deep trenches. Oceanic islands are either the above-water tops of volcanoes or coral that was formed in the shallow waters on undersea volcanic slopes (Figure 6.2). Polynesia ("many islands"), forms a vast triangle with the Hawaiian chain at the northern corner, New Zealand in the south, and Easter Island in the east. Except for New Zealand situated on the Indian plate, Polynesia contains many **high volcanic islands**, most of which lie south of the equator. Micronesia ("tiny islands") lies north of Melanesia and north of the equator. Micronesian islands occur primarily as islets on **coral atolls** formed from the reefs that fringed ancient, now submerged volcanoes (Figures 6.2 and 6.3).

Many factors affect the habitability of islands. Generally, large, high volcanic islands, such as those found in Melanesia and Polynesia, contain relatively more land resources than the small coral islands of Micronesia. High islands will support a larger human population and are likely to have several zones of natural vegetation, rich soils, and flowing freshwater. There may be significant environmental differences, however, between the moist windward side of high islands and the dry leeward side because mountain slopes form a rain shadow. There is also a general decline in biological diversity with increasing distance from Asia and Australia. For example, only a few reptiles, rats, and bats colonized the oceanic islands; even on New Zealand, there were no native land mammals, other than bats. The most remote islands would have only a few species of seabirds. This meant that unless human colonists brought animal domesticates with them, animal protein could only be obtained from marine life. Similarly, few if any edible plants occurred naturally on the smaller islands, and a reliable source of carbohydrates had to be introduced as domesticated plants.

The availability of marine resources is related to many details of the local environment, such as the extent of tidal flats where marine invertebrates can be collected. Generally, the larger islands and those nearer the continental areas are richer. Fishing is usually not as productive in the open ocean

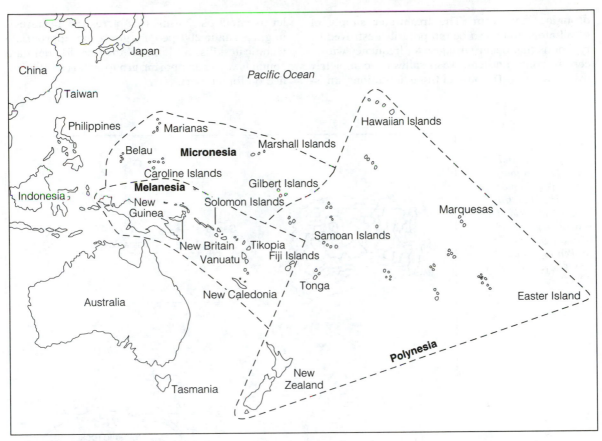

FIGURE 6.1   *Three Pacific island culture areas: Melanesia, Polynesia, and Micronesia, with the principal island groups and cultures discussed in the text.*

as it is along the reef and in the lagoons of atolls, but the extent of these areas can vary widely from island to island.

Perhaps the most critical limiting factors are related to climate and the absolute size of an island. The tiny coral islets might be no more than 6–8 ft (2–3 meters [m]) above sea level and lack flowing freshwater; but if they are at least 350 ft (107 m) in diameter, they might support an underground layer of freshwater, the ***Ghyben–Hertzberg lens***, which forms when rainwater percolates through porous coral and mixes only gradually with the denser seawater beneath. Many islets support a small fresh or brackish swamp in the center, but they depend on rainfall that is regionally variable and erratic, so that in some places serious

***Micronesia***   A culture area lying north of Melanesia in a region primarily of small, widely scattered atolls occupied by Austronesian-speaking peoples.

***Polynesia***   A central Pacific culture area in the great triangle defined by Hawaii, Easter Island, and New Zealand, where Austronesian-speaking peoples occupy mostly high volcanic islands.

***high volcanic island***   A large island formed by a volcanic cone and likely to be relatively rich in soil, water, and vegetation.

***coral atoll***   A coral reef structure formed in a ring around a submerged oceanic volcano. Atolls may contain small, very low, inhabitable islets.

***Ghyben–Hertzberg lens***   A rain-fed layer of freshwater that collects above the saltwater in the permeable coral underlying a large islet in an atoll; a requirement for human occupation.

droughts can occur. The freshwater supply of small atolls may also be temporarily destroyed by typhoons that occur with greater frequency within certain zones and can wash saltwater completely over low islets. Despite all these limitations, an is-let as small as .25 mi² (158 acres [67 hectares]) might sustain 200 people, given the appropriate technical skills, as long as they could maintain contacts with neighboring groups who could be re-lied on for support.

FIGURE 6.2
*Examples of island types. (a) Rarotonga, a high, reef-rimmed volcanic island; (b) Uvea (Wallis Islands), a small, high island with fringing coral reef; (c) Penrhyn, an atoll. (SOURCE: Cumberland 1956.)*

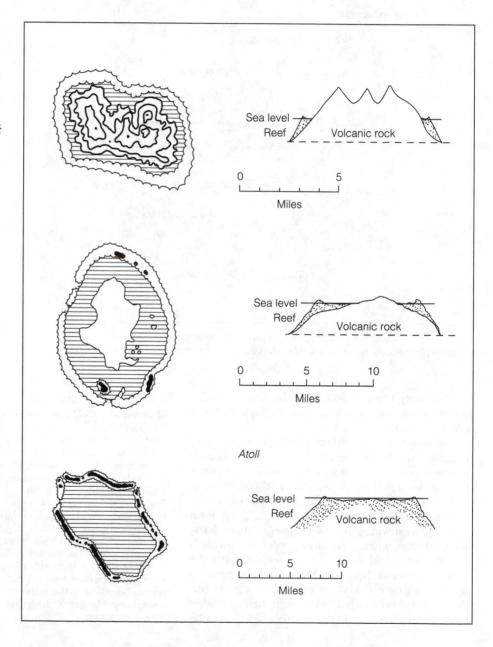

FIGURE 6.3    *Coconut palms on the shore of a Micronesian atoll.*

## Prehistory of Oceania

Speculation on the origin of the Pacific islanders began as soon as outsiders encountered them; in the absence of solid linguistic, archaeological, and biological data, many fanciful and mutually exclusive theories were devised (Howard 1967). Pacific islanders were variously thought to have come from North America, South America, Egypt, Israel, and India, as well as Southeast Asia. Many older theories implicitly deprecated the navigational abilities and overall cultural creativity of the Pacific islanders. For example, British diffusionists G. Elliot Smith (1928) and W. J. Perry (1923) (see Chapter 16) assumed that only Egyptians would have been skilled enough to navigate and colonize the Pacific. They inferred that the Egyptians even crossed the Pacific to found the

great civilizations of the New World. In 1947 Norwegian adventurer Thor Heyerdahl drifted on a balsa-log raft westward with the winds and currents across the Pacific from South America in order to prove his theory that Pacific islanders were American Indians. Later Heyerdahl (1952) suggested that the Pacific was peopled by three migrations: by Indians from the Pacific Northwest of North America drifting to Hawaii; by Peruvians drifting to Easter Island; and by Melanesians. In 1969 he crossed the Atlantic in an Egyptian-style reed boat to prove Egyptian influences in the Americas, thus indirectly supporting Smith and Perry but reversing the direction of diffusion to the Americas. Contrary to these theorists, the overwhelming evidence of physical anthropology, linguistics, and archaeology shows that the Pacific islanders came from Southeast Asia and were skilled enough as navigators to sail against the prevailing winds and currents.

The basic outlines of the prehistory of the Pacific islands and adjacent Island Southeast Asia are presented in Table 6.1. The island of Java, in what is now Indonesia, is famous as the site where the earliest hominid remains were found by Eugene Dubois in 1891. The so-called Java Man is now known as ***Homo erectus*** and is dated at 1.5 million years ago (mya) to 250,000 BP. No evidence suggests that any prehuman hominids ever reached any part of Oceania prior to approximately 60,000 BP. This would have been unlikely because (as discussed in chapter 2), even during periods of lowest sea level, a 44-mile (70-km) open-water gap separated Sundaland (the once connected islands of Southeast Asia) from Sahulland (Australia-New Guinea). Douglas Oliver (1989) calls the earliest peoples to cross to Sahulland ***Sundanoids***, implying some degree of physical and cultural continuity and a common origin in Sundaland. At this early date, these peoples were foragers and carried a relatively simple stone toolkit. Presumably, they were the ancestors

***Homo erectus***    A fossil hominid ancestor of modern *Homo sapiens*.
***Sundanoid***    The first peoples to occupy the Sunda region, which is now Island Southeast Asia, perhaps 60,000 BP; presumably included the ancestors of the first Australian settlers.

TABLE 6.1  *Prehistory of the Pacific Islands*

| | |
|---|---|
| AD 1522 | Magellan expedition crosses Pacific ocean |

**Polynesian Expansion (AD 800–300; 2000–3600 BP)**

| | |
|---|---|
| 800 | New Zealand settled |
| 500 | Sweet potato introduced from South America |
| 400 | Easter Island settled |
| 300 | Hawaii settled |
| 2000 | Marquesas settled |
| 2700 | Melanesian colonies in Fiji |
| 3000 | Lapita pottery in New Caledonia |
| 3200 | Lapita pottery in Tonga |
| 3250 | Lapita pottery in Fiji |
| 3000–3500 | Proto-Nuclear Micronesian divergence begins from northern New Hebrides |
| 3500 | Proto-Polynesian divergence begins |
| 3600 | Lapita cultural complex, New Britain |

**Proto-Oceanic Expansion (3800–5000 BP)**

| | |
|---|---|
| 3800 | Red pottery in Marianas, Micronesia |
| 3500–5000 | Cord-marked pottery, Philippines to Timor |
| 4000–5000 | Outrigger canoes enter Oceania |
| 5000 | Proto-Oceanic divergence begins maritime specialization |

**Proto-Austronesian and Domestication (6000–9000 BP)**

| | |
|---|---|
| 6000 | Proto-Austronesian divergence begins |
| 6500 | Domestic pigs in highland New Guinea |
| 7000 | Cord-marked pottery in Taiwan; Proto-Austronesian culture; taro, yams, banana, sugarcane, breadfruit, coconut, sago, rice, fishing, outrigger canoes |
| 9000 | Earliest horticulture in New Guinea, yams and taro |

*Homo Sapiens* **Foragers (15,000–60,000 BP)**

| | |
|---|---|
| 15,000 | Niah Cave, Sarawak: Edge-ground axes, adzes |
| 17,000 | Niah Cave: Intentional burials |
| 20,000 | Low sea level facilitates island hopping |
| 17,000–30,000 | Sundadonts develop in Sundaland |
| 26,000 | Kosipe, New Guinea: Stone tools |
| 32,000 | Niah Cave, Sarawak: Bone points |
| 40,000 | Niah Cave, Sarawak: *Homo sapiens* skull |
| 53,000 | Low sea level facilitates island hopping, likely first Sahul colonization |
| 60,000 | Sundanoid foragers in Sundaland; ancestral Australians and Papuans |

**Protohumans**

| | |
|---|---|
| 250,000 BP–1.5 mya | *Homo erectus* in Java; stone choppers, hand adzes, hand axes |

SOURCES: Bellwood (1980), Kirch (1985), Oliver (1989), and Turner (1989).

of Australian aborigines, Tasmanians, and the Papuan-speaking peoples of Melanesia. As early as perhaps 9000 BP in highland New Guinea, some of these peoples may have locally developed a gardening system based on taro and yams, but their primary adaptation does not seem to have been maritime.

The basic cultural requirements for the successful colonization of the Pacific islands include the appropriate boat-building, sailing, and navigation skills to get to the islands in the first place; domesticated plants and gardening skills suited to often marginal conditions; and a varied inventory of fishing implements and techniques. It is now generally believed that these prerequisites originated with peoples speaking **Austronesian languages** and began to emerge in Southeast Asia by about 7000 BP. The **Proto-Austronesian culture** of that time, based on archaeology and linguistic reconstruction, is assumed to have had a broad inventory of cultivated plants including taro, yams, banana, sugarcane, breadfruit, coconut, sago, and rice. Just as important, the culture also possessed the basic foundation for an effective maritime adaptation, including outrigger canoes and a variety of fishing techniques that could be effective for overseas voyaging. By about 5000 BP, Austronesian-speaking peoples began to expand toward the Pacific islands, first into Taiwan and the Philippines and then along coastal New Guinea. By 3000 BP, virtually all of Melanesia and much of Micronesia was occupied, and the *Proto-Polynesians* speakers had established a firm foothold in Fiji, Tonga, and Samoa on the western edge of what would become Polynesia.

Some of the best archaeological evidence for the sequence of colonization in the Pacific is based on the recovery of a distinctive red, stamped, and incised pottery style, known as *Lapita*, and associated domesticated plants and fishing technology. Lapita peoples were ultimately derived from the Proto-Austronesians of Island Southeast Asia but appear to have developed their distinctive style in the New Britain area off eastern New Guinea some 3600 BP before spreading through the closely spaced chain of Melanesian islands to New Caledonia (Kirch 1985). The crossing of the 528 miles (850 km) of open ocean between Vanuatu and Fiji, which took place about 3250 BP, judging by the appearance of Lapita pottery in Fiji at that time, was a major achievement that set the stage for expansion into the rest of the inhabitable Pacific.

Contrary to the arguments of some that much of the Pacific was settled by Polynesians accidentally marooned after being lost and adrift, it seems reasonable that this feat was accomplished by deliberate colonization expeditions that set out fully stocked with food and domesticated plants and animals. Detailed studies of the winds and currents using computer simulations suggest that drifting canoes would have been a most unlikely means of colonizing the Pacific (Levison, Ward, and Webb 1973). The 1000-mile (1600-km) crossing between Samoa and the Marquesas in central Polynesia, which took place approximately 2000 BP, was a logical continuation of the earlier voyages of discovery. Even longer voyagers from the Marquesas

to Hawaii, Easter Island, and New Zealand followed shortly thereafter. These expeditions were likely driven by population growth and political dynamics on the home islands, as well as the challenge and excitement of exploring unknown waters. Besides the evidence of the Lapita pottery, because all Polynesians, Micronesians, and many Melanesians speak Austronesian languages and grow crops derived from Southeast Asia, all these peoples most certainly derived from that region and not the New World or elsewhere. The undisputed pre-Columbian presence in Oceania of the sweet potato, which is a New World domesticate, has sometimes been used to support Heyerdahl's "American Indians in the Pacific" theories. However, this is only one plant out of a long list of Southeast Asian domesticates. As Patrick Kirch (1985) points out, rather than being brought by rafting South Americans, sweet potatoes might just as easily have been brought back by returning Polynesian navigators, who could have reached the west coast of South America.

The human biological evidence is less clear, but genetic traits show consistent separations between Australian aborigines, Tasmanians, and Papuan-speaking Melanesians as a group (descendants of Oliver's Sundanoids) and all Austronesian-speaking peoples (Bellwood 1985). Christy Turner (1989) has used genetically based dental traits to propose that a second major population group emerged in the Sunda region some 30,000–17,000 BP, which he calls *Sundadonts*. By approximately

---

*Austronesian language*  A group of several hundred related languages, also called malayo-Polynesian, whose speakers are found in Southeast Asia, Taiwan, the Philippines, and Madagascar and throughout the Pacific.

*Proto-Austronesian*  The parent language of all modern Austronesian languages, presumably present in Southeast Asia some 7000 BP.

*Proto-Polynesian*  The parent language of all modern Polynesian languages, presumably present in western Polynesia some 3500 BP.

*Lapita*  A distinctive pottery style that archaeologists use to trace the rapid spread of the early Austronesian settlers into Polynesia approximately 3000 BP.

*Sundadont*  A human population with unique tooth forms originating in the Sunda region of Southeast Asia some 30,000 BP and thought to be the first settlers of China, where they became Sinodonts.

20,000 BP, Turner suggests that the Sundadonts expanded northward into China where they developed other unique dental traits, including details of roots and tooth crown shape, and formed another population, which he called **Sinodonts**. The distribution of these distinctive dental traits suggests that Sinodonts settled China, Siberia, and the Americas, whereas the Austronesians who settled the Pacific islands were Sundadonts. Polynesian peoples are relatively homogenous physically, which is to be expected if they spread rapidly from a single source. They differ as a group from the coastal Melanesian Austronesian speakers from whom they presumably derived, but they are not beyond the range of Melanesian variation, allowing for the **founder effect** when a migrating subset of a larger population takes only a portion of the genetic variation of the parent population. There are similarities in blood proteins between Native Americans and Pacific islanders, as Heyerdahl observed, but these similarities are shared with other Asian populations and demonstrate only that both Native Americans and Pacific islanders had common ancestors.

The general picture of the settlement of Oceania seems to conform well with linguistic reconstructions based on **glottochronology**, or lexicostatistics, which suggests that most of the differentiation of Austronesian has occurred within the past 6,000–7,000 years (Figure 6.4). The Austronesian language family, or Malayo-Polynesian, as it has also been called, is one of the most widely distributed language families in the world and includes some 900 languages scattered from Madagascar to Indonesia, Malaysia, Taiwan, the Philippines, and throughout the Pacific (Ruhlen 1987). Most classification systems show the **Polynesian languages** to form a cluster of closely

FIGURE 6.4    *A family tree of Austronesian languages showing time depths of separations for the Oceanic branches.* (SOURCE: *Kirch 1985:62*)

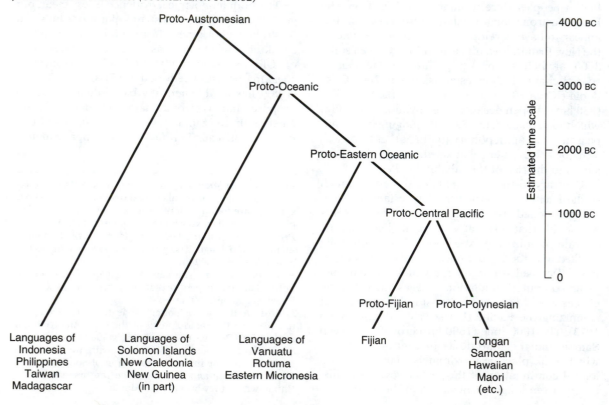

related languages, which are presumed to have separated with Fijian from a common Proto–Central Pacific ancestor language some 3500 BP. Most Micronesians are more closely related linguistically to Melanesians than to Polynesians, but both Micronesians and Polynesians shared a common ancestral language in Proto–Eastern Oceanic some 4000 BP. The Oceanic languages may have separated from their Austronesian ancestors in Southeast Asia some 5000 BP.

As a method of linguistic reconstruction, glottochronology is based on a number of ultimately unverifiable assumptions. It provides relative dates that are useful additions to chronologies derived from biological data and archaeology, but they are not precise and should not be accepted without question. Glottochronology assumes that all languages lose words from a common core vocabulary at a constant rate historically documented for Indo-European languages (Gudschinsky 1956). Groups of related languages likely do change at a constant rate, but many cultural factors may influence this rate and the specific Indo-European rate is not reliably applicable to all languages. The **core vocabulary** is a list of 100 or 200 words for cultural universals such as body parts and geographic features. The years since two languages separated from a common ancestor are calculated from the percentage of cognates identified in the core vocabulary. **Cognates** are words that are recognizably derived from a common source in a parent language, and thus their frequency is assumed to be a measure of their separation time. To cite a Polynesian example, Table 6.2 lists the words for *deity*, *chief*, and *taboo* in Tikopian, a member of the Samoic branch of Nuclear Polynesian, and Hawaiian, an eastern Polynesian language. The words in both languages are obviously similar enough to be considered cognates, implying a common ancestry, even though their speakers live more than 3000 miles apart.

Languages sharing more than 80 percent cognates are assumed to be separated by no more than 500 years and are considered dialects of the same language. Languages sharing 33 to 80 percent cognates suggest a separation of 500–2500 years and membership in a common language family. In theory, relationships as remote as 10,000 years might be suggested on the basis of extremely

**TABLE 6.2** *Cognates Between Tikopia and Hawaiian Languages of Nuclear Polynesian*

|  | Tikopian (Samoic Outlier) | Hawaiian (Eastern Polynesian) |
| --- | --- | --- |
| Deity | *Atua* | *Akua* |
| Chief | *Ariki* | *Ali'i* |
| Taboo | *Tapu* | *Kapu* |

SOURCES: Firth ([1936] 1957), Malo (1951), and Ruhlen (1987).

low percentages of shared cognates. However, the identification of "true" cognates is plagued with difficulties, such as the problem of deciding whether "cognates" are similar due to common ancestry or because of borrowing from a common source. Languages also do not always separate completely and may continue to share vocabulary even as they evolve in different directions.

Given the present interpretation of Pacific prehistory, Polynesia is a well-defined area with a common ancestry, language, culture, and physical type. Micronesia shows many cultural similarities to Polynesia but is physically and linguistically closer to Melanesia and Island Southeast Asia. Melanesia, with its Papuan and Proto-Oceanic foundation, is a more complex mix of language, culture, and physical type than Micronesia and Polynesia.

**Sinodont** A people thought to be earliest modern human inhabitants of China, who were distinguished by unique dental patterns and derived from Sundadonts some 20,000 BP.

**founder effect** The outcome that results when a small group of migrants who leave a larger population establishes a new population that contains only a portion of the parent population's genetic material.

**glottochronology** A method of estimating the relative date at which related languages separated from a common ancestral language, by calculating the percentage of cognates shared between the related languages.

**Polynesian language** A group of closely related Austronesian languages spoken in Polynesia.

**core vocabulary** A list of 100 or 200 words assumed to be universally present in all cultures and that are used by linguists to establish a glottochronology.

**cognates** Related words found in more than one language and that were derived from a common protolanguage.

# PACIFIC ISLANDER SURVIVAL SKILLS

## The Prerequisites for Island Colonization: Outrigger Canoes and Navigation

The outrigger canoe and very sophisticated knowledge of the sea and island ecosystems supported Pacific island societies. Seagoing Micronesian outriggers, which were routinely used to cross more than 300 miles (483 km) of open ocean were only 25 ft (8 m) long, whereas the huge double-hulled Polynesian canoes used in overseas colonization were nearly 100 ft (30 m) long and could easily accommodate supplies for an extended voyage. Canoes were designed to be extremely seaworthy and, unlike rafts, were highly maneuverable and could be propelled by both sail and paddles. The most widely distributed canoe type was the outrigger, which in Micronesia was usually constructed from a carved breadfruit-log hull, with wooden planks lashed on the side. The outrigger was a wooden float suspended approximately half a hull length off the windward side of the canoe and counterbalanced by a platform suspended off the lee side (Figure 6.5). The outrigger was always oriented so that the float would be lifted by the wind on the sail. When the float dipped into the water, it pulled the canoe back into the wind. The great advantage of the outrigger was that it maximized speed and stability, without a deep keel, which would impede passage over the reefs surrounding most Pacific islands, to counterbalance the sail.

The addition of an outrigger posed many design problems that traditional canoe builders solved in very sophisticated ways. The hull had to be asymmetrical in cross section, and its overall contours were shaped within very narrow tolerances to achieve a balance between seaworthiness, speed, and maneuverability (Gladwin 1970). Only a few specialists had the necessary skills to direct construction of such a complex craft. Bow and stern of the outrigger were reversible, and when a major change of direction was made in order to keep the float facing the wind, sailors shifted the sail from end to end.

The navigational techniques that allowed the Polynesian explorers to maintain a steady course across vast distances in search of islands are still being practiced by a few skilled navigators on some of the most isolated Micronesian atolls. Thomas Gladwin's (1970) research on Puluwat revealed the main features of the system. Gladwin found that Micronesian navigation was based on an elaborate body of formal knowledge, which was both empirical and mythical. A few titled specialists, known as Master Navigators, controlled the system and offered formal instruction to aspiring navigators. Out of the island population of 400 people, only six men were considered Master Navigators. Successful navigation depended on the ability to sail a steady course on a specific bearing while keeping a mental record of the distance traveled, for days or weeks at a time, at night, during storms, across changing currents, and in unfamiliar waters. The key to the system was a star chart (Figure 6.6) with thirty-two named bearing points based on the rising and setting points of specific stars. For each route traveled, a navigator had to commit to memory a unique sequence of bearing stars.

The navigators on Puluwat routinely sailed between twenty-six different islands using 110 different routes. To follow a given bearing, the navigators needed to know what stars would be observed en route, and they kept careful track of wave patterns and weather conditions. There was little margin for error on a long voyage because small atolls were only visible for 10 miles (16 km) at sea and might easily be missed in passing. Upon arrival, the navigator then had to find narrow passes through treacherous reefs.

Canoes and navigation were a vital part of Pacific island culture. Navigators were greatly respected, high-status individuals. Canoes were treated with great care. They were stored in special canoe houses, to prevent them from becoming waterlogged, and the lashings and caulking might be replaced every 2 years.

Long-distance voyages also depended on a reliable system of food storage. Whole coconuts were a ready, storable source of food and drinking water and were widely used, but there were elaborate ways of processing other important staples such as breadfruit, pandanus palm fruits, and taros, so that they could be stored indefinitely without canning or refrigeration (Schattenburg 1976). Micronesians had at least four different ways of preserving breadfruit, involving grating, pounding,

FIGURE 6.5
*Micronesian outrigger.*

soaking, fermenting, cooking, and sun drying. Under one method, raw ripe breadfruit could be stored in a pit for up to 2 years after processing: Peeled slices were soaked for 1½ days in the lagoon, fermented for 3 days on the ground, then squeezed and stirred with freshwater for 3 days to convert it into dough. When the dough was shaped into slabs and sun-dried, it could be stored indefinitely until being reconstituted by soaking again in water (Murai, Pen, and Miller 1958).

Breadfruit is more nutritious than potatoes and is rich enough in calories and vitamins to supply virtually all daily food requirements when supplemented with fish and coconut. Because many of the cultivated plants in the Pacific are grown from cuttings, special techniques were developed for transporting them. Schattenburg (1976) reports that the root balls of delicate young breadfruit trees were wrapped in rotted coconut husks, bound with dried leaves, and bundled in woven baskets. In this way, they could be protected from saltwater.

## Fishing and Gardening: The Island Technological Base

Pacific island subsistence was similar to that of Amazonia in that it was based on two rather dis-

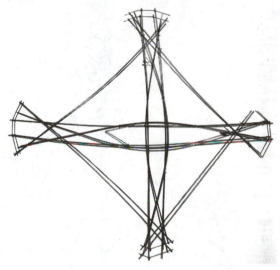

FIGURE 6.6  *Stick figure from Marshall Islands, used to teach the fundamentals of the Micronesian star chart.*

tinct systems: Fishing and gathering of marine animals was the source of protein, and gardening produced the bulk of dietary calories. According to the usual sexual division of labor, men did the fishing and heavy gardening work, whereas women gathered marine animals and did the daily garden cul-

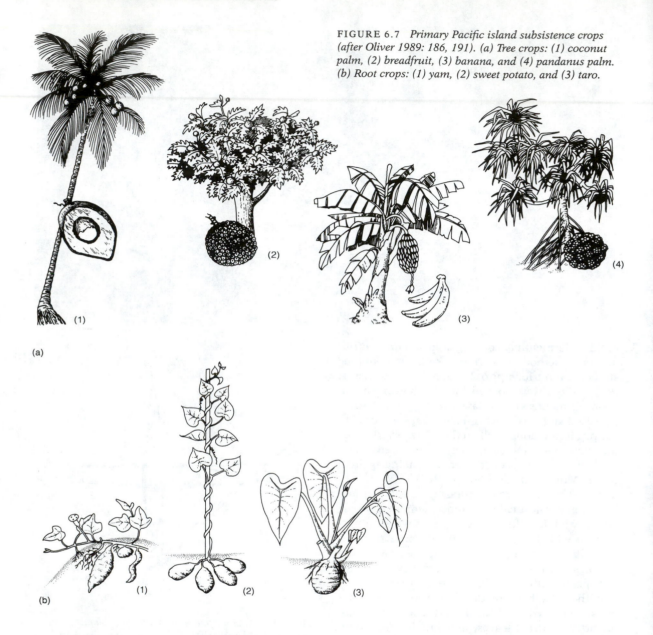

FIGURE 6.7 *Primary Pacific island subsistence crops (after Oliver 1989: 186, 191). (a) Tree crops: (1) coconut palm, (2) breadfruit, (3) banana, and (4) pandanus palm. (b) Root crops: (1) yam, (2) sweet potato, and (3) taro.*

tivating and harvesting. Three crop zones, which on small islands were often arranged in concentric zones according to altitude and proximity to the ocean, included **orchard crops**, **dry crops**, and **wet crops**. The orchard crops were the breadfruit trees and the relatively salt-tolerant coconuts and pandanus palms, which could grow near the beach (Figure 6.7a). All of these trees provided food as well as raw materials for canoe building, house construction, and basketry. On the smaller islands, they were the only significant sources of wood and fiber. The subsistence importance of coconuts is indicated by the fact that Polynesians named seventeen different stages of nuts according to their

## Taro

The arum family includes many familiar leafy tropical ornamentals, such as the philodendrons. The edible aroids grow large heart-shaped ears and are sprouted from cuttings. They produce starchy corms and bulbous underground stems and are highly productive, but they require large amounts of relatively fresh water. The true taro, *Colocasia esculenta*, is sometimes grown in terraced, irrigated ponds, on high islands given the availability of abundant water. It can be planted at any time and is harvested within a year, but it does not store well, either in the ground or after harvest. Another important aroid, *Cyrtosperma*, the swamp taro, produces a more fibrous corm and takes 3 years to reach full maturity, but it can be harvested over a longer period, allowing it to be stored in the ground, and it keeps for about 2 weeks after harvest. It is the preferred taro in much of Micronesia where it is grown in the swampy center of small coral islands where the freshwater lens reaches the surface. Another aroid, *Alocasia macrorrhiza*, giant taro (elephant ear), grows under drier conditions, but its corms require special processing to remove irritating crystals.

edibility (Handy and Handy 1972). Micronesians specialized in producing a fermented drink from the sap tapped from the unopened flower stem.

The dry gardens produced sweet potatoes, yams, and bananas, but the extent of such gardens was severely limited by soil conditions and rainfall, especially on the smaller coral islands and atolls. On many of these islands, soil, other than coral sand, was virtually absent, and humus had to be created and maintained by a continuous process of mulching. Throughout much of the Pacific, the most important food plants were the taros, members of the arum family (Araceae), known as aroids (see the box "Taro" and Figure 6.7b).

The productivity of taro and its subsistence importance are indicated by data obtained by William Alkire (1965) on the Micronesian atoll of Lamotrek in the central Caroline Islands. In Lamotrek, approximately 200 people live on a .25-mi$^2$ (158-acre [67 hectare]) islet. Alkire estimated that taro supplied approximately three-fourths of the average 2 lb (.9 kilogram [kg]) of plant food consumed daily by adults on the island. An estimated 500,000 taro plants grew on the island, with some 15,000 per acre in the 58 acres (23 hectares) of the island's swampy interior. Annual consumption was only about 20 percent of the total crop, but even if most of the plants were slow-growing swamp taro, the consumption rate still would have been well below potential production. However, if typhoons swept saltwater into the swamp and totally destroyed the crop, it would take at least 3 years for recovery.

Taro-based subsistence was a time-consuming woman's task on Lamotrek. During half of the year when breadfruit was not being harvested, Lamotrek women worked over 2 hours a day in the taro swamp, cultivating and harvesting. Taro processing took nearly an additional 3 hours a day. Breadfruit harvesting and processing required about 3 hours a day in season.

Fishing was a primary male activity throughout the Pacific. Alkire (1965) found that on an average

***orchard crops***   Pacific island tree crops such as breadfruit, the salt-tolerant coconut, and pandandus palms, which grow near the shore.

***dry crops***   Pacific island root crops such as sweet potatoes, yams, and bananas, which require well-drained soil.

***wet crops***   Pacific island root crops such as taros, which are grown in swampy areas.

day nearly one-fourth of the male population of Lamotrek would be out fishing. Men typically spent over 5 hours fishing at a time and brought back 9 lb (4 kg) of fish. Virtually every major fishing technique was used in the Pacific, including traps, nets, spears, and hook and line. Fish were also raised in fish farms—rock-lined pools in tidal shallows—where they were fed and allowed to reproduce.

Coral reefs are composed of rough limestone (calcium carbonate) built up from the skeletons of generations of tiny marine invertebrates. Coral grows under only very narrow tolerances of temperature (73°–78° F [22.7°–25.5°C]), salinity, and sunlight; but when conditions are right, they can grow at ocean depths of 150 feet (46 m). Coral reef ecosystems cover less than .1 percent of the globe, but they produce some 10 percent of the world's fish and support many other traditionally important food animals including sea turtles and edible marine invertebrates such as shellfish. Estimates for sustained productivity of these rich coral reef zones range as high as 22 tons (20 metric tons) of fish per square kilometer of reef per year (Kenchington 1985). If 50 percent of this amount is edible and is counted as 20 percent protein, than .4 mi$^2$ (1 km$^2$) of reef would produce 4400 lb (2000 kg) of protein per year, which would supply 110 people with a minimum annual protein requirement of 1.8 oz (50 grams) per day. As noted earlier, different islands varied greatly in the extent of available reef zones; for example, Bikini Atoll in the Marshall Islands of Micronesia contained some 30 mi$^2$ (78 km$^2$) of reef strung along a broken circle some 70 miles (113 km) around. The Ulithi Atoll in the Carolines enclosed a lagoon of 183 mi$^2$ (474 km$^2$). Protein was probably not a limiting factor for most Pacific islands.

The amount of specialized knowledge that successful fishing required was most impressive. Many important marine ecozones were exploited in different ways. Atolls, for example, included at least five broad marine zones (Knudson 1970): the lagoon in the center of the atoll, shallow waters, deep waters along reef edges and coral heads, intertidal reefs and flats, and the open ocean. The islanders themselves recognized many finer distinctions. The shallow waters, reef edges, and the lagoon were generally the most intensively exploited zones, where nets, traps, and weirs could be used most effectively (Figure 6.8). According to a study by Don Rubinstein (1978), the people of Fais, in the Carolines, named four broad marine zones and thirteen subzones ringing their 1-mi$^2$ (2.6-km$^3$) raised coral island. They located specific fishing areas by reference to some sixty submerged coral heads, which were individually named, and they identified eleven lines radiating from the island and aligned with named features on shore and at sea. Phil Lobel (1978) found that the Gilbertese Islanders in Kiribati have names for 254 fish species, ninety-five marine invertebrates, and twenty-five fish anatomical features.

Marine biologist Robert Johannes (1981) has documented the knowledge employed by native fishermen on Belau (Palau) in Micronesia. A critical element in organizing Belauan fishing activities was keeping careful track of the seasons. For this purpose, the Belauans used a 12-month lunar calendar that allowed them to predict with considerable precision changes in wind, weather, and

FIGURE 6.8    *In Micronesia, fish are frequently taken in traps.*

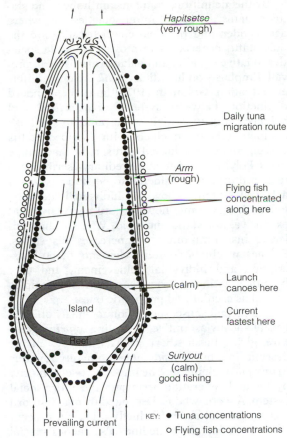

*Hapitsetse*
(very rough)

Daily tuna
migration route

*Arm*
(rough)

Flying fish
concentrated
along here

(calm)   Launch
         canoes here

Current
fastest here

Island

Reef

*Suriyout*
(calm)
good fishing

Prevailing current

KEY:  ● Tuna concentrations
      ○ Flying fish concentrations

FIGURE 6.9  *How Micronesians in Belau use their knowledge of ocean currents to locate fish (after Johannes 1981, fig. 3.).*

waves and the movements and breeding patterns of many pelagic fish, turtles, and seabirds. Belauans understood how ocean currents, when deflected for miles by islands and reefs, reacted, and they know where specific fish would concentrate seasonally in relation to the eddies and calm places (Figure 6.9).

Johannes (1981) shows how a profusion of fishing gear and techniques reflected an understanding of the specific feeding habits, life history, and anatomy of many different fish species. He points out that the curiously incurved shell fishhook, so widely used in the Pacific, works more effectively than the standard barbed steel hook, which Europeans assumed to be so superior. The

traditional shell hook is designed to slide to the corner of the fish's mouth after a light tug, then it rotates, penetrating and locking securely around the fish's jaw.

## PACIFIC ISLAND SOCIAL SYSTEMS

### The Polynesian Chiefdoms: Elementary Aristocracies

Irving Goldman (1970) undertook a systematic, controlled comparison of Polynesian societies because of his interest in the role of **aristocracy** in the development of civilization. He thought that aristocracy was the basic theme of Polynesian societies and they represented the sort of elementary aristocracies that formed the developmental foundation of all of the world's great civilizations. In Goldman's view, the underlying principle of aristocracy was a belief in the "inherent superiority of a line of descent" (1970:xvi). Chiefdom societies were thus preeminently kinship societies because they used genealogical principles to determine personal rank, prestige, and political leadership, in a far more systematic way than any of the small-scale societies considered in previous chapters.

Drawing a distinction between leadership based on pragmatic, or utilitarian, principles—as was the case in aboriginal Australia, Amazonia, and among the East African cattle peoples—and Pacific islander leadership based on aristocracy, Goldman (1970) observes that utilitarian leadership lacks continuity because it is limited to the personal qualities of individuals and specific crisis situations. The aristocrat bases his position on genealogy and religious authority and does not need to prove himself; at the same time, he will be supported by a group of close but lower-ranked kinsmen, and he will be succeeded by his descendants. Marshall Sahlins (1963) earlier drew a similar contrast between Melanesian big men, who—like some Amazonian headmen—were self-made leaders who had to constantly verify their positions by their generosity and success in warfare, and Polynesian chiefs, who were born to office.

***aristocracy***  A political system in which a small, privileged elite rule.

Aristocracies are based in both religion and history in a way that differs strikingly from small-scale tribal societies. Australian totemism was used to create exclusive groups and to regulate territories, but the Pacific aristocracies used religious sentiments to help expand the political community and to support the superiority of individual chiefs and their descent groups. Australian aborigines derived certain degrees of political authority from their relationships to totemic ancestors; however, it is significant that totemic ancestors were nonhuman, and when important men died, their souls were recycled, and they were forgotten as individuals. In this respect, which is typical of small-scale societies, aboriginal society could be considered ahistorical. Aristocracies are historical in that they keep lengthy genealogical histories that recount the names and acts of specific chiefs. Such genealogies are used to verify claims to rank and chiefly title and may be as historically "accurate" as chronologies based on archaeological dating and linguistic reconstruction. Goldman (1970) found that, using 25 years as the average life span of a chief in power, traditional dates for the original settlement of New Zealand, Easter Island, Mangareva, and the Marquesas were within 50–100 years of estimates based on archaeology and glottochronology.

According to Goldman's (1970) interpretation of Polynesian chiefdoms, they are best understood not in relation to political or economic processes as such. They are not simple results of the needs of a large or dense population for political administration to organize production; rather, they are fundamentally a system of **social status**, a scale of human worth, which has economic and political consequences. Goldman thinks that this is a more "realistic" way to view Polynesian societies than functionalist models, which consider the abstract goal of cohesion for a society as a whole, because status concerns directly influence individual actors. Goldman's definition of status system is as follows:

. . . the principles that define worth and more specifically honor, that establish the scales of personal and group value, that relate position or role to privileges and obligations, that allocate respect, and that codify respect behavior. (1970:7)

By this definition, status meant honor, and status systems are found in all societies; but where age, gender, and personal characteristics are the only status criteria, as in most small-scale societies, relative equality and balance are likely to prevail. Emphasis on hereditary **rank** creates a different situation. Goldman (1970) finds the standard distinction between systems of **ascribed** and **achieved status**, which correspond to Sahlins's distinction between chiefs with ascribed status and bigmen with achieved status, to be inadequate in the Polynesian context. Hereditary-ascribed systems are usually considered to be static, whereas achieved systems allow for individual mobility; Polynesian systems, however, are aggressive and expansive, not static and rigid. When a chief enlarges his community, he increases his status. Polynesian chiefs combine elements of both ascription and individual achievement, and they base their actions on sacred and formal principles as well as secular and pragmatic ones.

In a formal sense, succession to chiefly office is genealogically ascriptive, according to **primogeniture**, giving the firstborn priority and by rank of descent line, but considerable ambiguity remains in any particular case. The importance of seniority by age and generation permeates the entire social system. Anyone who is descended from a firstborn has a potential claim to chiefly rank, but descent through exclusively male lines also carries special distinction and deeper genealogies are more worthy.

The religious basis of Pacific island status systems appeared most conspicuously in the related concepts of mana and tabu (taboo), or tapu. Mana has been variously defined as an impersonal supernatural force, or power, that could manifest itself in people, objects, and spirits. The term **mana** was a Melanesian word, whose significance was first noted by the missionary ethnographer R. H. Codrington in 1891. Cognate terms occur throughout the Pacific, and the mana concept has close parallels in many parts of the world. It is sometimes referred to as **animatism** to distinguish it from the more elementary belief in souls, or animism.

Mana was inherited with chiefly rank, and its presence was demonstrated in the chief's objective ability to control his followers. A chief with powerful mana could give goods to his subjects in exchange for their labor services, and he could influence nature as an agent of the gods. Thus, in a circular fashion, the hereditary elite demanded respect because they had *mana*, and the presence of *mana* was expressed in the respect that they received. The elite could possess various degrees of *mana*, while commoners might have none. The Polynesian term ***tabu***, usually translated as "forbidden actions," refers to a wide range of ritual avoidances that lower-ranked individuals must observe as an acknowledgement of the sanctity of elite status. Deference toward chiefs included such things as bowing, keeping one's head below the chiefs' head, use of special respect language, and special offerings.

Chiefly prerogatives might also be marked by special forms of dress, badges, housing, and foods, which accrued to the chief by birth to the status; but perhaps more important were the claims that a chief could make in land, labor, and goods, as an expression of his personal power. Polynesian status inequality also appeared in honorific titles that were applied to outstanding warriors and to a variety of specialists, including priests and artisans, who displayed special skills. These individuals, especially if they were already elites with *mana*, were important challenges to chiefly authority.

Goldman (1970) distinguishes three levels of Polynesian status systems, which he calls traditional, open, and stratified. The traditional system defines status primarily by genealogical criteria, and the chief assumes relatively little power. Open systems add military and political power as a more important criteria for chiefly status, thus generating intense competition, or ***status rivalry***, and ultimately leading to stratified systems where status and power are equally important and commoners become a landless class.

The argument that status rivalry creates ***social stratification*** challenges both classical functionalist and cultural materialist explanations of Polynesian cultural development. In the functionalist view, chiefly powers arise as a means of increasing economic productivity, thereby contributing to the overall adaptability of a society. Sahlins (1958), who argued this view, tried to show a direct correspondence between ecologically determined levels of productivity in Polynesia and levels of stratification. He found that larger islands tended to have

more powerful chiefs, but Goldman (1970) points out that there are some outstanding exceptions. The New Zealand Maori, for example, had the most abundant resources available to them yet displayed only traditional status systems, whereas materially poor Mangareva was highly stratified. To give a clearer picture of how Polynesian chiefdoms worked, two case studies will be presented: first, Tikopia as a traditional system and, second, Hawaii as a stratified system.

## Tikopia: A Traditional Small Polynesian Chiefdom

Tikopia is 3 mi² (4.6 km²) of land, a miniature high island dominated by the jagged rim of an extinct volcano surrounding a crater lake. It is occupied by one of the best described traditional Polynesian cultures, thanks to the detailed monographs published by Raymond Firth ([1936] 1957, [1940] 1967, [1965] 1975), the British functionalist stu-

---

***social status***    A position that an individual occupies within a social system; defined by age, gender, kinship relationships, or other cultural criteria and involves specific behavioral expectations.

***rank***    Social position in a status hierarchy.

***ascribed status***    The social status that one is born into; includes gender, birth order, lineage, clan affiliation, and connection with elite ancestors.

***achieved status***    Social position based on a person's demonstrated personal abilities apart from social status ascribed at birth.

***primogeniture***    Preferential treatment to a couple's firstborn offspring or oldest surviving child; may be a basis for establishing social rank.

***mana***    An impersonal supernatural force thought to reside in particular people and objects. In the Pacific, *mana* is the basis of chiefly power.

***animatism***    Once thought to be a stage in the development of religion involving a belief in *mana*.

***tabu***    Actions that are forbidden under the sanction of supernatural punishment. *Tabus* may be imposed by chiefs and are supported by chiefly *mana*.

***status rivalry***    Goldman's explanation for the development of stratified Pacific chiefdoms from the intense political struggles between chiefs for greater personal power.

***social stratification***    A ranking of social statuses such that the individuals of a society belong to different groups having differential access to resources, power, and privilege.

dent of Bronislaw Malinowski. Firth conducted his initial fieldwork in 1928–1929 while Tikopia was virtually self-sufficient and returned for a restudy in 1952. Archaeological and ecological research was carried out in 1977–1978 by Patrick Kirch and Douglas Yen (1982). Tikopia is considered a Polynesian outlier because it is situated well inside Melanesia, some 1200 miles (2000 km) west of Samoa and Tonga in western Polynesia and just 130 miles (210 km) east of the Melanesian Santa Cruz and Banks islands. In 1928 Tikopia was inhabited by 1200 "healthy and vigorous natives," and Firth considered them "almost untouched by the outside world," although European explorers had landed on the island in 1798. It was included in the British Protectorate of the Solomon Islands in 1896, and Christian missionaries were introduced in 1911. However, in 1928 there were no European residents, and the traditional chiefs were clearly in control.

Archaeological research demonstrated 3000 years of continuous occupation of Tikopia, presumably initiated by Austronesian-speaking peoples carrying Lapita-like pottery (Kirch and Yen 1982). In their excavations, Kirch and Yen recovered 35,000 bones representing eighty-five different types of animals, 1800lb (1 metric ton) of shells, and thousands of artifacts. The record was complete enough to provide a reasonably clear picture of the human impact on Tikopia's ecosystem. The first settlers found a pristine environment teeming with wildlife. The island was covered with rain forest, and the crater lake was then a saltwater bay or lagoon. During the early centuries of settlement, the wild protein resources were decimated. Harvests of fish, shellfish, and sea turtles rapidly declined in volume and diversity, until they were augmented by domestic pigs and chickens. At least one wild bird, the megapod, a chickenlike scrub fowl, was locally exterminated, whereas according to local tradition sea turtles appear to have been protected by *tapu*.

Continuous slash-and-burn cultivation gradually led to severe deforestation that had the effect of enlarging the land base by some 40 percent at the expense of the reef zone, through infilling by eroded materials from the volcanic slopes. This greatly extended the gardening areas on the west end of the island, but it also cut off the lagoon, turning it into a lake, thus further reducing marine resources. In more recent centuries, people gradually abandoned shifting cultivation in favor of a system of permanent gardens and selectively planted domesticated forests. Tikopian arboriculture created a multistoried, multispecies forest-orchard of useful trees and shrubs that replaced virtually all the natural forest on the island. It also stabilized the slopes and dunes and helped buffer the damaging effects of typhoons. At the same time, according to their own accounts, the Tikopians decided to eliminate pigs, thereby reducing demands on their gardens because pigs, although they contributed protein, competed directly for garden produce.

As severely restricted environments, small islands such as Tikopia should be excellent testing grounds for cultural ecological theory. However, discussing carrying capacity and balance with resources on Tikopia is difficult because the relationship between people and resources is not simple. Since 1929 the resident population has fluctuated between about 1000 and 1700. Population growth was regulated in the past by numerous cultural means including ritual sanctions, abortion, and infanticide and by immigration. Firth reported that celibacy was required of younger brothers. Traditional history, verified by archaeology, records that bloody intergroup conflicts, exterminations, and expulsions of whole groups occurred a few centuries ago and were attributed to land conflicts. However, this cultural interpretation may have been a rationalization for what was actually a rivalry between competing chiefs. Furthermore, serious food shortages occurred after hurricanes hit the island in the 1950s. However, direct and indirect human action has improved the island's agricultural potential, but no effort has been made to intensify agricultural production through terracing or irrigation. The island continued to be virtually self-sufficient as recently as the mid-1970s.

The 1200 people living on Tikopia in 1928 were organized into two districts, or "sides," divided by the crater rim. Faena was on the lee side and Ravenga on the windward (Figure 6.10). Some twenty-five named villages were concentrated in the lowlands near the western and southern shores. Districts and villages acted as individual units in ritual and economic activities, although

**FIGURE 6.10**
*Map of Tikopia districts, villages, and temples. (Based on Firth 1957, and Kirch and Yen 1982.)*

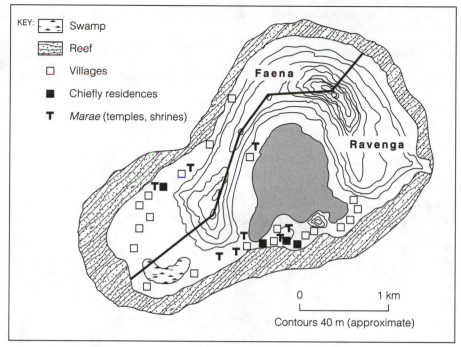

KEY:
- Swamp
- Reef
- □ Villages
- ■ Chiefly residences
- T *Marae* (temples, shrines)

Faena

Ravenga

0          1 km

Contours 40 m (approximate)

they were crosscut by descent-based groups that formed the status hierarchy and organized land tenure.

Each village consisted of a row of named hereditary house sites with attached orchards or garden sites. Houses were accompanied by canoe sheds and ovens. The houses themselves contained the graves of their former owners aligned along the "sacred" inside half of the house, facing the beach. This made each house, in effect, a temple, and long-abandoned houses of important chiefs were marked by upright slabs of stone and were recognized as *Marae*. They served as important temples and sites for major rituals. Land was so important that virtually every part of the island was under some form of ownership, which was inherited patrilineally. Boundaries between gardens were carefully demarcated, and every feature of the island was named. Even the lake and reef zones were under chiefly jurisdiction.

The status system, as described by Firth, was the key to understanding most claims of ownership and explained most personal interaction. Every person was assigned a position in the status

hierarchy, which was organized into units at four distinct levels: household; *Paito*, or lineage; *Kainanga*, or clan; and the entire island community (Figure 6.11).

At the highest level, the islandwide ritual community was presided over by a single chief, or *Ariki*, who controlled an elaborate series of rituals founded by the ancestral deity of the chief's descent group. These rituals, known as "the work of the gods," promoted the welfare of the entire island, ensuring productive gardening and fishing. Firth ([1940] 1967) devotes an entire book to their description.

At the second level were four named descent groups, or *Kainanga*, which were ranked by order of ritual precedence and ranged in size from 89 to 443 people (see Figure 6.11). Firth called these groups clans, and they claimed patrilineal descent from founding ***tutelary deities*** enshrined at spe-

***tutelary deity***  A supernatural entity thought to be an ancestral founder and guardian over a specific descent group; sometimes associated with specific shrines or temples.

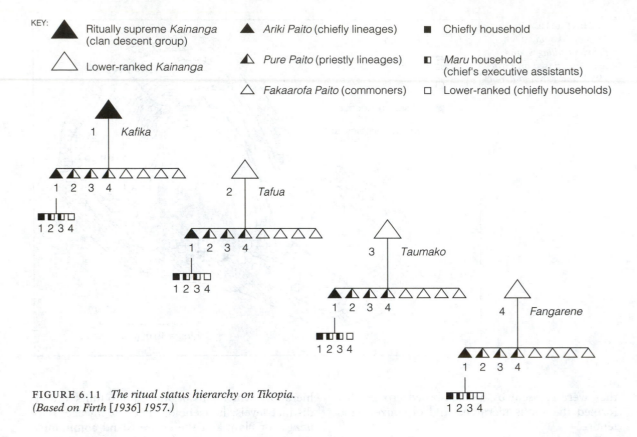

FIGURE 6.11   *The ritual status hierarchy on Tikopia.*
*(Based on Firth [1936] 1957.)*

cific clan "temple" sites; however, the clans were neither localized nor exogamous and only indirectly owned land of their constituent lineages and households. Membership recruitment was usually by patrifiliation, but it was also possible to marry in, as when a stranger would be adopted after marrying the chief's daughter. Each *Kainanga* had its own chief, named for his *Kainanga*, and participated as a unit in the islandwide "work of the gods." The *Kainanga* were linked in pairs for ritual food exchanges, and the chief of each *Kainanga* also had ritual responsibility for the fertility of one of four major food plants: taro, coconut, breadfruit, and yams.

At the third level, the *Kainanga* segmented into individual, named patrilineages called *Paito*, or houses. This is the primary property-holding unit. These groups averaged about forty persons each. There is no question about the cultural reality of these clan and lineage groups. Regardless of how

the rules of rank or recruitment worked, Tikopian culture had names for these groups, and they had clearly defined functions. The highest ranked *Paito* (lineage) in a *Kainanga* (clan) supplied the *Ariki* (chief) for that *Kainanga*. Below the *Ariki Paito*, chiefly lineage, were high-ranking lineages, Pure *Paito*, that supplied ritual specialists, or priests, known as "Pure." Lower-ranked *Paito* were *Fakaarofa Paito*, commoner lineages whose relative order was irrelevant.

The lowest-level unit was the individual nuclear family household, although polygyny, especially among higher-ranked people, might extend the size of this unit. The husband was the ritual head of the family. The rank of the household was determined by his seniority within the lineage, the seniority of its lineage within the clan, and the ritual precedence of the clan. Relative rank within the *Ariki Paito*, chiefly lineages, was most critical. The households most closely related to the chief supplied the assistants, or *Maru*, who helped carry out his directives.

The authority of the chiefs was derived from their religious position as hereditary representatives of important ancestral deities who were responsible for the welfare of the land. Clan chiefs held titular control over all the lands owned by the members of their clan. Chiefs were sometimes called upon to settle territorial disputes and could impose *tabus* to restrict use of local resources under certain conditions (Figure 6.12). It was assumed that they worked for the community's benefit, and they seem to have been genuinely respected. They often owned more land than other individuals, but this only helped them fulfill their ritual responsibilities. Chiefs might claim ritual ownership of the freshwater springs near their villages, but they did not deny community access. Wealth in land was generally independent of rank, and even commoners could be richer than chiefs. Land ownership did not mean exclusive use; upon request, individuals were often allowed to plant on or harvest resources from land they did not own in return for a token gift of food. There were no landless classes.

A visiting Australian aborigine would have been overwhelmed by the density and permanence of population on Tikopia and by the degree to which people manipulated the environment for productive purposes, but an aborigine would have understood many features of Tikopian culture. As in any small-scale society, kinship was certainly the most important organizing principle of domestic life on Tikopia, and households were largely self-provisioning units often working cooperatively with related households in the local settlement. Tikopian villages were similar in size to aboriginal bands, but the villages were circumscribed by their neighbors and were much less independent than the mobile bands. The belief that mythical ancestral beings continued to influence human affairs would have been familiar to an aborigine, but the sanctity of specific descent lines linked to the gods and the pervasive ranking of social units would have seemed strange. Even stranger to an aborigine would have been the islandwide authority carried by the Tikopian hereditary title *Ariki* and the extreme deferential behavior accorded the person of *Ariki* status. This calls to mind Firth's summary

FIGURE 6.12 *Statue of Hawaiian chief Kamehameha, who united rival chiefdoms.*

of the chief's role on Tikopia, which clearly has no parallel in small-scale societies:

> . . . the chief has been shown to be the most important single human factor in the economic life of the Tikopia. Not only does he play a part as a producer within his immediate household, but by initiative and example he gives direction to the productive work of the community; he is titular owner of the most valuable property of the members of his clan; he imposes far-reaching restrictions on production and consumption and in many important activities he acts as a focal point in the processes of exchange and distribution. ([1965:231] 1975)

## The Rise of the Chiefdom as a Theoretical Concept

According to Robert Carneiro (1981), chiefdoms, such as Tikopia, are a critically important cultural type representing multicommunity political units. In Carneiro's view, chiefdoms are the first step in supravillage political aggregation, "the first transcending of local autonomy in human history," which only occurred within the past 7500 years. Chiefdoms are thus considered qualitatively distinct from small-scale tribes and are thought to be an evolutionary stage on the way to states and empires. It is remarkable that, as a theoretical concept, chiefdoms are a relatively recent anthropological discovery. The use of the term *chiefdom* to refer to a hierarchy of villages and districts with a paramount chief, as distinct from autonomous villages, was introduced by Kalervo Oberg as recently as 1955 and was only popularized in the anthropological literature following Elman Service's (1962) adoption of "chiefdoms" as an evolutionary stage.

Sahlins (1958) did not use the chiefdom concept as such in his ranking of Polynesian societies by degree of social stratification, although he emphasized the role of the chief, and Carneiro suggests that Sahlins's typological system accurately identified the most critical political features of chiefdom systems. Sahlins (1958) noted that throughout Polynesia the chief was the "agent" of societywide redistribution of goods, whose generosity gave him prestige and direct control over social processes. For Sahlins, the key to the system was the economic power of the chief at the center point of a *redistribution* system in which he promoted the production of otherwise "surplus" food and goods, which were concentrated and then used to support communitywide rituals, public works for the common good, or the stratification system itself.

Sahlins's cultural materialist hypothesis was that "other factors being constant, the degree of social stratification varies directly with productivity" (1958:5). To measure productivity, he considered the size of the networks in which food was redistributed, the frequency of redistribution, and the number of *specialists* who were not directly involved in primary food production and who were therefore supported by "surplus" production.

To test his hypothesis, Sahlins grouped fourteen Polynesian societies into four ranked categories as a "rough and qualitative" measure of social stratification, focused on the economic, political, and religious power of the chief. This classification closely parallels Goldman's (1970) three-part

scheme, discussed previously, which was designed with a different theoretical perspective in mind. Sahlins placed Tikopia in midrange on his stratification scale as a Group II society, distinct from Group I societies such as Hawaii at the upper end, which were virtually small states, and Group III societies, which were simply elaborate small-scale societies. Carneiro (1981) thinks that Group II societies best represent the important features of chiefdoms as levels of evolutionary complexity.

In his elaboration of the chiefdom concept, Service (1962), borrowing from Sahlins, called chiefdoms "redistributive societies" and emphasized their "pervasive inequality." For Carneiro, the essential nature of chiefdoms was their political structure rather than their economic organization. By his minimal definition, "a chiefdom is an autonomous political unit comprising a number of villages or communities under the permanent control of a paramount chief" (Carneiro 1981:45). Carneiro follows the four-part structural classification of political systems into simple, compound, doubly compound, and trebly compound, originally proposed by nineteenth-century social philosopher Herbert Spencer (1967). This system begins with autonomous villages that would be characteristic of small-scale societies. Structurally, the great divide was the surrender of village autonomy in order to create a second level of political authority, with villages aggregated under a paramount chief to form a chiefdom. Adding a third administrative level to form a state and a fourth to form an empire would then follow logically (Figure 6.13).

Archaeologists have used a number of criteria to identify chiefdoms including *monumental architecture*, ceremonial centers; elaborate grave goods reflecting high social status, and the appearance of a few large settlements, as administrative centers, surrounded by small villages. The first two criteria would suggest that the coordinated activity of people from beyond local villages would be required. Many of these criteria would identify the Polynesian chiefdoms, and even on Tikopia the temples are visible as ceremonial centers, although with such a relatively small population they are not very monumental.

Theoretical explanations for the origin of chiefdoms have varied widely. Sahlins (1958) empha-

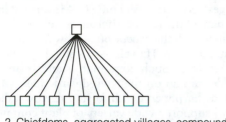

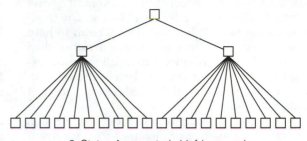

1. Autonomous bands and villages—politically simple

2. Chiefdoms, aggregated villages–compound

3. State:  Aggregated chiefdoms under a "king"—doubly compound

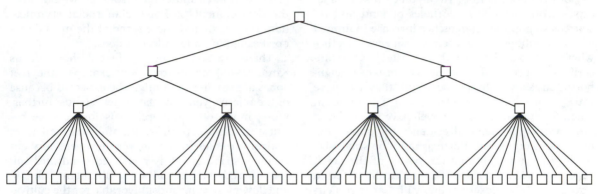

4.  Empire, aggregated states—trebly compound

FIGURE 6.13   *Levels of political complexity. (SOURCES: Carneiro 1981, Spencer 1967.)*

sized the causative role of surplus production, which in turn was largely a function of technoenvironmental variables, such that in Polynesia the islands with the richest natural resources would produce the strongest chiefdoms. In Carneiro's (1981) view, technology and ideological, or religious, factors played supporting, not causative, roles in the development of chiefdoms. Similarly, he thinks that status differences per se are aspects of chiefdoms, not causes. Carneiro emphasizes that significant surplus will not be produced regardless of technoenvironmental potential, unless there is either economic or political incentive. In Polynesia the strong political power of the chiefs could provide such incentive. Simple redistribu-

tion by a chief who gives away everything people donate to him may give him prestige, but his political power can only increase when he diverts

**redistribution**   A form of exchange in which goods, such as foodstuff, are concentrated and then given out under the control of a central political authority.

**specialist**   A full-time specialist is an individual who provides goods and services to elites in hierarchically organized societies. Such a specialist does not produce his or her own food but is supported from the surplus that is politically extracted by central authorities.

**monumental architecture**   Large-scale permanent constructions, such as temples, palaces, or tombs, that require large labor forces and central planning.

goods to his political supporters. By this means, simple gifts to the chief may eventually become tribute and then taxation as requests become more coercive and the return to the community is restricted. The more "advanced" Polynesian chiefdoms such as in Tahiti and Hawaii seem to have been based on tribute and taxation rather than community redistribution because little of the extracted "surplus" returned to benefit the community, contrary to the Sahlins and Service model of redistribution.

Carneiro (1981) derives chiefdom organization directly from warfare or threats of coercion, combined with environmental or social *circumscription* that prevented villages from escaping threats of political domination. He assumes that conflict arises from perceived shortages of land and resources as population densities increase in limited areas. If conquered or coerced villagers have nowhere else to go because their territory is circumscribed by geographic barriers or because neighboring areas are already occupied, they will have little choice but to pay tribute to a paramount chief. Such a scenario may well have been played out on Tikopia, but real evidence for population pressure is equivocal. Furthermore, the small size of the island has limited the power of the chief. Goldman's (1970) theory of status rivalry, referred to previously, is closely in line with Carneiro's circumscription theory; both views emphasize the political outcome of conflict. In general, these theories seem to be going in the right direction. Sahlins's original hypothesis about stratification may also be correct—that is, the power of the chief clearly expanded with the size of population that he could control, and population was ultimately limited by the richness of island resources. However, the specific relationships between these variables are very difficult to sort out as the following Hawaiian case study demonstrates.

## Hawaii as a Protostate

From the original settlement of Hawaii, perhaps as early as AD 300, the native Hawaiian population had grown to a conservatively estimated 200,000 people, organized into numerous complex chiefdoms, when Captain James Cook arrived in 1778. The Hawaiian Archipelago is extremely isolated from the rest of Polynesia, and indeed from everywhere else. Although there is considerable diversity because of differences in geological age, the major inhabited Hawaiian islands are high, volcanic islands and very large for Polynesia. Hawaii, the largest, contains 6500 mi² (10,458 km²) of land, more than all the rest of Micronesia and Polynesia combined, with the exception of New Zealand. The highest point on Hawaii is 13,800 ft (4206 m) above sea level. Such large high islands trap considerable rainfall on their windward sides, which are often sharply eroded into step narrow valleys, and they support a wide variety of plant communities from deserts to wet mountain forests with many endemic species. If, as Sahlins (1958) argued, rich environmental resources would favor the development of Polynesian social stratification, Hawaii should show some of the most developed examples, and indeed it does.

There are some limiting factors however, as Kirch (1985) points out. For example, the reef zones are smaller than might be expected because of the relative youth of the larger islands; furthermore, much of the shoreline is inaccessible because of the steep cliffs. Rainfall and soil were critical variables for crops, yet they were very unevenly distributed. Only restricted windward valleys offered the alluvial soils, abundant rainfall, and flowing streams most favorable for the cultivation of Polynesian crops such as taro, yams, and bananas. Forest clearing increased erosion and sometimes caused floods that destroyed crops. Droughts, seismic waves, and volcanic eruptions were also significant environmental hazards.

In comparison with Tikopia, the most obvious difference in Hawaiian subsistence patterns was in the elaborate complexes of ditches and terraced and irrigated pond fields for taro cultivation, as well as the extensive area devoted to permanent dry-field cultivation. Kirch (1985) also emphasizes that the Hawaiians developed true aquaculture, in which fish were raised on a large scale in special fish ponds constructed on reef flats. It has been estimated that the 449 fish ponds known to have existed prehistorically may have produced 1000 tons (907 metric tons) of fish annually.

The irrigation systems have the most interesting theoretical implications because many theorists have speculated that control of irrigation systems was the primary route to state formation for all the world's great civilizations. Hawaiian irrigation systems were well developed by Polynesian standards; as a significant form of **agricultural intensification**, they helped produce the surplus that supported the elites, but the construction of these systems seems not to have required either technical specialists or large labor forces. Archaeologist Timothy Earle (1978) examined twenty-nine modern, traditional-style irrigation systems still used to grow taro in the Halelea district of Kaua'i, and he mapped eight others that were in use in 1850. Earle concluded that these systems grew in gradual stages and were small enough in scale to be independently managed by local peoples. The Hawaiian irrigation systems, however, were vulnerable to floods, drought, and warfare, and some form of regional assistance would have been needed as a backup.

Many features of the traditional religious system were abandoned by the Hawaiian rulers in 1819 following the shock of contact with Europeans, but native Hawaiians who were closely connected with the highest chiefs have written detailed eyewitness descriptions of the system at its peak (Ii 1983, Malo 1951). Hawaii represented a dramatic expansion over the basic Polynesian status hierarchy system operating on Tikopia. The most striking differences involved the elaboration of the *tabu* system, which sharply demarcated the person of the chief, and the remarkable powers that chiefs, especially high chiefs, could exercise. The *tabu* system was complex, and chiefs could possess or impose several different types of *tabu*, but they all were expressions of the chief's personal power.

The highest chiefs were so *tabu* that people had to prostrate themselves on the ground when the chief passed or even if only his personal possessions were carried by. Special retainers ran ahead carrying a special staff signaling the *tabu*, and they shouted a warning to people to prostrate themselves. Chiefs sometimes traveled at night to minimize the inconvenience that the *tabus* created. No one could allow their shadow to fall across the chief or any of his personal possessions, including his house. No one, other than his immediate retainers, was allowed to approach closer than 12 ft (4 m) to the chief's back. When the chief ate, every-

one in his presence had to remain on their knees.

The paramount chiefs had completely arbitrary life or death powers over their subjects, including lower-level chiefs. They could kill them or expel them from their land at will. They apparently sometimes did so, although not all chiefs were considered to be abusive and oppressive. Infractions of *tabus* were strictly enforced by burning, strangulation, or stoning. Sometimes, people who violated seemingly minor *tabus* were put to death. John Papa Ii (1983), who became a personal attendant to high chief Liholiho, described a case in which three men were caught eating coconuts with women while a major ritual for the general welfare was being performed at the paramount chief's temple, or *luakini heiau* (Figure 6.14). Because there was a general *tabu* against men and women eating together and against women eating coconuts, the three men were seized and were sacrificed along with pigs on the altar before a row of images of the deities (Ii 1983). Human sacrifices of this sort apparently only took place at the temples of paramount chiefs and on special ritual occasions.

On Tikopia it was understood that the deities might be angered if rituals were neglected or improperly performed and might even take a human life as a sacrifice (Firth [1940] 1967), but it would have been unthinkable for a chief or any of his priests to carry out such an act themselves. Clearly, the high chiefs of Hawaii enlarged upon an underlying Polynesian belief that chiefs were descended from the gods, and they assumed the role of gods themselves.

Malo (1951) reported that it was preferable for the highest ranked chief to marry his full sister. The child of such a union was called a deity and possessed the most powerful *tabus*. Given the enormous powers that the high chiefs assumed

---

**circumscription** Carneiro's explanation for the development of political centralization. He argues that villagers may be forced to surrender their autonomy if they are unable to move away from authorities because of geographic barriers or neighboring societies.

**agricultural intensification** Changes in farming technology, such as shortening fallow periods, use of fertilizers, new crops, or irrigation, in order to produce more food per year in a given area, often at greater energy cost.

and the terrifying punishments they could inflict, it follows that "the people held the chiefs in great dread and looked upon them as gods" (Malo 1951:61). It is possible that these accounts, written by missionary-trained Hawaiians, may overstress the oppressive practices of the chiefs, but many of these details are corroborated by the earliest European observers.

FIGURE 6.14  *The Hawaiian* luakini heiau *paramount chief's temple where human sacrifices were performed.*

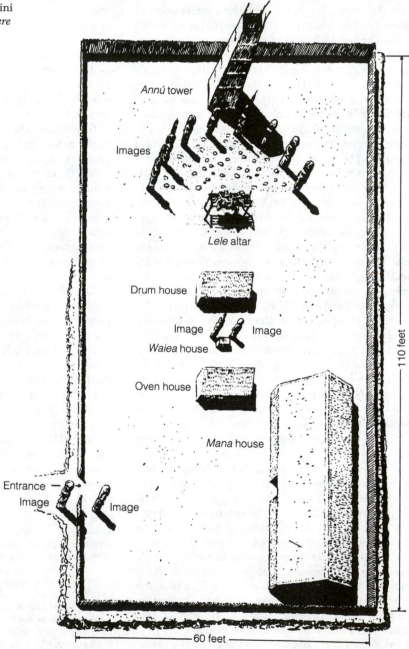

The ethnohistorical descriptions, written by Hawaiians in the nineteenth century, use language typically applied to state-organized societies to describe the Hawaiian system. Paramount chiefs are called kings; they have governments and royal courts, tax collectors, priests, temples, and armies; and they fight wars to conquer territory. The only difference between Hawaiian states, or proto-states, from states in other parts of the world was that the Hawaiian states were relatively small and lacked massive monumental architecture, urbanization, metal, and writing. Structurally, it is appropriate to call Hawaiian societies "states" because they clearly possessed at least two administrative tiers above the village level (Figure 6.15). The paramount chief, who in some cases controlled an entire island, surrounded himself with an elaborate court. Malo (1951) listed more than a dozen categories of specialists who were directly attached to the chief's personal household, including political advisors, military experts, architects, astrologers, food handlers, robe masters, priests,

masseurs, keepers of his images and paraphernalia, and servants to whisk away flies and stand over him as he slept, in addition to miscellaneous "hangers-on." It is unclear actually how many people this might have involved, but this is an obvious expansion over the Tikopian chief's *Maru*.

Below the paramount chief and his immediate court were numerous lower-ranked chiefs in charge of smaller territorial divisions. There were at least ten chiefly ranks distinguished below the highest, divine chief, based on diverse genealogical criteria, and land was grouped into as many as six administrative segments, with household plots as the lowest segment. The lowest potentially self-sufficient land unit was the *ahupua'a*, which was a long narrow strip of land, running uphill from the coast and thereby providing access to several environmental zones. It was further subdivided into family-size holdings, and the entire unit was supervised by a lower-level chief and his assistants.

Land rights at the household level were con-

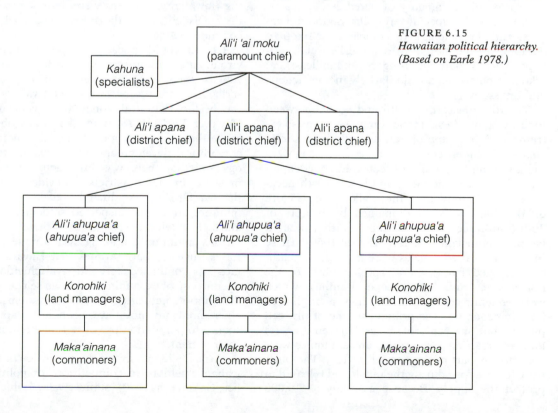

FIGURE 6.15
*Hawaiian political hierarchy.*
*(Based on Earle 1978.)*

trolled primarily not by local descent groups but by the local administrator, the *Konohiki*, who acted on behalf of the district chief and did not even belong to a local descent group. Land ownership was ultimately vested in the paramount chief, and use rights depended on payment of the annual taxes. The *ahupua'a* was probably equivalent in population to the clan on Tikopia, although the *ahupua'a* chief exercised much more power over his subjects than Tikopia's paramount chief.

In the Hawaiian bureaucracy, there was no place even for independent local clan chiefs. Hawaiian priests had their own ranking system and were grouped into various specialist orders. The commoners, called *maka'ainana*, were the most numerous segment of the population and were not further subdivided by rank. They supported themselves through basic subsistence activities, they produced the "surplus" food and luxury objects that supported the elites, and they were on call to provide labor service. Below the commoners, were the *kauwa*, who were sometimes called slaves, but were a despised category of hereditary outcasts. There were also special terms for vagrants, beggars, and the landless. In comparison, Tikopian commoners did not form a powerless class; Tikopia had no outcasts, beggars, or landless; and Tikopian chiefs remained relatively inconspicuous and unassuming.

The differences in wealth and power between the Hawaiian elites and the commoners was so extreme that it is appropriate to call them **social classes**. The most conspicuous class markers were the lavish and magnificent feathered short capes, long cloaks, leis, helmets, and whale tooth necklaces, which only the elite could wear (Figure 6.16). Chiefs were accompanied by bearers of 20-ft (6-m) poles topped with brilliantly feathered banners as insignias of rank (Feher 1969). These intricately crafted articles were made from feathers removed from several specific birds of the honey eater and honeycreeper families, which were endemic to Hawaii. The liwi, a bright red honeycreeper, was the primary source of tiny red plumes but was only 6 inches (15 centimeters) long and restricted to forested areas. Plumes were collected as part of the annual tax levy. The birds were live-trapped during the moult and released to protect the supply. Because as many as 10,000

birds might have been required to produce a single feathered cloak, it had major ostentatious value (Earle 1987).

The remaining key question is, How and why did the extreme Hawaiian status hierarchy develop? If, as Earle (1978) argues, the food requirements of an expanding population were met by agricultural intensification through irrigation and dry-field systems that did not require centralized bureaucratic management, perhaps the Hawaiian hierarchy developed because the chiefs redistributed resources from diverse environments, thus helping to integrate locally specialized economies for everyone's benefit. This interpretation is suggested by Service's (1962) model of the adaptive advantages of chiefdoms as redistribution systems. However, Earle stresses that the local *ahupua'a* administrative units were designed to be self-sufficient because they crosscut diverse ecological zones and virtually eliminated the community need for centrally administered economic exchange. The so-called redistribution functions of the Hawaiian chiefdoms were designed to benefit the chiefs' elites, not the subsistence needs of the commoners.

Hawaii would appear to support Carneiro's environmental circumscription theory because the islands themselves are geographically circumscribed, as are the narrow coastal valleys where the best agricultural zones were concentrated. However, Earle (1978) notes that many observers argue that great untapped potential remained for agricultural development given existing technology and that there was little actual population pressure. In many districts, no evidence suggests that warfare was conducted between local communities, given the dispersed settlement pattern and lack of defensive positions, or that it led to victorious communities taking over conquered territories. Instead, Earle argues that Hawaiian warfare was conducted between rival chiefdoms for the purpose of expanding their own self-serving redistribution networks, or tribute systems. Thus, chiefdoms may not have been an adaptive response to population pressure in a circumscribed environment.

Earle (1978) attributes the expansion of the Hawaiian chiefdom to competition for political office, Goldman's (1970) "status rivalry," which given

**FIGURE 6.16**
*Hawaiian feather work.*

a large enough population base, can result in the intentional development of a ***political economy*** dedicated to support the elite, alongside the ***subsistence economy***, which continues to support the commoners. This is a key feature of the politicization process. The political economy tends to promote its own expansion, whereas the subsistence economies of small-scale societies tend toward equilibrium. Two options seem to be open to a Polynesian population colonizing a new island: It could segment into many equal-sized units as it grows, or it could centralize by promoting a senior lineage to a higher management level (Flannery 1972b). Environmental conditions on Hawaii seem to have been especially suited for centralization because agricultural production was so easily expanded and thus readily supported expanding political economies. Chiefs use the "surplus" extracted from the commoners to maintain their control over potential political rivals by rewarding their loyalty with lavish gifts of expensive wealth objects such as feather cloaks. Capital investment by chiefs in expanded irrigation systems was a specific means to increase their political power by increasing their local labor population. Thus, in this case, population increase results from subsistence intensification, not the reverse, which is usually

thought to occur in unstratified small-scale societies. Expansive warfare directed by chiefs was another means of increasing a chief's wealth and total political power. Warfare of this sort was a form of capital investment because it was an expensive business requiring equipment produced by specialists and the commoner army had to be fed on campaign.

As Earle (1978) stresses, chiefdoms are not simple developments out of small-scale autonomous village societies. Chiefdoms are not just aggregated villages because villages lose their political and economic autonomy when they are subordinated to paramount chiefs in stratified chiefdoms such as Hawaii. Hawaiian commoners did not own their lands and had little control over their day-to-day lives. They became social isolates

---

***social class***  A group of people in a stratified society, such as elites and commoners, who share a similar level of access to resources, power, and privilege.

***political economy***  A cultural pattern in which centralized political authority intervenes in the production and distribution of goods and services.

***subsistence economy***  Production and distribution carried on at the local community level, primarily for local consumption.

with truncated kinship systems. Peace is imposed on local communities, self-help networks collapse, and individual households must depend on centralized authority for emergency aid and defense. Kirch's (1985) summary of Hawaiian archaeology shows that the most expansive phase of Hawaiian chiefdom development, which established the basic structure, occurred relatively quickly between AD 1100 and 1650, after some 800 years in which the Hawaiians—organized as more traditional, smaller-scale Polynesian societies—gradually settled into the most favorable environments.

## SUMMARY

The Pacific islands presented formidable obstacles to successful human occupation because they were so widely scattered and were often very small and resource-poor. They were settled by skilled Austronesian-speaking farmers, sailors, and navigators who originated in Southeast Asia some 6000 BP. The farthest reaches of Polynesia were settled during a period of approximately 1000 years ending by AD 800 with the settlement of New Zealand.

The societies of Polynesia and Micronesia represent a major contrast to the small-scale societies of Australia, Amazonia, and East Africa examined in earlier chapters. Pacific island societies were characterized by a great concern with rank, and they developed permanent political and economic structures above the level of local village communities. These island societies were chiefdoms, which elevated certain high-ranking individuals to permanent leadership positions as "chiefs." The example from the Polynesian island of Tikopia showed that chiefs in small chiefdoms coordinated ritual and economic activities between villages, but they had relatively little power and there were no social classes. On larger islands, such as in Hawaii, political struggles between chiefs led to the formation of powerful chiefdoms. These societies became divided by class into the elites who extracted tribute from the commoners who produced food and wealth objects. The highest-ranking chiefs claimed the supernatural power of deities and gained life-and-death control over lower-ranked people. Some of the Hawaiian chiefdoms were complex enough to be considered protostates, or small kingdoms.

## STUDY QUESTIONS

1. Characterize and distinguish between each of the following cultural areas: Polynesia, Melanesia, and Micronesia.

2. Discuss the physical constraints limiting settlement on Pacific islands, characterizing the cultural response.

3. Discuss the role of status rivalry, irrigation, redistribution, environmental circumscription, and economic productivity in the development of Pacific island chiefdoms.

## SUGGESTED READING

BELLWOOD, PETER S. 1987. *The Polynesians: Prehistory of an Island People.* London: Thames & Hudson. An authoritative archaeological overview of the original settlement of Polynesia and subsequent cultural developments.

FIRTH, RAYMOND. [1936] 1957. *We the Tikopia: A Sociological Study of Kinship in Primitive Polynesia,* 2nd ed. New York: Barnes & Noble. The basic ethnographic description of Tikopia, with an emphasis on social organization.

FIRTH, RAYMOND. [1940] 1967. "The Work of the Gods." In *Tikopia,* 2nd ed. London: Athlone Press. Describes in detail the system of ritual feasting on Tikopia.

FIRTH, RAYMOND. [1965] 1975. *Primitive Polynesian Economy.* Reprint. New York: Norton. An analysis of the subsistence economy and distribution system on Tikopia.

KIRCH, PATRICK VINTON. 1985. *Feathered Gods and Fishhooks: An Introduction to Hawaiian Archaeology and Prehistory.* Honolulu: University of Hawaii Press. A detailed prehistory of Hawaii.

# 7

# EARLY STATES: THE NEAR EAST AND THE ANDES

Although many Pacific island chiefdoms crossed the "great divide" from the social equality of small-scale societies into rank- and class-based social systems, a major gulf separates these island cultures from the larger-scale states and empires to be considered in this chapter. Early states created monumental temples, pyramids, palaces, and cities, which historians hail as major "achievements" and attributes of "civilization." However, the impressive monuments and museum-quality artworks produced by the early states clearly depended on pervasive social inequality and were characterized by an inherent instability not found in small-scale cultures. Urban civilizations drastically modify ecosystems and make enormous demands on natural resources. They intensify the political and economic implications of hierarchy such that human dependency and servitude may be institutionalized. They concentrate despotic power in a few hands, often creating a split between the economically dependent urban center, with its culturally distinct Great Tradition, and the more autonomous and stable rural village culture, with its own more egalitarian Little Tradition.

The contrasts between small-scale tribal cultures and civilizations are so extreme, and the comparative disadvantages of civilizations for all but the elite minority are so obvious, that explaining state origins and understanding how states function as cultural systems continue to be a major theoretical challenge for anthropology. Understanding the full implications of urban civilization for the long-term future of humanity is also a critical issue. It is important to remember that urban civilization has only existed for a mere 5000 years and could be considered a very shaky experiment when its short span and record of chronic collapse is compared with the 50,000-year record of small-scale foraging cultures in Australia. In this chapter, we will not resolve the issues surrounding urban civilization, but we will review these problems within the context of two major civilizations from different parts of the world: the Sumerians of Mesopotamia and the Inca of Peru.

The "early states" treated in this chapter are "early" in that—in the case of the Sumerian city-states of Mesopotamia, which date to approximately 3000 BC—they are among the very earliest states anywhere in the world. Chronological priority in itself need not be especially significant, but treating a clearly "pristine" state, which arose independently of previously existing states, helps isolate the distinctive features of state organization and to examine the process of its original development. The Andean states were also chronologically early and pristine, and they were fully functioning when Europeans conquered them in AD 1532.

## STATE AND CIVILIZATION: BASIC ISSUES

### Definitions

Social theorists have long recognized a difference between "civilized" and "uncivilized" societies—or as I prefer to call them, large-scale and small-scale societies—but *civilization* has usually been defined by the presence of a specific list of traits, with different theorists stressing different traits. A careful review of many of these trait-list definitions suggests that the centralization of political power is the most important underlying feature of civilization because it is functionally connected with many other "civilized" traits; this, in turn, suggests that explanatory theories that focus on political power will be most productive. Before treating the issue of the origin of civilization, let us consider in more detail the traits that have figured prominently in definitions of civilization.

Lewis Henry Morgan (1877) defined civilization by the presence of writing with a phonetic alphabet, whereas V. Gordon Childe (1936, 1950) emphasized the importance of cities and spoke of civilization as an *urban revolution*. Writing and cities do reflect an important increase in cultural scale, and both are directly connected to political power, as will be shown in later sections of this chapter. Table 7.1 lists many other intuitively convincing criteria of civilization. However, an obvious problem with such lists is that many "urban" traits can exist in the absence of large cities and not all urban cultures display all the traits. The Inca, for example, did not have writing, although they managed with a functional equivalent.

The problem of defining the state and/or civilization stems from two facts: Different researchers used differing conceptual approaches, and early state formation was a complex and gradual process along a continuum of increasing complexity and growing political power. For example, archaeologist Kent Flannery (1972b) has constructed a scale of cultural complexity showing an approximate temporal sequence for the development of selected cultural institutions or traits distributed along a continuum from mobile foragers ("bands"), to small-scale villagers, ("tribes"), through chiefdoms, and ending with the state. Figure 7.1 shows how this developmental sequence compares to the concept of culture scale used in this book and where specific cultures fit in both analytic schemes.

Robert Carneiro and Stephen Tobias (1963) have demonstrated that a number of cultural traits indicative of the move toward state organization demonstrate *scalability* as cultural complexity increases, such that the presence in a given culture of a more statelike trait (e.g., taxation) can be used to predict the presence of presumably earlier traits (e.g., agriculture or temples). Figure 7.2 clearly shows the cumulative nature of politically significant traits for all the institutions that first appear with chiefdoms and then continue after states develop.

Carneiro and Tobias (1963) sorted through a list of 354 potentially scalable traits and produced a

TABLE 7.1  *The Concept of Civilization as an Urban Revolution: Defining Features*

| Primary Features | Secondary Features |
|---|---|
| Large, dense population | Monumental art and architecture |
| Full-time specialists | Long-distance trade |
| Food surplus | Writing and mathematics |
| Class structures |  |
| State organization |  |

SOURCE: Childe (1950).

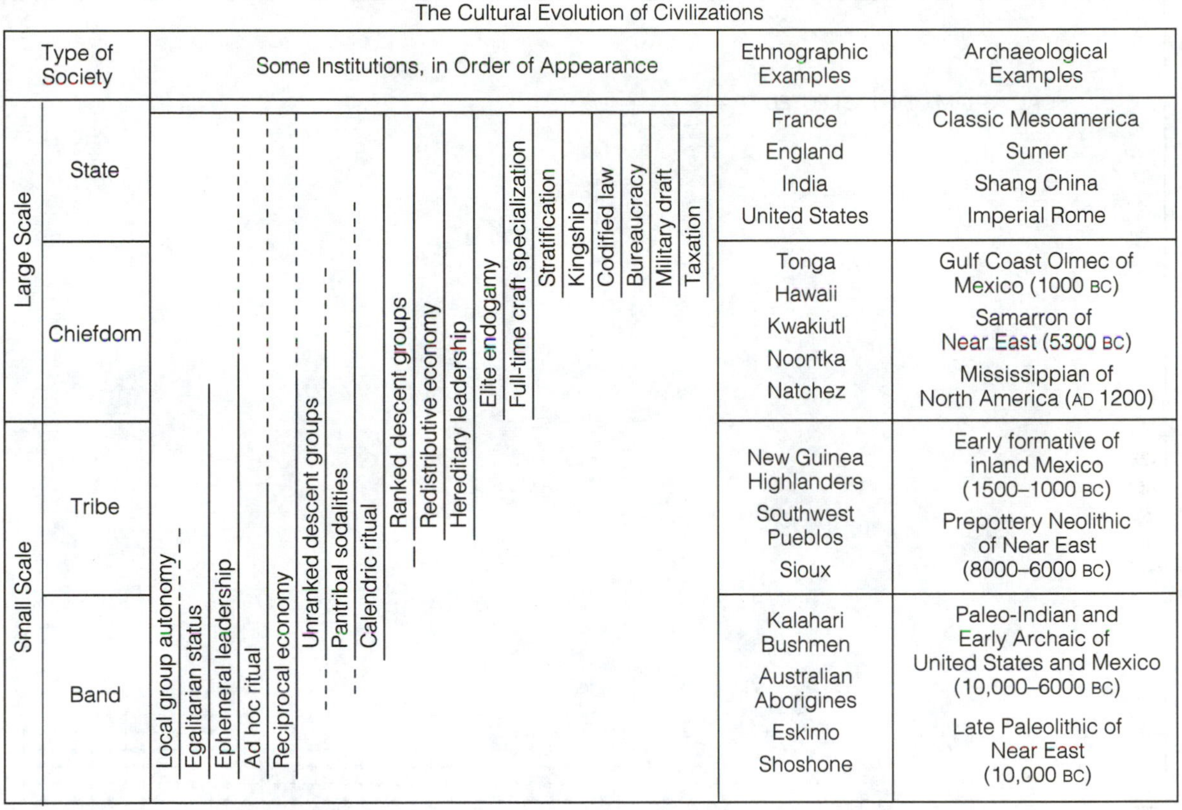

The Cultural Evolution of Civilizations

| Type of Society | | Some Institutions, in Order of Appearance | Ethnographic Examples | Archaeological Examples |
|---|---|---|---|---|
| Large Scale | State | | France<br>England<br>India<br>United States | Classic Mesoamerica<br>Sumer<br>Shang China<br>Imperial Rome |
| Large Scale | Chiefdom | | Tonga<br>Hawaii<br>Kwakiutl<br>Noontka<br>Natchez | Gulf Coast Olmec of Mexico (1000 BC)<br>Samarron of Near East (5300 BC)<br>Mississippian of North America (AD 1200) |
| Small Scale | Tribe | | New Guinea Highlanders<br>Southwest Pueblos<br>Sioux | Early formative of inland Mexico (1500–1000 BC)<br>Prepottery Neolithic of Near East (8000–6000 BC) |
| Small Scale | Band | | Kalahari Bushmen<br>Australian Aborigines<br>Eskimo<br>Shoshone | Paleo-Indian and Early Archaic of United States and Mexico (10,000–6000 BC)<br>Late Paleolithic of Near East (10,000 BC) |

Institutions, in ascending order of appearance: Local group autonomy, Egalitarian status, Ephemeral leadership, Ad hoc ritual, Reciprocal economy, Unranked descent groups, Pantribal sodalities, Calendric ritual, Ranked descent groups, Redistributive economy, Hereditary leadership, Elite endogamy, Full-time craft specialization, Stratification, Kingship, Codified law, Bureaucracy, Military draft, Taxation.

FIGURE 7.1   *Selected institutions appearing along the band–tribe–chiefdom–state continuum in ascending order of sociopolitcal complexity. (After Flannery 1972:401, Figure 1.)*

short list of 50 traits that represented what they considered to be part of a "main sequence" in the development of cultural complexity. In Table 7.2 on page 164, compare the organization of the Inca as a very complex state and the Hawaiians as a relatively simple state. The traits "social stratification" and "craft specialization" suggest a well-developed chiefdom, and "empires" and "two or more cities" would indicate a very large-scale state. The "three or more levels of territorial administration," which in Chapter 6 was proposed as the defining criteria for state organization, falls almost in the middle of the list and demonstrates the difficulty of drawing sharp lines to distinguish between large chiefdoms and small states. However, most traits in the upper two-thirds of this list clearly reflect the increasing use of political power.

Probably the most useful definitions of the state use the presence of government institutions, or administrative hierarchies, often characterized as having a monopoly on the legitimate use of force. Thus, kings, courts, judges, police forces, and armies might be considered the essential features of

*civilization*   Sometimes used synonymously with *culture* but more commonly refers to cultures with state organization, writing, and cities; generally equated with large-scale cultures.

*urban revolution*   Childe's concept that emphasizes the role of cities in the development of civilization.

*scalability*   A characteristic of a series of cultural traits that are assumed to be functionally related and that appear to be added and retained in a predictable sequence during the course of cultural development.

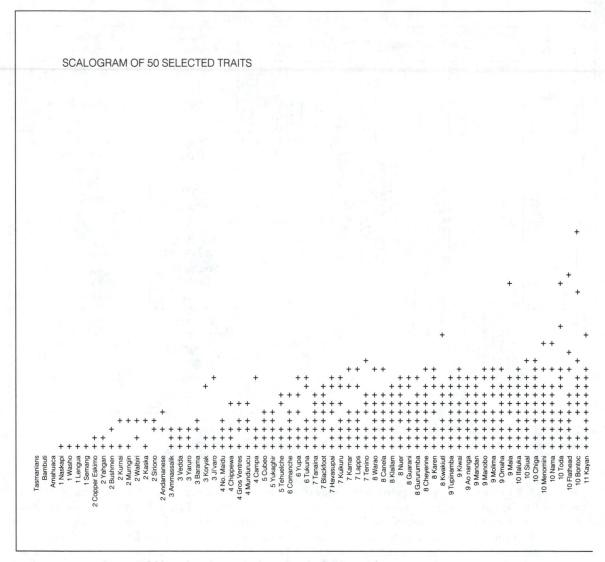

FIGURE 7.2    *Scalogram of fifty cultural traits and one-hundred cultures showing increasing levels of complexity. Numbers total pluses in columns and rows. Note the comparison between Hawaiians and the Inca.* (SOURCE: *Carneiro and Tobias 1963.*)

states. Such formal institutions are a uniquely important development because, as C. R. Hallpike (1986) notes, they have explicit goals, such as the preservation of the social order, and they can legitimately be analyzed in functional terms. Following this lead, the next section examines the functions of state institutions.

## State Functions

Childe (1936) argued that the purpose of the state was to protect upper-class economic interests from the oppressed lower classes. However, theorists are divided over whether the primary functions of government institutions were to protect the interests

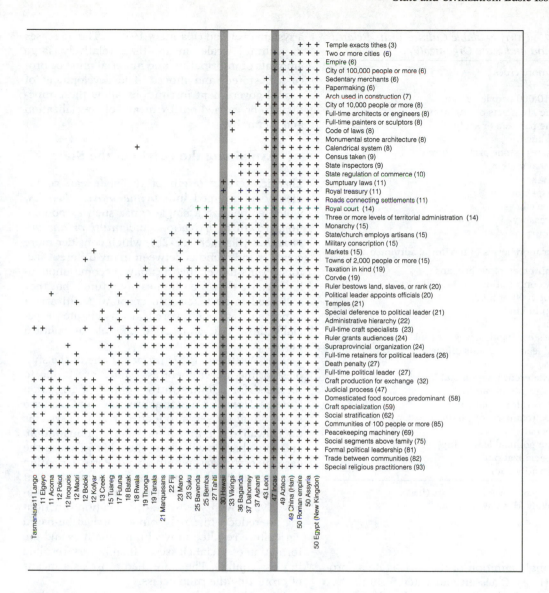

of the upper classes or to protect society as a whole. Elman Service takes the latter view but emphasizes that the government had to also ensure its own existence as an institution:

*Centralized leadership . . . in developing its administrative functions for the maintenance of the society, grew into a hereditary aristocracy. The nascent bureaucracy's economic and religious functions developed as the extent of its services, its autonomy, and its size increased. Thus the*

*earliest government worked to protect, not another class or stratum of society, but itself. It legitimized itself in its role of maintaining the whole society. Political power organized the economy, not vice versa. The system was redistributive, allocative, not acquisitive. . . . And these first governments seem clearly to have reinforced their structure by doing their economic and religious jobs well—by providing benefits—rather than by using physical force.* (1975:8)

As a relatively neutral starting point, we can use

TABLE 7.2  *Thirty Scalable Culture Traits Related to Civilization and State Organization**

+ Two or more cities
+ Empires
+ City of 10,000 people or more
+ Full-time architects or engineers
+ Full-time painters or sculptors
+ Code of laws
+ Monumental stone architecture
+ Calendrical system
+ Census taken
+ State inspectors
H+ Sumptuary laws
H+ Royal treasury
H+ Royal court

H+ Three or more levels of territorial administration

H+ State/church employs artisans
H+ Military conscription
H+ Towns of 2000 or more
H+ Taxation in kind
H+ Corvée
H+ Ruler bestows land, slaves, or rank
H+ Political leader appoints officials
H+ Temples
H+ Special deference to political leader
H+ Administrative hierarchy
  + Full-time craft specialists
H+ Full-time retainers for political leader
H+ Death penalty
H+ Full-time political leadership
H+ Craft specialization
H+ Social stratification

SOURCE: Data from Carneiro and Tobias (1963).
*+ = Inca culture; H = Hawaiian culture.

the functional definition of the early state as proposed by Henry Claessen and Peter Skalnik: ". . . the early state is the organization for the regulation of social relations in a society that is divided into two emergent social classes, the rulers and the ruled" (1978:21).

Because the state involves an increase in the scale of society as formerly autonomous smaller-scale units, such as villages and chiefdoms, are combined into larger structures, this makes information handling and decision making more difficult. Purely from an information standpoint, the state can be understood as a structural response to

a system overload (Flannery 1972b). The increases in cultural scale mean that relatively large amounts of information and material must be processed, stored, and moved. The development of formal government institutions allow these functions to be carried out by means of specialization and hierarchy.

## Explaining the Origin of the State

Theories on the origin of the state can conveniently be grouped into **prime mover theories,** which emphasize a single cause such as population growth or irrigation, and **multivariant approaches** (Flannery 1972b), which consider more complex interactions between many different factors. Prime-mover theories have become unpopular because they are often easily refuted, but they still need to be taken into account. Multivariant approaches will be favored in this chapter, especially those that emphasize the role of political power.

Karl Wittfogel (1957) proposed one of the simplest prime-mover theories—states arose due to the need for administrative control of irrigation systems. However, material presented in Chapter 6 showed that the very productive irrigation systems on Hawaii did not require state administration, and this chapter will show that this was also the case in early Mesopotamia and Peru. Irrigation can profitably be incorporated in a multivariant approach. For example, according to Igor Diakonov (1969), who sees state organization functioning to reduce internal conflict, irrigation-based agriculture resulted in wealth inequalities and the formation of social classes, which in turn resulted in class conflict. The state then arose as a means of protecting the ruling class.

Some theorists have used population growth as an independent variable, assuming that it drives agricultural intensification, conflict, and the need for bureaucratic control (Carneiro 1970, Smith and Young 1972, Steward 1949). All these variables are certainly associated, but the direction of causality is not always easily determined. Political factors need to be considered by any state-origin theory that focuses on population. For example, Carneiro's (1981) circumscription argument for chiefdom development (see Chapter 6) relied on population growth, but warfare and conquest were clearly political processes that rewarded polities with larger populations.

Hallpike (1986) stresses that *equifinality* characterizes the process of state origins, meaning that there are many possible routes to the same outcome. Hallpike argues that state organization results from unequal access to political authority that arises out of a given culture's preexisting "roots of authority," including such traits as lineage systems, primogeniture, military organization, or gerontocracies. These are necessary preconditions, or *preadaptations*, for state organization, but they require other factors such as circumscription, warfare, and large-scale trade, before the state would appear.

Clearly, there can be no single explanation for such a complex phenomenon as state organization. It will perhaps be most useful to move to specific case studies. In the following sections, we will examine early Mesopotamian civilization within the larger context of Near Eastern prehistory and environment. This case study will be followed by a concise comparative view of Andean civilization.

## NEAR EASTERN PREHISTORY

### Fertile Crescents and Hilly Flanks: Neolithic Origins

Culturally and geographically, Mesopotamia is party of the ancient *Near East,* or Southwest Asia as it is sometimes called, which includes Anatolia (the Asian portion of modern Turkey), Palestine, Syria, Arabia, Iraq, and Iran (Figure 7.3). The term *Middle East* covers the Near East but also refers to the larger region across North Africa occupied by modern Arab speakers. The Near East has long been a central focus for archaeological research on the origin of *Homo sapiens*, domestication, and urban civilization. The region has been continuously occupied by humans since the emergence of *Homo sapiens* (Table 7.3) and contains several famous archaeological sites from the Middle and Upper Paleolithic. For example, an important series of Neandertal skulls were found in excavations at the Mt. Carmel caves in Palestine, and some of the earliest fully modern humans are known from that re-

gion. The Near East is also famous as perhaps the earliest center of plant and animal domestication in the world.

The concept of the *Fertile Crescent* as the cradle of Near Eastern civilization originated with James Henry Breasted (1865–1935), the American classical archaeologist who founded the Oriental Institute of the University of Chicago in 1919. The Fertile Crescent is a 1500-mile-long (2414 kilometers [km]) curve of territory stretching from the mouth of the Tigris-Euphrates at the head of the Persian Gulf, northwest through Mesopotamia and Syria, south along the Mediterranean Levant to the lower Nile Valley in Egypt. Within this region began some of the world's earliest urban literate civilizations, which ultimately formed the bases of the Greek and Roman civilizations of Europe.

Archaeologists have long recognized that all the wild ancestors of the most important Near Eastern domesticated crops and animals, including sheep, goats, cattle, wheat, and barley, originated in this region. V. Gordon Childe (1892–1957), a University of London archaeologist, helped popularize the concept of a *Neolithic revolution* based on the development of agriculture in the Near East. Beginning in 1947, the pioneer excavations organized by

---

*prime-mover theory*   A theory that espouses a single powerful cause for or determinant of a cultural development such as the state.

*multivariant approach*   Flannery's theoretical approach that draws attention to many interacting factors that may be involved in the development of a complex cultural phenomenon such as the state.

*equifinality*   Hallpike's argument that there are many possible paths to the development of the state.

*preadaptation*   Cultural features that serve particular functions at a given level of cultural development but that may later make other developments possible.

*Near East*   An ancient culture area that included the earliest civilizations in the Fertile Crescent region.

*Middle East*   A modern culture area that includes predominately Arabic-speaking, Muslim peoples of the Near East and North Africa.

*Fertile Crescent*   Near Eastern region including Mesopotamia and Egypt where some of the earliest civilizations arose.

*Neolithic revolution*   Childe's concept that emphasizes the dramatic cultural changes brought about by domestication and settled village life.

Robert Braidwood of Chicago's Oriental Institute identified some of the earliest traces of domestic plants in the Zagros Mountains, at sites such as Jarmo on the **hilly flanks** of the Fertile Crescent (Braidwood and Howe 1960). However, the major issue, which is still being debated, was the how and why of the transition to settled farming life because the transition was obviously a long, gradual process with a revolutionary outcome and not a sudden invention.

This discussion will focus more on the Neolithic cultural change process, rather than on pinpointing precisely when and where the "first" domestication occurred. Many domesticates of the wild ancestors, especially livestock, are spread over large areas of the globe, and new "earliest" finds are regularly reported. The Fertile Crescent was likely not the original source of many of the major "Near Eastern" domesticates, and there may well have been multiple origins, with independent, roughly simultaneous domestications occurring in different places. Who was "first" is less important

than understanding the general process involved and the implications of farming for a drastic change in the scale of culture.

Many theorists have focused on demographic and environmental factors as the underlying causes of domestication. Flannery (1965, 1972a) argued that domestication and sedentary village life developed in the Near East as part of a **broad-spectrum subsistence revolution** that took place in response to resource-population disequilibriums following the Ice Age. Broad-spectrum subsistence means eating a wide range of food resources such as wild grains and small animals that might require significant labor costs to procure and process. As people specialized in producing and processing wild grains, sedentism might have encouraged population growth because the incentives for family planning related to nomadism were abandoned. Philip Smith and Cuyler Young (1972) follow a similar argument for the Near East, seeing local colonizing migrations and subsistence intensification occurring as people attempted to main-

FIGURE 7.3 *Map of the Near East showing the Fertile Crescent, Mesopotamia, and major archaeological sites referred to in text.*

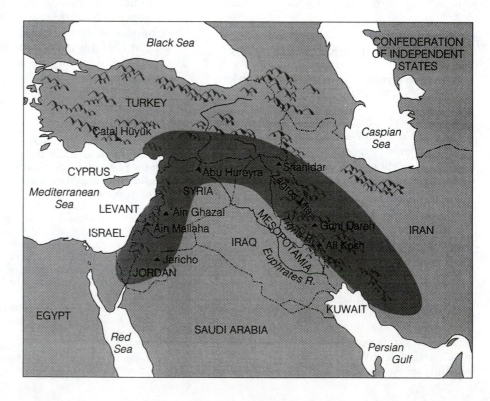

TABLE 7.3    *Near Eastern Prehistory and Early History: Mesopotamia and the Levant\**

| | | |
|---|---|---|
| 2300–600 BC | 1600–600 | Kassite and Assyrian dynasties |
| | 2000–1600 | Isin-Larsa and Old Babylonian dynasties |
| | 2100–2000 | Third Dynasty, Ur (Sumerian) |
| | 2300–2100 | Akkadian dynasties |
| | 2400–2100 | Ur I and II (Sumerian) |
| Early Dynastic (2900–2300 BC) | 2900–2300 | Early Dynastic I (Sumerian); urbanized city-states, cuneiform writing well established |
| Uruk (4000–3100 BC) (Mesopotamia/Khuzistan) | 4000–3100 | Large centers with temple mounds; use of cylinder seals; earliest writing systems; probable state organization |
| Ubaid (5500–4000 BC) (Mesopotamian/Khuzistan Chalcolithic) | 5500–4000 | Probable chiefdom organization; painted ceramics; some articles of copper |
| Neolithic (8500–3700 BC) (Levant) | 5000–3750 | Neolithic 4 (developed): Further population growth; ceramics, domestic pigs |
| | 6000–5000 | Neolithic 3 (developed): Climate increasingly hot and dry; full dependence on mixed dry farming and herding in upland forest zones |
| | 7600–6000 | Neolithic 2 (archaic): Farming and herding of domestic sheep and goats, supplemented by hunting and foraging; sites larger, steppe occupied; large, permanent egalitarian villages |
| | 8500–7600 | Neolithic 1 (archaic): Simple farming and herding |
| Epipaleolithic (18,000–8500 BC) (Levant) | 10,000–8500 | Epipaleolithic 2 (Natufian): Climate cool and wet; larger, semisedentary settlements; selective hunting; population increases; intensive use of wild grains, microlith sickles, ground-stone tools; possible simple cultivation and beginnings of animal domestication |
| | 17,000 | Persian Gulf dry land |
| | 18,000–10,000 | Epipaleolithic 1 (Kebaran): Climate cool and dry; mobile foragers and hunters; microlithic tools |
| Upper Paleolithic | | Upper Paleolithic: Fully modern humans; mobile foragers |

SOURCES: Moore (1983) and Voigt (1987).
\*Absolute chronologies for Near Eastern archaeology vary widely in different sources and are frequently recalibrated; thus, they must always be used with caution.

tain familiar cultural patterns despite steadily increasing population pressure.

The demographic explanation of domestication has had many critics, but, in general, it remains a compelling argument. However, recent archaeological work appears not to support some of its predictions. For example, studies of the strontium–calcium ratio found in human bone have been used to infer the proportions of meat and plant foods in ancient diets. Tests conducted on burials from the Levant revealed no indication of

nutritional stress during the period of incipient domestication (Sillen 1986). Of course, population pressure need not be taken as a sole cause of do-

---

**hilly flanks**  Foothills of the Zagros Mountains bordering Mesopotamia, believed by Braidwood to be the area where domestication first took place in the Near East.
**broad-spectrum subsistence revolution**  Flannery's characterization of the postglacial intensification of subsistence activities that ultimately lead to domestication in the Near East.

mestication, and as Smith and Young (1983) more recently observe, "population pressure" need not imply starvation. Like Marvin Harris's (1984) protein argument, population pressure may simply encourage people to make cultural adjustments to avoid more drastic changes in preferred ways of life.

Andrew Moore (1983), who excavated the early site of Abu Hureyra on the middle Euphrates of Syria, found extensive use of wild-type einkorn wheat, wild barley, and wild rye during the Natufian or Late Epipaleolithic by 9000 BC, suggesting that *incipient cultivation*, the gradual transition to farming, was well underway by that time, although the plants were still indistinguishable from the uncultivated forms. (This Early *Holocene* period between the Paleolithic and Neolithic is also referred to as the Mesolithic or Protoneolithic.) Cultivation was further suggested by the appearance of weeds that typically pioneer cultivated areas and because the site of Abu Hureyra was located in what would have been a prime farming area.

In this sequence, it is interesting that cultural changes seem to have been promoted by both favorable and unfavorable climatic-environmental conditions, interacting with demographic variables in somewhat different ways. Moore (1983) argues that intentional cultivation of wild grains might have begun as population increased under the improved, cool wet conditions of the late Epipaleolithic as people attempted to increase subsistence production to permit larger communities to remain together throughout the year. Settlement pattern data from the earliest Neolithic sites in the Levant (Table 7.4) show a continuing trend toward sedentism, cultivation, and herding because sites are larger and located in the best farming areas.

Recognizably domesticated forms of wheat, barley, and lentils are known from the Levant region by approximately 8000 BC. Although the precise causes of domestication can probably never be known with certainty, Solomon Katz and Mary Voigt (1986) argue that the strongest motivation for domestication might have been people's desire to increase the supply of grain to be used to brew beer because people appreciated the intoxicating properties of alcohol. A secondary benefit of beer was that the yeasts used in fermentation improved

the amino acid and vitamin content of the grain and made it a greater source of protein. Wheat grain and malt produced from sprouted barley would have been the ideal ingredients for brewing beer, and the yeasts involved in fermentation could have also been used to produce bread. No direct evidence proves when beer was first brewed in the Near East, but it does appear to have been important in the earliest Mesopotamian civilizations. This explanation of domestication is significant because it does not depend on demographic imbalances or climate but instead provides a sociopsychological motivation for human actors. However, it seems basically untestable and is not widely endorsed.

## The Neolithic and Indo-European Expansion

By the Late Archaic, or pre-Pottery Neolithic in the Levant at approximately 6000 BC, villages had become large and had presumably grown increasingly dependent on domesticates, farming, herding, and evermore intensive hunting and foraging. Some villages such as Jericho were dramatically larger than any previously seen in the region and may have had several thousand people. However, these societies apparently remained egalitarian because nothing indicates signs of rank or differential wealth in the residences or burial sites.

After 6000 BC, in the Developed Neolithic, Moore (1983) suggests that increased population, deforestation, and overgrazing, combined with an increasingly hot and dry climate, forced people to abandon foraging entirely and become full-time,

TABLE 7.4   *Settlement Size in the Epipaleolithic–Neolithic Levant, 18,000–3750 BC*

|  | Average Size | Maximum Size | Estimated Inhabitants |
|---|---|---|---|
| Neolithic 4 | — | — | — |
| Neolithic 3 | — | — | — |
| Neolithic 2 | — | — | + 2000 |
| Neolithic 1 | — | 4 hectares | — |
| Epipaleolithic 2 | <500 m² | 2000 m² | — |
| Epipaleolithic 1 | 300 m² | — | 30 |

SOURCE: Moore (1983).

mixed, dry farmers and herders in the moister upland forest zones. By this time, they had a full range of food crops and animals including sheep, goats, cattle, and pigs. Smith and Young (1983) present a very similar picture of cultural developments for the period through the Epipaleolithic into the Early Neolithic in the Zagros Mountains. Population growth is clearly associated with the shift to full dependence on domesticates, although the causal connections are not well understood.

As a continuation of the demographic expansion interpretation, Cambridge archaeologist Colin Renfrew (1989) attributes the spread of *Indo-European languages* to an advancing wave of colonial migration spreading out from Anatolia beginning about 6500 BC and carrying the Neolithic way of life across all of Europe over the following 2000 years. Farming dramatically increased carrying capacity over foraging and may have been adopted by indigenous European foragers as the arrival of farming colonists made foraging difficult. Earlier views of the spread of Indo-European languages assumed an invasion of mounted warriors out of Central Asia. The "wave of advance" model is based on the work of physical anthropologists Albert Ammerman and L. L. Cavalli-Sforza (1984) and assumes a rapid fifty-fold increase of population density as farmers moved peacefully into Europe at a rate of .6 mile (1 km) a year, with new homesteads spreading out 11 miles (18 km) at random every 25-year generation. Grover Krantz (1988) proposes a similar model of Neolithic expansion.

Renfrew (1989) suggests that *Afro-Asiatic languages* such as Semitic (Egyptian, Arabic, and Hebrew), Cushitic, and Berber may have spread into Arabia and North Africa and that Dravidian-speaking peoples migrated into India, all as part of the same Neolithic wave of advance. Renfrew also speculates that all Indo-European, Afro-Asiatic, and Dravidian languages separated from a single superfamily called *Nostratic*, located in the Near East about 8000 BC at the beginning of the Neolithic.

Villages built during the Near Eastern Neolithic were strikingly different from any settlements discussed in previous chapters because they were very permanent, consisting of closely clustered, rectangular stone or adobe structures. Such structures were often preceded by round structures, which were probably used by seminomadic peoples (Flannery 1972a). A tantalizing glimpse of what Near Eastern Neolithic villages may have looked like is provided by the site of Çatal Hüyük in south central Turkey (Mellaart 1967, Todd 1976). In about 6000 BC, Çatal Hüyük was a compact 32-acre (13-hectare) site, perhaps the largest Neolithic village in the Near East (Figure 7.4). There were specially decorated structures with likely religious functions, and craft production was well developed, but there is no evidence of full-time specialists or social stratification.

## THE EARLY MESOPOTAMIAN STATE

### Environment and Archaeology

The general region of Mesopotamia, one of the earliest centers of urban civilization, is a flat, 500-mile-long (805 km) alluvial plain, or basin, lying between the Zagros mountains of Iran on the east and the Arabian plateau on the west (Figure 7.5). For much of its length, the Mesopotamian plain is less than 200 miles (322 km) wide, and it is traversed by the parallel Tigris and Euphrates rivers. An arid region, it is best suited for pastoral nomadism except for the irrigation potential pro-

---

*incipient cultivation*  Early phase of the gradual process of domestication when it is difficult to distinguish between wild and domesticated forms but where settled village life, or sedentism, has begun.

*Holocene*  Geological period covering the 10,000 years since the end of the Pleistocene Epoch and the Ice Age up to the present.

*Indo-European language*  A very large language group with many major branches. Includes most modern European languages such as French, Spanish, Italian, and Portuguese, derived from Latin; Germanic languages such as English; Slavic languages such as Russian; and many languages in South Asia and Southwest Asia.

*Afro-Asiatic language*  Includes the Near Eastern Semitic languages such as Egyptian, Arabic, and Hebrew, as well as the Cushitic languages of Ethiopia and Berber languages of North Africa.

*Nostratic language*  The hypothetical language believed by some linguistics to have been the Near Eastern ancestor to Indo-European Afro-Asiatic, and Dravidian languages some 10,000 BP.

FIGURE 7.4 *Çatal Hüyük, a very large early Neolithic prestate village in what is now south central Turkey: (a) a reconstructed view of densely packed multistoried buildings in the village; (b) a reconstruction of a structure that is thought to have been a religious shrine.*

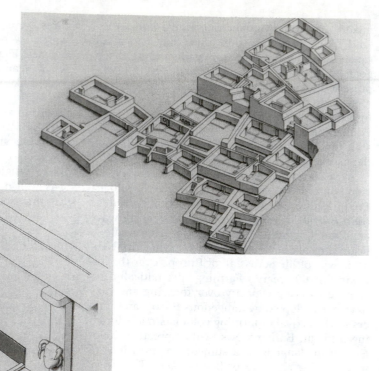

vided by the river systems. The Euphrates is less subject to flooding and tends to build natural levees, which elevate it above the level of the surrounding land, making it more amenable to irrigation than the Tigris (Adams 1981). The Euphrates is a braided and meandering river that has constantly changed its channel such that ancient cities may stand in barren desert miles from the modern riverbed.

Several hazards threaten subsistence activities in this region. Pastoralism is subject to great fluctuation in rainfall and periods of drought, along with the related possibility of overgrazing. Agriculture is dependent on irrigation, but crops can be destroyed by floods and yields can be reduced by salination due to an elevation of saltwater caused by overirrigation. The early states that developed in Mesopotamia were **primary states,** or pristine

states, arising independently of other states; therefore, they offer a good place to test theories of state origin. In this section, we examine the research of archaeologist Gregory Alan Johnson (1973), whose work was part of a team effort to explore the origins of the state in Mesopotamia. In 1970–1971, Johnson surveyed the remains of ancient settlements in southwestern Iran on the eastern margin of the Mesopotamian lowlands that were occupied during the **Uruk period** (approximately 4000–3100 BC) when the shift from chiefdom to state organization took place. Johnson wanted to learn if changes in settlement patterns would reflect the political and economic changes associated with the emergence of the state. Based on his analysis of potsherds, Johnson was able to measure the size of sixty-seven ancient settlement sites and assign them to a **relative chronology** within four sequen-

**FIGURE 7.5**  *Ancient settlement mounds in the Mesopotamian lowlands of southwest Iran, surveyed by archaeologist Gregory Allen Johnson.*

tial ***stylistic phases*** spanning a 1000-year period beginning roughly in 4000 BC (Table 7.5). His dates do not correspond precisely with the dates shown in Table 7.3 because there is considerable disagreement on the precise calibration of ***absolute dates*** in Near Eastern archaeology.

**TABLE 7.5**  *Settlement Pattern Changes in Mesopotamia, 4000–3000 BC*

|  | Terminal Susa A | Early Uruk | Middle Uruk | Late Uruk |
|---|---|---|---|---|
| **Sites** | 18 | 49 | 52 | — |
| **Large Centers** | 0 | 1 | 3 | 3 |
| **Small Centers** | 2 | 3 | 4 | 1 |
| **Large Villages** | 0 | 0 | 12 | 0 |
| **Villages** | 16 | 45 | 33 | 10 |
| **Area (hectares)** | 30 | 95 | 127 | 53 |
| **Population** | 6000 | 20,000 | 25,000 | 10,600 |
| **Density/km²** | 2 | 7 | 9 | 4 |
| **Village Land, (hectare/ person)** | — | .49 | — | — |
| **Center Land (hectare/ person)** | — | 2.12 | — | — |

SOURCE: G. Johnson (1973: 97–98).

The switch from the earliest phase (Terminal Susa A, equivalent to the Ubaid on the Tigris-Euphrates) to Early Uruk was dramatic. At first, there were relatively few villages, and they were clustered in relation to larger centers in a way that suggested chiefdom organization. During the Early Uruk, the population suddenly tripled in size, density increased, and the site of Susa became an "urban" center of 2400 people. This change in settlement pattern and population suggests that villages and small centers came under some form of central control.

Based on his assumption that each hectare of

***primary state***  A state that is assumed to have developed without direct influence from any other state.

***Uruk period***  The archaeological time period when state organization first appeared in Mesopotamia.

***relative chronology***  A sequence of events ordered relative to one another but that may not be reliably related to a universal calender.

***stylistic phase***  A relative archaeological time period based on distinctive design features or art styles expressed in material culture such as ceramics or textiles.

***absolute date***  Any date that can be expressed in a universal calender, such as BP (before present, before 1950) or BC (before Christ), and AD (*anno Domini*, year of our Lord) in the Christian calender.

FIGURE 7.6  *Mass-produced beveled-rim ceramic bowls from ancient Mesopotamia. Their presence suggests the existence of state organization because they were used to distribute rations to laborers.*

settlement area was occupied by 200 people, the total population of the region may have increased from 6000 people to 20,000 in the Early Uruk. The earlier 6000 people lived in sixteen villages under two small chiefdom centers. By Early Uruk times, there were forty-five villages under three small centers with Susa as an overall center. G. Johnson (1973) infers that Susa may have operated as a *central place* because villages were evenly spaced in a pattern that would support the most efficient communication to the center for the distribution of resources. The center contained workshops where artisans using pottery wheels produced large quantities of specialty ceramics for distribution to outlying villages. The villagers apparently produced their own food and a surplus to support nonfood-producing administrators and artisans.

During Early Uruk times, there was an increase in the use of identifying seals, or marks stamped in soft clay, to seal bundles and containers such as jars. Clay seals would be broken when a container was opened, and their use suggests that officials in the centers were becoming more concerned with controlling the production and distribution of goods. Given the settlement-pattern evidence of three administrative levels, it seems reasonable to treat Early Uruk as a small-scale state.

By the Middle Uruk period, there was further increase in settlement number, size, and total population (see Table 7.5) and an obvious elaboration of administrative functions. Monumental architecture appeared in large centers as large buildings, and residences were differentiated, suggesting an increase in bureaucracy, status differences, and wealth inequality. The presence of elite government administrators in outlying villages is suggested by the appearance of clay seals and small painted ceramic cones normally used to create lav-

ish decorative mosaics on walls in the centers. Further evidence of exchange between centers and villages can be documented by the appearance in the villages of pottery manufactured in the centers where the kilns and workshops were exclusively located.

The mobilization of significant village labor forces during the Middle Uruk is inferred from the most abundant form of pottery, a simple bowl with a distinctive beveled rim (Figure 7.6). These bowls were apparently mold-made by specialists using assembly-line procedures. They were produced in three standardized sizes and may have been used to distribute barley rations to pay workers in service to the state (see Table 7.6 and the box "The Mesopotamian Ration System"). Other evidence of elaborate administrative controls included the appearance of cylinder seals, which allowed identifying marks to be applied more efficiently by rolling instead of stamping, and the extensive use of

TABLE 7.6  *Rations in Mesopotamia by Age and Sex*

|  | Se-ba (Barley) (sila/month)* | I-ba (Oil) (sila/year) | Sig-ba (Wool) (ma-na/ year)† |
|---|---|---|---|
| Men | 60 | 4 | 4 |
| Women | 30 | 4 | 3 |
| Children | — | 1.5 | 1.5 |
| Boys | 20–30 | — | — |
| Girls | 20 | — | — |
| Infants | 10 | — | — |

SOURCES: Gelb (1965), G. Johnson (1973), Kramer (1963).
*Sila = .85 L, 705 g of barley.
†Ma-na = 500 g.

## The Mesopotamian Ration System

The early Mesopotamian city-state was based on a large number of full-time urban specialists, who included priests, scribes, overseers, and artisans. All these people were supported by monthly allotments of rations, which in Sumerian were called *Se-ba* (*Se* means "barley"; *ba* means "distribution"). According to I. J. Gelb's (1965) analysis of the textual evidence, standard rations included *Se-ba*, *I-ba* (oil), and *Sig-ba* (wool) and were distributed in standardized units according to a set formula specifying the amounts that people would receive by age and gender category. For example, barley was distributed by the *sila*, a volume measurement equivalent to .85 liter (L). Men normally received 60 *sila;* women, 30; boys, averaged 25; girls, 20; and infants, 10 (see Table 7.6). The rations were probably generous, and people no doubt bartered the surplus to acquire other basic needs. According to figures used by G. Johnson (1973), 1 L of barley contained 829 grams (g), and 100 g of barley produced 350 calories (cal). The average adult ration of 45 *sila* would have provided 3698 cal/day. Barley was the most important subsistence staple, but it probably supplied only 66 percent of people's average caloric consumption, the balance being supplied by animals products, fruits, and vegetables. Thus, people probably consumed directly only about half of their barley allotments. The oil ration was generally animal fat, although sometimes it might have been sesame oil, and it was used for consumption and in ritual anointings. Besides barley, oil, and wool distributions, there were also irregular distributions of wheat, bread, flour, and cloth. Standard rations were sometimes replaced with equivalent substitutes, such that 1 *sila* of oil could replace 2 *sila* of barley. On ritual occasions or to specific categories of people, there were also supplemental distributions of such articles as meat, dairy products, beer, wine, fish, dates, fruits, and vegetables.

---

counting devices known as *bullae*, which were marked with numerical notations and contained hollow clay balls, or tokens. Archaeologist Denise Schmandt-Besserat (1982) believes that these clay tokens represented specific quantities of goods that were collected as a tax to support centrally controlled rituals. Their use seems to be directly related to the development of writing systems in Mesopotamia, which is discussed in a later section. The presence of clay tokens by very early Neolithic times some 10,000 BP suggests that chiefdomlike political authority may have very ancient roots in the Near East.

The archaeological record from the Susiana plain seems to refute both the irrigation and the conflict theories of state origin. Uruk irrigation systems were small and apparently did not require state administrators. Conflict, whether internal or external, did not arise until after the state was in place. Similarly, long-distance trade seems not to have been an important factor in state formation during Uruk times, although regional trade cer-

---

**central place**    A settlement that serves as the focus of a regional communication network.

tainly occurred. Environmental circumscription due to population increase can also be discounted because similar densities were reached earlier in the same area without leading to state organization. G. Johnson (1973) concludes that the most critical factors may have been an increase in the demands for information processing on the relatively simple decision-making structures of the Susa chiefdoms, perhaps related to increasing interaction with adjacent pastoralists.

G. Johnson's (1973) emphasis on the administrative and distributive functions of the early Mesopotamian state correspond closely to Service's (1975) view that the state evolved as a society-maintaining system. Robert Adams (1981) challenges these conclusions with data from his own site survey from the central Mesopotamian floodplain. He finds no evidence for central-place redistribution functions and argues that the ubiquitous beveled bowls may have been used in rituals and not to distribute rations. Adams suggests that the earliest Mesopotamian urban sites were formed as cult centers augmented by political subordination and military coercion.

## Royal Tombs, Ziggurats, and Cylinder Seals

During the Early Dynastic (approximately 3000–2000 BC), Mesopotamian culture acquired the unmistakable marks of a well-developed, stratified, urban, state-organized system. Adams (1981) suggests that by the Early Dynastic, Mesopotamia had become the world's first predominantly urban society with 70 to 80 percent of the population living in urban centers of 1000 people or more. The city of Uruk for example, quadrupled in size between the Late Uruk and the Early Dynastic I, growing to perhaps 40,000 people or more. Because he found little evidence for subsistence intensification, Adams infers that dependent villagers must have worked under bureaucratic control to help support the nonfood-producing urban population.

The nature of early Mesopotamian society has been a subject of scholarly debate for many years. Wittfogel (1957) considered Sumerian society to be an example of **agromanagerial despotism,** in which the economy was based on "hydraulic agriculture" involving "large-scale and government-

managed works of irrigation and flood control" (1957:3). He thought that such systems required large-scale cooperation and a division of labor between managers and farmers. As Wittfogel explicitly declared,

*Thus a number of farmers eager to conquer arid lowlands and plains are forced to invoke the organizational devices which—on the basis of premachine technology—offer the one chance of success: they must work in cooperation with their fellows and subordinate themselves to a directing authority.* (1957:18)

The managers then gained absolute power over their populations and became tyrannical and despotic rulers who terrorized their subjects into absolute submission. The primary problem with this view, as was noted in our earlier discussion of Hawaii, is that effective irrigation systems apparently did not require the kind of large-scale coordination Wittfogel envisioned. In the Near East, there are examples of local villagers managing their own regional irrigation systems in a basically egalitarian way (Adams 1982). Furthermore, as G. Johnson's (1973) research demonstrated, bureaucracies and city-states developed in the Near East before the large-scale, labor-intensive irrigation systems that probably did require centralized administration.

There is general agreement that some kind of institutionalized temple-city, or temple-palace, bureaucracy controlled the urban centers in early Mesopotamia. Each city belonged to a founding god drawn from the rich Sumerian pantheon and contained temples dedicated to it. The Sumerian word for temple, *e-bitum,* meant "house," so the temple was the god's house and the temple personnel existed as the god's caretakers. The visible focal point of major Sumerian cities was the *ziggurat* (an Akkadian world for "temple tower"), a stepped pyramid of clay bricks built as a shrine to the city's deity. This was monumental architecture at its finest.

The Ziggurat of Ur, the best surviving example, was completed around 2000 BC during the third Sumerian dynasty. The Ziggurat of Ur, which was excavated by Sir Leonard Woolley (1982) between 1922 and 1934, is one of the best described early ziggurats. The base platform was 200 ft by 150 ft (61 m by 46 m) and 50 feet (15 m) high. Two other

FIGURE 7.7 *The central Ziggurat (temple tower) of Ur built around 2000 BC.*

levels were built on top of this, and they were topped by a small shrine to the moon god Nanna, so that the total height was at least 70 ft (21 m) (see Figure 7.7). Because the ziggurat was built on an elevated terrace, the whole structure must have been an imposing sight rising above the surrounding plain. The ziggurat was part of the *Temenos* (Greek for "sacred ground"), a sacred enclosure containing a major temple to Nanna, other shrines, storehouses, courtyards, and quarters for temple personnel. At this time, Ur was a walled city of some 321 acres (130 hectares) that might have contained 25,000 people, according to some estimates.

The spiritual head of the Sumerian temple bore the title *En*, and he or she resided in an elaborate complex within the *Temenos*, called the *Giparu*. The temple administrator was titled *Sanga*, and there were many other named temple or priestly offices. The temple claimed ownership of at least three named categories of land:

*Nigenna*, whose produce directly supported the temple;

*Kurra*, used to support those who worked *nigenna* land;

*Urulal*, lands that could be farmed by temple personnel for their own use, in exchange for a share of the produce.

Thus, the temple administration, besides conducting major religious activities, managed the production of farmland, collected and stored grain, and paid out rations to laborers.

Secular rulers apparently rose to prominence as military leaders in conflicts with neighboring city-states. As kings (*lugal*), they founded dynasties, built palaces and temples, raised armies, maintained the city walls, and were buried in royal tombs. In 1927–1928, Woolley found some of the most spectacular art treasures of the ancient Near East in the Royal Tombs of Ur. A series of royal burials dating to the Early Dynastic period were discovered in a cemetery just beyond the *Tenemos* wall (Woolley 1982). The burials contained a treasure trove of grave goods, including lyres decorated with golden bull heads (Figure 7.8), gold and silver weapons, jewelry, and headdresses.

Most remarkable was the discovery that the royal personages were accompanied in death by an entourage of soldiers and retainers, wagons, and oxen, all in full regalia. One tomb contained

**agromanagerial despotism** Wittfogel's explanation for the rise of the Mesopotamian state, arguing that the first rulers controlled irrigation and agriculture.

**ziggurat** A Mesopotamian temple pyramid containing a shrine to the city's principal deity and serving as a ritual focus for the state religion.

FIGURE 7.8   *A lyre decorated with a golden bull's head from the royal tombs of Ur.*

seventy-four additional people, including four male guards, four female musicians, and sixty-four women of the royal court in ceremonial dress. Woolley (1982) infers that many of the sacrificed attendants may have taken poison in a mass-suicide ceremony as part of the royal funeral. Human sacrifice on this scale certainly attests to the strength of the religious system, as well as the despotic power of the temple-palace complex. It makes the occasional human sacrifice associated with the Hawaiian temple cults seem almost trivial by comparison.

Henry Wright (1969) used a combination of archaeological evidence and inscribed tablets to reconstruct the complexities of the administrative bureaucracy of Early Dynastic Ur at about 2800 BC. He infers that at that time the city itself contained about 4000 people, while another 1800 people lived in the immediate vicinity. He finds direct archaeological evidence that ceramics, stone

bowls, copper vessels, spinning, and cylinder seal cutting all took place within the city. Inscribed tablets found in the city refer to bricklayers, carpenters, smiths, gardeners, cooks, kitchen supervisors, maltsters, and physicians, all of which are named as specialists. Tablets also attest to the distribution of bread and grain from the temple storehouse to various groups.

The most critical temple function was the management of agricultural production. Temple lands and lands held in large estates, perhaps as allotments from the temple, were all farmed at the lowest levels by small-scale farmers who cultivated plots of 7–17 acres (3–7 hectares). A work foreman supervised a 99–123-acre (40–50-hectare) unit of land, worked by perhaps ten small-scale farmers. Several foremen, in turn, reported to an overseer. Another official supervised the harvest, and the temple administrator controlled the stored grain. Wright (1969) estimates that the planting, harvesting, and irrigation maintenance involved in the annual cultivation of the land could have been readily accommodated by the 2500-person work force that could have been mobilized. This centrally managed production system could have supplied an average adult barley ration for 1200 urban specialists and the 2500 farmers (see Table 7.6).

Economist Karl Polanyi (1977) has described the Mesopotamian economy as a nonmarket redistribution system, emphasizing the managerial role of temple and palace. The Mesopotamian administrative system, however, was clearly different from the relatively small-scale redistribution described for Tikopia (Chapter 6), where independent, basically self-provisioning village farmers contributed to a chief who returned their contributions in the form of religious feasts. It is possible that much of the managed agricultural production in Mesopotamia was carried out by landless, dependent laborers working for rations. At the same time, abundant evidence suggests that there were "free" peasants, as well as large landholders and merchants, who may have operated independently of the central administration.

Adams (1982) stresses that the textual accounts of land ownership and agricultural production may be describing a formal urban code that had only limited applicability in the countryside, where more egalitarian practices may have continued to operate. Modern villages in the region have resisted government efforts to regulate their land-use systems and have used basically tribal systems, which periodically reallocate land in ways that minimize risk and help ensure equal access to land of different quality. Royal dynasties and elite families came and went, but villagers may have formed closed-corporate communities that effectively insulated them from many forms of state intrusion.

## Cuneiform Writing and the Literary Tradition

As the administrative bureaucracy in the Mesopotamian city-states grew, the requirements for information storage increased dramatically. The earliest written inscriptions appeared about 3100 BC in a pictographic script found in the city of Uruk and involved economic control functions such as bookkeeping of receipts, expenses, and goods. By 2400 BC, Mesopotamian writing had become a well-developed cuneiform system (Nissen (1986). The word *cuneiform* (*cunei* means "nails") refers to the distinctive nail shape produced when a stylus with a triangular cross section is pressed into a soft clay tablet at an angle. The early pictographs represented the names of naturalistically portrayed objects, but this limited and cumbersome system was readily improved by simplifying the pictographs into abstract forms and giving some of them phonetic meanings (see Figure 7.9). The basic cuneiform system was used throughout the Near East by the Sumerians, Babylonians, Assyrians, and Persians over a 2000-year period.

A scribal school, the *edubba*, became institutionalized as a formal means of standardizing the writing system and to produce a professional body of scribes needed to write and archive the great masses of clay tablets required for routine administration. Students memorized some 2000 different cuneiform signs by copying standard texts, which often consisted of word lists. One such list contained a ranked list of one hundred professions and titles. The writing system went through a rapid period of development over a period of about 150 years (Nissen 1986) and then became very stable. It was a medium for sacred temple literature, epic poetry, and royal decrees, but the bulk of the material concerned mundane administra-tive matters. Numeration was based on a sexagesimal (60s) system with place values, but it also used a numeral for 10. There was no concept of zero, but complex mathematical calculations such as multiplication, square roots, and area problems were still carried out.

## "Just So Stories" and the Origins of Mesopotamian Civilizations

Sumerologist Samuel Kramer (1963) attributes the development of Sumerian civilization to the special qualities of the Sumerian people. He describes them as "venturesome and resolute, clear-sighted, and level-headed" pragmatists, who had an "unusually creative intellect" and a "flair for technological invention." Kramer emphasizes that the Mesopotamian floodplain was initially an unpromising desert, devoid of trees and minerals. Thus, Sumerian civilization might be considered a classic example of the "challenge and response" theory of history championed by historian Arnold Toynbee (1934). However, such approaches are

FIGURE 7.9  *Clay tablet inscribed in cuneiform writing from ancient Mesopotamia.*

value-laden, circular, and untestable generalizations. Unfortunately, anthropological approaches to the problem are only somewhat better.

Julian Steward (1949) was a pioneer in the effort to place the development of civilization within a global scientific framework based on typologies and predictable causal sequences. Steward thought that civilizations in Peru, Mesoamerica, Mesopotamia, Egypt, and China all developed independently along similar, *multilinear, evolutionary lines.* He stressed the regularities in this process, noting that these early civilizations all developed in arid or semiarid environments. In Steward's view, irrigation was clearly a key to the development process because maximum agricultural production depended on irrigation, which in turn produced population growth, religiously based administrators, and social classes. As he states:

*there is no question that maximum production in these areas of critical and minimal precipitation required irrigation, and that in proportion as irrigation works develop, population will increase until the limits of water are reached. Social or political controls become necessary to manage irrigation and other communal projects. As early societies were strongly religious, individuals with supernatural powers—lineage heads, shamans, or special priests—formed a theocratic ruling class.* (Steward 1955:206)

The developmental sequence that Steward outlines for Mesopotamia overemphasizes the role of technology and population growth, but it is still endorsed by historians such as William McNeil who, in referring to Sumerian civilization, declares,

*Farmers had to be able to produce a food surplus for civilization to get started. Only then could a substantial number of persons free themselves from the task of finding food and begin to spend their time doing other things. This, in turn, allowed specialized skills and new ideas to multiply until society as a whole became sufficiently complex, wealthy, and powerful to be called "civilized."* (1987:31)

This all seems rather teleological and recalls earlier "just so" stories in which apes struggle to their feet in order to "free their hands" so they can become human and "build culture." Increased farming productivity "releases" subsistence farmers who then develop new technology, luxury goods, and monuments. However, continued population growth leads eventually to population pressure, interstate conflict, and empire building, with increased tribute, declines in productivity, and collapse of the system. This treats the whole process as too natural and inevitable and diverts attention from important political processes and complex interconnections.

Charles Redman (1978a, 1978b) has produced a more refined systems theory approach, which he applies specifically to Mesopotamia. Redman adds the dimension of positive-feedback loops that operate within a complex causal network to promote further growth (Figure 7.10). In 5500 BC, the Mesopotamian plain was an empty ecological niche with great agricultural potential waiting to be developed. Soon after the area was colonized by village farmers from the adjacent uplands, the following variables identified in Figure 7.10 acted as primary *positive feedbacks:*

A. Population increase
B. Food production by independent farmers
C. The need for imported raw materials
D. Warfare
E. Social stratification and bureaucratization

Items A–C led to craft specialization, unequal wealth distribution, and urbanization; items D and E resulted in the formation of regional empires.

These positive feedbacks, driven by individuals seeking politically based wealth and power, gradually transform the cultural system from farming villages, to temple towns, to city-states, to nation-states.

Redman (1978a, 1978b) is aware that his explanation for the development of Mesopotamian civilization is simply an "interpretive theory" and a "plausible story," which is "logical but not objectively confirmed." The obvious unanswered question in all of this is why previously small-scale cultures would have permitted such runaway growth to have started in the first place. Some specialists have argued that a major shift in the channel of the Euphrates River, which occurred during the Early Uruk period around 3300 BC, may have forced many independent villagers to move into

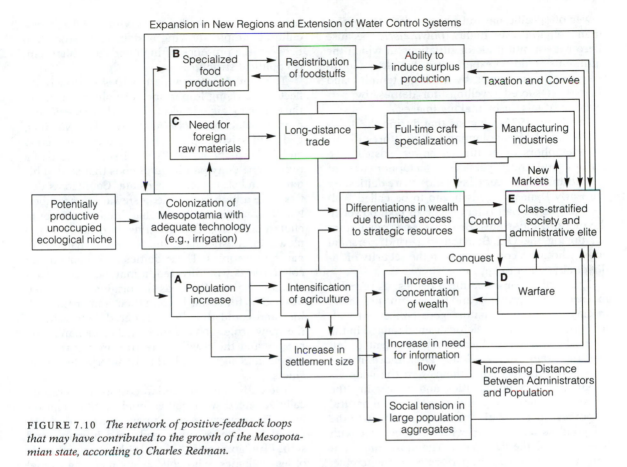

**FIGURE 7.10**  *The network of positive-feedback loops that may have contributed to the growth of the Mesopotamian state, according to Charles Redman.*

the urban centers (Gibson 1976). It may be that the growth potential of irrigation agriculture was simply unprecedented.

## Mesopotamian Religion in Service of the State

In his analysis of Mesopotamian religion, Sumer-ologist Thorkild Jacobsen defines religion as the human experience of the ***numinous,*** or "confrontation with power not of this world" (1976:3). Because the numinous is unworldly, it cannot be directly described; thus, people must resort to religious metaphors that are shared within a culture, for example, by imagining the numinous as specific gods in specific form. Mesopotamian religion

sees the numinous as immanent, as an intrinsic part of nature. So for example, the sun god *Utu* is the sun and the sun's numinous power, all at the same time. The gods thus represent the indwelling

***multilinear evolution***  Steward's theory that, given similar conditions, cultures can develop independently along similar lines. For example, he argued that irrigation agriculture led to state organization several times.

***positive feedback***  In systems theory, an increase in the quantity of a particular variable within an interconnected system that is caused by another variable in the system, such as an increase in population caused by increased food supply.

***numinous***  The aesthetic or emotional experience of religion as an encounter with supernatural, holy, or divine power.

power of specific natural phenomena. Mesopotamian religion was highly **polytheistic** because there were a multitude of situations in which the numinous could be experienced. People could invoke numinous power by building temples and shrines as sacred dwellings for deities, by performing rituals, or by making images.

Jacobsen (1976) suggests that during the 4000-year span of Mesopotamian culture, three different metaphors of numinous power existed. The earliest and most persistent metaphor was of the intransitive power of specific nature deities. By the Early Dynastic, gods began to be called "rulers," just as human rulers began to take power in the merging city-states. By the second millennium BC, during the Old Babylonian period, personal gods, who were concerned with the security of individuals, began to appear.

The earliest Mesopotamian deities, as revealed in a series of engravings and lyric poems preserved in clay tablets, were nature gods concerned with fertility. Initially, these deities were depicted in the form of the natural objects they represented, but over time they were gradually given more human form. Prominent among them were the gods associated with specific cities and expressing the power of economically important regional natural resources, such as *Enki* the water god, *Nanshe* the fish goddess, and *Dumuzi* who was concerned with livestock and the date palm. The most important annual rituals, no doubt performed at the temple, involved a sacred wedding, in which nature deities as bride and groom perpetuated the return of fertility in the spring and mourned the decline and death of fertility in the fall. The temple deity and associated storehouse were direct embodiments of nature's fertility.

By the third millennium BC, deities were referred to as "Lords" or "Masters" and mirrored the actions of human rulers. People were now impressed by the awe-inspiring energy and majesty of the numinous, not just their life-sustaining powers of fertility. The major city gods were viewed in new roles as spiritual estate managers, judges, and warriors. This sequence of development supports the general cultural materialist theoretical position that religion, as part of a culture's **superstructure**, changes in response to changes in the sociopolitical **structure**. G. E. Swanson (1960) provides

further support for this view with a global cross-cultural sample showing a statistical association between the presence of high gods and hierarchical political structures.

The new Mesopotamian deities obviously reflected the rising importance of political rulers in the emerging city-states of the Early Dynastic. For example, Jacobsen (1976) shows that *Ningirsu*, god of life-giving spring thunderstorms and flood and titular deity of the city of Girsu, was head of a twenty-one-deity pantheon of gods that staffed his temple and supervised his estate. Counted as deities were a high constable, a steward, a chamberlain, two musicians, seven handmaidens, a councilor, a secretary, two generals, two herdsmen, a plowman, a fisherman, and a general manager of natural resources. These deities had their human counterparts who directed human laborers in service to *Ningirsu*. Whereas the original nature deities had no functions beyond their immanent qualities and could thus be considered "intransitive," the new ruler-gods could make demands on people, and their wills were transmitted through dreams and signs that had to be interpreted by diviners.

The entire Mesopotamian cosmos is hierarchically arranged with deities holding titles and offices. There were seven primary gods, who determined the fate of other gods and humans, and some fifty "great gods," along with a vast multitude of lesser deities, who collectively met as a formal assembly of gods. City deities such as *Ningirsu* served the higher-ranking deity *Enlil*, Lord of the Wind and primary executive god. The water god *Enki*, Lord of the Soil and Owner of the River, is credited not only with establishing the seasonal regime of the Tigris-Euphrates system, but he also placed various deities in charge of a number of recognized occupational specialties such as farming, brickmaking, architecture, and weaving. *Enki* made *Utu*, the sun god and god of justice, responsible for boundary maintenance. Even the creation myths are brought in line with the realities of the political system. By the second millennium BC, the primary Mesopotamian creation epic, known as *Enuma Elish*, is a lengthy account of how the god *Marduk* becomes the permanent king of the universe and all the basic elements of the Mesopotamian cosmic politics are put in place.

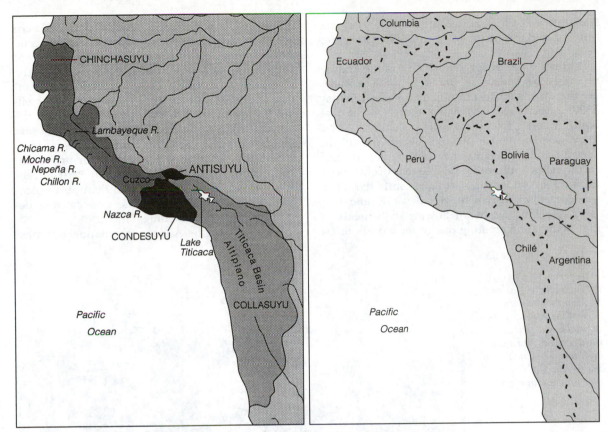

FIGURE 7.11 *Map of the Andean region and the Inca empire with its division into four quarters: Chinchasuyu, Antisuyu, Condesuyu, and Collasuyu. (After Conrad and Demarest 1984.)*

## ANDEAN CIVILIZATION

### Andean Environment and Prehistory

Eight thousand miles from Mesopotamia, in the central Andes and the adjacent Pacific coast of Peru, another major civilization developed independently and flourished for some 3000 years. The Inca empire, which reached its peak between AD 1476 and 1532, extended over an area of some 380,000 square miles (mi²) (984,000 square kilometers [km²]), covering the Andean regions of modern Ecuador, Peru, Bolivia, and the northern Andes of Chile and Argentina (Figure 7.11). Estimates of its population range from 6 to 32 million

people. The Inca empire rivaled the Roman empire in scale, yet it was maintained without wheeled vehicles, writing, or draft animals, by the effective mobilization of a vast labor force, within the

***polytheism*** A religious system based on belief in many gods, or deities.
***superstructure*** The mental, ideological, or belief systems, as expressed in the religion, myth, and ritual of a culture. According to Harris's cultural materialist theory, superstructure is shaped by the structure.
***structure*** The social, economic, and political organization of a culture, which is shaped by the technological base, or infrastructure, according to Harris's cultural materialist theory.

framework of an elaborate bureaucracy that was ordered and sustained by a compelling religious system.

The dominant geographic feature of the Andean region is the Andean mountain chain. The Andes are the world's longest mountain range, stretching 5500 miles (8800 km) along the west coast of South America from Venezuela to southern Chile. They were formed by tectonic uplift during the past 2.5 million years, and volcanic activity and earthquakes continue to be frequent occurrences. Because the Andes run north and south, they are a perpendicular barrier to global winds and currents, blocking westward flowing moisture from the Atlantic and creating one of the world's driest deserts in the rain shadow along the coast of Peru and Chile. A series of narrow, short valleys descend from the Andes to the Pacific and offer significant irrigation potential not unlike that offered by the Mesopotamian floodplain. An additional advantage of the Andean region is that the cold, upwelling *Peru current* lifts rich nutrients toward the ocean surface from the deep offshore trench and thereby supports one of the world's richest marine ecosystems. Unfortunately, during an unpredictable phenomenon called *El Niño,* the Peru current is replaced by warmer water that disrupts the ecosystem, destroying marine life and causing destructive rains and flooding.

The bulk of the Andean population occupied

FIGURE 7.12 *View of the Inca city of Machu Pichu on the eastern edge of the Andes, showing elaborate agricultural terraces and stone architecture, which were the products of a complex bureaucratic state.*

TABLE 7.7  *Andean Prehistory*

| AD 600–1532 | AD 1476–1532 | Inca empire |
|---|---|---|
| | AD 1000–1476 | Chimu state on north coast |
| | AD 600–1000 | Middle Horizon, Tiahuanaco, and Huari empires |
| 1400–2200 BP | 1400–2200 | Mochica and Nazca regional coastal states |
| 2200–2800 BP | 2200–2800 | Early Horizon; Chavin; metallurgy |
| 2900–4000 BP | 2900–3500 | Initial Ceramic period, city-states or advanced chiefdoms; ceramics, irrigation, population growth |
| | 3500–4000 | Late (Cotton) Preceramic chiefdoms; maize, manioc |
| 5000–6000 BP | 5000 | Sedentary coastal fishing villages; small-scale farming of cotton, gourds, beans, squash |
| | 5800 | Domesticated potatoes in highlands |
| | 6000 | Domestic camelids |
| 6000–32,000 BP | 6000–14,000 | Mobile foragers and hunters |
| | 14,000–32,000 | Earliest settlement |

SOURCES: Burger and van der Merwe (1990); Lanning (1967), and Wheeler (1984).

the *altiplano*, the high plateau, at elevations from 12,000 ft (3658 m) to over 16,000 ft (4877 m) (Figure 7.12). This is a cold, inhospitable region: The air is thin, it can freeze at any time, and it is subject to drought. The treeless vegetation, called *puna*, supports only the hardiest grazers such as the native camelids, the guanaco and vicuña.

The Inca empire was only the last in a series of large-scale pre-Columbian cultures that developed in the Andean region beginning approximately 4000 BP (Table 7.7). The earliest settlers in the high Andes were generalized hunters and gatherers for 7000 years or more. They began to specialize in hunting the wild camelids, guanaco and vicuña, by approximately 7200 BP, perhaps as a result of environmental changes following the end of the Ice Age, including the loss of the Pleistocene megafauna.

Domestic llamas and alpacas can be identified archaeologically by 6000 BP, based on changes in their teeth and mortality patterns (Wheeler 1984). Llamas and alpacas were valued for meat and wool and as pack animals capable of carrying up to 100 lb (4 kg). Dried llama dung was also an important fuel on the treeless *altiplano*. Another important animal domesticate, the guinea pig, appeared by approximately 4500 BP. Guinea pigs lived on kitchen scraps and were eaten. The potato was domesticated by 5800 BP and became the primary highland subsistence crop because it was

highly nutritious, tolerated frost, was readily stored, and could be grown at elevations of up to 14,000 ft (4267 m). Andean farmers developed some 3000 varieties of potatoes, selecting for differing tuber qualities and environmental tolerances (Brush et al. 1981). Another important early highland domesticate was quinua, which also grows well under the harsh conditions of the *altiplano* and produces a protein-rich, grainlike seed. Quinua was in use by 5000 BP, and some 200 varieties were developed (Cusack 1984).

Coastal peoples specialized very early in the rich marine resources and were living in sedentary fishing villages by 5000 BP. Edward Lanning (1967) suggests that the earliest inhabitants hunted and foraged in the *lomas*, a unique vegetation zone supported by the dense fog belt that blankets the coastal region from June to October. Climate

---

**Peru current**  A cold ocean current off Peru that is normally associated with an upwelling of nutrients that supports a very rich marine food chain and maintains a cool, dry, coastal desert.

**El Niño**  A warming of the ocean currents off Peru that causes rain and flooding on the normally desert coast and disrupts the marine ecosystem.

**altiplano**  The Andean high plateau and center of a large indigenous population, much of it over 12,000 ft (3658 m).

**puna**  The low, largely treeless vegetation of the *altiplano* region.

change apparently elevated the fog belt and drastically reduced the *lomas* zone, forcing people to move to the shore and river mouths in order to exploit more easily the abundant fish and shellfish resources. Cotton and gourds were cultivated initially to provide the raw materials for fish nets and floats.

Several archaeologists have argued that marine resources proved so abundant that they supported relatively large, permanent settlements, with ranked social systems, without cultivated food plants (Lanning 1967, Moseley 1975, Quilter and Stocker 1983). Thus, Andean civilization may have had a unique maritime foundation. The well-documented site of El Paraiso, or Chuquitanta, which may date to as early as 4000 BP in the Cotton Preceramic, was a complex of stone and mortar buildings that may have supported 3000 people. The structures contain an estimated 100,000 tons of quarried stone and may have taken one-hundred years to construct. The monumental constructions at the El Paraiso site suggest an advanced chiefdom society and invite comparisons with the Uruk period temple centers of Mesopotamia; El Paraiso, however, is a pre-Ceramic site with no evidence that any cultivated food crops other than cotton and gourds were important in subsistence. These were apparently grown by simple floodwater farming on low land near the river mouth. Irrigation agriculture could not have been causally related to either population growth or social stratification in this case.

Whereas some argue that evidence for subsistence agriculture was overlooked in these pre-Ceramic sites (Raymond 1981, Wilson 1981), other researchers have shown how important marine resources may have been during the pre-Ceramic. Elizabeth Reitz (1988) examined the animal remains from an early pre-Ceramic site on the central coast, dating between 7700 and 5000 BP, and found that 90 percent of the animal biomass was derived from marine sources. More than 75 percent of the biomass was from fish, mostly anchovies, which form vast schools and even today provide the bulk of Peruvian fishery.

The next major development in Andean prehistory was the farming of irrigated food crops in the desert farther up the river valleys. This development was perhaps encouraged by the arrival of pottery and new food crops, such as maize, peppers, and some squashes from Mesoamerica, and manioc, sweet potatoes, and some beans from Amazonia. It is also possible that the steady tectonic uplift or a particularly destructive series of *El Niño* episodes may have disrupted the marine ecosystem sufficiently to encourage alternative subsistence practices. Michael Moseley (1975) explains all these changes, from foraging to fishing to farming, as the result of population gradually expanding to the limits of the food supply. In this case, marine resources were so rich that they probably slowed the development of irrigation agriculture. Moseley suggests that the pre-Ceramic fishermen were preadapted for irrigation agriculture because they were already experienced cotton farmers and had large, well-organized labor forces and authority structures. Irrigation may have been seized upon and promoted by the political elites because it provided a more easily controlled source of political power than production systems based on marine resources.

By the late Initial Ceramic period, approximately 3000 BP, the basic elements of the Peruvian or **Andean cultural tradition** (Lanning 1967) were firmly established and rapidly evolved thereafter. The basic features of this tradition were the following:

State-level political organization

Intensive agriculture based on maize and potatoes

High-altitude llama pastoralism

Monumental architecture

Pilgrimages to shrines

Urban centers

Elaborate ceramics and textiles

Pre-Inca Andean peoples were masters at metallurgy, weaving, and ceramics. Andean peoples worked copper, gold, bronze, and silver, using a variety of techniques, including lost-wax casting, to produce elaborate jewelry and simple implements (Figure 7.13). Textiles, including tapestry and embroidery, were highly developed and along with jewelry became important markers of status. Very fine cotton and wool-dyed yarns were woven into extremely tight and colorful fabrics, with weft threads of 250 or more per inch and in sixteen

FIGURE 7.13 *Andean peoples were accomplished metallurgists, which is demonstrated by these Inca bronze tools and implements.*

shades. Nazca textiles from the south coast were some of the finest products, and many were used as long shrouds for mummy bundles. One such burial cloth measured 20 ft by 200 ft (6 m by 61 m). Ceramics were often beautifully painted in intricate polychrome designs. Mochica pottery is famous for its realistic depiction of everyday life.

The Chimu state on the north coast built an urban center at Chanchan, which covered 6 mi² (16 km²) and may have contained 50,000 people (Moseley and Day 1980, Moseley and Mackey 1973). The Chimu also built a 50-mile (80-km) intervalley canal system that included ten-storied embankments and 70-ft-high (21 m) aqueducts. It has been estimated that this project was under construction for 200 years and required extremely sophisticated hydraulics skills and ten times the labor that went into the great pyramid of Egypt (Hadingham 1987).

By 2800 BP (900 BC), Chavin, the first widespread Andean cultural style, spread from the temple site of Chavin de Huantar in the north central highlands to some thirty other temple centers throughout much of the coast and adjacent highlands. Chavin was an art style that featured distinctively styled snarling jaguars and birds of prey, appearing in stone carvings and on pottery. Representations of specific Chavin-style deities are recognizable over a 2000-year period, suggesting that the spread of Chavin established a pan-Peruvian religion, although Chavin deities were probably incorporated into local pantheons and perhaps reinterpreted in local terms (Keatinge 1981).

The temple of Chavin de Huantar was likely an important oracle shrine and a major site for long-distance pilgrimages. The temple contained a hidden inner sanctum, where the principal deity was housed, and public courtyards, where other images were displayed. The priests thus had privileged access to supernatural power, as was also apparently the case in Mesopotamia. Richard Keatinge (1981) argues that Chavin-style pilgrimage centers, which were scattered in diverse environments, would have guaranteed safe passage and may have fostered regional trade networks between coast, highlands, and Amazonia. Religion thus may have been an important integrating mechanism and provided further ways for the developing political elite to increase their power without using direct military force.

## Inca Society and Political Economy

The immediate beginnings of the Inca dynasty can be traced to a small Quechua-speaking chiefdom in the region of Cuzco at approximately 1200 AD. Quechua is a member of the Andean branch of *Amerind languages,* which also includes the foraging peoples of Patagonia and Tierra del Fuego (see also Mannheim 1991). The rapid expansion of

*Andean cultural tradition* Cultural patterns related to state organization in the Andean region, such as intensive agriculture, art styles, and religious patterns that have existed for some 3000 years.

*Amerind language* Language family of all pre-Columbian indigenous peoples of South and Central America and most of North America.

the Inca empire, which begun in 1438 under Pachacuti, is difficult to explain even though it is not totally unprecedented. The empire was a vast administrative bureaucracy that joined together pre-existing regional states, chiefdoms, and tribes into a centrally managed system. The ultimate ideological foundation of the empire was the religious belief in the supreme divinity of the Inca ruler, who was the sun god personified. The Inca's identity with the sun had a literal reality, given the vast energy resources at his control in the form of enormous quantities of foodstuffs stored in state warehouses throughout the empire. The Inca state also supported large numbers of craft specialists, **corvée laborers,** and military forces. Over a 60-year period, the state carried out innumerable monumental building projects, constructed and maintained a vast road network (Hyslop 1984), and developed large-scale agricultural projects.

The Inca empire was known as **Tawantinsuyu**, or the land of four quarters. It was directed from the capital of Cuzco, at the center of the named quarters: *Antisuyu* covered the tropical lowlands; *Chinchasuyu*, the north coast and highlands; *Collasuyu*, Bolivia; and *Condesuyu*, the south coast. Each quarter was directed by a member of the royal family and was subdivided into provinces, also ruled by the nobility. The eighty some provinces were further subdivided into paired **suyus**, or moieties, which were ranked as upper and lower, and contained **ayllus**, or kin-based groups. Territorial units were defined in part by the individual **huacas**, or cult shrines, for which they were responsible, reminiscent of the way that Australian aboriginal estate groups, or clans, were responsible for Dreamtime sacred sites. In theory, productive lands were owned by the Inca state, temples, and local communities. Much land was centrally administered, but the line between church and state was not always clear, and local elites administered many locally controlled estates. The empire was apparently not as monolithic as it might appear.

Much of the rural population was also organized as a labor force into a formalized hierarchy of workers in units that were subdivided alternately into units of two and five. The highest decimal unit was the *hunu*, which contained approximately 10,000 workers. It was divided into two

units of 5000 called *piska* (five) *waranqa*. Each *piska waranqa* contained five *waranqa* units of 1000 workers. The *waranqa* in turn were divided into two units of 500 called *piska pachaka*, which in turn contained five *pachaka* units of 100 workers (see Figure 7.14).

This bureaucratic system may have existed more in the mind of central administrators than it did in the hinterland, but it did have some functional reality and is closely connected with the *quipu*-recording system (see the box "The *Quipu*"). Decades after the Spanish conquest, local native leaders were still able to describe the system in detail, and the Spaniards immediately recognized its utility as a census and control mechanism.

Superimposed on the hierarchy of territories and labor units was a hierarchy of offices and social classes and a variety of named occupational specialties and ethnic groups. Social status was defined by a dress code and associated privileges and duties. The Inca god-king was personally sacred in the same way as the Hawaiian rulers. He also married a full sister and was the head of the **Capac Ayllu**, or Inca royal family, which consisted of a central patriline and nine ranked **cognatic lines**, or side branches. The members of the royal *ayllu* constituted the nobility, the highest social class, and were the most powerful officials in the bureaucracy. The Spanish called them *Orejones*, or "big ears," because they were privileged to wear enormous gold earplugs and distinguished headgear. Their social status was finely ranked by genealogical distance from the Inca king.

According to the analysis of R. Tom Zuidema (1990), the marriage of the Inca king to his sister was a cultural statement that symbolically used kinship categories and marriage form to dramatize the hierarchical nature of Inca society. All those men within the royal *ayllu* in Cuzco who could claim descent from the Inca king belonged to *ayllus*, which were ranked in several ways. Descent was calculated back five generations to a mythical founding Inca king ancestor, yielding a six-ranked generational system. The ruling Inca's direct line was considered to be a straight line, or **ceque**, and its members were most highly ranked, whereas those who belonged to a branch *ceque*, sister's-sons lines, were treated either as high-ranking "sons" with Inca mothers or as low-

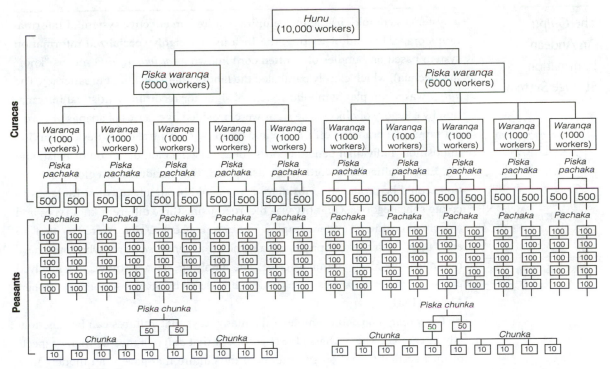

**FIGURE 7.14** *The Inca bureaucracy.*

ranking "nephews" with non-Inca mothers. These categories can also be distinguished as "older" and "younger" sons, with older being superior. Men of the highest genealogical rank, and thus closest to the ruling Inca, were called lords and were associated with eagles; the most distant were called skunks and stinkers, thus emphatically spelling out their relative social worth, even though they were all superior to commoners.

Depending on the genealogical depth of their closest link to the royal *ceque*, these men might be actual grandsons, great grandsons, and so on of the founding Inca ruler. Those called nephews were the children of the Inca's dozens of secondary non-Inca wives. Sons became administrators over the upper moiety of Cuzco, and nephews were placed in charge of Cuzco's lower moiety. Sons were associated with ruling lords, and younger sons or nephews were servants or priests and sometimes played ritual feminine roles.

Who the men of the royal *ayllu* were permitted to marry revealed their rank along a continuum from extreme endogamy to maximum exogamy, with marriage to the closest kin ranking highest. The marriage of the king to his sister represented the highest degree of endogamy and was reserved for the highest-ranking person. Individuals ranking immediately below the Inca were permitted to

*corvée labor*   Work done for the state on demand, usually for large public projects.
*Tawantinsuyu*   The Inca empire, land of four-quarters.
*yanacona*   Commoners who were trained as children to serve as retainers to the Inca nobility.
*suyu*   One-quarter, one of a four-part territorial division.
*ayllu*   A social unit larger than the individual family.
*huaca*   A sacred place, or shrine, often associated with a *ceque*.
*Capac Ayllu*   The Inca royal family, whose members constitute the Inca nobility.
*cognatic line*   A descent line traced to a common ancestor and that need not rely on exclusively male or female links.
*ceque*   A straight line, or line of sight, from a center to a point on the horizon; creates ranked territorial and social divisions.

## The *Quipu*: An Andean Information-Storage System

A system as complex as the Inca empire required an effective system of information storage. Instead of writing, the Inca used a highly specialized information system based on bundles of knotted cord known as *quipus* (*quipu* means "knot" in Quechua), which closely paralleled the labor system decimal bureaucracy. The *quipu* was a complex symbolic system of signs for recording statistical information by category of object. The signs were provided by a series of strings or cords, with multiple branches off the top and bottom of a central cord. Besides varying in position, individual pendant cords could vary in color, direction of twist, and ply. Even multicolored cords were used, such that hundreds of color combinations could be produced. Subsidiary cords could be attached to several levels to create subcategories. Quantity was recorded using three different knot types and a decimal positional system employing a zero concept. *Quipus* were "written" to and "read" by a class of professionals known as *quipu camayo*, who must have resembled the Mesopotamian scribe. The highly specialized knowledge involved in the use of the *quipu* has been described in detail by Marcia Ascher and Robert Ascher (1981).

The *quipu* is a good example of the many ways that cultures can be functionally integrated. The Aschers (1981) point out that *quipus* reflected many aspects of Inca aesthetics and other features of the culture that gave it a uniquely Inca ethos, especially the Inca concern with spatial relationships, fitting things neatly together, symmetry of pattern, portability of objects, a methodical and repetitive approach to design, and an overall conservatism, which can be seen in the Inca political system, architecture, ceramics, and textiles. On a much larger scale, the *ceque* system, which related *ayllu* social groups and *huaca* sacred places within a larger political whole, represented the same cultural reality.

A *quipu* might contain several thousand cords, but each cord occupied a specific place, oriented vertically along a horizontal axis. Like cloth, *quipus* were highly portable and based on spatial relationships. A *quipu* could be designed to represent different levels of the Inca bureaucracy and could record the quantities of goods such as various types of cloth, crops, and animals that were moved and stored, as well as the numbers of soldiers and workers of different types. It was an ideal device for keeping track of *mita* service and goods stockpiled in storehouses.

The Aschers (1981) emphasize the very close parallels between Sumerian writing and the *quipu* and argue that *quipu* makers were, in fact, writing. The *quipu* could be read verbally, and the act of tying knots was tactilely and visually comparable to using a stylus in clay or a pencil on paper. Furthermore, both systems recorded information in the service of the state.

marry half-sisters and parallel cousins. Third-ranking individuals could marry cross-cousins and so on until people more than five generational ranks removed from the ruling Inca married non-kin who represented the maximum of exogamy.

Zuidema (1990) shows that women of the royal *ayllu* were placed in six ranked **aclla** ("chosen women"), categories based on age grades that were associated metaphorically with an invidious ranking based on physical appearance. These age–beauty ranks apparently corresponded to the genealogically based male ranks, such that women of high-ranking genealogical standing relative to the ruling Inca were assigned to high-ranked *aclla* age grades. Those women who, because of their genealogical rank, were assigned to the most prestigious *aclla* group at approximately 20 to 24 years of age were considered "most beautiful" and remained in that category for life. They were never supposed to speak to men and performed ritual services in the most sacred shrines. Women of lower genealogical rank were selected for lower-ranked *aclla* age grades as they grew older, and they carried out lower-level ritual duties. For example, the three lowest *aclla* grades were joined at ages 35, 40, and 50 years, and these women wove textiles of increasingly lower quality and social worth. At age 35 years, an *aclla* could make very fine cloth for ritual in the most important *huacas*, whereas women who became *acllas* at 50 years of age were commoners who made the most ordinary textiles such as belts and bags.

Below the nobility were **curaca**, officials who were in charge of decimal units down to the *pichaka* (100s) level. These Inca appointees held positions that became hereditary offices. Leaders of lower-level units were commoners. The highest non-*curaca* status was that of **yanacona**, who worked as retainers to the nobility. Raised as children in royal households, they were trained to become servants and attendants in the palaces and temples. Sometimes they were rewarded with *Orejon* status.

Specialized laborers in full-time service to the state were called **camayo** (*camayoc*), with an additional designation to specify their duty. For example, there were *llama camayo*, who herded llamas; *coca camayo*, who raised coca; *chacara camayo*, who were farmers; and *pukara camayo*,

who garrisoned frontier fortresses (Rowe 1982). Another important group were the **mitima** (*mitmaq*), ethnic groups that were moved as colonists to work on large-scale agricultural projects. Commoner women might also become *acllas*, who worked full time to produce high-status textiles known as *kumpi*. *Acllas* might also be married to the *yanacona*. Nonspecialist commoners were called *suyu runa*, "people of the quarter," and were subject to periodic labor service, known as the *mita*.

The decimal hierarchy was well suited for labor mobilization, which was a primary and self-serving state function. For example, if a *hunu*-(10,000) level *curaca* needed to draft 1000 laborers, they could be readily assembled from the bottom up, if one man from the *chunka* (10) level was sent up the hierarchy. A typical labor assignment, which was documented for four *waranqas* (4000) men, showed nearly half assigned to permanent assignments as *camayo* craft specialists, in the military service, and as *yanacona*. The other half served on rotating *mita* in the mines, on construction projects, and as soldiers and carriers (Julien 1982).

The Inca state was a nonmarket political economy based on "supply on command" rather than the "supply and demand" of a market economy (La Lone 1982). An autonomous subsistence economy was operated in the background by the *suya runa* when they were not on state service. The subsistence sector has been characterized as a **vertical economy** in which self-sufficient villages exploited resources in different ecological zones at different elevations, rather than depending on trade or mar-

---

**aclla**  "Chosen women" who serve the state, functionally grouped by ranked age grades.
**curaca**  An administrator in the Inca decimal bureaucracy.
**yanacona**  Commoners who were trained as children to serve as retainers to the Inca nobility.
**camayo**  Full-time specialists who work for the state.
**mitima**  Settlers in a state-sponsored agricultural colonization project.
**mita**  Labor shared by rotation; applied to a variety of repetitive temporal events.
**vertical economy**  Village- and household-level subsistence production based on access to resources from different altitudinal zones.

ket exchanges. Four productive zones were distinguished by elevation (see the box "Productive Zones in the Andean Vertical-Economy").

The state economy was functionally divided into a staple economy and a wealth economy (D'Altroy and Earle 1985). The **staple economy** was concerned with the production and storage of potatoes and other primary foodstuffs to provision the army and the vast numbers of full-time state employees. The use of maize was highly ritualized, and it was used to brew *chicha* beer, which state officials provided to *mita* laborers as a ritual feast in reciprocity for their labor service (Murra 1960). The **wealth economy** involved the state-directed production of luxury goods such as gold and silver jewelry, featherwork, and fine textiles, which were used to reward the ruling class and served as status markers.

## Inca Cosmology

The Inca bureaucracy was based on traditional Andean cosmology and conceptions of spatial order and reciprocity, of which the Inca rulers were quick to make use. The concept of four quarters still organizes the space centered around rural Andean villages (Urton 1981). Conceptually, the quarters are derived from the great cross in the sky formed by the Milky Way as it shifts its position relative to earth between 6 PM and 6 AM. This sky cross defines a center and divides the night sky into quarters, which people imagine projecting to the ground. Each village contains its own center, called *chawpi* in Quechua, and the individual quarters, or *suyu*, are usually grouped into upper and lower divisions. Imaginary lines, called *ceques*, radiate from the village center toward sacred points situated on the mountain skyline and along the way align with specific shrines, or *huacas*.

Zuidema (1990) found that there were forty-two *ceques* in Cuzco, radiating as vectors or lines of sight toward the horizon as viewed from the main temple. There were 328 *huacas* located along the *ceque* lines. The *ceques* divided the province of Cuzco into territories, which were assigned to specific *ayllus*, *suyus*, and moities. This system was integrated with a ritual calendar established by astronomical observations in which special rituals were performed sequentially at specific *huacas* on a certain day during the year. The most important of these rituals concerned agricultural activities. The two most basic principles of interaction underlying the interaction between households within the village community and between house-

---

**Productive Zones in the Andean Vertical Economy**

Subsistence farmers in the Andean region traveled up-and-down the slopes to secure a variety of resources. In simplified form, the four most important zones were the following:

1. *Puna* zone: Grazing of llamas and alpacas on wet and frosty alpine pastures at the highest elevations, above 14,000 ft (4267 m)

2. *Puna/Jalka* zone: Frost-prone, relatively dry zones, suitable for potato cultivation, 11,000–14,000 ft (3353–4267 m)

3. *Kichwa* zone: Temperate region where maize and beans were grown, 7000–11,000 ft (2134–3353 m)

4. Tropical zone: Lowest elevations at the margins of the Amazon rain forest, where tropical products such as manioc, avocados, coca, and papayas were grown

SOURCES: Brush (1976) and Murra (1972).
Elevations vary from north to south in the Andes and are only approximate.

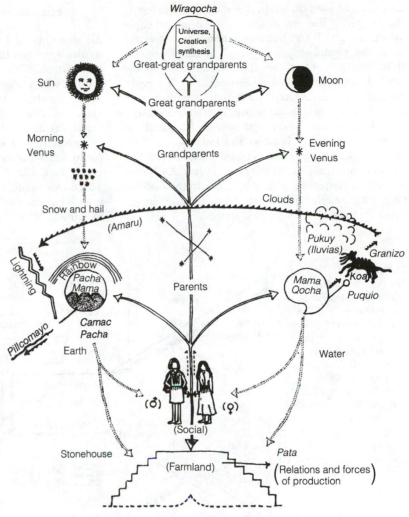

FIGURE 7.15 *An Andean model of the place of people, culture, and the flow of energy in the cosmos, based on a plaque in the Inca temple in Cuzco. (SOURCE: Adapted from Earls and Silverblatt 1978.)*

holds and nature and the Inca state were **ayni**, or reciprocity, and *mita*, which meant turn or share (Earls and Silverblatt 1978). *Ayni* referred to the exchange of services between a variety of entities and was considered essential to the orderly operation of the cosmos. It applied to marriage exchanges, food and drink given for communal labor within the village, gifts of drink to the earth mother at harvest, and water cycling between earth and sky. Labor service to the state was also *ayni* and was rewarded by ritual *chicha* distributions. *Mita* added temporal order to *ayni*. *Mita* referred to crop rotation, calving seasons, human generations, and an individual's share at labor ser-

vice to the state. *Ayni* and *mita* were thus ritually sanctioned as part of the natural order.

Figure 7.15 represents a native view of Andean

---

**staple economy**  The state-controlled production, storage, and distribution of subsistence staples, such as potatoes and maize in the Inca case, to support nonfood-producing specialist groups and for emergency aid.

**wealth economy**  The state-controlled production, storage, and distribution of wealth objects that support the status hierarchy.

**ayni**  The basic principle of reciprocal exchange that operated throughout the Inca cosmos.

cosmology based on a representation appearing in the temple of the sun in Cuzco, the imperial capital. Although all the elements cannot be analyzed here, the model employs complementary oppositions and presents a parallel hierarchy of divinities, showing male and female aspects. It clearly reflects the central elements of the state hierarchy, even to the detail of depicting *ayni* relationships and showing the state storehouse (*collqa*) and intensive agricultural land as the foundation. This cosmological system shares some features with the Amazonian tribal cosmology (see Figure 3.17) discussed earlier, with which it is no doubt historically connected, but departs from it radically in ways that support social inequality.

## Huanaco Pampa: An Inca City

All elements of Inca society are shown diagrammatically in the layout of Huanaco Pampa, a representative Inca city (Figure 7.16). Huanaco Pampa was a planned city, built about 1475 AD as an administrative center. It covered .8 mi² (2 km²) and was situated at an elevation of 12,471 ft (3801 m) in a prime potato-growing region. The city contained a special platform where the Inca could lead public ceremonies and a residence where he could be accommodated on royal visits. There were elite residences, barracks for rotating *mita* laborers, and great halls where they were entertained at ritual *chicha*-drinking feasts. The

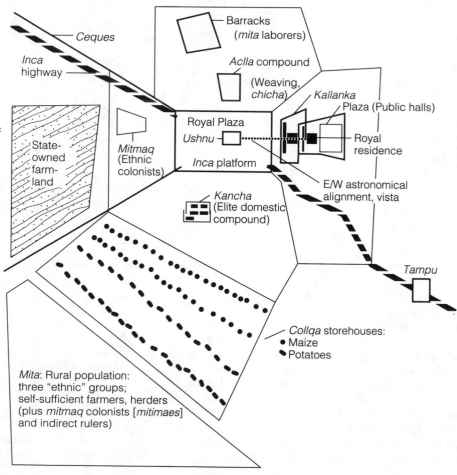

**FIGURE 7.16**
*The Inca administrative city of Huanaco Pampa: a .8-mi² (2-km²) planned city at 12,471 ft (3801 m), built around 1475; the Spanish took over in 1539. It had 4000 structures and 10,000 to 15,000 residents. (SOURCE: Adapted from Morris and Thompson 1985.)*

*Aclla,* chosen women, were securely sequestered within a walled compound (Morris and Thompson 1985). The city's primary function must have been warehousing great quantities of food, judging by the 30,065 cubic yards (yd³) (23,000 cubic meters [m³]) of storage space in storehouses devoted to potatoes and 18,301 yd³ (14,000 m³) for maize. The potato storehouses alone could have supplied more than 50,000 workers a year with 1 lb (.5 kg) of potatoes a day, which is more than the average daily consumption of potatoes by rural Andean peoples today (Orlove 1987). This calculation is based on a rough estimate of 36 lb (16 kg) of potatoes per bushel and 33 bushels/m³, less 25 percent for storage loss. If, as is likely, potatoes were stored in the form of freeze-dried *chuno,* then annual provisions for 100,000 might have been stored in Huanaco Pampa. Additionally, the stored maize could have been used to brew vast quantities of *chicha* beer.

Some authorities consider food storage to be perhaps the most important functional advantage of state organization in the Andean region (D'Altroy and Earle 1985, Isbell 1978). The state storehouses served to average out environmentally determined fluctuations in food production that occurred both seasonally and from year to year with *El Niño*–related events and unpredictable droughts and frosts. Large-scale storage might have raised the overall carrying capacity of the region. This food-energy averaging interpretation tends to support the redistributive social-benefits approach to state origins, and many observers have described the Inca system as a great socialist welfare state. The Inca state could equally well be considered despotic and totalitarian because individual freedom was constrained by the way in which wealth and power were distributed. The state moved whole communities at will and imposed a national language. The real advantage in expanding the scope of national control was that it increased the power of the privileged elite.

## SUMMARY

The early state shows a systematic pattern of social inequality and the concentration of power into relatively few hands. When modern scholars, who are themselves members of state systems, view these early states, they are impressed with the monumental architecture, great art, and massive technological achievements, and they minimize the social costs of such developments. Large-scale systems tend to expand to the limits, and sometimes beyond, what the natural environment can sustain because they reward individuals who manage to increase their personal power.

## STUDY QUESTIONS

1. In what way is centralized political power a fundamental element of "civilization" as it is usually defined?

2. Discuss the role of irrigation, population, and political factors in the origin of the state, distinguishing between prime-mover and multi-variant theories. Refer to Mesopotamian case materials.

3. Discuss the explanations that have been proposed to account for the gradual process of plant and animal domestication in the Near East.

4. What archaeological evidence can be used to trace the earliest development of the state in Mesopotamia?

5. Describe the role of religion in the early Mesopotamian city-state. Make specific comparisons with religion in the Inca state.

6. What was the role of record keeping, and how was it carried out in ancient Mesopotamia and the Inca empire?

7. Distinguish between wealth economy and staple economy and show how each operated in the Inca empire.

## SUGGESTED READING

**The Near East**

KRAMER, SAMUEL NOAH. 1967. *Cradle of Civilization.* New York: Time-Life Books. A well-illustrated, popular description of Mesopotamian civilization by a respected scholar.

REDMAN, CHARLES L. 1978. *The Rise of Civilization: From Early Farmers to Urban Society in the Ancient Near East.* San Francisco: Freeman. Presents a complete overview of the origin of Mesopotamian civilization.

WOOLLEY, SIR LEONARD. 1982. *Ur "of the Chaldees."* London: Herbert Press. A detailed account of the Royal Tombs of Ur by the original discoverer.

**Andean Civilization**

ASCHER, MARCIA, AND ASCHER, ROBERT A. 1981. *Code of the Quipu: Study in Media, Mathematics, and Culture.* Ann Arbor: University of Michigan Press. Explains how the *quipu* was used to encode information.

EARLE, TIMOTHY K. 1987. "Specialization and the Production of Wealth: Hawaiian Chiefdoms and the Inka Empire." In *Specialization, Exchange, and Complex Societies,* edited by Elizabeth M. Brumfiel and Timothy K. Earle, pp. 64–75. Cambridge, Eng.: Cambridge University Press. Compares the political use of wealth in Hawaii and the Inca empire.

HADINGHAM, EVAN. 1987. *Lines to the Mountain Gods: Nazca and the Mysteries of Peru.* New York: Random House. Shows how Andean ideology and astronomical observations were related to the landscape.

MORRIS, CRAIG, AND DONALD E. THOMPSON. 1985. *Huanaco Pampa: An Inca City and Its Hinterland.* London: Thames & Hudson. Uses archaeological analysis to describe an Inca city.

# 8

# THE CHINESE GREAT TRADITION

In this chapter and Chapter 9, we will examine the great cultural traditions of China, India, and Islam. All are important area-study specializations, which anthropology shares with history. Because these cultures continue to shape the lives of well over half of the contemporary world's peoples, understanding them is an essential part of understanding world cultures. Traditional China is the largest imperial state to survive into the twentieth century on a preindustrial base. With a population that probably numbered 400 million people by 1850, China is a dramatic example of an empire based on moral authority and a superintensive agricultural system using human labor. Yet it was also the largest early literate civilization with cities and a monetary economy continuously in place for more than 2000 years. Chinese villagers, as a tax-paying, rural peasantry, provide a sharp contrast with the egalitarian, politically autonomous tribal villagers of Amazonia seen in Chapter 3.

## CHINESE ENVIRONMENT AND PREHISTORY

China is a vast subcontinental area of 3.6 million square miles (mi²) (9.5 million square kilometers [km²]), approximately the same size as the United States. In the south, China reaches into the tropics, whereas in the north it reaches the subarctic. Much of the western half of the country, including the Tibetan Plateau and the Xinjiang (Sinkiang) region, is high altitude, relatively barren, and inhospitable and will not be treated in this chapter. Eastern China is divided into a northern, temperate zone and a southern subtropical zone, with a dividing line running midway between China's two great rivers, the Hwang Ho (Huang He), or Yellow River, in the north and the Chang (Yangtze River) in the south (Figure 8.1). The great Chinese civilizations developed along the lower reaches of these two rivers, primarily in the relatively flat plains and lake areas at elevations below 650 ft (200 meters [m]).

## Early People, Teeth, and Language

China is famous for the site of Zhoukoudian (Chou-k'ou-tien), west of Beijing (Peking), where fossils of the early hominid *Homo erectus*, dating to the Lower Paleolithic at approximately 1 million–200,000 BP (before the present), were discovered in the 1930s. *Homo erectus* began to look

FIGURE 8.1
*Major rivers and regions
of China.*

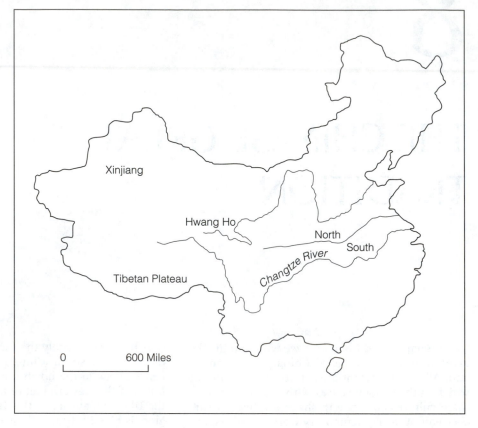

more like *Homo sapiens* beginning about 200,000 BP (see Table 8.1); by 20,000 BP, Southeast Asian peoples had developed the Sundadont dental characteristics, which are still recognizable in that region and were also present in prehistoric China (see Chapter 6 and Turner 1989). By 15,000 BP, the distinctive Sinodont dental pattern of Chinese, Japanese, and Native Americans was probably beginning to separate from the earlier Sundadont population. Sinodants show a higher frequency of **shoveling,** with upper incisors that have a thickened ridge on the inside edge, giving them a shovel shape in cross section.

The predominant Chinese languages are all classified as **Sino-Tibetan** and are probably spoken by more than 1 billion people. Sino-Tibetan includes 8 modern Chinese languages and more than 200 other languages scattered throughout southern and eastern China, Tibet, the Himalayas, and Burma. Japanese, Korean, and Mongolian are grouped in the **Altaic language** family, which also includes Turkish and Ainu (Ruhlen 1987). "Chinese" is not a single language, although there was a Proto-Chinese common ancestor language. The long use of a common writing system by speakers of related languages that are mutually unintelligible has led to the unfortunate use of the term *dialect* to refer to what are actually distinct languages. Chinese written characters are **logographic**—they refer to entire words and can retain their meaning with different pronunciation, in different languages. According to linguists, dialects must be mutually intelligible variations of a single language.

In China, the term *Han* is applied to all speakers of Chinese languages. Standard Chinese, or

TABLE 8.1    *Paleolithic China (10,000–200,000 BP)*

| | |
|---|---|
| 10,000–13,000 | Holocene begins, modern climate; terminal Paleolithic foragers, microlithic tools |
| 15,000 | Sinodont population develops in China |
| 20,000 | Sundadont population expansion into China |
| 12,000–50,000 | Upper Paleolithic, *Homo sapiens sapiens* |
| 50,000–200,000 | Middle Paleolithic, early *Homo sapiens* |
| 200,000–1,000,000 | Lower Paleolithic, *Homo erectus* in the Zhoukoudian caves |

SOURCE: K. C. Chang (1986).

Mandarin, is spoken in northern China, and official Chinese is based on the Beijing dialect. All Sino-Tibetan languages are based on monosyllable words, and most are tonal—that is, the tone of a syllable constitutes a phonemic distinction, which makes a meaning difference in words.

## The Chinese Neolithic

The pre-Neolithic of China is not well known, but this Late Pleistocene, Early Holocene period from about 15,000 to 7000 BP seems to mirror some of the general trends seen in other parts of the world, with foraging peoples steadily intensifying their subsistence activities. This trend is suggested, for example, by the appearance of **microlithic tools.**

The wild rice and millet, which became the foundation of Chinese civilization, are spread through a wide zone from the Ganges region of India to southern China. Millet, which includes several members of the grass family that produces small round seeds, was being cultivated in the Hwang Ho river basin by 6000 BC and rice in the lower Chang region by 5000 BC, but the details of the domestication process are not well understood. Peter Bellwood (1985) speculates that domestication in East Asia may have followed a similar path to that of the Near East. The wild ancestral rices and millets may have expanded during favorable climatic conditions during the Early Holocene. The availability of very rich and predictable resources may have encouraged mobile foragers to sedentarize, which resulted in gradual population growth. Subtle climatic changes might have threatened the natural supply of the wild grains and encouraged people to turn to intentional cultivation, selecting plants that produced larger, more numerous seeds that ripened at the same time and stuck together when harvested. T. T. Chang (1983) suggests that domestication may have occurred independently in China, at the limits of the natural range, where conditions would have been marginal and selection pressures most severe.

Early farming villages developed in China by 7000–5000 BC, only a few centuries after their Neolithic counterparts in the Near East (Table 8.2). These early villagers were represented archaeologically by seven regional cultures scattered throughout the north and southwestern portion of China (K. C. Chang 1986). They were apparently small-scale, basically egalitarian cultures, with a wide range of domesticates, including millet, pigs, dogs, chickens, and water buffalo. There were stone sickles, mortars and pestles, and ceramics, which included the three-legged pot, or *ting*, which later became such a prominent shape in bronze.

---

**shoveling**   A Sinodont characteristic found in many East Asian peoples, showing a ridge on the inside edge of the upper incisors.

**Sino-Tibetan language**   The language family that includes the major languages of China, Tibet, and Burma. By number of speakers, it is the world's second largest language group, after Indo-European.

**Altaic language**   A widespread group of Asian languages distributed from Turkey to Siberia and China, including Turkish, Mongolian, and Manchu.

**logographic**   A writing system in which the symbol represents a word.

**microlithic tools**   A small, thin piece of sharp stone, often a fragment of a long blade, which may be mounted on a shaft.

TABLE 8.2    *The Chinese Neolithic*

| | |
|---|---|
| **Yang-shao Culture (5000–3000 BC)** | Postglacial climatic optimum; north greener, wetter, warmer; shifting settlement, cultivation; domesticates—millet, wheat, dogs, pigs, cattle, sheep, silk, hemp; painted pottery, domestic crafts; inferred clan and lineage organization; burials show some status differences |
| **Regional Neolithic Expansion (5000–4000 BC)** | Increasing complexity, diversity, stratification; Yang-shao culture covers Hwang Ho, with new cultures in the north and south |
| **Regional Neolithic Cultures, Early Farming Villages (7000–5000 BC)** | *North China, Hwang Ho:* Four related clusters; semisubterranean round houses, sunken grain-storage pits; stone sickles, stone mortars and pestles, microlith tools; domesticates—millet, pigs, dogs, chickens; deer hunted; stamped and marked pottery, *ting* tripod pots <br> *South China, Chang River:* Three isolated cultures; domesticates—water caltrop (herbs), fox nut, lotus, arrowhead, water chestnut, rice, wild rice, bottle gourd, dog, pig, water buffalo |

SOURCE: K. C. Chang (1986).

## Tribe to State or State to Tribe?

According to archaeologist K. C. Chang (1986), the period from approximately 5000 to 4000 BC was characterized by steadily increasing cultural complexity, diversification, and emerging social ranking. This is approximately the same time period during which chiefdoms were emerging in Mesopotamia and in the Andean region. The best example of this development process in China is the **Yang-shao** culture (5000–3000 BC) in the lower Hwang Ho plain, which was apparently based on shifting cultivation of millet, with status differences indicating clan and lineage organization appearing in the burials.

K. C. Chang (1986) suggests that by the period from 4000 to 2000 BC a **Proto-Chinese interaction sphere** had emerged. He infers that the expanding regional cultures had begun to influence one another such that a pan-Chinese culture could be distinguished on the basis of shared art styles, burial practices, and inferred common religious beliefs involving shamanism and ancestor worship. The best example of this period is the **Lung-shan** culture (3000–2000 BC), which showed the first bronze work, divination based on **scapulimancy**

(see the box "Early Chinese Scapulimancy"), elaborate burials, craft specialization, and large villages fortified with walls of stamped earth. This **Chinese co-tradition,** or **horizon style,** like Chavin in Peru and the Andean Cultural Tradition, contained elements that are still prominent features of Chinese culture and directly preceded the first Chinese urban civilizations.

The notion that a "tribal" form of organization was a necessary stage on the way to states and civilization is firmly entrenched in much of the anthropological literature and classical scholarship on China. However, this view obscures the egalitarian nature of small-scale cultures and the qualitative transformation that occurs when they become large-scale cultures. As Morton Fried (1983) observes, many Chinese scholars were influenced by the theories of Karl Marx, Friedrich Engles, and Lewis Henry Morgan, all of whom identified some form of politically organized "tribe" as a precursor of the state. As these scholars defined it, the "tribe" is a loosely organized collection of villages or bands, united by common language and culture, under a centralized, noncoercive political leadership.

Fried (1983) criticizes this interpretation and

## Early Chinese Scapulimancy

The basic technique of divination by scapulimancy involves interpreting the pattern of cracks that develops in a heated piece of flat bone, such as a scapula or turtle plastron. In Shang China, scapulimancy was used to guide the conduct of official business in the royal court and was carried out by specialists at the request of the king (K. C. Chang 1980). A royal representative would submit an official yes or no question to the diviner, for example, asking the outcome of a proposed military campaign. The diviner would then apply heat to a specially polished, grooved, and notched bone, usually a turtle plastron or water buffalo scapula. The preparation helped direct the cracking into a center-line crack with intersecting side cracks. The angle of the side cracks and other details were then interpreted by an official prognosticator, who came up with a yes or no answer to the question. Each piece of cracked bone was inscribed by an official archivist with signs and pictographic characters, recording the date, the name of the inquirer, the question, the answer, and final outcome. These bones were then archived for future reference. Some 100,000 inscribed oracle bones have been recovered from An-yang, and they have provided detailed insights into the organization of Shang society.

uses Chinese material to argue that prestate cultures did not form politically discrete "tribes," but rather such tribal organization results when autonomous local communities are intruded upon and consolidated by states for their own purposes. Prestate societies may indeed have shared common features of language and culture, as suggested by the Proto-Chinese interaction sphere, but archaeologically defined cultures like the Lung-shan were not politically unified "tribes" under a central authority until ranked chiefdoms and states emerged. Thus, Fried would invert the sequence "tribe to state" to read "state to tribe." Discrete tribes are more easily exploited by states than the relatively amorphous and overlapping small-scale cultural systems that precede them. If tribes are not considered stepping stones to states, then it remains to explain how the pristine state arises.

Fried (1983) prefers a developmental sequence that runs from egalitarian (small-scale, in my terms) cultures, to ranked cultures (chiefdoms), to stratified cultures, which may become states. The Tikopia chiefdom discussed in Chapter 6 would be

a ranked culture in Fried's terms, whereas Hawaii would represent a stratified culture and simple

---

**Yang-shao**  A well-developed regional Neolithic culture, beginning approximately 7000 BP, that showed the first moves toward ranking, suggesting the emergence of simple chiefdoms.

**Proto-Chinese interaction sphere**  A region in the heartland of Chinese civilization where 5000 BP a common horizon style developed that emphasized religious elements that later became central features of the Chinese Great Tradition.

**Lung-shan**  A regional Chinese culture, beginning approximately 5000 BP, that suggested the beginnings of social stratification and probable chiefdom organization and perhaps small states.

**scapulimancy**  A very ancient divination technique involving the analysis of cracked animal bone and shell, which became an instrument of state decision making in the early Chinese state.

**Chinese co-tradition**  A distinctively Chinese archaeological culture that was in place some 5000 BP. See Proto-Chinese interaction sphere.

**horizon style**  An archaeologically recognized cultural pattern that occurs over a wide area during the same time period.

state. The status differences appearing in the Chinese burials of Yang-shao suggest the appearance of ranking and therefore chiefdom organization, whereas the larger mobilization of human labor implied by the monumental constructions and craft specialization of Lung-shan and in the later Shang cultures suggest social stratification and either large chiefdoms or states.

Egalitarian cultures have equal access to social status and basic resources, whereas ranked societies limit only the number of high-status positions. Stratified societies further limit access to key subsistence resources, making it possible for individuals to gain coercive political power. Fried (1983) sees the state arising because of the potentially disruptive contradictions between kinship-based sharing and the exclusion and exploitation of dependency relations created by social stratification. Contrary to the common explanations of state origin that rely on warfare, Fried argues that the state arises within individual communities, via stratification:

*The stratified local community that has gone into formal state organization looks like a city-state and utilizes its less well-organized surroundings as a source of manpower and raw materials. In its expansion it creates tribes in the hinterland and ethnic groups within its own polity.* (1983:480–481)

In this view, **ethnic groups** are formerly autonomous small-scale cultures that have been fully incorporated into the state, yet still retain distinctive linguistic or cultural characteristics. State-created tribes are dependencies that retain more autonomy than ethnic groups because they are relatively remote from the centers of state power. These tribes may still be permitted to run some of their own village-level affairs, but they are nevertheless subject to various forms of state control. Ethnic groups are likely to have little if any political and economic autonomy and may often be left with no unified territorial base.

## EARLY CHINESE CIVILIZATION

### The Shang Dynasty

During the millennium of approximately 2000–1000 BC, many of the local communities sharing in K. C. Chang's (1986) Proto-Chinese interaction sphere clearly crossed the boundary into state organization (Table 8.3). Towns became urban centers, chiefs became kings who founded dynasties,

TABLE 8.3    *Chinese State Formation*

| Early State, Urbanization, and Civilization (2000–1000 BC) | 1400 | Written records |
| | 1766–1045 | Late Shang dynasty: Highly elaborate mortuary cults, "mortuary taxes"; hereditary rulers; earliest writing, bronze; in Zhengzhou (Chengchou)—earliest urban center, rammed-earth construction, workshops, bronze foundry, distillery |
| Proto-Chinese Interaction Sphere (4000–2000 BC) | | State threshold; regional interaction sphere; cultural exchange |
| | 3000–2000 | Lung-shan culture: Permanent settlements; domesticates—rice, chickens; scapulimancy; burials distinguished by abundant wealth and elaborate ritual; ancestor cult; ceremonial crafts, ritual specialists, craft specialists; warfare, fortified villages, rammed earth walled towns; social stratification; copper objects, pottery wheel, earliest bronze implement (2500 BC), 139 signs on ceramics |

SOURCE: K. C. Chang (1986).

FIGURE 8.2
*Shang China, 1766–*
*1045 BC.*

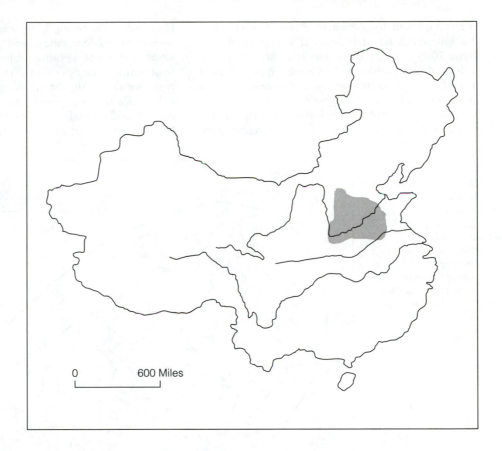

0          600 Miles

simple writing systems were developed, and production of crafts and specialized wealth objects
was greatly expanded. This was the beginning of
the period of initial Chinese civilization, which
historians refer to as the Three Dynasties—the
semimythical Hsia, the Shang, and Chou.

Shang (1766–1045 BC) is the earliest well-
described civilization of early dynastic China,
thanks to extensive excavations carried out since
1928 by Chinese archaeologists at An-yang, a
major Shang center north of the Hwang Ho in
Henan (Honan) province (Figure 8.2). An-yang
was a sprawling urban complex centered on a
palace–temple complex of elaborate wooden buildings constructed on low platforms of stamped
earth (Figure 8.3). The center was surrounded by
residential areas, cemeteries, and specialized
workshops (K. C. Chang 1980). The graves of commoners and the nobility were clearly distinguished
by the quality and abundance of grave goods. Besides the type and quantity of grave goods, rank
was indicated by the better quality of the dentition
in higher-status individuals. This suggests that social stratification, in the sense defined by Fried
(1983), operated such that the nobility enjoyed
better nutrition than commoners.

One of the most spectacular aspects of An-yang
was the royal cemetery where eleven Shang kings
and their consorts were buried. The royal tombs
were wooden-lined pits, up to 59 by 52 ft (18 by 16
m) at the top and 98 ft (30 m) deep, which were

---

***ethnic group***   A dependent, culturally distinct population that forms part of a larger state or empire and that
was formerly autonomous.

entered by four long excavated ramps oriented to the four cardinal directions. It is estimated that some 7000 working days may have been required in their construction (K. C. Chang 1986), but even more labor was incorporated in the treasure trove of bronze and jade grave goods.

Most royal tombs were looted over the centuries, but in 1976 an unlooted tomb belonging to Fu Hao, wife of a Shang king, was found to contain 440 bronzes, 590 jades, and many other bone, stone, ivory, and ceramic objects, along with sixteen human sacrifices and six dogs. Similar to royal tombs at Ur, the An-yang royal burials and palace foundations were often accompanied by human and animal sacrifices. Whole chariots with horses still in harness were buried. One An-yang

FIGURE 8.3
*Shang civilization, early dynastic China (1766–1045 BC). (a) Reconstruction of wooden palace building; (b) structural model of the An-yang urban network during the Shang Dynasty. (SOURCE: Chang 1980:130, Figure 38.)*

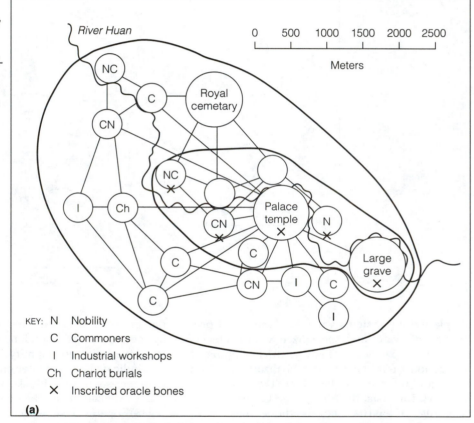

(a)

(b)

tomb contained 111 human skulls, and more than 600 people were sacrificed in the construction of a single Shang building (K. C. Chang 1980). Such large-scale sacrifices clearly foreshadowed the recently uncovered 7000-man, life-size terra-cotta army buried with the first Ch'in emperor about 210 BC (Figure 8.4).

Fried (1983) explicitly rejects the general interpretation accepted by many China specialists that Shang civilization, as the earliest Chinese state, developed out of the Shang "tribe" as a result of warfare against neighboring tribes. In Fried's view, there was never a discreet Shang tribe; rather, local small-scale village communities gradually became ranked and stratified as they grew. Fried cannot explain precisely how this transformation occurred but attributes it ultimately to the global environmental disruptions that accompanied the end of the Ice Age, making it part of the sedentarization–domestication process.

As Paul Wheatley (1971) points out, even though Chinese urban civilization emerged some 1500 years later than Sumerian city-states, urban developments in China appear to be independent. There was no colonial expansion from Mesopotamia into China that might have led to the founding of urban centers, nor was there any obvious *stimulus diffusion* by means of the large-scale introduction of economic, religious, or political influences from Mesopotamia that might have indirectly stimulated cultural development. Stimulus diffusion could be said to occur if the *idea* for some cultural trait, rather than its direct transfer, inspires its development in another culture.

In K. C. Chang's (1983, 1986) view, the Chinese state arose because emerging political elites were able to gain control of the religious system and used it to increase their political power, creating a self-reinforcing cycle of wealth and power that led to urban civilization. Such an interpretation shifts attention away from the Shang agricultural *infrastructure*, toward the political *structure* and ideological *superstructure*, emphasizing religion to an extent that would perhaps make a cultural materialist uneasy.

K. C. Chang (1983, 1986) calls the religious foundation of Chinese civilization **high shamanism** because it was a direct elaboration of the shamanistic communication with spirits that char-

FIGURE 8.4    *A view of the life-sized ceramic troops buried as part of the royal tombs of the first emperor (Ch'in Dynasty) over a unified China about 210 BC.*

acterizes small-scale cultures. The official cosmologies of early dynastic China incorporated concepts of a stratified universe connected by a world tree, animal intermediaries, and transformations. The critical difference, however, was that, unlike Amazonian or Australian shamanism, Chinese high shamanism involved highly exclusive communication with specific ancestors and deities who were sources of wisdom and supporters of the

---

**stimulus diffusion**    A theoretical concept suggesting that, in some cases, cultural *ideas* may spread rather than specific material items.
**high shamanism**    The transformation of shamanistic spirit beliefs derived from small-scale cultures into a state religion supported by a stratified social hierarchy.

social hierarchy. Communication with the ancestors was by means of scapulimancy, divination using animal bones, which was conducted by full-time ritual specialists (see the box "Early Chinese Scapulimancy" on page 199).

K. C. Chang (1983, 1986) thus rejects many established theories of state formation that rely on economic determinants as prime movers. In his view, early Chinese kings did not gain their positions because they controlled irrigation systems, trade, or the means of production, as Marxist theorists would argue, and not because social classes gained control over strategic subsistence resources as Fried suggests. Chang notes that no significant change in Chinese agriculture preceded state formation. Bronze was an important technological innovation, but it was used to manufacture ritual paraphernalia, weapons, and chariots, which provided religious and military support for elite political power.

## Shang Society

At the center of the Shang social hierarchy was the king who was a member of the royal lineage (*wang tsu*), within the ruling clan (*tsu*), a patrilineal descent group that was not strictly exogamous. In many ways, the Shang system shows striking parallels to the organization of the Inca royal *ayllus*, but the differences are striking enough that no direct connections need be posited. K. C. Chang (1980) believes that the Shang royal lineage was divided into ten ritual units named after the celestial signs naming the ten days of the week and structuring the ritual calendar. These units were arranged in two groups between which the kingship alternated according to specific rules of succession with the alternate group providing the king's counselors. The royal court contained the king's numerous wives or consorts, princes, and at least twenty categories of titled officials, such as priest, prime minister, and diviner. The court and dependents must have been large, because individual kings are known to have had up to sixty-four wives and 120 diviners (K. C. Chang 1980).

The political power of Shang rulers is shown by the standing armies of up to 10,000 men that they commanded, and there are reports of some 30,000 war captives being taken in a single campaign. The army was organized into 100-man foot companies, three companies to a regiment, and chariot companies of five chariots and 15 men, five companies to a squadron. Troops were armed with bows, bronze halberds, knives, and shields. Rural towns were also organized as militia units and could supply thousands of extra troops if needed. Military force was an important means of expanding the state and maintaining internal order.

Law, in its formal sense (see the box "The Law and the State"), supported the Shang social hierarchy, as in ancient Sumer, although no Shang law codes survive. Early historical texts referring to this period and fragmentary Shang records indicate that a well-developed court system must have existed. Subordinates were obligated to obey their rulers, and lawbreakers were harshly punished by various forms of mutilation, shackles, and execution. Rulers were obligated to not be too oppressive; if they failed, they faced supernatural punishments such as natural disasters or being overthrown by a rival state.

The underlying religious basis of the Shang state was the assumption that the king was the exclusive channel, via his personal ancestors, to *Ti*, the high god, who was responsible for the welfare of the entire population and the fertility of nature. The king was a key node in a supernatural communication network. He called himself "I, The One Man" or "I, the Unique One," assuming absolute power as the parental authority over the whole land. By means of his diviners and through proper ritual, prayer, and sacrifice, the king could persuade his dead ancestors to appeal to the high god on behalf of the whole community.

The status and prestige of Shang royalty was further affirmed by the king's physical possession of the symbols of royalty: banners, battle axes, and special bronze pots of specific size and shape, bearing specific decorations and inscriptions. Royal objects were often decorated with stylized animals such as tigers, which reinforced the king's religious role, because animals also served as supernatural messengers in Shang mythology.

The Shang state, like the Inca empire, was divided into four quarters, oriented to the cardinal directions. Beyond the capital, which was the political, economic, and ceremonial center, the hinterland population lived in walled towns (*yi*), ruled by lords. The king claimed formal title to all the kingdom and was responsible for its welfare but personally managed it to maintain and increase the power of the royal lineage. New towns were centrally planned and built as a unit by ranked lords to whom the king granted a clan name, town land, a title, ancestor tablets, and appropriate ritual paraphernalia. The townspeople constituted the working class or peasantry (*chung-jen*) and were organized into ranked patrilineages (*tsu*). Because numerous pictographic lineage names depict various economic activities, lineages may have been occupationally specialized. War captives (*ch'iang*) were the very bottom of the social pyramid (Figure 8.5) and served as laborers; they also were probably the primary source of human sacrifices because divination records list more than 7400 such victims (K. C. Chang 1980).

Modern Chinese scholars following Marxist terminology often refer to Shang as a slave society, whereas Western writers refer to a "free" peasantry. Only the war captives were probably slaves in a formal sense, but the bulk of the population enjoyed few of the benefits of their own labor. Even their semisubterranean housing symbolically separated them from the elite who resided on stamped-earth platforms.

It is difficult to see what benefits, other than protection, the peasantry derived from the Shang state. Goods and services flowed to the center to support the army and the royal court, although some wealth returned as rewards to the lords ruling the towns. Writing was not concerned with recording economic transactions but dealt only with divination records and the identification of clans and lineages. There was no market system or trader class. Kinship obligations and religious duty were the primary foundations of the social structure, which basically resembled a large-scale Hawaiian chiefdom.

## The Law and the State

Law, if broadly defined as social control, is a universal (Hoebel 1968). However, significant differences exist between social control in small-scale societies—where basic equality and low population density minimizes internal conflict to levels that kinship roles can easily manage,—and large-scale societies. Large-scale societies face more difficulties. Anthropologist Leopold Pospisil (1972) identifies four attributes of law:

*Authority:* the ability to enforce a decision
*Intention:* the assumption that legal decisions will be applied universally
*Obligation:* specific rights and duties between different categories of people
*Sanction:* punishment for lawbreakers

These attributes can be recognized in the conflict-resolution mechanisms of some small-scale societies. Law as a formal concept, however, is most appropriately applied to larger-scale, ranked-and-stratified societies and especially to politically organized states, where it serves a critical social control function. States have courts, judges, and formally codified laws, which may be written. The authority of a king comes from his executioners, the palace guard, and the standing army. Legal obligations specify what a ruler can demand of his subordinate subjects and what the subjects can expect from their rulers.

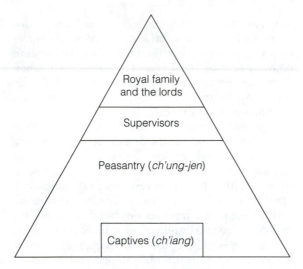

FIGURE 8.5   *Social hierarchy of the Shang state.* (*SOURCE: Chang 1980:231, Figure 60.*)

## The Nature of Early Chinese Civilization

Marvin Harris (1988) characterizes traditional China as an ***agromanagerial state*** resembling Mesopotamia and the Inca state: The Chinese ***peasantry*** was subject to large-scale conscript labor service but, in theory, received emergency aid from the state in times of scarcity. The peasantry was also subject to the local elite who extracted taxes and rents. A contrast can be drawn between this type of peasantry and European ***feudalism*** in which serfs were granted hereditary rights to use land in exchange for payment of rent and military service to local lords. Chinese peasants were potentially subject to exploitation by both local elites and the central government, although the peasant was allowed relative freedom to relocate and upward mobility was possible.

Historian David Keightley (1990) finds that the institutionalization of ***ancestor worship*** by the Shang state had important consequences that helped set the future direction of Chinese civilization. With ancestor worship, the king was the central religious figure who served as his own priest, and the kingdom was in effect a ***theocracy.*** All lineage heads also worshiped their ancestors, and the whole kingdom was integrated as a single, great politicoreligious family, leaving little room for conflicting loyalties. Ancestor worship, especially involving lavish mortuary gifts and human sacrifice, emphasized the permanence of social hierarchy and the kinship structure. There was no difference between the secular and the sacred, there was no ambiguity in the system, and everything was assumed to work as long as everyone followed their hierarchically structured kinship–ritual obligations.

Ancestor worship was thus a "strategic custom" that provided the foundation for the later elaboration of the concept of *hsiao*, or ***filial piety.*** In Mesopotamia, by contrast, there was a distinct priesthood, although temple and palace were not always in harmony and the clan and lineage system were not institutionalized. Even though one can speak analytically of social classes in early China, the emic view of the social system was kinship-based, and the dominant value was family harmony. This must certainly have minimized the potential for conflict that the grossly unequal flow of resources might otherwise have generated.

Wealth and power in the Chinese system derived from control of the labor force, as in Inca Peru. A vast conscript labor army was mobilized for the construction of the 1400-mile (2250 km) Great Wall along the northern boundary of China (Figure 8.6) during the Ch'in dynasty (approximately 215 BC). Significantly, the major river valleys, as Keightley (1990) notes, run east and west and thus remain in broadly similar ecological zones, reducing the importance of trade and providing little incentive for the development of a merchant class. The Grand Canal, only one of many monumental water-development projects, linked the Chang in the south with the Hwang Ho in the north by AD 610, providing a major boost to trade.

The imperial system of Chinese government was an expansion of the Shang system, and it remained in place with variations in detail until 1911 when the last emperor was removed from power. Historian Jack Dull (1990) distinguishes four stages in the development of Chinese government: patrimonial (1766–221 BC), meritocracy (221 BC–AD 220), aristocracy (220–906), and gentry (960–1911) (Table 8.4). Throughout the centuries, the political structure varied with cycles of civil war and conquest, with changes in the strength of the central government versus regional kingdoms and as the importance of local families changed. Important changes also occurred in the system of recruitment to political office. The patrimonial stage was described previously using the Shang example. The Chou dynasty, which overthrew the Shang, developed the concept of the **mandate of heaven** (*t'ien-ming*), as the formal legitimation of dynastic rule. Chou kings called themselves "The Son of Heaven" to emphasize that their rule was a mandate from heaven. This led to the related concept of the "bad last emperor" because a dynasty could only end when the mandate of heaven was withdrawn due to the emperor's misconduct.

The Ch'in rulers, who ushered in the imperial order in 221 BC, called themselves *Huang-ti*, literally "august god," which is usually translated "emperor" because the kings were not considered to be gods. The imperial bureaucracy under the Ch'in was territorially structured and more elaborate than the familial organization of the Shang, presumably because the former patrimonial system could not deal with the increased scale of empire. The emperor had three officials and nine ministers who ran the central government. The hinterland was divided into forty-two commanderies (*chun*), subdivided into prefectures (*hsien*); each territorial unit had an imperially appointed administrator, an inspector, and a police chief. Imperial officials were "outsiders," prohibited from operating within their home territories in order to minimize opportunities for corruption. Regional governments developed their own large bureaucracies with many positions that in theory, were filled by local individuals who were promoted on the basis of merit; thus, this entire period was characterized as a **meritocracy.** The constant struggle against corruption led to the creation of provinces to oversee the commanderies.

During the aristocracy period, recruitment to the bureaucracy was dominated by membership in

FIGURE 8.6  *The Great Wall of China constructed along the northern frontier during the Chi'in Dynasty, 215 BC.*

**agromanagerial state**  A politically centralized state where the peasantry are subject to taxation and conscript labor.

**peasantry**  Village farmers who provide most of their own subsistence but who must pay taxes and are politically and often, to some extent, economically dependent on the central state government.

**feudalism**  A political system in which village farmers occupy lands owned by local lords to whom they owe loyalty, rent, and service.

**ancestor worship**  A religious system based on reverence sometimes for specific ancestors and sometimes involving shrines, rituals, and sacrifice.

**theocracy**  State government based on religious authority or divine guidance. The Chinese emperor was the highest civil and religious leader.

**filial piety**  *Hsiao*, the ritual obligation of children to respect their ancestors, and especially the duty of sons to care for shrines of their patrilineal ancestors.

**mandate of heaven**  *T'ien-ming*, supernatural endorsement of the ruling Chinese emperor; in theory, dependent on performance.

**meritocracy**  Rule by those with demonstrated abilities. Chinese bureaucrats were selected through a highly competitive national examination system on Confucian literature.

TABLE 8.4   *Chinese Empires**

| | | |
|---|---|---|
| **Modern China** (AD 1912–   ) | 1949– | People's Republic of China |
| | 1912–1949 | Republic of China |
| **Gentry China** (AD 960–1911) | 1644–1911 | Ch'ing dynasty: Civil service exam abolished (1905); last Chinese monarchy |
| | 1368–1644 | Ming dynasty (Chinese rule) |
| | 1272–1368 | Yüan dynasty (Mongol rule) |
| | 960–1279 | Sung dynasty: civil service exam established; invention of movable type; Confucian-scholar officials |
| **Aristocratic China** (AD 220–906) | 618–906 | T'ang dynasty |
| | 610 | Great Canal built |
| | 265–420 | Tsin dynasty |
| **Meritocratic China** (221 BC–AD 220) | | Han dynasty: paper invented (AD 105), Buddhism introduced (AD 65); Confucianism established as state orthodoxy (141–87 BC) |
| | 202 BC–AD 220 | |
| | | Ch'in dynasty: Imperial rule; hereditary rule abolished; written language standarized; Great Wall built |
| | 221–206 BC | |
| **Patrimonial China** (1766–221 BC) | | Chou dynasty: Iron; cavalry; mandate of heaven established; written laws; era of Confucius (551–479), Mencius (371–289), Hzun Tzu (298–238); followed by Warring States (403–221) |
| | 1045–256 | |

SOURCES: K. C. Chang (1986) and Dull (1990).
*This is not an exhaustive list of all Chinese kingdoms and empires. Only the most prominent are shown corresponding to the major phases in political development. Precise dates used by different authorities do not always agree. There are gaps in the sequence and in the historically overlapping empires.

a nine-level hereditary hierarchy of social status. Recruitment during the gentry period was based on the examination system, which became highly elaborated and allowed more social mobility than under the aristocracy. Prospective bureaucrats took highly competitive examinations in the Confucian classics. There were three exam levels: provincial and national and at the imperial palace. The system was potentially open to anyone who could gain admission to the government schools. Only 2 to 3 percent passed their preliminary exams and were permitted to take the palace exam, successful passage of which was rewarded with entry to elite, or gentry, status and a position in the bureaucracy. The examination system, which was ultimately controlled by the emperor, reduced the potential conflicts between the aristocratic families and the government and gave more people an interest in maintaining the system.

## THE GREAT TRADITION

### Confucianism and Liturgical Government

Confucianism is a Western label for what the Chinese themselves referred to as *ju-chia*, "family of scholars." It is a scholarly tradition and moral order, based on the humanistic teachings of Confucius (K'ung-Fu-tzu, 551–479 BC). Confucianism was not a religion as such, but it became a virtual state cult because it advocated filial piety and a perpetuation of the ritual and political traditions of the Chou dynasty, which was at the core of Chinese civilization.

Confucianism taught that social order was based on virtue that came from ritual performance, beginning with household-level ancestor worship and moving up the hierarchy to the emperor. Confucius, whose teachings were preserved in the "Analects," and other major teachers who followed after, such as Mencius (Meng-tzu, 371–289 BC) and Hzun Tzu (298–238 BC), sought to promote practical ideals of good government, citizenship, and domestic life that would preserve a stable system of social inequality.

Confucianism was institutionalized by 124 BC with the creation of an imperial university focused on the *five classics:*

1. The *I Ching,* "Book of Change," is concerned with divination according to the principles of Confucian ethics and yin–yang complementary oppositions.

2. The *Shu Ching,* "Book of Documents," spells out the ideals of statecraft to be followed by the "Sage King" and all bureaucrats.

3. The *Shih Ching,* "Book of Songs," contains Confucian poetry.

4. The *Li Chi,* "Book of Rites," specifies the formal duties and rituals between social classes, kin, and husbands and wives.

5. The *Ch'un-ch'iu,* "Spring and Autumn Annals," deals with dynastic history (Wei-ming 1990).

Confucianism constituted the Chinese *Great Tradition*—elite culture, or high culture—because it was propagated by the literate elite and was directly involved with official ritual and the maintenance of the bureaucracy. Under Confucian ideals, which remained important until modern times, Chinese society was divided into a class system that was very similar to that of Shang times, but increased population meant that extreme social inequality operated.

By the end of the Ch'ing dynasty, under the Manchu rulers (1644–1911), some 700 people belonged to be emperor's clan at the top of the hierarchy (Figures 8.7 and 8.8). Perhaps 40,000 more people were part of the formal administrative bureaucracy. Beneath this group were four social classes: (1) scholars (*shih*), (2) merchants (*shang*), (3) artisans (*kung*), and (4) farmers (*nung*). The 7.5 million or so scholar-bureaucrats were part of the privileged elite (*kwei*) gentry, who controlled local affairs and were granted many special privileges (Stover and Stover 1976).

The elite were set apart by special dress and their rigid adherence to Confucian ideals, linguistic forms, and ritual. In all, elites and their families may have totaled 7.5 million by 1900, perhaps less than 2 percent of the total population (Michael 1964, Wolf 1969b). Some authorities distinguish between three elite subgroups: the upper gentry who were entitled to formal offices in the bureaucracy, the scholars who did not qualify for high office, and those nonscholars who derived elite status from independent economic or political power (Eastman 1988).

The bulk of the population, which may have grown to some 400 million by the mid-nineteenth century, constituted the commoners (*liang*), who were primarily farmers with very small landholdings. At the very bottom were outcasts, such as bandits and prostitutes.

Confucian concepts of formal ritual and etiquette, or **li,** regulated social conduct and helped people feel good about their social station. Leon Stover and Takeko Stover (1976) have characterized the Chinese system as *liturgical government,* or "culturalism," arguing that Confucianism created a form of moral nationalism that held the empire together in the absence of overt political or military force. The emperor occupied the ritual center of the world, where he held lavish state rituals and established a formal ritual calendar. The emperor lived a leisured life of conspicuous consumption, defining and legitimating the cultural ideal for the elite. In this view, which was probably only accurate during certain historical periods, the emperor was a politically weak figurehead, who supported himself from local tribute and the imperial monopoly on the Grand Canal connecting north and south China, the salt tax, and foreign trade. The emperor's primary political role was to

---

*five classics* Texts in Confucian ethics, poetry, etiquette, ritual, and history, which provided a formal model for ideal behavior at all levels of Chinese society beginning some 2000 BP.

*Great Tradition* The culture of the elite in a state-organized society with a written tradition that is not fully shared by nonliterate, village-level commoners.

*li* Confucian etiquette as specified in the *Li Chi,* "Book of Rites," covering the smallest details of proper ritual behavior between individuals of different social status.

*liturgical government* The use of ritually prescribed interpersonal relations and religious, moral authority as a primary means of social control in a state-level society.

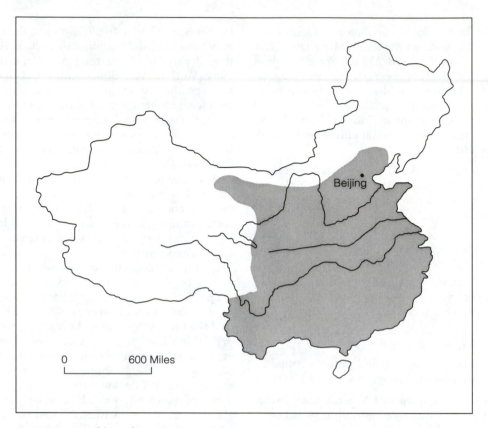

FIGURE 8.7    *Ch'ing China, 1900.*

FIGURE 8.8    *The structure of Ch'ing society, 1900. Of the total population, 7.7 percent (30.8 million people) was urban, and 92.3 percent (369.2 million people) was rural.*

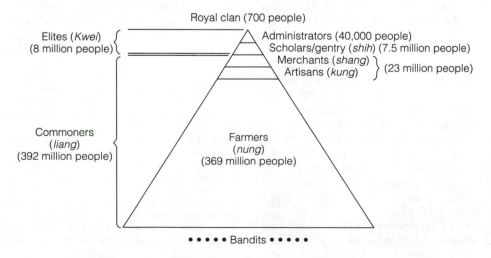

award scholarly degrees and official appointments and to maintain overall peace and security.

The local nobility and elite had virtually full political and economic autonomy in the countryside. They supported themselves by extracting taxes and rents from the peasantry because officials earned only token salaries. The provincial elite returned little material support to the center but acknowledged the superior status of the imperial court by following the centrally issued ritual calendar and by observing the **kowtow** (*k'ou-t'ou*), ritual prostration. Whenever an official received a message from the emperor, the official was required to bow to his knees three times, rapping his forehead against the floor three times for each bow. This was a small cost to pay to support a High Culture that quieted the peasantry with the sayings of Menicus and Confucius that "inequalities are in the nature of things" (Menicus) and that one should "seek no happiness that does not pertain to your lot in life" (Confucius) (Stover and Stover 1976:166, 170).

## The Li Chi, "Book of Rites"

The *Li Chi*, a Confucian classic, was compiled during the Han dynasty in the first century BC by Confucian scholars. It specified details of dress, diet, ritual, and interaction between all ranks, offices, and kinship categories. The Inca state was no doubt guided by a similar cultural code; however, in the Inca case, the details were part of the oral tradition and were not compiled in a formal book. The *Li Chi* provides a remarkable inside view of the cultural minutia of the Chinese Great Tradition. For example, for state rituals during the first month of spring, the *Li Chi* specifies the alignment of stars; which day names are to be used; which deities, animals, and musical notes, numbers, and tastes; in which temple room sacrifices are to be offered by the emperor; the bells on the royal carriage; the type of horse drawing the carriage; the color of flags on the carriage; the color of the emperor's robes; and the type of jade ornaments on his cap. According to the *Li Chi*, the emperor is also supposed to eat mutton and wheat from vessels carved to represent sprouting plants, during the first month of spring (Legge 1967, vol. 2 [Bk. 4, sec. 1, pt. 1]).

In excruciating detail, the *Li Chi* prescribes deference behavior between officials of different rank. For example:

*All (officers) in attendance on the ruler let the sash hang down till their feet seemed to tread on the lower edge (of their skirt). Their chins projected like the eaves of a house, and their hands were clasped before them low down. Their eyes were directed downwards, and their ears were higher than their eyes. They saw (the ruler) from his girdle up to his collar. They listened to him with their ears turned to the left.* (Legge 1967, vol. 2:17 [Bk. 11, sec. 3, pt. 1]).

The respective contributions of individual, family, officials, and the emperor to harmony is described as follows:

*When the four limbs are all well proportioned, and the skin is smooth and full, the individual is in good condition. When there is generous affection between father and son, harmony between brothers, and happy union between husband and wife, the family is in good condition. When the great ministers are observant of the laws, the smaller ministers pure, officers and their duties kept in their regular relations and the ruler and his ministers are correctly helpful to one another, the state is in good condition. When the son of Heaven [the emperor] moves in his virtue as a chariot, with music as his driver, while all the princes conduct their mutual intercourse according to the rules of propriety [Li], the great officers maintain the order between them according to the laws, inferior officers complete one another by their good faith, and the common people guard one another with a spirit of harmony, all under the sky is in good condition. All this produces what we call (the state of) great mutual consideration (and harmony).* (Legge 1967, vol. 1:390–391 [Bk. 7, sec. 13]).

When everyone does his duty, the living are fed, the dead are properly buried, and the ancestral spirits are taken care of.

## Taoism, Cosmology, and the Little Tradition

Taoism and Buddhism were other important religious and philosophical systems that were part of the Chinese Great Tradition; they had literate com-

---

**kowtow**   Exaggerated bowing, head to the floor, in ritual respect for the emperor.

ponents and shared many elements with Confucianism, but they did not enjoy the official support the state gave Confucianism.

Taoism shares much with Confucianism, most prominently a concern with the **tao,** or "way," which could be identified with the "way of heaven" and all the cosmic forces, as well as following one's social and ritual duty. However, unlike Confucianism, which is strongly secular, Taoism is a mystical religious system that appealed to disaffected commoners and contained messianic elements that sometimes mobilized the peasantry to oppose the established political system. Taoism traces its origins to Lao-tzu (Lao-tze), a religious sage and contemporary of Confucius during the Chou period, who wrote the primary sacred text of Taoism, the *Tao-te Ching.* As a formal religious institution, Taoism has its saints and divinities, diverse sects and schools, and is represented in temples throughout China. There are full-time Taoist priests, who are celibate and live in monasteries. Taoist thought has been an important influence on both Confucianism and folk religion.

Buddhism reached China from India by AD 65 during the Han dynasty and simply added another literate temple–monastic system and enriched the Chinese pantheon. It ultimately shaped the Taoist and Confucianist traditions and was absorbed into the folk religion, adding concepts of hell, sin, *karma,* and judgment. (Buddhism is also discussed in Chapter 9.)

The Confucian Great Tradition represented the power of the state in the form of great palaces, temples, rituals, literature, and artworks, which together must have encouraged feelings of awe and subordination in the commoners. This elite culture, together with the literate and institutionalized elements of Taoism and Buddhism, receives most attention from Western historians and students of comparative religion, art, and literature. However, commoners, who constituted 98 percent of the population, were passive participants in the Great Tradition, but they maintained their own **Little Tradition,** or popular culture.

In their daily lives, commoners directly perpetuated shamanistic cultural traditions, which were rooted in the Neolithic past, underlying both the Great and Little Traditions. Commoners practiced a syncretistic folk religion that drew freely on ele-

ments from formal Confucianism, Taoism, and Buddhism. Part-time Taoist priests, who did not live in the monasteries, were often called upon as ritual specialists to perform at marriages, funerals, and curing ceremonies. The most prominent cultural elements shared by elites and commoners alike included the basic family system, with its emphasis on patrilineal descent lines and the ancestor cult, and basic cosmological elements. The lowest-level deity, who operated at the household level, was the stove, or kitchen god, who symbolized the domestic unity of the family. The stove god represented the bureaucracy and could report directly to the god symbolizing the emperor in the supernatural bureaucracy (Wolf 1974).

Complementary opposition, a prominent element in Australian and Amazonian cosmologies, was also a basic feature of Chinese popular culture. Complementarity was represented in Chinese cosmology by the **yin–yang concept,** symbolized in Figure 8.9. Yin is female, earth, dark, cool, winter, valleys, tigers, and the color orange. Yang is male, heaven, light, hot, summer, mountains, dragons, and the color blue. The yin–yang concept was formalized by the Great Tradition during the early dynasties and combined with other philosophical features such as the concept of the **five elements:** metal, wood, water, fire, and earth, which were connected in a transformation cycle, emphasizing balance, harmony, change, and continuity. According to five element philosophy,

> Water produces Wood but overcomes Fire
> Fire produces Earth but overcomes Metal
> Metal produces Water but overcomes Wood
> Wood produces Fire but overcomes Earth
> Earth produces Metal but overcomes Water
> (Chai and Chai 1967:lxviii)

The five elements were correlated with colors, directions, musical notes, and periods of Chinese history, to produce an elaborate, often occult, cosmology. Color symbolism has also been important in Chinese popular culture. White, universally considered the color of mourning, was associated with west, and the east was blue-green. Red was auspicious and south, black was north, and yellow was associated with the emperor (Rawski 1987).

This popular belief system has sometimes been

FIGURE 8.9
*Yin-yang.*

called a ***correlative cosmology*** because it provided a framework that helped elites and commoners alike structure their daily lives in proper alignment with the cosmic forces to guarantee prosperity. Concern for proper alignments were reflected in the layout of cities, temples, tombs, and houses; in the timing of ritual events; the selection of mates; and the seating of guests. Specialists in *geomancy* took cosmic forces into account when they studied the topographic details of a particular locality in order to select the most auspicious location for houses and graves. Correlative cosmology also influenced popular medicine, diet, and astrology.

## CHINESE SUBSISTENCE AND DEMOGRAPHICS

### Permanent Agriculture: Farmers of Forty Centuries

U.S. Department of Agriculture soil scientist and agriculture professor F. H. King (1911) went to China and Japan during the first decade of the twentieth century to learn how these "farmers of forty centuries" could support dense populations and still maintain soil fertility after so many years of permanent agriculture. King found that Chinese farmlands were being cultivated so intensively that they directly supported 1783 people, 212 cattle or oxen, and 399 pigs per 1 mi² (2.6 km²), nearly thirty times the comparable human density for the United States at that time. He attributed the success of Chinese agriculture to favorable climate and soils and choice of crops, along with labor-intensive multicropping, intertilling, terracing, and highly efficient use of water and organic fertilizer. He estimated that some 200,000 miles

(321,800 km) of major canals supported rice cultivation (Figure 8.10). Soil fertility was maintained by composting, reclamation of canal mud, manuring, and extensive application of night soil, or human waste. Soil and subsoil were sometimes carried to the village to be mixed with compost and then returned to the field. King credited the Chinese with judiciously rotating legumes in their gardens to improve fertility, even though Western scientists failed to understand their nitrogen-fixing role until 1888. Most of all, King was impressed with the Chinese economy of resource use:

*Almost every foot of land is made to contribute material for food, fuel or fabric. Everything which can be made edible serves as food for man or domestic animals. Whatever cannot be eaten or worn is used for fuel. The wastes of the body, of fuel and of fabric worn beyond other use are taken back to the field; before doing so they are housed against waste from weather, compounded with intelligence and forethought and patiently labored with through one, three or even six months, to bring them into the most efficient form to serve as manure for the soil or as feed for the crop.* (1911:13)

Prerevolutionary China's 500 million people were supported by very small farms, usually of less than 5 acres (2 hectares), which were concentrated on just 8 percent of the land. As the Stovers (1976) note, the Chinese agricultural strategy was to apply human labor intensively to the lands that would yield the greatest return per acre. They

---

***tao*** The "way" or basic principle of Taoism, emphasizing proper conduct and alignment with cosmic forces.
***Little Tradition*** Ritual beliefs and practices followed by nonliterate commoners, especially rural villagers who are part of a larger state-level society.
***yin-yang concept*** A basic principle of complementary opposition in Chinese thought resembling a moiety system in which yin is associated with female and earth and yang with male and heaven.
***five elements*** Metal, wood, water, fire, and earth, which played a prominent role in Chinese correlative cosmology.
***correlative cosmology*** A belief system emphasizing the need to maintain proper time and space alignments between objects, people, events, and cosmic forces, to provide order and meaning to life.
***geomancy*** Divination based on alignments and topography, part of Chinese correlative cosmology.

FIGURE 8.10
*Chinese wet rice agriculture is highly labor-intensive but produces enormous per-acre yields on a sustainable basis.*

argue that in a sense, Chinese agriculture was a capital-maintaining, labor-absorbing, intensive hand-gardening system, in which the real crop was human beings. People were produced in the smallest possible space at the lowest energy cost. A similar intensification process in Java has been called *agricultural involution* (Geertz 1963).

The productivity of such a system is remarkable. In 1940 researchers investigated a village of 611 people, which they called Luts'un, in central Yunnan province, south China (Fei and Chang 1945). They found that when multicropped a standard 2688-ft² (250-m²) unit of land (called a *kung*) produced 821 lb (372 kilograms [kg]) of rice and beans per year, yielding approximately 1.147 million kilocalories (kcal) of food. This assumed good-quality land and an input of 152 hours of human labor (Table 8.5). This is more than sixty times the per-acre productivity from industrially grown American rice in 1975, which required enormous inputs of chemical fertilizers, pesticides, and fossil fuels. The Chinese production system yielded a return of 50 kcal of food energy for each kilocalorie of human labor expended, whereas American rice was grown at an energy

deficit because of the energy cost of the fossil fuels expended.

The Stovers (1976) further observe that the Chinese subsistence system is effective because it makes limited use of draft animals or animal protein. The Chinese diet is typically vegetarian, with only 2 to 3 percent of the caloric intake derived from meat (Eastman 1988). Only chickens, ducks, and pigs, which are scavengers, are raised to be consumed. They can also be fed rice hulls and bean stalks, whereas large draft animals are costly to feed, especially if valuable cropland is devoted to raising animal food. In some areas, fish ponds were also a significant source of food.

## Immiseration, Overpopulation, and Exploitation

With periodic wars and famines, the population of China fluctuated between 30 and 60 million people during most of the first millennium AD, jumping to 100 million by AD 1100, then moving steadily upward (Figure 8.11). The most dramatic change was the fivefold increase that began after 1400, during the Ming dynasty, and approached 500 mil-

TABLE 8.5  *The Productivity of Chinese Intensive Agri-culture (kcal/kung/year), Luts'un, Kunming, 1940*

|  | Picuals | kg/year | kcal/kg | Total kcal |
|---|---|---|---|---|
| Rice, Hulled | 3.8 | 192 | 3600 | 691,200 |
| Broad Beans | 2.6 | 130 | 3380 | 439,400 |
| Green Beans | 1.0 | 50 | 320 | 16,000 |

Total kcal produced: 1,146,600
Input: 20.3 days × 7.5 hours × 150 kcal = 22,837
Output–input ratio: 50.2 to 1

*Comparison with U.S. Rice Production*

|  | kg/Acre | kcal/Acre |
|---|---|---|
| **U.S., 1975** | | |
| **Hulled** | | |
| **Rice** | 828 | 298,080 |
| **Luts'un,** | | |
| **1940** | | |
| **Multicrop** | 5952 | 18,345,600 |

SOURCE: Fei and Chang (1945:70, Table 12).
NOTES: The caloric value of "waste" by-products such as bean stalks, rice hulls, and straw, which are used as animal feeds, are not included. 1 picual = 50.1 kg; 1 *kung* = 250 m² of land, 40 *kung* = 1 hectare, 16 *kung* = 1 acre; 1 *kung* of labor = 1 person day of labor, 7.5 hours; 1 hour of labor = 150 kcal expended.

lion by the end of the Ch'ing dynasty in 1911. By 1975 China's population reached 800 million, and it exceeded 1 billion by 1990. Several factors have been proposed to explain the Ming–Ch'ing increases, including a prolonged period of peace and stability; improvements in health, such as the development of smallpox vaccinations in the sixteenth century; the introduction of new food crops from the Americas; and a global warming trend that improved agricultural conditions (Eastman 1988).

Although population growth had fundamentally changed the scale of Chinese society by 1900, the culture remained basically the same, and many observers argued that the Chinese peasantry was undergoing a steady Malthusian *immiseration,* or impoverishment. The English demographer Thomas Malthus (1766–1834) theorized in his famous *Essay on the Principle of Population* ([1798] 1895) that populations naturally increased faster than their food supply and were limited by the misery that ensued when poverty set in. However, the Chinese case demonstrates that cultural factors significantly shaped how Malthusian pressures were felt. By 1900 China's population was ten times larger than during the 2000-year period between 1000 BC and AD 1000 when the basic cultural system of a stratified, agrarian state was established, with a ranked bureaucracy extracting taxes, rents, and labor from the peasantry.

Large-scale migration out of the lower Hwang Ho and Chang floodplains as well as further agricultural intensification during the Ch'ing dynasty helped the standard of living keep up with population growth. Pioneer expansion into the forested and hilly autonomous tribal areas of south and central China, and into Taiwan and Manchuria, accounted for a significant portion of the population increase. Large-scale deforestation and erosion accompanied this expansion, resulting in drastic changes in the Chinese landscape. Throughout the

**agricultural involution**  Geertz's concept of a labor-intensive agricultural system that provides an incentive for population growth.
**immiseration**  Malthusian impoverishment, a declining standard of living attributed to continuous population growth on a limited-resource base.

recent period, farmers tended to cultivate smaller plots more intensively. Maize, potatoes, and sweet potatoes from the New World complemented existing crops and certainly increased productivity. The fragmentation of plots was accelerated by the Chinese practice of giving each son an equal division of the family land. There were also incentives for population growth. Patriliny and ancestor worship provided strong cultural reasons for having sons; indeed, Confucian ideals stressed the importance of maintaining the lineage. Furthermore, agricultural intensification depended on greater and greater inputs of human labor, as discussed previously.

It is difficult to demonstrate the extent to which conditions for the peasantry deteriorated significantly with population increase. Albert Feuerwerker (1990) argues that per-capita economic productivity peaked during the Sung dynasty (AD 1000) and that there was no significant change in basic standard of living until after 1900, despite population increase. However, other researchers point to a steady reduction in the urban proportion of the population and the increasing fragmentation of land as evidence of overpopulation (Chao 1986). Kang Chao also argues that population growth prevented an early industrial revolution in China, even though China in AD 1000 was technologically more advanced than Europe, because there was no incentive to produce labor-saving machinery.

Lloyd Eastman (1988) suggests that immiseration was a myth because the lot of the peasantry had always been poor, although conditions reached a low during the political and economic upheavals of the 1930s and 1940s. However, the fact that population continued to increase suggests that, contrary to Malthusian predictions, conditions did not become absolutely intolerable. Perhaps the most important factor underlying the pervasive impoverishment of the peasantry was the operation of the market economy with a highly nonegalitarian system where most of the population were subsistence farmers. Peasants paid rent even to use communally owned clan land, and privately owned plots were often only tiny inheritances. Cash cropping to pay for land often proved risky and could undercut subsistence production.

The extent of social inequality at the household-level in village China by 1940 is clearly shown in the data collected by Hsiao-Tung Fei and Chih-I Chang (1945), showing three social classes in the village of Luts'un. At the top was a landowning leisured class that managed its land to produce enough subsistence and cash crops to ensure a minimum standard of living for the least effort.

FIGURE 8.11
*Chinese population growth, AD 100–1900. (SOURCE: Feuerwerker 1990.)*

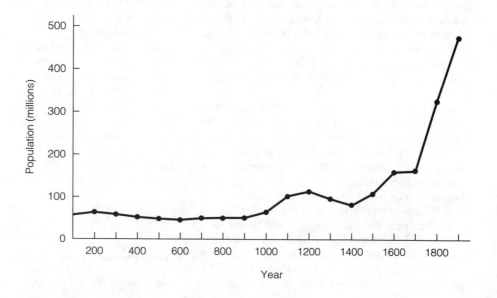

Men in this group often refused to engage in any agricultural labor and spent their time relaxing and smoking. The "middle" class was composed of owner-tenants who had to rent additional land to farm in order to produce a slim subsistence margin. At the bottom was the landless class—those who had to survive by hiring out their labor and purchasing basic necessities. In Luts'un, 41 percent of the farmland was owned by 15 percent of the households, and 31 percent of the households were completely landless. Nearly half of these non-land-owning households were too poor to even rent land.

Energetics analysis, comparing annual input–output ratios and energy-flow patterns between a modest landowning household in Luts'un village and a landless household, dramatically illustrates the physical dimensions of this social stratification (Bodley 1981b). The sample households differed in size, with five individuals in the landholding family and only two in the landless household. The landowning household controlled only 27 *kung* (1.6 acres [67 hectares]), which placed it in the lower range of the landowning class, but it still enjoyed a comfortable standard of living. When the caloric value of rice was used as a cash equivalent, the landed household showed a potential per-capita food consumption five times that of the landless household. On a per-capita basis, it also consumed more than four times the goods and produced at more than twice the energy efficiency of the landless household. The wealthy household had enough savings to last for 1 year and was able to support pigs with its garden waste. The poor household was just able to purchase enough rice to meet its minimal caloric requirements and would have had difficulty meeting its protein needs. There was little margin for housing, clothing, fuel, or medical needs. Significantly, the poor household paid enough in rent and taxes to support two additional people, and this was actually more than paid by the wealthy household. Inequality of this magnitude could not have existed in an unstratified tribal village.

It would seem appropriate to call the Chinese system exploitative, at least by late Ch'ing times, if *exploitation* is defined as the unjust or improper use of another person for someone else's benefit. In Harris's (1988) view, exploitation exists if the lower class is deprived of basic necessities relative to the upper class and if the upper class derives luxuries from the lower class, yet refuses to redistribute its wealth. By this definition, exploitation was probably a frequent social problem in Chinese civilization. Confucian teaching explicitly condemned such abuse of the peasantry because it was not good government, and Buddhist and Taoist sages spoke against it; however, inequities of wealth and power were inherent features of the Chinese state. Whether the Chinese peasantry conceived of themselves as an oppressed social class in an emic sense is another matter. From a social scientists' etic perspective, social classes existed in China for at least 4000 years, but the powerful ideology of ancestor cults and Confucianism made such inequality seem part of the natural order of things. Furthermore, the examination system always held open the possibility of upward mobility.

## VILLAGE, KINSHIP, AND FAMILY IN CHINA

### The Chinese Village System

The daily life of the Chinese peasantry was centered on the highly self-sufficient village, which probably contained an average of about 400 to 500 people, approximately the same number as in Australian "tribes" or the largest Amazonian village communities. Unlike these small-scale societies, which maintained essentially horizontal interaction links with structurally similar neighbors, Chinese villages were the lowest rural units in an organizational hierarchy ultimately linking them to the imperial center. This system of social, economic, ritual, and political ties linking the literate elites of the Great Tradition and the peasantry of the Little Tradition has been called the *folk-urban continuum* (Redfield 1941). Cultural elements of the Great Tradition are most prominent in the urban

---

*exploitation* Unjust use of someone to differentially benefit another, especially when one social class is deprived of basic necessities while the elites live in luxury.
*folk-urban continuum* Redfield's concept of a gradual distinction between the Little Tradition culture of rural commoners and the Great Tradition culture of the rural elites in a large-scale culture.

capitals and decline steadily as one moves toward smaller towns and villages where the Little Tradition becomes strongest.

In China, G. William Skinner (1964) has used central-place theory (see Chapter 7) to show that villages group themselves around local centers, which he calls standard market towns, in order to most efficiently exchange their produce for the limited range of goods and services that they cannot produce themselves. Villagers were usually self-sufficient in food, but they purchased such items as lamp oil, candles, incense, needles, soap, and matches and occasionally made use of blacksmiths, coffin makers, medical practitioners, scribes, and ritual specialists.

Skinner (1964) found that an average of eighteen villages were arranged about a standard market town within an area of some 19 mi² (50 km²), such that the most distant village was only about 3 miles (5 km) from the center; although where population density was low, the most remote villagers might need to walk 5 miles (8 km) to town (Figure 8.12). Markets were held in adjacent market towns according to a regular schedule following the lunar calendar that divides the month into three 10-day "weeks." A typical cycle would mean that a market would be held in the same town every 5 days; thus, an itinerant peddler or specialist could visit a different market every day and thereby greatly increase his potential customers. This system made it possible to efficiently sustain a very large and dense rural population without a costly and fuel-intensive transportation technology such as developed in industrial Europe and North America.

Skinner (1964) argues that the villages using a standard market town constituted the basic unit of the Chinese Little Tradition, or folk society. These 7000 or so people formed a relatively discrete social group that would regularly interact on market days and would be united by ties of kinship and marriage. They thought of themselves as a group and shared details of dress, ritual, and dialect and sometimes even used their own system of weights and measures. The market town was where the villagers paid their rents and taxes; it also contained religious shrines and teahouses where the members of secret societies and mutual-aid societies could meet. With its varied specialized functions,

market towns often served as the power base of a single large lineage or clan, whose various members might be localized in villages within the market district.

An average of six standard market towns was grouped in hexagonal territories around an intermediate market town where the local gentry conducted much of their business (see Figure 8.12). Intermediate market towns were often enclosed by walls and contained a temple to an urban deity. They might serve an overlapping area of 135 mi² (350 km²) with 50,000 people and were connected, in turn, with a central market town where the lowest-level officials of the official bureaucracy would be located. People maintaining connections between intermediate or central market towns were likely to be literate elites, whereas most peasants would never need to leave their local market districts.

In theory, Chinese social organization was based on the patrilineal *tsu*, usually translated as either clan or lineage. These genealogically defined units were segmented, localized, property-holding groups, with a specific surname and clan temples or halls, where tablets dedicated to specific clan ancestors would be kept. Villages or towns might be dominated by a single clan, with lineage segments occupying specific blocks. There might also be written genealogies showing remarkable depth. For example, a village of 1100 people examined in Guangdong (Kwangtung) province in 1957 contained members of two clans. The dominant clan preserved ancestor tablets back forty-two generations to the founding of the village in AD 1091 (Freedman 1966).

There are conflicting interpretations of how Chinese descent groups were organized and functioned. Francis Hsu (1963) probably presents an incomplete picture when he describes the "clan" as a large extended family, which forms a warm, peaceful, mutually self-contained unit. Maurice Freedman (1966) calls the same descent group a "lineage" and stresses that it was characterized by both internal conflict and harmony resembling the Nuer system of segmentary opposition. Freedman speculates that Chinese lineages may have gained special importance as landholding groups when lineage members cooperated in the development of local irrigation systems for wet rice agriculture

FIGURE 8.12 *Chinese market towns grouped about higher-level central places as predicted by central place theory: (a) map view of towns and the road network and (b) a diagramatic view on a hexagonal grid (numbers represent market days in 10-day weeks). (SOURCE: Skinner 1964.)*

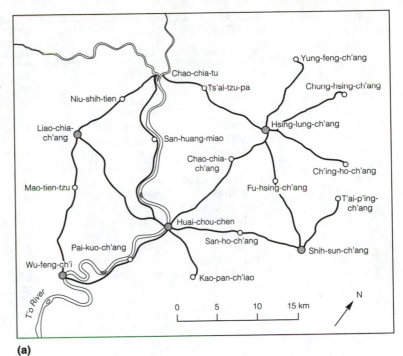

(a)

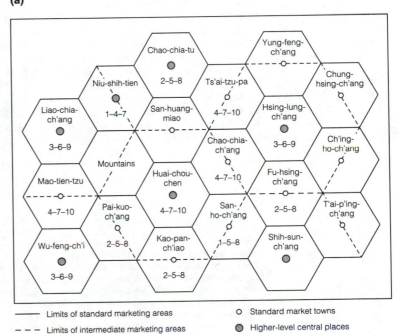

(b)

TABLE 8.6  *A Componential Analysis of Chinese Kinship*

| Description* | Chinese Term† | Components‡ | | | | |
|---|---|---|---|---|---|---|
| | | D | R | G | S | A |
| 1. F | *fu 4 thin 2* | M | L | +1 | M | |
| 2. FOB | *pak 2 fu 4/* | M | C | +1 | M | O |
| 3. FYB | *suk 2 fu 4/* | M | C | +1 | M | Y |
| 6. FZ | *ku 2 mu 5* | M | C | +1 | F | |
| 8. FBOS | *hong 3 hen 2* | M | C | 0 | M | O |
| 9. FBYS | *hong 3 ?ai 4/* | M | C | 0 | M | Y |
| 10. FBOD | *hong 3 tei 1* | M | C | 0 | F | O |
| 11. FBYD | *hong 3 moi 1/* | M | C | 0 | F | Y |
| 12. FZOS, MZOS, MBOS | *piau 1 hen 2* | C | 0 | | M | O |
| 13. FZYS, MBYS, MZYS | *piau 1 ?ai 4/* | C | 0 | | M | Y |
| 14. FZOD, MBOD, MZOD | *piau 1 tei 1* | C | 0 | | F | O |
| 15. FZYD, MBYD, MZYD | *piau 1 moi 1\* | C | 0 | | F | Y |
| 16. FF | *tu 1 fu 4* | M | L | +2 | M | |
| 17. FM | *tu 1 mu f/* | M | L | +2 | F | |
| 18. FFOB | *pak 2 tu 1 fu 4* | M | C | +2 | M | O |
| 19. FFYB | *suk 2 tu 1 fu 4* | M | C | +2 | M | Y |
| 22. FFZ | *ku 2 tu 1 mu 5/* | M | C | +2 | F | |
| 24. M | *mu 5 thin 2* | F | L | +1 | F | |
| 25. MB | *khiu 5 fu 4* | F | C | +1 | M | |
| 27. MZ | *i 3 mu 5/* | F | C | +1 | F | |
| 38. MF | *ngoi 4 tu 1 fu 2* | F | L | +2 | M | |
| 39. MM | *ngoi 4 tu 1 mu 5* | F | L | +2 | F | |
| 40. MFOB | *ngoi 4 pak 2 tu 1 fu 2* | F | C | +2 | M | O |
| 41. MFYB | *ngoi 4 suk 2 tu 1 fu 2* | F | C | +2 | M | Y |
| 44. MFZ | *ngoi 4 ku 2 tu 1 mu 5/* | F | C | +2 | F | |
| 46. OB | *ka 2 hen 2* | M | C | 0 | M | O |
| 47. YB | *pou 2 ?ai 4/* | M | C | 0 | M | Y |
| 50. BS | *cit 4* | M | C | −1 | M | |
| 51. BD | *cit 4 nui 1* | M | C | −1 | F | |
| 52. OZ | *ka 2 tei 1* | F | C | 0 | F | O |
| 53. YZ | *pou 2 moi 1/* | F | C | 0 | F | Y |
| 56. ZS | *sang 2 tu 1* | F | C | −1 | M | |
| 57. ZD | *sang 2 nui 1* | F | C | −1 | F | |
| 58. S | *tu 1* | M | L | −1 | M | |
| 62. D | *nui 1* | F | L | −1 | F | |

SOURCE: Modified from McCoy (1970).

*The numbers in this column are keyed to kinship terms in Figure 8.14.

†Linguistic symbols: tones 1–5, respectively, high, mid, low, mid-falling, low-falling; / = high-rising; \ = low-falling; ? = glottal stop.

‡D = descent line: M = male line, through F, S, or B; F = female line, through M, D, or Z. R = relationship of alter to ego's line: L = lineal, same line; C = collateral, off to side. G = generation of alter in relation to ego: 0 = ego's generation; +1, +2 = first and second ascending generations; −1 = first descending generation. S = sex of alter: M = male; F = female. A = relative age of alter: O = older; Y = younger.

or formed self-defense groups on the frontiers of pioneer settlement.

## Domestic Life and the Role of Women

Given the patrilineal descent system, the ideal Chinese nuclear family would produce many sons who would bring their wives to live in their father's house or, at least, to his village. This would increase the strength of the lineage and ensure its perpetuation. Wealthy families could also add new members by adoption. Freedman (1966) describes two broad types of Chinese families by size. The ideal was a large family containing two or more married sons and often called a *joint family*. The small family was either a nuclear family with no married sons or a *stem family* with only a single married son. Joint families were likely to be relatively wealthy, and they could form large lineage segments, whereas small families were usually poor members of disappearing lineages. The male members of the Chinese families, large or small, held joint property, which was usually divided equally.

The position of women in Chinese society is often portrayed in negative terms by Western observers. Sons were said to be preferred over daughters. Women did not own lineage property. A child bride was dominated by her mother-in-law. Such domination, which reinforced the control of the extended family by the elders, was reflected in the common practice of adopting a girl into the family for the son to marry (Wolf 1968). Marriages were often arranged, and even though monogamy was the pattern, concubinage occurred, divorce was difficult, and widow remarriage was discouraged. Upon marriage a woman was virtually absorbed into her husband's family. Marriage was so essential for women that if they died unmarried, their spirits could be married later in a pattern reminiscent of Nuer ghost marriage.

Footbinding produced small, stunted feet, leaving many women virtually crippled. This practice demonstrated a man's affluence because it meant that his wife did not do heavy domestic work. Foot binding was apparently not limited to the elite. It was thought to make women more attractive, but it also supported the ideal of wifely virtue by making it more difficult for women to venture unattended from the home (Ebrey 1990).

This picture of female subordination is incomplete. Freedman (1979) points out that Chinese women bring a sizable endowment of domestic articles and personal wealth with them when they marry. A woman can also manage her husband's share of the family estate, and she alone owns her private earnings. Although new daughters-in-law may be treated harshly, they will become mothers-in-law in turn. As a wife, a woman has important ritual responsibilities in domestic ritual, and her tablet will rest in her husband's ancestor hall.

## The Meaning of Chinese Kinship Terms

Chinese kinship terminology is complex because of the great diversity of terms that can be employed, but careful linguistic analysis reveals an orderly system that reflects the organization of Chinese society. In a study of the kinship terms used in Guangdong province by male speakers of Toishan, a Cantonese dialect of south China, John McCoy (1970) lists sixty-nine different terms used in indirect *reference* to kin and some fifty-three terms used in direct *address*. Table 8.6 presents a simplified list of thirty-five selected terms drawn from this list, but representing only terms used by men for five generations of consanguineal kin, excluding affines. The Chinese terms appear in column 2 in phonemic linguistic notation. The terms can also be written using Chinese characters to represent each syllable. The linguistic transcription used here differs from pinyin, the official Chinese romanization of the Chinese language introduced in 1958, but it resembles the 1859 Wade-Giles system's use of numbers to represent tones. Column 1 describes the terms using the ab-

---

*joint family*    A large, Chinese extended family with several married sons.

*stem family*    A minimal extended Chinese family with one married son to carry on the patriline.

*reference*    A term that ego uses to refer to a relative when speaking about them indirectly, such as "He, that man over there, is my *father*."

*address*    A kinship term used by ego when speaking directly to a relative, such as "Hello, *father*."

breviated primary kin terms introduced in Chapter 2 (two new abbreviations are O, which means "older," and Y, which means "younger").

The formal components of Chinese kin terms are coded in the right-hand columns and are diagrammed in Figure 8.13. *Componential analysis* is a formal way of exploring the meaning of kinship terms that linguistic anthropologists have applied to diverse systems (see, e.g., Goodenough 1965 and Lounsbury 1964). A kinship terminological system is a *lexicon,* a list of words applied to an individual's relatives. They constitute a formal linguistic system because the meanings of different terms can be described according to a logical set of rules that may not be immediately apparent to the speaker of the language. These underlying rules are based on specific contrasts in meaning. In the Chinese kinship system, just five points of contrast, or components, are used to define the meaning of each kin term: descent, *collaterality,* generation, sex, and *relative age.* For example, the Chinese term *fu 4 thin 2,* "father," means a male, related lineally to ego through the male line, one generation above ego. In this case, relative age does not need additional linguistic coding because father must be older than ego. An advantage of componential analysis is that terms can be described without reference to primary terms, such that underlying common elements, which were not intuitively obvious, may be revealed.

The genealogical distribution of the kin terms are diagrammed in Figure 8.14, which is keyed to the kin term numbers used in Table 8.6. Close inspection shows the importance of the male descent line and relative age, which is a very ancient pattern in Chinese culture. For example, FB's children, numbers 8, 9, 10, 11, are terminologically distinguished from all other cousins because they could share surnames as members of ego's patrilineal descent group, the *tsu,* which existed during the Shang dynasty nearly 4000 BP. Cross-cousins were not distinguished from parallel cousins, and no cousins were typically considered marriageable. Mates would normally have different surnames and would be unrelated, probably even unacquainted.

FIGURE 8.13   *Formal components of Chinese kinship terminology.*

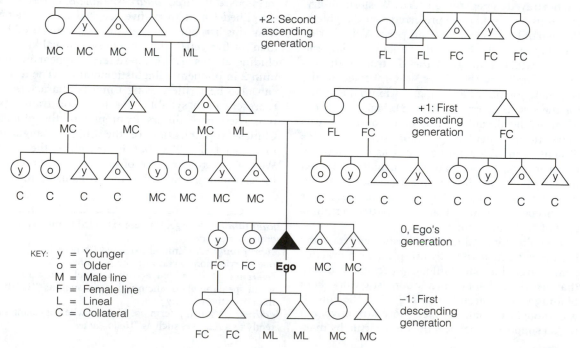

KEY:  y = Younger
      o = Older
      M = Male line
      F = Female line
      L = Lineal
      C = Collateral

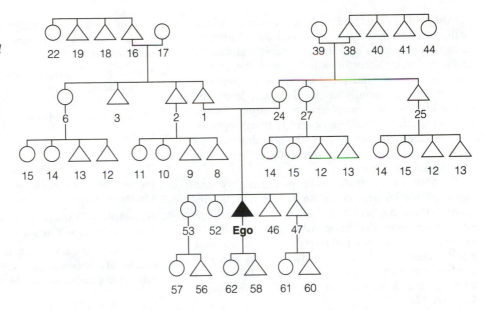

FIGURE 8.14
*Chinese kinship; the numbers here are keyed to those in Table 8.6.*

Older or younger age relative to ego is distinguished for everyone in ego's generation and for male siblings of ego's male lineal kin in higher generations. Concern with relative age reflects the increased ceremonial responsibilities of older siblings in carrying out the duties of *hsiao*, filial piety, and the preferential treatment that they might receive in many areas including inheritance.

*Lineal relatives,* who are ego's direct ancestors and descendants, are distinguished from all *collateral relatives,* who are off to the side. This distinction is important because it is lineal kin who must care for the elderly, play specific roles in mourning, and conduct ancestor rituals, all expressions of *hsiao*. Thus, an understanding of the meaning of Chinese kinship shows how important Chinese cultural patterns are acted out at the domestic level.

## SUMMARY

The Chinese Great Tradition began to develop some 7000 BP as a gradual transformation of the small-scale Neolithic farming cultures that had developed in the great river valleys of China 2000 years earlier. Their foraging ancestors can be traced to at least 15,000 BP in the same region. Many of the distinctive features of Chinese civilization were in place by the Shang dynasty, which began nearly 4000 BP and continued with only minor modifications until the last emperor was overthrown in 1911. Chinese civilization provides an important perspective on the debate over state origins because, in this case, control of religion by the political elite seems to have played a critical role in both the origin and long-term continuity of the state system. Chinese emperors were not deities,

*componental analysis* A form of linguistic analysis that sorts kinship terms into categories according to the different components of meaning that each term distinguishes.

*lexicon* A list of words.

*collaterality* A component of meaning in kinship systems that sorts kin terms into two categories: those that distinguish between collateral and lineal relatives and those that do not. For example, a term placing father and father's brother in the same category does not distinguish between lineals and collaterals.

*relative age* A distinction drawn between the younger and older of a pair of siblings.

*lineal relative* A relative who is one of ego's direct lineal ancestors, such as father and father's father, or a direct lineal descendant, such as son and son's son.

*collateral relative* A relative such as father's brother, who shares a common ancestor but is not a direct lineal ancestor.

but they ruled with the mandate of heaven, and the political order has been described as a liturgical government, based on moral authority backed by military force. Ancestor worship and the associated concept of filial piety were key elements in this system, especially at the domestic level; the entire ideology was expressed in a complex correlative cosmology based on complementary oppositions such as yin-yang and symbolism drawn from the five elements from colors, music, directions, and calendrical ritual.

Chinese agriculture was a gardening system powered by human labor on very small family farms, operating within a highly efficient village system that provided basic subsistence needs to a very large and dense rural population at a minimal energy cost. This labor-intensive system is a significant contrast to the industrial farming, fossil-fuel system described for the United States in Chapter 12.

Chinese culture tended to encourage large families and population growth, but the intensely hierarchical system kept living standards extremely low for most of the population. Chinese domestic life was structured around the patrilineage and extended family, which were dominated by men. The importance of men, relative age, and the patrilineage is demonstrated by a componential analysis of Chinese kinship terms.

## STUDY QUESTIONS

1. Identify, define, or discuss the following Chinese ideological concepts: Confucianism, Taoism, five classics, five elements, filial piety, *li*, mandate of heaven, august god, bad last emperor, sage king, yin-yang, stove god, ancestor tablet, and *kowtow*.

2. Discuss the following political concepts within the Chinese context: meritocracy, patrimonial, aristocracy, and gentry.

3. Discuss the following aspects of subsistence intensification using Chinese examples: multicropping, intertillage, permanent agriculture, labor intensive, capital intensive, and population density.

4. How does the Chinese state fit within the various theories of the origin of the state?

5. Discuss problems with the concepts of exploitation, immiseration, and Malthusian overpopulation, using Chinese material.

6. Discuss the role of ancestor worship as a central integrating device in Chinese culture.

7. Show how the components of descent line, relative age, lineal and collateral, sex, and generation are significant in Chinese kinship terminological systems.

## SUGGESTED READINGS

CHANG, KWANG-CHIH. 1986. *The Archaeology of Ancient China*, 4th ed. New Haven, Conn.: Yale University Press. An authoritative overview of Chinese prehistory.

ROPP, PAUL S. 1990. *Heritage of China: Contemporary Perspectives on Chinese Civilization*. Berkeley: University of California Press. An interdisciplinary collection of articles on China including such topics as Confucianism, the origin of Chinese civilization, and the development of government, economy, and family.

STOVER, LEON N., AND TAKEKO STOVER. 1976. *China: An Anthropological Perspective*. Pacific Palisades, Calif.: Goodyear. A wide-ranging analysis of Chinese culture.

WHEATLEY, PAUL. 1971. *The Pivot of the Four Quarters: A Preliminary Enquiry into the Origins and Character of the Ancient Chinese City*. Chicago: Aldine. Examines the physical organization of Chinese cities through time in relation to worldview and cosmology.

# 9

# GREAT TRADITIONS: HINDUISM AND ISLAM IN SOUTH ASIA

One-third of the contemporary world's people identify themselves as either Hindus or Muslims. These two Great Traditions arose independently more than 1000 BP (before the present) and are culturally distinct, but both are centered on formal religions with sacred texts. These religions provide charters for a hierarchically organized society and regulate the smallest details of daily life, including family structure, the relationships between men and women, and the food that people eat. Europeans, as members of the Christian Great Tradition, have been both fascinated and repulsed by Hindus and Muslims for centuries, but they have consistently misunderstood them. In this chapter, we focus on classical Hindu civilization, especially the relation between religion and society, and show how the ancient culture is reflected in modern India. The South Asian culture area is emphasized because it is the homeland of the Hindu Great Tradition and because Muslims and Hindus have coexisted here for 800 years. We will examine this area again in Chapter 13 in relation to contemporary issues of poverty and economic development.

## THE SOUTH ASIAN CULTURE AREA

### Languages of South Asia

The South Asian culture area covers modern Pakistan, India, Nepal, Bhutan, Bangladesh, Burma, and Sri Lanka. It is a complex mix of languages and culture types, with more than 1 billion people occupying an area less than two-thirds the size of the United States. South Asia is centered on the Indian subcontinent and is predominantly a Hindu and Muslim region, with important Buddhist elements as well as many coexisting small-scale cultures.

Most South Asian languages belong to one of three major language groups: Indo-European, Dravidian, and Sino-Tibetan (Figure 9.1). India alone recognizes fifteen official languages, including four of the twelve most populous languages in the world: English, Hindi, Urdu, and Bengali. Many other languages are spoken within the political boundaries of the country. The last three languages are members of the Indic branch of Indo-European, related to ancient Sanskrit, and are spoken by some 600 million people in the densely populated Indus Valley of Pakistan and the Gangetic Plain of India (Figure 9.2). Dravidian languages are spoken in southeastern India and Sri Lanka. They are presumed to have preceded the Indo-European languages in India and are spoken by many tribal groups (Figure 9.3). Sino-Tibetan languages are spoken in the Himalayan region, in Burma, and by many tribal peoples in extreme eastern India and Bangladesh.

The cultural Great Tradition that people identify with may be associated with a particular language. There are perhaps 60 million Buddhists in South Asia, primarily in India, Burma, and Sri Lanka, and some 200 million more in East Asia (Figure 9.4a). Buddhists are most likely to be speakers of Dravidian or Sino-Tibetan languages. Furthermore, many Dravidian and Sino-Tibetan peoples are tribal peoples who do not identify with any Great Tradition. The largest cultural group in

South Asia is composed of some 700 million Hindus centered in India, Bangladesh, and Nepal, who are primarily speakers of Indic languages. At its peak, the Hindu Great Tradition expanded into Southeast Asia as far as Java in what is now Indonesia (Figure 9.4). Approximately 300 million Muslims live in Pakistan, Bangladesh, and India. South Asian Muslims are predominantly speakers of Urdu and Bengali. There are more than 800 million Muslims worldwide, including some 170 million in Malaysia and Indonesia and more than 200 million in Africa and the Middle East (Figure 9.4c). The Islamic Great Tradition, although originated by speakers of Arabic, a Semitic language, is now practiced by more Indic speakers in South Asia than Arabic speakers in the Middle East. Furthermore, because not all Arab speakers are Muslim, the common stereotype that equates Muslim with Arab is misleading (compare Figures 9.4c and 9.4d).

FIGURE 9.1 *South Asian languages and geography.*

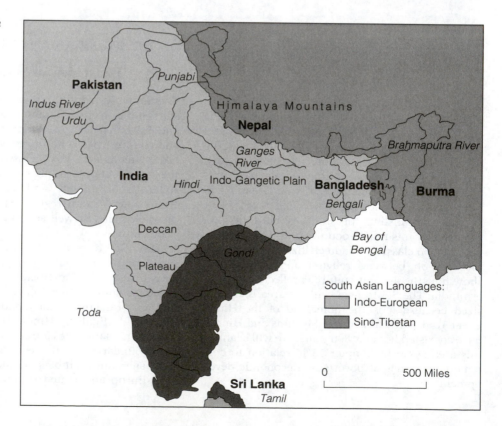

FIGURE 9.2  *Indic languages (Indo-Iranian branch, Indo-European). (SOURCE: Ruhlen 1987.)*

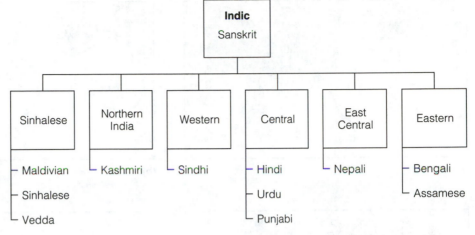

## South Asian Geography

The South Asian subcontinent (see figure 9.1) extends more than 2000 miles (3218 kilometers [km]) east to west and north to south, encompassing many sharply different environments. Because of this diverse expanse, cultures of very different scale have been able to interact with one another over the millennia while retaining their essential autonomy. South and central India lie within the tropics, whereas north India extends well into the temperate zones. Tropical rain forest is found along a narrow coastal strip of western India, Sri Lanka, and the hill tribe areas of Bangladesh, eastern India, and Burma. Much of southern India is an arid upland dominated by the *Deccan Plateau,* which is composed of vast tertiary basalt lava flows, perhaps formed when a giant meteor punched a hole in the earth's mantle. The Deccan region was not conducive to intensive agriculture and sheltered many Dravidian-speaking tribal peoples.

India is separated from China and Central Asia by the Himalayan–Hindu Kush mountains, which form the southern boundary of the vast Tibetan Plateau and contain the world's highest mountains and the largest permanent snowfields outside the polar regions. The 1500-mile (2414 km) east–west trend of the massive *Himalayan range* creates an enormous rain shadow to the north and funnels tropical monsoonal rainfall from Southeast Asia

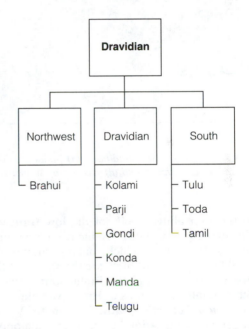

FIGURE 9.3  *Dravidian languages. (*SOURCE: *Ruhlen 1987.)*

---

***Deccan Plateau***  The interior of the Indian subcontinent south of the Indo-Gangetic Plain. Much of this area is over 2000 ft (610 m) in elevation and relatively dry.

***Himalayan Range***  A system of mountains between Tibet and the low Indo-Gangetic Plain. Contains many of the highest peaks in the world.

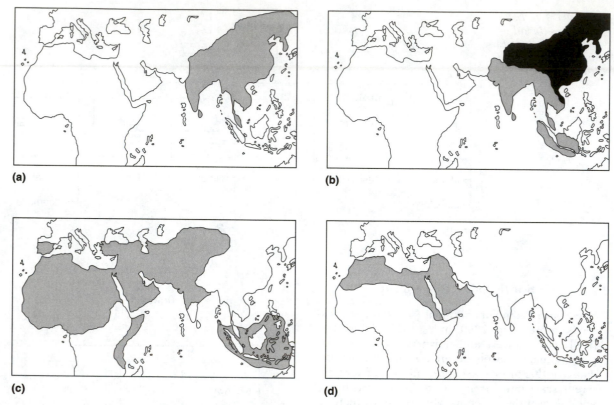

**FIGURE 9.4**    *Asian Great Traditions: (a) Buddhist, (b) Hindu (light screen) and Chinese (dark screen), (c) Islamic, and (d) speakers of Arabic.*

onto the rich alluvial soils of the low **Gangetic Plain,** making it a highly productive agricultural zone. The Himalayas, which contain many peaks over 20,000 ft (6096 m) high, are the source of the Indus, the Ganges, and the Brahmaputra rivers, which annually carry tons of Himalayan alluvium to the **Indo-Gangetic Plain.** The Indus Valley, where Indian civilization began, lies on the opposite end of the Iranian Plateau from Mesopotamia, which it ecologically resembles. The Indus Valley is an arid alluvial plain, bordered by mountains. The Indus, like the Euphrates, is a silt-laden, aggrading river, ideally suited to floodplain agriculture, yet frequently changing course.

Significant changes in the South Asian environment may have affected cultural development in ways that are still not understood. Changes in sea level and alluvial deposition on the floodplain have altered the area of prime agricultural lands. The Himalayas are still being pushed up by the northward-moving Indian continental plate colliding with the Eurasian plate, and this has happened rapidly enough to modify regional climate during the period of human occupation. In some areas of India since the Lower Paleolithic, the climate has been both wetter and drier than at present (Allchin and Allchin 1982).

## Early South Asian Prehistory

South Asia is not as well known archaeologically as the Near East, but cultural developments seem to have followed a closely similar pattern in both areas. The Lower Paleolithic is well represented by Acheulean hand axes and choppers found throughout India (Table 9.1). The Middle Paleo-

TABLE 9.1  *History and Prehistory of South Asia*

| | | |
|---|---|---|
| **British and Muslim India (1200–1947)** | 1818–1947 | British colony |
| | 1526–1761 | Mogul empire |
| | 1192–1526 | Early Muslim period |
| **Classic Hindu India (600 BC–AD 1200)** | AD 320–550 | Gupta empire |
| | 350–100 BC | Mauryan empire: Asokan edicts; writing; cities; Arthasastra, Dharma Sastra, Code of Manu compiled |
| | 540–468 | Mahavira, founder of Jainism |
| | 563–483 | Buddha (Siddhartha Gautama), founder of Buddhism |
| | 900–300 | Upanishads compiled |
| **Vedic India (1600–600 BC)** | 1000–600 | Early Iron Age |
| | 1000–800 | Brahmanas compiled |
| | 1500 | Indo-Aryan chiefdoms in Bramavarta; Rig-Veda Samhita compiled |
| | 1600 | Intrusion of Indo-European peoples |
| **Mature Indus Valley Civilization (2500–1500 BC)** | 2500–1500 | Harappan civilization; cities; writing; temples; trade |
| **State Formation (3500–2500 BC)** | 2800–2500 | Early Indus Valley Civilization: Incipient urbanism; regional interaction sphere; walled sites; cattle as religious icons |
| | 3500–2800 | Chalcolithic: Population expansion; increased use of copper |
| **Neolithic India (8000–5000 BC)** | 5000–3500 | Ceramic Neolithic: Mehrgarh painted pottery; copper beads; microlithic sickles; cotton |
| | 8000–5000 | Pre-Ceramic Neolithic: In Mehrgarh (Indus Valley)—permanent settlements; mud-brick architecture; grain storage; domesticates—wheat, barley, dates, cattle, water buffalo, sheep, goats; burials; figurines; long-distance trade in turquoise |
| **Mesolithic India (8000–12,000 BP)** | 8000–12,000 | Hunters, fishers, nomadic herders; possible domesticated sheep and goats in Hindu Kush valleys; microlithic tools |
| **Paleolithic India (17,000–1 million BP)** | 17,000–18,000 | Upper Paleolithic: Blade tools |
| | 25,000–200,000 | Middle Paleolithic: Flake tools; mobile foragers |
| | 200,000–1 million | Lower Paleolithic: Quartzite Acheulean hand axes and choppers |

SOURCE: Allchin and Allchin (1982) for prehistoric data.

lithic flake tools and Upper Paleolithic blade tools are also well represented. Archaeologists working in South Asia refer to cultures based on microlithic tools, foraging, fishing, and nomadic herding as Mesolithic. This adaptation began during the early Holocene about 12,000–8000 BP and continued in various parts of the subcontinent into the twentieth century. It is significant that this date for the earliest possible use of domestic animals corresponds to similar events in the Near East.

The South Asian Neolithic also goes through a pre-Ceramic phase of initial farming villages at about the same time as in the Near East (8000–5000 BC) and a full Ceramic Neolithic (5000–3500 BC), which includes paint decorated pottery. Be-

**Gangetic Plain**  A fertile alluvial plain in India and Bangladesh formed by the Ganges River and its tributaries. Receives high monsoonal rainfall and supports intensive agriculture and one of the world's densest populations.
**Indo-Gangetic Plain**  A vast alluvial lowland covering the northern part of the Indian subcontinent south of the Himalayas. Includes the Indus, Ganges, and Brahmaputra floodplains.

cause the earliest South Asian farming villages are known from the Indus region and the eastern edge of the Iranian Plateau in Baluchistan, especially the site of Mehrgarh, developments here were perhaps part of the same process that occurred in the Near East, especially given the similarities in ecological setting.

## Harappan Civilization: The Earliest South Asian State

After 3500 BC, the agricultural potential of the Indus floodplain began to be realized, and the settled population began to increase. Between 2800 and 2500 BC, small, walled urban sites appeared, and highly uniform ceramic styles over a wide area, together with further evidence of long-distance trade, indicates that a socioeconomic interaction sphere had developed. Over the next several centuries (approximately 2500–1500 BC), Harappan civilization flourished throughout the Indus region. This was the earliest state-level culture in South Asia.

*Harappa,* at the upper end of the Indus floodplain, and *Mohenjo-Daro,* in the lower, were major urban centers, both built according to a similar plan. Mohenjo-Daro may have had a population of 35,000 people. It contained an elevated brick-walled citadel with a great ritual bath, grain storehouses, and a probable temple. Near the citadel was a separate, lower, and much larger grid cluster of brick buildings, which were residences and workshops. Houses had bathrooms complete with drains that emptied into what appeared to be a public sewer system. The diversity of house plans and the presence of single-room barracks suggest differences in social class or wealth, but no royal tombs have been found and the Harappan elite remain anonymous.

The Harappans produced finely crafted utilitarian objects in bronze and copper, as well as jewelry and beads in gold, silver, and semiprecious stones. Because the floodplain lacked mineral resources, they maintained extensive trade contacts throughout India and as far as Central Asia and Mesopotamia. Standardized sets of weights and measures and numerous incised seals, resembling those from Mesopotamia but bearing unique Harappan markings, are further indications of the impor-

FIGURE 9.5    *An incised Harappan seal with undeciphered script.*

tance of trade (Figure 9.5). The Harappan language is unknown, and its unique writing system has never been successfully deciphered, but there does not seem to have been a developed literary tradition. Terra-cotta figurines and inscriptions of earth mothers, horned men, bulls, composite animals, and human-animals have been interpreted to be cult objects and forerunners of important Hindu deities such as Siva and Parvati. The Harappan civilization apparently collapsed completely around 1500 BC for reasons that are not well understood, as will be discussed in Chapter 10.

Sometime around 1600 BC, Indo-European speaking peoples apparently moved from the Iranian Plateau onto the Indus plains. These were the Aryans, who were probably seminomadic pastoral people, speaking an early form of Sanskrit, and organized in chiefdoms. These Aryans should *not* be confused with the imaginary north European "Aryan" superrace of Hitler's Nazi Germany and neo-Nazi racist political ideology. The Aryans of ancient Asia and the Neolithic settlers of Europe may well have had common ancestors in Southwest Asia some 8500 BP and belong to the Indo-European language family, but otherwise they were different peoples.

According to the religious hymns and verses preserved in the **Vedas,** especially the four Samhita Vedas compiled as oral texts between 1500 and 1000 BC, the Aryans of the Vedas were cattle herders and warriors who fought with the earlier, presumably Dravidian-speaking, peoples who they encountered. Some historians believe that the Aryans may have contributed to the collapse of the Harappan civilization, but this is difficult to establish. The Aryans settled initially in the Punjab and between the Indus and Ganges rivers, the region that was identified in the Vedic texts as Brahmavarta, the Aryan heartland. They then expanded steadily eastward into the fertile Gangetic Plain, such that by 600 BC they effectively occupied the entire region and were becoming increasingly sedentary and stratified. Over the next four centuries, classical Indian civilization became fully established, with cities, writing, states, empires, and the Great Traditions of Hinduism and Buddhism that continue to shape Indian culture to the present day (see Table 9.1).

## EARLY HINDU CIVILIZATION

### Origin of the Hindu State

A clear break seems to have occurred between the early Indus Valley civilization and the later Vedic–Hindu civilization centered on the Gangetic Plain. Pre-Aryan peoples, including members of the Harappan civilization, certainly contributed to what was, in effect, a second period of state formation, urbanization, and civilization in South Asia. The rise of early Hindu civilization between approximately 600 and 200 BC seems to have been primarily a political process that does not easily fit the Mesopotamian, Andean, or Chinese models of state origin examined previously. Hindu civilization developed after the Aryan invaders conquered the earlier small-scale residents of the Ganges region and incorporated them into larger-scale centralized polities, which then began to war against one another. Because the Ganges, as an incised river, was a difficult source of irrigation water, early Gangetic states were not hydraulic societies. Furthermore, because significant increases in population density took place only after political centralization, neither population pressure nor environmental circumscription could have been important causes of state formation. However, because Hindu civilization incorporated some elements of Harappan civilization and may also have been indirectly stimulated by contacts with Mesopotamian and Persian civilizations, it should not be considered an example of strictly pristine state development.

In his investigation of the development of Indian civilization, archaeologist George Erdosy (1988) focused on urbanization in the central Ganges region, following the approach that Henry Wright (1969) and Gregory Alan Johnson (1973) used with early Mesopotamian civilization. Erdosy defines cities as "the containers of those institutions that are required for the maintenance of increasingly complex and inegalitarian societies" (1988:5).

Small-scale societies did not need cities because small villages were self-regulating. Cities were places where the instruments of social control could themselves be developed and controlled, such that their appearance signals the arrival of state-level organization.

Erdosy (1988) surveyed settlement patterns at intervals covering the period from 1000 BC to AD 300, looking for changes in the size, distribution, and function of settlements that might serve as clues to changes in cultural complexity. During the first 400 years up to 600 BC, only two types of settlements could be distinguished: numerous small villages of perhaps 275 people and a small center of perhaps 1600 people, which was in a position to control the flow of imported mineral resources. Even in the absence of clear archaeological evidence of rank, this two-level settlement hierarchy

---

**Harappa**   The archaeological site of an ancient city associated with Harappan civilization, located in the upper Indus Valley approximately 4000 BP.

**Mohenjo-Daro**   The archaeological site of an ancient city associated with Harappan civilization, located in the lower Indus Valley approximately 4000 BP.

**Vedas**   Sacred texts of the Aryans, covering hymns, rituals, and esoteric knowledge. Assumed to be based on supernatural revelations and dating to approximately 3500 BP. Includes the Rig-Veda, Sama-Veda, Atharva-Veda, and Yajur-Veda.

suggests that simple chiefdoms existed at this time on the Ganges Plain (Figure 9.6a), but the institutions of social control must have been primarily religious and relatively unspecialized.

After 600 BC, an obvious change in political organization occurred, perhaps as high-ranking Aryans sought to enhance their control in the region. A functionally diversified, four-level settlement hierarchy emerged, clearly indicating the emergence of the state (see Figure 9.6b). The largest settlement within the study area became a small fortified city of perhaps 8000 people. It contained material evidence of formal administrative, economic, and religious functions, in the form of coins, beads, sculptures, and iron slag. After 350 BC, the Ganges Valley settlement hierarchy, as archaeologically detected, successively revealed the presence of the kingdoms and empires of early classic Hindu civilization, which have also left their own historic record.

### Kautilya's Hindu Kingdom: An Emic Political Model, 250 BC

The ideal organization of the early Hindu state is precisely detailed in Kautilya's *Arthasastra,* a written manual on ancient Indian statecraft. The Arthasastra is attributed to Kautilya, a minister in the Mauryan empire in 250 BC but was probably written by several people in the early centuries AD. It is a composite treatise on political science for kings and aspiring kings, written with candor, cynicism, and insight. As a manual for public administrators, it resembles the Confucian classics, but instead of professional ethics and ritual, the Arthasastra advocates the use of coercive power backed by the army, the police, the courts, and covert state security agents. The Arthasastra may be taken as a portrayal of the ideal structure and function of a hypothetical Indian kingdom during the early centuries of classic Hindu civilization. As an emic view, composed by elite political professionals, it may not be an accurate picture of any specific kingdom, and the ideal rules may not have been followed. However, the general system as described is probably valid and provides a useful model for comparison with the organization of small-scale tribes and other state systems.

The Arthasastra offers insider views on the use of state power for the king's personal advantage. It is filled with practical advice on palace intrigue—complete with how-to-do-it examples of the use of spies, sex, poison, and deception for political assassination—and to test the loyalty of government officials. In the Arthasastra, religion was simply another self-conscious tool of statecraft. Kings were advised to use rituals and pilgrimages as excuses to raise revenue. It was even proposed that

FIGURE 9.6    *Settlement patterns, Ganges Plain: (a) chiefdoms (1000–600 BC) and (b) early states (600–350 BC).*

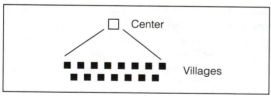

**(a)**

1 center = 1,600
15 villages of 275 = 4,125
    5,725 people

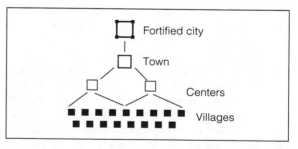

**(b)**

1 fortified city = 8,000
1 town = 1,920
2 centers of 1000 = 2,000
17 villages of 240 = 4,060
    16,000 people

FIGURE 9.7 *Settlement hierarchy within a Hindu kingdom, 250 BC. (SOURCE: Shamasastry 1960 [Arthasastra].)*

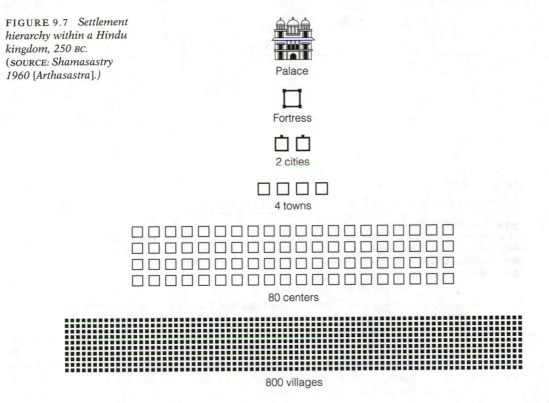

Palace

Fortress

2 cities

4 towns

80 centers

800 villages

omens, such as spirits speaking in trees, be deliberately staged in order to stir up fear so that people would increase their religious donations.

The difference between political leaders in Indian kingdoms such as this and tribal leaders who might also use deception and treachery to personal advantage was simply that small-scale cultures limited political power. Tribal leaders did not have standing armies, police forces, and secret agents at their disposal. They could not personally control the availability of basic subsistence goods to thousands of households. Tribal peoples feared and avoided those who abused their limited powers and thereby denied them control. Peasant villagers living in a world of rival kingdoms were pawns for the ruling kings, who tried to keep the levy just below the point at which disaffected villagers would join an enemy kingdom.

In 500 BC, there were some eighteen large kingdoms in northern India centered on the Gangetic Plain (Erdosy 1988). According to the Arthasastra, an ideally organized kingdom would have been di-

vided into four districts, each containing 800 villages dominated by a fortified city, with smaller cities, towns, and centers hierarchically arranged to facilitate administration and the flow of revenue. The government officials in two cities would have administrative responsibility for 400 villages each, officials in four towns would control 200 villages each, and some eighty local centers would each be responsible for very specific census taking, tax collecting, and police work in 10 villages within the district (Figure 9.7). Such an arrangement closely corresponds to the archaeological record, and combining Erdosy's population estimates based on site size (160 persons/2.5 acres [1 hectare]) with the Arthasastra model, the demographic parameters of a hypothetical Indian kingdom can be reconstructed (Table 9.2). These esti-

*Arthasastra* A text on statecraft from the classical period of Hindu civilization, detailing how the king could use political power to personal advantage.

TABLE 9.2    *Population of Model Hindu Kingdom, 350 BC*

| Per district | | Population in Each* | *Total* |
|---|---|---|---|
| 1 | Fortified city | 20,000 | 20,000 |
| 2 | Cities | 3,500 | 7,000 |
| 4 | Towns | 2,000 | 8,000 |
| 80 | Centers | 1,000 | 80,000 |
| 800 | Villages | 350 | 280,000 |
| *Total* district population | | | 395,000 |

| | | |
|---|---|---|
| 4 Districts | = | 1,580,000 |
| Capital city | = | 35,000 |
| Kingdom *Total* | = | 1,615,000 |

Urban population (cities over 2000 people) = 143,000 (8.8%)

SOURCES: Erdosy (1988) and Kautilya's Arthasastra (Shamasastry 1960).
*The Arthasastra states that villages ranged in size from 100 to 500 families. Erdosy estimates 3.5 persons per family and average villages of 240 people, assuming 160 people per hectare of archaeological site. Thus, villages of 350 people represent the lower range for the Arthasastra figures but are higher than predicted archaeologically.

mates suggest that a kingdom might have contained some 1.6 million people, with perhaps 143,000 people, 9 percent of the total population, living in cities of more than 2000 people.

A kingdom of 1.6 million people would have been much more amenable to management by direct political power than the 50 to 500 million people living in the vast Chinese empire. Traditional China and India make an interesting comparison because they are both preindustrial, agrarian-based civilizations, yet there were significant cultural differences. As shown in Chapter 8, China relied primarily on ethical principles, ritual, moral authority, and patrilineal descent groups to maintain social order. Hindu India, in contrast, used the moral authority of religion to support an endogamous caste system and relied on coercive political authority to a significant degree.

The most critical difference between India and China was probably total population size. There are no reliable census figures for ancient India, but the first British census of 1872 listed only 238 million people for all of India, while the population of China at that time exceeded 400 million people. More important, empires during the classic period of Hindu civilization were relatively short-lived, and the most permanent political unit was the small kingdom, which formed a relatively autonomous cultural system. All eighteen kingdoms of

the Gangetic Plain probably combined into an unstable empire of less than 30 million people.

The territory of an Indian kingdom was also relatively small. The total population of 1.6 million people, in theory, could have been supported by a minimum of 3991 mi$^2$ (10,336 km$^2$) of cultivated land, if we accept Erdosy's rough calculations that Indians consumed the caloric equivalent of 508 lb (230 kilograms [kg]) of grain per person per year and produced 795 lb/2.5 acres/year (360 kg/hectare/year), so that each person required 1.6 acres (.64 hectare) of cultivated land. However, the actual territory must have been much larger because the Arthasastra states that each village had a territory extending 1.2–2.5 miles (2–4 km) from the village. This extra land would have provided for pasture and forests and allowed for less intensive farming.

If village territories are assumed to have been hexagonal with sides averaging 1.7 miles (3 km), each territory would have contained approximately 8.9 mi$^2$ (23 km$^2$), which would yield a total village territory of 28,417 mi$^2$ (73,600 km$^2$). Farmers living in larger settlements might have used another 6287 mi$^2$ (16,284 km$^2$). Such a kingdom might have contained a total territory of approximately 34,749 mi$^2$ (90,000 km$^2$), 186 miles (300 km) on a side. In comparison, the 500 million people of the Chinese empire at its height were spread over a territory 1865 miles (3000 km) on a side. It is not surprising that Chinese civilization came to rely so heavily on moral authority.

The approximate social composition of a hypothetical Hindu kingdom is shown in Table 9.3, which suggests that a surprisingly small elite group maintained absolute power. Most of the population, probably about 85 percent, lived in farm households, which supplied basic subsistence for the other 15 percent. State-supported craft specialists did produce consumer goods for the villagers, but much of their production directly supported the state.

The Arthasastra gives a detailed picture of the revenue system and basic administrative structure of the Hindu kingdom. State-controlled wealth was concentrated in the capital and district fortresses. An underground royal treasury vault contained gold, jewelry, coins, and precious textiles. Special storehouses held grain and other products that were collected as taxes in kind or produced on crown land. Farmers paid an average grain tax of 16 percent, which was raised to 25 to 33 percent under emergency conditions. There were also village taxes, temple taxes, gate taxes, sales taxes, income taxes, tolls, fines, and excise taxes of various sorts. Some villagers submitted to corvée labor or military inscription in place of the grain tax.

Although there were no vast canal systems or irrigation works in ancient India, large armies were mobilized for frequent wars, and royal construction projects and defensive works required large labor forces. For example, Erdosy (1988) estimates that construction of the 49-ft (15-m)-tall earthen ramparts stretching for 3.7 miles (6 km) around one fortified city would have engaged 20,000 workmen for 250 days.

The state regulated commercial activities, mining, forestry, herding, and craft production, in order to extract the maximum feasible revenue (Figure 9.8). Even prostitutes were licensed and paid a monthly income tax. The supply of marketable consumer goods was centrally controlled. Only the Brahmans, who formed the religious elite, frontier villages, and state-supported colonization projects were exempt from taxes. A collector general attached to the royal palace was responsible for all revenue collection received from district and village tax collectors. There was also a high-ranking tax commissioner and a tax inspector, who used covert means to monitor the flow of revenue. Detailed bookkeeping was carried out at all levels, and all government expenses were further monitored by the central accounts office.

Many diverse functions were carried out in the fortified city, especially if it was also the capital. As described in the Arthasastra, the city was divided into twelve major sections, where specific categories of people were expected to live and where spe-

TABLE 9.3  *Estimated Population of Social Groups Within Model Hindu Kingdom, 350 BC*

|  | Salaried Elite | State Workers | Farm Workers | *Total* |
|---|---|---|---|---|
| **Capital** | 175 | 33,425 | 1,400 | 35,000 |
| **Fortresses** | 350 | 74,050 | 5,600 | 80,000 |
| **Cities** | 140 | 22,260 | 5,600 | 28,000 |
| **Towns** | 50 | 20,750 | 11,200 | 32,000 |
| **Centers** | — | 96,000 | 224,000 | 320,000 |
| **Villages** | — | — | 1,120,000 | 1,120,000 |
| *Total* | 715 | 246,485 | 1,367,800 | 1,615,000 |

NOTES: Salaried elites are palace officials and high-ranking government administrators receiving salaries of 1000 pana or more. State workers include all lower-level salaried officials, state-supported specialists, retainers, and merchants who pay taxes in cash. It is assumed that the capital and fortress cities each include the equivalent farm workers of four villages and smaller settlements include the equivalent of two villages each. All figures include all family members.

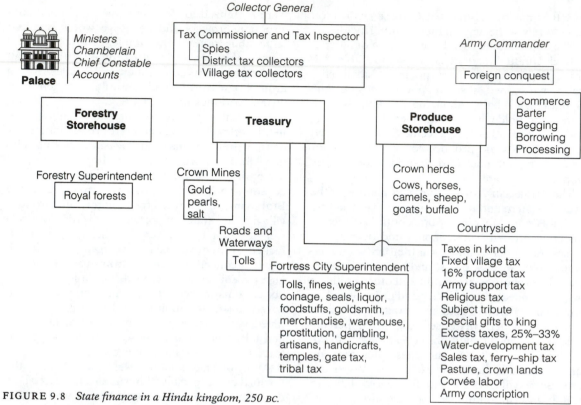

FIGURE 9.8  *State finance in a Hindu kingdom, 250 BC.*

cific activities and buildings were to be located (Figure 9.9). Each of the four **varnas,** or "colors," representing the four ranks of Hindu society—**Brahman, Kshatriya, Vaisya,** and **Sudra**—were assigned specific quarters within the city, grouped together with appropriately ranked economic activities. These social categories will be discussed in more detail in the later section dealing with caste.

The *varnas* were the early form of the **caste** system. During this early period of Hindu civilization, they were already associated with endogamy, relative purity, and occupation. For example, the Sudra, in the lowest-ranked *varna,* were assigned to the city's west quarter where leather working, an especially polluting activity, was carried out. The royal palace occupied one-ninth of the city and was to be located just north of city center, opening onto the sections occupied by Brahmans, jewelers, and the royal deity. Merchants and high-ranking specialist artisans were located in the west quarter

together with government ministers and the Kshatriya.

## Law in the Hindu Kingdom

The legal system in the Hindu kingdom upheld the authority of the state and the *varna* social system, which gave ritual priority and economic advantage to the upper ranks. Furthermore, fines imposed by the court were a source of state revenue and enforced the tax system. Law was based on tradition, or customary law, and on **dharma,** or sacred religious law, which resembled *li* in the Chinese system. Both dharma and *li* referred to duty, morality, and proper conduct; however, where *li* emphasized duty to emperor, ancestors, and family, dharma laid out different moral requirements for each *varna* and for individuals at different stages of the life cycle. Furthermore, the Hindu king was much more clearly a political ruler.

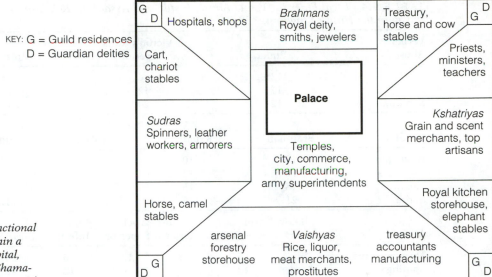

KEY: G = Guild residences
D = Guardian deities

G D | Hospitals, shops
Cart, chariot stables
Sudras Spinners, leather workers, armorers
Horse, camel stables

Brahmans Royal deity, smiths, jewelers
**Palace**
Temples, city, commerce, manufacturing, army superintendents

arsenal forestry storehouse
Vaishyas Rice, liquor, meat merchants, prostitutes
treasury accountants manufacturing

Treasury, horse and cow stables D G
Priests, ministers, teachers
Kshatriyas Grain and scent merchants, top artisans
Royal kitchen storehouse, elephant stables

G D

FIGURE 9.9 *Functional diversification within a fortified Hindu capital, 250 BC. (SOURCE: Shamasastry 1960 [Arthasastra].)*

All law in the Hindu kingdom was ultimately vested in the king, who was assisted by his political ministers and priestly authorities on dharma. According to the secular authors of the Arthasastra, the king's traditional law had legal priority over dharma, and the king was expected to use the state's power and physical punishment to "maintain both this world and the next" (Shamasastry 1960 [Bk. 3, chap. 1]).

Laws were explicitly designed to support the *varna* system and provided a quantified measure of the relative worth of each rank. For example, one could be fined for causing a Brahman to violate one of his food taboos, and a Sudra was to be burned alive for committing adultery with a Brahman woman. Brahmans were, in general, immune from taxes, fines, and punishments. The fine for selling a Brahman child into slavery was four times as severe as when the victim was a Sudra. The sons of a Brahman woman were to inherit four shares of their Brahman father's estate, but only one share if their mother was a Sudra. Twenty-four different terms existed to describe the conditions of birth according to the *varna* of the parents. Stanley Tambiah (1985) demonstrates that the caste system itself was generated by the legal classification and rank ordering of all the log-

ically possible types of marriage between people in different *varna* categories.

There was a broad three-level scale for fines in pana, the basic monetary unit, ranging from under 100 to 1000 pana. According to the government's salary scale, the highest officials were paid 24,000–48,000 pana a year, midrange officials earned 1000–12,000 pana, and the lowest retainers earned just 60 pana. Those unable to pay fines could substitute an equal number of lashes or body parts ac-

---

*varna*   The original four ranks, or "colors," of Aryan society: Brahman, Kshatriya, Vaisya, and Sudra.
**Brahman**   The highest-ranked *varna*, sprung from the mouth of Lord Brahman and assigned the roles of priests, teachers, sacrificers, and receivers of gifts.
*Kshatriya*   The second-ranked *varna*, sprung from the arms of Lord Brahman and assigned the roles of rulers and warriors.
*Sudra*   The lowest-ranked *varna*, sprung from the feet of Lord Brahman and assigned the role of servant to the other three *varnas*.
*caste*   An endogamous, ranked, occupationally defined group, known as *jati* in India.
*dharma*   Hindu religious law, or duty, based on the sacred Vedic texts and classical myths.

TABLE 9.4   *Legal Fines for Verbal Abuse, Insult, and Assault in Relation to Varna in the Hindu Kingdom, 350 BC*

| Verbal Abuse | | Victim's Rank | |
|---|---|---|---|
| | Equal | Superior | Inferior |
| Valid | 12+ | 6 | .5 |
| False | 12+ | 12 | 3 |
| Sarcasm | 12+ | 24 | 6 |

| Insultor | | Victim's Rank | | |
|---|---|---|---|---|
| | Brahman | Kshatriya | Vaisya | Sudra |
| Brahman | 12 | 10 | 8 | 6 |
| Kshatriya | 15 | 12 | 10 | 8 |
| Vaisya | 18 | 15 | 12 | 10 |
| Sudra | 21 | 18 | 15 | 12 |

| Assault | Below Navel* | | Above Navel | | Head | |
|---|---|---|---|---|---|---|
| | Inferior† | Superior† | Inferior | Superior | Inferior | Superior |
| Throwing mud | .5 | 6 | 3 | 12 | 6 | 24 |
| Spitting | 3 | 12 | 6 | 24 | 12 | 48 |
| Throwing feces | 6 | 24 | 12 | 48 | 24 | 96 |

SOURCE: Shamasastry (1960 [Arthasastra]).
*Target.
†Rank.

cording to a scale of equivalent values. A thumb was worth 54 pana; a right hand, 400 pana; and both eyes, 800 pana.

Verbal abuse or insults were scaled according to whether they were true, false, or sarcastic. For example, if you called a blind man "blind," that would be true abuse, but to tell a blind man that he had beautiful eyes would be false abuse. Generally, the fine was doubled if the victim was in a superior *varna* and halved if the victim was inferior (Table 9.4). More precise rank distinctions could also be made for if one's profession was insulted, with the severity of the fine increasing by three for each increase in the victim's relative rank and decreasing by two for lower-level ranks.

The legal severity of physical assault was measured along a graduated scale of violence reminiscent of that described for Amazonia because both considered the objects used and the body areas struck. The Hindu scale added relative rank. Throwing mud on a low-rank person's feet was a minor offense (.5 pana), whereas throwing feces on a high-ranking person's face was a very serious offense (96 pana). Extreme differences in rank

were the most serious. While striking with a hand or leg was normally a moderate offense, the Arthasastra declared "that limb of a Shudra with which he strikes a Brahmin shall be cut off" (Shamasastry 1960 [Bk. 3, chap. 19]).

To convince people of the "omniscient power of the state," the Arthasastra advocated routine use of undercover agents, entrapment, arrest on suspicion, torture to elicit confessions, severe punishment, and public display of criminals. Workers who failed to produce on time or fled their shops were fined. Theft of a minor commodity from a home or shop would be punished with public humiliation; but if an object of one-fourth the value were stolen from the government, it could bring banishment. Taking any government property worth more than 8 pana, spreading rumors, letting out prisoners, or unauthorized use of government documents could mean death. Beheading was reserved for those caught stealing government gems or rustling cattle. Insulting the king was punished by cutting out the criminal's tongue. The severest punishment, burning alive, was reserved for those creating dissatisfaction in the countryside.

# HINDU IDEOLOGY, SOCIETY, AND CULTURE

## Caste and Orthodox Hinduism: The Brahman View of Dharma

Hindu civilization is most widely known for the caste system with its emphasis on hierarchy and ritual *purity* and pollution, which continues to be a major fact of life in India. The caste system assumed its basic form in the Hindu kingdoms during the last centuries BC, as described in the preceding sections. The term *caste* is an English version of the Spanish and Portuguese word *casta,* meaning "race," "breed," or "family." The corresponding Indian term is *jati,* "birth" or "breed," which emphasizes that caste membership is assigned by birth; each caste is ideally an endogamous group. At its most general level, caste has been defined as a society "made up of birth-ascribed groups which are hierarchically ordered and culturally distinct. The hierarchy entails differential evaluation, rewards, and association" (Berreman 1979:73).

By this definition, caste could also describe race relations in the United States in the 1950s and the positions of blacksmiths in East Africa, as well as the Hindu case. French anthropologist Louis Dumont (1970) takes a more intellectualist approach, describing Indian caste is an ideological system of categories based on (1) hierarchically ordered social groups, (2) detailed rules of separation, and (3) a division of labor. The four *varna*—Brahman, Kshatriya, Vaisya, and Sudra—can be considered the most general castes, but castes are continuously segmented into many localized subcastes, which form finely ranked regional systems. The members of subcastes claim descent from a common founder and identify an original group specialty, such as herding, farming, blacksmithing, or weaving, even though it may not always be practiced.

Claude Lévi-Strauss (1966) offers an interesting structuralist comparison of caste and totemic clan as logically opposite systems. He points out that castes treat occupational differences as if they were natural. They exchange manufactured products and services between culturally created interdependent groups. This allows them to retain women within the endogamous caste. In contrast, exogamous totemic clans are based on the cultural myth that women are "naturally" different "species" who are therefore exchanged between social groups that are otherwise functionally the same. Clans lack an economic division of labor but nevertheless create a cultural basis for interdependence through exogamy. Lévi-Strauss condenses his comparison in the superficially enigmatic statement: "Castes naturalize a true culture falsely, totemic groups culturalize a false nature truly" (1966:127).

Caste organization and related concepts of ritual purity have a significant bearing on details of Hindu marriage and family life. Caste endogamy, the requirement that one marry within the caste, helps define caste boundaries, but subcastes are often further subdivided into exogamous lineages and clans. Marriage between different subcastes is often characterized by *hypergamy,* in which low-rank women marry equal- or higher-ranked men. This practice may severely limit choices for women in high-ranked subcastes, while down-marrying men (*hypogamy*) are unlikely to experience difficulty.

Marriage is one of the most important Hindu rituals. It involves great expenditure by the bride's family and is surrounded with extreme concern for ritual purity and status. Normally, all marriages are arranged by the families of the prospective bride and groom. Chastity is a ritual requirement, especially for the highest castes, and was related to infant marriage, prohibition on divorce and widow remarriage, and the practice of *sati,* widow self-immolation, in which a "virtuous woman" threw herself on her husband's funeral pyre to be transformed into a goddess. Many of these prac-

---

*purity*  Ritually superior status; a category in logical opposition to impurity.

*jati*  Caste in India; a ranked, endogamous group associated with a particular occupation.

*hypergamy*  Marriage to someone of higher rank. For example, Hindu women may marry men of a higher subcaste.

*hypogamy*  Marriage to someone of lower rank.

*sati*  The Hindu practice in which a woman burns herself to death on her husband's funeral pyre as a demonstration of her virtue.

tices were followed only by the strictest Brahman subcastes who were surrounded by the severest requirements for ritual purity. It must also be stressed that marriages did not always conform to the expected patterns, but when they didn't, a loss of ritual status could occur.

Dumont (1970) maintains that the three basic aspects of caste—hierarchy, separation, and division of labor—can all be reduced to the single principle of the opposition of pure and impure. The pure are defined as superior, and impure castes are impure because of their association with impure occupational specialties. ***Impurity*** for Hindus means a loss of status and is caused by association with "polluting" organic products and biological events such as birth, puberty, menses, and death. In tribal societies, such events may put individuals temporarily at supernatural risk, but Hindu ideology permanently associates particular social groups with impure biological events or organic products. The Hindu system is a logical reversal of the practice common in chiefdoms: The chief is considered to be endowed with sacred power (*mana*), which makes him dangerously *tabu* to lower-ranked individuals, but in India it is lower-ranked individuals who endanger higher ranks.

The mythical charter for caste is found in the purusha myth, an account of creation contained in the Dharma Sastra of Manu (Buhler 1886, Burnell and Hopkins 1884; see also the box "The *Purusha* Myth" box), which relates that Lord Brahma, the creator god, "for the prosperity of the worlds" created the four *varnas*—Brahman, Kshatriya, Vaisya, and Sudra—from his mouth, arms, thigh, and feet, respectively (Manu 1:31). Separate duties were assigned by the creator to each *varna*. The Brahmans (Figure 9.10) were the "Lords of Creation" and the perpetual incarnation of dharma (sacred law). They were the priests, teachers, sacrificers, and receivers of gifts, who, because of their "superiority and eminence of birth," were entitled to "whatever exists in the universe" (Manu 1:88–100). The Kshatriya were to be protectors of the people and took political roles as rulers and warriors. The Vaisya were responsible for cattle herding, farming, and trade. The Sudra were to serve the top three *varnas*, "without grudging." Similarly, only the top three were allowed to participate in a series of initiation rites that allowed them to be considered "twice born," and only the twice born could request the Brahman priests to perform sacrifices.

There are thousands of castes throughout modern India and many different ways of grouping and ranking them. It is common, particularly in census taking, to group them by the *varna* ranks, but caste clusters, castes, and subcastes can be dis-

---

## The Purusha Myth: A Mythic Charter for Varna and Caste

"But in order to protect this universe, He, the most resplendent one, assigned separate (duties and) occupations to those who sprang from his mouth, arms, thighs, and feet.

*To Brahmans he assigned teaching and studying (the Veda), sacrificing for their own benefit and for others, giving and accepting (of alms).*

*The Kshatriya he commanded to protect the people, to bestow gifts, to offer sacrifices, to study (the Veda), and to abstain from attaching himself to sensual pleasures.*

*The Vaisya to tend cattle, to bestow gifts, to offer sacrifices, to study (the Veda), to trade, to lend money, and to cultivate land.*

*One occupation only the lord prescribed to the Sudra, to serve meekly even these (other) three castes."*

SOURCE: Buhler (1886 [Manu 1:87–91]).

FIGURE 9.10 *A high-caste Brahman priest studying a sacred text.*

tinguished. Caste membership may be defined in a very general way by occupational specialty and endogamy, but food rules are also very important. Certain caste groups are distinguished by strict vegetarianism, avoidance of domestic pork and fowl, abstinence from alcohol, or the eating of pork or beef. At the village level, caste membership is also defined by the ***commensal hierarchy,*** according to which castes give or accept specific categories of food or water from one another or who smoke together (Mayer 1970). Accepting food implies either ritual equality or inferiority on the part of the receiving caste; thus, Brahmans may typically give food to all other castes but can accept it only from other Brahman-level castes. The commensal hierarchy would be displayed at any social gathering such as a wedding, where feasting occurred. Food restrictions are applied to food preparation, serving, eating arrangements, and who could enter a kitchen. The most common foods cooked in water, such as rice, are highly restricted, whereas rich foods cooked in clarified butter (*ghee*) and served on special occasions may be shared more widely between different castes.

The most extreme form of pollution could be transmitted by mere physical contact. This kind of impurity applied to the lowest caste, who Westerners called ***untouchables*** because any contact with such persons required some form of ritual purification such as sprinkling with water. In India untouchables are sometimes called Harijans, or "God's children," or "exterior castes." They are exterior because they are often excluded from many public activities due to their ritual disabilities. Untouchability was officially declared illegal by the Indian constitution of 1949 and by Pakistan's constitution of 1953, but it continues to be an important social phenomenon.

---

**impurity**  Low ritual status attributed to association or contact with polluting biological events or products.
**commensal hierarchy**  The differential giving and receiving of food between individuals, used as a demonstration of group rank. Recipients are equal to or higher than givers.
**untouchable**  The most ritually impure caste group, whose members pollute higher-caste members by any form of contact.

## Village-Level Caste and Exploitation

In 1954–1956, anthropologist Adrian Mayer (1970) studied caste relations in the village of Ramkheri in the Malwa district of Madhya Pradesh in central India. Ramkheri was a relatively large village with 912 people belonging to twenty-seven different castes. The castes were grouped by mutual consent into five groups and eleven ranks, with the Brahmans at the top and five untouchable castes at the bottom. Groups of castes at a similar rank tended to be localized in distinct quarters of the village. An interdependent division of labor, called the *jajmani system*, operated between the castes, with certain castes such as the barber, carpenter, blacksmith, potter, tanner-shoemaker, and sweeper castes providing communitywide services. For example, the sweeper caste was responsible for cleaning latrines and disposing of dead animals—highly polluting functions that benefited everyone. In exchange for their services, caste members received foodstuffs according to a regular schedule. Some caste members, such as farmers and tailors who sold their products in town, were paid in cash for their goods by their fellow villagers.

All castes could draw water from the village well except the Harijan, who used their own individual wells and even washed clothes and bathed at a separate place in the stream. The Harijan were expected to avoid the village temple and stood in the background during community meetings.

In the case of Ramkheri, the caste system had obvious implications for social stratification. Mayer (1970) found that the high-caste individuals owned more and tended to be more prosperous than low-caste people. However, wealth differences were not extreme and were partly attributed to expectations about their relative occupational abilities. The economic advantages enjoyed by the upper castes were to some extent offset by the mutual advantages provided by the caste division of labor, and people appeared to accept their traditional occupations as a religious duty. Basic Hindu beliefs in *karma* and reincarnation support such acceptance by implying that one's karma (deeds or action) in life reflects previous existences and shapes one's future lives. The next life might be more pleasant.

Researchers in other areas describe more extreme wealth inequities between castes. For example, Gerald Berreman (1979), who worked in the Himalayan foothills of Uttar Pradesh in 1957–1958, found that the Rajput and Brahmans enjoyed what M. N. Srinivas (1959) called "decisive dominance" in the region. At the district level, Brahmans and Rajput castes were not only the most numerous but also, politically and economically, the most powerful groups. The artisan castes were a small minority who were effectively dependent on and exploited by the higher castes. Jonathan Parry (1979), who worked in the Kangra district of Himachal Pradesh in 1966–1968, also found that the highest castes received the best educations, owned most of the land, and held the best jobs.

The conspicuous inequality inherent in the caste system has led Western observers to focus on its economic component and to see caste as an exaggerated form of social stratification and rank, perhaps designed by the Brahmans for their own benefit. Dumont (1970) acknowledges that there is an important material dimension to caste but argues that exclusive emphasis on this aspect is ethnocentric and obscures the native view in which caste forms a rational intellectual system. Dumont argues that it is most useful to examine caste as a "state of mind." He does not claim that mental facts cause the caste system, rather they make it intelligible.

British anthropologist J. H. Hutton, in his classic study of caste (1963), identified the functionalist advantages of caste at several levels. He argues that it provided the individual employment, a pattern for living, and personal security. The individual castes also function as self-reproducing corporate groups. They provide for themselves many services that the state might otherwise be required to supply. Hutton further argues that the caste system contributes to Indian national stability by creating a "plural society" capable of absorbing diverse groups into a single cohesive whole. Hutton is also critical of the inequities of caste—especially the disadvantages that women suffered under it—but as a functionalist, he cautiously concludes that it was too central to Hindu culture for reform-minded government administrators to attack directly.

The Hindu caste system is an extreme form of

institutionalized inequality, which as Berreman (1979:5) argues, arose in the process of state building by the Aryan invaders of India. Many castes are historically known to have been distinct tribal groups that were absorbed into expanding Hindu kingdoms. In the process, the hierarchical ranking of kin within tribal societies was replaced by the hierarchical ranking of castes within the state system, which was actually an incipient form of social stratification. The new ranking system helped secure the advantageous position of the political elites by making the former tribal groups dependent and divided against themselves.

Regardless of how it may be described in intellectualist or functionalist terms or how it may be understood emically, the caste system is a form of oppression and exploitation that benefits certain elite groups at the expense of other groups. Ultimately, it is political power that perpetuates the system. As Berreman observes,

*Poverty and oppression, whether rationalized by criteria of race, ethnicity, caste, or class, are endured not because people agree on their legitimacy, but because they are enforced by those who benefit from them.* (1979:221)

## Hindu Aesthetics: Divine Image and the Power of Religious Art

The caste system, with all its inequalities, is closely identified with and supported by the Hindu religion. However, beyond the belief in spiritual reincarnation, Hinduism also provides important emotional compensations for those wishing to escape the very real material inequities of caste. As self-conscious monotheists, Christians have great difficulty understanding the Hindu religion because, from a Christian viewpoint, it is based on the worship of "idols." Furthermore, the prominent use of erotic themes in Hindu religious art seems to blur the Western distinction between the sacred and the profane, thus making Hinduism appear very profane. Closer inspection of Hinduism shows that it contains an aesthetic system that makes culturally distinctive assumptions about art, worship, and the relationship between secular and sacred. Hinduism uses religious art as a powerful tool for helping individuals at all levels of the social hierarchy to emotionally experience a feeling of contact with an ultimate, eternal reality that transcends their daily mortal concerns. Christianity may accomplish the same objectives through different means.

Two key Hindu concepts, *rasa* and *darsan,* draw attention to some of the most important contrasts between Western and Hindu notions of religion and art. Richard Anderson (1990) notes that early Hindu philosophers felt that art was an important enough component of Hinduism to be considered a "fifth veda" on a par with the principal sacred texts but open to everyone, regardless of their *varna* level. Art in the Hindu context refers, first, to drama, poetry, music, and dance, all of which emphasize a temporal dimension, and, second, to painting, sculpture, and architecture, which are relatively static. According to classical Hindu scholars, art is supposed to be an unconscious vehicle for moral improvement and pleasure, which are assumed to be mutually reinforcing.

*Rasa* refers to the emotional pleasure that the experience of art can provide. Anderson (1990) shows that Hindu art is thought to be pleasurable because it helps people attain the most important goals of the Hindu good life: righteousness, spirituality, prosperity, and pleasure. It is this linking of pleasure with religion that offends some Christians, who at the same time would readily acknowledge that doing "good" should make one feel good. The Hindu concept of good merges the "sacred" goals of righteousness and spirituality with the "profane" goals of material prosperity and sensual pleasure. Thus, for Hindus, there is no contradiction in erotic religious art. The religious use of sensuality is even more obvious in *Tantrism,* which is a Hindu and Buddhist sect that uses food and ritualized sex as a form of religious meditation.

---

*jajmani system*  Complementary interdependence between castes, based on occupational specialization.
*karma*  The pattern of an individual's deeds in life and its impact on one's future existence.
*rasa*  Pleasure or satisfaction derived from experiencing art.
*Tantrism*  A Hindu and Buddhist cult that uses sensual pleasure as a form of ritual.

## Siva Iconography

Siva, or Shiva, the "Auspicious One" is one of the most prominent Hindu deities and illustrates the complexity of Hindu polytheism and iconography. Siva incorporates many universal complementary oppositions and ambiguities. He is a creator and a destroyer, a sensuous ascetic, benevolent and vengeful. He may be portrayed with multiple faces, three eyes, and four arms and sometimes as both male and female. He is often portrayed as a dancing figure in a ring of fire. Eck provides a concise exegesis of this image:

*The flaming circle in which he dances is the circle of creation and destruction called* samsara *(the earthly round of birth and death) or* maya *(the illusory world). The Lord who dances in the circle of this changing world holds in two of his hands the drum of creation and the fire of destruction. He displays his strength by crushing the bewildered demon underfoot. Simultaneously, he shows his mercy by raising his palm to the worshiper in the "fear-not" gesture and, with another hand, by pointing to his upraised foot, where the worshiper may take refuge. It is a wild dance, for the coils of his ascetic's hair are flying in both directions, and yet the facial countenance of the Lord is utterly peaceful and his limbs in complete balance. Around one arm twines the* naga, *the ancient serpent which he has incorporated into his sphere of power and wears now as an ornament. In his hair sits the mermaid River Ganga, who landed first on Siva's hair when she fell from heaven to earth. Such an image as the dancing Siva engages the eye and extends one's vision of the nature of this god, using simple, subtle, and commonly understood gestures and emblems*
(1985:41)

---

*Rasa* refers to the fleeting peak experience that art can inspire as distinguished from religious meditation, which also has an important role in Hinduism. In a more mundane sense, *rasa* also refers to culinary flavor, spice, or relish. Scholarly definitions of *rasa* identify eight universal human emotions: happiness, pride, laughter, sorrow, anger, disgust, fear, and wonder, which may be experienced as *rasa*. Some Hindu authorities add tranquility as a ninth *rasa* emotion. Thus, religious art uses culturally specific symbols to manipulate emotion to help people feel good. As Anderson explains, art in the service of religion

*. . . can sweep us away, transporting our spirits from the tedious cares and anxieties that beseige our daily lives. . . . It provides a means whereby we can transcend the sensory world around us and escape to a state of superior pleasure, practical betterment, and, ultimately, spiritual bliss.*
(1990:171–172)

Although Hinduism assumes the existence of one ultimate divine reality, it encourages great diversity in how this reality is culturally expressed and approached. Christianity, in contrast, is a very exclusive religion and recognizes relatively few images of divinity, such as the Father, Son, Holy Ghost, and the Virgin Mary.

*Darsan* refers to religious "seeing." For Hindus, viewing an image of the divine is in itself a form of worship or devotion (Eck 1985). It is expressed in pilgrimages to sacred places, in the special reverence for Hindu holy persons, and in the attention given to religious art, sculpture, temples, and shrines. Religious seeing, as Diana Eck (1985) points out, is a two-way process. The Hindu deity must "give" its image, and the observer receives it. Hindu polytheism is expressed in a vast variety of religious images, which may be called **icons**, when they take on a definite form, for example, as a representational painting or sculpture (see the box "Siva Iconography"). Often Hindu icons combine animal and human shapes with multiple arms, heads, or eyes to indicate different aspects of the deity. They are **aniconic images** when they are nonrepresentational, "formless" shapes, such as colored stones or a flame. Hindu religious images are not empty "idols" to Hindus; they are simply different forms, or manifestations, of the divine. Divine images are divine, and they focus the mind on the divine. Hindu devotion is expressed through the offering of humble gestures, flowers, food, and water or other special gifts, chants, and hymns to the divine images (Figure 9.11).

## Controversy Over the Sacred Cow

Cattle sacrifice, which was central to the ritual system, was a monopoly of the Brahman priests during the Vedic period in India. As Hinduism and the caste system developed, cattle were treated as deities and became an important feature of the ritual purity complex. The five products of the cow—fresh milk, sour milk, butter, urine, and dung—were important purifying agents, whereas eating a cow's flesh or leather working were polluting. According to the Dharma Sastra, cows were not to be disturbed or injured. The Arthasastra was blunt: "Whoever hurts or causes another to hurt, or steals or causes another to steal, a cow, should be slain" (Shamasastry 1960 [Bk. 2, chap. 29]). Under the influence of the **ahimsa** doctrine of nonviolence toward people and all animals, promoted by the **Jains** and Buddhists since the sixth century BC, this reverence for cows was carried to the point that special, templelike homes were maintained to care for aged and abandoned cattle. The sacred status of the cow was increased by the arrival of the beef-eating Muslims and the British because cow reverence became a conspicuous marker of Hindu culture.

The Indian Sacred Cow Complex has been the center of a theoretical debate between anthropologists, economists, and geographers over whether Indians keep too many cows for primarily religious reasons. Anthropologist Marvin Harris (1965, 1966) initiated the controversy by arguing that practical economic choices by poor farmers

FIGURE 9.11  *A richly costumed spirit dancer preparing to leap into a mound of white hot coals to demonstrate the purity of his devotion to a particular Hindu diety.*

were more important determinants of cattle practices in India than strictly religious considerations.

Harris (1965, 1966) was responding to numerous assessments by Indian public officials and development experts that Indians wastefully main-

---

**icon**  A representational likeness, such as a painting or sculpture of an object.
**aniconic image**  A nonrepresentational image, whose symbolic meaning is entirely arbitrary.
**ahimsa**  The belief that no life forms should be harmed, espoused by some Buddhists and Jainists.
**jainism**  A religious system that arose together with Buddhism as a challenge to the basic teachings of Hinduism.

tained vast numbers of useless cows because of irrational religious beliefs. Much of the criticism was over the poor quality of many of the animals and the quantity of fodder that they wastefully consumed. Harris challenges this interpretation, arguing that it was based on irrelevant market-economy cash accounting. He emphasizes that the relationship between people and cows in India was more likely to be symbiotic. Cattle subsist on the by-products of the grain-production system, which they in turn help sustain. He suggests that ecological pressures encouraged the maintenance of seemingly unproductive cattle as well as the ideology of *ahimsa*, which supports the practice.

Harris (1965, 1966) maintains that the most important contribution of Indian cattle was their support of the grain-based subsistence system as draft animals and through the production of dung for fuel and fertilizer. Bullocks pulling plows and carts help produce and transport the grain that supplies 80 percent of the calories people consume. For most peasant families, tractors would be prohibitively expensive to purchase and operate, and a pair of bullocks is an absolute necessity. There appears to be an actual shortage of traction animals during periods of intense plowing activity, which is determined by the annual cycle of monsoon rains. Furthermore, Harris argues, up to half of the cow dung may be used as a domestic cooking fuel, while the remainder serves as fertilizer. Considering the volume of energy involved in a country as densely populated as India, this resource would be very costly to replace with commercially produced fossil fuels. Harris concludes that

*. . . it should be obvious that without major technical and environmental innovations or drastic population cuts, India could not tolerate a large beef-producing industry. This suggests that insofar as the beef-eating taboo helps discourage growth of beef-producing industries, it is part of an ecological adjustment which maximizes rather than minimizes the calorie and protein output of the productive process.* (1966:57)

The Cattle Complex of India shows some striking contrasts with the pattern in East Africa, which are related to major differences in subsistence patterns. Indian cattle are managed primar-

ily to produce male traction animals, yet the direct production of animal protein remains an important secondary outcome. At 413 lb (187 kg) of milk a year, average milk production of Indian cattle is 26 percent of that produced by East African cattle (1606 lb [728 kg] and 8 percent of an intensively managed U.S. dairy cow (5000 lb [2265 kg]). However, even this relatively low production rate represents a significant contribution to the animal-protein intake of the Indian population. It is also important to remember that beef is consumed in India by Muslims, Christians, and members of the untouchable castes who can afford it, and cattle are an important source of leather, which is produced by the despised castes.

Critics such as Alan Heston (1971), Frederick Simoons (1979), and Stanley Freed and Ruth Freed (1981) charge that Harris unduly minimizes the role of religious ideology and the possibility that too many cows may be uneconomic. Most economists think that a cow surplus exists at the national level. For example, Heston (1971) looks at the well-being of the larger society in monetary terms. He argues that under different herd-management practices a smaller number of female animals, if better cared for, could produce the same number of traction animals and more milk because well-fed animals are more efficient. Harris (1965, 1966) agrees that cattle can be environmentally destructive and are part of the problem of increased human pressure on resources, but he still argues that poorly fed, relatively inefficient cattle can nevertheless be advantageous to individual poor farmers.

The problem with the approach of those who attack the apparent economic irrationality of Hindu religion, as Harris (1971a) points out, is that it ignores the inequities of the caste system and the difficult situation of the poorest Indian farmers who would be unable to maintain well-fed animals. Indian cattle are malnourished during the dry season; but when their services as draft animals are most required, they rebound when grazing improves with the monsoons. Like their East African counterparts, they tolerate drought conditions better than larger breeds, and they rebound more quickly. Free-ranging cattle feed themselves at public expense and no doubt, in some cases, at the expense of wealthy farmers and landlords;

thus, they may play a role in wealth redistribution where great economic inequality exists.

The origin of the Sacred Cow Complex has also been part of the debate. Harris (1966) proposes that it may have begun in the Ganges Valley by 1000 BC when population pressure resulted in decreased farm size and made cattle more valuable as draft animals. The religious taboo on killing cattle thus came about so that people would not be tempted to slaughter them for food and thereby threaten their agricultural system. Simoons (1979) argues that the ban on killing cattle may have been proposed by the early Hindu kingdoms in order to secure a surplus for the expanding urban centers, thus benefiting the elite rather than the peasants. This is in agreement with Harris's view that the prohibition on cattle killing was part of an "imperial cult" that supported the elite and is not incompatible with the view that the ban also benefited the peasants.

At the village level, evidence supports rational herd-management practices by farmers as well as decision making based on religious principles (Freed and Freed 1981). People do say that they protect cows as an act of worship, and there is no reason to doubt their sincerity. At the same time, as Harris observes (1988), from an etic point of view, Indians selectively starve unwanted calves, while emically they claim that all calves must be protected.

On balance, the controversy has drawn attention to the economic value of seemingly useless cows, but it also demonstrates the difficulty of positively determining why people do what they do. Contrary to what some observers have assumed, the sacred cow case does affirm the importance of religious belief. For example, as Simoons (1979) points out, many low-caste groups have stopped eating beef in order to avoid the ritual stigma of pollution and thereby enhance their social standing. The relationships between belief and actions are complex, and the best analysis would take a holistic ethnographic approach as recommended by the Freeds (1981). A full understanding of India's sacred cow must take into account both materialist and ideological factors. Assigning priority to one over the other may be useful as a research strategy, but it should not preclude a comprehensive understanding.

## WOMEN IN SOUTH ASIA

South Asian women, whether under Hindu or Islamic Great Traditions, are clearly at a cultural disadvantage in comparison with men. This disadvantage is based on myth and religious ideology recorded in sacred texts and is expressed in a ritual and physical separation between men and women in which men take leadership roles and enjoy relatively greater freedom outside the family. In the following section, we will concisely review the cultural-historical background of Islam to facilitate comparison with the Hindu Great Tradition. In later sections, we will consider the position of women under both cultural traditions.

### The Islamic Great Tradition

Striking parallels exist between the rise of Islam as an expansive state system and the development of Hindu civilization. Both cases are examples of secondary state formation from a pastoral tribal base in response to the influence of preexisting states. In both cases, a complex interethnic conquest state was integrated by means of a literate Great Tradition ideological system. It is remarkable that both traditions came to coexist in India even though the two systems were incompatible on fundamental issues of belief.

In contrast to Hinduism, the details of the founding of Islam are well known. Islam is a revealed religion, transmitted in Arabic directly by **Allah** to his messenger, the Prophet Muhammad (AD 570–632). God's message is recorded as sacred scripture in the *Qur'an* (**Koran**), and it is augmented by the **hadith,** or traditions surrounding the Prophet. *Islam,* which in Arabic means "surrender," refers to the need of the **Muslim** (believer) to surrender to the will of Allah, the one God. The

---

*Allah*    The one God, the Supreme Being in Islam.
*Koran*    The sacred text of Islam, based on God's message to the Prophet Muhammad.
*hadith*    Traditions relating to the life and teachings of the Prophet Muhammad as a source of religious doctrine.
*Islam*    Surrender to the will of Allah.
*Muslim*    A believer in Islam.

fundamental articles of faith are encompassed by the **Five Pillars** of Islam:

1. Recitation of the **Shahadah,** confession of faith: "There is no God but Allah and Muhammad is his Prophet"
2. The performance of five daily prayers
3. The giving of alms (*zakkat*)
4. The observance of the fast of Ramadan
5. Pilgrimage to Mecca (the **hajj**).

Muhammad was a member of the Quraysh, a sedentarized north Arabian Bedouin tribe that controlled the Red Sea trade from Mecca, which was already an important ritual center. Muhammad's religious visions began in about 610; after overcoming initial opposition to his message, by the time of his death in 632 he had succeeded in uniting all the Bedouin tribes of Arabia into a religious state based on the new faith. The pre-Islamic Bedouin tribes were relatively egalitarian, patrilineal segmentary systems, led by popularly supported "chiefs," or *shaykhs* (sheiks), who led raids, settled disputes, and enjoyed some prestige but were still considered "first among equals." An essential element in this tribe-to-state transformation was the replacement of tribal and kinship loyalties with membership in the **Umma,** the Islamic community, which created a united front by suppressing the blood feud that had characterized intertribal relations throughout Arabia (Lewis 1960).

The *Umma* was a nascent religious state, united by common belief and military opposition to unbelieving outsiders as expressed in the *jihad,* or holy war. Under Islam, the Prophet Muhammad was accepted as the divinely appointed head of state. However, Muhammad did not specify how his successor, the caliph, was to be selected. Conflict over the succession resulted in a sectarian split between the **Sunnites,** who believed they were following the *Sunna,* the Prophet's sayings in selecting the caliph, versus the **Shi'ites,** who favored keeping the **imam,** "foremost of the community," in the Prophet's closest line of descent and recognized their own line of imams. The caliph or imam, as the leader of the Islamic state and chief defender of the faith, was expected to lead prayer at the Friday service in the mosque. He was also responsible for settling disputes, collecting taxes,

and organizing the *jihad* against unbelievers.

After the death of Muhammad, a period of rapid military expansion began, which brought the Mesopotamian region—much of Persia, Egypt, and North Africa—under Islamic control by 700. Next, Muslims entered Spain and began to raid into northern India. Conquest was a major source of state revenue, whether directly as battlefield booty or as tribute or tax in agricultural production. During the expansion of Islam, unbelievers with literate sacred scriptures—such as Jews, Christians, and, by extension, Hindus—were granted protection as **peoples of the book** as long as they acknowledged Islamic political authority and paid their taxes. Small Islamic kingdoms, or sultanates, were established in India by 1200, and from 1526 to 1761, the Islamic Mogul empire ruled over most of the Indian subcontinent. Although the Mogul rulers generally tolerated Hindu practices, there were many areas of conflict between the two Great Traditions, as illustrated by the modern partitioning of British India into Muslim Pakistan and Hindu India in 1947 (Figure 9.12).

The Islamic state was based on the **shari'a,** which, like *tao* in Chinese, means "path" or "road." Like the Hindu concept of dharma, *shari'a* is God's Law as outlined in the Koran and the *Sunna* or the *hadiths* accepted by the Shi'ites (Levy 1962). Islamic law is a detailed prescription for all areas of life, specifying whether individual acts are required, forbidden, recommended, disapproved, and permitted. Islam, like Hinduism, constitutes a complete social system and has had a profound influence over preexisting cultural practices whenever Islamic states have been established.

## Women in Islamic Society

Any discussion of Islamic social practices must begin with a careful disclaimer acknowledging the great diversity of practices in specific countries and regions, at different historic times, between urban and village settings, and between different social classes. Furthermore, the Koran itself is interpreted in many different ways, but certain principles do stand out. According to fundamentalist Islamic interpretations, women are generally viewed as morally and legally inferior to men. They are to be protected by their husbands and

FIGURE 9.12  *This Pakistani mosque is a striking reminder that the Islamic Mogul empire ruled over much of South Asia from 1526 to 1761.*

represented an improvement in the position of women over the common practice of pre-Islamic times. Women's rights in marriage, divorce, inheritance, and property ownership are specified in ways that no doubt increased their security.

A modern expression of Islamic gender roles is a common tendency toward gender segregation in education and employment. Labor migration by men for extended periods, leaving wives to maintain the household, is a common pattern. Women are less likely to work outside the home than men, and when they are employed as professionals, women tend to work with other women as teachers or doctors. Both high-status and low-status positions in the complementary occupational pairs—such as doctor/nurse principal/teacher, executive/secretary, which are commonly seen as male–female sets in Western industrial countries—are more likely to be filled by men in Islamic countries (Papanek 1982).

When they address Western audiences, and especially Western feminists, Muslim female social scientists often stress that many of the cultural patterns that Western women take as evidence of Islamic oppression of women are misunderstood in ways that perpetuate the view that Muslim women are passive and ignorant, if not inferior. For example, Leila Ahmed (1982) argues that Westerners usually describe the ***harem*** entirely in male terms, as an institution for confining and controlling women to provide men with secure

close male kin and are to stay out of public life. In several respects, Muslim women are at a legal disadvantage by many interpretations of Islamic law in comparison with men. Daughters inherit less than sons. Women are permitted only one spouse at a time, whereas men may have up to four wives as long as they can provide for and treat all fairly. Muslim women are expected to marry only other Muslims, whereas men may marry unbelieving people of the book. It is more difficult for a woman to obtain a divorce. Furthermore, modesty and male honor often require female seclusion (discussed in detail in the following section).

Many observers stress that Koranic law actually

***Five Pillars***  The basic requirements of Muslim religion, including a profession of faith in Allah and the Prophet Muhammad, daily prayer, alms giving, fasting, and pilgrimage.
***Shahadah***  The Islamic profession of faith, "There is no God but Allah and Muhammad is his Prophet."
***hajj***  Pilgrimage to Mecca.
***Umma***  The Islamic community of believers.
***Sunnites***  Muslims following the *Sunna*, or sayings of the Prophet Muhammad.
***Shi'ites***  A Muslim sect endorsing the line of imams most closely related to the Prophet Muhammad.
***imam***  A religious and political leader of an Islamic state.
***peoples of the book***  Non-Islamic peoples such as Christians, Jews, and Hindus, who have their own sacred texts.
***shari'a***  Islamic law; also the "path" or "road."
***harem***  From the Arabic word for "forbidden," refers to physically segregated domestic living space for women.

sexual access to multiple wives. The harem system does segregate women from men; Islamic women themselves, however, recognize that such segregation need not be oppressive in itself. Ahmed notes that the English word *harem* is derived from the Arabic word *haram* meaning "forbidden." She suggests that it is women who forbid men from entering exclusively female space. The harem is a gathering place for women, where they can freely discuss and ridicule men and the world of men. It is also a place where a feminist critique of Islamic society can take place. Many Western women, isolated in nuclear families, do not enjoy such freedom. Thus, although Islamic women are in many ways discriminated against by their societies, seeing specific Islamic social institutions in entirely negative terms can be misleading. According to Ahmed,

... *to believe that segregated societies are by definition more oppressive to women, or that women secluded from the company of men are women deprived, is only to allow ourselves to be servilely obedient to the constructs of men, Western or Middle Eastern.* (1982:531)

It must be remembered, however, that the harem is part of a larger Islamic society, which is controlled primarily by men.

## Female Seclusion: The Purdah System

The practice of **purdah,** the veiling and seclusion of women, is a conspicuous South Asian cultural pattern, shared by Hindu and Moslems alike, and is related to the institutionalization of gender inequality shared by both cultures. Purdah means "curtain" or "veil" and refers to the physical separation of the living spaces used by men and women, as well as the actual veiling of a woman's face and body. This is a South Asian variation of the harem of the Arab Islamic world. The concept of purdah is also commonly extended to refer to a variety of avoidance or deference behavior practiced by women, including not looking at or speaking to certain people. Adherence to purdah restrictions is related to specific factors such as employment, education, social class, politics, and religion. Some Muslim sects have abolished or intensified seclusion by decree. Western observers often denounce purdah as another example of male oppression, but like the harem it plays an important functional role in the culture and is supported by many of the women who practice it.

In the strictest form of purdah, a woman must remain completely within the confines of her home throughout her adult life. Within a large house, there may be women's rooms and entrances that outside men cannot use, and special screens and partitions may be set up to hide women from view. In some cases, seclusion of women extends to otherwise public buildings and public transportation. Although there is considerable variation in the degree to which veiling is practiced, in extreme form, a Muslim woman in purdah can only leave the seclusion of her home when wearing the *burqa,* a full-length garment covering head and body (Figure 9.13).

FIGURE 9.13    *An Indian Muslim woman wearing* burqa.

Hanna Papanek (1982) considers purdah to be based on two interconnected principles in South Asian culture, which she calls *separate worlds*, and *symbolic shelter*. The principle of separate worlds is expressed in a sharp division of labor and workplace and in the corresponding economic interdependence between men and women. The principle of symbolic shelter is founded in the belief that women are especially vulnerable in a hostile outside world and therefore must be kept sheltered at home. The outside danger from which women need protection is the threat of uncontrolled sexual and aggressive impulses. The underlying assumption seems to be that people need close external supervision to control themselves; thus, purdah restrictions physically remove women from possible harm. Papanek suggests that Hindus and Muslims may view the dangers to women somewhat differently, with Hindu women seen as potential temptresses and Muslim women seen as potential victims, but either way they need to be protected. The dependency of women and supremacy of men are as deeply rooted in Hindu culture as they are in Islam. In certain details, the Hindu version of purdah has been influenced by Islamic traditions, but the principles of symbolic sanctuary existed prior to Islam in India. For example, Manu, in the Dharma Sastra, declares the following laws for women:

*No act is to be done according to (her) own will by a young girl, a young woman, or even by an old woman, though in (their own) houses. In her childhood (a girl) should be under the will of her father; in (her) youth, of (her) husband; her husband being dead, of her sons; a woman should never enjoy her own will. She must never wish separation of her self from her father, husband, or sons, for by separation from them a woman would make both families contemptible. She must always be cheerful and clever in household business, with the furniture well cleaned, and with not a free hand in expenditure. But him to whom her father gives her, or (her) brother with the father's consent, she must obey alive, and dead must not disregard.* (Burnell and Hopkins 1884:130–131).

Pananek (1982) stresses another important dimension of symbolic shelter: Women are "status demonstrators" for their husbands. The Muslim concept of **izzat,** family "honor" or "pride," extends to the modesty and virtue of a man's wife,

sister, and daughter, while the reverse is not the case. A woman's status is not determined by the virtue of her husband, brother, or father. This is the famous "double standard," which has also had a long history in Western civilization. The observance of purdah is an expression of modesty, social solidarity, and family respectability. The importance of feminine virtue is emphatically demonstrated by the ideal of Sita the heroine of the Ramayana, one of the best known Hindu myths (see the box "The Ramayana").

Anthropologist Manisha Roy (1975), a Bengali woman, has carefully documented how the experience of growing up in the Hindu extended family creates culturally conditioned expectations for women that are often unfulfilled. The popular Hindu myths, which stress the ideals of romantic love and self-sacrificing devotion to the husband, conflict with the realities of arranged Hindu marriages and generate psychological frustration for women. A woman's husband often turns out to be an emotionally remote protector who is close to his wife only when he relates to her as mother of his children. Upper-class, urban Bengali women are able to find some compensation for the frustrations in their domestic lives by developing a long-term relationship as a devoted disciple of a guru outside the extended family, but this is only possible after her children are grown.

There are significant differences between the way Muslim and Hindu women in South Asia practice purdah. For example, Muslim women are secluded from all outside men, whereas Hindu women are secluded from all male affines, especially from her husband's kinsmen (Papanek 1982, Vatuk 1982). The Hindu pattern has been described in detail by Doranne Jacobson (1982), based on her research in the Bhopal region of central India. In this area, Hindu women remain fully veiled before virtually all male affines in her husband's joint family. She must also be partially veiled before many of the senior women in her

---

***purdah*** Hindi word for "veil" or "curtain," generalized to refer to physical separation of daily lives of men and women.
***izzat*** Muslim concept of family honor in which a man is responsible for the modesty and virtue of his wife, sister, and daughter.

The Ramayana:
A Hindu Mythic
Charter of Feminine
Virtue

The Ramayana is one of the most popular Hindu myths, dating to 300 BC, during the early classic period of Hindu civilization. This epic romance is a part of the cultural identity of all Hindus. It is frequently recited in dramatic performances and is required reading in Indian schools. It presents a compelling role model of the ideal Hindu wife.

Briefly stated, the Ramayana (the Romance of Rama) tells the story of Rama, an incarnation of Vishnu, who weds the beautiful Sita, the heroine, after passing an heroic test. However, he is cheated out of his place as heir to his father's throne and banished to a 14-year exile in the forest. Out of devotion to her husband, Sita follows her husband into exile, even though he urges her to stay behind. Later, Sita is treacherously abducted by an evil king who wants to marry her, but she rejects his advances and is imprisoned. Meanwhile, her husband Rama recruits an army and rescues her, but he suspects that Sita was unfaithful to him during her imprisonment and forces her to pass an ordeal by fire to prove her loyalty before accepting her back. Rama takes his rightful place on the throne of his kingdom with Sita as queen. When his subjects gossip that Sita really was unfaithful after all, Rama sends her away again to the forest where she raises his twin sons. When Sita sends his grown sons back to him, he invites her to return but insists that she again prove her virtue. She has, of course, been totally faithful and totally devoted to him throughout her ordeal, but this time she accepts his rejection and asks the earth to swallow her up. This is a fitting gesture because in the myth she was born from the earth.

---

husband's joint family. However, when she visits her natal village, she is virtually free of purdah restrictions (Figure 9.14).

Before examining the possible functions of purdah, it is important to consider the emic view. Women who practice purdah often attribute it to feelings of shame, shyness, or embarrassment, and they relate it to parallel concerns for honor and respect. Their enculturation, especially through internalization of the heroic role models provided by mythic figures such as Sita, makes it an internal response that does not require outside sanctions. As Jacobson reports, "Most secluded women, too, pride themselves on their strict observance of purdah" (1982:96–97). This emic view supports the symbolic sanctuary interpretation, but women

also recognize that purdah can be a marker of elite status because only economically well-off households could afford to observe it fully.

Many functions of purdah have been proposed, and it seems clear that it is not caused by a simple conspiracy of men designed to oppress women. Purdah also restricts men and imposes responsibilities on them. It creates dependency between men and women because a woman who cannot leave her home must rely on her husband, children, or servants to perform outside errands, such as shopping. A man, in turn, might not do domestic chores such as cooking and cleaning. It has been suggested that Hindus might use purdah to reduce the danger of female ritual pollution and to safeguard the purity of caste endogamy (Yalman

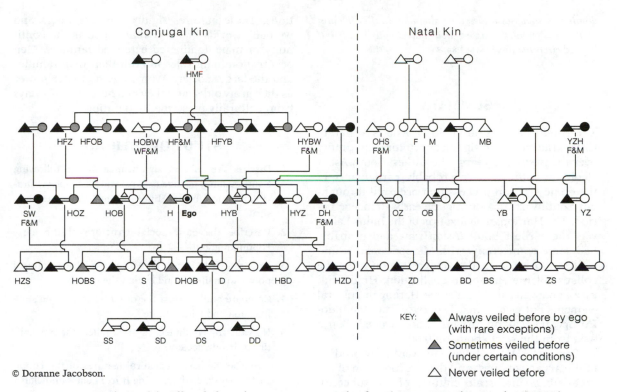

Conjugal Kin

Natal Kin

KEY:
▲ Always veiled before by ego (with rare exceptions)
◮ Sometimes veiled before (under certain conditions)
△ Never veiled before

© Doranne Jacobson.

FIGURE 9.14  *Hindu Purdah: Affines before when a woman covers her face. (SOURCE: Based on Jacobson 1982.)*

1963). The most direct function of purdah is that it helps sustain the integrity of the patrilineal extended or joint family, which is the most viable minimal social unit in stratified state societies based on plow agriculture (Boserup 1970, Jacobson 1982). This system requires careful control of small parcels of land and support from neighboring families and seems to work best with unambiguous lines of authority, a strict division of labor, and a maximum of domestic tranquility.

Purdah imposes social distance between men and women and intensifies their respective role differences. Purdah also minimizes the possibility for potentially disruptive incidents of adultery, both within and outside the extended family, and supports the common pattern of arranged marriages. Unmarried girls who are secluded in their homes are unlikely to find lovers to marry who might undermine established community-alliance

networks. In Muslim societies, marriage may be arranged between patrilateral parallel cousins (a man marries FBD), which helps to concentrate lineage resources and furthers a woman's seclusion by making even her affines relatively close kin.

In Jacobson's view, purdah has played a vital cultural role:

*However inimical such a system may be to the ideals of Westerners, urban-educated South Asians, or even to the preferences of a certain number of veiled women themselves, there can be no doubt that arrangements of this kind have allowed hundreds of millions of people to live—and sometimes even to prosper—over the course of several centuries in various corners of the earth. It should also be acknowledged that for many fortunate women, sequestered life in bustling and affectionate family units has provided security and satisfaction. Only as alternative family structures become economically feasible or necessary are male-*

*dominated societies undergoing alteration in the direction of allowing females to assert their individuality in any but limited circumstances.* (1982:84–85)

## SUMMARY

The Hindu civilization of South Asia is a literate Great Tradition with significant cultural continuity over the past 3000 years. The earliest South Asian Neolithic cultures were probably participants in the domestication process that occurred throughout Southwest Asia during the early Holocene period. The Harappan civilization of the Indus Valley was the earliest South Asian state and probably had some connections with Mesopotamia. Hindu civilization arose in the Ganges region after the collapse of the Harappan civilization. Hindu culture apparently drew on some Harappan cultural elements but was primarily derived from the Indo-European-speaking Aryans who invaded South Asia from the west about 1600 BC.

The early Hindu kingdoms were a by-product of the Aryan conquest and the incorporation of the preexisting small-scale cultures of the subcontinent. Classical Hindu kingdoms, as described in the Arthasastra, were organized around a complex government bureaucracy based on secular political power backed by a formal legal system with fines and physical punishments for offenders. It also relied on a religious system that divided society into four ranked groups, or *varnas*. The dominant structure of Hindu society up to the present time is the caste system, which assigns everyone to a ritually ranked endogamous occupational group. This generates great social inequality, but it is justified and supported by Hindu religious beliefs that emphasize religious duty, the hope of reincarnation at a higher level, and the opportunity for people at all social levels to enjoy transcendental contact with the divine. Hindu religious beliefs also provide ritual protection for cows that are an important source of fuel, food, and traction power for poor people who might otherwise have great difficulty supporting themselves.

Women are placed in inferior positions relative to men by both the Islamic and Hindu Great Tradi-

tions. These cultures rigidly separate men's and women's worlds in a way that supports the continuity of male-dominated extended families. Men occupy dominant roles in both their own families and the larger society. Women gain greater power as they grow older, and they benefit in certain ways from culturally prescribed separation.

## STUDY QUESTIONS

1. Discuss the cultural significance of the following South Asian language groups: Indo-European, Dravidian, Sino-Tibetan, Hindi, Bengali, Urdu, and Sanskrit.

2. Describe the basic social structure of the early Hindu kingdom.

3. How did early Hindu kingdoms use direct political power to maintain and extend the state?

4. Compare and contrast the organization of the state in China and Hindu India.

5. How did the Hindu legal system reflect the inequalities of Hindu society?

6. Describe the basic structural features of the Hindu caste system, distinguishing it from class and clan.

7. In what way was ritual purity a central feature of Hindu culture?

8. Distinguish between *varna*, *jati*, Brahman, Kshatriya, Vaisya, and Sudra.

9. Discuss the economic correlates of caste and weigh the arguments that it served positive social functions or was exploitative.

10. In what ways does the Hindu Sacred Cow Complex have positive adaptive functions?

11. What are the arguments for the religious explanations of the Sacred Cow Complex?

12. Describe the position of women according to fundamentalist Islamic principles.

13. Distinguish between the Islamic and Hindu cultural context of purdah, referring to the principles of separate worlds and symbolic shelter. What are the functionalist explanations of purdah?

14. Contrast the basic features of Islam and Hinduism, placing each system in its appropriate cultural-historical context.

## SUGGESTED READINGS

ALLCHIN, BRIDGET, AND F. RAYMOND ALLCHIN. 1982. *The Rise of Civilization in India and Pakistan*. Cambridge, Eng.: Cambridge University Press. An archaeological overview of South Asian prehistory and the early development of Harappan and Hindu civilization.

BASHAM, A. L. 1954. *The Wonder That Was India: A Survey of the Culture of the Indian Sub-continent Before the Coming of the Muslims*. London: Sidgwick & Jackson. A widely respected basic textbook on South Asian history and culture.

ECK, DIANA L. 1985. *Darsan: Seeing the Divine Image in India*. Chambersburg, Penn.: Anima Books. An in-depth treatment of the visual aspects of Hindu religion.

PAPANEK, HANNA, AND GAIL MINAULT (eds.). 1982. *Separate Worlds: Studies of Purdah in South Asia*. Dehli: Chanakya Publications. An interdisciplinary collection of papers on the seclusion of women in South Asia.

TYLER, STEPHEN A. 1986. *India: An Anthropological Perspective*. Prospect Heights, Ill.: Waveland Press. An anthropological overview of many aspects of Indian culture with an emphasis on linguistic and cognitive categories.

# 10

# THE BREAKDOWN
# OF STATES

A recurrent issue in Chapters 6–9 was how to explain the increases in social complexity that culminated in social stratification, state political organization, and Great Tradition "civilizations." The origin of the state has been a central research problem in anthropology for many years, but much less attention has been devoted to an equally important issue: the continuity of states and the reasons for their frequent collapse. Any consideration of the breakdown of states also forces us to more closely reconsider theories of cultural development and the nature of the state itself. History has shown that states are unstable entities, prone to collapse from internal conflict and external invasion. Considering the multiple, interconnected potential threats to which states are vulnerable, it is remarkable that they ever arose in the first place. The failure of deterministic origin theories to satisfactorily account for all cases suggests that state formation is not an entirely predictable process. Similarly, the frequent collapse of states helps demonstrate that evolutionary progress is neither irreversible nor inevitable, despite persistent popular beliefs in "progress."

## THE VIABILITY OF THE STATE

### The Concept of Collapse

The primary concern here is with understanding the process by which states and empires decompose into smaller political units. This kind of system collapse must be distinguished from the fall of particular dynasties and their replacement by other sets of rulers. Changing dynasties is a major topic for historians but will not be treated here, except where the change represents a major cultural discontinuity. The focus of this discussion is the fate of ancient, precapitalist systems because additional dynamics influence states in the modern world system; these new factors will be explored in Chapters 11–15.

In dealing with dynamic cultural and biological systems, defining when an entity ceases to exist and when it has changed into a different system is always a problem. As cultural ecologist Roy Rappaport observes (1977b), *processual continuity* is the most useful criterion, but some ambiguity will always remain and arbitrary judgments must be made about whether a particular culture, state, or civilization has been extinguished. The issue in this chapter is those conspicuous cases in which governments collapse and cities are abandoned. We will also consider a related but distinct issue, the less common problem of the total disappearance of particular Great Traditions.

Like any cultural system, a civilization is composed of the individuals or societies that perpetuate it, as well as the technologies, organizational patterns, and ideological systems that maintain it. States can break down, while the population may continue to transmit significant elements of the culture (Figure 10.1). The total disappearance of a people with their language and culture is an unlikely event, except where modern states have exterminated tribal peoples and cultures as a policy of national expansion (see Chapter 14).

It is important to ask, What changes when states collapse? The fall of states is not just an inconsequential change of political regimes; it also carries important human and environmental costs. State systems are based on social inequality and exploitation, but they do provide vital social services for very large populations. The government elite has a clear vested interest in maintaining a large, productive population because people are the main source of state revenue and the troops who will be used to extract booty from other states or to extend the boundaries of the state. People under state control may resent paying taxes, but, like it or not, their personal security depends on government institutions. State police, the law, and the courts protect their property from robberies and their persons from assault, while the army prevents foreign invasion. The state provides famine relief and promotes capital-intensive agricultural development. The state also develops and maintains the communications system and public services required by commerce and foreign trade. Living standards may be drastically reduced during periods of extreme political instability, as trade and marketing networks break down, and many people may be killed when social control mechanisms disappear or foreigners take over. Collapsing states may deplete valuable nonrenewable resources and leave behind seriously degraded ecosystems.

FIGURE 10.1  *Mayan civilization in Central America flourished for 600 years and then collapsed around AD 600; all administrative centers, such as Tikal in what is now Guatemala, were abandoned.*

## The Vulnerability of Inequality and Political Hierarchy

While no culture can claim perfect functional integration, focusing on the issue of collapse makes it clear that states are significantly more precarious than small-scale cultures. States are more complex systems with more pieces and more things to go

---

***processual continuity***   The continuation of the culturally established processes of government even though a change in dynastic leadership may occur.

wrong. However, this is not just a quantitative matter. Tribes cannot break down because there is no tribal political structure to collapse. Villages and bands undergo continuous reorganization and can be dissolved at any time with no particular impact on the larger society and culture. In contrast, large regional states break down into local kingdoms or city-states, which in turn may further split into chiefdoms or autonomous villages and bands.

States are especially vulnerable to collapse because they contain social classes based on major inequities in wealth and power. States create special-interest groups and give them a reason to risk bringing the whole system down in order to improve their own position. A limitation on the number of political offices generates perpetual rivalries. Inequalities of wealth and power may be the most critical defining feature of states and the single most important cause of their breakdown. The creation of wealth requires revenue, but revenue extraction by taxation is a doubly risky state function. State authorities will seek as much revenue as possible, but if they take too much from the citizenry, they may rebel. Too high a rate of revenue extraction also forces people to intensify their subsistence activities, which will increase the pressure on natural ecosystems.

Unequal concentrations of wealth, whether in the form of luxury goods, stored food, or labor-intensive construction projects, appear to be functional prerequisites for state organization; their presence, however, also causes dangerous instability. Warehoused food is required to support nonfood-producing specialists and to sustain dense populations that might be threatened by fluctuations in production. Luxury goods are necessary status markers and rewards for political service. Storehouses are prime targets for looters from both within and without a particular state, and their defense requires expensive walls and standing armies. The unequal distribution of luxury goods also makes police forces and court systems necessary.

Creating and defending state wealth was a primary reason for costly military campaigns against neighboring states. The maintenance of a full-time officer corps, palace guards, and frontier garrisons were permanent military expenses, and specific campaigns in which large numbers of peasant soldiers were mobilized could be extremely costly. Military expenditures may have been the largest category in many state budgets and created constant pressure for potentially destabilizing increases in revenue extraction.

In comparison with a cultural universe occupied exclusively by small-scale tribal cultures, states introduced a qualitatively different cultural dynamic into any regional system. Whereas chronic feuding was endemic in tribal systems, territorial conquest was a permanent characteristic of states. Tribal raids and blood feuds did not require permanent leaders or a standing professional army and thus were not incentives for increased production. However, the appearance of states in a nonstate area stimulated trade and raiding by tribal groups against the state. This sometimes pushed tribes into political developments leading to wealth inequality and instability within tribes.

## Explaining Collapse

The collapse of civilizations has been viewed from several different perspectives, as Norman Yoffee (1988b) has outlined. German philosopher historian Oswald Spengler (1880–1936) thought that civilizations, like organisms, inevitably went through regular life cycles in which they either slipped into a permanent state of stagnant "decline" or they died completely. British historian Arnold Toynbee (1889–1975) thought that civilizations arose in response to environmental challenges and declined as their creative spirit waned. Unfortunately, both approaches were highly subjective, personal interpretations and were not readily testable. Anthropologist Julian Steward (1955) identified "cyclical conquests" and "dark ages" as predictable final stages in the development of civilizations. In each case, he argued that collapse occurred when continued population growth and increased taxation reduced per-capita production rates, depressing living standards and raising mortality rates for the peasantry to the point of rebellion.

Elman Service has proposed that the rise and fall of states and civilizations is simply an example of the *law of evolutionary potential*, which de-

TABLE 10.1  *Hierarchical Adaptive Structures in Cultural Systems*

| Hierarchical Level | Function | Examples | Qualities |
|---|---|---|---|
| Highest | General purpose | Deities | Eternal principles, value-laden |
| Higher | Relations between lower-order regulators | Legal codes, economic systems, traditions ritual | Rules, general directives, arbitrary |
| Lowest | Special purpose, specific behavior | Subsistence practices, domestic routines | Rapid response, reversible, sensitive |

SOURCE: Rappaport (1977a).

clares: "The more specialized and adapted a form in a given evolutionary stage, the smaller is its potential for passing to the next stage" (1960:97). This means that a given state can become so over-invested in a particular Great Tradition pattern that it will be unable to convert to a new pattern that might offer important adaptive advantages. The corollary principle of *local discontinuity of progress* suggests that cultural "advances" are likely to occur in cultures that did not participate in earlier "advances" and are thus able to bypass their formerly more "progressive" but now over-specialized neighbors. These generalizations can be historically verified after the fact, but they do not identify the detailed causes of collapse.

Rappaport (1977a) offers a formal systems theory analysis of the adaptive structures operating in cultural systems in order to identify some of the inherently "maladaptive" aspects of large-scale cultures. Rappaport defines *adaptation* as the process by which cultures maintain equilibrium despite both short- and long-term environmental fluctuation. Equilibrium in this case refers especially to the well-being of human organisms, human population stability, and the maintenance of supporting ecosystems.

The *adaptive structures* of a culture can be arranged in hierarchical levels according to the amount of information and decision making they regulate (Table 10.1). Lowest-level regulators, such as individual farmers managing their domestic subsistence gardens, are responsible for very specific environmental details of soil and rainfall. They can respond quickly and precisely to changing conditions in their immediate environment. Higher-level regulators, such as a villagewide ritual, might control the individual farmer's produc-

tion decisions but would be less responsive to conditions in his specific garden. Higher-level regulators, such as remote rulers in a capital city, would also influence the farmer's actions but would be even more arbitrary and less responsive. Highest-level regulators, such as deities, would represent virtually eternal, and thus quite unresponsive, value-laden principles that would guide behavior at all lower levels.

*Maladaptations* are any factors within a culture's adaptive structures that impede the culture's ability to adjust to changes in its environment. Higher-level system regulators can only function if they selectively exclude very specific information; therefore, they are likely to misunderstand the conditions at the lowest levels. What Rappaport calls *hierarchical anomalies,* which undermine balancing functions, tend to increase as levels are added to the hierarchy. Higher levels are likely to either underreact or overreact, thereby disturbing the finely tuned responses of lower-order regula-

*law of evolutionary potential*  The postulation that highly specialized cultures may have difficulty making major adaptive changes.
*adaptation*  The long-term cultural process of maintaining a balance between population and natural resources within a given environment.
*adaptive structures*  Cultural features that contribute to adaptation by regulating decision making and the flow of information.
*—aladaptation*  A cultural feature that undermines the culture's response to environmental change.
*hierarchical anomaly*  Maladaptation caused by adaptive structures that influence decision making at the wrong level within the cultural system.
*usurpation*  A hierarchical anomaly caused when lower-level adaptive structures inappropriately gain control over the entire cultural system.

tors to environmental changes. An equally serious structural problem created by states is what Rappaport calls **usurpation,** or escalation, in which particular subsystems gain effective power over the larger system. According to Rappaport, this is maladaptive:

*Thus, for the narrowly defined short-run interests of some individuals to prevail over the long-run requirements of the societies and ecosystems of which they are parts is, it seems to me, maladaptive per se.* (1977b:83)

## STATE SYSTEMS THAT FAILED

In the following sections, we will examine possible causes of political collapse and the relationship between collapse and the continuity of particular civilizations of Great Traditions, using examples drawn from the cultures that were treated in previous chapters, which were focused on state origin and the basic cultural features of states. In Mesopotamia 3500 years of cyclical state building and collapse was definitely terminated by foreign invasion. Mesopotamian civilization disappeared a few centuries later. Andean civilization shows perhaps 4500 years of processual continuity, punctuated by frequent collapse of individual states and empires, until it is was halted by foreign invasion. In the Andes, however, there is major continuity up to the present after nearly 500 years, even though the political economy has been totally transformed. China, which is not examined in this chapter, also demonstrates nearly 4000 years of processual continuity, even though individual states and dynasties repeatedly collapse. In China the foreign invaders are absorbed by the Great Tradition, which persists despite political change. Harappan urban civilization collapsed after approximately 1000 years but contributed significantly to later cultural developments in India. These cases show the complexity of the issue of political collapse and the fate of civilizations. Cultural continuity is clearly stronger than political structure.

### Mesopotamia: The End of a Great Tradition

If state organization began in Mesopotamia with the Uruk period in 4000 BC and if as Yoffee (1988a)

suggests, the Persian conquest of Babylonia in 539 BC is taken as the end of the distinctively Mesopotamian political system, then the Mesopotamian political system based on the state lasted for approximately 3500 years. Yoffee dates the final termination of Mesopotamian civilization some 500 years later in AD 75 when the last cuneiform document is known to have been written. After that time, no recognizable Mesopotamian language, economy, or belief system persists, although certain specific cultural connections can still be traced in succeeding civilizations. This raises the question of whether Mesopotamian culture or civilization can be considered an entity. Yoffee defines Mesopotamian civilization as

*that fragile, but reproducible, set of cultural boundaries that encompass a variety of peoples, political and social systems, and geographies marked as Mesopotamian and that, importantly, include the idea of a political center.* (1988a:44)

It is clear that Mesopotamian civilization was a complex, multiethnic system, incorporating peoples speaking different languages, practicing different subsistence activities, and worshiping different gods. The written tradition and related religious beliefs gave the civilization great continuity. The Mesopotamian political system was based on a network of city-states, which at various times were combined into regional states or empires. There were constant power struggles between the rulers of different cities, and cities were abandoned or relocated after military defeats or changes in the course of major rivers. Dynasties were replaced by foreign invaders or following internal conflicts.

The Sumerian King List, shows how unstable the political situation was in Mesopotamia. The list is an official written record of the sequence of individual kings, together with their capital cities, who were entitled to rule over the Mesopotamian empire. The list begins in approximately 2900 BC in the Early Dynastic and continues through the last Sumerian dynasty in approximately 2000 BC. The list creates the fiction of perfect continuity and pretends that a single ruler was always in control of the entire region; thus, it cannot be accepted as literal history. The time span attributed to individual dynasties is purely metaphorical, and the list is an incomplete emic view, idealized for political purposes. Nevertheless, it provides a glimpse of the kind of upheavals that must have characterized the Mesopotamian scene.

The list names 146 rulers in twenty-six dynasties over the 900-year period (Table 10.2). This suggests an average of just 6 years per king and 35 years per dynasty, and the dynastic turnover is invariably attributed to military defeat. Some authors (Jacobsen and Adams 1958) have pointed out that overirrigation under state management may have played a role in the abandonment of southern Mesopotamian cities and the collapse of the third Ur dynasty, which effectively marked the end of the Sumerian period. The argument is that so much irrigation water was used that it inadvertently elevated the water table, causing subsurface saltwater to steadily contaminate the soil and inhibit the growth of crops. Evidence for salt damage is found in the records of declining crop yields, increased seed requirements reflecting poor germination rates, and specific references in ancient texts to salt-damaged fields. Documents show that barley yields declined by nearly two-thirds over 700 years, and wheat, which is more salt-intolerant, was virtually abandoned as a crop even though it had previously been as important as barley. Identifying such an ecological factor as a sole cause of collapse would be misleading because underlying political factors caused the mismanage-

TABLE 10.2   *Sequence of Dynasties Recorded in the Sumerian King List, 2900–2000* BC

| City | Source | Rulers | Cause of Loss | Putative Duration (years) |
|------|--------|--------|---------------|---------------------------|
| Eridu | Heaven | 2 | City abandoned | 64,800 |
| Badtibira | Transfer | 3 | City abandoned | 108,000 |
| Larak | Transfer | 1 | City abandoned | 28,800 |
| Sippar | Transfer | 1 | City abandoned | 21,000 |
| Shuruppak | Transfer | 1 | Flood | 18,600 |
| Kish | Heaven | 23 | Battle | 24,510 |
| Eanna | Conquest | 1 | Transfer | 324 |
| Erech | Transfer | 12 | Battle | 2,310 |
| Ur | Conquest | 4 | Battle | 177 |
| Awan | Conquest | 3 | Battle | 356 |
| Kish | Conquest | 8 | Battle | 3,195 |
| Hamazi | Conquest | 1 | Battle | 360 |
| Erech | Conquest | 3 | Battle | 187 |
| Ur | Conquest | 4 | Battle | 116 |
| Adab | Conquest | 1 | Battle | 90 |
| Mari | Conquest | 6 | Battle | 136 |
| Kish | Conquest | 1 | Battle | 100 |
| Akshak | Conquest | 6 | Battle | 99 |
| Kish | Conquest | 7 | Battle | 491 |
| Erech | Conquest | 1 | Battle | 25 |
| Agade | Conquest | 11 | Battle | 197 |
| Erech | Conquest | 5 | Gutian invasion | 30 |
| Gutians | Conquest | 21 | Battle | 91 |
| Erech | Conquest | 1 | Battle | 7 |
| Ur | Conquest | 5 | Battle | 108 |
| Isin | Conquest | 14 | — | 203 |

SOURCE: Kramer (1963).
NOTE: This is the "official record," the given length of particular dynasties.

ment of the irrigation system and created the demand for increased production.

Foreign invaders, or "barbarians," such as Amorites, Kassites, and Gutians, have sometimes been credited with bringing down Mesopotamian states. However, as Yoffee (1988a) observes, Mesopotamian civilization incorporated different ethnic groups that actually contributed to its persistence. It was only when the Persian invaders from a still larger empire conquered Mesopotamia that the established political system and later the entire civilization was brought down. Previous breakdowns did not prevent the city-states from being regrouped into regional states.

Thus, in the Mesopotamian case, we see a cultural tradition that maintained itself for a very long time despite chronic political instability. In the end, Mesopotamian civilization was superseded by a more powerful regional civilization, within what had become a western Asian world system based on extensive tributary empires. It appears that Mesopotamian civilization was so weakened when it lost its central position within the local world system that it was unable to recover from a routine dynastic collapse. This outcome could be considered an example of Service's (1960) law of evolutionary potential, but we are leaving out the specific historical details. The world-system concept will be discussed in more detail in Chapter 11.

## Harappa: Deurbanization and Cultural Continuity

By 1500 BC, the cities associated with the Harappan civilization in the Indus Valley were abandoned, perhaps 1000 years after their founding. Without the cities, the states also disappeared, along with the writing system. The best-known cities of Harappa and Mohenjo-Daro (Figure 10.2) were apparently rebuilt several times during that period; in the end, however, the civilization succumbed to a process that has been called **deurbanization** (Gosh 1982). As A. Gosh describes it, deurbanization would be the reverse of the urbanization process, and it implies a breakdown of political authority at the top. The population of cities would dwindle. Fewer full-time specialists, artisans, and administrators would be needed. Long-

distance trade in luxury goods would stop. Judging by the steady decline in the quality of housing, which is archaeologically documented, the city of Harappa seems to have turned into a slum before it was completely abandoned (Possehl 1977).

The cause of the demise of the Harappan civilization has been a long-standing "mystery" because there is no documentary account of the event. Three different explanations, however, have been posed: destruction by foreign invasion, natural destruction by Indus floods, or exhaustion of the resource base through overuse. The foreign-invasion theory has typically cited the Aryans as the principal villains, and skeletons piled in the streets of Mohenjo-Daro are presented as evidence of conquest and massacre. However, on close inspection, this interpretation seems weak. The Aryans did have a warrior tradition, but as noted earlier, their arrival cannot be correlated precisely with the fall of Harappan civilization. Furthermore, no hard evidence supports an invasion at either Harappa or Mohenjo-Daro.

The famous massacre is probably a myth, according to archaeologist George Dales (1964), who directed excavations at Mohenjo-Daro in the 1960s. Because the thirty-five skeletons were found in six different groups, which may not have been contemporaneous, and except for two of these groups, they were probably all intentional burials. It is likely that there were only two "bodies in the streets," and these were probably fortuitously buried on top of a much older street. There is no evidence of weapons or destruction to fortifications to indicate an assault ever took place and no evidence that the "victims" died of traumatic injury, according to Kenneth Kennedy (1982), who reexamined all the remains. Dales argues that bandits might have killed some people who remained in the city after it was abandoned for other reasons.

Perhaps the most dramatic single-cause explanation of Harappan collapse is the theory developed by Dales (1965, 1966, 1982; Dales and Raikes 1968) and his associate hydrologist Robert Raikes (1964, 1965): A series of great floods caused the cities to be abandoned. This theory, which Raikes (1964) admits is pure speculation, suggests that Harappan civilization was destroyed not by the normal fluctuation in the Indus seasonal flood re-

FIGURE 10.2 *Mo-henjo-Daro, one of the two urban centers of the Indus Valley civilization, which collapsed about 1500 BC.*

gime but by catastrophic tectonic uplift and associated earthquakes and flooding. They propose that uplift below Mohenjo-Daro caused perhaps several gigantic earth dams to block the flow of the Indus, flooding out the settlements immediately upstream and drowning them in a sea of mud. Earthquakes throughout the region would have destroyed other settlements and disrupted trade. Repeated attempts to rebuild or move the major cities ultimately failed. Dales summarizes this natural disaster view as follows:

> ... Flooding was the principal enemy of the Mohenjo-darians, and of all the Harappan period inhabitants of the lower Indus Valley. Bands of raiders from the nearby Baluchistan hills could well have taken advantage of the chaotic conditions following the floods, but they were apparently not the cause of such conditions. (1965:14)

The Dales-Raikes flood theory has been rigorously attacked by other researchers. H. T. Lambrick (1967) found insufficient geophysical evidence that an earth dam over 100 ft (30 meters [m]) high and more than 30 miles (48 kilometers [km]) long had formed across the Indus. He also argues that the sediment deposits in the Harappan cities could be accounted for in other ways. Greg-

ory Possehl (1967) also challenged the physical evidence for the dam and further argued that even if Mohenjo-Daro was so destroyed, that would be an insufficient explanation for the destruction of the entire civilization. Flooding was, after all, a normal problem along the Indus, and Possehl agrees that Mohenjo-Daro itself may have been repeatedly flooded out and rebuilt. Instead of flooding, Possehl favors the ecological argument that the Harappan civilization collapsed because of resource depletion.

Possehl cites conjectural evidence assembled by Walter Fairservis (1967) to suggest the level of resource demand posed by a city the size of Mohenjo-Daro. Based on data from contemporary Indus Valley villagers, Fairservis estimated that Mohenjo-Daro may have contained 41,250 people. The total population would have required at least 22,715 acres (9200 hectares) to supply 384 lb (174 kilograms [kg]) of grain per person per year. The necessary bullocks for plowing (one bullock plows 8 acres [3 hectares]) would require a herd of 8755

---

***deurbanization*** The decline and abandonment of cities.

cattle and another 3097 acres (1254 hectares) just to grow 25 percent of the fodder. Vast additional grazing lands would be required, but deforestation to supply building materials and fuel must have degraded much of the surrounding territory.

Dales and Raikes (1968) defended their "natural disaster approach" and rejected Possehl and Fairservis's "pre-conceived socio-economic model," by pointing out that there was no evidence for resource depletion, or "wearing out of the landscape," especially because the soil was seasonally renewed by the Indus flood.

Disregarding the specific causes of the breakdown of the urban phase of Harappan civilization, it is likely that it was largely expressed as a steady economic decline over a period of perhaps 200–300 years, with a reduction in the production of luxury goods (Rao 1982). Because, as some have suggested (Miller 1985), Harappa may have been less socially stratified than other ancient civilizations, the deurbanization transition may have been relatively smooth, with considerable cultural continuity. A recognized post–Harappan archaeological culture suggests that the Harappan peasantry "folk tradition" carried on much of the earlier culture and that significant cultural elements must have been reflected in the second urbanization that took place in the Ganges by 600 BC, culminating in the Hindu Great Tradition (Allchin 1982).

Like Mesopotamia, the Harappan case might also be considered an example of the local discontinuity of progress. However, the lengthy temporal gap between the fall of Harappa and the rise of classical Hindu civilization makes it difficult to argue that Harappa was outcompeted by a more "progressive" civilization. India provides numerous other examples of the rise and fall of states. After Harappa, over the centuries between 500 BC and AD 1970, sixty-two large regional states have successively arisen and collapsed in India (Figure 10.3).

## Andean Civilizations: Fragile Empire, Robust Culture

The Inca empire is as famous for the manner in which it collapsed as it is for its great size and wealth. The vast 380,000-square-mile (mi²)

(984,200-square-kilometer [km²]) empire, which may have had a population of 32 million people, was brought under foreign control within less than 5 years. Much of its wealth was subsequently extracted to benefit the even larger Spanish empire, whose capital was more than 5000 miles (8045 km) away. Even more remarkable was the fact that only 180 men comprised the conquering Spanish army. The Inca empire was, in fact, a very fragile political superstructure that had grown rapidly following the long-established tradition of Andean civilization. The basic nature of Andean civilization and the way in which political power was developed and empires expanded help explain the relative fragility of these complex systems, as well as their underlying cultural continuity. The following analysis is based largely on the work of Geoffrey Conrad and Arthur Demarest (1984).

According to Conrad and Demarest, the most critical factor underlying the dynamics of the Inca state was an ideological emphasis on ancestor cults. By AD 1000, ancestor worship as practiced by the kingdoms along the Peruvian coast began to assume forms that would set the stage for Inca expansion. A key cultural pattern related to the ancestor cult, and which the Inca shared with the north coast Chimu state, has been called *split inheritance* by Conrad (1981). Both the Chimu and Inca kings were worshiped as divinities after they died; even in death, they continued to hold title to the vast wealth that they had accumulated during their reigns. The office of kingship was inherited by the deceased ruler's principal son, but his other heirs were made trustees of the royal mummy and the deceased's treasury.

The practice of ancestor worship is very ancient in the Andean tradition, as indicated by the great attention devoted to funerary textiles and ceramics and by the fabulous treasure of gold and silver objects recently discovered in 2000-year-old unlooted Mochica royal burials (Alva 1990). The royal burials found in the Chimu city of Chanchan from the late empire period, immediately preceding the Inca, were contained within royal palaces, which were converted into royal temple-tombs upon the ruler's death. Ten such temple-tomb palaces have been identified in Chanchan, and it appears that the royal mummy was publicly displayed during repeated funeral ceremonies. This royal mummy

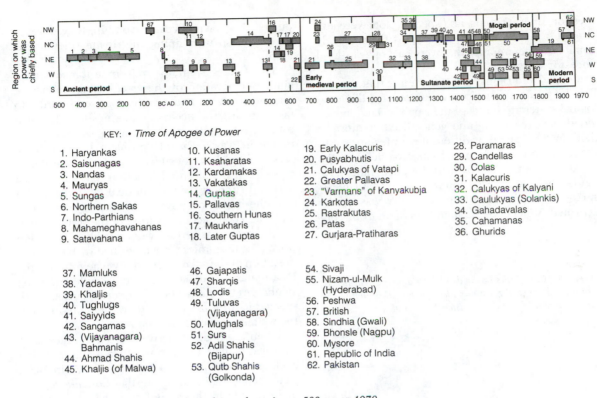

KEY: • *Time of Apogee of Power*

1. Haryankas
2. Saisunagas
3. Nandas
4. Mauryas
5. Sungas
6. Northern Sakas
7. Indo-Parthians
8. Mahameghavahanas
9. Satavahana

10. Kusanas
11. Ksaharatas
12. Kardamakas
13. Vakatakas
14. Guptas
15. Pallavas
16. Southern Hunas
17. Maukharis
18. Later Guptas

19. Early Kalacuris
20. Pusyabhutis
21. Calukyas of Vatapi
22. Greater Pallavas
23. "Varmans" of Kanyakubja
24. Karkotas
25. Rastrakutas
26. Patas
27. Gurjara-Pratiharas

28. Paramaras
29. Candellas
30. Colas
31. Kalacuris
32. Calukyas of Kalyani
33. Caulukyas (Solankis)
34. Gahadavalas
35. Cahamanas
36. Ghurids

37. Mamluks
38. Yadavas
39. Khaljis
40. Tughlugs
41. Saiyyids
42. Sangamas
43. (Vijayanagara) Bahmanis
44. Ahmad Shahis
45. Khaljis (of Malwa)

46. Gajapatis
47. Sharqis
48. Lodis
49. Tuluvas (Vijayanagara)
50. Mughals
51. Surs
52. Adil Shahis (Bijapur)
53. Qutb Shahis (Golkonda)

54. Sivaji
55. Nizam-ul-Mulk (Hyderabad)
56. Peshwa
57. British
58. Sindhia (Gwali)
59. Bhonsle (Nagpu)
60. Mysore
61. Republic of India
62. Pakistan

FIGURE 10.3    *Major powers of the Indian subcontinent, 500 BC–AD 1970.*

cult also included human sacrifices and is reminiscent of funerary patterns described earlier for Mesopotamia and Shang China. As in those cases, the Andean cult also must have functioned to reinforce the legitimacy of the rulers. More important for empire building, however, the added feature of split inheritance forced the newly installed ruler to engage in military conquest to build the personal wealth that would become the basis for his ancestor cult. Thus, an ideological pattern provided a clear motive for state expansion in the Andean area.

The Inca system of ancestor worship is well described in the ethnohistoric material recorded immediately after the Spanish conquest. It reveals the same functional connections between kinship, land, and political power that characterized Chinese ancestor worship. In the Inca case, as described by Conrad and Demarest (1984), the mummified bodies of the dead became sacred objects,

or *mallquis*, and specialist diviners, known as *mallquipvillac*, communicated with the ancestors through these mummies (Figure 10.4). The concept of *huaca*, shrine or sacred object, links the related concepts of *mallquis* (mummy), *ayllu* (descent group), and the kinship term *vilca* (great-grandfather or great-grandson, which also means ancestor). All these terms were used interchangeably. Furthermore, there are specific associations between specific ancestors and specific shrines. As in China, the well-being of the descent group was thought to depend on the proper ritual respect being accorded the *huaca* and mummy. In pre-Inca times, individual *ayllu* groups cared for their own mummies and *huacas*. Women wove special tex-

---

**split inheritance**  An Andean system of regulating succession to political office in which the principal son of a deceased ruler received political power and other heirs were given ritual power over the royal mummy.

tiles for funeral rituals, and specific plots were cultivated by *ayllu* members to support the relatively small-scale ceremonies that were part of *ayllu*-level ancestor worship.

Conrad and Demarest (1984) argue that the earliest Inca rulers consciously manipulated the ideological system to increase their power. They subdivided the preexisting and generalized creator/sky deity into at least four different manifestations, to make room for an imperial ancestor deity as the progenitor of the Inca dynasty. Because Andean religious beliefs were so interconnected and widespread, the divine–royalty concept was easily accepted. Whenever the members of an *ayllu* con-

ducted their own ancestor worship, they were, in a sense, also worshiping the divine ruler of the empire.

The Inca system of split inheritance was a simple elaboration of the established practice of ancestor worship and may have arisen in order to facilitate orderly succession to kingship. The earliest Inca rulers were probably war leaders, and factionalism was a chronic problem because there was no formal rule of succession. Split inheritance provided a major ritual function and guaranteed material support for the political faction that did not inherit political power. The Inca royal mummy cult was a conspicuous feature of the state religion and, as such, was certainly not a lowly consolation prize. The mummies were identified with the manifestation of the solar or sky deity who founded the Inca dynasty and, as such, were key legitimizing symbols of the state. They also were identified with specific natural forces and therefore could ensure the welfare of the general population.

When the Spanish arrived, the mummies of at least five earlier rulers in the Inca dynasty, dating back as far as Viracocha Inca, who died in 1438, were being maintained in the *Coricancha*, the main temple in the capital city of Cuzco (Figure 10.5). Each mummy was treated as lavishly as it had been in life. It was attended by its descendants, who served it as retainers and formed a corporate descent group, known as *panaqa*. *Panaqa* members were the *Orejones*, the Inca hereditary elite, who occupied the highest offices in the Inca bureaucracy. The *panaqa* was a special type of *ayllu*, a royal court focused on the deceased ruler who was treated as a *huaca*. The members of the *panaqa* paraded the mummy for important ceremonies, sacrificed food and drink to it, and managed its property.

The Inca system of split inheritance promoted imperial expansion because a ruler's personal wealth was derived from the production of his personal landholdings and the *mita* labor service that he could call up from his domain. The king needed to control land because labor service had to be rewarded with reciprocity in the form of food and drink as discussed in Chapter 7. All his personal royal estate remained with the *panaqa* of each ruler and significantly reduced the resources available both for the state as a whole and for suc-

FIGURE 10.4 *Cults of the dead were a prominent feature of Andean civilization as illustrated by this richly decorated skull from the pre-Inca Nazca culture.*

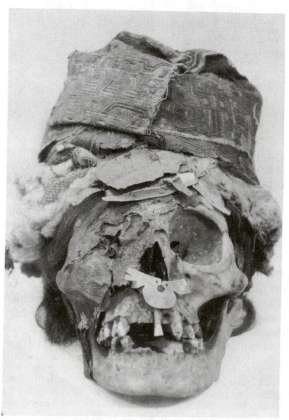

ceeding rulers. Therefore, the newly installed king was obligated to expand the total territory of the empire in order to finance the government and build his own wealth in food surpluses and subjects to support his *panaqa*.

While the underlying incentive for empire building was imposed on new rulers by split inheritance, successful conquest carried wide benefits. Conrad and Demarest (1984) point out that subsistence security improved for the population as a whole because new lands were opened up for agriculture and because state food stores could be stocked with staples from the new provinces. The hereditary elite *Orejones* derived additional wealth and power from war booty and must have formed a powerful interest group in support of further conquest. Individual citizens could also rise in the ranks as outstanding warriors and be rewarded with wealth and status as well as supernatural benefits.

In late pre-Inca times, the southern Andean highlands were divided into warring petty states or chiefdoms, which were the political units remaining after the fragmentation of the earlier Tiahuanaco empire. It appears that the institutionalization of split inheritance and the royal mummy cult, which began under the rule of Pachakuti Inca in 1438, gave the Inca rulers a decisive advantage in their struggles with their neighbors. However, Conrad and Demarest (1984) argue that continuous expansion quickly proved unsustainable. Within less than a century, the empire reached its maximum extent (see Figure 7.11). Beyond the limits of the familiar Andean environment, the Inca armies floundered at the edges of the Amazon rain forest, while further extension north or south along the Andean chain was hampered by communication difficulties. Administrative costs soared. The well-endowed *panaqa*, in effect, became rival kingdoms led by their mummy kings and were a constant challenge to the authority of the living Inca ruler. There were also problems with rebellious ethnic groups who were forcibly incorporated into the empire.

With no more frontiers open to easy conquest, the practice of split inheritance continued to push the elite to increase production, but now this meant confiscating prime land from the citizenry and increasing the labor tax to support the mummy cult. It also meant large-scale and costly

FIGURE 10.5 *Reconstructed view of the Coricancha, the main temple and center of the state religion in the Inca capital of Cuzco.* (SOURCE: *Conrad and Demerest.*)

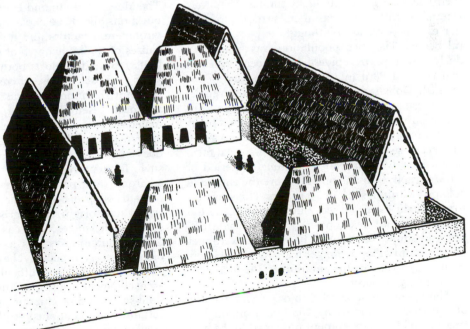

agricultural development projects on marginal lands subject to chronic crop failures. A further response to increasing economic pressures was the use of *yanacona* retainers and the *mitima* colonists as full-time agricultural laborers in service to the state and the nobility. Contrary to long-established Andean tradition, these changes made the rulers less obligated to maintain their reciprocal ties with the peasantry, and it undermined village self-sufficiency.

The final crisis began when the death of the Inca ruler Huayna Capac in 1525 resulted in controversy over the succession between two of his sons, Huascar, who assumed the throne in Cuzco, and Atahuallpa, who controlled the army. By this time, the economic deterioration of the empire had become so serious that Huascar attempted to abolish the royal mummy cult in an effort to stabilize the situation, but this move threatened the position of the *panaqa* elite and they joined with Atahuallpa in a civil war against Huascar. Atahuallpa won but was treacherously taken captive by the Spanish in 1532 before he could consolidate his victory.

Historians can cite many reasons for the remarkable success of the Spanish, but the secret of their success was simply lucky timing. They were veterans with steel swords, metal armor, guns, and horses, who were at first thought to be supernatural beings. The Inca population was being seriously disrupted by epidemic European diseases that reached Peru in 1524, 8 years ahead of the Spanish (Dobyns and Doughty 1976). However, despite these material and psychological advantages, the empire would have not fallen so easily if internal contradictions had not prepared the way. In the Inca case, split inheritance and a special form of ancestor worship caused a frenzied period of self-destructive expansion that drove the empire to collapse within less than 100 years. Huascar's reforms might have worked, but it was already too late. The empire was hopelessly divided against itself and simply fell apart. The Spanish were met by a peasantry that no longer had any vested interest in supporting the Inca mummies, the Inca elite, or the living emperor.

The Spaniards succeeded in destroying the last of the royal mummies by 1559, and although a fragmented Inca government remained in the hinterland until 1572, Inca civilization was effectively destroyed when the Spanish occupied Cuzco in 1533. The Andean cultural tradition, including subsistence practices, social organization, material culture, and beliefs, continued with little significant change at the village level. The Spanish replaced the Inca elite and turned the Inca labor tax into a harshly exploitative system that further impoverished the countryside. The Andean peasantry kept their language and culture, but they were forcibly incorporated into the emerging world system dominated by Europeans. The Spanish treatment of Atahuallpa was symbolic of the transformation. He was taken captive and held for ransom. To gain his release, he amassed a treasure of more than 13,000 lb (5889 kilograms [kg]) of gold and 26,000 lb (11,778 kg) of silver—three times the treasure that Cortez took from Mexico—but he was killed and the treasure went to Spain (Dobyns and Doughty 1976).

# THE LIMITS OF PROGRESS

## Diminishing Returns and Breakdown

The Mesopotamian and Harappan examples raise questions about the explanatory value of both environmental factors and foreign invasion as sole causes of the breakdown of states. Joseph Tainter (1988) explicitly rejects both explanations and instead proposes the use of **cost–benefit analysis** to pinpoint the inherent weaknesses of states. This approach resembles Rappaport's (1977a) "system maladaptation" approach, but Tainter treats states as general "problem-solving organizations" and does not focus on environmental equilibrium as such. Tainter stresses that it would be surprising if environmental problems were the primary cause of state collapse, because, according to some theories of state origin, states arise to help alleviate resource deficiencies. The case for the collapse of food-production systems as a cause of political breakdown is especially hard to make because cause and effect is difficult to establish from archaeological evidence. Furthermore, complex, state-supported production systems would almost certainly be abandoned in the event of political breakdown.

FIGURE 10.6 *The principle of diminishing returns.*

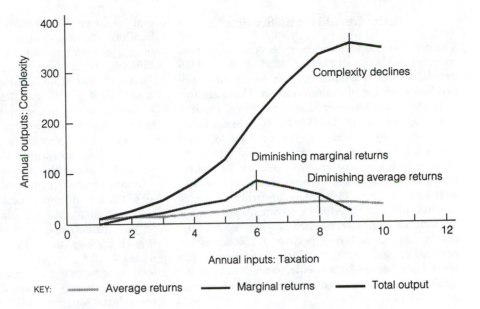

Tainter (1988) argues that environmental imbalance is only one example of a more general problem of *diminishing returns,* which affect virtually all state functions and most human endeavors. Technological or organizational changes that increase or maintain cultural complexity will eventually experience diminishing returns, and "collapse" will occur when the cost of maintaining cultural complexity becomes prohibitively expensive.

Diminishing returns apply to three conceptually distinct outputs, or products: *marginal returns, average returns,* and *total output.* Each output behaves somewhat differently, but marginal returns are most sensitive to the prognosis for the system. When marginal returns decline, more and more effort must be expended for less and less of whatever is being produced, whether it is food or cultural complexity. A decline in marginal returns means that average returns are also likely to decline soon, and, even though total output might continue to increase for a time, it too will experience a decline. Figure 10.6 shows diminishing returns on a scale of cultural complexity in relation to increases in tax revenues for a hypothetical state. This example arbitrarily assumes that average returns in complexity would increase for each added unit of revenue up to 8 units and

would then decline steadily. Such a decline would be due to rising inefficiency and corruption, as the bureaucracy became more cumbersome. In this case, marginal returns begin to decline when revenue inputs reach 6, but total complexity only declines when inputs reach 9. Thus, an inattentive ruler interested in rapid state building might be tempted to raise taxes too high by disregarding the warning sign of diminishing marginal returns.

---

*cost–benefit analysis*    Weighing the relative advantages of a particular course of action against its costs or disadvantages.

*diminishing returns*    The situation in which output values will decline as effort is increased in any production system.

*marginal returns*    The increase in the total output produced by the additional input; in subsistence production, the additional amount above what was produced the previous year, resulting from the increased effort.

*average returns*    The output divided by the input, the amount produced, or returned, for each unit expended; in subsistence production, the number of calories produced for each calorie expended on subsistence.

*total output*    The input multiplied by the average return. Marginal returns can be expected to decline first, followed by a decline in average returns, but total output may still continue to increase for a time before dropping.

## Agricultural Intensification

The primary problem for the ruler of a state is how to increase the production of food staples, which can be taxed to finance growth in the nonfood-producing sector of the population. There are two immediate ways to increase agricultural productivity: by increasing the number of peasant farmers and/or by increasing the amount of land farmed. Either approach, however, will ultimately require technological changes because of diminishing returns on labor. Danish agricultural economist Ester Boserup (1965) has argued that intensification of food production typically follows a predictable sequence of diminishing returns, involving shortened fallow periods, increased effort per unit of land, and technological change. People must work harder for a smaller return for their effort in order to increase the total production per unit of land.

The typical agricultural intensification sequence would begin with a shifting cultivation production system, such as the Amazonian example presented in Chapter 3. This is a *forest fallow system* because a plot must be allowed to return to forest before it can be recultivated in order to maintain soil quality. Productivity per unit of labor input with shifting cultivation is relatively high, but the output per unit of land is very low when the forest is counted as part of the production system. The forest fallow system can, in theory, remain stable if no additional demands arise from population increase or political pressure to extract a surplus. When increases are required, this can be accomplished by shortening the fallow period and thereby putting more land into production at a given time. The problem with this is that *secondary forest* is brushy and requires more work to clear than *primary forest;* thus increasing the labor input. As the fallow period is shortened further, hoes will be needed to dig out the weeds, and composting may be required to maintain soil fertility. When the fallow period is reduced to 1 year, a plow and draft animals will be needed to turn over the grass sod, which has replaced the forest.

The data presented in Table 10.3 and shown graphically in Figure 10.7 are largely conjectural, but they make more concrete the abstract principle of diminishing returns in agricultural intensification. Because documenting the intensification process for a single culture through time would be difficult, these figures were generated by using an Amazonian shifting cultivation system and a Chinese irrigated rice–growing village to define extreme points along a straight-line continuum. The intermediate values were simply extrapolated. Calculations of this sort are imprecise because the underlying data are estimates subject to sampling error and because the different systems themselves may not be strictly comparable. For example, not all of the potential production of a shifting cultivation system is ever harvested, and a garden plot may continue to be productive to some degree as it goes through the fallow process. Different estimates would generate different curves; nevertheless, the figures demonstrate the magnitude of difference between land-extensive systems, which make little demand on labor, and highly intensive systems, which require a very large labor force.

These figures also help explain why extensive systems are more likely to be found with small-scale egalitarian cultures. It could certainly be argued that people would not willingly move to the more intensive system, which clearly increases work loads, unless they were pushed by population growth or political pressure. Political factors, such as taxation, are probably the most important determinants of agricultural intensification because, when a ruler extracts a steadily increasing "surplus" from a peasantry with a fixed land base, the only way for the peasants to reduce their individual rise in labor costs is to raise a larger family and divide the work load. Thus, the population will tend to grow, but the underlying cause is the *political policy* of the state, not the inherent tendency of population to rise. In previous chapters, it was argued that diminishing returns in subsistence might provide a cultural incentive for limiting family size in a tribal culture where individual households are free to set their own production goals.

## State Institutional Functions and Costs

As a state system develops, a series of new problems arise, each of which offers further areas in which rising costs and diminishing returns occur.

**TABLE 10.3**  *Diminishing Returns in Agricultural Intensification*

| Subsistence Type* | Input/Hectare (in thousands of kcal) | Average Return (in kcal) | Total Output (in millions of kcal) | Marginal Return (in millions of kcal) |
|---|---|---|---|---|
| Forest fallow | 24 | 72 | 1.7 | — |
| Bush fallow | 250 | 68 | 17.0 | 15.3 |
| Short fallow | 475 | 62 | 29.0 | 12.0 |
| Annual crop | 700 | 56 | 39.0 | 10.0 |
| Multicrop | 912 | 50 | 45.8 | 6.8 |

*Forest fallow system is based on estimates for Amazonian shifting cultivation of manioc (30,000 lbs [13,590 kg] of manioc/acre/year for 1606 hours/year)/25-year fallow. Multicrop system is based on the Chinese village of Luts'un (Chapter 8). Data for the intermediate systems are based on extrapolations from the Amazonian and Chinese data. Bush fallow assumes hoe cultivation on an 8-year rotation. Short fallow assumes plow cultivation on a 2-year rotation.

**FIGURE 10.7**  *Diminishing returns in agricultural intensification.*

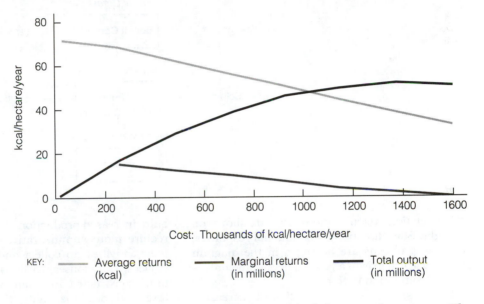

Cost:  Thousands of kcal/hectare/year

KEY:  Average returns (kcal)    Marginal returns (in millions)    Total output (in millions)

The state is composed of institutional responses to the special problems that it creates, but each response requires further increases in the number of nonfood-producing specialists and includes additional capital costs and maintenance costs. The states' institutional responses themselves generate new problems that call for new institutional solutions, in a continually expanding positive-feedback system with steadily diminishing returns.

Figure 10.8 illustrates some of these complex interconnections. The key functions that the state must support if it is to survive are staple production, wealth production, maintenance costs, technology, coordination, storage, transport, informa-tion, social control, defense, and conquest. The specialists carrying out specific functions—corvée laborers, artisans, and so on—are shown on the left in the figure, opposite the functions they serve. The physical constructions, or capital costs—pal-

***forest fallow system***  Using regrowth of the forest to restore soil fertility.

***secondary forest***  An immature forest containing pioneer species that will disappear as they are replaced by the shade-tolerant species that dominate the primary forest.

***primary forest***  A fully developed forest assumed to be in a steady state.

FIGURE 10.8 *State functions and costs.*

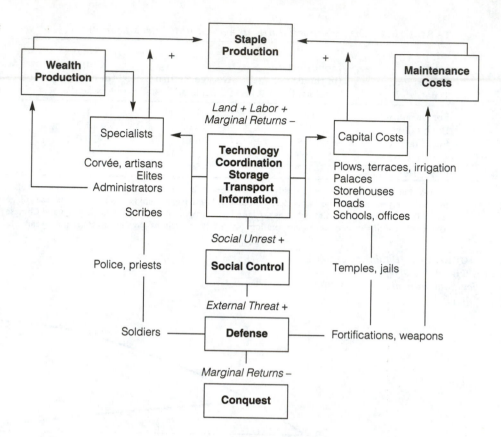

aces, irrigation systems, and so on—are shown on the right. State functions, institutional responses, and new problems are arranged in the diagram along a vertical axis in a general developmental sequence from top to bottom.

The most critical state function of increasing staple-food production is met at first through taxation that forces the peasantry to put more land into production, to shorten fallow periods, and to encourage larger families. However, increased pressure on land and labor generates the problem of marginal returns because the soil becomes depleted and cultivation is more difficult. The state must then finance a series of technological changes in order to apply more and more labor to each unit of land. Full-time artisans will be needed to manufacture new tools such as metal hoes and then plows. Eventually, large drafts of corvée labor must be mobilized to build terraces and irrigation canals. These developments will themselves re-

quire increased production of food staples and will require more administrative elites to coordinate their activities, to collect and store the revenue. Palaces, storehouses, roads, and offices will need to be constructed and maintained. The increased taxes and social inequality will generate social unrest, calling for social control functions provided by priests and police, temples and jails. A successful state with large storehouses and wealthy palaces will tempt neighboring states to invade; therefore, soldiers, weapons, and fortifications will be needed for defense functions. Eventually, as marginal returns decline in all areas, territorial expansion and looting through conquest will become an attractive means of perpetuating the system.

Table 10.4 gives some indication of the relative cost of state functions. Like previous estimates, these figures are largely conjectural, but they illustrate some of the constraints with which ancient rulers had to contend. This example shows the

TABLE 10.4    *State Finance in the Early Dynastic City-State of Ur, Mesopotamia*

| Capital Construction* | Total Cost (5 years) | Annual Cost |
|---|---|---|
| Irrigation canals | 1,544,825 | 308,965 |
| Storehouses | 500,000 | 100,000 |
| Palace | 965,515 | 193,103 |
| Ziggurat | 2,395,310 | 479,062 |
| City wall | 500,000 | 100,000 |
| *Total construction costs* | 5,905,650 | 1,181,130 |

| | |
|---|---|
| 1,181,130 | Total annual construction costs |
| + 253,500 | 500 workmen × 507 kg of grain per year |
| +1,102,000 | 5800 citizens × 380 kg of grain per year × 50% famine reduction |
| 2,536,639 | *Subtotal 1* |
| + 380,495 | Subtotal 1 × seed grain (15%) |
| 2,917,125 | *Subtotal 2* |
| + 729,281 | Subtotal 2 × storage loss (25%) |
| 3,646,406 | *Total annual cost* |

$$\text{Annual production} = \text{hectares} \times \frac{\text{kg of grain}}{\text{hectare}}$$

$$2,400,000 = 6000 \text{ hectares} \times \frac{400 \text{ kg of grain}}{\text{hectare}}$$

$$\text{Revenue} = \text{annual production} \times \text{tax rate (25\%)}$$

$$600,000 = 2,400,00 \times .25$$

SOURCES: Data for capital construction costs from Erdosy (1988) and Wheatly (1971). Estimates for storage, seed, population, and grain production from Wright (1969) and Adams (1981).
*Capital construction costs are expressed in kilograms of grain required to supply a workman's official barley ratio of 60 *sila*/month, 507 kg/year (see Chapter 7).

possible costs of capital construction in an early Mesopotamian city-state such as Ur. The values represent kilograms of barley, which was the basic ration used to pay laborers. With a combined population of perhaps only 5800 people, the small city of Ur and its support communities would have needed to draft large numbers of temporary laborers from outside to complete these projects within a short time. If the canals, storehouses, palace, ziggurat, and city walls were all built within 5 years as Table 10.4 assumes, more than 11,000 construction workers would have been needed each year. Shortening construction time would have been difficult.

Given potential grain production in the 14,815 cultivated acres (6000 hectares) surrounding Ur and a tax rate of 25 percent, grain stores would

have to accumulate for 6 years to finance each year of construction. In the meantime, losses in storage would taken an increasing toll. It would take the state 2 years just to accumulate enough surplus grain to supply half of the annual subsistence needs of its regular citizens in the case of a crop failure.

Because the capital costs of state functions are relatively high, they would probably only be taken on as they became absolutely necessary. Construction projects would probably be carried out in the order listed, with technological improvements in agricultural production coming first. Large-scale temple construction and expensive royal tombs would probably be later elaborations designed to reduce social unrest by lending greater religious legitimacy to the state apparatus.

Any increases in nonfood-producing elites or other government specialists would add to the state's financial burden. However, as C. Northcote Parkinson (1957) shows, bureaucracy exhibits an inherent tendency to expand, even as total output declines. According to **Parkinson's law,** administrative staffs will expand at a predictable rate of 5.75 percent a year, regardless of the actual work produced. This is because overworked officials prefer to add at least two subordinates rather than dividing their work with a potential rival. At the same time, new officials increase their work loads because they slow the flow of information. The potential growth rate of bureaucracy thus vastly outstrips population growth and helps explain the diminishing returns that occur with increases in cultural complexity.

Figure 10.9 illustrates the significance of **Parkinson's law** by demonstrating that in 300 years a staff of 10 people would, in theory, expand to more than 192 million people. At the same time, the base population would expand from 250 to under 1.8 million people if it grew at 3 percent a year, which is a very high but possible rate. Such an outcome would, of course, be impossible because if bureaucracy actually did increase at 5.75 percent a year, the system would collapse long before the demand for bureaucrats exceeded the total popu-

lation. Tax revenues to support the nonfood-producing administrators could not be sustained by the dwindling farm labor force. In this case, collapse could occur without environmental deterioration.

## SUMMARY

State breakdown, like the rise of states, is an overdetermined phenomenon. This means that it can be caused by many different, often interconnected factors, such that identifying the most important causes is often difficult. Because the state is a form of political organization, it could be argued that the best explanations for its demise will be political. However, as the examples demonstrate, specific environmental problems, ideological factors, and foreign invasion can all amplify the political weaknesses inherent in state organization. The best explanations in any particular case require detailed historical information. The most critical weakness of states is their vulnerability to diminishing returns in many important state functions.

## STUDY QUESTIONS

1. What does state breakdown mean? How can it be identified? Use specific examples.

FIGURE 10.9
*Growth of population
and bureaucracy.*

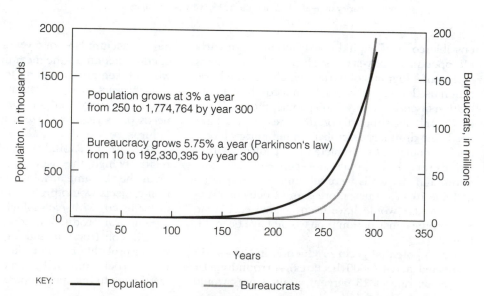

2. How can state organization be considered maladaptive from a systems theory perspective? Include the following concepts in your discussion: adaptive equilibrium, adaptive structures, maladaptation, system regulators, hierarchical anomolies, and usurpation.

3. Relate the principle of diminishing returns and Parkinson's law to the problem of state breakdown. Include the following concepts in your discussion: cost–benefit analysis, diminishing marginal returns, average returns, and total output.

4. Explain how diminishing returns in agricultural productions operate.

5. Critically discuss each of the following explanations for the demise of Harappan civilization: foreign invasion, floods, and resource depletion.

6. Why was the Spanish conquest of the Inca empire so easy?

7. Explain the law of evolutionary potential and the principle of local discontinuity of progress. Apply them to specific case material.

## SUGGESTED READING

LOWE, JOHN W. 1985. *The Dynamics of Apocalypse: A Systems Simulation of the Classic Maya Collapse.* Albuquerque: University of New Mexico Press. One of several interpretations of the Maya case.

PARKINSON, C. NORTHCOTE. 1957. *Parkinson's Law and Other Studies in Administration.* Boston: Houghton Mifflin. The classic study of why bureaucracy tends to expand and become unworkable.

TAINTER, JOSEPH A. 1988. *The Collapse of Complex Societies.* Cambridge, Eng.: Cambridge University Press. A nice review of explanations for collapse that includes many case studies and treats the Romans, Maya, and Chaco Couzon in detail.

YOFFEE, NORMAN, AND GEORGE L. COWGILL (eds.). 1988. *The Collapse of Ancient States and Civilizations.* Tucson: University of Arizona Press. A collection of case studies by specialists covering Mesopotamia, the Maya, Teotihucan, the Romans, and *Han* China.

***Parkinson's law*** Predicts the endless expansion of bureaucracy because, as work increases, individual bureaucrats will invariably add at least two new subordinates, whose presence will increase the work load.

# 11

# THE EMERGING WORLD SYSTEM

In this chapter and Chapters 12–15, we look at the contemporary world as it has been shaped by the Industrial Revolution and related changes in political economy into the interconnected, economically stratified, global system of nation-states that we see today. Clearly, industrialization must be seen as something more than a shift to fossil fuels and assembly-line factory production, which began in western Europe and North America at the end of the eighteenth century. This change transformed the world, drawing small- and large-scale cultures into a single global system. In the process, world population increased nearly sixfold from some 800 million people in 1750 to 5.3 billion in 1990, while per-capita rates of resource consumption and standards of wealth soared to unprecedented levels for many in the industrial centers and declined for the majority elsewhere.

## THE NATURE OF CAPITALISM

### Systems of Production and Exchange

The modern capitalist economy is radically different from all previous systems of production and exchange, and the distinctive features of capitalism created the global political economy. The concept of *political economy* emphasizes the fact that economics cannot be separated from politics. This shifts attention from the technological and ecological foundations of "economic" activity to a consideration of cultural factors such as political organization and ideology, which ultimately determine the ways in which humans exploit the earth. Capitalist economic organization uses social inequality to promote wealth accumulation and political expansionism on a scale unequaled in human history (Figure 11.1).

To understand the global impact of European colonial expansion, which was driven by capitalism, anthropologist Eric Wolf (1982) adopted the Marxian concept of *mode of production.* This is a useful concept, even though it has unfortunately been identified with *Marxism* as a political ideology. Karl Marx (1818–1883), the nineteenth-century German sociologist and political theorist, originally used mode of production to refer to the various ways in which people organize their labor (the *relations of production*) and technology (the material *forces of production*) to meet their physical needs and to reproduce society. Marx believed that capitalism would ultimately be superseded by communism, and he invented a specific historical sequence of modes of production to support his theory. The details of his developmental theory have been rejected by many scholars, but the underlying concept of a mode of production remains useful because it helps identify the specific ways in which cultures at different positions within the world system affect one another.

For his purposes, Wolf (1982) distinguishes just three modes of production: **kin-ordered, tributary,** and **capitalist**. Each type will be examined below.

Wolf's kin-ordered mode of production characterizes the small-scale cultures treated in Chapters 2–5. In these systems, kinship constitutes the culturally defined social categories around which productive activities are organized. Relationships between individuals established by marriage or family connections, real or fictive, determine the form of food-producing and -sharing groups. In all systems that are ordered exclusively by kinship, production is primarily for direct consumption, or **use value,** rather than for **exchange value.** From a Marxist perspective, political power in kin-based systems is derived from the age hierarchy and male control over women, which in theory could give older men greater control over the organization of labor. Significant inequalities and conflict can arise in a kin-based political economy when intensive agriculture or herding increases the importance of land and labor.

Kin-based groups fluctuate in size as a result of random demographic processes, and conflict may lead to fissioning, but small-scale cultures tend to resist overall changes in the basic mode of production. However, as we have seen, under certain conditions descent groups may become ranked, and the heads of politically more powerful branches may become the basis for chiefdom organization. Wolf's (1982) emphasis on mode of production clarifies the distinction between relatively small-scale chiefdoms such as on Tikopia, where production is ordered by kinship, and larger-scale systems such as in Hawaii, where social classes appear based on tribute payments.

Under the tributary mode of production, which characterized the ancient civilizations examined in Chapters 6–10, the peasantry remained in control of their basic resources and produced their own food, while the state supported itself by extracting the surplus as tribute. Title to land was often claimed by the state, but it was political power and ideology that compelled the peasantry to turn over surplus production to the state. The structure of surplus extraction was maintained by placing primary producers in subordinate status positions relative to the nonfood-producing elites. Much of the accumulated wealth went into maintaining status differences by means of the conspicuous display of luxury goods or in the construction of awe-inspiring temples and funerary ritual. Bureaucratically organized tribute extraction often existed alongside of long-distance market-oriented exchange systems managed by merchants or traders. Developed market systems helped the state acquire exotic luxury goods, but a fully commercialized distribution system would have undermined the status structure that supported the tribute system and would, in theory, have transformed it into a capitalist mode of production.

Marx considered the emergence of a monetary market for labor to be the key distinguishing feature of the capitalist mode of production. He ar-

---

**mode of production**    Marx's term for the way in which a society organizes its labor and technology.

**Marxism**    A political ideology based on Marx's theories that focuses on material conditions and class struggle and that assumes capitalism will be superseded by communism.

**relations of production**    Marx's term for the organization of labor.

**forces of production**    Marx's term for technology as a component of mode of production.

**kin-ordered production**    A mode of production organized at the domestic or kinship level and producing primarily for domestic use rather than exchange.

**tributary production**    A mode of production in which products are extracted as surplus from a self-supporting peasantry and used to support the state.

**capitalist production**    A mode of production in which a few people control the means of production and purchase the labor of those who could not otherwise support themselves.

**use value**    The value of goods produced for domestic consumption, usually within a kin-ordered mode of production.

**exchange value**    The value of goods when used as commodities.

FIGURE 11.1    *The New York Stock Exchange is one of the central institutions of the capitalist market economy, which drives the global-scale culture.*

increased by depressing the wage of the laborers and by raising the level of technology. The self-interests of capitalists to increase their profits by keeping the labor wage low is opposed to the interest of laborers to increase their own share of the products of their labor. Individual capitalists also compete with one another to increase their individual profits. This incentive to increase profits, as well as the contradiction of interests between social classes, accelerates the inherent tendency of states to promote technological development and territorial expansion.

Anthropologists and economists also describe economic systems according to the predominant form of exchange. For example, Karl Polanyi (1957) distinguished between kin-based sharing, which he called "reciprocity," and the "redistribution" exchanges carried on in ancient, tribute-collecting kingdoms and empires. These are nonmarket systems even when money is involved because exchanges are based on the status of the participants rather than legal contracts drawn up between them.

## Capitalism: An Emic View

Adam Smith (1723–1790), Scottish philosopher, political economist, and founding father of capitalism, presents an insightful and remarkably frank, emic view of the early capitalist market economy. In his famous book *Wealth of Nations* (1776), Smith identifies labor specialization and private ownership of land, together with the related emergence of landlords, manufacturers, laborers, rent, and profit, as the fundamental elements of a market, or "commercial" economy. In this system, the landlord received his share of production as **rent** and advanced part to laborers as **wages** for their maintenance. Labor specialization in manufacturing required that the manufacturer accumulate stock, or capital, but permitted dramatic increases in production. Wealth inequality was an important feature of the system.

Smith (1776) thought that most laborers "naturally" needed masters to maintain them between harvests and to carry out productive tasks. The relative poverty of laborers gave the manufacturers and landlords a strategic advantage in any disputes over wages. Even though they were ulti-

gued that the labor market emerged historically when capitalists separated the peasantry from their land and other resources that constituted their means of production, thus compelling the peasantry to sell their labor in order to secure basic subsistence. Laborers came to constitute a social class characterized by their separation from the means of production. Land and tools became **capital,** which was owned by a few, and basic products became **commodities** to be marketed. As a social class, capitalists, or the owners of capital, made a profit by appropriating surplus production above the costs of labor and capital. In this mode of production, the capitalist seeks to accumulate surplus in order to increase profit. Surplus can be mately dependent on their laborers, most manufacturers and landlords, with their larger stockpiles of wealth, could last more than 1 year if the laborers stopped working to enforce a demand for increased wages. Smith estimated that most laborers would not have enough stores to hold out more than 1 week without their wages.

Smith argued that as long as government did not intervene unduly, economic competition caused by people's natural desire for self-improvement would maintain orderly economic growth, as if by an *invisible hand*. Smith advocated that workers receive the lowest wage "which is consistent with common humanity" (1776:103). This minimum wage was determined by the short-run maintenance needs of individual workers combined with approximately double that amount to provide enough for workers to reproduce. He did not quantify this amount precisely but assumed that a worker would support a wife and four children, only two of which would reach adulthood. According to Smith, a direct feedback operated between increasing demand for labor during times of economic growth and an increase in the labor supply because wages would necessarily go up. This would mean that the poor could better support their children so that more would grow up to become workers. If there were too many workers, wages would go down, and the ensuing poverty would increase infant mortality, thereby reducing the number of workers and raising wages.

Smith thought that improved wages would increase production because it would give workers hope and make them work harder. Thus, continuous growth seemed to be the most desirable condition, as Smith explained:

*. . . It is in the progressive state, while the society is advancing to the further acquisition . . . that the condition of the labouring poor, of the great body of the people, seems to be the happiest and the most comfortable. It is hard in the stationary, and miserable in the declining state. The progressive state is in reality the cheerful and the hearty state to all the different orders of the society. The stationary is dull; the declining, melancholy.* (1776: 123)

Implicit in Smith's work is the concept of the *economy* existing apart from the rest of society. This ideology that linked social well-being with economic prosperity represented the ultimate disembodiment of the economy, especially because it assumed that prosperity was achieved by individuals pursuing their own self-interest with the least interference by government (Dumont 1977).

The contrast between the market-capitalism conception of economy and the ancient tributary economy can be demonstrated by a modern textbook critique of the economic theory of Greek philosopher Aristotle (384–322 BC). According to economists Robert Ekelund and Robert Hebert (1983), the Greek concept of economy was unprogressive because ancient economies were socially *embedded*.

Aristotle advocated a production and exchange system that, in theory, was remarkably reminiscent of the "original affluent society" of foragers as described by Marshall Sahlins (1968). Aristotle thought that human wants were limited and that economic scarcity was not a problem. This ideal was probably not actually realized in the Greek city-state, but it represents a view that is in direct opposition to the modern definition of a *disembodied economy*, which assumes limited means and unlimited wants. Aristotle's ideal city-state assumed a small community based on reciprocal exchange, self-sufficiency, and justice. In this system, an individual was not supposed to make a profit at

---

*capital*   Marx's term for land and tools as the means of production; also refers generally to accumulated wealth used for productive purposes.

*commodities*   Basic goods that are produced for their exchange value in a market economy to generate profit to be accumulated as capital.

*rent*   According to Smith, production or labor provided to a landlord by his laborers in exchange for the use of his land.

*wages*   Cash or commodities advanced by the landlord to his laborers to provide for their maintenance in exchange for their labor.

*invisible hand*   The capitalist belief that market forces, operating through supply and demand, will lead to continuous economic growth.

*embedded economy*   An economy that can only be observed and understood within the context of the social, political, and religious systems of the culture.

*disembodied economy*   The concept of an economy as something that can be understood apart from the rest of society and culture, especially with a capitalist mode of production.

his neighbor's expense because this would lead to inequality that would threaten community solidarity. Aristotle accepted money as a medium of exchange but argued that too much market trade would undermine the good life, and he considered wealth accumulation to be contrary to natural law.

Ekelund and Hebert (1983) are quick to point out the "apparent wrongheadedness" (p. 17) of Aristotle's economic theory, observing that it "is not economics as we know it" (p. 15) because it lacks an institutional economic framework and makes the wrong assumptions about human behavior. After all, as followers of Adam Smith, we now know that people are "naturally" self-seeking, individualistic, and acquisitive.

Economists Robert Heilbroner and Lester Thurow (1987) point out that earlier, noncapitalist societies did not institutionalize private property and had no organized markets for land, labor, and money. Production and trade was conducted on command, and people became wealthy because of their political power. Furthermore, people lacked the concept of economic freedom and were bound to their occupations. In contrast, "the capitalist employee has the legal right to work or not work as he or she chooses"(Heilbroner and Thurow 1987: 12–14), as well as the right to buy up farmland and turn it into a shopping center. Presumably, this allows one to find the most profitable arrangement.

Heilbroner and Thurow (1987) consider capitalism to be "utterly alien" and a "volcanic disruption" in comparison to the "tradition and command" systems that preceded it. In their view, there were no "factors of production" in precapitalist societies because "labor, land, and capital were not commodities for sale." Instead, these factors

*. . . are the creations of a process of historic change, a change that divorced labor from social life, that created real estate out of ancestral land, and that made treasure into capital. Capitalism is the outcome of a revolutionary change—a change in laws, attitudes, and social relationships as deep and far-reaching as any in history.* (1987: 15–16)

These emic views of the capitalist economy accurately highlight the cultural features that generate economic and sociocultural expansion on an unprecedented scale. The disembodied capitalist economy is no longer merely at the service of political rulers; it is a system of creating endlessly increasing profits for a new wealthy elite and is itself now supported by political power. Under capitalism, production and distribution are separated from the satisfaction of basic human needs, and social inequality promotes further economic growth. The following section shows how capitalism created a distinctive world system that brought together diverse societies into what has now become a global hierarchy of wealthy and poor nations.

## Immanuel Wallerstein's Capitalist World System

Modern social science theorist Immanuel Wallerstein helped found an important new, interdisciplinary approach to world culture with his 1974 publication of the first volume of *The Modern World System*. Wallerstein observed that the emergence of capitalism in sixteenth-century Europe created a uniquely organized global world economy by the early twentieth century. In his view, capitalism succeeded as a social system because it proved to be a more effective means of appropriating surplus production than the earlier tributary empires. Empires that used coercion to extract surplus were expensive to maintain and very fragile. Earlier, noncapitalist states were, in effect, "homeostatic systems," in that they tended to rise and fall within certain limits set by their unstable political organization. In comparison with tribal cultures, the early states and empires functioned at a much higher density and total size, but they were still limited in absolute scale.

In the capitalist **world system**, expansion to the limits of the globe became theoretically possible because the system can function without a centralized state political authority. Individual states are needed only to maintain internal order and to encourage the international market economy. The key to the success of capitalism was that the market economy provided incentives for technological improvements that increased productivity, while a world division of labor allowed costs and benefits to be unequally apportioned.

In an argument anticipated in André Gunder

Frank's (1967) model of the modern world divided into a developed *core* of wealthy capitalist nations and a *periphery* of dependent, underdeveloped nations, Wallerstein (1974) proposed that the emerging capitalist world system was a multilayered economic hierarchy divided into a European core, a southern European semiperiphery, and an eastern European and New World periphery. Each zone was defined by distinctive geography, political organization, economic production, and its form of labor control, but the zones were all linked to the center by *unequal exchanges* that contributed to *capital accumulation* in the core. The exploited lower classes were concentrated in the periphery and *semiperiphery*, where they were coerced to work as slaves and serfs for European managers. Conditions were somewhat less coercive for the tenant farmers in the semiperiphery. In the core, laborers worked for wages, and small farmers worked their own land, while merchants and industrialists profited enormously from their privileged positions as the ultimate beneficiaries of the unequal exchange.

It is important to note the distinctions between *world* and *globe* in this context. The world system initially does not encompass the globe; it begins in Europe and expands outward. Wallerstein (1974) distinguishes four distinct historical phases in which the world system originates in an economic crisis that undermined European feudalism by 1450 and encouraged capital accumulation at the expense of the peasantry. The system was spurred on by the gold and silver extracted as booty from the New World and was consolidated as a system between 1640 and 1815. The Industrial Revolution, utilizing coal as a new energy base, facilitated further expansion, which transformed the world system into a global system between 1815 and 1917. Since 1917 the system has consolidated further.

Albert Bergesen (1990) thinks that Wallerstein overemphasizes the role of unequal exchange relations in forming the modern world system. This makes the expansion of capitalism seem too "natural" and too narrowly an economic process. Instead, Bergesen argues, unequal exchange was an outgrowth of a political process. The periphery was a conquered world that did not join the capitalist world system voluntarily. This emphasis on conquest applies equally well to the breakdown and incorporation by the world system of the great New World empires, such as the Inca, the preindustrial kingdoms of Africa and Asia, and most small-scale tribal groups. Wallerstein (1974) documents the role of colonialism and conquest in the expansion of the world system, but he is reluctant to assign causal priority to either political or economic processes. However, his emphasis on market processes and commodity chains perhaps inadvertently suggests the operation of Smith's "invisible hand."

Wallerstein (1990) lists six destabilizing realities that characterize the modern world system:

1. A hierarchical division of labor
2. Periodic expansion and incorporation
3. Continuous accumulation
4. Continuous progress
5. Polarization of individuals and groups
6. The impossibility of perpetual growth

These characteristics imply critical contradictions in the system and have generated particular ideologies that tend to obscure the realities and help keep the system functioning.

According to Wallerstein (1990), the global division of labor integrates the world into a single production system based on exploitation and inequal-

---

**world system**  An international hierarchy of diverse societies and cultures integrated into a single economic system based on unequal exchange that allows wealth to accumulate in the core.

**core**  The wealthy industrial countries at the center of the world system where the recipients of unequal exchange reside.

**periphery**  Capital poor areas that supply raw materials and labor to the core; this area was integrated into the early capitalist world system through conquest and coercion.

**unequal exchange**  Market-based exchanges in which one party is consistently able to accumulate a disproportionate share of the profit or wealth.

**capital accumulation**  Expanding wealth and the means of production that can be devoted to further production.

**semiperiphery**  The intermediate area where labor was incorporated into the capitalist world system through sharecropping and serfdom rather than slavery.

FIGURE 11.2 *A cotton mill in Lancashire, England, 1900. Factory workers in the industrial core of the global system worked long hours, but they were encouraged by their religious faith that hard work was the key to salvation and by their belief in continuous economic growth.*

ities that paradoxically are supported by ideologies that stress universal values of peace and world order. Racist ideologies are also used to justify the disadvantaged position of peripheral groups with the argument that economic rewards are apportioned differentially according to the intrinsic merit and ability of different groups.

Since 1450 the world system has gone through cycles of expansion marked by the steady incorporation of external cultural groups into the periphery. This trend has been supported by the ideology calling for all peoples to be assimilated into a universal Western culture, on the assumption that other cultures were simply incapable of "advance." A universalist countertheme arguing for cultural diversity could also be used to justify an exploitative division of labor, in which newly incorporated groups would be encouraged to retain their ethnic identities while working at specific poorly paid jobs and perhaps living in ghettos. Continuous capital accumulation requires workers to accept increases in work load in exchange for reductions in pay. This is made easier when workers also accept a "work ethic" ideology, extolling the virtues

of hard work and competitiveness to overcome inequality (Figure 11.2). German social scientist Max Weber (1864–1920) was the first to point out that extreme Calvinist forms of Protestantism encouraged capital accumulation, in his famous book *The Protestant Ethic and the Spirit of Capitalism* (1930 [1904–1905]). According to Weber, German Calvinists believed that continuous hard work and self-denial was the best way to demonstrate that one was predestined for salvation. Such a belief was a religious endorsement for precisely the behavior that the capitalist economy needed.

Wallerstein (1990) observes that the capitalist quest for continuous progress and change contains a contradiction because it implies that even the political system should be changed. This can be countered by extreme nationalist ideologies emphasizing patriotism, which if pushed too far lead to destructive wars.

According to Wallerstein (1990), capitalism tends to polarize people by steadily widening the gap between rich and poor. However, such a reality is destabilizing and is therefore vigorously denied by the world system's "central myth of the rising standard of living." Wallerstein argues that elites in the core countries use "math tricks" to persuade peripheral peoples that wealth inequality is decreasing. Such myths ignore population increase, work loads, and environmental impacts, which might show a declining standard of living. Core elites also exhort the periphery to greater "development" efforts, while implying that failure to achieve development must be due to racial or cultural inferiority. The most serious contradiction of the capitalist world system is its failure to acknowledge that the system as constituted cannot expand forever.

## EARLY INDUSTRIAL CAPITALISM

### The Industrial Revolution and the Culture of Consumption

The most outstanding physical transformations accompanying the modern world system were the dramatic increases in population and resource consumption, which began in England between 1760 and 1830. Immediately prior to the Industrial Revolution, world population growth was relatively slow, with a doubling time of approximately 250 years. However, with industrialization well established, the European population doubled in just 80 years after 1850, while the European population of the United States, Canada, Australia, and Argentina tripled between 1851 and 1900, thanks in part to large-scale immigration. Between 1851 and 1900, some 35 million people left Europe (Woodruff 1966).

This growth in population was accompanied by a shift in consumption patterns that marked a radical break with the relative stability of prior large-scale cultures. Capitalist economic growth requires continuous per-capita increases in consumption, which would inevitably deplete resources, at least in the core countries. For example, by 1850 England was unable to satisfy its needs for grain, wood, fibers, and hides from within its immediate borders (Woodruff 1966). Newly industrializing countries initially secured more resources by the expansion of trade networks and colonial territories to draw resources from throughout the world. Equally important

was the switch in energy resources from the renewable, solar-driven fuels, such as wood, wind and water, and a reliance on traction animals and human labor, which had characterized ancient civilizations, to the use of nonrenewable *fossil fuels*, such as coal, to power industrial machines. Many earlier civilizations used a complex division of labor; assembly line, mass-production techniques; and a wide variety of simple machines; their reliance on *renewable energy* sources, however, was compatible with relative stable consumption patterns.

Coal fueled the factories, ships, and trains of western Europe and North America in the nineteenth century and prepared the way for the age of oil. In the short run, use of fossil fuels allowed the industrial, capitalist, world system to consume global resources at unsustainable levels, subsidizing otherwise impossible growth. Industrial civilization has become unique in human history as a *culture of consumption* (Bodley 1985). In such a culture, economy, society, and belief systems are geared to "nonsustainable levels of resource consumption, and to continual, ever-higher elevation of those levels on a per-capita basis" (Bodley 1985:67). Biologically, this is overconsumption, as ecologist Howard Odum explains:

*In the industrial system with man living off a fuel, he manges all his affairs with industrial machinery, all parts of which are metabolically consumers. . . . This system of man has consumption in excess of production. The products of respiration—carbon dioxide, metabolic water, and mineralized inorganic wastes—are discharged in rates in excess of their incorporation into organic matter by photosynthesis. If the industrialized urban system were enclosed in a chamber with only the air above it at the time, it would*

---

*fossil fuels*  Energy sources such as petroleum, natural gas, and coal, which are the geologically processed remains of ancient biomass; considered nonrenewable because they are consumed more rapidly than they are naturally produced.

*renewable energy*  Power derived from contemporary solar-driven natural processes such as wind, water power, and direct solar heating or processing biomass through burning and fermentation.

*culture of consumption*  A culture that stimulates continuous increases in per-capita consumption of natural resources at rates at nonsustainable rates.

*quickly exhaust its oxygen, be stifled with waste, and destroy itself since it does not have the recycling pattern of the agrarian system.* (1971:17)

This biological imbalance in its urban centers and the pressure to increase consumption force the industrial civilization to be a world and global system because it would have difficulty sustaining itself in any other way.

The label *Industrial Revolution* that historians apply to this great cultural transformation overemphasizes the role of technological factors; but as with the Neolithic, more than technology changed. It was not simply the "inventive genius" of a particular people that caused the Industrial Revolution. It was cultural changes in social organization and ideological systems that called forth technological innovation. In the view of Nathan Rosenberg and L. E. Birdzell (1990), the European institutionalization of science ultimately supported the technical achievements of the Industrial Revolution, but the partnership between formal science and economic interests developed slowly. Scientific organizations, formed in Europe during the seventeenth and eighteenth centuries, began to hold meetings and publish reports to share information based on a standard scientific method of observation, experimentation, and replicability. This was an important step, but many early technological innovations were not made by professional scientists. Research institutes, laboratories, and the specialized branches of Western science were not founded in many European countries until the early nineteenth century, and formal science made little significant contribution to economic growth until later. Many research laboratories were not directly linked to private industries until early in the twentieth century.

Rosenberg and Birdzell (1990) argue that scientific achievements by themselves do not explain the Industrial Revolution. What really count, in their view, are the "institutional characteristics" of a country, especially the presence of a free-market economy and active participation in international trade. This combination encourages competition and allows new firms to easily form to exploit new innovations that optimize *economies of scale* and specialization. These organizational changes upset the equilibrium of earlier states and imperial systems.

Rosenberg and Birdzell (1990) assume that decentralized and unregulated science and marketing systems are the best way to organize production and consumption in ways that will "optimize human welfare." They emphasize that wages and prices were regulated by preindustrial governments according to "subjective criteria" of social justice. The Industrial Revolution required "ethically neutral devices for keeping supply and demand synchronized" in ways that promote capital accumulation. Smith said the same thing in 1776. This assessment may well be correct as an explanation of the processes that led to the rise of industrial civilization, but it describes a cultural system that magnifies the instabilities and inequalities of the ancient civilizations that preceded it.

The overall pattern of population increase and increased consumption with the Industrial Revolution is clear, but there is disagreement on many details of the transformation process. British historian T. S. Ashton (1969) attributes the sudden tripling of the population of England and Wales between 1700 and 1831 to a decline in the mortality rate due to improvements in food supply, hygiene, public health, and medicine, which were presumably caused by industrialization. However, demographic changes also likely reflected changes in labor requirements and family organization. Furthermore, similar population increase occurred in other areas of Europe, which were not yet industrialized. Ashton correctly observes that population growth did not cause industrialization because growth in many areas of the world, such as India and China, did not lead to industrialization but instead caused a reduction in living standard.

Like most economists, Ashton (1969) argues that organizational and technological changes, rather than population growth, accelerated production during the Industrial Revolution in England. Increased production was initiated by organizational changes that brought more land into production and facilitated the adoption of technological changes, such as new crops and cropping systems. Agreeing with Smith, Ashton argues that social inequality, perhaps even "injustice," was the key that encouraged the accumulation of capital that funded the technological innovations of the Industrial Revolution:

*It is generally recognized that more saving takes place in communities in which the distribution of wealth is uneven than in those in which it approaches more closely to modern conceptions of what is just.* (1969:7)

Technological innovations are not chance discoveries. They involve repeated trial and error and are often based on combinations of previous inventions. This is a panhuman process, but it is accelerated by specific cultural conditions. Invention was especially encouraged by specialization and the complex division of labor that emerged with the first states, but the unprecedented pressures for perpetual growth in the emerging capitalist world system set in motion the positive feedback between technical innovation and capital accumulation that became the Industrial Revolution.

Historians identify the **enclosure movement** as an important organizational change leading to the Industrial Revolution. In Europe during the seventeenth and eighteenth centuries, the shift from village self-sufficiency to market-oriented agriculture was accompanied by the transformation of open communal pastures and woodlands into numerous, enclosed, privately controlled plots dedicated to the production of wool, meat, and hides.

Many historians urge us not to dwell on the fate of the formerly self-sufficient villagers who were forced off the land and impoverished by the enclosure process, which was supported by government decrees. These peoples were surely being victimized by industrial progress; but according to the ideology of capitalism, we should focus on "the constructive activities that were being carried on inside the fences" (Ashton 1969:20). The historical interpretation of this dispossession process is that it was used to increase agricultural productivity while reducing the rural population, in order to raise the national standard of living. Those who were pushed off the land were considered to be "free to devote themselves to other activities," which meant they could either become vagrants or accept poorly paid jobs in the newly appearing industrial factories in the cities.

The enclosure movement was only the beginning of a series of vast cultural disruptions that ultimately spread throughout the globe as the capitalist world system began its expansion. In the following section, we examine the second phase of this expansion process using the production, distribution, and consumption of sugar as a specific case study.

## Sugar Eaters and the World System

As anthropologist Sidney Mintz (1985) details in his book *Sweetness and Power*, refined sugar, or sucrose, played a major role in the rise of the modern world system, contributing to the accumulation of capital and helping the English lower class adjust to their changed life conditions. During the Industrial Revolution, sugar was transformed from being a rare European luxury before 1750 to its new status as a household necessity by 1850. In this process, the English subsistence system changed from its traditional reliance on a local, inexpensively produced **complex carbohydrate,** primarily wheat, to a system in which an imported, energy-intensive **simple carbohydrate,** sucrose, became a virtual staple for the lower and middle classes. England became a nation of sugar eaters, not because people naturally like sweet things but because of the cultural forces associated with expansive capitalist development.

Sugarcane is a tropical plant that was probably domesticated in Melanesia by 8000 BC for its sweet sap. By 400 BC, it was grown in India, where the earliest processed sugar is known to have been prepared by at least AD 500. Muslims spread sugarcane growing and sugar processing throughout the

---

**economy of scale**   Savings in the unit cost of production gained through mass production; for example, it may cost less per item to produce 10,000 items than 10 items.
**enclosure movement**   The conversion of community grazing lands used by self-sustaining peasants into privately owned fields dedicated to market production; an early phase in the industrialization of western Europe.
**complex carbohydrate**   A large starch molecule stored in the stems, roots, and seeds of plants, which humans can digest to produce glucose.
**simple carbohydrate**   A sugar such as glucose, fructose, or sucrose, which forms small molecules and can be metabolized very rapidly.

Mediterranean region by AD 1000. In medieval Europe, sugar was treated as a spice and had many medical uses, but it was too scarce to be available to any but the most wealthy. In medieval England, sugar was used in the royal court to prepare edible decorative works of art, which served as symbols of power and status. Such objects were a special expression of power because they could be conspicuously consumed as a valuable on a ritual occasion. By 1500 sugar decorations were an important part of ritual feasts throughout the upper classes, and within 200 years such use was becoming common even among the middle classes as sugar became more readily available.

During the early phase of capitalist development in England, from approximately 1650 to 1750, sugar was the single most important product imported from its colonies. Produced by slave labor on plantations in the British West Indies, sugar supported a major trade triangle that contributed to the accumulation of profits in the capitalist core. Shipments of manufactured goods such as cloth, tools, and iron shackles moved from England to Africa; slaves were carried from Africa to the West Indies and sugar from the West Indies to England, where it was further refined (Figure 11.3). Thus, sugar helped generate direct profits while providing a market for manufactured goods. In the process, millions of African slaves were forced to work 12-hour days, often while supplying their own provisions. After slavery was abolished in the British colonies in the 1830s, perhaps 50 million Asians, primarily from India, were carried to sugar-producing areas as contract laborers during the nineteenth century.

Perhaps as important as sugar's role in the trade triangle was the nutrition and comfort it gave to the English working class who supplied the human energy for the Industrial Revolution. This support role for sugar developed gradually as the plantation system expanded to make sugar more available and as sugar proved to be an ideal complement to the tropical "drug foods" such as tea, coffee, and chocolate, which begin to reach England in the seventeenth century. These are all bitter, calorie-free, hot, stimulating drinks that are sweetened and calorie-fortified by the addition of sugar. Tea had been imported from China by an English trading monopoly beginning in 1660, but it became the most popular English drink only after tea plantations were established in British India by 1840. In combination with sugar from the British West Indies, tea from British India became cheaper than beer as a stimulating and nourishing drink for the English working class.

As Mintz (1985) explains, sugar consumption by the English working poor grew in stages. At first it was used in tea, then in rich puddings, which by the nineteenth century became a dessert course to end a meal. Sugar was combined with wheat flour in sweetened baked goods; by the end of the century, bread and jam became a meal, especially in households where both parents were employed. At the national level, per-capita sugar consumption tripled from approximately 30 lb (14 kilograms [kg]) per year in 1800 to approximately 90 lb (41 kg) per year by 1900. By the 1970s, per-capita consumption seems to have peaked at about 115 lb (52 kg). As a proportion of total caloric consumption, sugar rose from 2 to 14 percent over the course of the nineteenth century (Mintz 1985). Such an increase was possible because the price of sugar in England decreased by 50 percent between 1840 and 1870 (Mintz 1985). Sugar became a relatively cheap source of calories and tended to supplement and replace more expensive grains, fruits, vegetables, meat, and dairy products.

The per-capita consumption figures mask the important role that sugar played in the diet of the working poor because actual rates varied by class and by age and gender within households. By 1850 sugar consumption by the English working class exceeded that of the upper class. Increased sugar intake was accompanied by a decline in bread consumption, from which some historians infer that more meat must have been eaten and nutrition improved. However, Mintz argues (1985) that in most lower-class households the workingman ate the meal while his wife and children were left with the sugar as empty calories and were thereby systematically malnourished. This was justified by the householders because the husband had to remain in top physical condition in order to be an effective worker. This nutritional inequality, however, must have elevated infant mortality rates.

Sugar was especially important in the capitalist transformation of the world system because its capacity to stimulate perpetually increasing con-

FIGURE 11.3 *The sugar trade triangle.*

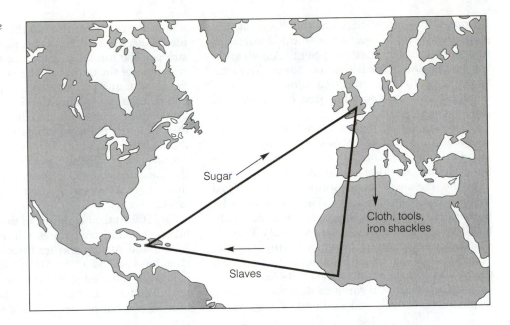

Sugar

Cloth, tools, iron shackles

Slaves

sumer demand neatly supported the endless-growth ideals of capitalism in opposition to the equilibrium theories of mercantilist economists. Sugar became the first great consumer product. It was a substance of which people never seemed to get enough, and it proved that basic human "needs" could be expanded as an instrument of national policy. Precapitalist economic theory held that most wage laborers were "target workers" who worked only long enough to satisfy their fixed needs. Alcohol consumption was potentially elastic, but alcoholics made poor workers. Sugar, on the other hand, made for contented workers and was especially attractive at first because its use was a marker of high social status. However, in the long run, it was the factory system itself, with its physically demanding work schedule, that helped increase sugar consumption by raising both demand and supply.

Mintz (1985) argues that England was converted into a nation of sugar eaters, at least in part, because such a change served the interests of individuals who were in a position to exercise political power. Many of the early West Indian sugarcane planters were themselves members of Parliament; along with the investors who supported them and those in slaving, shipping, refining, and marketing,

who benefited from sugar, they formed a significant interest group that influenced government policy. It is not surprising that sugar was issued to the inmates of English poorhouses, and a half-pint of rum made from West Indian molasses became an official daily ration of the British Navy in 1731 and was soon raised to a pint a day. The British government gained revenues from the sugar trade and indirectly subsidized the Caribbean planters by helping keep prices high. By the 1850s, the government shifted in favor of a free-trade policy to reduce the price of sugar and thereby increase the supply, thus making it more widely available.

In the following sections, we examine the colonial system in more detail, especially its impacts on the small-scale cultures that were incorporated into the expanding world system.

## COLONIALISM AND SMALL-SCALE CULTURES

### Ethnocide, Genocide, and Ecocide

During the first, preindustrial phase of capitalist expansion, which was underway by 1450, several

European powers, such as Spain, Portugal, England, and France, gained political domination over large areas in North and South America, the Caribbean, and in the islands of the eastern Atlantic. This was the beginning of a colonial process of conquest and incorporation that continued into the twentieth century.

Historian Alfred Crosby (1986) notes that the Guanches, the original inhabitants of the Canary Islands in the Atlantic 200 miles (322 kilometers [km]) off the northwest coast of Africa, were perhaps the first small-scale culture to be conquered by the advancing Europeans. The Guanches, who numbered some 80,000, appear to have been egalitarian village farmers with no metal tools. They resisted successive waves of French, Portuguese, and Spanish invaders from 1402 until the Spanish gained full control of the islands in 1496.

The Guanches who survived the conquest were dispossessed, exiled, and enslaved. Their culture was destroyed, and by 1540 the Guanche had virtually disappeared as a people. The Spaniards stripped the forests and sold the timber and other resources of the Canaries. They replaced the native flora and fauna with European species and established sugarcane plantations based on slave labor. Deforestation initiated flooding and erosion and then caused the local climate to become arid. All the negative impacts of colonial expansion—***ethnocide, genocide,*** and ***ecocide***—were underway in the Canaries when Christopher Columbus passed through in 1492 on his first crossing of the Atlantic.

In 1800, at the beginning of the Industrial Revolution, preindustrial states still existed in China, Japan, and Africa, and traditional kingdoms and chiefdoms in India, the Middle East, and the Pacific still retained considerable autonomy. The great Western colonial powers had made claims over 55 percent of the world's land area but exer-

FIGURE 11.4   *Autonomous tribal peoples, approximately 200 million people (20 percent of the global population), 1800.*

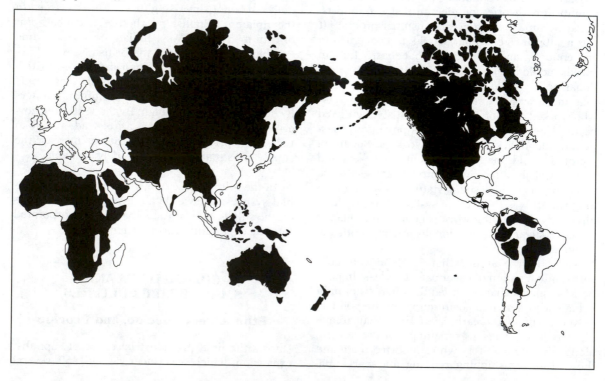

cised effective control only over 33 percent of the world (Clark 1936). Approximately half the world was still controlled by relatively autonomous and largely self-sufficient small-scale tribal cultures, with perhaps 200 million people, roughly 20 percent of the global population (Figure 11.4). Over the next 150 years, virtually all tribal territory was conquered by colonizing industrial states, and some 50 million tribal peoples probably died. This process created the modern world system but at an enormous cost in ethnocide, genocide, and ecocide suffered by the peoples and territories that were forcibly incorporated by the new system.

*Incorporation,* in this context, means that natural resources and/or human labor begin to flow into the world system from formerly "external" areas. From the viewpoint of the peoples and cultures being incorporated, incorporation sets in motion a process of **demographic disruption** and destroys political and economic autonomy. Demographic distribution first appears as drastic depopulation when people are enslaved and killed by invaders and when they die from newly introduced diseases to which they have little immunity. Mortality is increased when culturally established support networks are interrupted and food systems disturbed. Epidemic diseases that make everyone sick at once can be devastating in a small-scale culture.

Much of the increased mortality occurred as a direct result of violence perpetrated against tribal peoples during their conquest by outsiders. In rare cases, governments followed a policy of deliberate genocide in an effort to totally exterminate a tribal population, and many governments organized military campaigns against tribals. The largest tribal loss of life probably resulted from the actions of individual colonists who sought to profit from tribal territories before governments established formal political control. On the **uncontrolled frontier,** colonial governments, as a matter of policy, allowed their citizens to systematically kill and exploit tribal peoples (Bodley 1990) (Figure 11.5). Where tribal groups were not needed as a source of labor, they were classified as "nonhuman" savages and were killed with impunity in order to remove them from the land.

Increased mortality is a special threat to the survival of tribal cultures that rely on fertility-

FIGURE 11.5    *The uncontrolled frontier phase of capitalist expansion often involved direct physical violence against indigenous peoples, as illustrated by this contemporary engraving of an attack against Australian aborigines.*

limiting cultural practices to maintain their small, low-density, low-growth populations. Many of these groups simply disappeared when the frontier

---

**ethnocide**    The forced destruction of a cultural system.
**genocide**    The extermination of a human population.
**ecocide**    The degradation of an ecosystem.
**demographic disruption**    Depopulation due to the impact of an uncontrolled frontier, followed by extinction or rapid growth due to disruption of prior fertility controls.
**uncontrolled frontier**    A tribal territory that is invaded by colonists from a state-organized society but where the government chooses not to regulate the actions of the colonists.

overtook them, and only their territories remained to be incorporated.

The *loss of political autonomy* by tribal peoples occurs when state governments gain enough power over a tribal territory to prevent tribal peoples from acting in their own defense to expel outsiders. This can occur following military conquest, or it can be accomplished by formal treaty signing or some less formal process by which government control is extended over a formerly autonomous tribal area. In most cases, the relative difference in power between tribal cultures and states is so extreme that the state can impose control over a tribal territory virtually at will, although it can be a costly and time-consuming process.

State political control is usually symbolized by the appointment of political authorities and the introduction of a police force. State functions such as taxation, military recruitment, and census taking usually follow, along with the imposition of a legal system, courts, and jails. Administrative issues to be dealt with by colonial officials would concern specifying the differential rights of the native population and the colonizing population to land and other natural resources. Special regulations would define the conditions under which natives would be employed and how native culture could be expressed.

The *loss of economic autonomy* is fostered by political conquest because tribal groups must maintain control over their subsistence resources in order to remain self-sufficienct. Drastic depopulation can reduce the economic viability of a tribal group, but competition with colonists over resources, especially when the tribal land base is reduced by government decree, is often the decisive factor. Any factors that undermined the traditional subsistence base would push tribal peoples toward participation in the market economy, whether as wage labors or *cash croppers*.

There was also a desire to secure some of the manufactured goods, such as metal tools and factory clothing, produced by the world system's industrial centers. However, the "pull" forces in themselves were insufficient to compel tribal peoples into large-scale participation in the market economy without a strong "push." Whenever the subsistence economy remained strong, tribal peoples were often poorly motivated *target workers*, and colonial administrators resorted to legal measures such as special taxes and planting laws to force reluctant tribal groups into the market economy. Once initiated, involvement in the market economy can become self-reinforcing because wage labor leaves little time for subsistence activities and cash cropping can degrade the local ecosystem and reduce its potential for subsistence production.

The cost of industrial expansion was minimized or ignored by the economists and politicians who championed growth and "differential benefits," but anthropologists who conducted fieldwork on the colonial frontiers observed the devastation firsthand and often attempted to minimize it.

## The British Empire

By 1878 a political hierarchy in the global system was clearly established. More than half of the world's land area was claimed by just four giant states and their related territories: Britain, Russia, China, and the United States (Figure 11.6). Together with seven other colonial countries (Turkey, France, Belgium, Denmark, the Netherlands, Portugal, and Spain), these major states held claims over two-thirds of the world (Clark 1936). Most of Africa was still under the control of traditional kingdoms, chiefdoms, and tribal systems, while minor independent modern states were located primarily in Latin America, where vast areas were still occupied by autonomous tribal groups.

Beginning in the 1880s, the major colonial powers scrambled to extend their political control over Africa and the Pacific, and by 1913 more than three-fourths of the world's land area was controlled by just thirteen countries. During the 35 years between 1879 and 1913, only Japan and Italy were added to the list of colonizing states. After the rearrangements caused by World War I, which removed Germany and Turkey as colonial powers, the world territorial pie was still dominated by a few major countries (see Figure 11.6).

Throughout the modern colonial period from 1800 to 1945, a single power, Great Britain, remained a clear dominant. At its height in the 1930s, the British empire spanned the globe, encompassing roughly one-fourth of the world's land

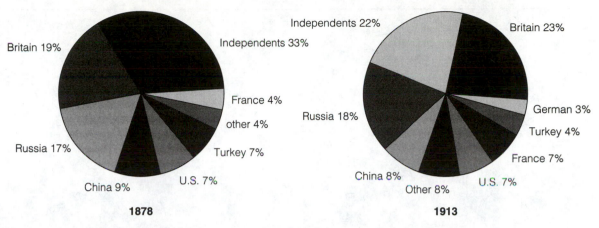

**FIGURE 11.6**  *Territorial claims of major states, 1878 and 1913. (SOURCE: Clark 1936.)*

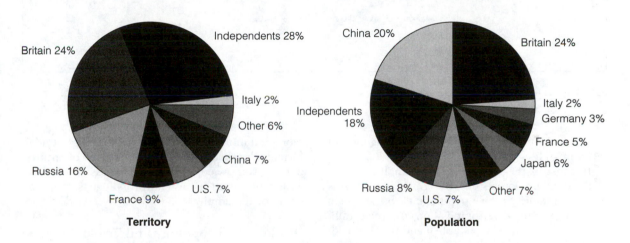

**FIGURE 11.7**  *Territorial claims and population of major states, 1933. (SOURCE: Clark 1936.)*

area and population (Figure 11.7). The empire included the United Kingdom; British India; the relatively independent Dominions of Canada, Newfoundland, and New Zealand; the Commonwealth of Australia; the Union of South Africa; and the various crown colonies, dependencies, and protectorates—for a total of more than 12 million square miles [mi²] (31.3 million square kilometers [km²]) and 500 million people (Figure 11.8). The British empire was primarily a loose federation held together by diverse political connections and the

***loss of political autonomy***   The loss of self-government due to foreign military conquest and the extension of government control.

***loss of economic autonomy***   The loss of self-subsistence due to territorial reduction and resource depletion, followed by market dependency and impoverishment.

***cash cropping***   The raising of crops for market sale rather than domestic consumption.

***target workers***   People who work only long enough to earn a specific amount of money, such as to pay taxes or buy certain basic necessities.

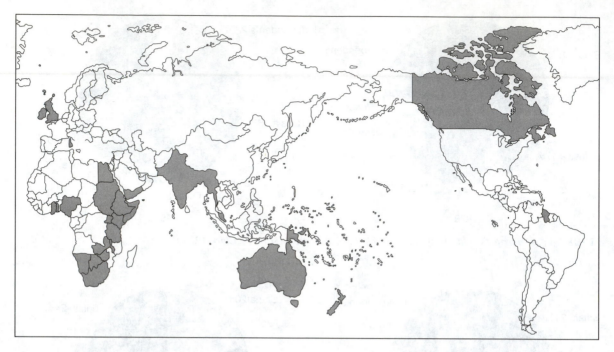

FIGURE 11.8    *The British empire in the 1930s.*

common British origin and English language of the ruling elites in each political unit.

In most of the colonies, a very small minority of European colonists enjoyed a privileged status over the majority native population who was held in a structurally inferior position. Coercive military power was used to establish and maintain administrative control, but the common objective was the capitalist development of productive resources, growing markets, and the expansion of trade, not the extraction of tribute as in ancient empires. Some 35 percent of the empire was controlled at least indirectly by London, but local colonial governments often enjoyed considerable autonomy. Depending on its size, a given colony might be governed by a governor general, governor, lieutenant governor, administrator, high commissioner, or commissioner. Some colonies elected their own parliaments, and their legislation was subject only to a rare veto by the crown. This promoted the "uncontrolled frontier" and allowed colonists to deal with tribal groups in their own way.

As the British colonial system matured and more and more tribal peoples were brought under formal administrative control, the value of anthropological knowledge became obvious to colonial authorities, and many anthropologists went to work for the empire.

## Applied Anthropology and Tribal Peoples

In many respects, anthropology, as an academic discipline and as a profession, was a product of colonial expansion. It was no accident that major anthropological associations were formed in Great Britain, the United States, and France during the nineteenth century and that their publications, such as the *American Anthropologist* and the *Journal of the Royal Anthropological Institute of Great Britain and Ireland*, were filled with ethnographic notes gleaned from native peoples on the colonial frontiers by administrators, missionaries, military men, and ethnologists.

The practical utility of anthropological knowledge for imperialist countries was recognized quickly. For example, Colonel A. H. Lane-Fox Pitt-

Rivers, in his opening address to the anthropology section of the British Association for the Advancement of Science in 1871, declared,

*Nor is it unimportant to remember that Anthropology has its practical and humanitarian aspect, and that, as our race is more often brought in contact with savages than any other, a knowledge of their habits and modes of thought may be of the utmost value to us in utilizing their labour, as well as in checking those inhuman practices from which they have but too often suffered at our hands.* (1872:170–171)

From the 1870s through the 1930s, as the colonial empires reached their height, two themes were frequently discussed at the meetings of anthropological associations: how to salvage the ethnographic data that was being destroyed by colonial expansion and how to increase the practical value of anthropology for the empire. In response to the first issue, several expeditions were sent out to save the data, and in 1873 a committee for the British Association for the Advancement of Science drafted a checklist of anthropological topics to guide "travellers, ethnologists, and other anthropological observers" who would be encountering native groups on the colonial frontier (Lane-Fox Pitt-Rivers et al. 1874). This instruction manual eventually became the classic handbook on anthropological field methods known as *Notes and Queries on Anthropology*.

Lane-Fox Pitt-Rivers (1882) coined the term ***applied anthropology*** to catalog a "valuable paper" read by Sir Bartle Frere before the institute in 1881. As high commissioner in South Africa, Sir Bartle prosecuted the 1879 war against the Zulu. To protect native welfare, Sir Bartle advocated "a strong and stable Imperial Government" that would enforce British law while extinguishing the political autonomy of tribal groups. Institute President Lane-Fox Pitt-Rivers endorsed Bartle's paper, commenting that it "deserves to be read by all anthropologists," and he reaffirmed that "no subject is more capable of being turned to useful account than the scientific study of mankind" (1882:507).

By the turn of the century, British anthropologists had become enthusiastic imperialists. In 1901 C. H. Read, by then president of the Anthropological Institute, specifically emphasized the utility of anthropology for "private enterprise" such as the great trading and colonization companies, observing,

*We should . . . be in a position to give the officers of such companies valuable information for the conduct of their affairs with natives, and thus be of distinct value to commercial enterprise.* (1901:15)

Anthropologists of the Anthropological Institute and the Folklore Society intervened directly in colonial policy in 1900 when they addressed a formal memorandum to the colonial secretary in London, proposing the creation of a special commission, including anthropologists, to study native culture in areas of South Africa where colonial development was creating serious tensions between colonists and native peoples. The memorandum blamed native unrest on misunderstanding of native culture and argued that, besides its obvious scientific value, anthropological knowledge would facilitate colonial administration because

1. *It will enable the Government to ascertain what customs may be recognized, and what customs must be forbidden or modified, and how to effect this object with the least disturbance to tribal conditions and native prejudices.*

2. *It will save time and ensure certainty in the administration of justice, and obviate many difficulties in other departments of government.*

3. *It will afford the Government authoritative materials for legislation adjusting the arrangements for native labour in the mines, and generally dealing with the relations between the natives and European settlers.* (Anthropological Institute 1903:70–74)

Joseph Chamberlain, the colonial secretary, politely tabled the proposal, and 2 years later a follow-up deputation of forty-five anthropologists again approached the Colonial Office. This delegation represented a cross section of British anthropologists of the day and shows that they generally supported colonialism, although they believed that it could be carried out with less damage to native peoples. Among the delegation was Professor E. B. Tylor, who is still widely known for his definition

---

***applied anthropology*** The nonacademic employment of anthropologists for government, commercial, or humanitarian purposes.

of culture and often considered the founder of academic anthropology.

After numerous further petitions and endorsements by various scientific committees, colonial administrations finally began to hire government anthropologists and recommended anthropological training for administrators. In a short period of time in the 1920s and 1930s, applied anthropology became institutionalized in the British empire. In 1921 A. R. Radcliffe-Brown was appointed to an anthropology professorship in South Africa where he became a popular lecturer on the "native problem." Like Sir Bartle Frere, Radcliffe-Brown stressed that understanding the "laws" of cultural development would give administrators "control over the social forces." More specifically, in 1923 he argued that knowing

*the functions of native institutions ... can afford great help to the missionary or the public servant who is engaged in dealing with the practical problems of the adjustment of the native civilization to the new conditions that have resulted from our occupation of the country.* (Radcliffe-Brown 1958:32)

In 1926 Radcliffe-Brown became professor of anthropology at the University of Sydney in Australia in order to promote anthropological training and practical research in the Pacific region, from a functionalist perspective. The Rockefeller Foundation of New York and the Australian government established a fund for anthropological research, and several anthropologists were soon in the field. The results of their work began to appear in 1930 in the new journal *Oceania*, which was at first edited by Radcliffe-Brown.

Applied anthropologists did not expect to be too directly involved in policymaking, for that was to be left to administrators. Applied anthropologists avoided value judgments about colonialism, while hoping that anthropological knowledge would be used to minimize the damage that imperialist expansion was causing to native peoples. Aside from standard functionalist analysis, the major object of research for applied anthropologists was **acculturation** or culture change, both of which were ethically neutral concepts that masked the harsh political realities of imperialism. According to a formal definition proposed by American anthropologists Robert Redfield, Ralph Linton, and

Melville Herskovits, acculturation is the culture change that occurs when groups with different cultures enter into ". . . continuous firsthand contact, with subsequent changes in the original cultural pattern of either or both groups" (Redfield, Linton, and Herskovits 1936:149)

Acculturation studies inventoried highly visible changes such as the adoption by tribal peoples of European clothing, crops, implements, language, and Christianity and the corresponding abandonment of traditional cultural features. The loss of political and economic autonomy was not usually examined as acculturation. In reality, firsthand contact meant conquest and dispossession of native peoples by colonial soldiers and settlers. Acculturation was forced culture change and was primarily an unequal process in which tribal peoples were subordinated and exploited. However, applied anthropologists in the service of the empire could hardly be expected to draw attention to the negative side of imperialism.

The real **native problem** that perplexed colonial administrators was how to keep the natives from resorting to armed resistance while settlers were depriving them of their lands and how to turn them into docile taxpayers and willing and effective laborers on their former lands. Culture change was supposed to be slow in order to avoid detribalization, which would make control more difficult and could lead to depopulation and labor shortages.

The primary recommendation from applied anthropologists was for administrators to use **indirect rule** to maintain political control. This meant using local native chiefs to serve as government agents and intermediaries and creating the positions when they did not already exist. **Direct rule** by European officers was culturally insensitive and prohibitively expensive.

Bronislaw Malinowski, a prominent British functionalist, was emphatic on the advantages of indirect, or dependent, rule:

*In fact, if we define dependent rule as the control of Natives through the medium of their own organization, it is clear that only dependent rule can succeed. For the government of any race consists rather in implanting in them ideas of right, of law and order, and making them obey such ideas.* (1929:23)

## The Native Problem in Kenya

Kenya colony in East Africa illustrates the political domination and economic exploitation that occurred as European powers forced much of Africa into the capitalist global system in the late nineteenth and early twentieth centuries. As discussed in Chapter 4, Nilotic-speaking cattle peoples and Bantu farmers effectively adapted their small-scale cultures to the distinctive ecosystems of East Africa some 2000 years ago. Around AD 800, the expanding Islamic empire reached the East African coast and established small coastal centers that remained important conduits for the slave and ivory trade into the nineteenth century. There was no Arab settlement in the interior, and the indigenous peoples retained their economic and political autonomy despite the disruption of the slave trade. The Maasai dominated the best pasturelands centered in the Rift Valley and raided their neighbors for cattle.

By the 1870s, European explorers ventured into the East African interior in increasing numbers. In 1886 Germany declared a protectorate over part of what is now Tanzania, taking advantage of a series of treaties arranged between African "chiefs" and German colonists. In the same year, Britain and Germany agreed to divide the entire East African region between themselves. Officially, the justification for British intrusion was to help end the slave trade and improve the condition of the Africans. These objectives were endorsed by the General Act of the Berlin Africa Conference of 1884–1885, in which the principal imperialist states set the international rules for the European partition of Africa and pledged themselves to a civilizing crusade ". . . to educate the natives and to teach them to understand and appreciate the benefits of civilization" (Figure 11.9).

In 1896 the British government created the East Africa Protectorate and established fortified outposts and used punitive expeditions, frequently pitting Maasai allies against their Bantu neighbors, to impose a *Pax Britannica*. The administrative arrangements that followed gave the European minority complete political power over more than 2 million disenfranchised Africans who were expected to serve as units of labor and pay their taxes while learning the "benefits of civilization."

The process of using political and economic force to create a dependent underclass of laborers resembles the enclosure movement that prepared the way for industrial capitalism in England.

As soon as the protectorate administration was firmly in control, construction was immediately begun on the Kenya-Uganda railroad designed to link the old Arab port of Mombasa with the highland interior. Completion of the railroad in 1902 provided Europeans easy access to the cool and fertile highlands that straddled the Rift Valley just east of Lake Victoria. This attractive region was considered to be ideal for European colonization, although it was also the center of Maasai territory. Much of this prime land was disingenuously declared by the government to be uninhabited and thus open for European colonization. The Maasai were weakened by smallpox and a rinderpest epidemic, which had devastated their herds in the 1890s, but their long-term interest in their grazing lands was obvious.

The consolidation of political and economic control over the protectorate was a complex process that the British administration carried out in stages as specific legislation was drafted. Seven provinces were set up, each directed by a subcommissioner. Each province was divided into districts, controlled by tax collectors and subcollectors. In 1924 areas of European settlement were given a separate administrative system, while "native" provinces and districts were placed under a chief native commissioner, senior provincial commissioners, and district commissioners—all Europeans. Under the Village Headmen Ordinance of

---

***acculturation***  The concept used by colonial applied anthropologists to describe the changes in tribal culture that accompanied European conquest but that minimized the role of coercion and the loss of tribal autonomy.

***native problem***  The difficulty faced by colonial authorities who attempted to control and exploit very large and potentially rebellious native populations for the disproportionate advantage of a European minority.

***indirect rule***  The situation in which European colonial administrators appointed local natives to serve as mediating officials, or "chiefs," to help them control local communities.

***direct rule***  The use of European colonial administrators to control a native community at the local level.

1902 and the Native Authority Ordinance of 1912, village "chiefs" were appointed by the administration and treated like government employees with very limited authority. A simple system of native courts, based on councils of elders, was established in 1913 and given limited authority to maintain order at the local level. In the 1920s, district-level native councils were given an advisory role.

From the start, the political structure was designed to favor European interests at the expense of Africans. Beginning in 1905, the protectorate was administered by the Colonial Office in London through a resident governor, who had full veto powers and was assisted by executive and legislative councils composed of appointed Europeans. In 1920, after pressure from settler associations, the protectorate became the Crown Colony of

Kenya, and the legislative council was expanded to forty members, half of which continued to be appointed European administrators. The unofficial half of the legislature contained an elected European majority of eleven members, while seven positions were reserved for Indians and Arabs who constituted nearly three times the European population. Indigenous African interests were represented by two European appointees.

In 1911 there were only 3175 Europeans in the East Africa protectorate, which also contained an indigenous African population that was estimated at between 2.5 to 4 million. The number of Europeans increased fourfold, to 12,529 by 1926, but even after the European population reached 30,524 in 1948, it still constituted barely .05 percent of the total population (Buell 1928, Hailey 1950).

Europeans were drawn to the protectorate by promises of low taxes and abundant resources, cheap land, and cheap African labor, all waiting to be exploited. Lumber, grain, livestock, rubber, copra, and gold were soon flowing to world markets, along with the hides, horns, and ivory of big-game animals that were being slaughtered in great numbers by European hunters. By 1908 the value of exported East African natural resources exceeded 400,000 pounds sterling annually (Great Britain Board of Trade 1909) (Figure 11.10). Nearly one-fourth of these resources was destined for the United Kingdom, and two-thirds of the total went to the world's major industrial powers: the United Kingdom, the United States, France, and Germany (Great Britain Board of Trade 1909) (Figure 11.11).

The British administration gained control over African land by simply enacting the necessary legislation. The only concern was that the appearance of justice and legality be maintained so that humanitarians in London would not protest in Parliament. Before the railroad cleared the way for large-scale colonization, government land regulations specified that African lands could not be deeded to Europeans if such alienation would be prejudicial to African interests. However, the Crown Lands Ordinance of 1902 simply specified that the government could not sell land that the Africans were actually occupying but provided that "unoccupied" lands could be "leased" to colo-

FIGURE 11.9   *This 1892 political cartoon of Cecil Rhodes, prime minister of Britain's Cape Colony in southern Africa, astride the African continent, symbolizes the arrogance of European colonialism.*

THE RHODES COLOSSUS

STRIDING FROM CAPE TOWN TO CAIRO

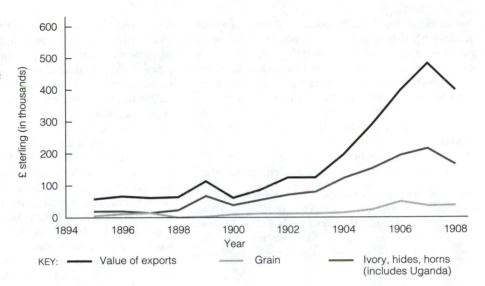

FIGURE 11.10 *The East Africa protectorate in the world system, 1894–1908.* (*SOURCE: Great Britain Board of Trade 1909.*)

KEY:    ——— Value of exports    ——— Grain    ——— Ivory, hides, horns (includes Uganda)

nists in lots of 1000 acres (405 hectares) for 99 years. The Crown Lands Ordinance of 1915 left no doubt about who would control the land by declaring that all African lands were "crown lands" and could be confiscated by the government. This policy permitted the very small minority of the European elite to systematically acquire the best agricultural lands while dispossessing the indigenous owners.

More than 40,000 Maasai were forced to give up more than half of their territory under the terms of a treaty in 1904, by which they agreed to move into a northern and southern reserve, abandoning the central Rift Valley to a handful of European settlers. The Maasai reserves were supposed to last "so long as the Maasai as a race shall exist" (Buell 1928:312). However, in 1911 the northern reserve turned out to be good farmland, and by 1913 the protesting Maasai were consolidated on the much poorer southern reserve.

Harvard political scientist Raymond Buell examined the Maasai case and concluded that the government's action was legally unjustified but thought that the Maasai themselves were partly responsible for the loss of their land because their culture was unsuitable. In exaggerated and ethnocentric terms that showed a complete misunderstanding of Maasai culture, Buell described them as

*. . . aimless and wandering pastoralists, owning economically worthless but continually increasing cattle. Their military organization was a constant menace to other natives, while their warrior villages were a corrupting influence inside of the tribe.* (1928:315–316)

Between 1907 and 1912, a series of native reserves were proposed on "crown land" for African

FIGURE 11.11 *Destination and value, in pounds sterling (in thousands), of exports from the East Africa protectorate, 1908. (SOURCE: Great Britain Board of Trade 1909.)*

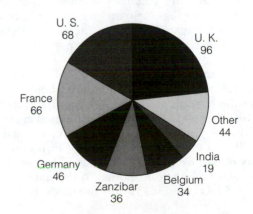

use in order to officially open land for European settlement. However, colonists objected that such reserves might be self-sustaining and Africans would not need to work for Europeans in order to support themselves. Government commissions recommended that reserves be drawn up to suit the needs of only the immediate African population with the expectation that population growth would soon force people to seek wage labor. In 1919 Governor Northey justified such a policy with an appeal to the ideology of capitalist economics:

*No one wants to take away any land that natives occupy or are using productively, but we can say, in these days of productivity and development, and world-wide shortage of food and raw materials, that Crown lands not made productive, may, by law, be made so as required.* (Buell 1928: 319)

This emphasis on productive use was somewhat misplaced, in view of the fact that in 1922 Europeans were only cultivating 6 percent of the land that they had appropriated. The inequities in the land system were obvious. Some 9000 Europeans were occupying 3.8 million acres (1.5 million hectares), with 422 acres (171 hectares) of prime land per person. By 1926 twenty-three native reserves were actually established, and 2.5 million Africans were crowded into 29.9 million acres (12.1 million hectares), leaving them with only 12 often very poor acres (5 hectares) per person.

African people who wished to develop their land along European lines faced significant difficulties. They could not legally purchase land outside the reserves or individually own land within the reserves. The colonists encouraged dispossessed Africans to remain on their former lands as squatters because African squatters were legally required to work 6 months a year for the landowners.

The taxation system was designed to provide revenue to help fund the administration and to force the Africans to find wage labor on European farms. A hut tax of 1 rupee was introduced in 1901, and by 1909 it was increased to 3 rupees, and a poll (head) tax was extended to all men over 16 years of age who were not heads of households. The total African contribution to the state's revenue in direct taxes was twenty-five times the Euro-

pean contribution between 1900 and 1925 (Ross 1927). Africans also paid indirect taxes in the form of 10 percent custom duties that were added to the price of cloth and beads and other trade goods. Because the total value of cash-crop farming on the native reserves covered barely two-thirds of the African tax, Africans were compelled to seek outside employment. The 3 rupee tax was roughly equivalent to 1 month's wages, although most labor contracts were for 3–6 months. Professional labor recruiters toured the reserves and paid local chiefs for rounding up workers. These efforts met with success because the number of employed Africans rose from 12,000 in 1912 to over 185,000 in 1927— approximately 14 African laborers for every man, woman, and child in the European population.

The attitude of Europeans toward African labor is illustrated by the British Masters and Servants Ordinances of 1906, which made it a crime punishable by a fine of 1 month's wages and up to 1 month in prison for a "servant" to be late to work, to be absent without permission, or to insult or disobey an employer. The punishment for quitting was 6 month's imprisonment. In 1922, 2187 Africans were punished for violating this ordinance. In 1915 a Native Registration Ordinance was passed, which required all African men over 16 years of age to register with the government, be fingerprinted, and carry identity papers. This procedure helped, but desertions remained enough of a problem, because of low wages and poor working conditions, that in 1925 the government approved a proposal to establish special detention camps for labor offenders.

British colonial policies were unusually harsh in Kenya because European settlement was a primary objective, unlike in West African British colonies where the climate was considered unsuitable for European settlement. Indirect rule was also more easily practiced in West Africa where traditional kingdoms were more common. In Kenya, indigenous peoples found it difficult to follow traditional cultural patterns in the absence of political and economic autonomy, and they were legally excluded from effective participation in the capitalist economy introduced by their British conquerors. The obvious inequities of the situation ultimately led to the Mau Mau armed rebellion of

1952–1959 and political reforms culminating in Kenya's independence from colonial rule in 1963.

Even before the modern era of decolonization began, Grover Clark (1936) carefully examined the economic balance sheets of imperialism and concluded that by the 1930s colonial expansion was no longer an economic gain for colonizing countries. Up to 1800, while colonial territories were still easily grabbed, imperialism proved profitable for both governments and private business interests. Between 1800 and 1880, costs began to increase, and governments had to subsidize the colonial enterprise, but private profits remained high. After 1880 colonial expansion became very costly, not only because of rebellions by colonized peoples but also because rivalries between competing colonial powers forced them to maintain very large armies and navies and contributed to World War I.

Clark (1936) also challenged the standard defense of imperialism, that it provided an outlet for excess population and was necessary to ensure the flow of resources to the imperial centers. The territories conquered in the Western Hemisphere by the Spanish, Portuguese, French, and British during the first round of expansion before 1800 became important outlets for colonizing European populations from the metropoles, as did South Africa, Australia, and New Zealand. However, Clark showed that only 2.6 percent of European immigration since 1880 had been to the tropical colonies. Clark also showed that modern trade depends more on communication links than political control. Trade monopolies are difficult to maintain, and most colonies and their major colonizing powers were not dependent on each other for markets.

## SUMMARY

In this chapter, we examined the concept of industrial civilization and the various attempts to understand it as something distinctive from the smaller-scale systems that preceded it. The wealthy elite who most benefit from the capitalist market economy have used industrial production and unequal exchange to integrate the diverse societies and cultures of the world into a single global economic system. An ideology of continuous economic expansion and high rates of consumption are central features of this system.

The global process of sugar production and consumption illustrates the early expansion of the global system. The initial involvement of anthropology in the colonial enterprise was examined within the context of British colonialism, while a detailed view of the specific process of colonial development was presented using material from East Africa. This example could be paralleled with similar material documenting the conquest, exploitation, and marginalization of Native Americans in the New World, both under the first colonial powers and later under independent countries such as the United States.

The global world-system approach forces us to consider the possibility that virtually all small-scale cultures that anthropologists have described ethnographically have been shaped by the existence of capitalist, large-scale cultural systems. Our discussion of these cultures in Chapters 2–5 largely ignored this possibility, by treating small-scale cultures as if they existed only within tribal worlds. However, more complex cultures clearly have varied impacts on smaller-scale cultures. In Chapters 6–10, it was pointed out that ancient kingdoms and empires often absorbed tribal cultures or forced them to organize into states in their own defense. In the modern era, industrial civilization has exerted enormous influence by means of economic and political forces as small-scale cultures are drawn into the emerging global system.

Since the breakdown of the colonial system after World War II, many supranational political and economic institutions such as the United Nations and the World Bank have taken over formal leadership of the global system, but the policies of these institutions are influenced by powerful nations and the giant multinational corporations that benefit from the global structure of inequality. In the next chapter, we will examine the United States as an example of one of the most dominant national cultures in the present global system; in Chapter 13, we will explore the problem of poverty in the countries that are peripheral to the wealthy industrial core.

## STUDY QUESTIONS

1. Define the following concepts: embedded economy, kin-ordered mode of production, market economy, means of production, mode of production, reciprocity, surplus, and tributary mode of production.

2. Distinguish between a market and nonmarket economy.

3. Define a capitalist political economy and explain how it differs from the economic systems of ancient states. Refer specifically to the interpretations of Polyani, Smith, Wolf, and modern economists such as Heilbroner and Thurow.

4. Describe the modern world system as defined by Wallerstein, referring to core, periphery, and semi-periphery, labor control, division of labor, unequal exchange, and accumulation.

5. What are the principal ideological features of the capitalist world system? Draw illustrations from Smith and modern economists and discuss the contradictory realities listed by Wallerstein.

6. Discuss the specific changes in cultural organization that accompanied the Industrial Revolution in England. Refer to the role of technology, population, capital accumulation, inequality, and the enclosure movement.

7. Explain how dietary change (sugar and tea) in England was related to the Industrial Revolution and the expanding world system.

8. Describe the process of the incorporation of tribal peoples and tribal territories into the world system and discuss its consequences. Refer to demographic, political, and economic aspects; genocide, ethnocide, ecocide, cash cropping; "push–pull" factors, target workers, taxation, and government control.

9. How was the development of British anthropology related to colonialism? Refer to applied anthropology, acculturation, the native problem, detribalization, culture change, depopulation, and indirect rule.

10. Describe the political and economic structure of modern colonialism in contrast to the empires of the past. Make specific comparisons between the Inca empire in the Andean world and the British empire in the modern world.

11. Using the East Africa protectorate and Kenya as an example, explain how political and economic power was used by colonial administrators to create structural inequalities and unequal accumulation.

## SUGGESTED READING

BODLEY, JOHN H. 1990. *Victims of Progress*, 3rd ed. Mountain View, Calif.: Mayfield. Examines the impact of global-scale culture on small-scale cultures worldwide.

CROSBY, ALFRED W. 1986. *Biological Imperialism: The Biological Expansion of Europe, 900–1900*. Cambridge, Eng.: Cambridge University Press. A historian views the biological consequences of European colonialism on ecosystems and people throughout the world.

DUMONT, LOUIS. 1977. *From Mandeville to Marx: The Genesis and Triumph of Economic Ideology*. Chicago and London: University of Chicago Press. A French anthropologist documents how "the economy" came to be treated as an independent reality within the global culture.

EKELUND, ROBERT B., JR., AND ROBERT F. HEBERT. 1983. *A History of Economic Theory and Method*, 2nd ed. New York: McGraw-Hill. A modern emic view of the capitalist economy that serves as a good comparison with Adam Smith.

SMITH, ADAM. 1776. *An Inquiry into the Nature and Causes of the Wealth of Nations*, Vol. 1. London: Strahan and Cadell. The classic formulation of the key features of the early capitalist economy.

WALLERSTEIN, IMMANUEL. 1974. *The Modern World-System: Capitalist Agriculture and the Origins of the European World-Economy in the Sixteenth Century*. New York: Academic Press. The pioneer statement of world-system theory.

WOLF, ERIC R. 1982. *Europe and the People Without History*. Berkeley: University of California Press. An anthropological treatment of European expansion since 1400, focused on the political economy and showing how the capitalist system incorporated tributary and kin-based systems.

# 12

# THE AMERICAN INDUSTRIAL STATE

Thanks to the enormous success of both its ideological and material culture, the United States is often a model for the rest of the world and is certainly an appropriate anthropological subject. For many, the United States represents the ideals of freedom, democracy, equality, and material abundance. Its size and economic power give the United States enormous influence; that means even such seemingly trivial matters as the American food preference for beef can have a profound impact on peoples in distant parts of the globe. Furthermore, its economic success makes the United States a critical source of stress in the global ecosystem; in the 1980s, Americans made up less than 5 percent of the world's population but consumed more than 25 percent of the world's commercial energy.

Attempting to understanding a country as large and complex as the United States is a formidable task, which has engaged anthropologists and other social scientists for a very long time. Studying the United States is a significant shift from anthropology's earlier role in support of colonialism. It means that American anthropologists must ask basic questions about their own culture and its place in the world. In this chapter, we focus on aspects of American culture that offer the strongest contrasts with small-scale cultures and the large-scale, tributary states discussed in Chapters 6–10. In the first section, we examine the demographic and ecological impact of the adoption of industrial technology in order to add a further dimension to the treatment of early industrial capitalism in Chapter 11. In the second section, we consider the functional consequences for American culture of giving high priority to the logic of "free" market forces and commercialization. In the final section, we examine the contradiction between America's ideals of democracy and equality and the realities of social class and poverty.

## THE INDUSTRIALIZATION OF AMERICA

### An American Profile

With a total territory of 3.6 million square miles (mi²) (9.3 million square kilometers [km3]), the United States is the world's fourth largest nation by land area, after the former Soviet Union, Canada, and China. By 1990, when the United States had grown to approximately 250 million people, America ranked as the fourth largest national population in the world, after China, India, and the Soviet Union. The United States is large enough to support great cultural diversity and is truly a complex culture. There are eight U.S. cities with more than 1 million people each.

The United States contains many subcultures representing diverse nationalities, speaking distinct languages, and practicing diverse religions. Roughly 75 percent of the population is of European ancestry, some 12 percent is of African, 8 percent Hispanic, and about 2 percent of Asian ancestry. Native Americans constitute only about .5 percent of the total population. Over 50 percent of the population are members of Christian churches, but there are important Jewish, Muslim, and Buddhist minorities. In many respects, the most significant cultural distinction in the country is by class, or level of wealth and power.

As an object of anthropological investigation, the United States is unique among all the cultures examined in earlier chapters, in the great wealth of information available. Federal, state, and local governments have continuously generated vast volumes of statistical material covering all aspects of American life. Newspapers, films, and books abound and constitute a cultural record of unprecedented detail. The challenge for the cultural anthropologist is to sift and sort through the existing data to reach useful conclusions about this complex culture. The analysis that follows draws on statistical data from national, county, and city levels in order to offer a more precise and ethnographically realistic picture for comparison with small-scale cultures.

## Urbanization and the Demographic Transition

Demographic variables are the most basic information to consider in examining any culture and are an important dimension of cultural scale. The *vital statistics* of the U.S. population provides an instructive contrast with tribal populations and illustrates basic concepts of demographic analysis. The obvious difference in size between the American population of 250 million people and the average tribal population of perhaps 500 to 1000 people should not obscure other fundamental demographic contrasts. Autonomous small-scale

tribal cultures, at least before the intervention of larger-scale cultures, contained generally low-density, rural populations. The archaeological record suggests that over the long run tribal populations were characterized by stable *fertility* and *mortality rates,* were little affected by immigration, and were relatively *stationary*—neither growing nor declining.

The dynamic aspect of U.S. demographic patterns presents a striking contrast to the tribal pattern. In 200 years, the 1790 nonnative population of 3.9 million increased sixty-fourfold (Figure 12.1). Much of this expansion was natural increase, reflecting the net effect of the birth rate exceeding the death rate. Population growth was augmented by large-scale immigration from Europe, which accounted for nearly 40 percent of the increase during the first decade of the twentieth century. Such phenomenal growth was supported by the systematic conquest of small-scale Native American cultures and the subsequent occupation of tribal lands.

The industrialization of American culture is dramatically illustrated in the shift in population from 95 percent rural in 1790 to 51 percent urban by 1920 (see Figure 12.1). Urban, as defined by the census bureau, refers to residence in settlements of 2000 people or more. By 1970 the American rural population had shrunk to just 26 percent of the total. In comparison, imperial China was still 92 percent rural in 1900; even by 1975, revolutionary China remained 80 percent rural (Cotterell and Morgan 1975). The American population moved to the cities because the rise of factory production created new demands for labor while mechanization and commercialization of farming reduced labor demand in the countryside. This shift reflected a profound change in the American food system.

American industrialization and urbanization are also related to important changes in vital statistics, which demographers refer to as the *demographic transition.* Improvements in public health related to water-purification and sewage-treatment systems, vaccination programs, and the introduction of antibiotics brought about a significant decline in annual mortality rates from infectious disease. Overall mortality declined from nearly 15 per 1000 in 1910 to under 9 per 1000 by 1975. Birthrates also declined from over 30 to un-

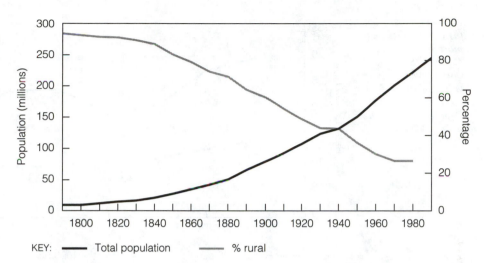

**FIGURE 12.1**
*Dynamics of the U.S. population, 1790–1990. (SOURCE: U.S. Department of Commerce 1990b.)*

KEY:  —— Total population    —— % rural

der 16 per 1000 during the same period, in part because the economic value of children declined as immigration and lower mortality rates meant that more adults were seeking jobs. Because city children could not help their families with the farm chores, there were overall fewer incentives to raise a large family. Demographers suggest that birthrates also declined because reduced infant mortality rates made it unnecessary to produce "extra" children to make sure that any would reach adulthood.

Broad national-level trends, such as changing demographic patterns, assume greater reality when a smaller, more ethnographically manageable region is examined in greater detail. For this purpose, illustrative material will be drawn from two counties of eastern Washington state in the Pacific Northwest. Spokane County is a U.S. Bureau of the Census Standard Metropolitan Statistical area (SMSA) and contains a major urban center, which is often used for marketing research because its ethnically diverse population is broadly representative of the country as a whole. Adjacent Whitman County occupies one of the world's richest wheat-producing areas and mirrors national-level trends in agriculture. This region did not attract significant Euro-American settlement until the 1870s, and most of its urban centers were not incorporated until the 1880s. By 1910 Spokane County had attracted immigrants from Canada and eighteen European countries. The

county grew from 37,000 people in 1890 to 341,000 people in 1980.

Spokane's vital statistics follows national trends in fertility and mortality rates and clearly illustrates the demographic transition (Figure 12.2). The most dramatic change was in infant mortality rates, which plunged from 93 per 1000 live births in 1910 to 10 per 1000 in 1981. The obvious explanation for reduced infant mortality was the decline in deaths due to infectious diseases. In 1910 nearly half of the infant deaths in Spokane were attributed to diarrhea, typhoid, scarlet fever, diphtheria, whooping cough, and various respiratory conditions that would be largely eliminated by public health measures and antibiotics. By 1981 almost

---

***vital statistics***   Data on births, deaths, and marriages that relate to total size and rate of change of a population.

***fertility rate***   Number of births per 1000 people per year, births per 1000 females, births per 1000 females of reproductive age, or births per reproductive females of age-specific categories.

***mortality rate***   Number of deaths in a population per year per 1000 people.

***stationary population***   A no-growth population in which the annual fertility rate equals the annual mortality rate.

***demographic transition***   A change in a population from preindustrial high mortality, high fertility rates to low mortality, low fertility rates following industrialization.

FIGURE 12.2
*(a) U.S. fertility and mortality rates, 1910–1980; (b) Spokane County, Washington, vital statistics, 1910–1981. (SOURCE: U.S. Department of Commerce 1990b.)*

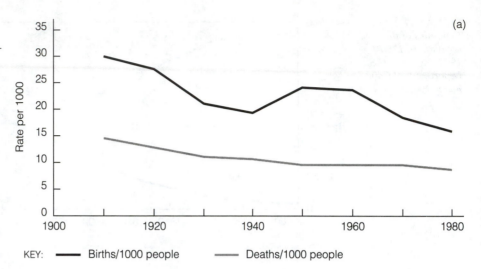

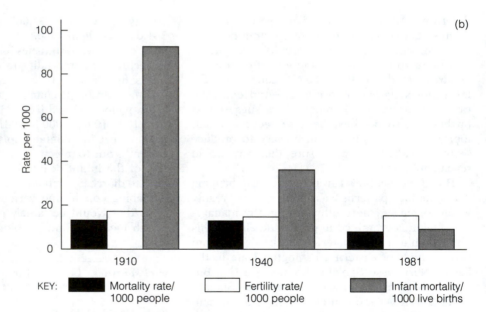

no one died of these diseases, and cancer and circulatory disease had become the leading causes of death as life expectancy increased.

Demographic processes can be clearly observed in **population pyramids,** which display age groups that trace the effects of mortality and fertility over a period of 85 years or more. Figure 12.3 presents a pyramid graph of a hypothetical, stationary tribal population, which was generated by a computer using fixed mortality and fertility rates

(K. Weiss 1973). The model assumed an average adult *life expectancy* at age 15 of 25 years and a life expectancy at birth of 30 years. The adult mortality estimate is probably representative of small-scale cultures living under fully independent conditions (see Table 5.3). A life expectancy at birth of 30 years assumes an *infant mortality* rate of 400 per 1000 live births, or 40 percent dying within the first year. A rate this high is impossible to verify for tribal groups and may be exaggerated, but many

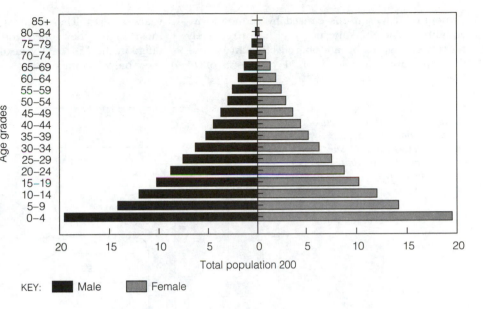

**FIGURE 12.3**
*Population pyramid of a hypothetical stationary small-scale culture with 200 people.*
*(SOURCE: Weiss 1973:142.)*

KEY:  ■ Male     ■ Female

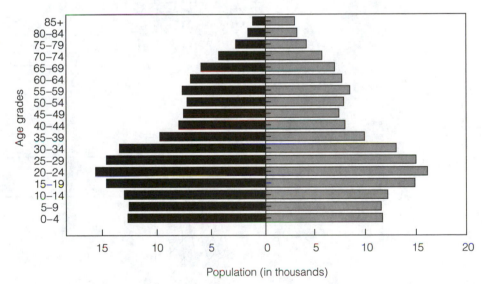

**FIGURE 12.4**
*Spokane metropolitan area, white population pyramid (157,218 males and 168,418 females), 1980.*

authorities consider it representative of tribal conditions. The pyramid produced by these rates has a very broad base and tapers rapidly and uniformly to a sharp peak showing less than 3 percent of the population over age 65.

By comparison, Figure 12.4 displays an age pyramid for the white population of Spokane in 1980. Ethnic whites are shown separately to control for

***population pyramid*** A bar graph showing successive cohort survivorships, often divided by sex and 5-year age intervals.

***life expectancy*** Average years of life remaining for people of a given age, often expressed as average age at death, $E(0)$, for life expectancy at birth, or as $E(15)$ for an adult life expectancy, at age 15.

***infant mortality*** Number of deaths of infants up to 1 year of age per 1000 live births.

demographic variations caused by economic in-equalities. The Spokane pyramid has a relatively narrow base and a broad top, reflecting an average life expectancy at age 15 of 61 years and of 74

years at birth. These figures are representative of most highly developed industrial nations. The bulge in the 15- to 34-year-old **cohorts** represents the "baby boom" increase in births following

**FIGURE 12.5**
*Energy flow in shifting agriculture where natural processes and especially the forest (successional plants) maintain crop productivity.*

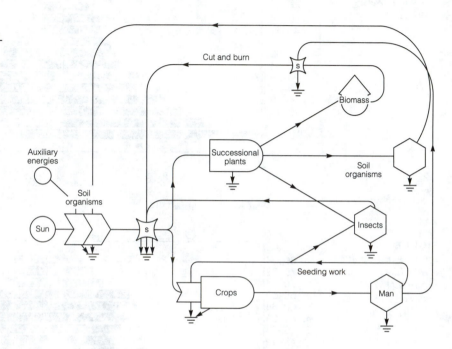

**FIGURE 12.6**
*Energy flow in factory farming.*

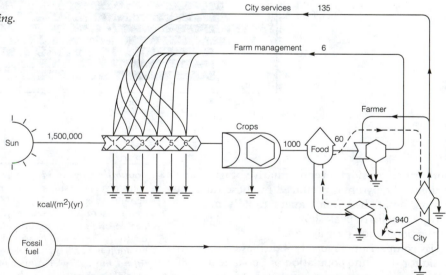

World War II (see Figure 12.2a) and demonstrates the constant variations that occur in real populations that have been artificially smoothed over in the tribal "model."

## The Rise of Factory Farming

The industrialization of farming and the general commercialization of the food system, which was well underway in Europe and the United States by the mid-twentieth century, must rank as a cultural transformation as significant as the domestication of plants and animals during the Neolithic. This great change is a continuation of the broad trend toward subsistence intensification that has accompanied each increase in the scale of human culture—more food is produced at greater energy cost and ecosystem degradation. This characterization may seem counterintuitive, but the true costs of industrialization have been masked by the cultural accounting system that emphasizes human labor and monetary cost. In an industrial culture such as the United States, farms are operated like factories. Often the emphasis is on a single crop that is mass-produced at the lowest possible monetary cost for the maximum cash return. Economic imperatives compel the farmer to use labor-saving machinery to reduce cost and to employ chemical pesticides and fertilizers to increase production.

When viewed from a cultural ecological perspective, *factory farming* raises troubling questions for the long-term viability of industrial civilization. As ecologist Howard Odum (1971) observes, the factory farm replaces *self-maintaining biological processes,* which are fueled by renewable solar energy, with urban-based cultural processes that require vast *energy subsidies* in the form of nonrenewable fossil fuels. The contrasts between a shifting cultivation production system, such as described for Amazonia in Chapter 3, and factory farming is illustrated in energy-flow diagrams in Figures 12.5 and 12.6. Factory farming simplifies natural ecosystems, making them less stable while extracting a larger energy share for human consumption. An obvious problem with this system is that it also rapidly depletes fossil fuels and soils and thus cannot be sustained indefinitely.

Because it requires relatively few farm laborers and produces very high per-acre yields, factory farming appears deceptively productive. In 1970, when viewed at the national level, each kilocalorie of U.S. farm labor returned 210 kilocalories (kcal) of food—four times the yield of intensive Chinese rice farming as discussed in Chapter 8. However, when the full energy costs of production were calculated, including fuel, electricity, fertilizer, and farm machinery, 2 kcal of energy were expended to produce 1 kcal of food energy (Steinhart and Steinhart 1974).

Such *deficit production* is only possible when subsidized by vast inputs of solar energy stored in nonrenewable fossil fuels. Furthermore, when food production costs are calculated to include the costs of industrial processing and marketing, which necessarily precede domestic consumption in a highly urbanized society, then a minimum of 8–12 kcals were expended in the production of 1 kcal of food (Table 12.1). Even this figure underestimates the actual energy costs of the U.S. food system because it does not include all transport costs, especially the use of private automobiles in trips to the grocery store, and the costs of advertising commercialized food products and disposing of the trash by-products. A more realistic total would probably approach 20 kcals expended for each one consumed.

U.S. farm production was not fully industrialized until fossil fuel–powered farm machinery and agricultural chemicals became widely used after 1940. The social corollary of these technological changes was the decline in the rural population

---

*cohort*   A group of people of the same age, usually those born within the same 5-year period.
*factory farming*   Commercial agriculture based on fossil-fuel energy subsidies, mechanization, pesticides, chemical fertilizers, and large-scale monocropping.
*self-maintaining biological process*   Natural cycle of energy and materials through a food chain of organisms fueled by solar energy through green plants and solar energy.
*energy subsidy*   The use of fossil fuels to increase food production above the rate that could be sustained through use of renewable energy sources.
*deficit production*   The situation in which more calories are expended in food production than are produced for human food.

**TABLE 12.1**  *Energy Use in the U.S. Food System (in 10¹² kcal)*

|  | 1940 | 1970 |
|---|---|---|
| Farm production* | 124.5 | 526.1 |
| Food processing† | 285.8 | 841.9 |
| Distribution‡ | 275.2 | 804.0 |
| *Totals* | 685.5 | 2172.0 |

SOURCE: Steinhart and Steinhart (1974).

*Farm production includes fuel, electricity, fertilizer, and irrigation and the costs of producing agricultural steel, farm machinery, and tractors.

†Processing includes production, machinery, packaging, transport fuel, and trucks and trailers.

‡Distribution includes commercial and domestic refrigeration and cooking.

described previously. The number of individual farms actually declined, but those that remained became much larger than before.

## Wheat for Topsoil: Erosion and Plenty in Whitman County

The impact of farm industrialization at the local level can be illustrated using census bureau statistics for Whitman County in eastern Washington. Whitman County is the heart of the Palouse region, an area of steep, dunelike hills composed of deep loess soils, which were deposited by the wind 100,000 years ago (Figure 12.7). Climate and soil conditions in the Palouse are ideally suited for *dry farming* and help make Whitman County one of the world's leading wheat-producing regions. *Monocrop farming* of wheat was well underway in the Palouse by the 1880s.

According to census bureau figures, 27,000 people lived in rural Whitman County in 1910. Approximately 75 percent of the cash value of farm production was in grain. There were some 3000 farms, averaging 383 acres (155 hectares) (Figure 12.8). The primary farm-production inputs were human labor and horses. Because much of the feed for the 38,000 horses and mules was grown locally, the county enjoyed a high degree of energy self-sufficiency.

By 1987 the switch to industrialization in Palouse farming was strikingly apparent in the cen-

sus bureau data that showed a drastic reduction in human labor inputs, the virtual disappearance of horses, and an enormous increase in fossil fuels and chemical fertilizers (Figure 12.9). Yields of wheat per acre suddenly doubled and tripled. Between 1910 and 1940, approximately 30 bushels were produced per acre, but by 1987 yields averaged 69 bushels and sometimes reached 100. Such increases resulted from the use of newly developed "miracle grains," genetically engineered to take maximum advantage of agricultural chemicals and machinery. This energy-intensive production system became known as the *Green Revolution* and was widely exported to the developing world in the 1970s and 1980s.

FIGURE 12.7
*Active soil erosion on cultivated wheat field in Whitman County, Washington. Note the soil slumping on the steep hillside in the background.*

FIGURE 12.8
*Palouse farming trends,
1910–1987.*

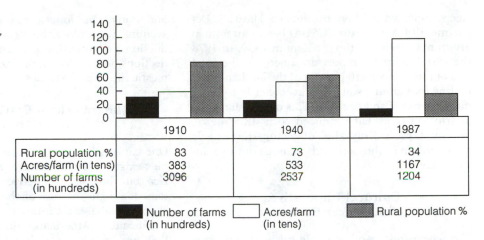

| | 1910 | 1940 | 1987 |
|---|---|---|---|
| Rural population % | 83 | 73 | 34 |
| Acres/farm (in tens) | 383 | 533 | 1167 |
| Number of farms (in hundreds) | 3096 | 2537 | 1204 |

Legend: ■ Number of farms (in hundreds)   □ Acres/farm (in tens)   ▨ Rural population %

FIGURE 12.9
*Palouse farm inputs,
1910–1987.*

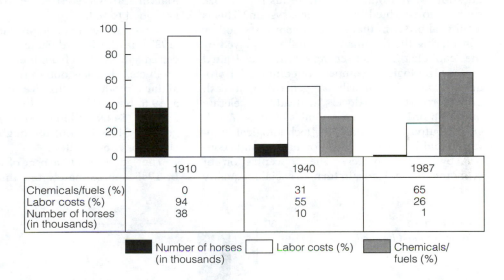

| | 1910 | 1940 | 1987 |
|---|---|---|---|
| Chemicals/fuels (%) | 0 | 31 | 65 |
| Labor costs (%) | 94 | 55 | 26 |
| Number of horses (in thousands) | 38 | 10 | 1 |

Legend: ■ Number of horses (in thousands)   □ Labor costs (%)   ▨ Chemicals/fuels (%)

The social and environmental consequences of the technological changes in Palouse wheat farming were equally striking. As the demand for labor declined, by 1987 the total rural population had shrunk to less than half of what it had been in 1910. More significantly, the number of farms declined even more steeply, while total farm acreage remained approximately the same. This meant that individual farms tripled in size. Land became concentrated in fewer and fewer hands, such that 15 percent of the farms came to control 46 percent of the land (Figure 12.10).

The most ominous change was the steady loss of soil due to erosion caused by deep cultivation of

---

**dry farming**  Rain-fed farming without artificial irrigation.

**monocrop farming**  Growing one plant species, sometimes only a single variety, often in very large continuous stands.

**Green Revolution**  Dramatic increases in agricultural production from genetically engineered hybrid grains that produce high yields in return for high inputs of chemical fertilizers and pesticides.

steep slopes with heavy machinery. The U.S. Department of Agriculture (USDA) began an annual program to monitor the problem in 1939. In 1978 the USDA issued a report documenting the total loss of topsoil from 10 percent of the land and estimating that annual soil losses averaged 14 tons (13 metric tons) of soil per acre. This means that each metric ton of wheat produced costs 13.5 metric tons of topsoil. This kind of factory farming is truly "mining" the soil and cannot continue indefinitely.

## Cultural Imperatives of a Market Economy

The wheat-for-topsoil example raises the obvious question, Why would any culture institutionalize such a short-sighted technological system? This is a cultural problem that can best be understood by considering the dominant cultural role played by the capitalist market economy in the United States. The logic of competitive commercial production aimed primarily at generating a cash profit forces U.S. producers to steadily accelerate output in order to gain economies of scale. Accelerated output is facilitated by technological innovation and by the concentration of economic control by a wealthy few. The concentration of economic power leads, in turn, to social inequality

and many other long-term costs. In the following sections, we explore this process using cattle production, consumption patterns, and the interconnections between economic concentration and domestic life as case studies.

## The American Cattle Complex: Good to Sell

One can easily make the case that a Cattle Complex exists in the United States just as in East Africa, but the contrasts between the two cattle systems highlight the role of the market economy in shaping global-scale industrial cultures. Cattle are significant in American culture not only because they are "good to eat" but more importantly, as Marvin Harris (1985) emphasizes, because cattle are "good to sell."

According to figures produced by the USDA (1987), in the United States in 1986, farmers received $46.7 billion from the sale of beef and dairy products. This was one-third of the cash value of all farm products sold. Livestock wholesaling was a $9.6 billion business in 1987, meat packers grossed $44.9 billion, and meat wholesalers grossed $47.3 billion, although these figures include pork and mutton.

The "good-to-eat" aspect of cattle is also clear. In 1985 approximately one-third of the calories

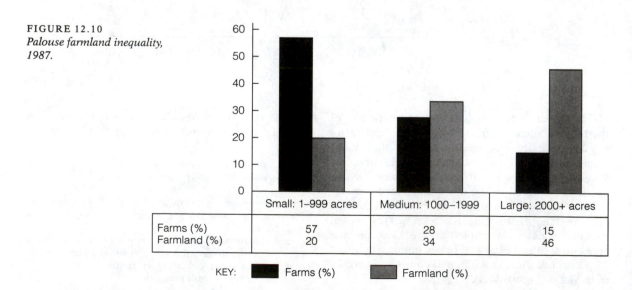

FIGURE 12.10
*Palouse farmland inequality, 1987.*

| | Small: 1–999 acres | Medium: 1000–1999 | Large: 2000+ acres |
|---|---|---|---|
| Farms (%) | 57 | 28 | 15 |
| Farmland (%) | 20 | 34 | 46 |

KEY: ■ Farms (%)　■ Farmland (%)

Americans consumed, two-thirds of the protein, and one-half of the fat came from animal products in general (Table 12.2). Two-thirds of the animal products consumed by weight were derived primarily from cattle in the form of beef and dairy products (Table 12.3).

The USDA estimated that there were 102 million cattle in the United States in 1987, .4 head per person, including beef and dairy animals, calves and adults. Approximately 40 percent of this national herd was slaughtered to provide meat, while some 10 percent of the herd produced milk. In comparison, East African cattle people, such as the Karimojong, need 4 animals per person to supply an approximately equal proportion of its subsistence requirements (see Table 4.3).

The greater efficiency of American cattle production requires a significant energy subsidy as discussed in Chapter 4. American cattle must be brought to maximum weight and marketed as quickly as possible, or cattle raising will not be profitable. The high level of beef consumption in the United States also requires a high level of beef imports from throughout the world. Approximately 8 percent of the beef consumed in the United States in the mid-1980s was imported, mostly from twenty-one countries (USDA 1987). Beef imports exceeded exports by approximately four to one.

Extreme specialization and inequality is a striking feature of the subsistence role of cattle in American culture. Remarkably few specialists are involved in producing and marketing the bulk of the nation's cattle products. Focusing on beef cattle, for example, the National Cattlemen's Association estimated that 45 percent of America's cattle were owned by only 6.7 percent of the producers in 1988 (Pietraszek 1990). This pattern was reflected in eastern Washington's Whitman County where twenty-nine farms, just 7.4 percent of the farms with cattle, owned 51 percent of the county's 31,000 cattle in 1987 (U.S. Department of Commerce 1989).

At the national level in 1987, an estimated 71 percent of the 10 million cattle fattened at feedlots passed through just 1.4 percent of the nation's

TABLE 12.2    *U.S. Food Consumption/Person/Day by Category, 1985*

|  | Kilocalories | % | Protein (g) | % | Fat (g) | % | Carbohydrates (g) | % |
|---|---|---|---|---|---|---|---|---|
| Animal | 1224 | 34 | 69 | 68 | 88 | 51 | 25 | 6 |
| Plant | 2376 | 66 | 33 | 32 | 84 | 49 | 388 | 94 |
| *Total* | 3600 | 100 | 102 | 100 | 172 | 100 | 413 | 100 |

SOURCE: U.S. Department of Agriculture (1987). These are crude estimates of apparent food consumption based on the disappearance of agricultural commodities from inventories.

TABLE 12.3    *U.S. Consumption of Animal Food/Person/Year, in 1985*

|  | Animal Products (lb) | Cattle Products (lb) |
|---|---|---|
| Red meat | 143.0 | |
| Beef (79.1) | | 79.1 |
| Pork (62.1) | | |
| Mutton (1.8) | | |
| Fish | 14.4 | |
| Poultry | 102.1 | |
| Dairy products* | 289.3 | 289.3 |
| *Total* | 548.8 | 368.4 |

SOURCE: U.S. Department of Agriculture (1987). These are crude estimates of apparent food consumption based on the disappearance of agricultural commodities from inventories.
*Cheese, milk, and ice cream, all processed primarily from cow's milk.

commercial feedlots, which were often vertically integrated with livestock wholesaling and meat-packing enterprises (Pietraszek 1990). A mere 188,750 people worked throughout the country in some 6000 establishments as livestock wholesalers, meat packers, and wholesalers (Table 12.4). In 1988 the four largest meat packers, just 4 percent of the total, processed nearly 70 percent of all of the cattle slaughtered, while three wholesalers sold nearly 90 percent of all the meat sold in the country (Table 12.5). This degree of control, by so few, over all aspects of such a major element of subsistence, is a remarkable cultural arrangement that certainly has *no* parallel in any small-scale cultures or ancient civilizations.

Inequality and concentration of this magnitude are driven by the economic logic of production in a highly industrialized market economy. The production of market cattle is a costly process that can only succeed if producers take advantage of economies of scale. For example, agricultural economists in eastern Washington concluded that even with the most careful management, a beef cattle enterprise based on only 25 animals would be uneconomical (Carkner, McReynolds, and Clark 1983). In East Africa, a Karimojong household supports itself comfortably on a herd of 33 cattle, but researchers in eastern Washington found that even when cattle production was treated as a sideline to grain production, and with a herd increased to 80 animals, farmers were barely able to cover operating costs (Hinman et al. 1988). Thus, over half of the cattle in Whitman County were on individual ranches with over 200 animals, while the largest ranches had over 1000.

Market forces shape how cattle are handled, categorized, graded, slaughtered, and butchered and how the meat is named, packed, and distributed. In the small-scale cultures of East Africa, cows are highly personalized, and slaughtering is a public and ritual act. The meat is distributed according to kinship relationships and is consumed immediately. In the United States, market cattle and meat are depersonalized commodities, whose production is left entirely to specialists, such that few people have more than a vague idea of where their meat even comes from.

The production process is designed to move the

TABLE 12.4    *U.S. Production and Distribution of Cattle and Meat, 1986–1987\**

|  | Establishments | Workers |
|---|---|---|
| Farms | 2,173,410 | 2,718,000 |
| Livestock wholesalers | 1,383 | 9,441 |
| Meat packers | 446 | 112,900 |
| Meat wholesalers | 4,212 | 66,409 |
| Grocerers and meat markets | 148,948 | 2,561,512 |

SOURCES: U.S. Department of Agriculture (1987) and U.S. Department of Commerce (1987a and 1987c).
\*Cattle, 40.7 million; consumers, 241.6 million.

TABLE 12.5    *Economic Concentration in the Cattle Industry, 1988*

45% of cattle owned by 6.7% of producers
71% of cattle fed by 1.4% of feedlots
69% of cattle slaughtered by four largest packers
89% of wholesale beef sold by three largest packers
30% of wholesale beef sold by one packer\*
35%–40% of retail sales of beef by twenty largest retailers

SOURCES: National Provisioner (1990) and Pietraszek (1990).
\*Estimate for 1990 (*Spokesman Review* 1991).

animal to full slaughter weight as quickly as possible—usually within 24 months, although milk-fed calves may be slaughtered as veal at under 3 months. Calves may receive appetite stimulants and ear-implant hormones to speed their growth and are weaned at 6–9 months, either to be returned to the range as "stockers" to grow further or vaccinated and sold to feedlots as "feeders" to be "finished" for slaughter. At the feedlot, cattle receive more vaccinations and growth-hormone implants and are fattened on a weight-gain diet of grain, molasses, beef fat, and plant protein supplements, laced with antibiotics, vitamins, and growth steroids (Thomas 1986). Cattle feed is also likely to contain animal protein concentrates derived from slaughterhouse trimmings and rending-plant "tankage," which would otherwise be inedible by-products. Some researchers even propose that feedlot manure be recycled as cattle feed to extract the maximum energy value and reduce waste (Dyer 1986).

The entire production process is highly regulated by federal and state laws. Live cattle are sorted by federal inspectors into classes by sex condition, such as steer, bullock, bull, cow, and heifer and into grades such as prime, choice, select, standard, commercial, utility, cutter, and canner. Grades relate to anticipated carcass quality and reflect age, body shape and size, muscle development, and fat distribution.

The Code of Federal Regulations requires humane slaughtering. Cattle are stunned, or "anesthesized," with gunshot, electrical shock, or carbon dioxide gas and quickly hoisted, stuck, and bled. Regulations specify every detail of the slaughtering process, even prescribing the rate in head per hour at which inspectors can examine specific parts of animals. For example, one inspector can examine the viscera of fifty-seven to eighty-four steers and heifers per hour, but only that of fifty-six to seventy-seven cows and bulls. Inspectors look for obvious diseases or injuries that would damage the meat, and they must test for unacceptable levels of drug residues. Parts of some diseased animals may be processed only as cooked meat, while carcasses condemned as human food move to the rendering plant where they may become animal food. Such detailed regulation and classification are necessary to ensure quality standards when animals move rapidly through a complex chain of buyers and sellers, each seeking to maximize their monetary return.

Economies of scale are a major factor in slaughtering. Larger plants, using highly specialized technology, were able to increase the hourly kill-and-butcher rate from 100 head per hour during the 1970s to 300 to 350 head per hour in the 1980s, thereby reducing the unit price of processing by 25 percent (Pietraszek 1990). At the same time, with intensive use of feedlot fattening, average carcass weights increased nearly 50 percent. Faster butcher rates required a multitude of mechanized tools such as dehorners, dehiders, carcass splitters, brisket opener saws, bone saws, and primal cut saws. Further meat-processing operations use mechanical trimmers, dicers, massagers, tumblers, grinders, collagen films, patty machines, and vacuum stuffers. Meat cutting is a highly intensive, technical occupation, where the demand for increased efficiency produces a high rate of injuries in the workers.

Virtually every part of the animal finds some use. A beef carcass is split and quartered and then quickly reduced to six to ten primal and subprimal cuts for wholesale. Dozens of specialized cuts are marketed at the retail level. "Variety meats" include organs such as liver, brains, kidneys, hearts, tongues, and tripe (beef stomach). People who are offended by the East African practice of eating cattle blood may be surprised that beef blood routinely finds its way into American meat food products, along with tiny bits of meat that are mechanically removed from beef heads. Only lungs, tonsils, and thyroids are not considered human food. Cattle bladders and intestines are used as sausage casings. Numerous other edible by-products include gelatin, marshmallows, and canned meat. Inedible by-products include leather, buttons, and soap from beef tallow, as well as pet foods and animal feeds. A wide range of pharmaceuticals such as insulin, estrogen, and thyroid extract are also derived from cattle.

## Promoting Beef as Real Food

The market-centered and highly specialized American subsistence system creates a situation in which food producers often find themselves opposed by antagonistic groups in the larger society who confront them on a variety of issues. For example, some environmentalists would like to reduce livestock production on public lands to benefit wildlife, natural vegetation, and watersheds (Wuerthner 1989). Cattle ranchers see themselves pitted against an anticow conspiracy directed by "tree-huggers" and the "environmental elite" led by the nation's largest environmental organizations such as the National Wildlife Federation and the Sierra Club. Cattle ranchers argue in extreme terms that any move to raise grazing fees or limit access to lands would be a threat to the livelihood of "literally thousands of ranching families" and would be an unprecedented economic disaster for the country (Wortham 1990).

Cattle groups also worry that the "diet/health establishment" will assault "virtually anything edible," generating "anti-meat food-faddism" and "anti-meat propaganda," thereby causing consumers to eat less meat out of unnecessary fear (*National Provisioner* 1990a-3, 7). Animal rights "extremists" are also a concern. Many small ranchers and packers operating on narrow profit margins are clearly threatened by any fall in demand or price. Health groups are working to reduce the total fat and cholesterol intakes of Americans, and meat is an obvious target. There can also be legitimate public concerns over the long-term biological, environmental, and social impact of a highly intensive bioindustry, such as beef production, which is driven primarily by market forces.

Beef associations exist to protect the interests of the beef industry. For example, there is the National Cattlemen's Association, the American Meat Institute, and the National Livestock & Meat Board. These organizations influence legislation and direct advertising programs at the public, promoting the safety and nutritional virtues of lean beef, in order to increase consumption of their products. The Beef Industry Council began a major market research and promotional effort in 1982, which led to the televised campaign featuring celebrities and small-town settings with the message "Beef: Real Food for Real People." Beef industry organizations have also developed "issues management" strategies to confront and preempt antimeat activists.

Anthropologist Marvin Harris (1985) argues that cultural preferences for specific meats are largely determined by utilitarian, ecological, and economic factors. He attributes the American preference for beef to the forced removal of the bison and the Native Americans from the Great Plains in the 1870s and their replacement by cattle. The ranchers were, in turn, displaced by grain farmers, and cattle had to be grazed on the arid lands and in the logged-over forests farther west. The real boom for beef, according to Harris, came after World War II when large numbers of American women began to work outside the home and fast-food dining on hamburgers suddenly opened a vast new market for beef. The key to the success of hamburger, which legally must be all beef, is that it can contain added beef fat, up to 30 percent. The added fat helps bind the meat when it is cooked. Thus, hamburger can be ground from relatively tough, range-fed steers, combined with the abundant fat trimmed from feedlot-fattened beef, which otherwise supply tender, marbled, and very expensive cuts of meat.

## The Cultural Construction of Consumption

*Conceiving the creation and movement of goods solely from their pecuniary quantities (exchange-value), one ignores the cultural code of concrete properties governing "utility" and so remains unable to account for what is in fact produced. . . . The structure of the economy appears as the objectivized consequence of practical behavior, rather than a social organization of things, by the institutional means of the market, but according to a cultural design of persons and things.* (Sahlins 1976b:166–167)

The preceding analysis focused on the economic utility of the way in which cattle are produced, processed, and marketed as commodities. Anthropologist Marshall Sahlins (1976b) observes that this "utilitarian" bias is a dominant feature of American culture, shared by economists, producers, and consumers, as well as by many anthropologists. Americans assume that the choices they make about production and consumption are entirely rational, logical, and naturally economical. Such **utilitarianism** also explains U.S. politics and social class, at least in the minds of the participants. In complementary opposition to this utilitarian cultural bias, Sahlins stresses that the physical and biological limits of human social existence leave considerable space for cultural variation, and thus a wide variety of "rational" cultural systems can be constructed. In this view, production becomes a "cultural intention," and there must be a "cultural account of production" before it can become fully intelligible.

In pursuing a cultural view of American production and consumption, Sahlins (1976b) considers the cultural place of meat. He argues that in American culture, because of its long cultural association with virility and strength, beef, and especially steak, has a central place in the diet. Pork takes second place, as a less preferred meat, while eating dogs or horses is virtually tabooed. Harris's (1985) ingenious utilitarian interpretations help explain these practices, but they do not provide a full cultural understanding. Sahlins emphasizes the limitations of utilitarian interpretations of meat preferences by pointing out that during the early 1970s, even though food prices were rising rapidly, people resisted the suggestions of government officials that the poor should buy variety meats, such as beef heart, liver, and kidney, which were inexpensive yet highly nutritious. There were also some unsuccessful moves to market horse meat as an alternative to beef. These proposals were economically rational, but they violated American cultural structures.

Sahlins (1976b) shows that, in their culturally defined levels of edibility, cattle, pigs, horses, and dogs form a structural metaphor on cannibalism that makes a statement about rank in U.S. society. Using symbolic analysis, like that developed by Claude Lévi-Strauss and discussed in Chapters 2 and 3 in reference to Australian and Amazonian cultures, Sahlins observes that in American culture cattle and pigs form a structured set in opposition to horses and dogs (Figure 12.11). Cattle and pigs are treated as unnamed objects and are eaten, whereas dogs and horses are named subjects and are not eaten. Dogs and horses are seen as more "human." They are talked to and petted, and dogs may live in the house and are buried. Eating dogs would be like eating kin and implies cannibalism. Horses are more like servants, and eating them is only slightly less tabooed. Pork is less preferred than beef, in part because pigs scavenge human food and are thus closer to people than cattle, such

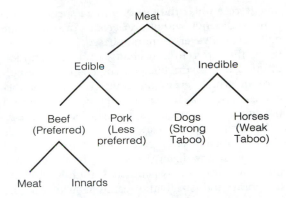

FIGURE 12.11  *The cultural structure of meat edibility in the United States. (SOURCE: Sahlins 1976b.)*

that eating pigs would be slightly cannibalistic. The relative ranking between beef and pork is illustrated by 1991 grocery store prices that showed the higher beef steaks and roasts ranging from $4–$7/lb, while pork ranged from $1.40–$2.70/lb.

A further cultural code of edibility is imposed on beef itself. Meat is culturally distinguished as the most edible part of the animal, in opposition to "innards" such as heart, tongue, and liver, which, like pork, imply cannibalism. Cuts of beef are subdivided into dozens of named categories and products such as chuck roast and T-bone, sirloin, and flank steaks, each is priced according to its culturally defined desirability, such that eating a given cut reinforces one's social rank. Only a few can eat tenderloin at $6.99/lb, while liver at $1.39/lb could be much more widely consumed. Sahlins (1976b) stresses that pricing and desirability are not obviously related to supply and nutritional quality because liver is highly nutritious and relatively scarce yet is much cheaper than steak, which is more abundant per animal. Demand in this case seems to be shaped, at least in part, by symbolic cultural categories.

The use of cultural products, such as "meat," to encode social differences among categories of

---

***utilitarianism***  The use of economic profit, direct material advantage, or physical welfare, such as food and shelter, as an explanation for cultural practices.

people resembles the use of animal species as totems to distinguish cultural groups in small-scale cultures. However, in market-based, industrial cultures, the differential exchange and consumption of culturally distinguished products create a culture in which ever-expanding consumption becomes a cultural imperative and goes far beyond the egalitarian categories that tribal societies use.

Anthropologists Marshall Sahlins and Jules Henry both consider consumption patterns and their institutionalized supports to be the decisive point of contrast between tribal cultures and contemporary industrial cultures. In his wide-ranging critique of American culture, Henry (1963) stressed that Americans assume that wants are infinitely expandable, whereas tribal peoples assume fixed wants and produce only what is wanted. Tribal peoples culturally dampen wants and enjoy a complementarity between production and needs, whereas Americans deliberately create a disequilibrium by increasing needs above the level that can ever be satisfied. Sahlins makes the same point in his famous statement on foragers as "the original affluent society," in which he observes that foragers easily satisfy their wants by desiring little, whereas for Americans,

*Scarcity is the peculiar obsession of a business economy, the calculable condition of all who participate in it. The market makes freely available a dazzling array of products all these "good things" within a man's reach—but never his grasp, for one never has enough to buy everything. To exist in a market economy is to live out a double tragedy, beginning in inadequacy and ending in deprivation. All economic activity starts from a position of shortage . . . one's resources are insufficient to the possible uses and satisfactions.* (1968:86)

Scarcity or poverty is thus not strictly a technological problem, and it is not inherent in nature; it is a cultural creation, which is most elaborated by global-scale, industrial cultures. According to Henry (1963), the dependence of American culture on the deliberate creation of needs for goods and services constitutes a "psychic revolution" with far-reaching impacts on human thought and behavior.

Henry (1963) examines advertising as the primary means of stimulating consumption, suggesting that advertising is a distinct, pecuniary,

philosophical system, a mode of thought, and a quasi-moral institution, operating with its own language. Henry draws examples from an influential "how-to" manual for professional advertisers by Rosser Reeves (1961), one of advertising's most successful practitioners. Reeves assumes that people can remember only some 30,000 product names, and advertisers must fight for the limited space within a consumer's brain. Products are treated like natural species that proliferate and are threatened by extinction. The language of advertising extolled by Reeves is based on what Henry calls "pecuniary pseudo-truth," according to which, false advertising claims are supported by "pseudo-proof" and "shadowy evidence" presented as truth. Advertising is called "education," and it seeks to promote impulsiveness, fuzzy thinking, and fantasizing because cautious, thoughtful people might be slow to buy. The pecuniary philosophy defines truth as "what sells" and as what the seller wants people to believe. Immorality in such a system, or bad advertising, is what destroys products.

Since Henry's analysis of American culture, the influence of advertising has steadily increased. Expenditures on advertising have expanded tenfold from approximately $12 billion annually in the early 1960s to more than $125 billion by 1989. This is because "advertising does work," as a member of the poultry business explained, when he linked advertising directed at children, with increased consumption and profit: "We need to increase communication [advertising], which drives purchase, which drives consumption, which drives profits for egg producers" (*National Provisioner* 1990b:13).

This is the "cultural design of persons and thing . . . by the institutional means of the market" that Sahlins (1976b:166–167) referred to in the quote at the beginning of this section. Such a cultural design is a central feature of global-scale cultures, but it is not "natural," even though it might be quite profitable for certain interest groups to pretend otherwise.

## Family, Inequality, and Oligopoly

Harris (1981) uses his cultural materialist theories to explain the decline in the quality of American life, which became strikingly obvious during the 1970s, as evidenced by rising crime rates, inflation, poor service, shoddy production, and the breakdown of the family. Harris attributes all these problems to two major changes in the U.S. economy: the rise of *oligopolies* and conglomerates in U.S. business and a shift in emphasis from the production of goods to the production of services and information. These changes are a continuation of economic trends that became apparent shortly after World War II.

The quality of American goods may decline because many giant corporations, because of their size, can eliminate competition and control markets to such an extent that corporate directors can be relatively unconcerned with the quality of their products. Large corporations also derive a significant proportion of their profits from buying and selling smaller corporations, rather than directly from production, and this could further reduce production quality. Large "parent" corporations may contain so many small companies and produce so many diverse products that the top executives are far removed from either the day-to-day operation of a factory or the concerns of consumers.

The scale of giant corporations can be illustrated by Philip Morris, the seventh largest industrial corporation in the United States. In 1989 Philip Morris sold a staggering $39 billion worth of products, an amount far exceeding the national budgets of many countries. As a giant conglomerate, Philip Morris contained some thirty-three additional operating companies, subsidiaries, units, and divisions in the United States and seventy-two others in twenty-nine foreign countries. From top to bottom, there were at least four major organizational levels, such that the corporation, with its 111,000 American employees, was structurally as complex as a political state. Philip Morris produced hundreds of food items, including Kraft and General Foods brands, Miller beer, Oscar Meyer meats, and a wide range of cigarettes, sea foods, bagels, pizzas, and frozen foods (Directory of Corporate Affiliations 1991, International Directory of Corporate Affiliations 1990–1991).

Harris also maintains that the quality of goods is likely to decline in large-scale industrial cultures. The reason for this decline is that there is no longer a direct connection between producers and consumer:

*In our era of industrial mass production and mass marketing, quality is a constant problem because the intimate sentimental and personal bonds which once made us responsible to each other and to our products have withered away and been replaced by money relationships* (1981:23)

The expansion of giant corporations is related to the tremendous increase in the service and information sector of the U.S. economy, which occurred in the twentieth century. Large corporations need large bureaucracies to keep track of their operations, while expanding markets require many special services, along with vast numbers of retail clerks and low-level managers. Many of these jobs require little training, and the increasing demand is filled primarily by women and minorities, who are willing to take temporary, part-time, often poorly paid jobs.

Census data for Spokane County in eastern Washington document this rise of employment in the service sector in relation to employment in agriculture, manufacturing, and transportation. In 1920, 55 percent of the employment in the county was in management, technical professions and clerical, support, and domestic services. Women held 38 percent of these jobs. By 1980, services accounted for 72 percent of all employment in the county, and women held 55 percent of these jobs. Thus, a significantly larger proportion of employment was in the service area, and more of these jobs were held by women. Such a change would indeed be likely to influence family patterns and the relation between men and women.

Harris (1981) argues that during the nineteenth century the leaders of industrialized nations, most of whom were men, and working men in general, preferred keeping women out of the factory labor force for a variety of reasons. Government officials and business leaders feared that, if women worked, the birth rate would decline, as would the labor force, markets, and tax revenues. Men also did not want women to work because working

*oligopoly*  Concentrated economic power when a market is dominated by only a few producers—like a monopoly, which is controlled by a single producer.

**FIGURE 12.12**
*In the 1950s, women were increasingly drawn into the work force to help pay for new consumer goods, yet they were also expected to be housewives as this stereotyped view of a "typical" American family illustrates.*

women would undermine male dominance in the family, and it was feared that working women would reduce wages by increasing the work force as Adam Smith predicted.

In 1890 women were only 17 percent of the work force, and most women who worked were divorced, widowed, or still unmarried and were thus already outside the reproductive force. In the 1940s, women moved into the labor force to replace the men at war; in the 1950s and early 1960s, many women continued to work in order to help buy new consumer goods, which represented improvements in living standard (Figure 12.12). After 1965 rising inflation rates meant that more and more wives had to find jobs in order to maintain what was becoming a declining standard of living. Men were now seeing their buying power decline and welcomed the extra income from a working

wife, but they still wanted a "housewife" in the home.

Women's dissatisfaction with this situation, according to Harris (1981), was largely responsible for the feminist movement of the 1970s and 1980s. These developments changed the shape of the American family, causing divorce rates to soar, such that by 1980 only 6 percent of families fit what was long considered to be the ideal and normal pattern of working father, housewife mother, and two or more children. By 1987 women constituted nearly 45 percent of the work force, and by 1988 only 56 percent of all households were composed of a married couple, whereas in 1966 over 72 percent of all households fit this ideal.

Some of the most striking changes in the quality of life and family structure are directly related to economic inequality and can be seen in national statistics on poverty, welfare, and crime. An impoverished lower class has always been part of American society, but it is difficult to show historical changes in the proportion of the impoverished population. For example, in 1910 in Spokane County, Washington, only .5 percent of the population lived in workhouses, were officially listed as "paupers" in "almshouses," or were residents of prisons, orphanages, old people's homes, or other benevolent institutions. At that time, many impoverished people were taken care of by relatives or lived as farm hands in the rural area. In 1980 more than 8 percent of the households in the county were officially considered to be living in poverty, and 1.4 percent of the total population was institutionalized.

In 1964 the federal government established an official minimum income level that would be sufficient for a family of a given composition to purchase a nutritionally adequate diet. For example, in 1987 the poverty threshold stood at $11,200 for a family of four. This "poverty line" is often readjusted to reflect changes in inflation and political considerations but nevertheless provides a broad measure of inequality. Since 1965 roughly 13 to 17 percent of the total American population has been considered to be officially "poor," but many homeless people are likely not being counted. In 1989 more than 10 million Americans were receiving federal assistance under the Aid to Families with Dependent Children program.

From health statistics showing poor nutrition, higher infant mortality rates, and lower life-expectancy figures for economically disadvantaged groups, it appears that public assistance programs do not adequately provide for all impoverished people in the country. Harris (1981) points out that public welfare programs encourage the formation of single-parent households because limitations on income levels make it disadvantageous for husband-fathers to remain in the household if they begin to earn too much.

In 1960 the rate of violent crimes (murder, forcible rape, robbery, and aggravated assault) in the United States stood at 161 per 100,000 people. In 1989 it was 663 per 100,000. Crime statistics are tricky to interpret because they can be skewed by differential reporting and changes in the age and sex composition of the population, but there have clearly been dramatic increases as economic power has become more concentrated in giant corporations and social inequality has increased. Correlations of this sort do not prove causation, but they do suggest that a closer look at American social structure, personality, and value systems would be helpful.

## THE STRUCTURE OF AMERICAN SOCIETY

### Margaret Mead and the American National Character

Many prominent anthropologists such as Franz Boas (1928), Margaret Mead (1942), Jules Henry (1963), and Marvin Harris (1981) have analyzed American culture, but the issues these researchers focused on and their interpretations have differed widely through time. The anthropological enterprise is shaped by the contemporary events and issues of which it is a part. As Eric Wolf (1969a) has observed, American anthropologists abandoned racist nineteenth-century cultural evolutionary theory and shifted their attention to *culture and personality, national character, values,* and *socialization,* under the influence of Franz Boas, between 1890 and 1940. Wolf characterizes this latter period in U.S. history as the liberal reform era during which many political leaders attempted to

place some moderating constraints on capitalist expansion and to make American society more democratic. At the same time, the United States was absorbing large numbers of foreign immigrants, like German-born Boas himself, and Boasian anthropologists shared the widespread belief that people could change rapidly so that everyone would share in the American Dream of progress and plenty. With the rise of what President Eisenhower called the *military–industrial complex* after World War II, Wolf argues that the problem of how to control this unprecedented concentration of enormous power emerged as the dominant issue in the United States, but anthropologists have had difficulty developing effective perspectives to understand such a complex issue.

Mead's (1942) analysis of American culture typifies anthropological views of the United States during the liberal reform era of U.S. history. Mead's book centered on American national character, which she maintained was generated by a distinctively American pattern of socialization or child rearing. Her intuitive concept of "national character" referred to how individual personality traits might be used to characterize the average personality of an entire national society. Thus, it often resembled both popular ethnic stereotypes and emic value systems and worldviews.

Mead's work was solidly within the Boasian tradition, and she did not treat political and economic power as a specific issue, even though her

---

*culture and personality*  Psychological anthropology, a subfield of cultural anthropology, dealing with the relation between cultural patterns and individual personality.
*national character*  An average personality pattern or value system projected onto an entire country abstracted from the study of individuals; often reflects normative statements about idealized behavior and simple ethnic stereotypes.
*values*  Beliefs about ideal behavior and goal expectations shared by the members of a culture.
*socialization*  Learning the rules of one's society, especially the way children are raised, with an emphasis on appropriate interpersonal behavior; related to enculturation, which refers more broadly to learning one's culture.
*military–industrial complex*  The very large defense-related industries that emerged in the United States during World War II and that became a major force in economic and political affairs during the postwar period.

book was written in support of the war effort. Mead attributed the rapid urbanization and material progress of the United States to American "character" and side-stepped issues of power and social class by declaring that in the United States people were "more nearly equal than they had ever been before" (1942:204). In her view, social class was really a ladder that people moved up. Mead emphasized that the United States was uniquely egalitarian because its colonial founders had abandoned the European class system. She refused to explain American culture by referring to underlying economic causes, rejecting **economic determinism** as a "mythological substitute for taking responsibility for our lives" (1942:160). She did not deny the importance of material conditions in shaping American character but argued that all such external factors were "mediated to the child" by the family in the socialization process, which was so "deeply ingrained" as to be relatively unaffected by the forces of history and economics. As Mead explained, "Americans are what they are because they have been reared in America by parents with certain ways of behaving" (1942:120–121).

The primary elements of the American character, which Mead identified, were conformity, a drive for success, and a belief in progress. According to Mead, these character traits were derived from the insecurity and disillusionment engendered in the child by American child-rearing practices in which parents punish their children and hypocritically pretend to be completely virtuous. Insecurity was caused by the small child's perception that parental love was conditional upon the child's achievements. Disillusionment set in when the adolescent realized that its parents had not achieved as much as they had pretended.

## Social Class in Yankee City

Other anthropological observers of the United States during the liberal reform era took a much broader view of social class and even included economic and political dimensions. However, even these studies failed to adequately address the problem of inequality and power in the United States because they emphasized an emic concept of social class that focused on the community level, as if the country could be studied like a small-scale culture. For example, the famous five-volume *Yankee City* monograph series (Warner 1959; Warner and Low 1947; Warner and Lunt 1941; Warner and Srole 1945) provided a rich ethnographic account of social class in a single American community, but it treated class as interpersonal relationships and thus overlooked the national-level dimensions of class-based power.

Yankee City was a pseudonym for a New England manufacturing town of 17,000 people, which was studied over a 5-year period from 1930 to 1934 by a team of thirty Harvard University social anthropologists, directed by W. Lloyd Warner. Warner was inspired by the structural-functionalism of Bronislaw Malinowski and A. R. Radcliffe-Brown and had just completed a 3-year field study of an Australian aboriginal group. He was anxious to analyze the social structure of an American community using the theoretical tools that had worked so effectively in Australia. His team used the standard range of anthropological field methods including participant observation and formal and informal interviews. They collected life histories and genealogies and gleaned additional data from the local newspaper and the published U.S. census.

Warner and his researchers found that at the interpersonal level people in Yankee City ranked one another into superior and inferior social statuses based on "education, occupation, wealth, income, family, intimate friends, clubs and fraternities, as well as . . . manners, speech, and general outward behavior" (Warner and Lunt 1941:83). This convinced him that social class was not a simple reflection of economic level. Six social classes ranging from "upper" to "lower" appeared to cover all the culturally significant social statuses that the Yankees identified. Warner then distinguished seven key social structures in the community: family, informal clique, formal associations, schools, churches, economic institutions, and government.

Detailed analysis involved enormous effort. For example, there were 357 **associations** in the community, including a variety of social clubs, fraternal lodges, and veteran organizations. Because an individual could belong to several associations, thousands of memberships had to be sorted out.

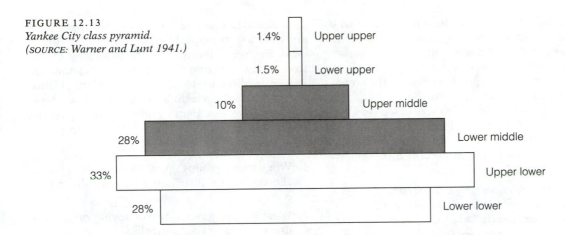

**FIGURE 12.13**
*Yankee City class pyramid.*
*(SOURCE: Warner and Lunt 1941.)*

| | |
|---|---|
| 1.4% | Upper upper |
| 1.5% | Lower upper |
| 10% | Upper middle |
| 28% | Lower middle |
| 33% | Upper lower |
| 28% | Lower lower |

Warner grouped associations into nineteen different types based on the social class of their members and showed that association and class defined fifty-four unique status positions, each of which reflected distinct and predictable behavioral patterns. Type 1 associations contained only members of the upper-upper class, whereas type 9 associations included people from all classes. When the individual members of all seven key social structures were sorted by social class, a complex chart of community social status emerged.

Contrary to Mead's expectations, Warner's picture of American social class showed a very small upper class that was relatively endogamous and socially exclusive. It was also predominantly white, Anglo-Saxon, and Protestant and controlled a disproportionate share of the wealth. Warner's data showed that the 3 percent of the population belonging to the upper class (upper-upper and lower-upper) received over 17 percent of the community's total annual income. Various ethnic groups were concentrated at the lower half of the class pyramid (Figure 12.13). The bulge in the middle of the Yankee City class pyramid is strikingly different from the class pyramids typical of preindustrial states and empires such as China and India and indicates that economic progress does contribute to social mobility in the American class system. However, social class is still a reality in the United States.

The technological and social changes that industrialization brought to rural America were overshadowed by even more profound changes taking place in the urban centers. Technological changes in the cities occurred in the steady mechanization and specialization of production and in a corresponding increase in the proportion of workers devoted to management, sales, service, and information.

### The American Ruling Class

A much broader view of social class in the United States appears in the work of G. William Domhoff (1967, 1983), which first appeared some 25 years after the studies by Mead and Warner. Domhoff directly confronts the issue of power by identifying a *national upper class* and examining its institutional role within the country. Examining the American elite is what anthropologist Laura Nader (1972) has called "studying up." Research of this sort reverses anthropology's historic focus on the least powerful villagers in the poorest countries, by

*economic determinism*  The argument that economic factors are the primary influences shaping other aspects of culture; similar to utilitarianism and infrastructural determinism.
*association*  An organization that individuals join voluntarily as opposed to groups, such as clans and lineages, where membership is normally assigned at birth.
*national upper class*  The highest socioeconomic class in the United States, which also operates as a governing class.

asking who is in control at the top, how and why decisions are made, and who benefits from them. Studying up is seldom a mere intellectual exercise; it may be stimulated by indignation over the inequities of power and is a good example of the potential scope of applied anthropology.

In his original study, which was based on a detailed analysis of the Social Register in twelve major cities and various national institutions for the period 1932–1967, Domhoff described the American upper class as

closely knit by such institutions as stock ownership, trust funds, intermarriages, private schools, exclusive city clubs, exclusive summer resorts, debutante parties, foxhunts, charity drives, and, last but not least, corporation boards. (1967:4)

Domhoff, who was trained as a psychologist, draws on perspectives from anthropology, sociology, economics, and political science. Like Warner, Domhoff defines a **social class** as a group of intermarrying families bounded by a variety of cultural devices. However, Domhoff suggests that at the national level less than 1 percent of the American population who comprise the American upper class form an aristocracy, or a **governing class.** In this view, the American upper class constitutes a social group with common economic interests. As a socioeconomic group, the upper class enjoys strategic ownership and control over the key institutions in the country, including the most important banks, corporations, foundations, universities, the mass media, and other policy-shaping associations, including the federal government. This etic view deserves careful consideration because it is contrary to the popular emic view of the United States, such as Mead and Warner presented, which emphasizes American core values of freedom, equality of opportunity, democracy, and social mobility.

Power is the key concept in Domhoff's analysis of social class. In this case, **power** refers to the ability of members of the upper class to shape events. Domhoff argues that the upper class **co-opts** upwardly mobile members of lower classes such that they must take on upper-class values before they are admitted into the upper class. The **power elite** consists of people who are in the most important leadership positions in the country; it

also includes many members of the upper class and others who support the objectives of the upper class and serve its interests as managing executives in the government and major corporations. Power is difficult to investigate in the United States because, according to the emic view, power and class are not significantly linked. Therefore, Domhoff (1983) uses indirect indicators of power, asking

1. What social groups enjoy the most benefits, as shown by the distribution of wealth and income?

2. What groups govern, by occupying or controlling positions of authority?

3. What groups win in disputes over public policy?

In American culture, data on income are notoriously unreliable. Furthermore, it is impolite to ask Americans directly about their wealth, and there are many reasons why people would wish to hide such information, but the imprecise data that are available indicate dramatic wealth concentration in a few hands. Domhoff (1983) estimates that for most of the twentieth century approximately .5 percent of the population owned 20 to 25 percent of the wealth, but he cautions that this may be a gross underestimate. The compensation that top executives in major corporations received in the mid-1970s was ten to forty times the salaries of average workers, and this made it easy for rising executives to assume upper-class lifestyles and assimilate as wealthy individuals.

Most telling for Domhoff's argument is the role played by the upper class in controlling America's largest corporations. Since the mid-nineteenth century, the corporation, rather than individually owned proprietorships and partnerships, has become the most important form of business organization in the major industrial countries. A corporation has a formal constitution and is legally registered with the state. A corporation is owned by its shareholders in proportion to the stocks that they individually own, and it is controlled by its board of directors, who are the largest stockholders. The chief executives of a corporation manage daily affairs but may not themselves be owners. Stockholders enjoy limited liability for the corporation's debts and receive a share of the annual dividends declared by the board of directors. The business corporation is uniquely suited to promote industrial expansion and the accumulation of vast family fortunes.

Since the end of World War II, U.S. corporations have grown to enormous size, creating Eisenhower's military–industrial complex, despite antimonopoly efforts by the federal government. The size and economic power of the largest corporations are difficult to comprehend. For example, in 1975 there were 14,657 commercial bank corporations in the United States, but the 10 largest, .06 percent of the total, owned 20 percent of the total assets, while the largest 50 banks, representing just 2 percent of the total, owned 35 percent of the assets. By 1989 there were fewer banks, but the 10 largest still owned 20 percent of the assets. In 1972 there were 313,000 manufacturing corporations, but the largest 50, representing a tiny fraction of the total, accounted for 25 percent of all value added in manufacturing. The trend toward corporate mergers during the 1980s further enhanced the power of a few giant corporations, which can now be called oligopolies to emphasize their enormous control over the market.

Many observers argue that the United States is a pluralistic society and cannot be controlled by any social class. However, Domhoff (1983) maintains that, because a few giant corporations have come to dominate American life and because members of the upper class own the largest share of stocks in these corporations and disproportionately sit on the boards of directors, the upper class can legitimately be considered a governing class. Estimates of concentration in stock ownership suggest that 1 percent of American adults owned 61 to 76 percent of all privately held stocks from 1922 to 1953, and in 1962 1 percent owned 63 percent of public stocks (Domhoff 1983). More important, control by a few large stockholders is facilitated by further concentration of their holdings, for management purposes, into a few family-owned offices, trusts, and holding companies. Domhoff refers to such extended families that form wealth-centered, relatively closed kin networks and economic interest groups as *kinecon groups.* They are reminiscent of the royal lineages of the ancient empires and imply that many

features of state organization have remained constant despite recent democratic reforms in political structure.

Domhoff's findings support the earlier conclusions of C. Wright Mills (1956) that the upper class forms a "power elite" of "corporate rich" business people that dominate the corporate community and thus indirectly influence what happens throughout the culture. As Mills expressed it,

*. . . They [the power elite] have secured their privileges and prerogatives in the most stable private institutions of American society. They are a corporate rich because they depend directly, as well as indirectly, for their money, their privileges, their securities, their advantages, their powers on the world of the big corporations.* (1956:148)

Members of the upper class often simultaneously occupy multiple positions on the boards of directors of several of the largest corporations, foundations, and universities, where they can make strategic decisions that will promote their interests. Complex interlocking directories occur when the same individual sits on more than one corporate board, creating an "inner group" of face-to-face acquaintances representing diverse corporations. Such individuals meet regularly in private social clubs where they can share inside information to benefit their common interests. For example, in 1990 fifteen of the largest industrial corporations, the four largest banks, the two largest insurance companies, and two of the largest pri-

---

*social class*   A clearly bounded group of intermarrying families.

*governing class*   The socioeconomic upper class that enjoys a disproportionate share of wealth and political and economic power in the country.

*power*   "The capacity of some persons to produce intended and foreseen effects on others" (Wrong 1979:2).

*co-optation*   A process of social mobility in which lower-class individuals are socialized into the values of the dominant class.

*power elite*   Members of the governing class and co-opted members of lower social classes, who are in controlling positions within leading national institutions.

*kinecon group*   Extended families formed by the wealthy American elite, based on common economic interests in formal corporate organizations such as family trusts and holding companies that protect and manage their wealth.

vate foundations were interconnected by thirty-five individuals who sat on more than one board (Figure 12.14). Each of four individuals were on three different boards and formed a tight cluster connecting such industrial giants as General Motors, IBM, Texaco, Du Pont, and Philip Morris; two of the largest banks, Citibank and Morgan Guaranty; one of the largest insurance companies, Metropolitan Life; and the Rockefeller Foundation.

In addition to the key role played by the American upper class in the corporate community, Domhoff (1983) argues that the upper class also maintains strategic control over foreign and domestic social and economic policies and public opinion because they have substantial influence over the institutions that set the parameters within which policy is formulated. The upper class financially supports and sits on the governing boards of elite universities, charitable foundations, and many influential public policy associations. The upper class also exerts broad control over the federal government itself, by guiding the process by which political candidates and appointees and special commissions are selected and by using lawyers and lobbyists to influence regulatory agencies. This amounts to "domination" of the government, which Domhoff defines as "the ability of a class or group to set the terms under which other classes or groups within a social system must operate" (1983:150).

## America from a Chinese Perspective

The preceding sections implied that American culture could best be understood through an analysis of its economic organization and class structure. This materialist emphasis is hardly surprising because it is also a prominent theme in American culture and would appeal to American anthropologists, but it provides a very incomplete view. Fortunately, American culture has also been analyzed by a Chinese anthropologist, Francis Hsu, who grew up in China and has lived for many years in the United States. Hsu is a psychological anthropologist and, like Mead, is interested in socialization, values, and personality. Hsu's deep familiarity with both Chinese and American culture allows him to make very insightful comparisons between the two cultures and provides an effective balance to the materialist bias of many American anthropologists.

Hsu (1972, 1981) argues that many of the key differences in economic life and class structure between Chinese and American culture can be attributed to what he considers to be the American core value of individual self-reliance in contrast to the Chinese pattern of family dependence and filial piety. The exaggerated emphasis that Americans place on self-reliance is represented by the ideal of the "rugged individualist" and a corresponding fear of dependence. For example, American chil-

FIGURE 12.14
*Interlocking directories in the largest U.S. corporations and foundations, 1990.*

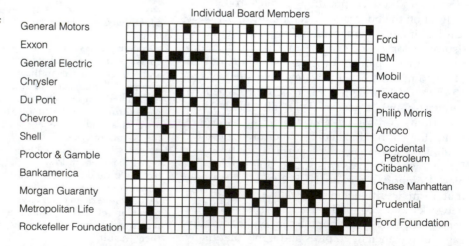

FIGURE 12.15 *This American Chinese family illustrates the central importance of the interdependent, multigeneration, extended family.*

dren are socialized to value privacy, independence, and self-expression, and American parents are not supposed to "interfere" in the domestic lives of their adult children.

The Chinese emphasis on kinship and continuity of patrilineage highlights the virtues of dependency. Chinese children are socialized within families that include at least three generations and in-laws (Figure 12.15). They are cared for by a variety of elders. There is little individual privacy within a Chinese household, but individuals are always surrounded by many people who can be called upon for physical and emotional support. There is little cultural incentive for an individual to pursue perpetual economic profit. An individual's primary responsibility is to parents and extended family, not self. Indeed, it is a source of pride for an aging Chinese parent to be taken care of by a child, whereas in the United States one is expected to make it alone and accepting economic aid from one's children might be embarrassing.

Realistically, humans do depend on other people for many of their needs, and according to Hsu, culturally denying such dependence can generate psychological problems. Hsu maintains that the American ideal of self-reliance is likely to cre-

ate emotional insecurity, which helps explain other seemingly contradictory American characteristics such as racial and religious intolerance coexisting with an expressed belief in equality. Hsu suggests that personal insecurity drives Americans to accumulate material wealth as compensation and to demonstrate their self-worth. This not only makes Americans enormously competitive and intolerant of others but is also well suited to the imperatives of a growth-centered capitalist economy. In contrast, the Chinese plow their earnings into family ceremonies, such as funerals, birthdays, and ancestor shrines, confident that they will be taken care of by their descendants.

The realities of American life pose some problems for Hsu's theory of self-reliance as a core value. It is likely that the poorest classes in the United States survive by sharing with kin. Furthermore, the existence of kinecon groups among the American elite suggests that extended-family dependency relations can be compatible with capitalist accumulation.

The role that Hsu ascribes to the American value on self-reliance fits well with the view that commercialization and profit making is the dominant cultural process in global-scale cultures. Chinese civilization was created by the politicization process that does not require perpetual economic expansion. In support of this interpretation, Hsu observes that the small wealthy class in preindustrial China was composed of government bureaucrats, not merchants, and modern China has been very slow to industrialize. He also notes that most large Chinese cities are political capitals, whereas most large U.S. cities are commercial centers. American acquisitiveness generated economic growth and a relatively large middle class. This is not to argue that American values in themselves shaped the rest of American culture, but it suggests that values and personality are functionally connected to other economic and social variables.

## SUMMARY

In this chapter, we examined the following broad topics that facilitate cross-cultural comparison: demography, the American food system, inequality and social class, and cultural aspects of consumption. The analysis of the food system explored the implications of a subsistence system that is fully based on a market economy and dependent on fossil fuels and mechanization in contrast to self-sufficient tribal systems and labor-intensive peasant systems. The discussion of inequality examined the cultural ideal of equal opportunity and the free market against the ethnographic realities of poverty and privilege.

As shown in this chapter, inequality in the United States involves differential access to status and prestige, productive resources, income, and economic and political power generally. The existence of this kind of inequality is an objective contradiction in a country that enjoys formal democracy and a high degree of personal freedom. American culture demonstrates that the human problem of social inequality, which seems to be an intrinsic feature of states, is not necessarily solved by capitalist market economies and continuous economic expansion. It is important to understand the cultural significance of inequality in the United States and the way in which production and consumption are carried out because, at a global level, the wealthiest industrial nations occupy the top of an international hierarchy of nations in which most of humanity is desperately impoverished.

## STUDY QUESTIONS

1. Describe the demographic trends that characterize the growth of the United States from 1790 to 1990. Refer specifically to total size, natural increase, immigration, industrialization, and the demographic transition.

2. Make specific comparisons between the demographic characteristics of small-scale tribal cultures and a representative industrial population such as the United States. Use a population pyramid to illustrate your points.

3. Identify the following demographic concepts: "baby boom," cohort, fertility rate, infant mortality, life expectancy, mortality rate, population pyramid, and stationary population.

4. Define and explain the demographic transition using specific data on U.S. fertility and mortality patterns.

5. Discuss the cultural ecological features of factory farming in comparison with less intensive subsistence systems. Refer to monocrop, Green Revolution, energy input–output ratios, energy subsidy, social consequences, stability, and ecosystem degradation.

6. In what way did the theoretical approaches toward American culture used by American anthropologists reflect the dominant historical processes of the time? Refer to Mead, Boas, liberal reform, and the military–industrial complex.

7. Discuss the limitations of Mead's national character studies as she applied them to the United States.

8. How did Warner define social class in Yankee City? What were the limitations of his approach? How did the social hierarchy Warner describe differ from that found in ancient civilizations?

9. What concept of social class does Domhoff use? What evidence does he present for the existence of an American ruling class? Refer to the following terms: social class, co-optation, governing class, power, power elite, national upper class, domination, kinecon group, holding company, and corporate rich.

10. Describe the organization of the U.S. business corporation and discuss its role in contemporary American society. Refer to military–industrial complex, oligopoly, concentration, conglomerate, multinational corporation, stockholders, board of directors,

interlocking directory, chief executive officer, manager, vertical integration.

11. In what sense is it legitimate to speak of a Cattle Complex in the United States? Make specific comparisons between the role of cattle in the United States and their role in an East African cattle culture. Briefly describe the pathway that American cattle follow as commodities from production to consumption.

12. Using the U.S. beef industry as an example, show how market forces influence specific production and processing practices and promote inequality and social conflict. Refer to economies of scale, commodity, specialization, issues management, and the Beef Industry Council.

13. Describe Harris's utilitarian explanation for the importance of beef in American subsistence, in contrast with Sahlin's "cultural" interpretation. Describe the way in which the edibility of meat can be used to encode differences in social class.

14. Describe how scarcity and consumption are culturally constructed in the United States. In what sense does Henry refer to advertising as a distinct cultural institution?

15. According to Harris, how do economic factors explain changes in the quality of American life during the second half of the twentieth century? Refer to sex roles, family structure, poverty, and service sector.

## SUGGESTED READING

DeVita, Philip R., and James D. Armstrong (Eds). 1993. *Distant Mirrors: America as a Foreign Culture*. Belmont, Calif.: Wadsworth. Fourteen foreign scholars, primarily anthropologists, offer interpretations of American culture and describe their experiences as outsiders.

Domhoff, G. William. 1983. *Who Rules America Now? A View for the '80s*. Englewood Cliffs, N.J.: Prentice Hall. An updated version of Domhoff's 1967 book about the domination of the American political economy by the upper class.

Harris, Marvin. 1981. *America Now: The Anthropology of a Changing Culture*. New York: Simon & Schuster. A wide-ranging analysis of American culture by a prominent cultural materialist anthropologist.

Hsu, Francis L. K. 1981. *Americans and Chinese: Passage to Difference*. Honolulu: University Press of Hawaii. A comparative analysis of American and Chinese culture by a Chinese psychological anthropologist.

Spradley, James P., and Michael A. Rynkiewich. 1975. *The Nacirema: Readings on American Culture*. Boston: Little, Brown. A collection of ethnographically based studies of diverse aspects of American culture.

# 13

# THE IMPOVERISHED WORLD

During the decades following World War II, the disparity in material welfare between the wealthy industrial nations and the rest of the world steadily widened, as did the gap between rich and poor within individual countries. Even as decolonization and technological progress proceeded, millions of people throughout the world increasingly came to live in absolute poverty. By 1980 an estimated 730 million people (excluding China) were living on diets considered inadequate by international standards and had extremely limited access to material resources. By the late 1980s, dramatic increases in poverty were occurring throughout the world. Real living standards plunged while public spending for social services declined as many countries found themselves precariously in debt to first-world lenders.

Development, as it has been practiced throughout most of the twentieth century, has systematically undermined the self-maintenance abilities of small-scale peasant communities, leaving them highly vulnerable to outside exploitation. The primary ideological justification for externally planned development was that it would ultimately raise rural living standards, but the outcome of

decades of development suggests that a fundamental reassessment of the entire issue is called for. The barriers to progress are more likely to lie beyond, rather than within, local communities.

In the following sections, we begin by examining the development of the international development establishment since 1945, focusing on the United Nations, its related agencies, and the United States. A close view of the complex structure of development at the global level, considering the flow of resources, costs, and benefits, shows why development often works against the interests of small-scale communities. Bangladesh is presented as a case study of a poor nation to show how village-level poverty can be increased by technologically based development programs that leave unequal power structures in place. Next, we examine diverse anthropological perspectives on development, peasantries, and poverty. Finally, a famous anthropological experiment in community development in the Andes shows that, even when local power structures are altered, development that undermines the unique strengths of small-scale culture may still leave rural communities impoverished.

# THE GLOBAL INSTITUTIONALIZATION OF DEVELOPMENT

## The United Nations and Development Decades

The United Nations (U.N.) is the most prominent international organization concerned with global development issues. The U.N. Charter, which was formally adopted in 1945 by fifty-one nations, specifies that the promotion of "social progress and better standards of living" as well as "economic and social advancement of all peoples" are among the principal aims of the United Nations. Over the years since its founding, the United Nations has focused on a changing series of development issues and has proposed a variety of development strategies (Table 13.1). To formulate and implement its development effort, the United Nations has also constructed an elaborate institutional framework of specialized agencies, councils, commissions, funds, and programs, each chartered by formal resolutions (Table 13.2).

By the end of World War II, it was obvious to world leaders that much of the world was seriously impoverished. Vast numbers of people in many countries were living under conditions that were intolerable from a humanitarian perspective. Furthermore, because impoverished peoples made poor producers and consumers in the global economy and were potential sources of political instability, it was in their "enlightened self-interest" for wealthy industrialized countries to attempt to alleviate world poverty. War-caused impoverishment could be solved by reconstruction, but most authorities assumed that global poverty was caused by a vicious cycle of disease, ignorance, and poverty and would be eliminated by the transfer of industrial technology and education from rich to poor countries. In 1948 the United Nations began the international campaign to improve the human condition by issuing the Universal Declaration of Human Rights, which stated "Everyone has the right to a standard of living adequate for the health and well-being of himself and of his family, including food, clothing, housing and medical care . . ." (United Nations 1952:22).

As its first major development initiative, in 1949

TABLE 13.1  *U.N. Development Issues and Strategies, 1950–1999*

| Decade | Issues | Strategies |
|---|---|---|
| 1950–1959 | Disease<br>Proverty<br>Ignorance | Public health programs<br>Public education<br>Technology transfer<br>Promote economic growth |
| 1960–1969 | Population<br>Urban growth<br>Income inequality | Integrated economic and social growth |
| 1970–1979 | Social equity<br>Global disparity<br>Human environment | Unified economic–social–political approach |
| 1980–1989 | Foreign debt<br>Energy cost<br>Economic downturn | Human development<br>Popular participation<br>Grassroots development<br>Appropriate technology<br>International development cooperation |
| 1990–1999 | Poverty | Labor-intensive development<br>Human-capital improvement |

SOURCE: United Nations (1952, 1963, 1974) and World Bank (1988, 1989, 1990, 1991).

TABLE 13.2    *The Institutional Framework for U.N. Development Programs, 1945–1989*

| Years | Charter | Institutions |
|---|---|---|
| 1945–1959 | 1945: U.N. charter<br>1948: Universal Declaration of Human Rights<br>1949: General Assembly Resolution 200 (iii)—Expanded Program of Technical Assistance for Economic Development of Under-Developed Countries | 1945: U.N. Food and Agricultural Organization (FAO); International Bank for Reconstruction and Development (IBRD), the World Bank<br>1946: U.N. Educational, Scientific and Cultural Organization (UNESCO)<br>1948: World Health Organization (WHO)<br>1958: U.N. Economic and Social Council (ECOSOC); U.N. Regional Economic Commissions; U.N. Special Fund |
| 1960–1969 | 1960: U.N. General Assembly Resolution 1496 (xv)—assistance to food-deficient peoples<br>1961: First U.N. Development Decade | 1960: FAO, Freedom from Hunger campaign, International Development Association (IDA)<br>1963: U.N. World Food Programme (WFP)<br>1966: U.N. Development Programme (UNDP); U.N. Industrial Development Organization (UNIDO) |
| 1970–1979 | 1971: U.N. General Assembly Resolution 2626 (xxv)—Second U.N. Development Decade<br>1974: U.N. Charter of Economic Rights and Duties of States; Declaration and Programme of Action of the Establishment of a New International Economic Order | 1971: Consultative Group on International Agricultural Research (CGIAR) |
| 1980–1989 | 1980: U.N. General Assembly Resolution 35/56—Third U.N. Development Decade | |

SOURCE: *Yearbook of the United Nations.*

the United Nations began its "Expanded Program of Technical Assistance for Economic Development of Under-Developed Countries." In 1950 the United Nations placed fifty technical experts in sixteen countries and expended $20 million on projects, while a U.N. affiliate, the International Bank for Reconstruction and Development (IBRD), or the **World Bank,** loaned $279 million to governments for large-scale development projects. This action showed that global poverty was considered to be a technical and an "economic" problem that would respond to increased technical proficiency and economic expansion.

Because, according to the U.N. Charter, the Economic and Social Council (ECOSOC) was expected to "help solve international problems in the economic, social, humanitarian and cultural fields," it was asked by the General Assembly in 1949 to prepare a general report on the world so-

cial situation. The U.N. council report, which was issued in 1952, emphasized standard of living and was based on existing data drawn from official government sources. Researchers examined basic demography, health, food, housing, education, and labor and found that conditions were shockingly "inadequate" for more than half of the world's people. The council compiled data showing dramatically higher fertility, crude mortality, and infant mortality rates and much lower life-expectancy rates for populations in Asia, Africa, and Latin America, in comparison with North America. For example, infant mortality in some African countries was more than five times the North American rate, and life expectancy throughout much of the world was half that of North Americans (Table 13.3).

The council report offered no absolute definition of *underdevelopment* or *poverty* but provided

TABLE 13.3   *Social Conditions in North America, Asia, Africa, and Latin America, 1947-49*

|                              | North America | Asia | Africa | Latin America |
|------------------------------|---------------|------|--------|---------------|
| Birth rate/1000              | 25            | 42.5 | 42.5   | 40            |
| Death rate/1000              | 10            | 30   | 27.5   | 17            |
| Natural increase             | 15            | 12.5 | 15     | 23            |
| Infant mortality/1000 births* | 31.8         | 88   | 177    | 119.9         |
| Life expectancy at birth†    | 68.7          | 27   | 33     | 39            |

SOURCE: U.N. (1952).

*National averages in the Asian countries Ceylon, Federation of Malaya, and Singapore; in the African country Sierra Leone; and in the Latin American countries Chile, Mexico, and Venezuela.

†National averages in the North American country United States (whites), in the Asian country India (1921–1931), in the African country Mauritius, and in the Latin American country Peru (Lima, 1933–1935).

TABLE 13.4   *Average Social Conditions in Developed Versus Underdeveloped Countries, 1947–1949*

|                                        | Developed | Underdeveloped |
|----------------------------------------|-----------|----------------|
| Percentage of world population         | 20        | 66             |
| Annual/person income (U.S. $)          | 461       | 41             |
| Food supply (daily calories/person)    | 3040      | 2150           |
| Physicians/100,000 people              | 106       | 17             |
| Life expectancy at birth               | 63        | 30             |

SOURCE: U.N. (1952).

figures showing that two-thirds of the world's population had only 17 physicians/100,000 people and earned only $41 dollars/person/year, while the "developed" 20 percent of the world earned $461/person and had 106 physicians/100,000 people (Table 13.4). Such inequality had obvious implications for public health.

During the 1950s, U.N. experts treated the economic and social aspects of development as separate issues, and they focused on improving specific target indicators at national levels, especially in the area of public health. Initial efforts focused on relatively easily combated mass diseases such as malaria, yaws, hookworm, tuberculosis, and gas-

trointestinal diseases, which accounted for much of the elevated mortality in the world and which responded readily to DDT and penicillin. Nutritional diseases, such as beriberi (vitamin B deficiency) and kwashiorkor (protein deficiency), were considered to be more intractable because they were caused by "ignorance and poverty" rather than microbes. For many development planners, disease was the most basic problem. As the council report explained,

*... A community burdened with ill-health is an impoverished community. There is a vicious circle: disease—underproduction—poverty—poor health services—more disease, which is manifest in those underdeveloped countries where the majority of a people are afflicted with gross diseases which rob them of vitality and initiative and which create social lethargy.* (United Nations 1952:22)

*The control of disease ... is a precondition of economic and social development. The advance of any community depends on the extent to which it reduces the burden of ill*

**World Bank**   Also known as the International Bank for Reconstruction and Development (IBRD). The World Bank is a U.N. affiliate established in 1945 and owned by the governments of 144 countries. The United States owns 20 percent of the capital stock. The IBRD makes development loans to governments or government-guaranteed loans to the private sector. Loans must be repaid within 20 years, although payments need not begin for 5 years. Loans can have no trade or political preconditions.

*health which squanders human resources, wastes food in nourishing bacteria and parasites, produces social lethargy, and prevents people and countries from developing their full capacities.* (United Nations 1952:36)

This emphasis on technical progress steadily accelerated over the decade of the 1950s, until in 1960 the U.N. Special Fund for Development, which was created in 1958, spent $27.9 million to provide 3308 technicians for seventy-one projects in 108 countries. However, the cash value of this effort was dwarfed by the World Bank's loans in 1960 of $602 million to 54 countries for large-scale infrastructure development.

By 1960, after a decade of major development effort and steady improvement in highly visible areas of public health and formal education, several ominous global trends had become inescapably obvious. In its "Report on the World Situation" in 1963, the U.N. Economic and Social Council observed that global population increased by 19 percent during the 1950s. Such a dramatic increase was partly due to a rapid decline in death rates. At a global level, the crude death rate dropped from an estimated 26 per 1000 people in 1937 to 18 by 1960, while fertility rates remained approximately constant. A demographic change of this magnitude was absolutely unprecedented in human history and gave rise to the term *population explosion.* In specific countries, the figures were truly remarkable. For example, in Ceylon (Sri Lanka) the overall mortality dropped from 25 to 10.1 per 1000 people and infant mortality from 183 to 69 per 1000 live births. The global impact of these changes was much higher than most demographers had at first expected and led to a doubling in world population between 1950 and 1990.

Ironically, the world population increase experienced by 1960, in the absence of changes in wealth distribution, meant that the absolute number of impoverished people actually increased, even though the proportion of impoverished may have declined as a percentage of total population in certain countries. The U.N. report also observed that the gap between developed and less developed countries had widened in regard to consumption of material goods and per-capita national income,

while inequality within individual developing countries increased. The U.N. report was emphatic on this point:

*In many less developed countries, growth in national income appears to have been shared disproportionately by the minority already well-to-do, while in richer countries certain disadvantaged minorities have continued to lag behind the majorities in growth of income.* (1963:2)

Even before the official report detailing the failures of previous development efforts was released, U.N. planners called for "integrated development" and initiated a 10-year plan designating the 1960s as the *U.N. Development Decade.* The Development Decade Resolution, adopted unanimously by the U.N. General Assembly in 1961, specified that each developing country should achieve a target annual growth rate of 5 percent in national income by 1969. To help reach this goal, annual U.N. development expenditures were further accelerated, until by 1970, the U.N. Development Programme (UNDP), created in 1966 as the U.N.'s coordinating agency for its development work, spent $206 million to send 8848 technical assistants to work on 3500 projects in 130 countries. In 1970 the World Bank loaned $1615 million to governments, while the bank's affiliates, the International Development Association (IDA) and the International Finance Corporation (IFC), gave out an additional $723.4 million. Much of this money went into giant dams, power plants, and highways—all major symbols of technological progress.

During the 1970s, a "unified" or "holistic approach" was recommended by development planners to solve the inequality problems recognized a decade earlier. A Second U.N. Development Decade was proclaimed in 1971, calling on poor countries to increase their annual growth rates of gross national product (GNP) per person by 3.5 percent, their annual agricultural output by 4 percent, and their manufacturing output by 8 percent. (For a definition of GNP and related concepts, see the box "National Income Accounting.") Developing countries were asked to contribute at least 1 percent of their own GNPs to help reduce the technological gap between rich and poor nations. A new institution, the Consultative Group on International Agricultural Research (CGIAR), was given

## National Income Accounting

**Disposable income**   Personal income less taxes.

**Gross domestic product** (GDP)   The total output of goods and services produced within a country, by monetary value.

**Gross national product** (GNP)   The total output of a country's goods and services, by monetary value; includes profits from foreign activities.

**National income**   All wages, salaries, and profits received by the members of a country, calculated by subtracting various indirect taxes from NNP.

**National product**   Goods and services in the market economy. Normally excludes unpaid housekeeping and child care performed by family members. May include monetary values imputed to wages paid in kind and household production-consumption of food and fuels.

**Net national product** (NNP)   Calculated by deducting capital used up, or depreciated, in the production process, from gross product, either GNP or GNP.

**Personal income**   All income received by individuals, calculated from national income by adding government transfer, or welfare, payments to individuals and by subtracting corporate profits that are not paid out as dividends.

**Public debt**   Amount owed by governments and paid off according to a specified scale and interest rate. External, or foreign, debt is payable to creditors outside the country.

SOURCE: "National Income Accounting," *Encyclopaedia Britannica* 1975, Vol. 12:847–850.
NOTE: Because national-level income accounting may be carried out differently in different countries, detailed comparisons must be made cautiously.

---

the task of building a global network of agricultural research stations to develop energy-intensive, factory-farming technologies to help poor countries increase food production.

Midway through the Second Development Decade, the original goal of a better standard of living for all peoples was still far out of reach. A new U.N. report found that development had not achieved "any significant narrowing of disparities in income or levels of living" (United Nations 1975:1) either within individual countries or between different countries at the global level. For example, a survey of income distribution in forty countries showed that the top 20 percent of the population received from 43 to 50 percent of the total national income, while in many poor countries the top 5 percent received 25 to over 30 percent of the national income (United Nations 1975). National development was helping create wealthy national elites, while the absolute number of severely impoverished people continued to grow. Frustrated U.N. planners were forced to conclude that "policies geared to national or macro-growth

**population explosion**   The sudden increase in rate of global population growth and the rapid rise in total population following the decline in mortality rates since 1950; related to improvements in public health.
**U.N. Development Decade**   Ten-year periods beginning in 1961 for which the United Nations specifies development goals.

objectives do not of themselves give rise to a more equitable distribution of income" (United Nations 1975:13).

During the 1970s, people became more aware that the global market economy made conditions in the developing world different from conditions existing in Europe during the Industrial Revolution; this implied that technological changes by themselves would not achieve development. In 1974 the United Nations even recommended the creation of a "New International Economic Order" based on more equitable trade relations between nations. During the 1980s, however, the rise in energy costs, the burden of development debts, and the related problems of inflation and economic recession put hopes for a new economic order in the background.

Although the implications of expanding impoverishment were still not fully understood, new development issues continued to emerge. By the mid-1970s, the obvious failure of many projects

**TABLE 13.5**  *Annual Development Effort by the United Nations and Related Agencies, by Decade, 1950–1980*

|  | 1950 | 1960 | 1970 | 1980 |
|---|---|---|---|---|
| Projects | — | 71 | 3,500 | 5,000 |
| Technicians | 50 | 3,308 | 8,848 | 12,200 |
| UNDP expenditures (in millions) | $20 | $27 | $206 | $708 |
| Loans, IBRD, IDA, and IFC (in millions) | $279 | $602 | $2,338 | $11,747 |

SOURCE: *Yearbook of the United Nations.*

at the local level made it desirable to refer to the need for "popular participation" in development. This meant some degree of decentralization and involvement of local target populations in planning. A further issue that began to emerge at this time was the environment because many large-

**FIGURE 13.1**
*At the end of the third U.N. Development Decade in 1990, there were more than 1 billion people living in absolute poverty. In 1988 the World Bank considered El Salvador, where this peasant family lives, to be a lower-middle economy country based on GNP per capita.*

scale development projects were degrading the "human environment," simplifying ecosystems, lowering the quality of soil and water, and generating pollution.

The third U.N. Development Decade began in 1981 with the announcement that the goals of the Second Development Decade remained "largely unfulfilled," even though the United Nations and its related agencies were expending annually more than $12 billion in development loans and direct assistance, more than forty times the level of expenditure in 1950 (Table 13.5). As the Third U.N. Development Decade came to an end in 1990, the World Bank estimated that more than 1 billion people were living in absolute poverty with annual incomes of less than $370 per person (Figure 13.1) (World Bank 1990).

The wealth disparity between nations after four decades of concerted development effort is dramatically illustrated by the World Bank's international rank order of nations by annual per-capita GNP based on 1988 data (Table 13.6). The wealthiest nation, Switzerland, showed a per-capita GNP of $27,500, which was 275 times greater than that of the poorest nation, Mozambique, with $100 per capita. These dollar GNP figures cannot be directly compared with the figures presented in Table 13.4 for 1947–1949 because of inflation. GNP figures also do not consider wealth distribution within a country and can disguise great inequities.

The World Bank ranking shows that only 25 nations, with 15 percent of the world's population, were high-income nations with per-capita GNPs of over $6000, while 42 nations, more than one-third of the 121 nations listed, were considered low income with GNPs of under $545. Low income correlated with poor scores on many indicators of social well-being. For example, the average infant mortality rate in low-income countries was 72 per 1000 live births, eight times the rate of high-income countries. Four African countries showed infant mortality rates of over 140 per 1000. The 42

TABLE 13.6   *The Per-Capita GNP International Rank Order, 1988\**

| Income | Country |
| --- | --- |
| High: $6000+ | Switzerland, Japan, Norway, United States, Sweden, Finland, Federal Republic of Germany, Denmark, Canada, France, United Arab Emirates, Austria, Netherlands, Belgium, Kuwait, Italy, United Kingdom, Australia, New Zealand, Hong Kong, Singapore, Israel, Ireland, Spain, Saudi Arabia |
| Upper Middle: $2200–$5999 | Romania, Iraq, Iran, Libya, Oman, Greece, Portugal, Republic of Korea, Trinidad, Venezuela, Gabon, Yugoslavia, Argentina, Uruguay, Hungary, Algeria, South Africa |
| Lower middle: $546–$2199 | Nicaragua, Lebanon, Angola, Brazil, Panama, Malaysia, Poland, Mauritius, Mexico, Costa Rica, Syria, Chile, Jordan, Peru, Turkey, Tunisia, Paraguay, Colombia, Ecuador, Jamaica, Cameroon, Botswana, Thailand, El Salvador, Congo, Guatemala, Honduras, Morocco, Papua New Guinea, Cote d'Ivoire, Dominican Republic, Egypt, Zimbabwe, Senegal, Yemen, Philippines, Bolivia |
| Low: $545 or below | Viet Nam, Sierra Leone, Liberia, Kampuchea, Myanmar, Afganistan, Sudan, Mauritania, Indonesia, Yemen PDR, Guinea, Sri Lanka, Lesotho, Ghana, Benin, Haiti, Central African Republic, Togo, Kenya, Pakistan, India, China, Rwanda, Niger, Zambia, Nigeria, Uganda, Burundi, Mali, Burkina Faso, Madagascar, Nepal, Lao PDR, Bhutan, Zaire, Somalia, Malawi, Bangladesh, Tanzania, Chad, Ethiopia, Mozambique |

SOURCE: World Bank (1991).
*Not all countries are listed because not all report GNP. Highest per-capita GNP is Switzerland with $27,500; lowest is Mozambique with $100.

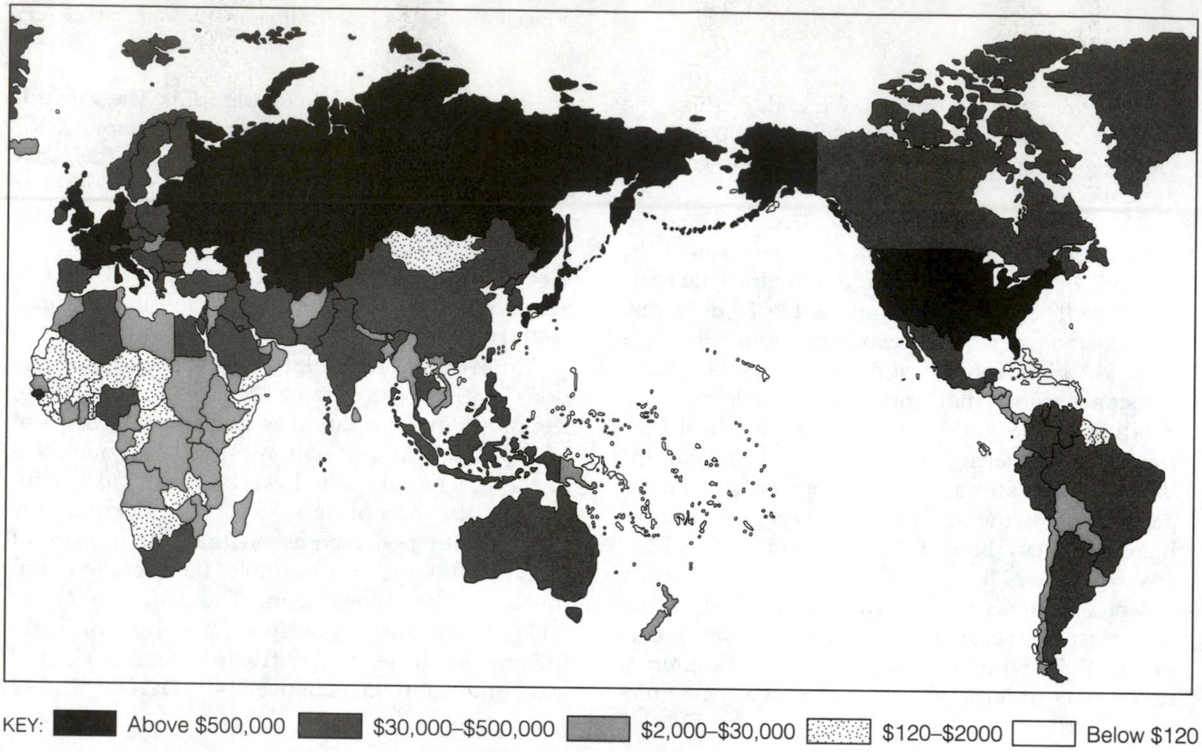
KEY:
Above $500,000
$30,000–$500,000
$2,000–$30,000
$120–$2000
Below $120

FIGURE 13.2 *Per-capita gross national product (U.S. dollars), 1988.*

FIGURE 13.3 *Female life expectancy (in years), 1988.*

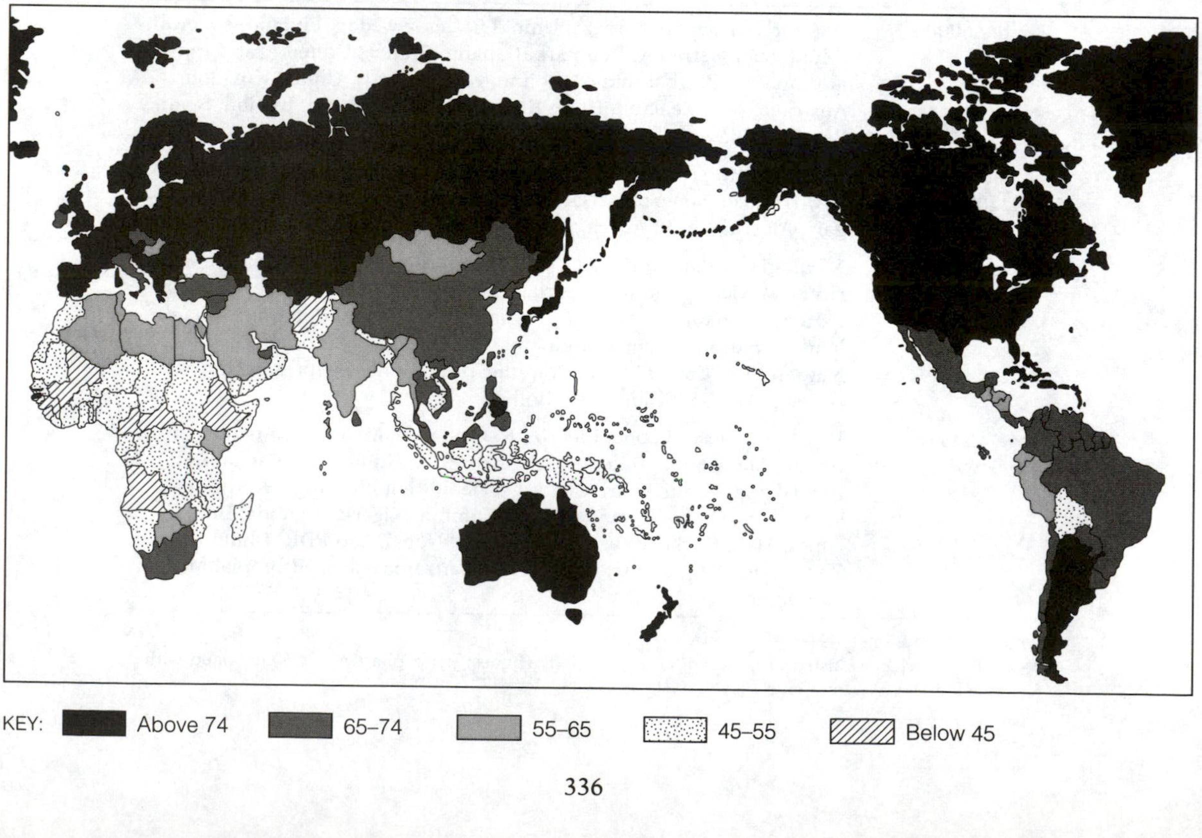
KEY:
Above 74
65–74
55–65
45–55
Below 45

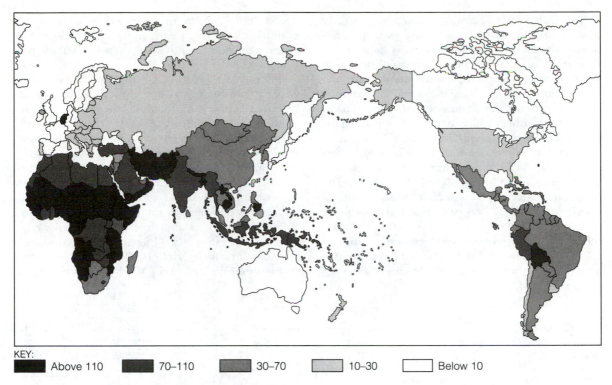

KEY:

■ Above 110    ■ 70–110    ■ 30–70    ▨ 10–30    □ Below 10

**FIGURE 13.4**  *Infant mortality (per 1000 births), 1988.*

poorest nations included some 2.8 billion people, approximately 55 percent of the world's population in 1988. Figures 13.2–13.4 show the global distribution of inequities in GNP, female life expectancy, and infant mortality by nations.

In 1988, near the end of the Third U.N. Development Decade, there were more impoverished people in the world than ever before. Although global averages showed some improvements, the U.N. goal of an adequate standard of living for everyone had clearly not been realized. Obviously, poverty is not a problem of technological "underdevelopment" or "ignorance"; it is an amplification of the inherent inequities in the social hierarchies of large-scale cultures. These inequities are intensified by the operation of the global market economy. If eliminating poverty were the sole objective of technologically focused development programs, an impartial observer in 1988 might have concluded that the wrong course was being followed, but by then development efforts had come to serve many other interests.

## The United States, AID, and the Development Industry

The formal structures through which technical assistance and development finance reach the developing world consist of many complex bureaucracies linked in a ponderous network. Priorities are set by relatively few key organizations at the top that make decisions that affect the smallest details of life for millions of people living in remote villages throughout the impoverished world. Development decisions pass through so many hands before actually being implemented that the entire enterprise is extremely costly and often proves counterproductive. The development establishment itself is a classic example of the maladaptive process described by Roy Rappaport (1977a, 1977b) in which high-level regulators take over lower-level functions (see Chapter 10). Understanding how this can happen requires some knowledge of aid categories, specific organizations, their functions, and interconnections.

The United Nations and related agencies offer what is called ***multilateral development assistance*** because it is financed by many nations and thus must offer assistance without political considerations or special trade preconditions. All development assistance given by individual countries is called ***official development assistance*** (ODA). It must be either a gift, or grant, or it must be loaned at less than commercial rates. Multilateral development assistance accounted for only 22 percent of the $40.3 billion in aid that developing countries received in 1987 (World Bank 1990). The largest aid category, 64 percent of the total, or approximately $25 billion, was bilateral assistance, or ODA supplied directly from one country to another. ***Bilateral development assistance*** can, and often does, have political and trade conditions attached and thus can serve the interests of the do-

nor. A donor country might give only to "friendly" countries and require them to spend their aid money on goods and services provided by the donor.

Figure 13.5 presents a simplified view of the network through which technical assistance is channeled from the United States and the Organization for Economic Cooperation and Development (OECD) countries to developing nations as bilateral aid and through the major multilateral aid organizations. This figure emphasizes agricultural technology. The acronyms appearing in the figure are identified and additional organizational details are provided in the accompanying boxes. Figure 13.6 shows the flow of development finance. (See the box "International Assistance Agencies" for a description of the agencies listed in Figures 13.5 and 13.6.) Much of this money is

FIGURE 13.5
*The structure of international technical assistance.*

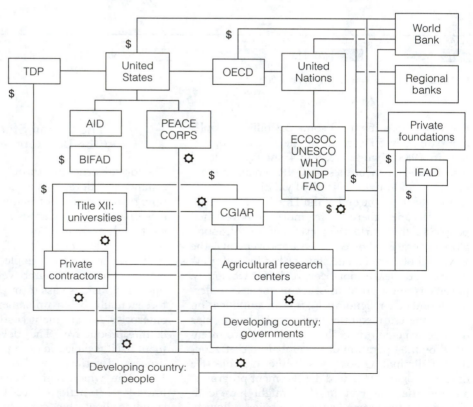

KEY:    ✿ Technical assistance     $ Financial assistance

FIGURE 13.6
*The structure of
international develop-
ment finance.*

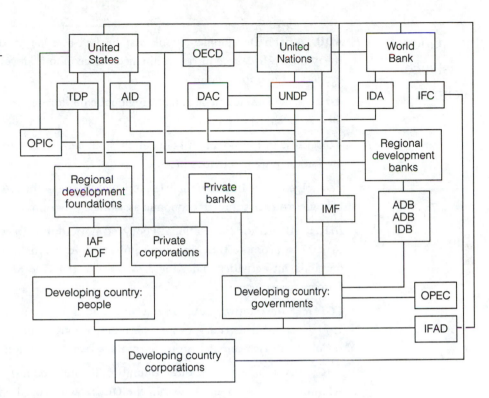

in the form of loans for massive construction projects. For example, nearly two-thirds of the $120
billion in cumulative lending by the World Bank
by 1983 had gone for capital construction projects
in agroindustry, irrigation, energy, heavy industry,
telecommunications, and urbanization (World
Bank 1983).

Global poverty has been consistently treated as
a technological problem partly because professional elites who are far removed from the daily
realities of poverty formulate and finance development policies. Development is much more than a
humanitarian concern; it has become a thoroughly
institutionalized and highly complex industry with
important political and economic functions for the
wealthy donors, which may be unrelated to the
needs of the poor.

Thousands of people have found employment
as development technicians, and hundreds of development contract firms have sprung up around
the world. A 1986–1987 survey found 595 U.S. organizations offering technical assistance to developing countries, primarily on contracts for

the U.S. Agency for International Development
(USAID, AID) and the major development banks
(Vickery 1988). Half of these organizations were
profit-making businesses, while the remainder
were private, nonprofit, volunteer groups or U.S.
colleges and universities. Together these organizations reported holding contracts worth $5.7 bil-
lion. The inequality that characterizes other U.S.
businesses appeared in the development contractors, where just 5 percent held nearly half of all the
contracts. These dominant contractors generally
shared a vested interest in expensive technological

---

***multilateral development assistance*** Aid that is donated by several countries and channeled through a
single international agency such that it can be free of political favoritism.
***official development assistance*** (ODA) Aid given by a
government for development purposes, including both
direct gifts and low-rate loans.
***bilateral development assistance*** Aid that is given directly from one country to another and that may be given
under conditions that favor the donor.

## International Assistance Agencies

**ADB**   African Development Bank: Established in 1964 by the governments of thirty-three African countries to finance the economic development and social progress of member countries.

**ADB**   Asian Development Bank: A regional bank formed in 1965; lends at commercial rates.

**ADF**   African Development Foundation: Founded in 1984 to assist community-level development activities in Africa.

**AID**   Agency for International Development: Founded in 1961 to administer the U.S. government's foreign economic assistance program.

**BIFAD**   Board for International Food and Agricultural Development: Founded in 1977 to promote U.S. land-grant university involvement in AID agricultural development activities under the provisions of the Title XII amendment to the Foreign Assistance Act.

**CGIAR**   Consultative Group on International Agricultural Research: Formed in 1971 to coordinate and sponsor international agricultural research centers in various countries; a major promoter of the Green Revolution.

**DAC**   Development Assistance Committee: Established in 1960, the primary development lender countries within the OECD, who coordinate OECD development activities.

**ECOSOC**   Economic and Social Council: An official body of the U.N. organization with primary responsibility for coordinating development activities in the United Nations and related agencies.

**FAO**   Food and Agricultural Organization of the United Nations: The U.N. special agency formed in 1945 to promote food production, directs the Freedom from Hunger campaign.

**IAF**   Inter-American Foundation: Created in 1969 to promote the development activities of private, nonpolitical, democratic organizations in Latin America; often assists very small, local organizations.

**IDA**   International Development Association: A World Bank affiliate, established in 1960, that provides interest-free, 50-year development loans (credits) to governments of the poorest countries (1986 per-capita incomes of $790 or below). Loans must be repaid within 50 years, although payments need not begin for 10 years.

**IDB**   Inter-American Development Bank: A regional bank formed in 1959.

Owned by forty-four member nations and makes development loans in Latin America, at varying interest rates.

**IFAD**   International Fund for Agricultural Development: Founded in 1976 to assist the poorest countries make technological improvements in food production.

**IFC**   International Finance Corporation: A World Bank affiliate, established in 1956, that provides development loans (investments) to the private sector in developing countries.

**IMF**   International Monetary Fund: A U.N. affiliate, founded in 1944, that regulates currency exchanges between countries, assists developing nations with balance-of-payments shortfalls.

**OECD**   Organization for European Economic Cooperation and Development: Formed in 1961, composed primarily of wealthy industrial nations.* Its member countries provide official development assistance (ODA) to developing countries, either individually (bilateral assistance) or on a multilateral basis.

**OPEC**   Oil Producing and Exporting Countries: Formed in 1960, primarily provides aid to Muslim countries.*

**OPIC**   Overseas Private Investment Corporation: Established in 1970, provides private U.S. corporations with guaranteed loans and investment insurance to promote their business activities in developing countries, in ways beneficial to U.S. economic interests.

**TDP**   Trade and Development Program: Created in 1980 to help U.S. technicians conduct feasibility studies for development projects in middle-income developing countries that might not otherwise qualify for technical assistance. This will promote the export of U.S. technology.

**UNDP**   U.N. Development Programme: Established in 1966 to coordinate all development activities of the United Nations and related agencies.

**UNESCO**   U.N. Educational, Scientific and Cultural Organization: A U.N. special agency, established in 1946, that promotes international welfare.

**WHO**   World Health Organization: A U.N. special agency, established in 1948, that promotes public health in developing countries.

NOTE: Multilateral development agencies provide support that has been pooled from many sources. OECD members in 1990: Australia, Austria, Belgium, Canada, Denmark, Finland, France, West Germany, Greece, Iceland, Ireland, Italy, Japan, Luxembourg, Netherlands, New Zealand, Norway, Portugal, Spain, Sweden, Switzerland, Turkey, United Kingdom, United States, and Yugoslavia. Principal OPEC members: Algeria, Iran, Iraq, Kuwait, Libya, Nigeria, Qatar, Saudi Arabia, United Arab Emirates, and Venezuela.

approaches to development, as demonstrated by the three large engineering companies that netted 14 percent of the total development contracts.

There were striking inequities in the amount of ODA supplied by individual countries in 1987, such that just four countries, the United States, Japan, France, and Germany, provided 67 percent of the world total ODA, while the United States by itself provided 22 percent. Because more than 80 percent of America's ODA was in the form of bilateral aid, this country was in a powerful position to use its aid to serve its own interests. At the same time, the United States had played a major role in the largest multilateral agencies since their founding and could thus influence development agendas

FIGURE 13.7   *The Peace Corps, initiated by President Kennedy in 1961, has played an important role in America's development aid program. This Peace Corps volunteer is inspecting a rural water system in the Bolivian Andes.*

in directions favorable to the American elite. For example, in the 1980s, the United States was the largest contributor to the U.N. Development Programme, providing roughly 18 percent of the total, and was a controlling stockholder in the World Bank and the Inter-American Development Bank (IDB), while the United States split control of the Asian Development Bank (ADB) with Japan.

The assistance policies of the United States deserve a closer view since it plays such a major role in the development process. U.S. development policies and programs were formally initiated by **Point Four** in President Truman's 1949 inaugural address, in which he declared, "We must embark on a bold new program for making the benefits of our scientific advance and industrial progress available for the improvement and growth of underdeveloped areas."

This was at the beginning of the Cold War, and the objective of Point Four development assistance was to use U.S. technology to advance U.S. interests in the world as part of Truman's policy of Soviet "containment." The U.S. development effort received a major boost in 1961 under President Kennedy when the Agency for International Development (AID), the **Peace Corps,** and the Alliance for Progress were all launched (Figure 13.7). In the same year, Kennedy urged the U.N. General Assembly to create the U.N. Development Decade program. Between 1962 and 1969, a staggering $33.5 billion worth of food commodities and economic assistance flowed directly to developing countries and through development banks and the Peace Corps (Statistical Abstract of the United States 1990).

Significant changes were brought about in U.S. policies by the 1975 Freedom from Hunger **Title XII** amendments to the Foreign Assistance Act of 1961, further reinforcing the narrow view that world hunger was primarily a technological problem. Title XII amendments directed AID to recruit U.S. universities to apply "science to solving food and nutrition problems of the developing countries" (U.S. Code 1982, Title 22, Section 2220a). The assumption of this legislation was that because agricultural research, especially by the land-grant universities, had successfully increased farm productivity in the United States, this was the best way to deal with hunger in the impoverished

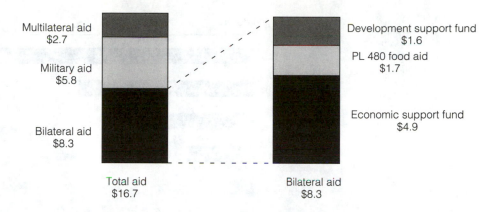

**FIGURE 13.8**
*U.S. foreign aid (in billions of dollars), 1986. (SOURCE: U.S. Department of Commerce 1990b.)*

Multilateral aid
$2.7

Military aid
$5.8

Bilateral aid
$8.3

Total aid
$16.7

Development support fund
$1.6

PL 480 food aid
$1.7

Economic support fund
$4.9

Bilateral aid
$8.3

world. The potential cost in energy, resources, and social inequality of implementing American-style factory farming in the developing world were disregarded.

U.S. development policy shifted again in the 1980s under the Reagan administration. Although continuous economic growth and technological advance remained the primary development objectives, "free-market forces" and the "private sector" were now considered "the principal engines of sustainable development" (United States AID 1985:iv). AID's new development objectives were, in some cases, perhaps realistically, less than the goals set by the United Nations for the Third Development Decade. For example, the United Nations wanted infant mortality rates to be 50 per 1000 live births or below by the year 2000, but AID set below 75 as the target. *Privatization* called for the increased commercialization of agricultural systems, while emphasizing biotechnology. Seed and fertilizer companies were to become "extension agents," and many poor farmers were encouraged to produce export crops instead of locally consumed subsistence crops. The problem with applying this approach to the impoverished world is that market forces select for large-scale enterprises and inequality. In the United States, as shown in Chapter 12, this process makes small farms "uneconomical" and forces much of the rural population into the cities. Furthermore, many poor peasants simply lack the financial resources to take the expensive risks that producing for the international export market requires (Lappe, Schurman, and Danaher 1987).

It is important to recognize the underlying political motivation behind U.S. foreign-assistance programs. Anticommunism has been the dominant element in U.S. assistance programs for four decades, since the first days of Point Four. This is clearly seen in the fact that approximately 33 percent of the $16.7 billion expended in all U.S. aid programs in 1986 went directly to military assistance (Figure 13.8). Furthermore, the $8.3 billion spent for bilateral economic assistance was divided into three categories: (1) *economic support fund* (59 percent), (2) *PL 480 Food Aid* (21 percent), and (3) development assistance (20 percent). By law, economic support funds must be used to strengthen countries whose instability might threaten U.S. security or foreign policy interests as perceived by the American elite. Because these

---

***Point Four***   The first major U.S. effort at postwar development assistance begun by President Truman in 1949.
***Peace Corps***   Established in 1961 to place skilled American volunteers to serve in developing countries.
***Title XII***   The 1975 amendment to the Foreign Assistance Act of 1961 that created a partnership between AID and U.S. universities to transfer American agricultural technology to developing countries.
***privatization***   The use of commercial incentives and "free enterprise" as a development tool.
***economic support funds***   U.S. foreign assistance that must go specifically to support countries whose stability is considered vital for the United States.
***PL 480 Food Aid***   Public Law 480, the U.S. Agricultural Trade Development and Assistance Act of 1954, provides for the distribution of surplus farm commodities to developing countries.

FIGURE 13.9
*The top eight recipients
of U.S. regional eco-
nomic assistance (in
millions of dollars),
1988. (SOURCE: U.S.
Department of Com-
merce 1990b.)*

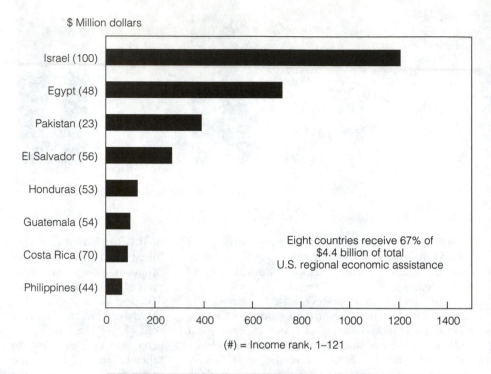

$ Million dollars

Eight countries receive 67% of
$4.4 billion of total
U.S. regional economic assistance

(#) = Income rank, 1–121

FIGURE 13.10
*The top ten recipients
of official development
aid from all sources
(in millions of dollars),
1988. (SOURCE: World
Bank 1990.)*

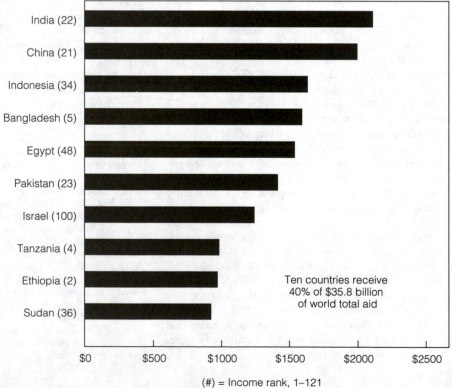

Ten countries receive
40% of $35.8 billion
of world total aid

(#) = Income rank, 1–121

**FIGURE 13.11**
*The structure of international food aid.*

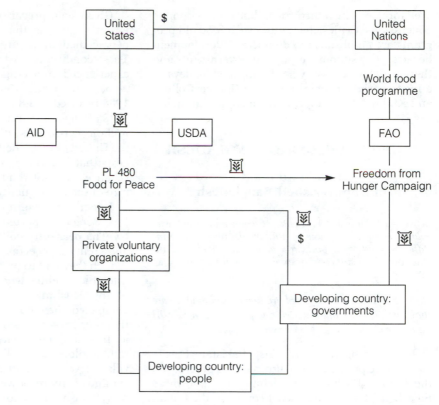

KEY:  ☒ = Food commodities    $ = Financial assistance

funds constitute well over half of U.S. bilateral assistance, politics override humanitarian considerations. Figures 13.9 and 13.10, which compare U.S. bilateral economic aid priorities with multinational development priorities, illustrate this politicization of development policy. Figure 13.9 shows that U.S. assistance is inequitably distributed and is overwhelmingly political. In 1988 just eight countries received more than two-thirds of U.S. development aid. Israel, the top recipient, received more than one-fourth of U.S. aid, even though it was ranked by the World Bank as a high-income, developed country and contained only 4.2 million people. Egypt and Pakistan, important Muslim allies of the United States, together received another one-fourth. Most other top recipients were Central American countries then considered vital in the

U.S. struggle against leftist Nicaragua. Multinational assistance is more egalitarian and more directed to poor countries such as Ethiopia, Tanzania, and Bangladesh (Figure 13.10).

Even U.S. food aid, which may appear to be entirely humanitarian, was designed as a price-support program begun in 1954 to help U.S. farmers find a market for the overproduction caused by high-energy factory farming. U.S. farm commodities continue to play a major role in the international food aid network (Figure 13.11), but in 1986 less than 20 percent was given as free gifts to the United Nations and voluntary organizations to be distributed as emergency aid to famine victims (IDCA 1987). Most U.S. food aid is actually purchased by foreign governments with low-interest loans from the United States. Many of these loans are "forgiven" in return for political or economic concessions. Critics charge that such food aid programs are an obstacle to democratic development because they support unpopular governments and thereby delay necessary land reform while devaluating the products of local farmers (Lappe, Collins, and Kinley 1981; Lappe, Schurman, and Danaher 1987).

## UNDERDEVELOPING BANGLADESH

### Land and Food in Impoverished Bangladesh

*Between 1933 and 1960 the village became poorer, and was polarized into two groups of households, one owning insufficient land to support an average household, and another owning a sufficient or excessive amount of it.* (Van Schendel 1981:82)

*Thus, international systems of production and finance are changing the ways that the rich and poor [of Bangladesh] eat and lead their lives.* (Lindenbaum 1987:436)

Bangladesh, formerly East Pakistan (1947–1971), is a primarily Muslim nation centered on the Ganges–Brahmaputra delta region known as East Bengal, in the northeast corner of the Indian subcontinent at the head of the Bay of Bengal. In 1990 the World Bank listed Bangladesh as one of the world's poorest nations, fifth from the bottom with a per-capita GNP rank of $170 (World Bank 1990). In line with its status as an impoverished nation, average life expectancy in Bangladesh stood at 51 years, infant mortality at 118 per 1000 live births, and 57 percent of its population, or 62 million people, were considered impoverished (World Bank 1990). By FAO (Food and Agricultural Organization of the United Nations) caloric standards (2122 calories/day), 85 percent of the population was living on an inadequate diet. Nutritional deficiencies related to poverty were reflected in the low birth weights (under 5.5 lb [2.5 kilograms, kg]) of 39 percent of Bangladeshie babies due to a high rate of maternal malnutrition. Roughly 90 percent of the population was rural, and nearly 50 percent of all rural households were landless. Some 67 percent of the population was either unemployed or underemployed (Jansen 1986).

Given such precarious economic conditions, it is not surprising that several hundred thousand people died in famines in Bangladesh in 1974. These conditions existed even though Bangladesh experienced an average annual growth in GNP of .4 percent during 1965–1988 and from 1982 to 1988 received $13.8 billion in ODA. From 1985 to 1988, Bangladesh received 4.6 million tons (4.2 million metric tons) of food aid, much of it from the United States. The Bangladesh experience suggests that economic growth and development assistance may not reduce poverty when the structure of social inequality remains unchanged.

Under the Muslim rulers of the Mogul empire, East Bengal supported a prosperous cotton industry. The peasantry collectively controlled the land and remained economically self-sufficient, although they had to pay taxes to the zamindars, the title of local elites who were the appointed agents of the Muslim state. Shortly after the British completed their conquest of the region in 1765, they legally recognized the zamindar tax collectors as the rural landowners. Turning the zamindar into landlords, as well as tax collectors, amplified village-level inequalities; however, by giving the zamindars more power, it made it easier for the new British rulers to maintain political stability and assured a steady flow of taxes. The British also suppressed the indigenous cotton industry and converted the peasantry into agricultural laborers for the production of jute as an export crop to supply British-owned mills in Calcutta and England.

Thus, preexisting social structures created by state authority laid the foundation for the profound impoverishment of Bangladesh in the twentieth century. Despite various changes in the central government and apparent reforms in land laws, the rural elites have tenaciously maintained their grip over the best agricultural land in Bangladesh. Their favored social standing, which is ultimately supported by the state, has permitted them to benefit at the expense of their less favored fellow villagers since agricultural development programs became important during the 1970s. Thus, Bangladesh demonstrates that the incorporation of a regional state into the global system can increase internal inequality and reduce the quality of life for much of the population (Figure 13.12).

The impoverishment process in Bangladesh

is well documented at the village level in some two dozen modern ethnographic studies (e.g., see Hartmann and Boyce 1983, Jansen 1986:22, Van Schendel 1981). As a representative case, we will examine Goborgari, a single village described by Dutch researcher Willem van Schendel (1981). Goborgari is a Bengali-speaking, mixed Hindu and Moslem village situated on a level alluvial plain north of the Ganges and west of the Brahmaputra River in northern Bangladesh.

The village of Goborgari was primarily settled by immigrants during the nineteenth and early twentieth centuries. A government survey showed that in 1933 Goborgari was a small village of nineteen relatively egalitarian and self-sufficient farming households. There were no landless households, few large landholders, and the average acreage per household stood at approximately 4.3 acres (1.7 hectares), which was adequate for basic needs (Table 13.7). The situation had changed dramatically by 1977. The population had increased from 30 people to 392. Total acreage increased, and cultivation was greatly intensified with irrigation and with double, even triple, cropping, but most people were impoverished.

It might appear that natural population increase was the primary cause of impoverishment in Goborgari, but a closer look shows that this was not the case. Much of the growth of Goborgari since 1933 was because landless villagers moved in from other areas. More important, even with a tenfold population increase, subsistence resources would have still been marginally adequate if land were equitably distributed. If Goborgari had been organized as an egalitarian, small-scale culture, land resources and the risks of food production would have been shared equally. The primary crop in Goborgari by 1977 was the newly introduced Green Revolution **high-yield variety** (HYV) of rice, which increased production by a third. The problem with the new HYV rice, which was promoted by government extension agents, was that it required access to land and high levels of water and chemicals. Despite these technological improvements, the village was still relatively impoverished in comparison with earlier conditions. Average household acreage dropped to 1.5 acres (.6 hectare), which was insufficient to meet basic household needs. Thirty-three percent of the households

FIGURE 13.12  *Bangladesh was the fifth poorest nation in the world in 1990 according to the World Bank. Millions of impoverished people, such as these villagers, live in the flood-prone Ganges Brahmaputra delta.*

were suddenly landless, and the top richest 10 percent of households owned 46 percent of the land. A full 70 percent of the households were at or below the 2-acre (.8-hectare) line, which was the minimal acreage needed to produce what villagers considered to be a "moderately contented living" derived from full-time farming.

Van Schendel (1981) arrives at this poverty-line figure based on a minimal basic needs requirement of 3.86 lb (1.75 kg) of rice per person per day. The latter figure is set at two and one-half times

---

***high-yield variety***  High-yield plant varieties developed by selective breeding as part of the Green Revolution.

TABLE 13.7    *Change in a "Developing" Bangladeshi Village,*
*Goborgari, 1933 and 1977*

|  | 1933 | 1977 |
|---|---|---|
| Population | 30 | 392 |
| Households | 19 | 75 |
| Average household size | 1.5 | 5.2 |
| Total land owned, acres | 83 | 122 |
| Total land controlled | — | 136 |
| Total land cultivated | — | 148 |
| Total plows and teams | — | 31.5 |
| Average acres/household | 4.3 | 1.5 |
| Average fragments/household | — | 6.5 |
| Households landless (%) | 0 | 32 |
| Households 0 Control (%) | — | 16 |
| Households own <2 acres (%) | — | 70.6 |
| Land control top 10%–12% | 10 | 46 |
| Households own full plow (%) | — | 34.7 |
| **1977 Villagewide Rice Production-Consumption** | | |
| Rice production/person/day | | 0.8 kg |
| Rice production/person/day (HYV rice) | | 1.3 kg |
| Nutritional requirement/person/day | | 0.7 kg |
| Basic needs requirement/person/day | | 1.75 kg |
| Acreage to produce basic needs/household | | 2.1 acres |
| Households not self-sufficient in rice | | 60% |

SOURCE: Van Schendel (1981).

the daily nutritional requirement of 1.6 lb (.7 kg), in order to allow for a marketable "surplus" for the purchase of other food items and basic material needs.

The land situation was more complex than the facts of legal ownership suggest because land quality and productivity varied and land fragmentation made cultivation difficult. An average household might own 1.5 acres (.6 hectare) in six and one-half separate pieces. A significant amount of land was also either mortgaged or sharecropped under an arrangement in which the sharecropper could keep half of the production. Holding a mortgage or rights to sharecrop a given piece of land gave a degree of control over "unowned" land and made it considerably more difficult to assess the actual degree of poverty and inequality in the village. Virtually as critical as control over land was ownership of a plow and team of draft animals, yet only 33 percent of the households owned a full team. A farmer who did not own a team could not sharecrop, and hiring a team to plow one's own land

meant reduced yields and increased expenses. To a limited extent, sharecropping gave the poorest villagers a chance to make up their deficiencies, but, nevertheless, 60 percent of all households were not self-sufficient in rice. They could not produce enough rice to meet their minimal nutritional requirements and were even further short of producing a marketable surplus to help meet their physical needs for moderately contented living by local standards.

Because agricultural self-sufficiency was out of reach of two-thirds of the villagers, they were forced to supplement their incomes with seasonal part-time labor; petty, sometimes illegal, business operations; and whatever irregular and poorly paid service employment they could find. Under these conditions, most villagers faced continual economic emergencies and scarcity, and serious poverty and inequality appeared to be steadily increasing.

When he attempted to estimate the actual economic status of Goborgari households, Van Schendel (1981) found that cash values were inadequate to cover all the significant economic exchanges that took place in the village and the varying requirements of individual households. Instead, Van Schendel used a 4-point scale based on the villager's own estimate of monthly household-maintenance requirements and standard of living. Villagers implicitly recognized at least four standards of living within the village, which Van Schendel labeled A (substandard), B (low), C (moderate), and D (comfortable) (Table 13.8), according to a household's ability to produce sufficient rice for its total annual needs. The poorest 20 percent of households (category A) often went hungry and could not afford respectable clothing. The top 16 percent of households (category D) enjoyed an annual surplus that would allow them to maintain their modest comforts and simple luxuries for more than 3 months beyond a given agricultural year. Households in the two middle categories existed on a very narrow margin. The villagers themselves explicitly named only three wealth categories within the village, based on rice production, and two additional categories of "rich" landowners that were known in neighboring villages.

The economic position of the village as a whole could be affected by war, famine, and fluctuations in the price of cash crops. Upward or downward mobility of individual households was determined by a variety of specific factors. Where the margin of economic viability is so narrow, illness, a single poor crop, an expensive wedding or funeral, a robbery, or litigation could all push a household into extreme poverty.

The local rural elite were wealthy landowners who could live relatively comfortably, even though in comparison with the national-level urban elite they did not appear wealthy. The rural elite were heavily dependent on the labor of sharecroppers who worked their land, and they made significant profit from lending money to the chronically indebted peasantry at exorbitant rates. The rural elite thus had a vested interest in maintaining the long-established peasant landholding system, which was defined by a large, high-density agrarian population living under very marginal conditions. The system's basic features, especially landless laborers, sharecroppers, mortgages, and high rates of indebtedness, severely inhibit upward mobility.

## Bangladesh and the Green Revolution

The Green Revolution refers to the use of institutionalized agricultural research, large-scale capital resources, and energy-intensive technology to increase per-acre food productivity in the developing world. This approach to agricultural development began in 1943 when the Rockefeller Foundation

TABLE 13.8    *Household Economic Categories in Goborgari, 1977*

| Category* | Households (no.) | Households (%) | Population (no.) | Population (%) |
|---|---|---|---|---|
| A: Substandard | 15 | 20 | 74 | 19 |
| B: Low | 32 | 43 | 147 | 38 |
| C: Moderate | 16 | 21 | 90 | 23 |
| D: Comfortable | 12 | 16 | 81 | 20 |

SOURCE: Van Schendel (1981).
*Etic categories distinguished by Van Schendel: (A) Substandard: virtually landless, tattered clothing, hungry; income insufficient for year. (B) Low: plow, less than 2 acres, basic annual food and clothing. (C) Moderate: more than 2 acres, 1–3 month's surplus. (D) Comfortable: metal-roofed house, tube well, expensive clothes, bicycle, wristwatches, as status symbols; surplus of 3 months or more. *Native economic categories within Goborgari:* (1) *Chhotolok:* laborers, cannot produce rice. (2) *Moidhom:* sharecroppers, must also buy rice. (3) *Dewani:* eat rice they produce. Wealthy landowners in other villages. (4) *Mashari:* wealthy, owners of 10–25 acres. (5) *Adhoni:* very wealthy, owners of more than 25 acres.

funded a special project in cooperation with the Mexican government to improve the yield of grain crops by selective breeding. By the early 1960s, the program successfully produced a dwarf hybrid wheat capable of tripling yields. In 1966 the Mexican research center became an international agricultural research institute known as CIMMYT (International Center for the Improvement of Wheat and Maize). By 1977, after an intensively funded international campaign, Mexican dwarf HYV wheat was being grown on half of the wheatland throughout the developing world and was replacing many indigenously produced varieties and other crops (CGIAR 1980). CIMMYT became a model for a dozen other similar centers, which are now spread throughout the developing world under the sponsorship of CGIAR (Consultative Group on International Agricultural Research; see Figure 13.5).

HYV grains are often presented as the primary factors behind the large per-acre yields of the Green Revolution; however, these production increases are won at a cost. The local domesticates that the new plants replace were produced by many generations of local people to fit local environmental conditions and the requirements of small-scale, self-sufficient production techniques. The new plants can be called ***high-response varieties*** (HRVs), to emphasize that they depend on expensive inputs (Palmer 1972). The "miracle grains" are extremely demanding plants. They only produce high yields under optimum conditions. They require much water, but not too much, and large quantities of chemical fertilizer. They are also vulnerable to disease and pests because they are a genetic monocrop; thus, successful production also requires generous applications of chemical pesticides. They are often dwarf forms because a short stock is needed to support the heavy head of grain, but this leaves the plants more vulnerable to flooding and means that they can not be grown in many otherwise favorable areas. The special requirements of the new varieties mean that only the largest farmers with the best land and the best connections with the government are able to take advantage of the new technology and can afford the risk of occasional crop failure (Lappe, Collins, and Fowler 1978).

Joining the Green Revolution means that small farmers are linked to a complex global political economy in which the seeds they plant, the tools they use, and the most critical factors affecting their security, such as land, marketing, wages, and credits, are all removed from effective village control. Ultimately, the fate of "developing" rural villagers is determined by the heads of governments, banks, corporations, foundations, and other international development agencies, all operating through many interconnected bureaucracies. Under the Green Revolution, village-level agricultural production is connected to global-level institutions by way of national-level institutions through a series of unequal exchanges, or inputs and outputs, in which power is concentrated at the top at each level and costs and benefits are unevenly distributed.

Figure 13.13 illustrates the three levels, global, national, and village, at which the Green Revolution is organized and lists some of the exchanges between levels. Although the public purpose of this kind of agricultural development is "to help poor peasants feed themselves," at the global level it can be seen that important political and economic benefits return to the elites of the donor nations. Many elites at the national level also derive important benefits in the form of food surpluses, land, profits, cheap labor, bribes, and votes. National elites, including government officials at all levels in the bureaucracy and the wealthy in private enterprises (who are often also in government), control the technological and financial inputs, as well as the natural resources of land and water, that make the HYVs produce. In exchange the developing countries have accepted an increasing burden of debt to international donors and often find that they must submit to specific conditions in order to keep up their payments. Thus, a form of international debt peonage has become part of the development process. Ironically, at the village level, the local elite repeat the unequal exchanges of higher levels, such that the majority of the rural population becomes impoverished, not nourished and empowered, by the Green Revolution.

Impoverishment was one of the unintended secondary outcomes that accompanied increased production as the Green Revolution reached the village level (see Figure 13.13). This occurred as part

FIGURE 13.13
*Input–output structure of the Green Revolution.*

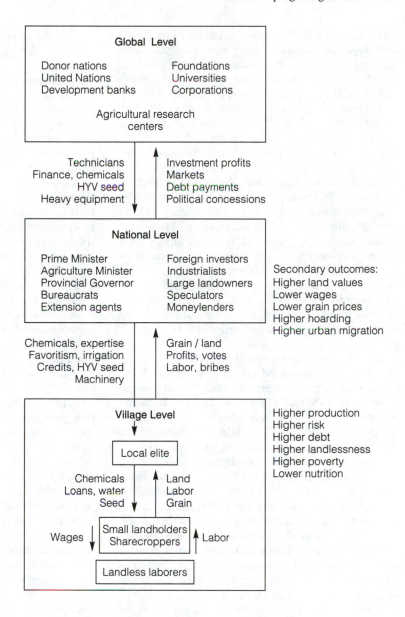

of an interconnected process in which the new technology was linked to increased debt and landlessness and reduced nutrition in the villages. Nutrition declined because the monocrop HYVs replaced other food crops, while declining incomes made it more difficult for no longer self-sufficient villagers to buy food. At the national level, land values increased, along with grain hoarding by speculators, while grain prices fell. Many rural people forfeited their small landholdings when they were unable to pay off their debts. Increased

---

**high-response variety** High-response plant varieties designed to produce high yields when grown with chemical fertilizers and pesticides.

mechanization reduced the demand for farm labor and wages fell, driving many people to seek low-paying jobs in the cities. Elites at every level benefited from all of this, while the total level of poverty increased (Lappe, Collins, and Fowler 1978).

Green Revolution impoverishment is well illustrated in Bangladesh. The local elite used their political connections to gain control of the tube wells required for irrigating HYV crops. They also "cultivated" the government extension agents with bribes to make sure that the seeds, expertise, chemicals, and machinery came to them first. The elite dominated village agricultural cooperatives and effectively controlled whatever technological inputs reached the lower-class small landholders and sharecroppers. Skillful manipulation of their political and economic advantages helped the local elite systematically appropriate the land of less fortunate fellow villagers, while extracting their labor and grain. The landless laborers at the bottom of the village hierarchy had only their labor to exchange for inadequate wages.

Wheat has steadily displaced rice and other crops as a primary food staple in Bangladesh because HYV wheat proved more suitable in Bangladesh than HYV rice. This crop change, however, has also had unexpected cultural consequences (Lindenbaum 1987). The traditional Bangladeshi diet consists of rice, lentils, fish, and vegetables. As inexpensive HYV wheat has become widely available, however, it has become the dominant food. The poor, who can afford little else, must abandon their preferred foods and eat wheat three meals a day even though this means a decline in the caloric and nutritional quality of their diet. Culturally, rice remains the most important food and is considered the essential element of a meal, whereas wheat is treated as a foreign snack food and is understandably associated with disease by villagers.

Some development experts have argued that the expansion of wheat production in Bangladesh benefits women because many women, who were formerly employed as rice hullers but were displaced by machines, may now find employment harvesting and threshing wheat. However, this work is taken only by the poorest women because it violates purdah restrictions, is very heavy and difficult work, and must take place during the hottest time of year.

# ANTHROPOLOGY AND DEVELOPMENT ISSUES

## Development Anthropology and Peasants

Cultural anthropologists enthusiastically supported post–World War II international development efforts by turning their attention to rural peasantries and the urban poor. Many researchers shifted their focus from the functional equilibrium of small-scale cultures to the realities of poverty, the process of cultural change, and the "obstacles" to modernization or development progress. This research shift corresponded to changes within anthropology itself. Since 1950 many anthropologists have found full-time employment in development. In 1968 roughly 75 percent of the new PhDs in American anthropology still took academic positions; but by 1982, when there were few new academic positions, only 28 percent found teaching positions, and many of the others took positions as development anthropologists (Weaver 1985). For example, in 1980 there were fifty anthropologists doing development work as full-time employees of AID. This was probably greater than the total number that ever worked as colonial anthropologists for the British empire. In the 1980s, many more American anthropologists conducted temporary contract work through universities or private firms (Hoben 1982). One such firm, the Institute for Development Anthropology, held contracts with AID and the FAO for over $5.8 million in 1987 and had conducted projects in forty-eight countries. "Development" is clearly what many contemporary anthropologists do, often within an academic framework.

The anthropological approach to development and poverty has gone through significant changes since the 1950s. Initially, some prominent anthropologists uncritically accepted the established view that poverty was caused by ignorance and disease—in effect, blaming the poor, or their culture, for poverty, while ignoring the inequalities of economic and political power that sustained poverty. For example, Margaret Mead (1961) argued that people everywhere would be modernized and enriched simply by exposure to "obviously better" ways of life. Thus, culture change involved "seeing a light and following it freely" (Mead 1961:19–20).

Such a "poverty is ignorance" view did not at first acknowledge that "development" might require outside coercion and might generate legitimate resistance from its intended beneficiaries. Mead's narrow view of cultural development made it easy for planners to overlook the ways in which small-scale cultures were already designed to satisfy basic human needs.

Anthropologists Conrad Arensberg and Arthur Niehoff (1964) presented a similar tone of technological arrogance. They emphasized the superiority of industrial technology and compared change agents to "brain surgeons" who were introducing "new ideas, which constitute the medicine of social change" (1964:6). This inherently ethnocentric view of change implicitly denigrated traditional cultures for their backwardness, while endorsing bureaucratically planned, technologically based development projects that ignored the views of the target population. Such an approach directly supported the official position of the international development establishment of the time and certainly had widespread popular support; but in the 1960s, few Americans questioned the wisdom of high-energy factory farming or worried about the social or environmental impacts of giant hydroelectric projects.

Many anthropologists have long been aware of the complex ethical issues they must face when working for development agencies (Manners 1956). Applied anthropologists now subscribe to formal codes of ethical conduct, but many difficult judgments must still be made. Development contractors necessarily have a dual, sometimes irreconcilable, responsibility to their employers and to the people who will be affected by development projects. They must consider the political agenda of funding agencies and the differential costs and benefits at all levels. Predicting all consequences of development changes is not possible, and even the most well-intended programs can still increase poverty and inequality.

Because target populations, the assumed beneficiaries of development programs, often have little power, it is vital that their views be taken into account. When small-scale cultures control their own resources and are able to support relatively self-maintaining communities, they often resist development programs designed to integrate them into large-scale national systems. This can create a dilemma for anthropologists who disavow the use of force in development projects. Some early development writers attributed resistance to ethnocentrism on the part of the target people, suggesting that they mistakenly believed their own culture to be superior (Arensberg and Niehoff 1964). Other social engineers even recommended that change agents try to make people feel inadequate so they would desire change (Goodenough 1963). Development anthropologists, however, have increasingly recognized that resistance to change is often justified.

As development efforts were first beginning, some anthropologists correctly identified critical features of peasant culture that acted as apparent obstacles to the kind of development progress envisioned by government planners. However, these researchers also emphasized the rationality and practicality of peasant culture. For example, Robert Redfield (1947) used his "folk society" concept as an ideal type, to draw a contrast between peasants and urban societies. Redfield's folk society was defined by cultural features that also characterize small-scale tribal societies, such as small population, homogeneity, high social solidarity, simple division of labor, and economic self-sufficiency. In Redfield's view, *peasants* were former tribal societies that had been incorporated by states. State intervention, however, caused significant cultural changes in the folk society, including inequality, loss of autonomy, and impoverishment.

Focusing on political economy, Eric Wolf (1955, 1957) defined peasants as subsistence agriculturalists who control their own land but do not produce primarily for the market to make a profit. Wolf suggested that a common characteristic of peasants in Latin America and Island Southeast Asia is their organization as *closed corporate communities* in defense against conquest and exploitation by outsiders backed by state authority. Closed corporate communities either own land communally

---

*peasants* Subsistence farmers who pay taxes to the state but own their own land and produce primarily for their own use rather than for a commercial market.
*closed corporate community* Communally organized peasants who exclude outsiders and limit the acquisition of wealth and power by their own members.

or regularly redistribute ownership of individual plots to ensure equal access of all members. To protect their lands, peasants also try to exclude outsiders and discourage members from becoming too involved with the larger national society. Peasant communities are corporations in that they seek to be self-perpetuating and self-sufficient (Figure 13.14). They promote internal security by means of **wealth-leveling devices** such as expensive rituals and feasting that tend to reduce economic inequality, while inhibiting economic growth and capital accumulation by consuming potential surplus within the community.

When cultural features of the closed corporate community are practiced by peasants, they are a defense against state exploitation. These same features may also be found in small-scale tribal societies where they inhibit the concentration of inter-

FIGURE 13.14  *Many small-scale subsistence agriculturalists engage in rituals and feasting that promote cohesiveness. These women are making corn tortillas during a fiesta in San Pedro Chenalhó, Chiapas, Mexico. Corn, a symbol of fertility and regeneration, is the primary food eaten and circulated in fiestas.*

nal political and economic power that leads to the state in the first place. Given this self-defense emphasis, peasants often prefer to grow their own locally adapted crops for their proven hardiness, and they emphasize domestic food crops over market crops. They are also likely to reject exotic and expensive agricultural technologies in order to avoid debt and loss of independence. Peasants maximize subsistence security, and they value social support networks and strategic reserves over risk taking. Such cultural objectives may be conservative, but they are not ignorant or irrational.

George Foster (1965, 1969) identified the "image of limited good" as the key cognitive orientation in peasant societies. **Limited good** refers to the assumption that "all desired things in life . . . exist in finite and unexpandable quantities" (Foster 1969:83). This view was a direct expression of a stable, egalitarian, predominately nonmarket economy and meant that a wealthy peasant was gaining his wealth at the expense of his less fortunate neighbors. The contrasting principle of **unlimited good** assumes that "with each passing generation people on average will have more of the good things of life." Unlimited good reflects a capitalist market economy and is compatible with poverty and inequality. Unfortunately, many development planners mistakenly concluded from the limited-good concept that peasants were poor because they believed in equality, not because they were oppressed and exploited.

## Urban Anthropology and the Culture-of-Poverty Controversy

As rural areas became more impoverished, the peasantry moved increasingly into urban centers, and anthropologists began to focus on the urban end of the folk–urban continuum. Anthropologist Oscar Lewis studied Latin American urban poor in Mexico, Puerto Rico, and New York and described some seventy specific features which he called the **culture of poverty.** Lewis (1959, 1966a, 1966b) found the poor to be relatively unorganized, yet "disengaged" from and suspicious of the political and economic institutions of urban society, even though they lived within cities. The poor lived in crowded slums (Figure 13.15), were chronically unemployed and short of food and cash, and were

FIGURE 13.15
*The slums of Bombay are an extreme example of urban poverty conditions. Whatever cultural patterns the world's urban poor may share, they are a response to conditions imposed by dominant classes and institutions. (SOURCE: Bernard Pierre Wolff/Magnum Photos.)*

forced to make small expensive purchases and borrow at exorbitant rates. Marriages were often not legalized and easily dissolved. Poor families were unstable, often matricentered, and children quickly assumed adult roles. Lewis fond that as individuals the poor tended to be fatalistic, with feelings of inferiority and dependency. They were present-oriented, unwilling to defer gratification, and had little sense of history or their place in society.

Lewis argued that the culture of poverty served "adaptive functions" in response to economic deprivation. He thought that poverty traits defined a subculture, which he attempted to describe in positive terms, as Redfield had successfully done with the folk society. The culture of poverty, however, proved to be a very slippery and controversial concept. It had no obvious roots in small-scale culture, and many poverty traits corresponded to popular negative stereotypes about the poor and lended further credibility to development planners who blamed the "ignorance" of the poor for their own poverty. Lewis himself often acknowledged the negative aspects of poverty traits and even referred to them as pathologies.

Lewis (1969) documented the extreme material poverty of the urban poor by conducting an inventory of the possessions of fourteen households in a complex of windowless one-room adobe apartments in Mexico City. The eighty-three people in the complex shared a common water trough and outdoor toilets. The average value of all possessions was $338 per household, with the richest household owning $937 worth and the poorest $119. Furniture and clothing accounted for 59 percent of the total value, and every household owned at least one bed, a mattress, table, and shelves; however, because there were only twenty-three

---

**wealth-leveling devices**  Any cultural means, such as ritual feasting, used to redistribute wealth within a community and thereby reduce inequality.

**limited good**  A belief often found in peasant communities that total wealth is limited and anyone who acquires too much is taking away from others. This is a justification for wealth-leveling.

**unlimited good**  The belief in continuous economic growth often used to justify wealth inequality.

**culture of poverty**  Lewis's concept of a complex of culture traits that both help the urban poor adapt to and help perpetuate poverty.

beds, many people slept on the floor. Not all households could afford to own a chair, wardrobe, or a radio, even though these were all considered essential. Articles were often purchased secondhand and had to be pawned so frequently that even something as important as a bed was only owned for an average of less than 5 years. Jewelry and personal adornments consisted primarily of quickly pawned wristwatches. None of the women owned necklaces or bracelets.

Like Wolf, Lewis (1969) attributed the culture of poverty to specific conditions in the political economy, especially a capitalist economy with high unemployment, inadequate government assistance, an absence of supportive descent groups, and a dominant class that prizes wealth and attributes economic achievement to personal effort. However, a certain ambiguity remained. Lewis argued that the culture of poverty is not just a response to deprivation because not all impoverished groups share these traits. Furthermore, he considered poverty culture to be an inadequate solution to poverty conditions. Lewis also suggested that poverty culture was self-perpetuating through socialization and may actually prove more difficult to eradicate than poverty itself. Thus, the culture-of-poverty concept, perhaps inadvertently, gave support to those who would blame the poor for their poverty.

Critics found serious deficiencies with the culture-of-poverty concept. Charles Valentine (1968, 1971; Valentine et al. 1969) objected to Lewis's use of the culture concept because Lewis's (1959, 1961, 1966b) prolific published data consisted almost exclusively of autobiographical oral histories of a few individual poor families. It is difficult to determine what, if any, actual subculture they represented. This is especially the case because it is obvious that these families, like all other families in complex urban settings, displayed idiosyncrasies such as particular occupational specialties or common personality traits that made them atypical. In many cases, the families that Lewis portrayed revealed patterns incompatible with the culture-of-poverty model. The poor neighborhoods they were part of were also more organized than might be expected; larger organizational patterns, however, do not stand out when analysis remains at the family level. The individuals in

the sample families were often more "engaged" with the world around them than the model of passivity and ignorance suggests. Valentine argues that regardless of the distinctive traits the poor may share, poverty does not constitute a self-perpetuated subculture and poverty traits are a response to conditions imposed by the dominant classes and institutions. Lewis certainly would have agreed with the last part of this interpretation.

## ANDEAN DEVELOPMENT

### Andean Peasantry and the Cornell–Peru Project

The Cornell–Peru project conducted at the hacienda of Vicos in the Peruvian Andes from 1952 to 1963 is one of the best-known development anthropology projects (Dobyns, Doughty, and Lasswell 1971). This was a unique, long-term development effort, planned and directed by anthropologists as a *participant intervention* experiment in cultural change designed to empower the peasantry. Using research funds provided by the Carnegie Corporation of New York, the project codirectors, American anthropologist Allan Holmberg, then of Cornell University, and Peruvian anthropologist Mario Vazquez, rented the traditional colonial-style hacienda of Vicos where some 2000 peasants lived as virtual serfs on a 60-square-mile (mi²) (155-square-kilometer [km²]) estate. The anthropologists then used their position as managers of the hacienda to gradually turn political power back to the peasants and help them regain control over their ancestral land. This was a novel approach to development and was widely considered a success; however, as an externally imposed solution, the project did not enhance the potential of small-scale Andean cultures.

The *hacienda* system in the Peruvian Andes in 1952 was a continuation of colonial social structures created by the Spanish following their conquest of the Inca empire in the sixteenth century. It is necessary to understand the colonial background to put the Vicos project in proper perspective. The original Spanish conquerors created great landed estates for themselves out of the best lands. These estates were known as **encomiendas** and included rights to extract labor and produce from the natives who were already residents on the land. After Peru became independent from Spain in 1821, the descendants of the conquerors, who called themselves *criollos*, retained their dominant position in Andean society, and many of the *encomienda* estates remained in place as vast **latifundia** haciendas and plantations.

The Andean haciendas, like similar haciendas throughout Latin America, were agricultural estates with a dominant landowner and a dependent native labor force that produced primarily for subsistence and local markets (Miller 1967, Mintz and Wolf 1957). In contrast, **plantations** were designed to produce for large-scale markets in order to accumulate capital. In the twentieth century, haciendas were often administered by absentee owners who intentionally kept the resident natives impoverished so that many would be forced to provide cheap migrant labor to the plantations and mines. The hacienda was divided sharply into two classes, which were each further stratified. Power was concentrated at the top with the *hacendado*, the Spanish owner, and his hired administrators who were usually *mestizos* of mixed Spanish–Native Andean ancestry and identified with the dominant *criollo* culture. The *hacendado*, or *patron*, used his landholding to enhance his personal wealth and status and was supported in his power by regional and national political authorities and church officials.

Hacienda natives, or *peones,* were granted small subsistence holdings, often on marginal lands, and were allowed to graze their livestock on the estate. As rent, the *peones* were obligated to work 3 days a week for the hacienda for which they received a token wage. They were also required to provide the hacienda free service and the labor of their animals on demand. Indigenes were treated as ignorant children by the *patron* and his managers. As serfs, the natives were expected to show exaggerated, hat-in-hand respect for those in charge. Uncooperative natives were subject to imprisonment and fines, although formerly they might have been beaten. Hacienda officials created support by dispensing small favors and sometimes acted as godparents to specific native families. Ritual co-parenthood, the institution of **compradazgo,** es-

tablished an informal alliance between families of different social ranks.

Indigenes exercised only limited political power within their own community. Their political action was focused primarily on a **civil–religious hierarchy** known as the *varayoc* system, which had counterparts in native communities throughout Latin America, and was instituted by the Spanish as a form of indirect rule. The term *vara* referred to the official wooden staff held by officials in the *varayoc* system. In Vicos there were nine hierarchical statuses, such as mayor, treasurer, and councilman, occupied by some seventeen officials. These officials coordinated public works such as road maintenance, carried out the *patron's* orders, and organized religious events, which were under the priests' control. *Varayoc* officials served for specific terms and derived considerable status from their offices, although the rituals associated with each status were costly and it took many years to work up in the hierarchy. The *varayoc* system is an example of wealth-leveling mechanisms in peasant societies.

## The Vicos Experiment

When the Vicos participant intervention experiment began, the anthropologist-*patrons* immedi-

---

**participant intervention**  A form of culture change in which those in control become members of the system they seek to change.

**hacienda**  A Latin American agricultural estate with dependent laborers that produced for local rather than global markets and was designed to maintain the social status and lifestyle of the *hacendado* landowner.

**encomienda**  A land grant made by Spanish colonial authorities to individual Spaniards, which included rights over the indigenous residents.

**latifundia**  Very large Latin American landholdings, usually under private control by the wealthy elite.

**plantation**  A large agricultural establishment designed to generate capital by producing for the global market.

**compardazgo**  The ritual institution of co-parenthood with godparents and godchildren; in Latin America, often reinforcing dependency relationships between *hacendado* and *peone.*

**civil–religious hierarchy**  A wealth-leveling mechanism in Latin American peasant communities in which expensive feasts must be given by those moving up a ranked hierarchy of offices.

ately began to move the native-*peones* into administrative positions in the hacienda, replacing their *mestizo* managers. Next they abolished free service and began to pay decent wages to their new native employees. Profits from agricultural production were returned to the community in the form of agricultural improvements and schooling. A formal group of community leaders was organized to participate directly in the planning of the entire project, and weekly meetings were held with all workers to discuss problems. In 1957 the project leaders petitioned the government for a decree of expropriation that would allow indigenes to obtain full ownership of the hacienda. This action aroused the ire of the local elite, who accused the project of being a Communist plot. After 5 years of persistent effort and the intervention of the U.S. ambassador and supportive officials within the Peruvian government, the Vicos hacienda was sold to its former serfs in 1962 (Figure 13.16). The Cornell–Peru Project terminated the next year. Holmberg attributed the apparent success of his experiment to its approach to political power:

*The element of power proved to be the key that permitted the Cornell Peru Project to open the door to change; the devolution of power to the people of Vicos proved to be the mechanism that made the new system viable.* (1971:62)

The emphasis on changing the local power structure in Vicos was certainly innovative in development anthropology; in retrospect, however, precisely evaluating the long-term impact of the project is difficult. Surveys conducted up to 1964 showed measurable improvements in nutrition, education, and some indicators of material prosperity (Dobyns, Doughty, and Lasswell 1971). Nevertheless, the project and the economic opportunities it presented were designed to favor the "most progressive" community members, and it is possible that a new elite was created. More cash wealth was flowing into the community, and agricultural production had apparently increased, but it is unclear how the new wealth was being distributed or how long the community could remain competitive in the national economy.

The community did make some critical trade-offs in their "modernization." Responding to the program's directives, they formed an agricultural cooperative organized along capitalist lines as a profit-making agricultural corporation. This move carried significant risks because it weakened or replaced many pre-Inca subsistence practices, and this may explain why researchers found that by 1963 household heads showed a substantial increase in several clinical measures of anxiety (Alers 1971). To buy the land, the new Vicos corporation assumed a substantial long-term debt with the government for half of the total purchase price. Many Vicos families also assumed large individual debts with the Peruvian government's agricultural bank to pay for the expensive new agricultural inputs required for profitable market production.

Even the new production technology involved additional trade-offs, but the project planners treated the development process as "enlightenment," virtually disregarding the centuries of accumulated agricultural knowledge already present in Vicos and the genetic value of local crop varieties. Stephen Brush and his associates (Brush, Carney, and Huaman 1981) have shown that high-yield hybrid potatoes produced by agricultural scientists have many disadvantages for Andean communities. The new potatoes are grown as a monocrop that requires exotic, debt-producing inputs, and the crop must be sold on the national, government-controlled market. In contrast, local communities control all the skills and other "inputs" required to produce and distribute native potatoes. Oxen and footplows are locally produced and maintained. Unlike tractors, they require no imported fuel and are highly reliable. There are more than 2000 varieties of traditional potatoes, each developed for special qualities of taste, storability, and hardiness under specific local conditions. These potatoes, greatly preferred by Andean people, are readily bartered and sold in the local markets.

The Vicos project closely resembled Peru's later agrarian reform program of 1969, which also expropriated haciendas and promoted commercial agriculture. However, it is significant that, although many Andean communities were eager to gain control over their lands under the new land-reform program, they stubbornly and sometimes violently refused to form cooperatives and resisted agricultural "modernization." Diane Hopkins (1985) suggests that this refusal to cooperate with the government program was not because the peasants were ignorant and backward. They simply did not want the government to become their new *patron,* and they rationally preferred their own forms of agricultural production.

At the local level, the Andean system is based on barter of food products between communities; exchanges of labor based on *ayni,* or simple reciprocity; and household ownership of widely dispersed plots. This form of land ownership is a distinctively small-scale cultural pattern and assumes relative equality and self-sufficiency while it minimizes risk and makes effective use of local resources. In the Andean setting, small, intensively utilized plots, though disparaged by agricultural economists as **minifundia,** can be highly productive. The Andean vertical economy, described in Chapter 7, provides individual households access to land in three distinct and complementary ecological zones.

The national agrarian reform plan calls for the peasants to be integrated into the national economy by means of agricultural cooperatives in debt to the government and dependent on the market economy. The advantage for the government of such an arrangement is that it gives them greater control over the peasantry and provides inexpensive food to support urban industrialization. This kind of rural development might make some farmers wealthy, but it brings substantial risks and means that local control systems would be effectively lost.

## SUMMARY

Since the 1950s, poverty has been conceptualized as a "development" or "modernization" problem. Development planners assumed that people were poor because they were "underdeveloped," and they were underdeveloped because they were technologically backward and culturally conservative. Hoping to reduce poverty, the "developed" countries optimistically financed the transfer of agricultural technologies, dam and highway construction, and other large-scale developments designed to promote economic growth throughout the world. Unfortunately, these efforts have not significantly reduced poverty.

Initially, anthropologists enthusiastically endorsed this development model and worked in small communities to identify the "cultural barriers" to economic progress. It became apparent, however, that traditional cultures were not the primary cause of poverty. National and international level efforts to raise GNP in many cases actually further impoverished local communities by promoting debt and dependency, and intensified internal inequalities that reduced access to basic resources. Anthropological data also show that many cultural traits, which development planners may consider to be causes of poverty, are actually rational coping mechanisms to conditions of extreme deprivation. Similarly, overpopulation cannot be a sole cause of poverty. Although population growth has certainly intensified poverty, the relationship is complex. Poverty and the development process itself have both fostered population growth.

FIGURE 13.16    *The Cornell–Peru Project was an applied anthropology experiment designed to turn control of the Andean hacienda of Vicos over to its former serfs. These Vicos farmers are sorting their harvest of traditional potatoes grown for local consumption. (SOURCE: Dr. Paul Doughty, University of Florida.)*

---

**minifundia**    Tiny landholdings of the Latin American peasantry.

The concept of culture scale offers a different perspective on the problem of poverty. Poverty is not entirely a technological problem to be cured by evolutionary progress. The evidence presented in previous chapters showed that poverty was essentially absent in autonomous small-scale cultures but was created by the inequality inherent in the social stratification of large-scale cultures. Poverty was further intensified by the process of colonialism and the global system of stratification, which emerged with industrialization. To be effective, development efforts designed to reduce poverty must deal with the inequalities of wealth and power that exist at all levels of the global system.

## STUDY QUESTIONS

1. How did U.N. experts conceptualize the problem of global poverty in 1950? What specific indicators of underdevelopment did they refer to? What was the vicious cycle? What solutions did they call for?

2. In what sense can it be said that poverty has increased since 1950? Refer to poverty indicators, absolute numbers of impoverished people, and GNP rankings between nations.

3. Describe the official charter and the institutional basis for the U.N. approach to development, referring to the following: U.N. Charter, Universal Declaration of Human Rights, technical assistance, integrated development, Development Decades, Economic and Social Council, World Bank, FAO, U.N. Development Programme.

4. Define the following development related concepts: official development assistance, multilateral assistance, bilateral assistance, and gross national product.

5. Describe how the issues and strategies of the U.N. approach to development has changed in the decades since 1950.

6. Define underdevelopment and poverty, discussing the conceptual and cultural problems that limit the usefulness of your definitions.

7. In what sense can development itself be considered an industry?

8. Describe the major categories of U.S. foreign assistance and the institutional pathways that it follows in order to reach impoverished villagers in the developing world. Refer to multilateral aid, bilateral aid, military aid, development aid, food aid, and the economic support fund. What evidence is there that factors other than humanitarian concerns influence foreign aid?

9. In what way do the following concepts—Point Four, Freedom from Hunger, privatization, free market, and biotechnology—reflect changing priorities in official American approaches to development?

10. How does U.S. food aid benefit U.S. interests?

11. Discuss how colonialism, social structure, population growth, and technological advance were related to poverty in Bangladesh at both national and village levels.

12. Describe village social structure in Bangladesh, emphasizing access to land, labor, technology, food, and cash income, in relation to standard of living.

13. What is the Green Revolution? Discuss the advantages and disadvantages of HYVs. In what way can the Green Revolution contribute to the impoverishment of village-level people? Describe the organization of the Green Revolution at global, national, and village level, referring to the differential flow of costs and benefits.

14. In what way did the conceptual approach of some early development anthropologists reflect dominant trends in the development establishment at the same time?

15. What ethical decisions do applied anthropologists confront? Refer to conflicting responsibilities and the problem of resistance.

16. Discuss cultural "obstacles" to development programs, referring to folk society, closed corporate community, and limited good.

17. What was the culture of poverty, according to Lewis? Why was this concept so controversial, and how was it related to public policy issues? What conceptual and methodological problems have been identified?

18. Define the following related to Latin American and Andean peasantries: *encomienda, criollo, hacendado, mestizo, patron, peone, compradazgo, varayoc* system, civil–religious hierarchy, hacienda, plantation, *latifundia, minifundia, ayni,* and vertical economy.

19. Describe the social structure of the Vicos hacienda when the Cornell–Peru Project began in 1952. Ex-

plain how the participant intervention experiment was conducted and discuss the results.

20. Why did some Andean communities refuse to participate fully in Peru's agrarian reform program? Identify specific points of conflict, referring to production technologies, cooperatives, *ayni*, vertical economy, risk, debt, market economy, subsistence economy, barter exchange, and land ownership.

## SUGGESTED READING

HARTMANN, BETSY, AND JAMES K. BOYCE. 1983. *A Quiet Violence: View from a Bangladesh Village*. San Francisco: Institute for Food and Development Policy. A detailed case study of development in Bangladesh, which expands on the coverage provided in this chapter.

LAPPE, FRANCIS MOORE, JOSEPH COLLINS, AND CARRY FOWLER. 1978. *Food First: Beyond the Myth of Scarcity*. New York: Ballantine Books. This and the following two books provide the essence of Lappe's critique of development policy and emphasize the importance of food self-sufficiency.

LAPPE, FRANCES MOORE, JOSEPH COLLINS, AND DAVID KINLEY. 1981. *Aid as Obstacle: Twenty Questions About Our Foreign Aid and the Hungry*. San Francisco: Institute for Food and Development Policy.

LAPPE, FRANCES MOORE, RACHEL SCHURMAN, AND KEVIN DANAHER. 1987. *Betraying the National Interest*. New York: Grove Press.

# 14

# INDIGENOUS PEOPLES

Indigenous peoples are members of small-scale cultures who are engaged in a contemporary struggle for autonomy and survival in a world dominated by national governments and international markets. Previous chapters detailed the cultural background of these peoples as they existed under independent conditions (Chapters 2–5) and the genocide and ethnocide that they suffered along the frontiers of national expansion (Chapter 11). In this chapter, we examine the conceptual, philosophical, and political issues involved in defining the place of small-scale cultures within the global system. In the first section, we discuss the complexities of devising a nonethnocentric concept of indigenous peoples. In the remaining sections, we examine the history of the great humanitarian policy debate carried on by anthropologists, missionaries, and government officials since the 1830s over how states should relate to tribal peoples and their cultures.

To maintain maximum cultural context, we discuss these complex issues using extended case studies drawn from Australia (see Chapter 2) and Amazonia (see Chapter 3). We examine the background of the International Labour Organisation's controversial Conventions 107 and 169 and the promising new United Nations Universal Declaration on Rights of Indigenous Peoples in detail because these are the most important, modern international conventions on indigenous peoples.

## INDIGENOUS PEOPLES AND THE POLITICS OF LABELS

The labels that one employs in any discussion of "indigenous peoples" is a critical matter because use of any specific label implies a particular understanding of what indigenous people are like and how they should be treated. Choice of labels may also be an expression of political domination or superiority. For example, use of such labels as "Stone Age tribe" implies that an indigenous group is an anachronism, perhaps lost, or at least in the wrong time and place. A "Stone Age tribe" may also be seen as especially weak, childlike, helpless, and naive. In the interests of cross-cultural understanding, anthropologists generally prefer to use the self-selected terms that specific cultural groups use themselves.

TABLE 14.1   *Labels for Indigenous Peoples and Small-Scale Cultures*

| | Ethnolinguistic Distinctiveness | Politicoeconomic Distinctiveness | Original Inhabitants | Self-Appelation | Oppressed | Pejor- ative |
|---|---|---|---|---|---|---|
| Indigenous | +/− | +/− | + | + | + | − |
| Indian | + | + | + | +/− | + | +/− |
| Native | + | +/− | + | +/− | − | +/− |
| Aborigine | + | + | + | +/− | − | +/− |
| Stone Age | + | + | + | − | − | + |
| Savage | + | + | + | − | − | + |
| Uncivilized | + | + | +/− | − | − | + |
| Preliterate | + | + | +/− | − | − | + |
| Tribal | + | + | +/− | +/− | − | +/− |
| Small Scale | + | + | +/− | − | − | − |
| Ethnic Minority | + | − | − | +/− | + | − |
| Primitive | + | + | +/− | − | − | +/− |
| Folk | + | + | +/− | − | − | − |
| Fourth World | + | + | + | +/− | + | − |

NOTE: + means the characteristic is implied by the label; − means the characteristic is not implied; +/− means the characteristic is sometimes implied, sometimes not.

## Who Are Indigenous Peoples?

As threatened small-scale cultures became politically involved in self-defense movements early in the 1970s, many native leaders gradually adopted the term *indigenous* as a self-designation to use in pressing their claims in international forums such as the United Nations. Within the political arena, *indigenous* means the original inhabitants of a region and is posed in opposition to the colonists, usurpers, and intruders who came later in search of new resources to exploit. As a political category, indigenous people includes peasant groups and ethnic communities who have been absorbed by states but who still strongly identify with their cultural heritage and claim special rights to territory and resources on that basis.

Many other terms, which anthropologists and others have applied to peoples and cultures, have carried a variety of different meanings and connotations, such that these terms must all be approached with care, giving attention to context, connotation, and the intended audience. Table 14.1 sorts out fourteen such terms in English according to the degree to which they emphasize ethnolinguistic distinctiveness, specific cultural features of the political economy, priority of settlement in a territory, and oppression, as well as

whether the terms are applied by the people themselves or may be used pejoratively. Many of these terms are ambiguous, and the meaning may vary dramatically depending on who is using them.

In reference to most areas of the world, indigenous is an appropriate label for international discourse. However, if priority of residence in a territory is considered the most critical aspect of the concept indigenous people, then the term *indigenous* must be applied cautiously in specific areas because indigenous peoples have sometimes displaced or absorbed other, more indigenous inhabitants. Archaeological evidence would be needed to sort out the details of settlement priority in some areas of Africa and South America. In general, however, the priority of indigenous groups relative to modern invaders connected with modern states and global culture is obvious.

Unfortunately, the term *indigenous* does not identify the specific cultural characteristics that underlie the political struggle of indigenous peoples (see Table 14.1). *Indigenous* does not distinguish between people living in small-scale cul-

**indigenous**   Peoples who are the original inhabitants of a territory and who seek to maintain political control over their resources and their small-scale cultural heritage.

tures or large-scale chiefdoms or who were incorporated as peasants into states and empires. However adherence to such traits of small-scale cultures as community-level resource management, high levels of local self-sufficiency, and relative social equality makes indigenous peoples distinctive. These traits also generate conflict with larger-scale cultures that seek to extinguish local control systems and create dependency in order to extract resources. Indigenous peoples are likely to resist any external pressures for change that undermine their autonomy, yet their small size and lack of political organization make them especially vulnerable to outside intervention and give them special claims before the international community. The term *indigenous* is usually preferable to similar terms such as *native*, which in some settings carries negative connotations because of its use by colonial powers. In other areas, native may be a self-designation used interchangeably with indigenous. Indigenous, now a self-appellation, has no

negative connotations for the people who use it. This usage, which is rapidly becoming internationally accepted, calls attention to both cultural uniqueness and the political oppression, or at least the disadvantage, that indigenous peoples must often endure from the larger-scale cultures surrounding them.

Colonizing peoples also used generic labels such as *Indian* or *aborigine* in much the same way as the term *native*, to refer to original inhabitants. Indigenous peoples themselves also used these terms, but in this case, a negative connotation is not implied. The disadvantage of *Indian* and *aborigine* is that they are regional terms and lack specific cultural content.

Historically, anthropologists have used the terms *savage*, *primitive*, *uncivilized*, and *preliterate* to call attention to cultural differences. These terms have sometimes enjoyed a certain scientific respectability, but they have not successfully avoided the popular negative connotation of back-

FIGURE 14.1.  *Estimated populations of indigenous people, 1980. (SOURCE: IWGIA.)*

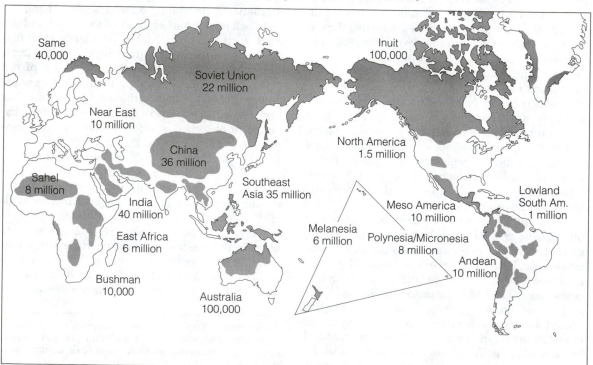

wardness. Some writers used *primitive* in the sense of *primary* or *original* and emphasized positive cultural features (Bodley 1975, 1976; Diamond 1968), but the term has now been abandoned.

## Tribes, Nations, and the Fourth World

*Tribal* is sometimes used synonymously with *indigenous* and is an acceptable self-designation in many areas of the world. In this chapter, *tribal* will refer to indigenous groups who maintain significant degrees of independence. However, the term is usually avoided in Africa because in modern political circles *tribal* may be used pejoratively to imply backwardness and ethnic division. Many anthropologists also reject the term on technical grounds because tribes, as political divisions, were created by colonial administrators (see discussion in Chapter 2, "The Band–Horde Controversy"). Furthermore, as was shown in earlier chapters, small-scale cultures were not organized into discrete polities under centralized leadership. *Tribe* is also used to refer to a stage in cultural evolution, and missionaries often use the term to mean "ethnic group."

The problem of terminology also applies to labels applied to specific cultural groups. Ethnic group names that find their way into the anthropological and popular literature may be pejorative labels applied by neighbors who despise the group in question. For example, the term *Eskimo* is an outsider term applied to people who call themselves "Inuit." Other names, like tribes, may be artificial creations of colonial governments.

Indigenous people self-identify as members of small-scale cultures and consider themselves to be the original inhabitants of the territories that they occupy. Perhaps 200 million or more indigenous peoples are scattered throughout the world, often in remote areas containing valuable natural resources (Figure 14.1). They are self-conscious of the advantages of their cultural heritage in comparison with life in the larger-scale systems surrounding them.

Because indigenous people claim a territorial base and a history of independence, they resemble politically organized states and sometimes call themselves "nations." Geographer Bernard Nietschmann (1988) adopts the term **nations** in place of tribes, to refer to indigenous people, pointing out that nations have a common territory, language, and culture, in contrast to modern states that are often composed of diverse ethnic groups. Further emphasizing the dimension of political struggle, Nietschmann also refers to indigenous people as the **Fourth World,** to distinguish them from the developing states of the Third World. The First and Second Worlds represent the old Cold War division into Western, capitalist countries and Eastern, Communist countries. Many Third World states were created out of former colonies with little regard for the integrity of the Fourth World nations, which they incorporated and turned into internal colonies as their territories were thrown open for development.

## HUMANITARIAN CONQUEST

Since the beginning of European colonial expansion, authorities on international law maintained that indigenous peoples held legitimate group rights to political sovereignty and territory that could be taken from them only by treaty or military conquest. Tribal groups were considered to be autonomous sovereign nations. Of course, tribal nations were often militarily weaker than the colonial powers that invaded their territories and were often easily defeated in war, but the important, internationally acknowledged legal point was that a formal written document had to define the relation between the invading power and the tribal nation. Such a document would specify the details of landownership and the degree of independence that the indigenous group might enjoy. This left room for the legal abuses of ethnocide, genocide, and ecocide that accompanied colonialism (see Chapter 11) and sparked the great debate over humanitarian policy. At the same time, failure to sign treaties, as was the case in Australia, deferred the question of specific rights and provided a basis for modern negotiations. Former agreements may also be renegotiated in reference to the higher in-

---

**nation**  A people with a common language, culture, and territory and who claims a common identity.

**Fourth World**  Indigenous peoples and small-scale cultures.

ternational standards of conduct toward indigenous peoples that have steadily evolved along with the emergence of the global system.

## Las Casas: "Indians Are Human"

The enormous human suffering caused by the commercially driven expansion of European civilization generated humanitarian concern almost immediately. One of the earliest and most outspoken advocates of humane treatment of indigenous people was Bartolome de Las Casas, a Catholic priest who accompanied the Spanish conquistadores to the New World in 1502. He participated in the conquest, attempting to convert the indigenes to Christianity, and was even awarded an *encomienda*. By 1514 he became convinced by experience that the Spanish system of colonialism was unjust. He freed the Indian serfs on his *encomienda* and began a life-long campaign against the exploitation and mistreatment of the indigenes. Las Casas composed a series of works condemning the worst abuses of colonialism, especially the *encomienda* system. In public debates with leading Spanish intellectuals, he championed the basic humanity of indigenous peoples, successfully challenging the concept that un-Christian Indians were subhuman inferiors who could be mistreated with impunity. Las Casas gained royal support in Madrid for his views, but the reforms that he proposed were never effectively implemented in the New World (Dussel 1975).

## The Select Committee and Aboriginal Protectors

Throughout their expanding colonial empire, the British used military force against resisting indigenous peoples, but they consistently drew up formal treaties to legalize the transfer of political authority and tribal lands to Europeans. British policy in Australia was a striking exception because the legal presence of the aborigines as mobile foragers was never acknowledged and no treaties were signed. The abuses of British colonialism, which flourished under such legalism, inspired a dedicated group of British humanitarians lead by Thomas Fowell Buxton, who formed the Anti-Slavery Society in 1823 and successfully campaigned for a ban on slavery throughout the empire by 1833.

In 1835 Buxton, like Las Casas, turned his attention to the larger humanitarian issue of the negative impact of colonialism on tribal peoples. Buxton, as a member of Parliament, persuaded the House of Commons to appoint a fifteen-member Select Committee to formulate official policies to protect the rights of tribal peoples and ensure their just treatment. The committee conducted an extensive survey of the impact of European civilization on tribal groups throughout the empire in order to document the existing injustices. Over a 10-month period, the committee interviewed more than forty witnesses from South Africa, Canada, Australia, New Zealand, the South Pacific, and British Guiana. The final published report was definitive. Issued in two volumes in 1836–1837, it contained more than 1000 oversize pages, weighing some 8 lb (3.6 kilograms) (an extract appears in Bodley 1988:63–69). The bulk of the report was a monotonous recital of physical atrocities, exploitation, and dispossession. The evidence overwhelmingly demonstrated that European colonialism was "a source of many calamities to uncivilized nations." The report elaborated:

*Too often, their territory has been usurped; their property seized; their numbers diminished; their character debased; the spread of civilization impeded. European vices and diseases introduced among them....* (House of Commons 1837:5)

The committee recommended nine specific corrective measures that it hoped would bring justice to tribal peoples without hindering the growth of British colonies. The first and most important measure acknowledged the inherent conflict between invading settlers and indigenous peoples and recommended that colonial governors in consultation with Queen and Parliament, and not local legislatures, should safeguard the rights of indigenous peoples. The committee also called for curbs on alcohol, strict controls on contract labor to prevent debt slavery, and a prohibition on the acquisition of tribal lands by settlers, arguing that there was enough empty land to satisfy the needs of settlers. Legal dispossession of tribal groups could still take place, but it required an act of Parliament; in such cases, dispossessed natives were to be protected and educated by missionaries who would be supported by the revenues the crown received from the sale of tribal lands. Thus, under the most liberally envisioned form of British justice at the time, the rights of natives were narrowly defined and remained secondary to the economic needs of the colonizers. This was a policy approach that could be characterized as **realist** because it advocated no major changes in the existing political relationship between a dominant state power and a subordinate indigenous people. Even these enlightened policies, however, were seldom effectively enforced.

After the Select Committee issued its report, the committee's work was continued by the Aborigines Protection Society (APS), an advocacy group formed by committee members under the direction of Thomas Hodgkin in 1836 to "promote the advancement of Uncivilized Tribes." The APS was a model humanitarian organization that played a decisive role throughout the nineteenth century in keeping government attention focused on the painful human cost of colonialism for tribal peoples and lobbying for protective policies. The first issue of the society's journal, the *Colonial Intelligencer; or Aborigines' Friend*, published in 1847, described the organization's purpose and activities:

*. . . To collect and diffuse information regarding the feeble and injured races in the various dependencies of the British Empire, and also in some parts of the globe not so connected with it. It has earnestly pleaded in their behalf with each successive Administration with which it has been contemporary; and scarcely a Colonial Governor has entered upon his important functions, without receiving from that Society a personal or written appeal in favour of those Aborigines who were likely in an especial manner, to come under his notice and influence.* (Colonial Intelligencer 1847, no. 1:4)

Through its network of branch societies and corresponding members, the APS was able to closely monitor the condition of native peoples throughout the empire and directly petition government officials to take humanitarian action. Appeals by the APS led to the establishment of aboriginal reserves and Protectors of Natives in Australia by 1850. These actions did not prevent the wholesale extinction of aborigines in many areas of Australia, but they did demonstrate that such injustice was officially disapproved. Aboriginal reserves at this time were not considered to be aboriginal lands where aborigines could live independently; instead, they served a dual protecting and "uplift" role. Reserves were to contain mission schools and farms where aborigines were to learn "civilized" skills.

Proimperialist humanitarian concern for the welfare of indigenous peoples did not envision the persistence of independent small-scale cultures and tended to discourage any cultural diversity. The APS did not go beyond the Select Committee's 1837 charter and remained a firm supporter of British imperialism, but even this limited application of the principle of human rights to indigenous people was an important development in the ideological system of the emerging global system.

## The Civilizing Crusade

Early international conventions containing humanitarian provisions designed to protect indigenous people were sometimes outrageously ethnocentric. For example, when the major imperialist powers met in Berlin in 1884–1885 to facilitate the colonial partitioning of Africa, they described their action as a "civilizing crusade" and pledged to support all efforts "to educate the natives and to teach them to understand and appreciate the benefits of civilization" (General Act of the 1884–1885 Berlin–Africa Conference). Because Africa was the last major world area colonized by Europeans, some 50 years after the Select Committee's report, it was already obvious that colonialism was unavoidably destructive. It would have been more humanitarian to have left Africa independent, but instead Europeans took control to protect their political and economic interests, justifying their action as an effort to end the illegal slave trade (Figure 14.2). By 1892 the Brussels Act effectively mandated ethnocide as part of the "uplift," or civilization, process by declaring that the colonizing powers should civilize tribal peoples and "bring about the extinction of barbarous customs."

---

***realist***  A policy position that maintains that indigenous peoples must surrender their political and economic autonomy and be integrated into dominant state societies.

In 1907 the APS tried to persuade the international Hague Peace Conference to ban wars of extermination and punitive military raids against relatively defenseless tribal groups. This would have been a logical extension of the rules of war covered in the various Geneva Conventions, which began in 1864 with the establishment of the International Red Cross. Unfortunately, the APS proposal was not placed on the agenda because the British prime minister objected.

Toward the end of World War I, the APS had another opportunity to promote the rights of indigenous people during international discussions on the fate of Germany's former colonies. These territories were scattered throughout Africa and the Pacific and contained some 30 million indigenous people, many still living independently. The APS recognized that ideally, if humanitarian considerations were primary, this would have been the time to grant full political sovereignty to existing tribal nations and grant self-determination to detribalized groups. However, the APS had now merged with the Anti-Slavery Society, and key people within the combined leadership, which included a member of Parliament, considered tribal independence impractical because it would threaten the colonial system. The vice-president of the new organization, Sir Harry Johnston, was a pioneer explorer and colonial administrator in East Africa, whose first loyalty was solidly with the empire. His rejection of tribal independence was emphatic:

*Supposing we consulted their [tribals] wishes and they did not want to come under Germany or any other foreign flag, but wanted to be left to themselves? I have seen too much of Africa, and of tropical America, to be able to subscribe to that. I feel that these backward races have to undergo a considerable period of tutelage before they can be safely left to themselves.* (Anti-Slavery Reporter and Aborigines' Friend 1917:53)

By this time, it was obvious that the humanitarian measures proposed by the Select Committee 80 years earlier, and all the "protection and uplift" efforts of the APS, had not prevented massive depopulation of tribal areas. The APS recognized that such large-scale loss of life threatened the labor supply and the success of the colonial venture, but they argued that it was still a problem that

could be corrected by policy reforms that left unchallenged the basic "civilizing" process of colonialism. These discussions, which ultimately determined the fate of countless tribal groups, were permeated with paternalistic, racist, and demeaning language. Tribal peoples were variously referred to as backward races, subject races, and child races. Under the mandate system, established by the League of Nations Covenant in 1919 to administer former German colonies, tribal peoples were called "peoples not yet able to stand by themselves under the strenuous conditions of the modern world." They were to be administered according to the principle that "the well-being and development of such peoples form a sacred trust of civilization" (League Covenant, Article 22).

## THE AUSTRALIAN ABORIGINAL POLICY DEBATE

The political fate of tribal groups is often determined by government policies, which are in turn shaped by the demands of varied special-interest groups exercising political power. As was shown in Chapter 11, anthropologists, and anthropological theory, have often played a role in shaping and supporting government policies toward indigenous peoples. This was certainly the case in Australia until the late 1960s, where some anthropologists helped sustain a colonial policy that denied aboriginal rights, while others urged policy reforms.

### Genocidal Protection and Uplift

The European invasion of Australia began in 1788 with the founding of Port Jackson, now Sydney, as a penal colony. Because the aborigines were not settled farming peoples and had no chiefs, colonial administrators declared Australia to be an "empty wasteland" and dispensed with treaty signing. The aborigines were given no legal existence and no official claim to their land. As elsewhere, genocide and ethnocide followed the Australian frontiers of European settlement. Except where aborigines were useful as labor, they were systematically eliminated by poison, disease, and shooting as if they were wild animals. Tasmania's aboriginal popula-

FIGURE 14.2   *This 1895 photo of Sir William E. Maxwell (seated on right), governor of the British Gold Coast colony, and a contingent of native police represents the political and military power used by Europeans to carry out the "civilizing crusade" formalized by the Berlin–Africa Conference of 1884–1885. (SOURCE: M. W. Sexton, Peabody Museum of Salem.)*

tion was reduced from 5000 to 111 within 30 years. In western Victoria, 4000 aborigines were reduced to 213 within 40 years, and 10 years later no one remained who could reliably describe the culture (Corris 1968). Witnesses before the Select Committee in the 1830s reported "many deeds of murder and violence" committed by settlers on the Australian frontier. This situation persisted well into the twentieth century. According to A. G. Price, in the Northern Territory in 1901, "It was notorious, that the blackfellows were shot down like crows and that no notice was taken" (1950:107–108).

The fact, which no one disputed, was that aborigines were facing extinction as a result of fron-

tier violence and dispossession. In contrast, from 1788 to 1880 the European population had increased from under 1 million to 3 million. By 1920 there were 5 million Europeans and barely 60,000 aborigines, just 20 percent of the widely accepted estimate of 300,000 for the pre-European population. All authorities anticipated a continuing decline in the aboriginal population, and many predicted their total extinction. Everyone agreed that the European invasion was responsible, but the government still followed the inadequate "protection and uplift" approach devised by the House of Commons Select Committee and the APS in the 1830s.

By 1880 the sparsely settled Northern Territory,

which contained 17 percent of Australia's land area, had become the last great frontier. There were fewer than 700 Europeans throughout the territory's 500,000 square miles (mi²) (1.3 million square kilometers [km²]) stretching from the desert center of Australia to the tropical north coast. This vast, seemingly inhospitable region was the ancestral homeland of unknown thousands of aborigines still living independently. European Australians saw the territory as a great pastoral frontier. There was still no national policy to allow the aborigines to defend themselves, their resources, and their culture against the final invasion that was just beginning.

The government encouraged immigration into the territory to promote economic development, fully aware that the aborigines would be victimized. To minimize the damage, humanitarians such as Sydney's Archdeacon Lefroy (1912) recommended federal control of all aborigines by a permanent Native Commission and urged the formation of reserves on which aborigines could be preserved and uplifted by becoming cattle ranchers. A committee of the Australasian Association for the Advancement of Science, which included pioneer central Australian ethnographers Spencer and Gillen, drafted a resolution to the government that followed Lefroy's proposals. The committee emphasized that aborigines were "a valuable labor asset" in the pastoral economy as a justification for a preservation policy. There was no attempt to protect aboriginal culture, except in museums, or to defend aboriginal political autonomy; instead, the emphasis was on "the well-being and preservation of the native race," presumably as units of labor (ANZAAS 1914). But even these modest ameliorative proposals were ineffective.

By 1920 there were some 4000 Europeans and 600,000 cattle in the Northern Territory, steadily advancing against an aboriginal population estimated at 17,000 who faced a grim future. A mere 30,000 mi² (77,770 km²), barely 6 percent of the territory, had been designated for aboriginal reserves, even though the aborigines were the majority population, still outnumbering Europeans more than four to one. The reserves contained cattle stations and missions where the aborigines were to be "civilized," just as the APS envisioned in the nineteenth century.

## Reserves, Assimilation, and Land Rights

As the situation for aborigines in the Northern Territory became increasingly desperate, anthropologist Frederic Wood Jones (1928) issued a stinging condemnation of the established policy of limited protectionism and uplift. In an emotional presidential address to the anthropology section of the Australasian Association for the Advancement of Science in 1926, Wood Jones declared that civilizing the aborigine, whether on missions or cattle stations, meant extermination. Using missionary reports, he showed that aborigines in the best condition were the most remote from civilization. Missionized aborigines were unhealthy and ill-housed and continued to die. Arguing that the missions were a form of humanitarian euthanasia that had failed in every sense, Wood Jones concluded, "I fail to see any sort of justification for a belief that salvation for the Australian native can ever lie in this direction" (1928:504).

Wood Jones was just as critical of the government effort to provide welfare to the aborigines on the fringes of civilization. He suggested that it was a form of conscience money that served to hide the fact that aborigines were being dispossessed. He also challenged the belief that the aborigine could be converted to a "coolie" population to provide cheap labor for the pastoral stations. He pointed out that although individuals might become successful station hands, they did not reproduce to replace themselves. There seemed to be no substitute for the traditional independent life.

Wood Jones argued that the existing reserves were "fictions and frauds" because they existed only on paper and were revoked whenever outside economic interests demanded entry: "There are no real reserves in Australia where the aborigine is free to live, what everyone is agreed on calling, a life uncontaminated by the white man" (1928:513).

A "real reserve" in Wood Jones's terms would be one that allowed the continuation of tribal "culture and traditions." Melbourne anthropologist Donald Thomson (1938) proposed making Arnhem Land, in the far north of the Northern Territory, just such a reserve after he conducted a government-commissioned field investigation there in 1935–1937. Some 1500 aborigines were still living independently in Arnhem Land, and

FIGURE 14.3
*Big Bill Neidjie and his son Jonathan Yarra-marna visit a sacred site on their clan land in Kakadu National Park, Northern Territory, Australia. The park was created in 1979 as part of an agreement permitting uranium mining on aboriginal land in Arnhem Land.*

when five Japanese fishermen and a policeman were killed in the reserve, the government hoped Thomson could help settle the matter peacefully. Thomson was trained in functionalist applied anthropology by A. R. Radcliffe-Brown at Sydney, but he was also a close associate of Wood Jones. Thomson's sympathies were clearly with the aborigines. He concluded that the killings were self-defense, and he recommended that Arnhem Land be made an absolutely inviolable reserve, with missionaries and ranchers excluded, in order to allow the aborigines freedom to maintain their nomadic settlement pattern, culture, and social structure (Figure 14.3). This was perhaps the first time that an *idealist* policy approach was seriously proposed for Australia.

This approach was soundly rejected by Sydney anthropologist A. P. Elkin (1891–1979), who represented the vested interests of the government and missionary organizations. Elkin was an influential and outspoken advocate of "justice" for aborigines, but he also wanted to secure a place for both anthropology and missions in the business of smoothing what he considered to be the inevitable *assimilation* of aborigines from their independent tribal life into a settled existence within civilized Australian society. Trained by Radcliffe-Brown and Bronislaw Malinowski in functionalist applied anthropology, Elkin became a leading expert on aboriginal culture but also accepted Radcliffe-Brown's ominous dictum that "the Australian Aborigines, even if not doomed to extinction as a race, seem at any rate doomed to have their cultures destroyed" (1930:3).

As an anthropologist, Elkin clearly understood the centrality of totemism in aboriginal culture but considered it an obsolete and ignorant belief that was to be replaced by ". . . a religious and philosophical outlook which will enable them [the aborigines] to see that their own spiritual life and the future of natural species is not bound up with the integrity of particular spots on the earth's surface" (1934:7).

Oblivious to his own ethnocentrism and convinced that the culture was doomed, Elkin went on

---

*idealist*  A policy position that advocates cultural autonomy for indigenous peoples as a basic human right.
*assimilation*  Ethnocide without genocide; the loss of distinctive cultural traits as a population surrenders its autonomy and is absorbed into a dominant society and culture.

to suggest, "Wise teaching on religion and in the rudiments of science should do much to enable the natives to pass through the difficult transition period for which we are responsible" (1934:7).

The irony of this is that the aborigines were right on this very critical issue. Totemism was not a matter of tribal ignorance over which the aborigines needed to be "educated." The spiritual life of aborigines and the future of their natural resources are literally tied to the ultimate integrity of their sacred sites, but it was nearly 40 years before government policy grudgingly came to acknowledge this point with the Northern Territory Land Rights Act of 1971. Accepting the validity of the totemic system would have meant also acknowledging the legitimacy of the aboriginal claim to full control over their land, resources, and political and economic independence.

Rather than advocating aboriginal rights, Elkin called for a "positive policy" for aborigines, based on close collaboration between church and state to promote "education as well as law, order, harmony, and pacification." Elkin was a religious man, ordained in 1915 as an Anglican priest, and was in charge of a parish until 1937. Combining his religious role with his training as an applied anthropologist, he advised missionaries to "build on the religious life of the natives, modifying it where necessary, and seeking its fulfillment along Christian lines" (Elkin 1933:6).

Elkin opposed any aboriginal claim to the land that would stand in the way of outside development interests. In his view, keeping whites off the reserves, "of course, cannot be done once gold or valuable land be found in them." Elkin's policy approach was probably related to his position in the Sydney anthropology department, which he began to chair in 1934. The department developed an applied program under Radcliffe-Brown's earlier direction and with Rockefeller Foundation grants. The Sydney program was designed to support the government's colonial development policies, and Elkin emphatically disassociated his department from any support for aboriginal autonomy:

*It should be stated quite clearly and definitely that anthropologists connected with the Department in the University of Sydney have no desire to preserve any of the aboriginal tribes of Australia or of the islands in their pristine condition as "museum specimens" for the purpose of investigation; this charge is too often made against anthropologists . . . for change is coming, and anthropologists, like all good members of a "higher" and trustee race, are concerned with the task of raising primitive races in the cultural scale.* (1934:3)

Twenty years later, Elkin's assimilation approach was still the government's solution to the "aboriginal problem." In 1952 Paul Hasluck, minister for territories, publicly attacked "a few," unnamed anthropologists whose "mystical" belief in "changeless primitive culture" had led them to advocate strict inviolability of aboriginal reserves. Hasluck declared contemptuously, "My view is that no society can live in such an isolated dreamland as that" (Hasluck 1953:156).

Of course, the real issue was not the existence of culture change but the political independence of tribal peoples and whether outsiders should be allowed to dictate the kind of changes that occur on tribal land. Hasluck inadvertently admitted that the government had no intention of respecting the boundaries of tribal reservations when he rhetorically asked, "Do we expect that they can remain static even if protected by imaginary lines, drawn around reserves, when a new and active society and culture are brought into their country?" (1953:157).

Hasluck knew the reserves were a sham, that the government would not permit tribal autonomy, yet he shamelessly argued that good social science culture change theory had led him to such a conclusion. The ethnocentric policy that Hasluck promoted was uncompromising assimilation, which he described in the following terms:

*A policy of assimilation means, to my mind, that we expect that, in the course of time, all persons of aboriginal blood or mixed-blood in Australia will live in the same manner as white Australians do, that they will have full citizenship, and that they will, of their own desire, participate in all the activities of the Australian community.* (1953:163)

The government continued this rigid policy of rejecting aboriginal **self-determination** and land rights into the 1970s when politically active aboriginal organizations began to publicly demand legal ownership of traditional lands. The protest began in 1971 when the government rejected aboriginal claims of ownership to the Arnhem Land Reserve. The aboriginal landowners wanted to protect their sacred sites by preventing a multinational mining company from strip mining bauxite inside the reserve. By 1973 the protest began to take on international dimensions, and the government appointed an Aboriginal Land Rights Commission to find a solution. The result was the Aboriginal Land Rights (Northern Territory) Act of 1976, which provided a legal mechanism for aboriginal communities to gain title to their traditional lands. This was a major victory for aborigines, although the act provided only limited protection from outside development and was later weakened by amendments. The real significance of the act was that it meant that the government was finally acknowledging the legitimacy of aboriginal culture and the right of aborigines to maintain themselves as independent communities.

## DECOLONIZATION AND HUMAN RIGHTS

The decolonization era, which began with the founding of the United Nations in 1945, was also the beginning of a gradual shift away from the paternalistic and ethnocentric basis of even the most humanitarian of colonial policies toward indigenous peoples. The United Nations and affiliated organizations such as the **International Labour Organisation** (ILO) provided an international framework within which the concept of human rights was steadily expanded to include indigenous peoples as cultural groups and to legitimize their struggle for self-determination. The extension of fundamental human rights to indigenous peoples has been a slow and difficult process, which required decisive participation by indigenous peoples themselves.

### The United Nations and Indigenous People

The U.N. Charter provided an opening for indigenous rights, but it still contained ethnocentric thinking. Article 1 of the charter proclaimed support for "the principle of equal rights and self-determination of peoples," but it did not define

peoples. The only provision in the charter specifically applicable to indigenous peoples were in Chapters XI–XIII describing the international **trusteeship system.** The "Declaration Regarding Non-Self-Governing Territories" in Article 73 ethnocentrically speaks of "territories whose peoples have not yet attained a full measure of self-government." This language was obviously ethnocentric when applied to Pacific islanders with functioning chiefdoms, but it was equally patronizing to call small-scale cultures "nonself-governing" when they clearly managed their own internal affairs without formal government. Many "nonself-governing territories" were already under the League of Nations mandate system, and the framers of the U.N. Charter borrowed from the League of Nations Covenant when they referred to a "sacred trust" to promote "the well-being of the inhabitants of these territories." There are demeaning references to "stages of advancement" and "constructive measures of development," which were direct carry-overs from the "protection and uplift" civilizing policies of the colonial era.

From the perspective of indigenous peoples, the early institutionalization of international development under the U.N. system represented a direct continuation of the old colonialism under new leadership. Fortunately, additional international covenants helped expand the concept of human rights, providing a framework that indigenous political leaders could build on. For example, Article 22 of the 1948 U.N. Declaration of Human Rights states that everyone is entitled to the realization of the "cultural rights indispensable for his dignity and the free development of his personality." This was amplified by the International Covenant of Human Rights, adopted by the U.N. General Assembly in 1966:

*. . . In those states in which ethnic, religious or linguistic*

---

**self-determination**   The right of any people to freely determine its own cultural, political, and economic future.
**International Labour Organisation**   A specialized agency of the United Nations concerned with work and living conditions in member states; originally founded in 1919 as a League of Nations affiliate.
**trusteeship system**   U.N. supervision designed to convert former colonial territories into independent states.

*minorities exist, persons belonging to such minorities shall not be denied the right, in community with the other members of their group, to enjoy their own culture, to profess and practice their own religion or to use their own language.*

This is a significant statement because it refers specifically to the human rights of cultural groups, as group rights, whereas most earlier international declarations have referred to individual human rights.

## ILO Convention 107

The first attempt to write an international convention devoted entirely to the relationship between indigenous people and governments was undertaken by the ILO in 1946 in cooperation with the United Nations, UNESCO, FAO, and WHO. Anthropologists were directly involved in this historic, 11-year effort, which culminated in 1957 when the General Conference of the ILO adopted "Convention (No. 107) concerning the protection and integration of indigenous and other tribal and semi-tribal populations in independent countries" (United Nations 1959).

ILO Convention 107, a curiously ambiguous document that attempted to raise a new standard for the rights of indigenous people, fell short of its goal because it failed to incorporate the viewpoint of indigenous peoples themselves. Convention 107 made a strong statement in support of the human rights of tribal individuals while endorsing government programs that directly undermine tribal cultures. The key contradiction is found in Article 7:

*These populations shall be allowed to retain their own customs and institutions where these are not incompatible with the national legal system or the objectives of integration programmes.*

This convention merits careful study because the issues that it defined are still being debated. The following section details the background to the writing of Convention 107 in order to show how ethnocentric misunderstanding of small-scale cultures can weaken even the most well-intended humanitarian efforts.

The ILO was created at the end of World War I as a League of Nations affiliate concerned with international labor conditions and standard of living. It became a U.N. affiliate, and by 1980 its membership included 144 countries. The ILO's original interest in indigenous peoples were restricted to labor problems in colonial territories. In 1946 the ILO expanded its concerns to include general issues of economic development and indigenous people, and it established a Committee of Experts on Indigenous Labor.

The general approach to "the problem of Indigenous populations" expressed at the committee's first meeting in 1951 indicated that indigenous peoples would be treated ethnocentrically as impoverished and underdeveloped people in need of development. This narrow interpretation closely followed the U.N. Economic and Social Council (ECOSOC) view of global poverty and underdevelopment, which launched the United Nation's development campaign at precisely the same moment (see Chapter 13). According to ILO experts, indigenous people were disadvantaged because they were backward and ignorant. Their legal "rights" were being denied because they were not able to participate fully in development progress. The solution was formal education, economic development, new forms of political organization, and special legislation.

ILO experts identified *integration* of indigenous people into the national society as the best policy objective. Integration would help tribal groups "progress" and raise their "cultural level" so that they would overcome their social and economic "inferiority," but integration left little room for the existence of independent small-scale cultures. The committee noted that tribal culture might already seem "attractive" and change might disturb prior ecological balances, but they concluded that "the scientist must accept the fact that social change is inevitable as a result of the general economic and social development of the community" (ILR 1951:64).

At the same time, the committee expressed confidence that applied social science could overcome any problems. However, recognizing the potential for damage, efforts were to be made to set "standards that would prevent the indigenous groups from being overwhelmed" by change. Governments were to create special vocational training programs to provide

*. . . the aboriginals with proper opportunity to develop fully their occupational abilities, so as to improve their conditions of life, to obtain the greatest benefit to the national economy and to assist in their assimilation into the cultural life of the nation.* (ILR 1951:65)

It was argued that vocational training could be used to improve the existing subsistence economy of a tribal group in order to raise their living standard, but it could also be used to modify the culture more directly (Figure 14.4). The report specifically recommended that, in some cases, "an attempt should be made to change the direction of the traditional activities of the group" (ILR 1951:65). It was suggested that special extension agents could deliver "oral advice" to tribal groups on such matters as agricultural methods, handicrafts, and "good habits of living" (ILR 1951:66).

A second ILO Committee of Experts was convened in 1954 to discuss how to protect and integrate forest-dwelling indigenous groups such as Amazonians. This fifteen-member committee was also flawed by ethnocentric preconceptions, even though it was chaired by New Zealand anthropologist Ernest Beaglehole and included two other prominent anthropologists, Horace Miner, an American, and Darcy Ribeiro, a Brazilian. The committee's agenda was limited to helping forest-dwelling "populations" adapt to forced development change. The committee acknowledged that the expansion of "technologically advanced societies" into formerly isolated tribal refuges was disturbing ecological balances and cultural patterns and breaking up tribal communities, marginalizing tribal individuals and leaving them easy prey to economic exploitation. However, instead of condemning the invasion of tribal lands, the experts blamed the victims by declaring that tribal peoples were "marginalized" because "they have failed to identify themselves with the values of technologically advanced societies" (ILR 1954:422).

By accepting the state's right to invade tribal areas in the interest of economic development, the Committee of Experts was placed in an ambiguous and contradictory position, and this contradiction was incorporated into ILO Convention 107. The experts endorsed a tribal right to self-fulfillment, to retain their traditional lands, and to move freely across national boundaries, but the committee re-

FIGURE 14.4
*An Ashaninka shaman processing sheets of raw rubber for sale at a mission station in the Peruvian Amazon.*

fused to condemn the greatest threat to these noble objectives—the state's right to "integrate" tribal peoples on its own terms.

The Committee of Experts described all tribal groups as occupying various stages on their way toward "inevitable" integration with national society. Totally independent tribes represented the first stage of integration. When the integration process was inadequately directed, stage two was characterized by violence, disease, disorder, ecological disruption, and other direct assaults on tribal culture. Stage three involved collapse of the tribal system and social disintegration, followed by margin-

---

***integration*** The absorption of a formerly autonomous people into a dominant state society with the possible retention of ethnic identity.

alization of former tribal individuals in stage four. The experts argued optimistically that these negative outcomes could be avoided by more carefully planned integration programs, backed by special protective legislation. They envisioned a limited "cultural autonomy" for tribal groups who would be integrated into a pluralistic national society, where economic development would mutually benefit all groups. Successfully integrated tribal peoples would "identify themselves with the values of technologically advanced societies." This positive outcome mirrored the "benefits of civilization" approach advocated by the nineteenth-century humanitarians and was equally prone to failure.

Like the anthropologists who identified the obstacles to economic progress in peasant cultures, ILO experts recognized that successfully adapted indigenous groups might resist imposed integration. The committee found that "isolated" tribal groups were healthy and self-sufficient, yet this was called "an undesirable state of segregation" (ILR 1954:424) because it perpetuated tribal culture, thereby blocking successful integration. Committee chairman, Ernest Beaglehole was explicit on the value of applied anthropology in implementing culture change programs:

*The anthropologist, through his detailed knowledge of indigenous life, can note the areas of resistance, blockage and susceptibility to change, so that local patterns will be circumvented or utilised in order to reduce friction and resistance.* (1954:432)

Because force was not supposed to be employed in helping tribal groups realize their "inexorable destiny," the central problem for planners was "how to produce a shift from the satisfactions that indigenous forest dwellers find in their own societies to the satisfactions normally found in modern society" (Beaglehole 1954:424).

The experts proposed a 4-point program for a combined "protection–integration" action plan:

1. *The safeguarding, preservation and development of the indigenous forest-dwelling population's economic base*

2. *The raising of its standard of living*

3. *The development of medical and health action with the object of maintaining at least the same health conditions as existed before contact with the invading society*

4. *The development of fundamental education* (Beaglehole 1954:425)

This program may have sounded promising, but it supported external conquest and invasion and was founded on outrageously ethnocentric assumptions. In a series of resolutions, the committee declared that tribal groups were socially and economically "impoverished," their subsistence was "inadequate," and they were unhygienic. They needed outside technical experts to teach the "best agricultural, stock-rearing, forestry and handicraft techniques." They needed to be taught how to work efficiently, maintain subsistence reserves, and prevent waste and resource depletion and "irrational" deforestation. Tribal groups needed to be told how to ensure the equitable distribution of water resources. They needed to grow more crop varieties and increase their economic independence.

Ironically, undisturbed tribal peoples were doing just fine in all of these areas before outside intrusion, whereas "integration" created the very conditions of impoverishment that it intended to prevent. This negative view of tribal culture likely resulted, in part, because the first Committee of Experts was primarily concerned with the most depressed and exploited Andean peasantry and tended to generalize their unhappy condition to *all* tribal peoples, while attributing its cause to the indigenous culture rather than the national political and economic structures that encouraged oppression.

The committee's final resolution was contradictory because, although they advocated respect for tribal culture "as a legitimate way of life," they accepted the self-fulfilling prophecy that tribal peoples were "doomed to change." Committee members were divided over whether change should be rapid or slow, but they all agreed that development would be imposed. As Horace Miner explained, "The realist recognizes the inevitability of increasing encroachment of civilization on the remaining outposts of preliterate culture" (1955:441).

The drafting of Convention 107 presented anthropologists with a golden opportunity to create a blueprint for the independence of small-scale cultures, but the momentum of global economic development was too strong. Convention 107 failed to support indigenous rights because it made the economic goals of global-scale state cultures the primary objective.

## Indigenous Organizations and ILO Convention 169

In the 1960s and 1970s, indigenous peoples throughout the world began to form political organizations to press their demands for full control over their traditional lands and communities. Indigenous organizations emerged at local, national, and international levels. In Amazonia, the Shuar of Ecuador were among the first to organize when they formed a federation in 1964 to unite communities fragmented by land invasions. Similar groups exist in other Amazon countries, including Peru. At the international level, the **World Council of Indigenous Peoples** (WCIP) was formed in 1975, with delegates drawn from indigenous organizations from throughout the world. The WCIP is one of the only indigenous organizations to have **nongovernmental organization** (NGO) status with the United Nations. This allows it to play a consultative role in deliberations before ECOSOC and U.N. affiliates such as the ILO. The primary objective of the WCIP is "to ensure political, economic, and social justice to indigenous peoples."

At the Fourth Assembly of the WCIP, which was held in Panama in 1984, some 300 indigenous people from twenty-three countries drew up a Declaration of Principles of Indigenous Rights. This declaration clearly defines the international standards that should define their position relative to state governments and international institutions. Three of the most critical principles are the following:

*Principle 1. All indigenous peoples have the right of self-determination. By virtue of this right they may freely determine their political status and freely pursue their economic, social, religious and cultural development.*

*Principle 9. Indigenous peoples shall have exclusive rights to their traditional lands and its resources; where the lands and resources of the indigenous peoples have been taken away without their free and informed consent such lands and resources shall be returned.*

*Principle 12. No action or course of conduct may be undertaken which, directly or indirectly, may result in the destruction of land, air, water, sea, ice, wildlife, habitat or natural resources without the free and informed consent of the indigenous peoples affected.*

Indigenous organizations are supported by various religious, environmentalist, and human rights groups in many countries. International organizations such as **Cultural Survival,** the **International Work Group for Indigenous Affairs** (IWGIA), and **Survival International,** which are directed by anthropologists, have played important support roles for indigenous organizations as fund-raisers and by helping them establish national and international contacts where their views can be expressed.

A new possibility for raising the international standard on the rights of indigenous peoples arose in 1985 when the ILO decided to revise its 1957 Convention 107 on the protection and integration of indigenous peoples. Even though Convention 107 was only ratified by twenty-six states, it remained the principal international convention on indigenous rights. The ILO hoped to remove the integrationist tone of the old convention, while keeping the basic document intact. Indigenous groups and their supporters wanted a revised convention to be a strong statement in support of indigenous rights to self-determination and urged removal of the old convention's ethnocentric emphasis on integration and development and its ambiguity concerning indigenous land rights.

---

**World Council of Indigenous Peoples**   An organization of indigenous peoples, founded in 1975, who represent indigenous organizations and political leaders from many parts of the world.

**nongovernmental organization**   A group that is formally recognized by the United Nations and allowed to participate in certain U.N. functions, even though it does not represent governments.

**Cultural Survival**   A proindigenous people organization formed by American anthropologists in 1972 and based in Cambridge, Massachusetts.

**International Work Group for Indigenous Affairs**   A Copenhagen-based organization formed by anthropologists in 1968 to support indigenous peoples.

**Survival International**   A London-based organization formed in 1969 to support indigenous peoples.

A new "Committee of Experts" took up the question in Geneva at formal meetings in 1986, 1988, and 1989. This time indigenous people were permitted at least token representation, but the final wording and approval of the revision rested with the one hundred or so "experts" who represented employers, governments, and workers, and not with indigenous people. The WCIP, IWGIA, and Survival International were allowed to speak as NGOs, but they could exercise only indirect influence. The proceedings were also attended by official and unofficial indigenous observers representing various native groups from North and South America, India, and Australia, but they remained on the sidelines (Gray 1987).

As discussion proceeded, two familiar arguments emerged, and the specific terms used and precise definitions became critical matters. Experts representing the ILO, employers, and some governments urged realism and proposed that indigenous peoples be granted the right to participation and consultation in the process of integration and development. Indigenous people assumed that participation and consultation still meant integration, and they insisted on self-determination with indigenous consent and control over government policies that might affect them. They wanted the power to veto undesirable development programs and refused to be seen as passive participants in programs already designed by others. The realists also wanted to retain the original language of 107 that referred to "populations," thereby avoiding references to specific cultural characteristics that defined *peoples* as groups. Recognizing that cultural uniqueness was the most fundamental issue, indigenous people insisted that the term *people* should replace *population* in a new convention.

The indigenous representatives objected to the old convention's derogatory references to "stages" of development and integration. They also wanted to greatly expand references to "land" to refer to "territories of the earth," to emphasize their claims to land, water, ice, and air. Indigenous people considered themselves to be "custodians" of inalienable resources, not *owners* in the market economy sense. When the final deliberations appeared to be supporting the old integrationist approach, the Australian aboriginal delegation withdrew in protest. Delivering an impassioned speech, aboriginal representative Geoff Clarke declared,

*. . . We define our rights in terms of self-determination. We are not looking to dismember your States and you know it. But we do insist on the right to control our territories, our resources, the organisation of our societies, our own decision-making institutions, and the maintenance of our own cultures and ways of life. . . . Do you think that we are unaware of the actual meaning of words like consultation, participation and collaboration? Would you be satisfied with "consultation" as a guarantee for your rights? Unless governments are obligated to obtain our consent, we remain vulnerable to legislative and executive whims that inevitably will result in further dispossession and social disintegration of our peoples. The victims are always the first to know how the system operates. (IWGIA Yearbook 1988, 1989:184)*

A final revision was approved by the ILO in 1989 as Convention 169. It did eliminate most of the ethnocentric language, but the contradictory emphasis on integration remained. The term *people* was introduced but was avowed to have no legal significance. Over the objections of indigenous leaders, governments retained responsibility for development and policymaking, with indigenous peoples relegated to "participation" and "cooperation." There were references to respect for indigenous culture and recognition of land rights, but the qualifications and escape clauses were so numerous that, in many respects, less real protection was provided than in the original covenant. Not surprisingly, the new convention has been widely rejected by indigenous peoples (Gray 1990).

## The Universal Declaration on Rights of Indigenous Peoples

Indigenous political organizations have presented their viewpoints on indigenous rights before a variety of U.N. human rights forums, beginning in 1977 when more than fifty indigenous leaders were invited to attend the International Conference on Discrimination Against Indigenous Populations in the Americas, organized in Geneva by the special U.N. Committee on Human Rights. Similar conferences followed, and in 1982 a special Working Group on Indigenous Peoples

(WGIP) was established by the U.N. Sub-Commission on the Prevention of Discrimination and Protection of Minorities, of the U.N. ECOSOC Commission on Human Rights. The WGIP was directed to draft a Universal Declaration of Indigenous Rights for final adoption by the U.N. General Assembly in 1992. In this case, there was direct involvement of many indigenous groups in the proceedings and in the drafting of the declaration. In contrast to the ILO Convention, the real concerns of indigenous peoples with guaranteeing self-determination and preventing genocide, ethnocide, and ecocide were specifically addressed. The first revised draft, issued in 1988, listed thirty rights of indigenous peoples, including:

3. *The (collective) right to exist as distinct peoples and to be protected against genocide. . . .*

5. *The individual and collective right to protection against ethnocide. This protection shall include, in particular, prevention of any act which has the aim or effect of depriving them of their ethnic characteristics or cultural identity, of any form of forced assimilation or integration, of imposition of foreign life-styles and of any propaganda derogating their dignity and diversity.*

12. *The right of collective and individual ownership, possession and use of the lands or resources which they have traditionally occupied or used. The lands can only be taken away from them with their free and informed consent as witnessed by a treaty or agreement.*

16. *The right to protection of their environment and in particular against any action or course of conduct which may result in the destruction, deterioration or pollution of their traditional habitat, land, air, water, sea, ice, wildlife or other resources without free and informed consent of the indigenous peoples affected. . . .*

23. *The (collective) right to autonomy in matters relating to their own internal and local affairs, including education, information, culture, religion, health, housing, social welfare, traditional and other economic activities, land and resources administration and the environment. . . .* (IWGIA Yearbook 1989, 1990: 151–158)

These rights represent a significant departure from the ethnocentric uplift and limited protectionism of the colonial era. They are also a clear repudiation of the forced integration policies that were called "inevitable" by the realists during the modern era of economic development. These new indigenous rights, if they are recognized by the international community, will provide a firm basis for the coexistence of small-scale cultures within the global system. However, as the draft declaration declares in Article 29, "These rights constitute the minimum standards for the survival and the well-being of the indigenous peoples of the world."

The following case study from Amazonia shows how indigenous groups are continuing to be dispossessed by national development and integration programs that ignore these most basic of human rights.

## NATIONAL INTEGRATION IN AMAZONIA

Because ILO Convention 107 was written with the welfare of Amazonians specifically in mind and because most Amazonian countries signed the convention, it is especially relevant to examine the effects of national integration programs that have been carried out in Amazonia and to consider policy alternatives.

Historically, the European invasion of Amazonia nearly annihilated the indigenous populations. In 1500, when Amazonia was first claimed by Europeans, there may have been as many as 6.8 million native residents (Denevan 1976), but by 1970 the population had declined by nearly 90 percent to less than 1 million. Ribeiro (1957) reported that in Brazil more than one-third of the indigenous groups known in 1900 were extinct by 1957, the year ILO 107 was adopted. In 1968 the Brazilian government revealed that officials of the Indian Protection Service had conspired with wealthy landowners to remove indigenes from their lands using machine guns, dynamite, poison, and disease. Thousands must have died in an extermination process that rivaled the worst abuses of the early colonial period. Native dispossession and deaths were accelerated when construction of the transamazon highway system began in 1970, followed by large-scale colonization, agricultural development, mining, and hydroelectric projects (Davis 1977).

## The Ashaninka Versus Global Development

The Ashaninka (Campa) of eastern Peru, who were introduced in Chapters 1 and 3, provide a useful case study of the integration process in Amazonia. In the 1960s, some 21,000 Ashaninka were still the principal occupants of their vast homeland in the forested eastern foothills of the Andes in central Peru. They were highly self-sufficient and only minimally involved with the market economy. Their first contacts with Europeans occurred in the 1500s, and over the next two centuries, Franciscan missionaries gradually established outposts throughout the region and imposed their own culture change program. However, the Ashaninka resented Franciscan disapproval of polygyny and other restrictions on their freedom. They destroyed the missions in 1742 and enjoyed complete independence for more than 100 years, demonstrating that the integration process was reversible, not inevitable.

The situation began to change in the 1870s when the Republic of Peru turned to Amazonia as a frontier of national expansion. Ashaninka territory was critical to government planning because it controlled the river pathways to the Amazon, but explorers and missionaries entering the area were frequently met with a rain of Ashaninka arrows. Military force and gift giving eventually overcame most Ashaninka resistance and cleared the way for colonists. A regional economic boom began after the Pichis Trail was successfully opened in 1891 as a mule road through the Ashaninka homeland to a navigable point on the Pichis River, and a huge tract of Ashaninka land was deeded to an English company for a coffee plantation. This development activity caused many Ashaninka to experience all the negative aspects of the uncontrolled frontier and led to further hostilities. In 1913–1914, frustrated Ashaninka warriors armed themselves with guns and attacked missions and outposts in the Pichis Valley, killing 150 settlers before they, in turn, were defeated by troops.

After these events until the 1960s, the government took little interest in the region. Scattered groups of fully independent Ashaninka dominated the remote areas, while the more accessible riverine zones were only lightly settled by outsiders who established missions, small cattle ranches, and farms, following successive economic waves of rubber and lumber extraction. The Ashaninka still maintained a viable culture after more than 400 years of colonial intrusion, but their future began to be seriously threatened by a shift in government policy that began in 1960 with the Plan Peruvia, which selected some 45,000 mi$^2$ (116,550 km$^2$) in Amazonia, including most of the Ashaninka area, for a long-term economic development plan. A special unit (ONERN) was established, with U.S. AID funds, to evaluate the natural resources in the zone and to formulate a detailed development proposal. Military engineer units, supported by U.S. military-assistance programs, began constructing a network of "penetration" highways that would provide the primary infrastructure for the project.

In 1965 Peruvian President Fernando Belaunde-Terry (1965) announced a definitive economic "conquest" of Amazonia. Ignoring the native population, he characterized the region as underpopulated and underexploited and promised that developing Amazonia would solve the overpopulation, poverty, food shortages, and land scarcity of the Andean and coastal zones. Indeed, Peru's population had tripled since 1900 and exceeded 10 million by 1965. However, the real issue was inequality, not population growth, because the Inca empire had supported an even larger population without invading Amazonia. The government's development program was simply an accelerated eastward extension of the national market economy, which had already generated Andean poverty and was now impoverishing the rain forest Amazonians. The new, multimillion-dollar program was eventually cofinanced by U.S. AID, the U.N. Development Programme, the World Bank, and the Inter-American Development Bank, contributing to a vast increase in Peru's external public debt from $856 million in 1970 to $12.4 billion in 1988. This debt arrangement helped make Peru a poor client state and made the fate of Amazonians and the forest ecosystem ultimately dependent on management decisions made at the global level.

My own investigations in the region between 1965 and 1969 (Bodley 1970, 1972b), showed that when Belaunde's project began some 2500 Ashaninka still remained fully self-sufficient, whereas

FIGURE 14.5
*A newly recruited Asha-ninka labor crew being interviewed by the author in 1969.*

many others were drawn into exploitative **debt bondage** with **patrons** who offered cheap merchandise in exchange for labor (Figure 14.5). Many Ashaninka had already joined Protestant mission communities and were establishing a marginal and precarious niche in the expanding regional market economy. These new mission communities did not control an adequate land base and were quickly depleting local subsistence resources, increasing their dependence on purchased goods. This placed the Ashaninka at an enormous disadvantage in economic competition with the wealthier and more sophisticated colonists who were invading their lands.

The Ashaninka were largely ignored by development planners. For example, air-photo planning maps had "empty wasteland" printed over plainly visible Ashaninka garden plots. In the Tambo–Pajonal planning unit, a 5500-mi² (14,245-km²) roadless area occupied by 4000 Ashaninka, plans called for 560 miles (901 km) of roads and the introduction of 145,000 settlers (ONERN 1968). There were legal provisions for granting limited land titles to the Ashaninka in accord with the general principles of ILO 107, but no provision for those who preferred not to be integrated into the national economy.

Because these events coincided with the widely publicized Brazilian massacres, many anthropologists began making public statements on indigenous rights at this time. The 39th Americanist Congress, assembled in Lima, Peru, in 1970, issued "recommendations" condemning ethnocide and calling threatened Amazonian communities "oppressed peoples" in need of "national liberation." In 1971 Stefano Varese, a Peruvian anthropologist who had also worked with the Ashaninka, joined with Ribeiro and nine other anthropologists to draft the Declaration of Barbados (Bodley 1990). They stated that native lands were being treated as **internal colonies,** and they called on governments, the missions, anthropologists, and especially the tribal peoples themselves to work for tribal "liberation." Varese (1972), optimistic that Peru's new approach to agrarian reform would re-

---

**debt bondage**  An exploitative economic relationship that is managed to keep an individual in virtually perpetual indebtedness.
**patron**  A Spanish term for someone who extends credits or goods to a client who is kept in a debt relationship.
**internal colony**  A territory within a state containing an indigenous population that is denied the right of self-determination.

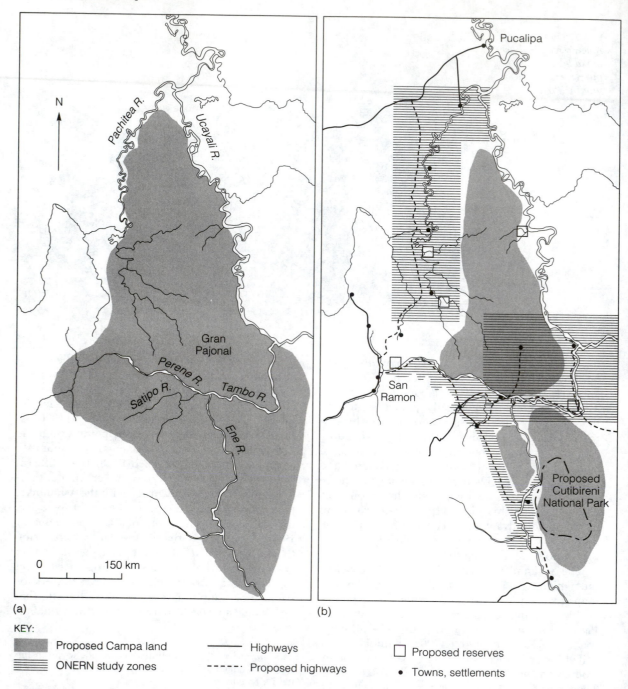

KEY:

| | | | |
|---|---|---|---|
| ▓ Proposed Campa land | —— Highways | ☐ Proposed reserves |
| ☰ ONERN study zones | - - - Proposed highways | ● Towns, settlements |

FIGURE 14.6  *(a) Ashaninka territory in 1850 before the most recent wave of colonization and development by outsiders. (b) The Ashaninka land cultural autonomy alternative proposed in 1970 shown in relation to new colonization and economic development zones.*

duce the exploitation and dependency of the forest Amazonians, proposed that special government teams encourage native groups to mobilize politically in their own defense. Precisely what form "liberation" would take was unclear.

## The Cultural Autonomy Alternative

In 1972 I proposed that the government demarcate the entire interfluvial upland zone as inviolable "Ashaninka land" (Figure 14.6). Development by outsiders would have been permanently prohibited in this vast 29,000-mi² (75,110-km²) territory, which encompassed most of the traditional Ashaninka homeland (Bodley 1972b). This was realistic given that the ONERN studies showed that most of this area was unsuitable for commercial agriculture, contained no important mineral resources, and was best maintained as a protected watershed. In lowland areas where integration was already underway, I recommended that very large reserves be established on the best agricultural soils to give market-oriented Ashaninka a competitive advantage. Later I called this approach the *cultural autonomy* alternative because it would allow small-scale cultures the opportunity of maintaining their independence; it specified three key points:

1. *National governments and international organizations must recognize and support tribal rights to their traditional land, cultural autonomy, and full local sovereignty.*

2. *The responsibility for initiating outside contacts must rest with the tribal people themselves: outside influences may not have free access to tribal areas.*

3. *Industrial states must not compete with tribal societies for their resources.* (Bodley 1975:169)

Granting this degree of autonomy to the Ashaninka would have forced drastic modifications in the government's programs, but the institutional momentum for large-scale development was so strong that the proposal was ignored. However, some aspects of cultural autonomy were coincidentally incorporated in Manu Park, a 5800-mi² (15,022-km²) environmental sanctuary established in the southern Peruvian Amazon in 1973. Independent tribal groups already living within the park were allowed to remain undisturbed as long

as they did not exploit park resources for commercial purposes (d'Ans 1972, 1981). The cultural autonomy alternative was rejected by some anthropologists who argued that it was based on an idealized concept of traditional cultures and would prevent the necessary political mobilization and economic development of indigenous peoples. For example, Danish anthropologist Peter Aaby stated, ". . . The 'cultural autonomy alternative' is only a policy against the nation state and not for any definite strategy of development for the marginal groups" (1977:71).

Of course, cultural autonomy must be implemented by governments. It is a strategy for allowing indigenous groups to chart their own course, not a strategy that nonindigenous experts can use to impose their own concept of development on target groups.

Varese opposed any "isolationist" policy in the Peruvian Amazon, declaring,

*. . . We must dissociate ourselves entirely from isolationist types of protective action on behalf of the natives. At bottom, these spring from an ethnocentric ideology which regards the tribal groups as culturally incapable and limited.* (Varese 1972:135)

Actually, "isolation" and "cultural potential" are irrelevant issues; what matters is whether indigenous peoples are allowed to control their own resources and cultural destiny. The anticultural autonomy arguments repeated the earlier Australian debate over aboriginal policy. Some missionaries firmly opposed native autonomy in Amazonia, arguing that it was "unrealistic" and "romantic" and would artificially deny indigenous people the benefits of Christianity (Wise, Loos, and Davis 1977). Like Elkin, Mary Ruth Wise and colleagues maintained that missionary intervention would help natives overcome maladaptive culture traits such as infanticide and shamanism and that Christianity would provide "spiritual help in facing the difficult life of the 20th century" (1977:521).

In 1974 anthropologist Richard Chase Smith (1977) proposed a development plan that would have allowed significant autonomy for the Yanesha

---

*cultural autonomy*  Self-determination by a cultural group.

(Amuesha), western neighbors of the Ashaninka, while protecting the vulnerable rain forest environment. Smith recommended creation of a 1200-mi² (3108-km²) zone, divided into three blocks as follows:

180 mi² (466 km²) in contiguous communal reserves, deeded to specific Yanesha communities to protect natural resources for their exclusive use

240 mi² (622 km²) in tribal territory for all Yanesha as a cultural group

780 mi² (2021 km²) in a national park as an environmental preserve

Smith's plan was initially approved by the Peruvian Ministry of Agriculture but was tabled by 1980 when the government actually began to implement its project to bring 150,000 agricultural colonists into the Pichis–Palcazu valleys and create a city of 20,000 people. No territory was deeded to the 12,000 resident Ashaninka and Yanesha for them to control as cultural groups, and less than half of the fifty-one scattered indigenous communities were given discrete village titles. This left the original inhabitants either landless or with fragmented blocks of land that were inadequate for either traditional subsistence activities or long-term commercial agriculture (Swenson and Narby 1986). Protests by a coalition of native organizations, religious and human rights groups, and anthropologists (*Amazonia Indigena* 1981) brought only token reforms represented by village land titles, community development advisors, and agricultural credits that fostered debt.

The World Bank, which provided $46 million for the Pichis Valley Project and cosponsored many similar projects that deprived indigenous groups of their resources and autonomy, responded to critics by issuing a position paper, "Tribal Peoples and Economic Development," by World Bank ecologist Robert Goodland (1982). The paper acknowledged that mistakes had been made in the past but argued that with "interim safeguards" it was possible to promote large development projects and still defend tribal people. Goodland reported that the Bank supported "cultural autonomy . . . until the tribe adapts sufficiently." Thus, they seemed to reject genuine cultural autonomy as a permanent policy.

Anthropologists Sally Swenson and Jeremy Narby, who investigated conditions in the Pichis Valley in the mid-1980s, observed that development policies at international, national, and regional levels need to be changed if indigenous groups like the Ashaninka are to benefit from development. They urged that indigenous political organizations be allowed to participate directly in planning affecting them and declared,

*A more appropriate approach would discourage colonization and place priority on the participation in development by current inhabitants; recognize native rights to, and title land sufficient for, subsistence and commercial production; and recognize the rationality of current native land use, incorporating native knowledge of the rainforest environment into development.* (Swenson and Narby 1986:24).

## SUMMARY

Since the policy debate began over how states should deal with tribal peoples, only two basic positions have been argued. A fundamental philosophical conflict exists between the realists, who advocate policies to help indigenous people adjust to the "inevitable" changes brought by colonialism or postcolonial national integration and economic development, and the idealists, who oppose the state-sponsored invasion of indigenous territories by colonists or externally imposed development projects. This philosophical split has obvious political implications for indigenous peoples. If the realists set national and international policies, indigenous peoples are likely to disappear as distinct cultural groups, whereas the idealist position will foster indigenous self-determination that will make cultural survival possible.

Throughout the nineteenth century and the first half of the twentieth century, the realist policy approach of adjustment and integration clearly dominated. However, since World War II, a more evolved international concept of human rights, fostered by the U.N. system, for the first time created conditions under which indigenous peoples themselves could develop their own formal political organizations and promote their own idealist perspective. This has given them the opportunity to directly shape international standards for the interaction between small-scale cultures and the larger state- and global-level forces surrounding them.

## STUDY QUESTIONS

1. Distinguish between the realist and the idealist position on policy toward indigenous peoples. Refer to specific examples, organizations, individuals, policies, or international conventions.

2. Define *indigenous people*. Differentiate between indigenous people and indigenous population. What are the limitations of the term *indigenous*? In what sense is *indigenous people* a political concept?

3. Why are the terms *tribal* and *primitive* sometimes avoided by anthropologists?

4. What features of small-scale cultures can be identified with indigenous peoples?

5. In what sense can indigenous peoples be referred to as *nations*? What is the *Fourth World*?

6. Describe the philosophical position and the policy recommendations of the Select Committee and the Aborigines' Protection Society. How were they actually applied?

7. In what way did colonial policy toward Australian aboriginals depart from standard British practice? How do you account for this?

8. Describe the different policies advocated by Wood Jones, Thompson, and Elkin in Australia. How did they defend their views?

9. In what way could the League of Nations mandate system, the U.N. Charter, and ILO Convention 107 be said to endorse ethnocentric policies that might be used to undermine the human rights of indigenous peoples?

10. What U.N. declarations or covenants provide a basis for the human rights of indigenous peoples?

11. Distinguish between the human rights of individuals and groups.

12. What were the assumptions of the anthropologists involved in drafting ILO Convention 107? How were they expressed in the convention?

13. Describe how Peru's economic development policies affected the Ashaninka and their neighbors. What alternative policies were proposed?

14. What is meant by *internal colonialism*? Use examples from Australia and Peru.

15. What are the most important human rights that indigenous peoples themselves define as the minimum conditions for their survival?

## SUGGESTED READING

BODLEY, JOHN H. 1988. *Tribal Peoples and Development Issues: A Global Overview*. Mountain View, Calif.: Mayfield. An edited collection of materials including case studies, policy positions, assessments, and recommendations on indigenous peoples and development issues throughout the world from the nineteenth century to the present.

BODLEY, JOHN H. 1990. *Victims of Progress*, 3rd ed. Mountain View, Calif.: Mayfield. Examines the official policies and underlying motives that have shaped the interaction between indigenous peoples and the members of global-scale culture since early in the nineteenth century. Includes many case studies drawn from throughout the world.

DAVIS, SHELTON H. 1977. *Victims of the Miracle: Development and the Indians of Brazil*. Cambridge, Eng.: Cambridge University Press. A critical analysis of the Brazilian government's development policies in the Amazon region and their impact on the native peoples.

# 15

# BEYOND 2000: THE FUTURE IN THE GLOBAL GREENHOUSE

As Bronislaw Malinowski (1944) pointed out long ago, culture is a mixed blessing because, in providing for basic human needs, it creates new, culturally derived needs and new problems for people to solve. Culture is both problem and solution, and the problems increase as culture scale increases. For example, farming as a means of subsistence intensification helped feed more people in a smaller area, but it also made it more difficult to maintain population stability and social equality. The problems generated by large- and small-scale cultures were often highly localized and occurred so imperceptibly that cultural adjustments were readily found and the tendency was toward equilibrium. The emergence of global culture, however, has completely changed the problem of human adaptation. The rate of culture change has become so rapid and its scale so vast that it is becoming increasingly difficult to respond effectively to new problems.

Today the world is threatened simultaneously by social and political conflict, impoverishment, resource depletion, and environmental deterioration on a level that few would have expected at the beginning of the twentieth century. These problems arise at global, national, and local levels and are so serious that the future of humanity and the biosphere itself is at risk for the first time in human existence. It would not be too dramatic to say that a global crisis exists. Major cultural adjustments will be required to see us through the twenty-first century.

The commercialization process that created the global culture has totally transformed and homogenized the planet in an astonishingly short time. Many of the most pervasive items of daily life such as computers, television, jet aircraft, nuclear power, and mass-produced organic compounds have come into worldwide use only since 1950. The scale and quality of fossil-fuel based industrial production and the unprecedented increases in global population and consumption within the past 200 years are depleting resources and altering the biosphere in ways that threaten the future viability of the global culture itself (Figure 15.1).

Previous cultural processes—whether the sapienization that generated language and small-scale culture, settled village life, farming and herding, or the politicization process that created social stratification, cities, and states—did not have such a sudden destabilizing effect. Small-scale cultures manipulated natural ecosystems in order to satisfy basic nutritional needs, but the changes they induced occurred over millennia and the tendency was toward equilibrium of population and resource consumption. Large-scale cultures promoted population growth and intensive food production in order to support political structures and social inequality. The environmental alterations produced by traditional states and empires were often drastic, but they occurred over centuries and were regional, not global, in their effects. The rise and fall of particular empires was a common and relatively insignificant event in the broad sweep of culture, but the breakdown of global culture would be devastating.

Global culture, driven by its consumption-based market economy, dominates the world's large- and small-scale cultures with its perpetually expanding quest for new resources and markets. This cultural domination is itself a problem because it leads to cultural homogeneity, which can reduce human adaptive potential. A multicultural world is not only a more diverse and interesting place, but it is also a way to develop and test alter-

native cultural solutions to common problems. Since 1950 vast resources have been dedicated to national defense, international development, and environmental protection, but many of these problems have only become more severe. Much of this problem-solving effort has been directed by specialists who offered purely technical solutions for what they assumed were isolated technical problems. The example of world poverty, examined in Chapter 13, suggests that the problems of global culture are actually cultural, not technical, problems. They are related to the most fundamental aspects of global culture and are thus best approached by a generalist anthropological perspective that takes cultural scale and diversity into account.

In this chapter, we assess the outlook for the world's peoples and cultures in the future beyond the year 2000 by focusing on three major issues: the potential for serious resource shortfalls, environmental deterioration such as through global warming and deforestation, and how a sustainable world might be designed.

FIGURE 15.1
*Steam rising from a nuclear power plant cooling tower in New Jersey dramatically symbolizes the sudden transformation of the planet brought about by the commercialization process. (SOURCE: Jeff Leone/Photo Researchers.)*

## LIMITS TO GROWTH IN A FINITE WORLD

### Energy, Adaptation, and the Evolution of Culture

One of the most widely held ideological features of global culture is the deceptive belief that evolutionary progress has given people greater control over nature, while increasing human security and adaptability. For example, anthropologist Yehudi Cohen (1974) treated hunting-gathering, cultivation, and industrialism as technological stages toward "freedom from environmental limitations." Cohen argued that progress meant a more secure food supply, suggesting with a seemingly trivial example that the ability to produce and market frozen strawberries represented "perhaps one of man's greatest achievements."

When viewed from a culture scale, rather than a strictly technological perspective, frozen berries illuminate some of the critical problems of global culture because commercialized berries primarily exist to make a profit for the stockholders of large food corporations, not to increase human food security. Nonrenewable fossil fuels are expended in berry production, refrigerated transport, and storage. Even more significantly, when Cohen wrote, many of America's supermarket strawberries were being produced by giant U.S. agribusinesses using Mexican land and labor in an exploitative international system that perpetuated poverty and inequality while damaging the environment (Feder 1978; Lappe, Collins, and Fowler 1979). Arguing that this is culturally "adaptive," either locally or globally, would be difficult.

Many older anthropological concepts of cultural evolution were based on inadequate concepts of **adaptive success.** For example, in 1949 Leslie White proposed that culture evolved "as the amount of energy harnessed per capita per year increased" (1949:368–369) and proposed that a more highly evolved culture would be better adapted. White's energy theory reflected the general optimism of his day that technology would remove all limits to continuous growth and economic progress. A more cautious observer later pointed out that within 200 years a mere 5 percent annual increase in world energy production would produce a "Sun Day" in which waste heat would equal solar radiation and burn up the planet (Luten 1974). Obviously, increased energy consumption by itself is not the best measure of successful cultural adaptation.

In White's (1949) materialist view, foragers were "underdeveloped" because they were restricted to human energy, whereas farming made additional sources of energy available that permitted states to "arise." However, not all village farmers developed states, and the archaeological record demonstrates the adaptive success of low-energy foragers and independent villagers. White's interpretation overemphasized the importance of purely technological innovation and ignored the advantages of moderate use of renewable energy sources. However, as will be shown later, White was aware that small-scale cultures enjoyed important long-run advantages.

Marshall Sahlins (1972), however, argued that monumental, state-funded construction projects became possible because political controls were used to increase the scale of society and concentrate "surplus" energy. He suggested that per-capita energy use in preindustrial states was not significantly higher than in tribes. This is confirmed by Earl Cook's (1971) estimate of the daily per-capita consumption of all forms of energy (food, fuels, wind, water, and electricity) by culture scale, suggesting that small-scale cultures used 5000–12,000 kilocalories (kcal), whereas the most technically advanced preindustrial states barely doubled this amount to 26,000 kcal/person/day. In contrast, the magnitude of energy use by global-scale cultures is qualitatively unique. By drawing heavily on fossil fuels, Americans in 1970 consumed 230,000 kcal/person/day (Figure 15.2). This was more than eight times the amount used in preindustrial states and can be attributed primarily to commercialization.

Continuing his emphasis on the technological determinants of evolutionary "progress," White (1949) applauded the use of coal and oil as the **fuel revolution** that led to industrialization and suggested that the discovery of nuclear energy would bring another great evolutionary advance. What was missing in White's concept of progress was a time perspective that included the depletion of energy sources and the full environmental cost of ac-

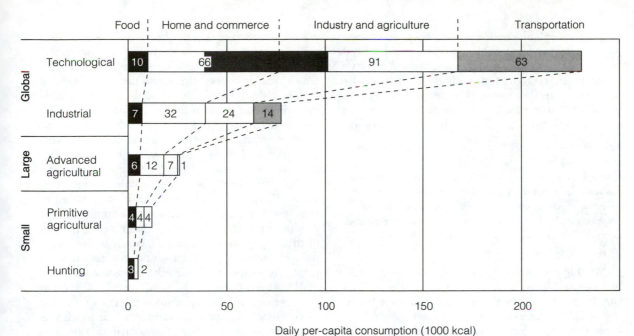

FIGURE 15.2  *Daily consumption of energy per capita by culture-scale level. Cultures identi-fied by Earl Cook as "hunting" and "primitive agricultural" are equivalent to foraging and shifting cultivation. (SOURCE: "The Flow of Energy in an Industrial Society," by Earl Cook. Scientific American 224(3):136. Copyright © by Scientific American, Inc. All Rights re-served.)*

celerated energy use. Historically, both large- and small-scale cultures relied primarily on solar energy. This was highly adaptive because it contributed to stability and set some limits on total growth. Since White wrote, it has become embarrassingly obvious that increasing energy use can be extremely maladaptive, especially when the primary energy base is not renewable and when it is expended at rates that exceed the biosphere's ability to recycle the waste by-products.

The adaptive success of global culture is sometimes defined by its "natural" ability to expand in population and territory at the expense of less "advanced" cultures. This has even been offered as an indirect explanation for the genocidal destruction of the members of small-scale cultures. For example, in 1915 Paul Popenoe assured the members of the 19th International Congress of Americanists that Native Americans were a "weak stock" that was being "killed off by natural selection." In 1960

anthropologist David Kaplan formulated a *law of cultural dominance* to explain the spread of industrial civilization: "That cultural system which more effectively exploits the energy resources of a given environment will tend to spread in that environment at the expense of less effective systems" (1960:75).

This "law" was offered as an ethically neutral scientific generalization, but it implied that ethnocide was inevitable and did not adequately define "effectiveness" of energy exploitation. Significantly, Kaplan acknowledged that in certain es-

---

**adaptive success**  The continuous survival of a given cultural system in a given environment over the long run.
**fuel revolution**  The large-scale adoption of fossil fuels such as coal and oil.
**law of cultural dominance**  Kaplan's generalization that cultures that use more energy will displace lower-energy cultures.

pecially marginal environments, such as deserts and the Arctic, small-scale cultures could indeed be considered adaptive successes, even in an environment that might temporarily be invaded by outsiders. In the same volume where Kaplan wrote, Sahlins agreed and commented in reference to peoples like the mobile foraging Inuit (Eskimo):

*Nor are those cultures that we might consider higher in general evolutionary standing necessarily more perfectly adapted to their environments than lower. Many great civilizations have fallen in the last 2000 years, even in the midst of material plenty, while the Eskimos tenaciously maintained themselves in an incomparably more difficult habitat. The race is not to the swift, nor the battle to the strong.* (1960:26–27)

Writing somewhat later, anthropologists Richard Lee and Irven DeVore, who organized in 1966 the first major international conference on foraging people, expressed concern over the "unstable ecological conditions" created by industrial civilization and were even more emphatic about the adaptive achievements of mobile foragers, declaring that they were "the most successful and persistent adaptation man has ever achieved" (Lee and DeVore 1968:3).

*Reproductive success* may be a very poor measure of human adaptive success because beyond a certain point the growth of any population must cease. There were ten times as many people in the world in 1990 as in 1650, but the world in 1990 was measurably less secure. Humans are **consumers** ultimately dependent on the energy produced by green plants through **photosynthesis,** which is powered by a fixed quantity of solar energy. Biologist Isaac Asimov (1971) estimated that the planet could support a maximum of 2 million million tons of consumer **biomass.** Any expansion in the human population must inevitably displace other species. The global culture with its 1990 population of 5 billion people makes far different demands on the biosphere than the .5 billion people in the large- and small-scale cultures that existed in 1650. In 1986 it was estimated that humans were already appropriating some 40 percent of the food energy produced by green plants (Brown and Postel 1987, Vitousek et al. 1986). The pinnacle of cultural evolutionary achievement, if narrowly defined by short-term human reproductive success,

would be reached when all natural "competitors" are eliminated and every gram of living material is available for human consumption. Asimov projected that, in theory, this could occur by 2436.

The sudden planetary dominance of the global culture has initiated a dramatic decline in biodiversity that may equal in magnitude the mass extinctions of the geological past, including the disappearance of the dinosaurs at the end of the Cretaceous and the loss of marine animals at the end of the Permian (Wilson 1989, Wilson and Peter 1988). Foraging peoples may have contributed to the more recent extinctions of some of the megafauna such as the wooly mammoth at the end of the Ice Age (see Chapter 2), but it is likely that natural changes in climate and vegetation were primarily responsible for those losses (Webster 1981). There is no doubt that since 1800 habitat destruction, or ecocide, caused by the expansion of commercial ranching, farming, and logging is now destroying species at a catastrophic rate. The bulk of current extinctions can be attributed to destruction of the tropical rain forest, where more than half of the world's species are found. In the 1980s, tropical forests were being removed at the rate of 1 to 2.6 percent a year (Grainger 1980, Wilson 1989). At that rate, Edward Wilson estimated that 4000 to 6000 species were disappearing every year—more than 10,000 times faster than would be expected "naturally."

Much of the world's present wealth of species was produced over the past 200 million years. Extinction is an irreversible process. Loss of biological diversity is maladaptive for humans because it makes the biosphere less able to support human life. It also involves an economic loss because it is often more costly to replace natural goods and services with their cultural counterparts. Species are now disappearing before they are even scientifically described and their possible uses identified. The extensive biological knowledge accumulated by small-scale cultures for many otherwise "unknown" species is unfortunately also disappearing as genocide and ethnocide continues.

## Global Culture and Resource Depletion

Because the global culture is most distinguished by its elevated rates of resource consumption, the question of resource balance is critical for any assessment of the future of global culture. In theory, culture growth, like the growth of any organism, must be limited by the essential material that is in shortest supply, as predicted in 1840 by German chemist Justus von Liebig's *law of the minimum.* Identifying any single, irreplaceable natural resource required by the global culture, however, would be difficult, although petroleum would be a likely candidate. Resource depletion by itself is an inadequate predictor of cultural viability because resources are culturally defined and major economic and social instabilities are produced by more comprehensive changes in ecosystems or climate, as will be examined later.

From the very beginning of the industrial era, a number of scholars including economist Adam Smith (1776), demographer Thomas Malthus ([1798] 1895), and pioneer conservationist George Marsh (1864) warned that the earth would not support endless economic progress. In 1873 scientists from the American Association for the Advancement of Science even petitioned the U.S. Congress to legislate conservation measures. However, the colonial expropriation of the resources controlled by large- and small-scale cultures postponed the inevitable shortages and fostered an ideology of unlimited growth.

The global issue of resource depletion was not even seriously addressed at the international level until 1949 when the United Nations convened 700 scientists from fifty nations to assess the resource demands of global economic development. At that time, H. L. Keenleyside, Canadian deputy minister of mines and resources, reported that between 1900 and 1949 more world mineral resources had been consumed than at any time in the past. Keenleyside thought that the mineral situation was not yet critical but warned that

*. . . It is clear that the combination of an increasing population and rising standards of living will place a strain on our metal resources which will almost certainly in the end prove beyond the capacity of man and nature to supply. . . . [Unless] there is a fundamental change in the economic fabric of human society we will ultimately be faced with the exhaustion of many of our mineral resources.* (1950:38)

Since the 1940s, American planners and resource scientists have kept a careful eye on the supply of strategically significant resources. This was prudent, given America's disproportionate consumption levels, as was demonstrated as early as 1952 in a study commissioned by President Truman, which amplified the Keenleyside report. Truman's commission estimated that between 1914 and 1950 Americans by themselves had consumed more of the world's fuels and minerals than the combined total of *all* previous consumption.

Given the inequities built into the global system, resource shortages will likely not be shared equally by peoples in different regions. Most U.S. assessments of resource limitations have been remarkably optimistic. For example, a major study to predict "America's Needs and Resources" up to 1960, commissioned by the Twentieth Century Fund in 1947, acknowledged that domestic mineral resources would eventually be exhausted, but it assumed that free access to foreign resources would support an "expanding American economy" for many decades (Dewhurst 1947). Another study in 1963 concluded that, given continued imports and substitution of synthetics for natural materials, no critical shortages would prevent Americans from tripling their consumption of natural resources by the year 2000 (Landsberg 1964). However, a 1975 report, "Mineral Resources and the Environment," issued by the National Academy of Sciences, was much more pessimistic and called on the government to establish a national policy of resource conservation, recycling, and reduced energy consumption. The report ominously declared, "Man faces the prospect of a series of shocks of varying severity as shortages occur in one material after another, with the first real shortages perhaps only a matter of a few years away" (National Research Council 1975:26).

---

**reproductive success**  The differential increase of a given population in relation to another.
**consumer**  An animal that eats plants or other animals.
**photosynthesis**  The process by which green plants use sunlight, water, and carbon dioxide to produce oxygen and energy-storing organic compounds.
**biomass**  The total weight of biological organisms living in a given area.
**law of the minimum**  von Liebig's generalization that the growth of an organism or population is limited by the supply of the least available essential nutrient or resource.

Theoretically, solar-based cultures can last perhaps 5 billion years, when the sun is predicted to burn out, but a fossil fuel–dependent global-scale culture is mining a limited energy source that is rapidly being depleted. There are no absolute figures on the total supply of fossil fuels, but a study commissioned by President Jimmy Carter in 1977 to guide government planning up to the year 2000 estimated that, at 1976 production rates, oil would be depleted within 77 years, natural gas in 170 years, and coal in 212 years (Barney 1980, vol. 2). Any such estimates are purely hypothetical and are based on assumptions about population, consumption, production technology, use efficiencies, prices, and politics; nevertheless, the magnitude of the supply problem is inescapable and has been acknowledged by geologists for many years. Petroleum expert M. King Hubert (1969) estimated that, even with the most optimistic supply estimate, oil production would peak about the year 2000 and would essentially stop by the end of that century. Remarkably, 80 percent of the total production would occur within a brief 64-year period (Figure 15.3).

Curiously, the commercial economy is designed to thrive on resource depletion, while theoretically denying its existence. According to an influential text, *The Economics of Natural Resource Availability*, by resource economists Harold Barnett and

Chandler Morse (1963), there can be no limits on economic growth because market forces and technological advance will inevitably create new resources. Barnett and Morse argue that industrial progress makes nature "subservient to man." They emphatically declare, "The notion of an absolute limit to natural resource availability is untenable when the definition of resources changes drastically and unpredictably over time" (Barnett and Morse 1963:7).

Such an economic ideology, when uninhibited by political controls, allows resources to be systematically depleted. Historically, different types of trees, whales, and fossil fuels have been exploited as long as prices and production costs made it profitable. Orthodox market theory suggests that a given resource will be replaced by a cheaper substitute the moment that it becomes too scarce or expensive to harvest. This makes economic sense, but it can lead to extinction.

## Limits to Growth and the Global Environment

The Club of Rome study, *The Limits to Growth* (Meadows et al. 1972), published in 1972, was the first comprehensive predictive model of the global system to incorporate the interaction of cultural and biological components and to look relatively

**FIGURE 15.3**
*Petroleum is perhaps global culture's most vital nonrenewable resource, yet its total availability is strictly limited as this chart of complete cycles of world crude-oil production demonstrates.* (SOURCE: Hubert 1969:196.)

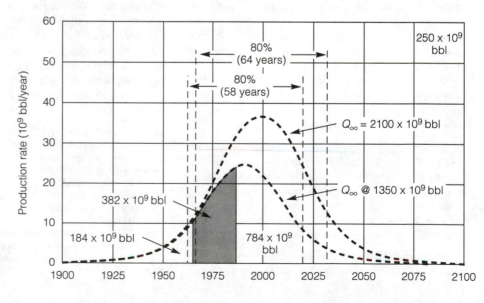

**FIGURE 15.4**
*According to this famous computer projection from the 1972* Limits to Growth *study, if historical trends in population and economic growth continued with no change, the global culture would collapse well before 2100.*
*(SOURCE: Meadows et al. 1972:124.)*

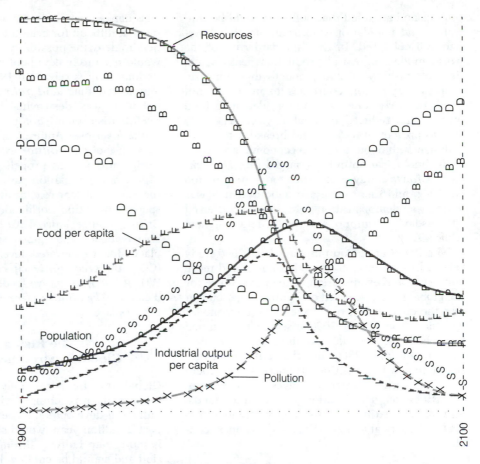

KEY: B = Crude birthrate (births per 1000 people per year)
D = Crude death rate (deaths per 1000 people per year)
S = Service per person (dollar equivalent per person per year)

far into the future. The Club of Rome is unusual among futurist groups because it is an informal international organization formed in 1968 under the sponsorship of an Italian industrialist to study the global system and the "predicament of mankind." *The Limits to Growth* study was produced by a seventeen-member international team of experts who worked with a sophisticated "world model" computer program developed by Jay Forrester of the Massachusetts Institute of Technology. The model took a systems approach and considered the positive and negative feedbacks between population, agriculture, industry, natural resources, and pollution. The objective was to see how long

the global system could function if the ***exponential growth*** trends already observed in the world economy and population from 1900 to 1970 were to continue indefinitely.

The Club of Rome study consistently predicted a system collapse before 2100 because of the seemingly inescapable limits to growth (Figure 15.4). Even when the researchers doubled world re-

---

***exponential growth*** The situation in which a population increases by an annual percentage rate and grows more and more rapidly in total size. This can be graphed as a steeply climbing curve and described by a mathematical function with an exponent.

sources and assumed that pollution could be controlled and population stabilized, the global system still collapsed. In the "standard run" of the world model, industrial production peaks sometime after the year 2000, due to dwindling resources. Population continues to increase until death rates rise due to pollution, declining food output, and reduced medical services. The only way to prevent *overshoot* and breakdown was to stabilize both population and economic growth.

Technological optimists charged that *The Limits to Growth* study was either too simple or too complex, and there were accusations that it was simply a demonstration of the preconceived "doomsday" assumptions of the model's designers (Cole 1973).

The 1977 Carter Commission *Global 2000* study referred to earlier was an independent and more conservative reexamination of the near future for the global system, carried out with a larger budget and the cooperation of thirteen U.S. government agencies. The *Global 2000* researchers assumed fewer negative feedbacks and limited their projections to the year 2000, but they still found that population would continue to increase and there could be serious water shortages, deforestation, desertification, deterioration of agricultural lands, and massive extinctions, together with more poverty and political tension. The commissioners concluded,

*The most knowledgeable professional analysts in the executive branch of the U.S. Government have reported to the President that, if public policies around the world continue unchanged through the end of the century, a number of serious world problems will become worse, not better . . . the world in 2000 will be more crowded, more polluted, less stable ecologically, and more vulnerable to disruption. . . . Serious stresses involving population, resources, and environment are clearly visible ahead . . . the world's people will be poorer. . . .* (Barney 1977, vol. 1:xvi, l)

## OVERSHOOT AND BIOSPHERE ALTERATION

Human-induced changes in global climate, which many experts conclude are now underway, are an ominous indication that critical natural thresholds may already have been crossed. During the 1980s,

a sequence of environmental events occurred that made it difficult for even the most optimistic planners to deny the possibility that the global culture would need to make major adjustments to ensure its long-term survival. In 1982 German scientists announced that **acid rain** caused by industrial pollution was destroying European forests. In 1985 British scientists reported a thinning in the **ozone layer** over Antarctica, which was attributed to release of **chlorofluorocarbons** (CFCs) used in refrigerants and as propellants in spray cans. In 1986 world population passed the 5 billion mark; the Soviet nuclear reactor at Chernobyl exploded, spewing radiation worldwide; and an article in the British science journal *Nature* reported measurable evidence that global warming was taking place due to elevated levels of carbon dioxide ($CO_2$), the **greenhouse effect** (Jones, Wigley, and Wright 1986). Negative feedbacks of the sort predicted by *The Limits to Growth* model may well be taking place.

## The Rising Tide: Global Environmental Change

Global warming is probably the single most dramatic and far-reaching environmental impact of industrial development. The natural cycles of the past 2 million years would suggest that the world is more than halfway through an interglacial period and should be cooling, but instead it appears that the world has actually warmed by 1°F (.5°C) on the average over the past 100 years (Edgerton 1991, Schneider 1989). The greenhouse effect, which has been recognized as a theoretical possibility since the nineteenth century, assumes that increased atmospheric $CO_2$ gas from the burning of fossil fuels would heat the earth like the glass of a greenhouse by trapping solar heat near the earth's surface. Precise measurements show an increase of nearly 8 percent in atmospheric $CO_2$ between 1958 and 1984 (Landsberg 1989). Scientists estimate that $CO_2$ levels have increased by 25 percent since the beginning of the Industrial Revolution, while $CO_2$ gas bubbles trapped in Antarctic ice show relative stability over the previous 10,000 years (Graedel and Crutzen 1989).

Carbon is stored in natural "sinks," or reservoirs, either as organic matter, especially in forest

**FIGURE 15.5**
*Tropical deforestation reduces biodiversity and releases stored carbon into the atmosphre where, in the form of carbon dioxide gas, it can contribute to global warming by increasing the greenhouse effect.*

biomass, or in coal, oil, or the ocean. In the natural **carbon cycle,** $CO_2$ is taken up by plants during photosynthesis. It is also stored chemically in the ocean. Carbon is released back into the atmosphere as $CO_2$ by respiration, decomposition, and other chemical and biological processes. Large-scale human burning of fossil fuels and forests imbalances the cycle by withdrawing carbon from storage faster than it can be reabsorbed by the forests and oceans (Figure 15.5).

In the 1980s, $CO_2$ was considered to be responsible for more than half of the predicted global warming, while other less common but more active greenhouse gases such as methane, CFCs, and nitrous oxide contributed the remainder. Although methane is produced naturally as swamp gas and by termites, significant quantities are also produced by fermentation in rice paddies and in the digestive tracts of domestic cattle (Cicerone 1989). CFCs are a commercial product that chemists synthesized in the 1920s. Their ability to destroy the ozone that screens the earth from ultraviolet radiation has been suspected since 1974 (Rowland 1989).

It is impossible to predict with absolute confi-

dence how much warming will occur; however, the Intergovernmental Panel on Climate Change (IPCC), established in 1988 by the World Meteorological Organization and the U.N. Environment

---

*overshoot*   The situation in which a population exceeds its carrying capacity.
*acid rain*   Acidic precipitation, often dilute sulfuric acid produced in the atmosphere from sulfur dioxide that is frequently emitted when fossil fuels are burned. Acid rain can kill trees.
*ozone layer*   Concentrations of ozone gas, $O_3$ (a triatomic form of oxygen), found in the stratosphere where it absorbs potentially dangerous ultraviolet solar radiation.
*chlorofluorocarbon*   A synthetically produced chemical compound, used as an aerosol propellant and in refrigeration, that can destroy atmospheric ozone.
*greenhouse effect*   An increase in global temperature caused by solar heat being trapped near the earth's surface by atmospheric carbon dioxide and other greenhouse gasses.
*carbon cycle*   The natural movement of carbon when it is incorporated into plant tissue from atmospheric carbon dioxide during photosynthesis, metabolized by consumers, and released again into the atmosphere by respiration.

FIGURE 15.6
*Global sea-level rise,
1985–2100, for policy
scenario A (no limita-
tion of greenhouse
gases). (SOURCE: IPCC
1991.)*

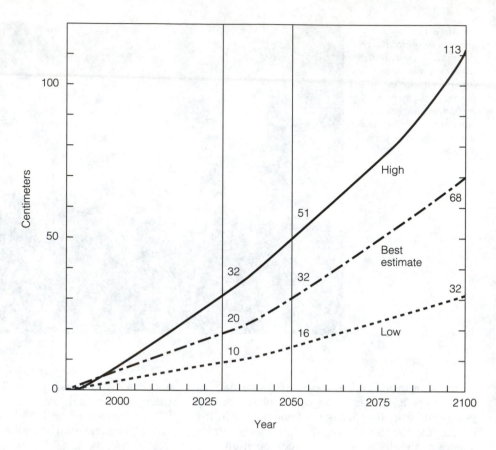

Program, calculated that if no preventive action is taken, the global mean temperature could rise by 5.4°F (3°C) over the next century (IPCC 1991). There are substantial uncertainties with these projections because, like earlier global models, they depend on many variables that interact in complex ways. Skeptics argue that climate models rely too heavily on aggregate data and suggest that increased cloud cover and dust in the air may have a cooling effect that will balance any warming. Predicting the temperature-moderating effect of the oceans is also difficult. However, the consensus opinion is that some degree of warming is very likely to occur within a range of (3.6°–9°F (2°–5°C), depending on the *rate* of climate change and the human response.

The possible impact of global warming is also conjectural, but sea-level rise and regional changes in rainfall and vegetation would be virtually cer-

tain. Some experts believe that sea level has already been rising at the rate of .04–.08 inches (1–2 millimeters) a year over the past century and that rate is expected to increase (Edgerton 1991). The IPCC projected a rise in sea level of 2 ft (60 centimeters [cm]) over the next century, within a range of 1–3 ft (30–100 cm) (Figure 15.6). Critical variables include thermal expansion of the oceans and the speed at which the vast ice fields stored in Greenland and Antarctica might melt. Rapid warming could produce 3-ft (1-m) rise in sea level by 2050 (Edgerton 1991), while a breakup of the West Antarctic ice sheet could by itself cause a rise of 5–7.5 yards (5–7 m) (Kellogg 1989). Large uncertainties remain because the models are based on global averages; with increased precipitation, ice could accumulate in Antarctica and certain alpine glaciers, while it retreated elsewhere.

Sea-level rise is an especially dramatic threat

because many of the world's largest cities, densest populations, and richest agricultural zones are located in low-lying coastal areas. Very low island groups and atolls would be quickly overwhelmed. Flooding would cause great economic loss everywhere. It has been estimated that a 3-ft (1-m) rise in sea level would displace 50 million people worldwide. Bangladesh would be especially vulnerable because most of its population is concentrated in a vast delta region, which is already chronically subject to storm-surge flooding (Jacobson 1989). Shifts in regional climates would disrupt agriculture worldwide, causing political and economic stress and population dislocation, but the precise impacts would be variable. Rapid environmental change would probably accelerate species extinctions because plants and animals would have difficulty moving to suitable environments quickly enough, especially when migration routes are blocked by developed areas.

## Food Production and the Malthusian Dilemma

Many researchers and policy planners have examined food production as a key variable limiting global population, but this is not a simple matter. Theoretically, treating global limits as a subsistence carrying-capacity issue should be possible, but carrying capacity can only be defined for a specific cultural system and technology in a given environment. This is difficult to do even for small-scale cultures, where food is produced directly to satisfy human needs, because neither environment nor technology are constants, as the long history of subsistence intensification demonstrates. In the global system, food production is only indirectly concerned with human nutritional requirements; it is primarily directed by political and economic objectives. Indeed, when food and the means to produce it are controlled by governments, multinational corporations, and market economies, the connection between food production and carrying capacity must be approached with caution. Hungry people and empty granaries in a given country do not necessarily mean that environmentally defined production limits have been exceeded. Similarly, steadily increasing grain output at the global level may not mean that technology has defeated

nature. Diminishing returns and environmental deterioration are real and can be described at both local and global levels.

In 1798 the English economist and demographer Thomas Malthus (1766–1834) correctly observed that human population has the biological capacity to grow faster than food production, but he did not realize that small-scale cultures can maintain a relative balance between food and population without suffering chronic hunger. Ignoring the culturally determined demographic imbalances and inequities that were generating hunger in the newly emerging global system, Malthus mistakenly concluded that misery worked "naturally" as the primary check on population growth. He supported his findings with historical data demonstrating that famine and hunger elevated mortality in states and empires, but he did not realize that he was also observing the action of cultural variables acting together with natural limits.

The Malthusian argument conveniently provided nineteenth-century policymakers with a justification for keeping public welfare low because it implied that only a certain level of human suffering would prevent overpopulation. This aspect of **Malthusian theory** has since been widely discredited, especially by "demographic transition" theorists. During the early post–World War II decades of economic development, some technological optimists argued that Malthus was also wrong about the ultimate limits of food production. However, granted that poverty and misery are "cultural," not "natural," checks on population, Malthus was indeed correct about the general relationship between food and population, even if it is difficult to define. Because of diminishing returns and the limits of water, soil, and energy, there are practical limits to subsistence intensification in any given region and at a global level. However, determining what the actual limits are is complicated by the intervention of governments, markets, and the fossil-fuel subsidy in the food-production process.

Any estimates of a maximum sustainable global population must consider not only physical limits

---

**Malthusian theory**  Malthus's generalization that populations can grow faster than their food supply and are naturally limited by misery and starvation.

but also cultural variables such as political and economic organization, as well as technology. In 1905, when world population stood at 1.5 billion, Harvard geologist Nathaniel Shaler (1841–1906) warned that world food production could not support a threefold increase to 4.5 billion people. That was probably a realistic estimate for the early twentieth-century world in which agricultural production was not fossil-fuel based and remained largely self-sustaining. This was still the situation at midcentury, when world population reached 2.5 billion and only marginal or highly erodible lands remained undeveloped (Brown and Postel 1987). Given that poverty-inducing colonial inequities were perpetuated in the decolonized world, massive Malthusian crises were probably delayed by the introduction of the expensive technological inputs that began with the post–World War II campaign for economic development. During the technological optimism of the 1950s, there were projections that world population might reach 30 billion by 2075, but geochemist Harrison Brown (1956) calculated that such a population would literally eat up the world, even if it could feed directly on rock and seawater.

At a global level, food production has kept pace and even exceeded population growth since 1950, judging by world grain-production figures (Table 15.1). Per-capita grain production actually increased by one-third between 1950 and 1986, and total production and yield per hectare more than doubled, seemingly disproving Malthus on the general relationship between food and population. Because grain directly provides about half of the world's food and feeds much of the world's livestock, such figures suggest significant improvement in world living standards. However, because grain is distributed as a commodity and is used to political and economic advantage, global production averages mask the realities of world hunger and inequality, which were examined in Chapter 13. Furthermore, a few countries hold decisive control over world oil production, which ultimately fuels agricultural intensification.

The rate of increase in grain per person has been declining, just as Malthus might have predicted. Grain production grew at 1.2 percent/year/person during the 1950–1973 period; but during 1973–1986, the annual rate of increase dropped to

0.4 percent (Brown 1987). Total grain production fell in 1987 and 1988. By 1988 world grain output per person had dropped 14 percent from its 1984 peak (Brown 1989). Per-capita production in Africa has actually fallen steadily to 27 percent below its 1967 peak (Brown 1989), and some authorities think that population growth is outstripping food production in many areas of Asia, the Middle East, and Latin America (Keyfitz 1989). Short-term production shortfalls can be compensated for by use of stored grain or by diverting grain from cattle feed directly to human consumption. However, any redistribution of this sort would be mediated by the global grain market and the political economy, and in 1989 only the United States, Canada, western Europe, Australia, and New Zealand were net grain exporters. Any long-term declines in the world food balance will compel the global culture to institute profound adjustments.

Numerous lines of evidence suggest that food production is already badly overextended in many countries, under prevailing cultural conditions. Food scientist Georg Borgstrom (1965) pointed out that developed countries were supplementing their agricultural production by drawing extensively on marine fisheries and market-based international trade. Borgstrom used the concept of **ghost acres** to refer to land that a given country

TABLE 15.1  *World Population and Agriculture, 1950 and 1986*

|  | 1950 | 1986 |
|---|---|---|
| Population (in billions) | 2.5 | 5.0 |
| Cropland (in millions of hectares) | 590 | 715 |
| Irrigated cropland (in millions of hectares) | 94 | 271 |
| Fertilizer use (in millions of metric tons) | 14 | 131 |
| Fertilizer/person (kgs) | 5 | 26 |
| Energy use (in millions of barrels of oil equivalent) | 276 | 1903 |
| Grain production (in millions of metric tons) | 624 | 1661 |
| Grain/person (in millions of metric tons of grain/billion people) | 249.6 | 332.2 |
| Barrels of oil/tons of grain produced | .44 | 1.14 |

SOURCES: Brown (1987) and Brown and Postel (1987).

would need to put into production to produce an amount of animal protein equal to its net food imports and fishery production. Ghost acres allow a country to subsidize what might otherwise be unsustainable economic growth, by shifting production costs to the oceans or the farmlands of other countries. Obvious examples are Middle East desert countries that trade oil for food, but richly endowed agricultural countries such as the United States also take advantage of favorable trade conditions to import large amounts of food from poorer countries. In the 1960s, Borgstrom estimated that Japan's ghost acres were six times greater than its agricultural acreage. Since then, innovations in the fishing industry—such as the use by Japan, Taiwan, and South Korea of miles-long monofilament drift nets that sweep all fish from vast areas of ocean—have extended ghost acreage to clearly unsustainable lengths.

The concept of ghost acres also applies to Peru's export of fish meal to the United States where it is used as chicken food, to native-grown oilseed cakes fed to European cattle, and to beef that is raised in former Amazonian rain forests and shipped to the United States. These seemingly irrational economic exchanges occur because they generate profit in a market system that does not count all production costs.

Diminishing returns to agricultural inputs seem to be an inescapable law of nature (see Chapter 10). The rapid early increase in food production after 1950 can be largely attributed to a 22 percent increase in world cropland, as previously undeveloped marginal lands were plowed and irrigated. These were lands that were undeveloped because they would not support intensive use or because the cost of their development was previously considered too high. Further production increases required large amounts of fossil-fuel energy and chemical fertilizer. Between 1950 and 1986, irrigated land increased nearly threefold, world fertilizer use increased ninefold, and energy use in agriculture increased nearly sevenfold (see Table 15.1). Much of this increase in agricultural effort was a result of the intervention of the global institutions of development examined in Chapter 13.

As diminishing returns theory would predict, increased yields have required steadily larger inputs of energy and fertilizer. In 1950 a ton of grain

required .44 barrel of oil to produce, but in 1986 the same ton cost 1.14 barrels. Declining yields in relation to fertilizer inputs, despite the widespread use of high-yield variety hybrids, suggest that many crops may be reaching the limits of photosynthetic efficiency, beyond which no further gains can be achieved regardless of the input (Brown 1989).

Such intensive production systems cannot be sustained for long because energy and fertilizer will inevitably become more costly. Elevated production is also mining highly erodible soils and withdrawing irrigation waters from underground aquifers at greater than replacement rates (Brown 1987, Brown and Postel 1987). Many marginal areas that were pushed too quickly into production have since been abandoned due to desertification, waterlogging, salination, and erosion. It now appears that world grain acreage has been declining since its peak in 1981 (Brown 1989). Acknowledging the problem of land degradation, in 1986 the United States initiated a federally legislated 5-year program, the Food Security Act of 1985, designed to convert the most erodible 12 percent of America's total cropland into permanent grass and woodland.

## Technological Optimism

Taking a more optimistic approach, some experts suggest that world food production might still support up to 10 billion people, given full application of environmentally "appropriate" technology. Economist Pierre Crosson and soils and climate specialist Norman Rosenberg, both of Resources for the Future, are skeptical of "apocalyptic scenarios," suggesting that damage to marginal soils may be overestimated. They point to the Green Revolution grain-yield achievements of the 1965–1985 period and a continued slowing of the annual growth rate of world population as cause for optimism. Advocating more high tech progress they call for ". . . a steady stream of new agricultural technologies that can only come from the CGIAR

---

***ghost acre***   Borgstrom's term for the amount of agricultural land that would be required for a country to produce the animal protein obtained from its marine fisheries.

system [see Chapter 13] and national research institutions in both the developed and the developing countries" (Crosson and Rosenberg 1989:132).

Many agricultural scientists hope that accelerated application of biotechnology will lead to new nitrogen-fixing plant varieties that will require less fertilizer or to plants that will tolerate salt and drought (Figure 15.7). Such genetically engineered plants might thrive in the warming global greenhouse, and some climatologists point out that increased atmospheric $CO_2$ may even make plants grow 5 percent faster (Kellog 1989). Lasers and mechanical improvements might increase irrigation efficiency. New cropping techniques might reduce pesticide requirements.

Lester Brown (1989) warns that biotechnology is unlikely to yield further dramatic production increases and many genetic "improvements" may be accompanied by trade-offs that will actually lower yields. Robert Chandler, founding director of the International Rice Research Institute, CGIAR's oldest research center, is also cautious about the long-term potential for continued yield expansion. Chandler was a leading architect of the Green Revolution in Asia and in 1988 was awarded the Kraft General Foods Foundation prestigious "World Food Prize" in recognition of his contribution to improving the world's food supply. In a 1989 address to a Smithsonian Institution–sponsored colloquium, Global Perspectives on Food, Agriculture, and Rural Development, Chandler (1990) predicted that Indian rice production might keep pace with population for another 20 years, given a 50 percent increase in irrigated acreage and a quadrupled application of fertilizer. He found the longer-term prospects for Asia as a whole "not at all bright," especially since the Rice Institute discovered that yields declined when rice was grown continuously on the same land for 20 years, even with the best management practices. Finding it "extremely unlikely" that Asian rice yields would ever be increased to more than double then current levels, Chandler cautioned,

*... It must be realized that the greatest gains in varietal improvement have already been made. There are limits not only to the amount of arable land and to fresh water supplies for irrigation but to the genetic improvement of plants. It is impossible at this stage to predict what advances in potential yield will come from genetic engineering and from other areas of biotechnology.... We should remember that we cannot increase average world precipitation or the quantity of solar radiation, the two most important factors limiting crop production.* (1990:174)

## TOWARD A SUSTAINABLE WORLD

Most global planners agree that significant cultural changes will be required if the global system is to remain intact through the end of the twenty-first century. Sustainability is now a widely endorsed planning goal, as shown by frequent use of the expression "sustainable agriculture" and the oxymoronic phrase "sustainable economic growth." Institutionalized planning, however, still sets relatively short-term goals often focused on single technologically defined issues such as global warming or food production. More fundamental problems such as the need for a redistribution of political and economic power to create a more balanced and equitable world are not adequately addressed.

### Emission Permits: A Market Response to Global Warming?

In 1991 the Response Strategies Working Group (RSWG) of the IPCC proposed an "integrated package" to reduce greenhouse gases while helping people adapt to rising sea levels and global warming. The RSWG recommended a "flexible and progressive approach" involving dozens of technical options to increase energy efficiency or reduce $CO_2$ emissions in electricity generation, industry, transportation, and construction. It was hoped that the necessary technologies would be in place by 2005–2030. They also called for expansion of forests and changes in agriculture production that would demand even more herculean efforts from the agricultural scientists attempting to increase yields. The ultimate object was to stabilize atmospheric $CO_2$ and prevent it from doubling by 2090. However, because the IPCC thought that, even if greenhouse gases were reduced, some sea-level rise was unavoidable, they recommended that emergency- and disaster-preparedness programs be instituted (Figure 15.6).

Planners are increasingly recognizing that the market economy as presently organized does not adequately respond to resource depletion or other environmental costs. Crosson and Rosenberg (1989) suggest that individual farmers are unlikely to adopt expensive "appropriate" technologies, which might improve yields while protecting limited soil and water resources, because the market does not reflect the true social costs of deteriorating resources. Many resource economists consider government regulation to enforce sustainable agricultural practices to be undesirable because they would require farmers to act against their short-term economic self-interest. Instead, they favor private ownership of land and water rights, such as often practiced in the United States as a free-market alternative, that might better represent the scarcity of these resources. However, even in the United States, the market has not operated with the theoretical freedom to fully protect the environment, and protective regulation has been required.

The IPCC also favored a market approach to slowing global warming. The panel proposed a series of market measures, or "economic instruments," that would use "price signals" that would make it profitable to reduce greenhouse gases. They recognized that government regulations might be required in some cases but thought that regulations would be cumbersome and expensive. The preferred free-market approach would involve permits, taxes, trade sanctions, and subsidies to limit gas emissions. Emission permits would be owned and traded like stocks or commodities and would grant permit holders a "right to pollute" up to a specified amount. Pollution budgets could be allocated at national and international levels, and maintenance of major carbon sinks, such as rain forests, might be rewarded with extra emission entitlements. The disadvantage of such a system is that the permits would be controlled by the wealthiest bidders.

The IPCC planners recognized that the industrialized countries produced the largest share of the world's greenhouse gases and would need to make changes in their economies. However, because their proposals needed to be politically acceptable, they did not seriously deal with the issue of global inequality. In contrast, the *Second Report to the Club of Rome*, issued in 1974 to examine alterna-

FIGURE 15.7
*The Biosphere 2 complex in Oracle, Arizona, where people seek to design completely self-contained ecosystems represents the extremes of human intervention and direction of natural systems.*

tive solutions to the problems posed by their earlier *Limits to Growth* study, did not hesitate to call for "drastic, unprecedented changes in the world system" (Mesarovic and Pestel 1974:127). This new report insisted that world problems were not purely technological and emphatically rejected exclusively "technological fixes," even to deal with expected shortfalls in energy and food production. The second Club of Rome report called "developed" countries "overdeveloped" and emphasized that a balanced world would require greater equality. The report declared, "A more equitable long-term allocation of global world resources would require that the industrialized regions put a stop to further overdevelopment by accepting limits on per-capita use of finite resources" (Mesarovic and Pestel 1974:69).

## Cultural Ecological Perspectives on Global Issues

The problem with the preceding solutions, is that, with the exception of the Club of Rome approach, they promote a similar concept of "development" and they assume that the world will continue to be dominated by the global system as presently structured. This narrow, technological, market economy–oriented approach serves the immediate interests of existing corporate and political interest groups but leaves unresolved the basic contradictions of inequality and infinite economic expansion in a finite world. Piecemeal solutions might help the existing system muddle along from crisis to crisis for another century or so, but they are unlikely to lead to genuine sustainability. In a sense, the "development" path that the world has followed for the past 6000 years requires some fundamental rethinking. What is needed is a holistic, cross-cultural view, with a long-time perspective. Cultural anthropologists who focus on cultural ecology have frequently applied their insights to global issues. Some of their views are examined next.

In a discussion of the "cultural ecology of development," drawing on a variety of sources, anthropologist Billie DeWalt (1988) enumerated the following specific problems with economic development as presently defined:

1. Disorder and control problems increase.

2. Consumption and growth become ends in themselves.

3. Other societies and species are endangered.

4. Cultural material is lost.

These are the broad-trend problems of inequality, poverty, ecocide, genocide, and ethnocide that have been underway since large-scale systems first appeared. They were greatly intensified by the emergence of the global system, but they are either strikingly absent or vastly reduced in small-scale cultures. This list neatly summarizes many of the issues that were prominently discussed in earlier sections of this chapter and in previous chapters dealing with the global system. All these trends were present in the large-scale cultures discussed in Chapters 6–10, but they were treated as local, not global, problems. The first two trends are directly connected with the most fundamental maladaptive features of large- and global-scale cultural systems, whereas the last two trends follow as secondary consequences. In this section, we explore different anthropological interpretations of these problems in relation to culture scale, as background for a rethinking of development alternatives.

Paradoxically, disorder and control problems increase as structures become larger and more complex, even though, as the discussion in Chapter 7 on the origin of states showed, structural complexity is a system response to increasing disorder. Richard Adams (1985) identifies hierarchy and market-exchange systems as new features of a cultural macroframework, which intrude between people and nature. Hierarchy and market economies arose with large- and global-scale cultures, respectively. They organize production and distribution and thus indirectly function to satisfy basic human needs; but as examples of Malinowski's culturally **derived needs,** they create new problems. State organization and global systems may offer humanity greater "control over nature," but as Adams (1985) points out, hierarchy and market economies are themselves inherently uncontrollable cultural "controls" that people must adapt to and work to maintain. Some of the maladaptive aspects of hierarchy were referred to in Chapter

TABLE 15.2   *Ideal Types of Societies Based on Degrees of Ecological Equilibrium* (SOURCE: *Bennett 1976*)

|  | Societies in Equilibrium with Environment | Societies in Disequilibrium with Environment |
|---|---|---|
| Population dynamics | Small, controlled | Large, expanding, weakly controlled |
| Contact with environment | Direct contact by maximum number of people | Direct contact by minimal number of people |
| Range | Restricted to local resources | Resources available from external sources |
| Sustenance needs | Close to minimal; defined largely by physiological needs | Maximal; defined in large part by cultural wants |
| Gratification expectations | Low; controlled | High; promise of continued expansion |
| Technological capacity | Low | High |
| Feedback loop 3 | Functioning to control resource use | Functioning only to promote resource use |

10, especially under Roy Rappaport's "hierarchical anomalies."

The primary problems of the market economy have appeared throughout this chapter and Chapters 11–14. Market systems, whether operating at national or global levels, are difficult to control, and it is not surprising that partisan arguments over the relative merits of free markets versus various forms of government regulation have continued for more than two centuries. Special interests, monopolies, and other inequalities mean that markets are seldom "free"; yet if the market is neither perfectly self-regulated or effectively controlled by government regulation, poverty and social disorder increase, along with environmental disruption. In an inadequately regulated market economy, consumption and growth become ends in themselves. This is problem 2 from the preceding list, which leads directly to problems 3 and 4 as economies expand and "development" pressures increase.

What is popularly conceptualized as the environmental problem—that is, deterioration of ecosystems, species extinction, resource depletion, and *biosphere* disturbances—is an aspect of all

four of the problems listed previously. Cultural ecologist John Bennett summarizes these trends under the term *ecological transition*, which refers to a "progressive incorporation of Nature into human frames of purpose and action" (1976:3). Bennett describes the ecological transition as a continuum between two idealized cultural types representing societies that are either in equilibrium or disequilibrium with the environment (Table 15.2). *Equilibrium societies* harvest natural resources on a sustained-yield basis, and are

---

**derived needs**   Malinowski's term for the culturally determined requirements for maintaining and reproducing a specific culture as distinguished from the biological requirements or basic needs of individuals.

**biosphere**   The area on and near the surface of the planet that supports life, cyclical flows of energy and materials, and ecosystems, as distinguished from the abiotic atmosphere, hydrosphere, and lithosphere.

**ecological transition**   Bennett's term for the increasing cultural incorporation of natural processes that transforms equilibrium societies into disequilibrium societies.

**equilibrium society**   Bennett's term for a society that is in balance with its natural resources.

locally self-sufficient. They are small-scale cultures, whereas *disequilibrium societies* are by definition out of balance with their resources and the environment in general and are best represented by global-scale cultures. "Feedback loop 3" in Table 15.2 is a key feature of Bennett's cultural ecological analysis because it condenses a number of variables such as population, values, and social organization that control the flow of energy and goods.

Bennett's equilibrium–disequilibrium typology closely resembles a distinction drawn simultaneously by conservation ecologist Raymond Dasmann (1976) between ecosystem and biosphere peoples. *Ecosystem peoples* are members of small-scale cultures that draw their resources from local ecosystems and, in Dasmann's view, are thus more likely to manage them for sustained use. *Biosphere peoples* are members of the global culture who extract resources from throughout the globe and can, in the short-run, disregard the damage this might cause.

Not wanting to be identified with "noble savage romanticism," Bennett stresses that people of all cultures have the same "behavioral propensities," are involved in similar technical processes, and have the ability to "modify and pollute Nature" (1976:12, 139–140). This is surely the case, but by using an evolutionary stage perspective, Bennett may have too quickly disregarded small-scale cultures as "only pauses in the overall historical tendency toward exponential increases in environmental use and impact." Bennett specifically warns against ". . . the 'ethnological fallacy' of locating desirable remedies for our own environmental ills in the specialized systems of tribal societies" (1976:12).

When the focus shifts from evolution to scale, however, quantitative differences between cultures can also be critical qualitative differences. Small-scale cultures may indeed point to important remedies that can help solve present problems in a multicultural world. Bennett (1976) recognizes that cultural conditions and institutions can reduce the tendency toward overexploitation, and he even asks whether certain features of equilibrium and disequilibrium cultures might be combined to produce a stable, high-tech, nonpolluting, high-living standard society. This is a reasonable question, but it may be too technocentered and does not give enough weight to cultural diversity.

DeWalt (1988) argues that what is needed is an alternative development paradigm to set new goals. He proposes a list of "precepts for survival," moral principles, which if adopted by the major development agencies, would transform the way development is presently being practiced to make it both achievable and sustainable throughout the world. Specifically he proposes that development must emphasize the following:

Long-term community goals

Nature–culture balance

Local regions and ecosystems

Local resource self-sufficiency

Basic human needs

Decentralization and local autonomy

Local cultural integrity

Justice and equity

Reduction of resource competition

Gradual change, diversity

This kind of development would, in effect, return power to small- and large-scale cultures, while reducing the role of the global market economy and the international political hierarchy. DeWalt notes that the goals he outlines are not new. Many international development agencies already acknowledge the validity of many of the precepts as individual goals, but they have had difficulty actually implementing them as a comprehensive development strategy.

## Small-Scale Cultures, Small Nations, and Global Equity

Many scholars have concluded that the most promising solution to global problems would build on the adaptive advantages of small-scale cultures. The basic principle, alluded to in DeWalt's ten precepts, would be to create a global system with economic and political power concentrated at the lowest levels, in cultural units of the smallest feasible scale. This would reverse the present trend toward centralization, scaling down the problem-causing macroframework, while maximizing democracy, independence, and diversity at all levels. Economist Leopold Kohr presented a pioneer proposal for such a world in his obscure book *The Breakdown of Nations* (1957). Kohr argued that size, or *scale*, was the key to understanding and solving most of the world's problems: ". . . A small-state world would not only solve the problems of social brutality and war: it would solve the equally terrible problems of oppression and tyranny. It would solve all problems arising from power" (1978:79).

In Kohr's view, nations generate "social misery" and tend to break down when they became too large and uncontrollable. He thought that a world composed of small nations of relatively equal power would be safer and more humane. Taking the ethnolinguistic map of Europe as an example, he argued, like Bernard Nietschmann in Chapter 14, that small nations already exist as ethnic groups. They have simply been submerged by the larger, more artificial political units that comprised the old empires or were created during the twentieth-century decolonization process. Anticipating the modern struggle of indigenous peoples and other ethnic "nations" for political autonomy, Kohr proposed that large countries and empires break themselves down into more manageable-sized nations, by offering local "nationalities" equal voting power within a federal system, which would then dissolve itself after a transitional period. He was not optimistic that this would ever happen and wrote a chapter entitled "The Elimination of Great Powers: Can It Be Done?" that contained one word—"No!" (Kohr 1978:229). This is precisely the course that the Soviet Union undertook in 1991–1992 after granting autonomy to the other Warsaw Pact nations.

Kohr's proposal was premature, and his book was largely ignored at the time because it ran counter to the dominant economic development and national integration trends of the late 1950s as the Cold War was intensifying. His work did inspire economist E. F. Schumacher to explore the advantages of small-scale solutions to economic problems in his important book *Small Is Beautiful* (1973).

American anthropologist Sol Tax, working independently, came up with a similar culture scale solution to global problems with his 1977 proposal that the world be divided into 10,000 relatively self-sufficient, politically autonomous "localities" averaging 500,000 people. This world of 5 billion people would be connected by an egalitarian global communication network (Tax 1977). Even in the late 1970s, when world affairs were still dominated by the seemingly static great power blocks of the Cold War, such a devolution of power seemed inconceivably idealistic. However, political events in eastern Europe in the 1990s have demonstrated the continued importance of small ethnic "nations" and have shown that large political and economic structures can scale down relatively peacefully. Perhaps the most difficult problem is the reality that ethnic groups are so frequently intermixed within a common territory.

A more detailed application of the **small-nation alternative** to solving environmental problems was developed in 1972 by a group of British ecologists, who borrowed ideas directly from tribal cultures. Their *Blueprint for Survival* (Goldsmith et al. 1972) spelled out in some detail how Britain could transform itself into a stable and sustainable society, which would "give the fullest possible satisfaction to its members." They proposed a series of measures to be carried out over a 200-year period that would reduce and then stabilize the population at 50 percent its present size. The tax system would be restructured to phase out unsustainable technologies and reward energy- and materials-conserving alternatives. For example, biological controls and organic fertilizers would gradually replace agricultural chemicals. They wanted to decentralize the political and economic system

---

**disequilibrium society**  Bennett's term for a society that consumes natural resources faster than they are produced over the long term.

**ecosystem peoples**  Dasmann's term for societies in small-scale cultures that live in relative balance with their ecosystems.

**biosphere peoples**  Dasmann's term for societies in global-scale cultures that draw resources from throughout the biosphere and thus may be insensitive to local ecosystem damage.

**small-nation alternative**  A proposal for restoring ecological balances and social equity by returning maximum autonomy and self-reliance to small-scale cultural communities within a framework of regional and global institutions.

by creating maximally self-sufficient and self-regulating local communities of 5000 people, grouped into regions of 500,000 with national representation. The local communities were consciously modeled after anthropological descriptions of tribal societies. They would be composed of "neighborhoods" of 500 people that would reproduce face-to-face tribal relationships. The *Blueprint* planners argued that small-scale societies would offer personal satisfactions that would compensate for the reduction in consumption that stability would require. At the same time, such an arrangement would reduce the importance of individual self-reliance as a driving force behind capitalist accumulation (see the discussion of Francis Hsu's theory, Chapter 12). Furthermore, the *Blueprint* planners argued that decentralization, self-sufficiency, and self-regulation would greatly reduce the need for and the costs of transportation, urbanization, and political bureaucracy.

The *Blueprint for Survival* thus envisioned a world composed of small-scale states, combining the best elements of large- and small-scale cultures. Such a solution would not imply that the global system and industrial technology would disappear but that the world would certainly be structured around different goals. A global system of decentralized nation-states would not only be able to respond more effectively to environmental problems, but it would also create ideal conditions for cultural diversity, equality, and democracy (Figure 15.8).

The devolution of political and economic power would promote the kind of "food self-reliance" that researchers at the Institute for Food and Development Policy advocate as a solution to world hunger and poverty. Frances Moore Lappe, Joseph Collins, and Carry Fowler (1978) argue that control over agricultural resources needs to be returned to democratically based communities, to give rural peoples greater economic power. Genuine democracy would also promote greater equality at both community and national levels and would allow the initiative for development to come directly from the people it was designed to benefit. Lappe, Collins, and Fowler are not opposed to international trade but argue that placing food self-reliance, or local self-sufficiency, as a first priority

FIGURE 15.8
*A world of relatively small-scale highly self-sufficient states would perhaps be more egalitarian and secure than a world system dominated by a few giant powers, but the breakup of large multiethnic states can be a painful process as shown by this view of the flight of refugees from Bosnia to Croatia during the fighting that followed the breakup of Yugoslavia in 1992–1993.*

would mean that trade would be more responsive to local needs and would not undermine local markets. Locally based food systems would also be more concerned with the direct nutritional value of food, rather than with its commercial value.

It is significant that moving political power downward to small-scale social units is precisely what indigenous political organizations are asking for, as outlined in Chapter 14. Planners who are dominated by evolutionary stage thinking might see this as a regressive move "back to the Stone Age." However, the issue is not any particular technology by itself; rather, it is how cultures are organized. Contemporary indigenous communities may optimize small-scale cultural features while still operating within a market economy. They make wide use of many types of industrial technology, often using them effectively to protect and extend their independence.

The restructuring envisioned by decentralization really means restoring a more stable balance between the three broad levels of culture scale. This is not a rejection of market-based exchanges, international trade, or state political structures as such. Each organizational level can contribute to human well-being, and a truly stable world probably requires the presence of all three levels. The goal is to create a world that enhances the best aspects of each level. Some form of international organization for conflict resolution, coordination of exchange, and protection of the biosphere will certainly be needed. Before the global system became the dominant level, small-scale cultures continued to thrive and trade with states. Politically independent small-scale cultures often occupied buffer zones between rival states. States can be stable, and they may be effective organizations for managing regional resources and reducing conflict between small-scale cultures. Given democratically chosen political hierarchies, it is also possible for states to minimize the inequalities and inhumanities that historically have been so common.

The most important adjustment in a sustainable world will be establishing social equality and justice in the absence of long-term economic growth. Using the language of capitalist economics, anthropologist Robert Textor (1991) suggests that it may be possible use a **peace dividend** created by the end of the Cold War to deal with the problems of injustice and inequity, which he refers to as the **social deficit**. As was shown in Chapter 11, perpetual growth has always been a fundamental ideological assumption of market economies, and many fear that no growth would mean stagnation and would condemn the impoverished to perpetual poverty. However, "stationary-state" economist Herman Daly (1971) and *The Limits to Growth* study (Meadows et al. 1972) point out that *distribution*, rather than production and growth, will become the most important global issue when production and population are both stabilized at constant levels. Zero growth would mean that social equality would become the highest-priority development goal. When this happens, it will be obvious that small-scale cultures are already highly developed. It would be well to recall that even the evolutionary anthropologist Leslie White, who measured culture advance by increasing energy use, called small-scale mobile foraging cultures "the most satisfying kind of social environment that man has ever lived in":

"[T]heir social systems . . . were unquestionably more congenial to the human primate's nature, and more compatible with his psychic needs and aspirations than any other of the cultures subsequent to the Agricultural Revolution, including our own society today. (1959:277–278)

Developments in the global culture's ideological system beginning with the 1948 Universal Declaration of Human Rights and its expansion to include group cultural rights demonstrate that global institutions can help restore equity and sustainability in a world that has become dangerously imbalanced by the dominance of its commercially driven political economy and energy-intensive technology. Small-scale cultures may yet point the way to a more secure world because a world that can be made safe for small-scale cultures will also be safe for large- and global-scale cultures.

---

**peace dividend** Resources that could be freed from military uses because of the end of the Cold War and could be used to solve social and environmental problems.
**social deficit** Textor's term for a country's failure to provide social equity and environmental quality, as distinguished from national monetary deficits.

## SUMMARY

This chapter explored the most fundamental issue facing humanity: How can a global culture based on perpetual growth and inequality survive in a finite world? In the first section, we found that truly successful cultural adaptation demands a long-term balance between available resources and consumption. In theory, there are measurable limits beyond which cultures cannot expand without degrading their resources and threatening their own existence. Industrial systems that rely primarily on fossil fuels will necessarily be a short-lived phenomenon lasting a few centuries at best; in contrast, cultural systems designed for lower levels of consumption can maintain a balance with renewable sources of solar energy and thus could exist for millions of years.

In the second section, we considered the ominous possibility that critical carrying-capacity limits may already have been exceeded, given the present structure of the global culture. Whether or not human-induced global warming is already underway, people now clearly have the capability to disrupt the life-support systems of the planet in a way that would have been inconceivable a mere 200 years ago. Food-production systems are being strained in many areas of the world; unless distribution systems and consumption patterns can be modified, it is unlikely that even the most optimistic technological solutions will prevent Malthusian crises.

In the final section, we considered alternative solutions to create a more secure human future. Our comparative analysis of cultural systems from an anthropological culture scale perspective suggests that an equitable and secure world needs to combine the best features of small-, large-, and global-scale cultural patterns. Social justice and preservation of the biosphere will require effective management by highly autonomous local communities, democratic regional governments, and fully representative global institutions.

## STUDY QUESTIONS

1. In what sense can cultural development be called a "mixed blessing" that both solves problems and creates new ones? Use specific examples from each level of culture scale.

2. Explain White's law of cultural evolution and discuss its limitations as a measure of human progress. Refer to Sun Day, Liebig's law of the minimum, and the cycle of world oil production.

3. What are the problems with using increasing cultural control over nature and human reproductive success as measures of greater human adaptability? Refer to consumer biomass, biodiversity, and resource depletion.

4. What is the basis for the optimism of resource economists and futurist planners who argue that there are no limits to the availability of resources?

5. Compare the Club of Rome, *The Limits to Growth Study*, and *The Global 2000 Report*, referring to basic assumptions, methods, and conclusions.

6. Discuss the dynamics of global warming, referring to the greenhouse effect, greenhouse gases, fossil fuels, carbon cycle, carbon sinks, sea-level rise, and thermal expansion. What degree of warming and sea-level rise is predicted over the next century?

7. Why is there uncertainty about the rate and pace of global climate and sea-level changes? Why do some challenge the consensus view?

8. What are the likely consequences of global warming?

9. Why is it difficult to apply a carrying-capacity model to the global system? What variables need to be considered in setting a global maximum for human population? What different estimates have been proposed?

10. Critique the Malthusian model of food production and population growth. Refer to natural and cultural checks on population, diminishing returns, and absolute limits on food production.

11. What evidence is there that global food production may already be overextended? What factors set absolute limits to food production?

12. Distinguish between predominately technological approaches to world problems from those that are more broadly cultural. Provide specific examples.

13. Discuss the problematic broad trends in cultural development enumerated by DeWalt. Refer to cultural scale, macroframework, hierarchical anomaly, and ecological transition.

14. Distinguish between equilibrium and disequilibrium cultures and ecosystem and biosphere peoples, relating both sets of concepts to culture scale.

15. Describe DeWalt's alternative development paradigm, specifying how it is different from current patterns of development.

16. What is the argument in favor of the devolution of political and economic power as a solution to world problems?

## SUGGESTED READING

BARNEY, GERALD O. (ED.). 1977–1980. *The Global 2000 Report to the President of the United States*, 3 vols. New York: Pergamon. A study of global trends and predictions to the year 2000, commissioned by President Carter in 1977.

BROWN, LESTER R. (ED.). 1987–. *State of the World* (annual). New York and London: Norton. Annual surveys of global conditions and prospects covering such issues as food, health, environment, and economics.

IPCC (INTERGOVERNMENTAL PANEL ON CLIMATE CHANGE). 1991. *Climate Change: The IPCC Response Strategies*. Washington, D.C., and Covelo, Calif.: Island Press. Presents the findings of an international panel assembled by the United Nations in 1988 to examine the long-range issue of global climate change.

KOHR, LEOPOLD. 1978. *The Breakdown of Nations*, reprint. New York: Dutton. Economist Kohr's argument that global problems are primarily a result of nations being too large.

KOTLER, NEIL G. (ED.). 1990. *Sharing Innovation: Global Perspectives on Food, Agriculture, and Rural Development*. Washington, D.C., and London: Smithsonian Institution Press. The proceedings of a conference on the world food problem sponsored by the Smithsonian Institution in 1989, exploring the technological limits to production.

MEADOWS, DONELLA H., DENNIS L. MEADOWS, JORGEN RANDERS, AND WILLIAM W. BEHRENS, III. 1972. *The Limits to Growth*. New York: Universe. The first widely publicized computer simulation of the global system, designed to diagnose problems and seek solutions.

SINGER, S. FRED (ED.). 1989. *Global Climate Change: Human and Natural Influences*. New York: Paragon House. An overview of the climate-change issue by a distinguished panel of specialists.

# 16

# HISTORY OF THEORY IN CULTURAL ANTHROPOLOGY

In this chapter, we introduce the most important theoretical perspectives that have dominated the history of anthropology since the late nineteenth century and illustrate them with several case studies. How and why cultures differ and change are two of the biggest anthropological questions that have been answered by different theories. These very broad questions are the central theme of this book, which seeks to understand the differences between tribes, states, and the global system and the how and why of culture scale changes. Culture change questions are focused on the three great historical divides, which were introduced in Chapter 1: sedentary living, political centralization, and commercialization. For example, an obvious culture change question is, If small-scale foraging peoples were well adapted and living comfortably, why did they ever settle down and become farmers? What were the social consequences of this change? Another major question is, Why did any independent and egalitarian villagers ever surrender their freedom to chiefs and then go on to pay taxes and build pyramids? We have no definitive answers to such questions, but it is the search for answers that makes anthropology so exciting. The

chapter ends with a discussion of the place of anthropology as an academic discipline.

## ANTHROPOLOGICAL MODES OF EXPLANATION

Just as any attempt to understand another culture is colored by the biases of one's own culture, the explanations that anthropologists devise are shaped by their theoretical preconceptions about cultures and how they work. Some understanding of different theoretical approaches is important because they can lead to very different answers to basic questions. For example, an anthropologist who assumes that religious belief is more important than food getting will have a different view from someone who thinks that people are more concerned with keeping their stomachs full than with fulfilling ritual obligations.

The modes of explanation, or the theories, that anthropologists have used have changed over time like fashions, often reflecting changes in national politics and the global culture itself. Anthropologists have accounted for cultural variation and change using at least five broad modes of explanation: biological, cultural materialist, mentalist, historical, and functionalist. These explanation modes are sometimes so strongly identified with specific theoretical schools or scientific paradigms that they may be called "-isms." In some cases, an entire subculture of anthropologists may conduct all their fieldwork, write all their ethnographies, and train students using one particular approach. Some British anthropologists certainly did this with functionalism at one time. Some modes of explanation may be compatible and even overlapping, whereas others dramatically conflict and have led to spirited public debates between their proponents. Each explanation mode will be briefly introduced in this section, but throughout the book examples have been drawn from all these modes. They will be specifically identified, and their relative utility will be critically evaluated. Although I have tried to strike a balance between rival theorists, sometimes my favorites have been championed. Intellectual conflicts are what anthropology is all about.

Prior to 1945, when the modern colonial era ended, *biological explanations* were closely linked with European notions of cultural superiority. At that time, this approach could be called *racist* because it equated cultural differences with racial differences that were assumed to be inferior. In extreme cases, biological determinism took the form of *social Darwinism,* applying Charles Darwin's (1809–1882) natural selection, "survival of the fittest" theory of biological evolution to cultures. Social Darwinists concluded that the peoples and cultures that European colonialists were destroying were culturally and biologically "unfit" and therefore doomed to disappear. Modern sociobiological explanations are much more sophisticated and avoid racist categories, while focusing on the genetic consequences of specific cultural practices. For example, as was discussed in Chapter 3, Napoleon Chagnon argues that the aggressive behavior of bigmen in Amazonia is a genetic advantage. He maintains that success in intervillage conflict allows bigmen to have more wives and more offspring than ordinary men.

*Cultural materialist explanations* emphasize the technological and environmental base of culture. Culture may be variously seen as determined,

or limited, by the environment and shaped by the technological system. From this perspective, cultures are composed of discrete technological, social, and ideological subsystems, with the technological component determining the social system and the social system determining the ideological system. Thus, it has been argued that the cattle-based technology of East African cattle herders predisposes the culture to male dominance because men control the cattle, which provide the most critical food and raw materials. Materialists also explain cattle herding as an adaptation to an arid environment that will not reliably support settled farming.

*Mentalist explanations* reverse the materialist argument, instead treating cultural values, ideas, psychological processes, and symbolic systems as the prime determinants of cultural variation. For example, some have suggested that East Africans herd cattle because they value cattle highly or have a psychological fixation on them.

During the colonial era, many social Darwinist anthropologists interpreted cultural differences according to their own biased assumptions about culture history. In this *historical explanation,* these anthropologists typically viewed small-scale cultures as living fossils representing the earlier stages of evolutionary development that Europeans had "advanced" beyond. This theory of culture history helps explain Staniland Wake's treatment of Australian aborigines as backward children, but it was extremely ethnocentric and made it difficult

---

**biological explanation** The use of evolutionary biology, physical type, or genetics to explain cultural variation.

**racism** Attributes differences between cultures to physical differences in human populations and assumes that some peoples and cultures are inherently superior.

**social Darwinsim** Assumes that only "superior" peoples and cultures are fit to survive.

**cultural materialist explanation** Assumes that material conditions, especially environment, resources, and technology, are the most important factors shaping cultures.

**mentalist explanation** Considers ideas, values, and symbols to be the primary force in cultural development.

**historical explanation** The existence of particular cultural traits is attributed to general theories of evolutionary development or historical events such as diffusion or borrowing.

to understand the positive achievements of small-scale cultures. Lewis Henry Morgan's theory of culture history, which will be examined later in this chapter, provides a more sophisticated example of the **cultural evolutionism** historical approach.

Other historically oriented anthropologists have been called diffusionists. They attempt to reconstruct the origin of individual culture traits, often attributing them to accidents of diffusion or borrowing from other, presumably more creative, cultures. For example, some theorists supposed that certain basic traits such as writing or pyramid building were invented only once by superior peoples and then spread to less capable peoples. The **diffusionism** of Grafton Elliot Smith and W. J. Perry will be presented in later sections as an example of such an approach. A major shortcoming of diffusionism is that borrowing is not always easy to distinguish from independent development. Furthermore, diffusionism is not concerned with how cultures actually work and, like evolutionism, can often be very ethnocentric.

**Functionalist explanations** refer to the way in which cultural practices are assumed to contribute to the survival of a culture. For example, a functionalist might argue that witchcraft beliefs existed as a means of controlling internal aggression. Such analysis can lead to useful insights and understanding. Functionalist anthropologists produced some superb ethnographies because they viewed other cultures as integrated systems, but functionalist explanations are circular and logically unsatisfactory, as will be discussed in a later section.

The relative popularity of different explanations may reflect contemporary political concerns. For example, racist biological explanations and evolutionary and diffusionist historical explanations supported an ideology of European racial and cultural superiority. Functionalist explanations facilitated the colonial administration of native peoples, and materialist explanations were related to issues of class conflict, environment, and resources that have become especially prominent since the 1960s. Given today's critical global problems, it is not surprising that materialist perspectives are especially prominent in this book, especially in Chapters 11–15 where the global system itself was considered.

In the following case studies, we examine some of the earlier theoretical perspectives that have been superseded by recent concerns but retain historic interest.

# Lewis Henry Morgan and Cultural Evolution

*. . . Portions of the human family have existed in a state of savagery, other portions in a state of barbarism, and still other portions in a state of civilization . . . these three distinct conditions are connected with each other in a natural as well as necessary sequence of progress.*   (Morgan 1877:3)

The book *Ancient Society* (1877), by pioneer American anthropologist Lewis Henry Morgan (1818–1881), is the classic example of nineteenth-century cultural evolutionary interpretations of world cultural development. Morgan occupies a unique place in the history of anthropology because, besides his important work in cultural evolution, he laid the foundation for the study of kinship systems (1871), conducted original fieldwork (Figure 16.1), and wrote the first modern ethnographic monograph (1851).

Morgan was a firm believer in the inevitability of progress and set out to classify and rank all the "branches of the human family" by the stage of their relative advancement toward the achievements of Euro-American civilization, which for him represented the highest type of humanity. Even though he believed that his Aryan and Semitic branches were the "central stream of human progress" and the world's most advanced peoples, Morgan was more open-minded than many anthropologists of his time. He argued emphatically for the essential unity of humankind, assuming that people's minds everywhere worked the same way and all people had the same potential for development. Peoples differed in their relative cultural achievements simply because they had not yet had sufficient time or favorable enough circumstances to move ahead.

Morgan was a lawyer and a New York state congressman and became modestly wealthy from his investments in mines and railroads, but he was also an adopted member of the Seneca tribe and remained a firm supporter of the political rights of Native Americans.

FIGURE 16.1 *American lawyer and pioneer anthropologist Lewis Henry Morgan (1818–1881) developed his theories of progressive cultural evolution in the last half of the nineteenth century as the global culture was invading territories occupied by small-scale cultures throughout the world.*

TABLE 16.1  *Cultural Evolution Stages*

| Thomsen's Ages (1836) | Archaeological Stone Ages | Morgan's Stages (1877) |
| --- | --- | --- |
| Iron | | Civilization |
| Bronze | | |
| | Neolithic | Barbarism |
| | ⇑ | |
| | Domestication | |
| | Foraging | |
| | ⇓ | |
| | Mesolithic | |
| Stone | | Savagery |
| | Paleolithic | |

As labels for his global stages of human progress, Morgan rejected the earlier European technological sequence of *Stone, Bronze,* and *Iron,* proposed by Danish archaeologist Christian Thomsen in 1836. Instead, he employed the terms *Savagery, Barbarism,* and *Civilization* for the three major stages (see Table 16.1), distinguishing and subdividing them by a mixed criteria of subsistence, settlement, and technological traits and using the invention of writing as the sole measure of civilization. He assumed 100,000 years of human existence and allowed 60,000 years for the stage of uninterrupted savagery, which was characterized by nomadic life with plant collecting, fishing, and hunting. Lower Barbarism began with settled village life, which Morgan associated with pottery making. Middle Barbarism involved food production and pastoralism, and Upper Barbarism, the use of iron. Within 15,000 years, Barbarism led to Civilization.

Critics called Morgan's approach **unilinear evolution,** arguing that it was unduly rigid because it required every culture to follow an invariant sequence of stages on its way to civilization. He was also criticized for giving insufficient attention to historical factors such as the diffusion of traits between cultures. Morgan did allow for such borrowing, but his main interest was **general evolution** by progressive stages, rather than **specific**

**evolution,** which involves the details of individual cultures adapting to local conditions. In reconstructing his stages, he relied on the **comparative method,** which involves using contemporary peoples arranged by order of complexity to reconstruct earlier stages. This technique is still widely used, but it means making assumptions about earlier conditions that may not be verifiable.

There has been considerable controversy over which mechanisms, or determinants, of cultural development Morgan considered most important. Many scholars have been impressed by his emphasis on material factors, especially subsistence, and they call him a "materialist." Certainly, he thought

**cultural evolutionism**  Concerned with the historical development of culture through sequential stages.

**diffusionism**  Considers borrowing to be the primary force in cultural development.

**functionalist explanation**  The existence of particular cultural traits is attributed to their role, or survival value, in maintaining the culture.

**unilineal evolution**  A variety of general evolutionary theory that assumes that all cultures must go through the same progressive stages of development.

**general evolution**  Broad levels of evolutionary "progress" measured by complexity, energy use, subsistence, adaptability, and so on. May be applied to development of culture of humanity as a whole.

**specific evolution**  The culture history of a single culture or a group of related cultures and their adaptation to local environments.

**comparative method**  Using ethnographically described cultures to reconstruct culture history and to infer earlier stages of development.

that "enlarging the basis of subsistence" was a fundamental prerequisite for human progress, and he devoted the first three chapters of *Ancient Society* to inventions and discoveries. The bulk of his book (twenty-three chapters), however, covers the growth of "ideas" or social and political institutions, which he treated as mental and moral improvement. In his scheme, monogamy, private property, and the territorially organized state were the real indicators of progress. Although Morgan was not a strict economic determinist, his work gave a boost to the politicoeconomic theories of revolutionary socialist philosophers such as Karl Marx and Friedrich Engels and was a major inspiration for later cultural anthropologists such as Leslie White who considered per-capita increases in energy use to be a basic measure of evolutionary progress.

Although many of the details of Morgan's sequence were based on inaccurate data and his moral evaluations may seem inappropriate, many of his basic assumptions about progress can be seen in the continuing use of sequential archaeological stages such as **Paleolithic, Mesolithic,** and **Neolithic.**

## Evolutionary Progress or Complexity Scales?

The notions of ranking and the inevitability of progress that are associated with evolutionary models can obviously stand in the way of a genuine understanding of world cultures. The ranking of cultures along a developmental scale may involve the ethnocentric assumption that the most "developed" cultures are somehow "higher" and "better" than the "lower" and therefore "inferior" cultures. The belief that all cultures must progress may be equally unwarranted. Sympathetic understanding of other cultures requires careful consideration of the criteria for ranking, or the measures of "progress," and a recognition of the actual causes of changes in complexity.

The criteria for evolutionary progress listed by Marshall Sahlins (1960) include greater energy use, greater adaptability, and higher levels of integration, measured by more parts, more specialization, and more effective integration. Thus, more evolved cultures are larger and more complex, exploit more ecosystems, and deplete resources at a faster rate. Whether life is better, more humane, or more secure for individuals is another matter. "Advanced" cultures may have more social inequality and great potential for environmental degradation than "lower" cultures.

Cultures can certainly be arranged by order of complexity, and this may be useful for certain purposes. Robert Carneiro and Stephen Tobias (1963) examined one hundred cultures for the presence of fifty culture traits presumably related to complexity and demonstrated that traits were indeed added in a predictable sequence. For example, if a culture had a legal code, it would also have craft specialists (see Figure 7.2). Carneiro (1967) has also shown a direct mathematical relationship between the population size of independent local communities and the number of traits related to social organization—the larger the community, the greater the organizational complexity. The undoubted existence of such sequences does not mean that all cultures will inevitably, or even should, increase in complexity. The specific causes of increase in cultural complexity is a major theoretical problem for anthropology and have been examined in detail in earlier chapters.

The persistent notion of the inevitability of evolutionary progress can have important political implications. Inevitability suggests that cultures can never remain at a given "level" unless they are stagnant or retarded. Such thinking is reflected in the common tendency to speak of tribal peoples as children on their way to adulthood. If they remain too long as "children," they must be "retarded." This notion of "savages" as children was implicit in Morgan's work and was unfortunately the basis of colonial policies that made tribal peoples legal wards of the state, incapable of controlling their own lives and natural resources. Today, the pervasive belief in the inevitability of progress makes it difficult to defend Amazonians against highways, dams, mining, and other development projects.

In the following two sections, we present case studies of racist and diffusionist theories that are part of the history of anthropology, although they have been thoroughly discredited. Today these examples may seem quaint and absurd, and even embarrassingly offensive, but they appeared in respectable scientific forums in their day, and their underlying ethnocentric assumptions have not entirely disappeared.

## Griffith Taylor's Race, Climate, and Migration Zones

Perhaps the most sophisticated racist view of world cultural development in the tradition of social Darwinist evolutionary thought was the antiquated "migration zones theory" proposed by Australian geographer Griffith Taylor (1937). Taylor wanted to explain the origin and global distribution of the human "racial types" that he distinguished, while he sought to account for variation in cultural development. Both a "scientific" racist and an environmental determinist, he was very aware that his interpretations had direct political implications. In hindsight, Taylor's views are absurdly misguided, and most of his basic assumptions had already been disproven decades earlier by American anthropologists; nevertheless, he found sympathetic supporters.

Taylor broadly distinguished five racial types and their corresponding language and culture types that he ranked by their order of emergence and migration outward from an unorthodox "cradle of humanity," which he supposed to be in central Asia. His racial types were identified by head shape, skin color, stature, and hair form. He inferred that each type was a product of the cyclical fluctuation in climate during the past million years of the Pleistocene geological epoch. He picked central Asia as the center because of its environmental complexity and because it could be considered the geographical center of the world with Africa, Australasia, and the Americas radiating out as peninsulas.

According to Taylor, racial and cultural development was in direct proportion to climatic stimulation and environmental resources. Central Asia and the adjoining temperate zones, including Europe, the Mediterranean, China, and India, were considered to be dynamic "regions of stimulus," but they were surrounded by the tropical zones, which he labeled "zones of stagnation" because the seasons were relatively uniform. The Arctic was a "zone of privation" because, although it was stimulating, it was simply too severe to promote proper development. Each racial type supposedly arose during the favorable interglacial periods and then was pushed out of central Asia by the successive ice ages at roughly 200,000-year intervals. Each new group was progressively superior, both physically and culturally, and simply pushed aside and dispossessed the "inferior" peoples that preceded them. For Taylor, the best measure of racial identity and superiority was head shape as measured by cephalic index (maximum skull width-length × 100), which increased with brain size and presumably reflected increased mental ability. Actually head form can be molded by cultural practices, and for normal humans, there is no relationship between brain size and intelligence. Today no reputable anthropologist would equate cephalic index with cultural or intellectual potential.

Taylor identified the first, most "primitive" race with the Acheulean artifacts of the Lower Paleolithic and considered the Tasmanian aborigines, Bushmen, Pygmies, and so-called negrito foragers scattered throughout Southeast Asia to be their modern representatives. He thought that these peoples were so childlike and inferior that they were all doomed to extinction. The "Negro" races were archaeologically identified with the Mousterian and Neandertaloids of the Middle Paleolithic and in Taylor's earliest schemes included the modern Australian aborigines, South Asian tribal peoples, and tropical Africans. In his later refinements, Taylor elevated the Australoids to a higher level and demoted the Africans and Melanesians because of their "cruelty, superstition, and ignorance" (1937:127). As lower races and residents of the "zones of stagnation," Negro peoples were unable to reach a "high state of civilization," and any apparent exceptions were attributed to admixture with higher races. Mediterranean peoples were credited with developing Upper Paleolithic art and technology and the early Neolithic. Only the Mediterranean types and the late arriving "Alpine"

---

**Paleolithic**   Archaeological Old Stone Age stage of mobile foraging.
**Mesolithic**   Archaeological Middle Stone Age stage of initial sedentism and subsistence intensification preceding domestication.
**Neolithic**   Archaeological New Stone Age stage distinguished by ceramics, domestication, and settled village life.

peoples, the Asians and Europeans, were truly "progressive" folks capable of developing worthwhile civilization.

The political agenda behind Taylor's work was made explicit in the final chapters of his 1937 work *Environment, Race, and Migration,* in which he assessed the potential of the world's resources and environments to sustain an expanding European population. He mapped the world into "habitability" zones ranked for suitability for settlement by his "white" races. For example, he projected a future white population in southern Africa of 82 million, while conspicuously ignoring the possible fate of the prior population. Taylor's work had little appeal for American anthropologists, thanks to the antiracist, antievolutionist influence of Franz Boas, but by 1937 Taylor was pleased to note that German ethnologists were working along similar lines. Ironically, he hoped that his work would promote human brotherhood. Taylor thought that race prejudice would be reduced by his form of ethnological knowledge and world peace would follow when "each nation realizes the place in the world's 'order of precedence' for which its racial, intellectual, and economic status equips it" (1937:468).

## The Diffusionists: Great Waves and Fantastic Archaeology

There have been many popular explanations of cultural diversity that attribute key cultural developments to diffusion from one or more special creative sources, rather than appealing to development in place. Many of these theories are totally lacking in scientific credibility and can easily be relegated to the "lunatic fringe." For example, Erich van Daniken (1970) assumed that ancient astronauts visited the earth and influenced the development of various civilizations (Figure 16.2). More recently, "New Age" writer José Arguelles (1987), drawing on crystals and channeling, has proposed that Maya civilization was similarly of extraterrestrial origin. Other writers have appealed to cultural origins from mythical sunken continents, such as Atlantis or Mu in the Pacific (see Wauchope 1962). Marine biologist Barry Fell (1976) claimed to have deciphered a series of rock markings and concluded that North America received

major Old World "cultural input" from Egyptians, Libyans, the Basques, and Celts over millennia before the arrival of Columbus. Psychic "archaeologist" Jeffrey Goodman, in his book *American Genesis* (1981) makes southern California the original Garden of Eden from which humanity populated the world.

Generally, such theories can easily be recognized as unscientific and cultlike because they are narrow, oversimplistic, and too often appeal to belief and special authority in opposition to established fact (Cole 1980, Williams 1988). The problem with many of these claims is that they are simply not supported by the evidence and must be accepted on faith. For example, the "mysterious" rock art figures that van Daniken (1970) takes as evidence of ancient astronauts are more plausibly interpreted as dancers wearing headdresses. These writers see mysteries everywhere because they selectively ignore more direct interpretations.

Although these unorthodox interpretations may be in fashion only briefly, they sometimes enjoy enormous popularity. Van Daniken's *Chariots of the Gods* (1970) sold some 40 million copies during the 1970s. Recognizing and critically evaluating such works is important because, even though they are justifiably rejected by the scientific establishment, they may be continually rediscovered by naive readers.

In the remainder of this section, we briefly examine the "great wave theory" of British anthropologists Grafton Elliot Smith (1928) and W. J. Perry (1923). This diffusionist theory assumed that all but certain favored people were uninventive and prone to degeneration or cultural loss. Such extreme diffusionist interpretations of cultural development were rejected by anthropological critics of the time because they were unsupported by the evidence; however, they are useful examples of the excesses of "scientific" ethnocentrism.

Smith and Perry believed that all significant cultural developments, from farming to pottery making, originated in Egypt and spread in a "great wave" from that center throughout the world. In their view, there were two types of preindustrial world cultures: Lower Cultures and Archaic Civilization. People in the Lower Cultures were "improvident and conservative" and simply could never have developed farming, or much of any-

FIGURE 16.2   *In his* Chariots of the Gods, *Erich Von Daniken suggests that the gigantic lines and figures drawn on the desert floor of Peru's south coast were navigational aids for ancient astronauts, but they are actually a feature of traditional Andean cosmology. (SOURCE: Bates Littlehales © 1964 National Geographic Society.)*

thing else, without outside help, as Perry asserts: ". . . Not one particle of evidence exists to warrant the belief that any food-producing people of lowly culture can be shown independently to have invented any of those fundamental arts and crafts that they possess" (1923:113).

They simply ignored the abundant archaeological evidence of long and gradual in-place cultural development throughout the world. Perry maintained that the Archaic Civilization was entirely developed by the Egyptians, "the master people of antiquity" (1923:53). Archaic Civilization was identified in its original form by a list of fifteen culture elements that included irrigation agriculture, stone pyramids and tombs, pottery, metal working, stone images, polished stone tools, mummifi-

cation, a sun cult, war chiefs, human sacrifice, a mother-goddess, matriliny, totemic clans, moieties, and exogamy. As discussed in previous chapters, there is no reason to treat these elements as a single complex or to believe that they could not occur independently.

Smith and Perry claimed that irrigation agriculture based on Nile flooding was the earliest and sole source of agriculture *anywhere* in the world. Building on their agriculture base, Egyptians then became master artists, shipbuilders, and artisans who excelled at everything. Archaic Civilization spread as Egyptians explored and colonized the world looking for mineral resources. Smith and Perry considered the appearance anywhere in the world of any of the fifteen culture traits identified with their Archaic Civilization to be positive evidence of Egyptian influence. They also inferred that when other peoples borrowed these elements, they were never as capable as the Egyptians and often degenerated, losing key elements. This accounted for the presence of farming among members of the Lower Cultures.

Their theories were couched in scientific language referring to "theorems, principles, and rules," which were simply highly subjective, untestable assertions. The most important "general principle" was Perry's claim that ". . . nothing is rarer, in the history of the world, than invention." Perry also proposed a "general theorem . . . of practically universal application . . . that the Egyptians invariably excelled all other ancient peoples in their skill in the manipulation of raw materials" (1923:21).

This "theorem" lended itself to circular arguments and was unfalsifiable because any counterclaims would be seen as proof of Egyptian influence. Another "rule" stated that a borrowed craft or skill is always degraded by the borrowers.

It is not surprising that Smith and Perry selected Egypt as the cradle of world civilization because Egyptology was a very popular interest at that time and the general outlines of Egyptian ar-

chitecture, writing, calendrics, arts and crafts, and religion were fairly well known. Major new archaeological discoveries were also taking place in Egypt and sparking wide speculation. For example, Tutankhamen's spectacular tomb was uncovered by British archaeologist Howard Carter in 1922. Moreover, world archaeological sequences were still poorly known, although the broad outlines were clear, and it was not immediately possible to refute all diffusionist claims with counter-evidence.

## Functionalism, Colonialism, and Ethnocentrism

Fortunately, by the 1920s, the predominant theoretical paradigm in cultural anthropology shifted from evolution to functionalism. Anthropologists began to examine living small-scale cultures in their own terms, rather than seeing them as survivors of inferior developmental stages. The leading functionalist anthropologists, such as A. R. Radcliffe-Brown and Bronislaw Malinowski (Figure 16.3), treated cultures as organisms and demonstrated how specific customs and institutions were interconnected and "functioned" to maintain the total system. Lists of the basic needs of individ-

FIGURE 16.3
*Polish-born Bronislaw Malinowski (1884–1942), shown here in New Guinea, was a leading developer of functionalist anthropology who advocated extensive fieldwork.*

uals and societies were drawn up. The goal became to show how cultures worked, or functioned, at a given time, not how they came to be.

Functionalist analysis forced anthropologists to make detailed studies of individual cultures from the inside and to follow out connections that a superficial observer might easily overlook. This approach requires extensive field research, knowledge of the language, work with informants, genealogies and life histories, and direct participation in the culture. These ethnographic techniques still distinguish cultural anthropology from sociology, which relies more on survey questionnaires.

Functionalism, used by all social sciences, is a valuable research strategy, though logically flawed as an explanation for why cultures have particular features. Its assumptions are inherently teleological—culture traits are assumed to exist by design to serve a specific end—but it can rarely be shown that an alternative trait might not function just as well. This leads to tautologies, or circular arguments, in which a trait is explained by its function, which is explained in turn by the trait. Cultures are also treated as if they existed as closed systems in timeless equilibrium, even though change is known to be a continuous process and cultures are rarely isolated.

The functionalists considered their work to be objective science, as the title of Malinowski's book *A Scientific Theory of Culture* (1944) suggests, but they were also driven by the need of colonial administrators to control the diverse peoples in their newly expanded empires. The working assumption that the various elements of culture are integrated and that culture may be thought of as a system of interconnected parts had immediate practical implications. Researchers could show that even well-intended outside intervention in another culture could have wide-ranging, even disastrous effects. Functionalist anthropologists soon found themselves advising colonial governments on how best to minimize the disruption of taxation and labor recruitment of native peoples. They also suggested ways of replacing "offensive" customs with acceptable alternatives that would preserve a culture's prior equilibrium. Administrators realized that it made economic sense to maintain self-sufficient local communities to provide their own social welfare while reproducing a cheap labor force.

FIGURE 16.4   *German immigrant Franz Boas (1858–1942) was the primary architect of the four-field approach to anthropology (archaeology, cultural, linguistics, and physical) as taught in the United States to overcome racial prejudice and ethnocentrism.*

## Franz Boas: Anthropology Against Racism and Ethnocentrism

The approach of American anthropologists to the understanding of cultural differences was profoundly influenced by Franz Boas who, during his years as professor at Columbia University from 1899 to 1937, trained many of the researchers who became the most prominent anthropologists throughout the country. Boas and his students founded a distinctive school of American anthropology that has been called historicist, or historical particularist (Harris 1968), because it focused on the specific historical complexity of cultural development, emphasized facts over ethnocentric speculation, and argued that grand scientific "laws" of cultural evolution would probably never be found (Figure 16.4).

A German immigrant with a Jewish heritage, Boas was especially sensitive to cultural and racial discrimination. Throughout his career, he remained emphatically opposed to any theories of racial superiority or that attributed cultural difference to racial type. He also brought with him a distrust of materialist theories, whether environmental or economic, and any historical explanations that relied on lawlike sequences of evolutionary stages.

The Boasian position on race and culture remains the standard anthropological orthodoxy and led to a universal repudiation of earlier racist theories. His arguments were laid out very clearly in his early classic *The Mind of Primitive Man* (1911). In that book, Boas used two approaches in his attack on racism. First, he picked examples to show that different popularly recognized racial types, such as Asians and Europeans, could both support civilized cultures, and within a single racial type, both civilized and "primitive" cultures could be found. Furthermore, he showed in the same way that there was no absolute connection between language, nationality, and race.

Second, Boas systematically demonstrated that the popular concept of "race" was scientifically invalid except when applied to the inherited characteristics of a specific family line. He used many examples to show that there were no sharp lines between "races" because the inherited traits of different populations overlapped widely and often varied along continuums. He also pointed to cases in which unrelated populations resembled one another through convergence. Human groups were constantly moving and their genetic composition was changing, thus there were no "pure" or stable races. Environmental and cultural factors, especially nutrition, could also modify body form and size, quite apart from heredity. Even the cephalic indexes, which Griffith Taylor thought were so important, were not reliable measures of genetic inheritance.

Boas (1911) argued that it was impossible to rank different human groups by relative closeness to a prehuman ancestor because different populations showed different "primitive" traits in no consistent pattern. Similarly, he showed that mental traits were related to cultural, not biological, differences; therefore, IQ tests were not measuring innate ability. His primary point was that there were no significant biologically inherited differences between human populations that would reduce the cultural potential of any group or that would offer any justification for labels of racial inferiority or superiority. Pointing to the universality of many common cultural traits, such as fire, the incest taboo, and belief in spirits, Boas assumed the emotional and mental unity of all modern humans. Many common cultural patterns were simply "elementary ideas," likely to recur independently among different peoples. Other traits he attributed to historical factors such as diffusion or to a common inheritance from the very origins of humanity, assuming a single origin. He considered environment to be a limiting influence, not a determining factor. In regard to stages of cultural evolutionary development, he generally rejected the notion of universal evolutionary sequences and emphasized that similar institutions could arise for different reasons and many institutions considered to be the same are actually unique when examined emically.

Boas was very aware of the political implications of his work, and it was no surprise when the German translation of *The Mind of Primitive Man* was burned by the Nazis and his doctorate degree from the University of Kiel was "rescinded." His later book *Anthropology and Modern Life* (1928) was written to reduce racial prejudice in the United States and as a critique of racially based U.S. immigration policies. He also opposed then-popular eugenics programs, arguing that criminals, alcoholics, and other "degenerates" were the products of social conditions including "abject poverty" that pushed people into "helpless and hopeless misery," rather than productions of inferior genetics.

Historical particularism has been criticized as nonexplanation (Harris 1968) because Boas and many of his students seemed reluctant to generalize and avoided evolutionary models. However, Boasian anthropologists did group similar cultures into culture areas on the basis of shared traits in order to simplify the task of describing the cultures of entire continents. Culture areas were subjective, implied no great time depth, and were geographically bounded, often reflecting adaptive responses to natural environments. They were intuitive, descriptive statements rather than explanatory devices. Culture areas are still widely used to organize ethnographic survey courses and museum displays, and they do provide a rapid sample of the cultural diversity of a region (see Figure 1.5).

The cultural "patterns" or "configurations" described by Boasian anthropologist Ruth Benedict in her famous book *Patterns of Culture* (1934) are similarly not really explanatory. Benedict simply declared that cultures differed in their "patterns" because they stressed different things. Although Benedict was an advocate of cultural relativity, her characterizations of other cultures were often curiously ethnocentric and derogatory. In her view, certain cultural behavior, such as sorcery and revenge killings, that we would recognize as "reprehensible" or even "psychotic" might be the central focus of another culture. Benedict identified cultures by what she considered to be their dominant personality types. She portrayed the Pueblos of the American Southwest in positive terms as "Apollonian," moderate, middle-of-the-road types, whereas Plains and Northwest Coast natives were presented negatively as "Dionysian," prone to extreme, sometimes violent behavior. Benedict's work made a wide audience aware of cultural differences, but much of it was unfortunately impressionistic stereotyping that did little to promote cross-cultural understanding.

Despite Benedict's ethnocentric slant, Boasians promoted objectivity and careful fieldwork and helped popularize the concepts of culture and cultural relativity. They were instrumental in exposing the racism of earlier evolutionary theories.

## ANTHROPOLOGY AS A DISCIPLINE

### Anthropology and the Social Sciences

Disciplines such as sociology, economics, political science, and social psychology analyze various aspects of contemporary human social behavior, and until its recent discovery of "social history," history chronicled the unique events of specific literate civilizations. Only anthropology is concerned with all aspects of human life, society, and culture, everywhere, since the earliest prehistory. The breadth of anthropological interests is dramatically illustrated by the 224 subject categories that were used to index the specialties of the 4765 anthropologists listed in the *Fifth International Directory of Anthropologists* in 1975. In comparison, the American Sociological Association's 1986 *Directory of Members* needed only 24 categories to index the specialties of its 12,192 members. Nearly all the sociological specialities would also be covered by

anthropology. Social or cultural anthropology retains close ties to sociology, given their mutual interest in society, and some academic departments combine both fields. However, anthropology is more consistently concerned with culture, prehistory, and cross-cultural research.

American anthropologists are often trained in human biology, archaeology, and linguistics, along with cultural anthropology. Cultural anthropologists developed many of their basic concepts and research techniques through participant observation of small scale-tribal cultures for months or years at a time. Today anthropologists study all types of cultures and borrow freely from the methods and theories of all the social sciences (Figure 16.5).

As an organized scholarly activity, anthropology was a direct outgrowth of industrialization and colonial expansion, which after 1800 suddenly brought Europeans into economic competition with exotic cultures throughout the world. The flood of strange artifacts and volumes of ethnographic description that soon filled the libraries and museums of Europe and the United States invited systematic interpretation. The first scholarly anthropological associations that formed, beginning in the 1830s, brought together researchers interested in human evolution, race, ethnology, archaeology, linguistics, comparative sociology, and comparative religion. Anthropologists used their rich new sources of data to explain universal cultural development in terms that placed Europeans at the pinnacle of human achievement and justified colonialism. Nineteenth-century sociology was also concerned with the stages of evolutionary progress, but it focused primarily on social surveys of Euro-American societies and the problems of poverty and social class that industrialization itself was intensifying.

### Anthropology: Science or Humanity?

Academic anthropology in the United States is considered a social science, but it also has a strong humanities element, as shown in the description and analysis of individual cultures from an internal, or emic, view. The use of the traditional scientific methods of systematic observation, data collection, and hypothesis testing is certainly ap-

FIGURE 16.5
*University of Florida anthropologist Maxine Margolis illustrates the diversity of anthropological research interests. She has conducted fieldwork on frontier agriculture in Brazil and on women's roles in the United States and is shown here interviewing a Brazilian immigrant in New York City.*

propriate for anthropology. Throughout much of this century, it was fashionable to call anthropology "the science of man" and to speak of the "science of culture." Cultural anthropology's claim to be a science, however, must be viewed cautiously.

As a science, the purpose of anthropology was considered to be the search for the "laws" that would explain human development and behavior, and many of the techniques of science, such as the use of mathematics and statistics, were adopted. However, a basic problem with the scientific approach in anthropology is that the cultural uniqueness of emic categories may be lost if they are forced into the observer's etic categories in order to formulate lawlike cross-cultural generalizations. Furthermore, some researchers may too easily use "scientific objectivity" as a reason to ignore the humanitarian, evaluative, or political implications of anthropological research, which may be anthropology's most important responsibility.

References to scientific principles or laws of culture often seem either overly pretentious or hopelessly naive given the dynamics of culture and the complexity of human behavior, but they have nevertheless generated useful research. George Murdock (1949), for example, used mathematical theorems and a series of propositions to organize his landmark cross-cultural study of kinship, which founded an entire subfield of cultural anthropology. Leslie White reduced his law of cultural evolution to the formula $E \times T \rightarrow C$, which reads ". . . culture evolves as the amount of energy harnessed per capita per year is increased . . ." (1949:368).

White's "law" was ridiculed as trivial, but it inspired an entire generation of energetics research that led to important insights on cultural adaptation. Marvin Harris has attracted many researchers to test his cultural materialist principle of infrastructural determinism, which states "The etic behavioral modes of production and reproduction probabilistically determine the etic behavioral domestic and political economy, which in turn probabilistically determine the behavioral and mental emic superstructures" (1980:55–56). In less ponderous language, this principle simply suggests that, in order to explain cultural variation, it makes sense to look first at how people sustain themselves.

The "science" in cultural anthropology can more modestly be characterized as an interest in empirical generalizations and explanatory hypotheses or causal explanations. Empirical generalizations, such as "patrilocal residence is associated with patrilineages," are often encountered in the anthropological literature, and they may be supported by carefully controlled comparisons, or cross-cultural survey data, and statistical tests of significance. For example, David Levinson (1977) examined 289 cross-cultural studies and filled a five-volume catalog with 1379 "theories" or statements about "the cause, prediction, or measurement of some phenomenon. . . ." Such theories rest on associations, or correlations, between variables and do not in themselves directly prove causation. There are actually far more correlations than theories to account for them, as demonstrated by Robert Textor's (1967) computer-generated compendium of 20,000 statistically significant correlations drawn from 400 cultures and thirty-eight variable categories.

Most anthropologists strike a balance between science and humanistic concerns. This is fortunate because anthropology is not just academic anthropology in the classroom. It is also practiced as applied anthropology under contract with government and international agencies, where it can have impact on millions of people.

## SUMMARY

The modes of explanation that anthropologists have historically used to answer the broad questions about cultural differences and how cultures change were grouped into five categories: biological, cultural materialist, mentalist, historical, and functionalist. Aspects of all these theoretical approaches continue to be used today, and although anthropologists still debate the relative utility of different modes of explanation, the earlier assumptions of racial or cultural superiority have been abandoned. Reflecting the prevailing colonial attitudes of the time, many nineteenth-century anthropologists were racist and ethnocentric, assuming the superiority of Europeans and European culture. However, early in the twentieth century, American anthropologists under the influence of Franz Boas persuasively argued that all human populations were genetically capable at the same levels of cultural development and advocated that

each culture was worthy of respect. Anthropology is both a science and a humanity and remains one of the most useful of academic disciplines because it is the broadest, most cross-cultural discipline, with the greatest time perspective on the human condition.

## STUDY QUESTIONS

1. In what ways can anthropology be considered both a science and a humanity?

2. In what ways have anthropological modes of explanation been influenced by their historical context? Use specific examples. Refer to biological, historical, and functionalist modes of explanation.

3. Identify the following anthropologists, associating them with a particular mode of explanation or theoretical school: Benedict, Boas, Kroeber, Malinowski, Mead, Morgan, Radcliffe-Brown.

4. What are the major advantages of functionalism in comparison with evolutionary interpretations?

5. Define the following concepts: general evolution, specific evolution, band, tribe, chiefdom, state, Paleolithic, Mesolithic, Neolithic, and comparative method.

## SUGGESTED READINGS

Bohannan, Paul, and Mark Glazer. 1988. *High Points in Anthropology*. New York: Knopf. A collection of representative works by twenty-nine leading anthropologists; includes useful biographical information and critical introductions.

Harris, Marvin. 1968. *The Rise of Anthropological Theory*. New York: Crowell. Still one of the best surveys of the history of anthropology, written from a cultural materialist perspective.

Langness, L. L. 1987. *The Study of Culture*. Novato, Calif.: Chandler & Sharp. This history of anthropological theory emphasizes the concept of culture.

Silverman, Sydel (Ed.). 1981. *Totems and Teachers: Perspectives on the History of Anthropology*. New York: Columbia University Press. A collection of personal appraisals of eight historically prominent anthropologists (Boas, Kroeber, Radin, Malinowski, Benedict, Steward, White, and Redfield), written by students who had worked directly with them.

# TOPICAL GLOSSARY

## CULTURAL ECOLOGY

**acid rain** Acidic precipitation, often dilute sulfuric acid produced in the atmosphere from sulfur dioxide that is frequently emitted when fossil fuels are burned. Acid rain can kill trees.

**adaptation** The long-term cultural process of maintaining a balance between population and natural resources within a given environment.

**adaptive structures** Cultural features that contribute to adaptation by regulating decision making and the flow of information.

**adaptive success** The continuous survival of a given cultural system in a given environment over the long run.

**agricultural intensification** Changes in farming technology, such as shortening fallow periods, use of fertilizers, new crops, or irrigation, in order to produce more food per year in a given area, often at greater energy cost.

**agricultural involution** Clifford Geertz's concept of a labor-intensive agricultural system that provides an incentive for population growth.

**altiplano** The Andean high plateau and center of a large indigenous population, much of it over 12,000 ft (3658 m).

**average returns** The output divided by the input, the amount produced, or returned, for each unit expended; in subsistence production, the number of calories produced for each calorie expended on subsistence.

**band** A group of twenty-five to fifty people that camp and forage together.

**biological productivity** Food energy stored by green plants in organic compounds; expressed as the weight of organic material (biomass) or in kilocalories.

**biomass** The total weight of biological organisms living in a given area.

**biosphere** The area on and near the surface of the planet that supports life, cyclical flows of energy and materials, and ecosystems, as distinguished from the abiotic atmosphere, hydrosphere, and lithosphere.

**biosphere peoples** Raymond Dasmann's term for societies in global-scale cultures that draw resources from throughout the biosphere and thus may be insensitive to local ecosystem damage.

**broad-spectrum subsistence revolution** Kent Flannery's characterization of the postglacial intensification of subsistence activities that ultimately led to domestication in the Near East.

**carbon cycle** The natural movement of carbon when it is incorporated into plant tissue from atmospheric carbon dioxide during photosynthesis, metabolized by consumers, and released again into the atmosphere by respiration.

**carrying capacity** The number of people who could, in theory, be supported indefinitely in a given environment with a given technology and culture.

**cash cropping** The raising of crops for market sale rather than domestic consumption.

*chlorofluorocarbons*  A synthetically produced chemical compound used as an aerosol propellant and in refrigeration, that can destroy atmospheric ozone.

*cohort*  A group of people of the same age, usually those born within the same 5-year period.

*complex carbohydrate*  A large starch molecule stored in the stems, roots, and seeds of plants, which humans can digest to produce glucose.

*consumer*  An animal that eats plants or other animals.

*coral atoll*  A coral reef structure formed in a ring around a submerged oceanic volcano. Atolls may contain small, very low, inhabitable islets.

*deficit production*  The situation in which more calories are expended in food production than are produced for human food.

*demographic disruption*  Depopulation due to the impact of an uncontrolled frontier, followed by extinction or rapid growth due to disruption of prior fertility controls.

*demographic transition*  A change in a population from preindustrial high mortality, high fertility rates to low mortality, low fertility rates following industrialization.

*desertification*  The process by which a savanna is converted into arid desert by overgrazing and/or climate change.

*diminishing returns*  A decline in output for each increase in effort that accompanies an attempt to increase total production beyond a certain point. Overhunting often produces diminishing returns.

*disequilibrium society*  John Bennett's term for a society that consumes natural resources faster than they are produced over the long term.

*dry crops*  Pacific island root crops such as sweet potatoes, yams, and bananas, which require well-drained soil.

*dry farming*  Rain-fed farming without artificial irrigation.

*ecocide*  The degradation of an ecosystem.

*ecological transition*  John Bennett's term for the increasing cultural incorporation of natural processes that transforms equilibrium societies into disequilibrium societies.

*ecosystem*  A community of plants and animals interconnected to one another and the physical environment by a flow of energy and materials.

*ecosystem peoples*  Raymond Dasmann's term for societies in small-scale cultures that live in relative balance with their ecosystems.

*El Niño*  A warming of the ocean currents off Peru that causes rain and flooding on the normally desert coast and disrupts the marine ecosystem.

*energy subsidy*  The use of fossil fuels to increase food production above the rate that could be sustained through use of renewable energy sources.

*equilibrium society*  John Bennett's term for a society that is in balance with its natural resources.

*exponential growth*  The situation in which a population increases by an annual percentage rate and grows more and more rapidly in total size. This can be graphed as a steeply climbing curve and described by a mathematical function with an exponent.

*factory farming*  Commercial agriculture based on fossil-fuel energy subsidies, mechanization, pesticides, chemical fertilizers, and large-scale monocroping.

*fertility rate*  Number of births per 1000 people per year, births per 1000 females, births per 1000 females of reproductive age, or births per reproductive females of age-specific categories.

*foraging*  Subsistence based on harvesting naturally occurring plants and animals by hunting, gathering, and/or fishing.

*forest fallow system*  A system of cultivation in which soil nutrients are restored by allowing the forest to regrow.

*fossil fuels*  Energy sources such as petroleum, natural gas, and coal, which are the geologically processed remains of ancient biomass, considered nonrenewable because they are consumed more rapidly than they are naturally produced.

*fuel revolution*  The large-scale adoption of fossil fuels such as coal and oil.

*genocide*  The extermination of a human population.

*ghost acres*  Georg Borgstrom's term for the amount of agricultural land that would be required for a country to produce the animal protein obtained from its marine fisheries.

*Ghyben–Hertzberg lens*  A rain-fed layer of freshwater that collects above the saltwater in the permeable coral underlying a large islet in an atoll; a requirement for human occupation.

*greenhouse effect*  An increase in global temperature caused by solar heat being trapped near the earth's surface by atmospheric carbon dioxide and other greenhouse gasses.

*Green Revolution*  Dramatic increases in agricultural production from genetically engineered hybrid grains that produce high yields in return for high inputs of chemical fertilizers and pesticides.

*hierarchical anomaly*  Maladaptation caused by adaptive structures that influence decision making at the wrong level within the cultural system.

*high-response variety*  High-response plant varieties designed to produce high yields when grown with chemical fertilizers and pesticides

*high volcanic island*  A large island formed by a volcanic cone and likely to be relatively rich in soil, water, and vegetation.

*high-yield variety*  High-yield plant varieties developed by selective breeding as part of the Green Revolution.

*house garden*  An assortment of useful plants, often including semidomesticates, that are cultivated around the house.

*immiseration*  Malthusian impoverishment, a declining standard of living attributed to continuous population growth on a limited-resource base.

*incipient cultivation*  Early phase of the gradual process of domestication when it is difficult to distinguish between wild and domesticated forms but where settled village life, or sedentism, has begun.

*infant mortality*  Number of deaths of infants up to 1 year of age per 1000 live births.

*interfluvial environments*  A forest on high ground (terra firma) between major rivers, where fishing is poor and animal protein is relatively scarce.

*law of cultural dominance*  David Kaplan's generalization that cultures that use more energy will displace lower-energy cultures.

*law of evolutionary potential*  The postulation that highly specialized cultures may have difficulty making major adaptive changes.

*law of the minimum*  Justus von Liebig's generalization that the growth of an organism or population is limited by the supply of the least available essential nutrient or resource.

*life expectancy*  Average years of life remaining for people of a given age, often expressed as average age at death, $E(0)$, for life expectancy at birth, or as $E(15)$ for an adult life expectancy, at age 15.

*maladaptation*  A cultural feature that undermines the culture's response to environmental change.

*Malthusian theory*  Thomas Malthus's generalization that populations can grow faster than their food supply and are naturally limited by misery and starvation.

*manioc*  The most important cultivated food plant in Amazonia, grown for its starchy edible tuber. Also known as yuca and cassava, genus *Manihot*.

*marginal returns*  The increase in the total output produced by the additional input; in subsistence production, this is the additional amount above what was produced the previous year, resulting from the increased effort.

*monocrop farming*  Growing one plant species, sometimes only a single variety, often in very large continuous stands.

*mortality rate*  Number of deaths in a population per year per 1000 people.

*orchard crops*  Pacific island tree crops such as breadfruit, the salt-tolerant coconut, and pandandus palms, which grow near the shore.

*overkill*  The theory that overhunting by human hunters contributed to the extinction of the Pleistocene megafauna.

*overshoot*  The situation in which a population exceeds its carrying capacity.

*ozone layer*  Concentrations of ozone gas, $O_3$ (a triatomic form of oxygen), found in the stratosphere where it absorbs potentially dangerous ultraviolet solar radiation.

*pastoralism*  A way of life based on raising livestock.

*Peru current*  A cold ocean current off Peru that is normally associated with an upwelling of nutrients that supports a very rich marine food chain and maintains a cool, dry, coastal desert.

*photosynthesis*  The process by which green plants use sunlight, water, and carbon dioxide to produce oxygen and energy-storing organic compounds.

*population explosion*  The sudden increase in rate of global population growth and the rapid rise in total population following the decline in mortality rates since 1950; related to improvements in public health.

*population pyramid*  A bar graph showing successive cohort survivorships, often divided by sex and 5-year age intervals.

*positive feedback*  In systems theory, an increase in the quantity of a particular variable within an interconnected system that is caused by another variable in the system, such as an increase in population caused by increased food supply.

*primary forest*  A fully developed forest assumed to be in a steady state.

*puna*  The low, largely treeless vegetation of the *altiplano* region.

*range*   The territory occupied by an Australian aboriginal band.

*renewable energy*   Power derived from contemporary solar-driven natural processes such as wind, water power, and direct solar heating or processing biomass through burning and fermentation.

*reproductive success*   The differential increase of a given population in relation to another.

*riverine environments*   A large river that is rich in fish, turtles, and other aquatic life; includes seasonally flooded lowlands with rich alluvial soils.

*root crop*   Domesticated plants that reproduce from cuttings such as manioc or from root bundles such as bananas; often cultivated with hoes or digging sticks.

*savanna*   An ecosystem dominated by grasses, often with scattered trees or shrubs, and frequently maintained by frequent fires, sparse rainfall, and poor soils.

*secondary forest*   An immature forest containing pioneer species that will disappear as they are replaced by the shade-tolerant species that dominate the primary forest.

*seed crop*   Domesticated plants such as beans and maize that reproduce from seeds; sometimes cultivated by plow.

*selective female infanticide*   According to cultural materialist theory, a cultural pattern in which infant girls are selectively killed or neglected in favor of boys who will become hunters and warriors.

*self-maintaining biological process*   Natural cycle of energy and materials through a food chain of organisms fueled by solar energy through green plants.

*simple carbohydrate*   A sugar such as glucose, fructose, or sucrose, which forms small molecules and can be metabolized very rapidly.

*slash and burn*   A farming technique in which forest is cleared and burned to enrich the soil for planting; a forest fallow system depending on forest regrowth.

*stationary population*   A no-growth population in which the annual fertility rate equals the annual mortality rate.

*subsistence*   The production of basic survival resources such as food and shelter.

*subsistence intensification*   Technological innovations that produce more food from the same land area but often require increased effort.

*swidden*   A garden cultivated by the slash-and-burn technique.

*total output*   The input multiplied by the average return. Marginal returns can be expected to decline first, followed by a decline in average returns, but total output may still continue to increase for a time before dropping.

*tragedy of the commons*   Destruction of a communally held resource, such as grazing lands, by unchecked individuals seeking their own self-interest.

*transhumance*   Seasonal movement of livestock herds to maintain optimum grazing conditions; often involves altitudinal shifts.

*trypanosomiasis*   Sleeping sickness, a disease caused by a parasitic protozoan in blood and spread by biting flies. Can be fatal to both humans and livestock.

*tsetse fly*   A blood-sucking African fly that lives in brushy areas. Its bite can spread trypanosomiasis.

*usurpation*   A hierarchical anomaly caused when lower-level adaptive structures inappropriately gain control over the entire cultural system.

*utilitarianism*   The use of economic profit, direct material advantage, or physical welfare, such as food and shelter, as an explanation for cultural practices.

*vertical economy*   Village- and household-level subsistence production based on access to resources from different altitudinal zones.

*vital statistics*   Data on births, deaths, and marriages that relate to total size and rate of change of a population.

*wet crops*   Pacific island root crops such as taros, which are grown in swampy areas.

## ECONOMIC SYSTEMS

*bilateral development assistance*   Aid that is given directly from one country to another and that may be given under conditions that favor the donor.

*bride-service*   The cultural expectation that a newly married husband will perform certain tasks for his in-laws.

*bride-wealth*   Goods, often livestock, that are transferred from the family of the groom to the family of the bride in order to legitimize the marriage and the children of the couple.

*capital*   Karl Marx's term for land and tools as the means of production; also refers generally to accumulated wealth used for productive purposes.

*capital accumulation*   Expanding the wealth and the means of production that can be devoted to further production.

**capitalist production**   A mode of production in which a few people control the means of production and purchase the labor of those who could not otherwise support themselves.

**cash cropping**   The raising of crops for market sale rather than domestic consumption.

**civil–religious hierarchy**   A wealth-leveling mechanism in Latin American peasant communities in which expensive feasts must be given by those moving up a ranked hierarchy of offices.

**closed corporate community**   Communally organized peasants who exclude outsiders and limit the acquisition of wealth and power by their own members.

**commensal hierarchy**   The differential giving and receiving of food between individuals, used as a demonstration of group rank. Recipients are equal to or higher than givers.

**commercialization**   The process in which profit making in the market economy becomes a dominant cultural process, as under capitalism (see Chapter 11).

**commodities**   Basic goods that are produced for their exchange value in a market economy to generate profit to be accumulated as capital.

**core**   The wealthy industrial countries at the center of the world system where the recipients of unequal exchange reside.

**corvée labor**   Work done for the state on demand, usually for large public projects.

**country**   English term used by aborigines to refer to their estate territories.

**culture of consumption**   A culture that stimulates continuous increases in per-capita consumption of natural resources at nonsustainable rates.

**culture of poverty**   Oscar Lewis's concept of a complex of culture traits that both help the urban poor adapt to and help perpetuate poverty.

**debt bondage**   An exploitative economic relationship that is managed to keep an individual in virtually perpetual indebtedness.

**deferred exchange**   A form of trade in which a gift is reciprocated with a return gift at a later time, thus providing an excuse for maintaining contacts and establishing alliances between potentially hostile groups.

**delayed-return system**   A subsistence system requiring food storage because production must be preceded by a significant investment of labor as with farming.

**disembodied economy**   The concept of an economy as something that can be understood apart from the rest of society and culture, especially with a capitalist mode of production.

**disposable income**   personal income less taxes.

**economic determinism**   The argument that economic factors are the primary influences shaping other aspects of culture; similar to utilitarianism and infrastructural determinism.

**economic support funds**   U.S. foreign assistance that must go specifically to support countries whose stability is considered vital for the United States.

**economy of scale**   Savings in the unit cost of production gained through mass production; for example, it may cost less per item to produce 10,000 items than 10 items.

**embedded economy**   An economy that can only be observed and understood within the context of the social, political, and religious system of the culture.

**enclosure movement**   The conversion of community grazing lands used by self-sustaining peasants into privately owned fields dedicated to market production; an early phase in the industrialization of western Europe.

**encomienda**   A grant of land made by Spanish colonial authorities to individual Spaniards, which included rights over the indigenous residents.

**estate**   Property held in common by a descent group and might include territory, sacred sites, and ceremonies.

**exchange value**   The value of goods when used as commodities.

**exploitation**   Unjust use of someone to differentially benefit another, especially when one social class is deprived of basic necessities while the elites live in luxury.

**factory farming**   Commercial agriculture based on fossil-fuel energy subsidies, mechanization, pesticides, chemical fertilizers, and large-scale monocropping.

**feudalism**   A political system in which village farmers occupy lands owned by local lords to whom they owe loyalty, rent, and service.

**forces of production**   Karl Marx's term for technology as a component of a mode of production.

**generalized reciprocity**   Distribution of goods and services by direct sharing. It is assumed that in the long run giving and receiving balances out, but no accounts are maintained.

**governing class**   The socioeconomic upper class that enjoys a disproportionate share of wealth and political and economic power in the country.

**gross domestic product**   (GDP) The total output of goods and services produced within a country, by monetary value.

**gross national product** (GNP) The total output of a country's goods and services, by monetary value; includes profits from foreign activities.

**hacienda** A Latin American agricultural estate with dependent laborers that produced for local rather than global markets and was designed to maintain the social status and lifestyle of the *hacendado* landowner.

**household** A social unit that shares domestic activities such as food production, cooking, eating, and sleeping, often under one roof, and usually based on the nuclear or extended family.

**immediate-return system** A subsistence system that does not normally require storage because production occurs daily without special advance labor inputs.

**industrialization** Mechanized mass production using assembly-line techniques for commercial purposes.

**invisible hand** The capitalist belief that market forces, operating through supply and demand, will lead to continuous economic growth.

**jajmani system** Complementary interdependence between castes, based on occupational specialization.

**kinecon group** Extended families formed by the wealthy American elite, based on common economic interests in formal corporate organizations such as family trusts and holding companies that protect and manage their wealth.

**kin-ordered production** A mode of production organized at the domestic or kinship level and producing primarily for domestic use rather than exchange.

**latifundia** Very large Latin American landholdings, usually under private control by the wealthy elite.

**limited good** A belief often found in peasant communities that total wealth is limited and anyone who acquires too much is taking away from others. This is a justification for wealth leveling.

**loss of economic autonomy** The loss of self-subsistence due to territorial reduction and resource depletion, followed by market dependency and impoverishment.

**Marxism** A political ideology based on Karl Marx's theories that focuses on material conditions and class struggle and that assumes capitalism will be superseded by communism.

**military–industrial complex** The very large defense-related industries that emerged in the United States during World War II and that became a major force in economic and political affairs during the postwar period.

**minifundia** Tiny landholdings of the Latin American peasantry.

**mode of production** Karl Marx's term for the way in which a society organizes its labor and technology.

**multilateral development assistance** Aid that is donated by several countries and channeled through a single international agency such that it can be free of political favoritism.

**national income** All wages, salaries, and profits received by the members of a country, calculated by subtracting various indirect taxes from NNP.

**national product** Goods and services in the market economy. Normally excludes unpaid housekeeping and child care performed by family members. May include monetary values imputed to wages paid in kind and household production-consumption of food and fuels.

**net national product** (NNP) Calculated by deducting capital used up, or depreciated, in the production process, from gross product, either GNP or GDP.

**nonmarket economy** Goods and services distributed by direct exchange or reciprocity in the absence of markets and money.

**official development assistance** (ODA) Aid given by a government for development purposes, including both direct gifts and low-rate loans.

**oligopoly** Concentrated economic power when a market is dominated by only a few producers—like a monopoly, which is controlled by a single producer.

**ownership rights** Among foragers, the right to grant to others permission to use certain property.

**patron** A Spanish term for someone who extends credits or goods to a client who is kept in a debt relationship.

**peasants** Subsistence farmers who pay taxes to the state but own their own land and produce primarily for their own use rather than for a commercial market.

**periphery** Capital-poor areas that supply raw materials and labor to the core; this area was integrated into the early capitalist world system through conquest and coercion.

**personal income** All income received by individuals, calculated from national income by adding government transfer, or welfare, payments to individuals and by subtracting corporate profits that are not paid out as dividends.

**plantations** A large agricultural establishment designed to generate capital by producing for the global market.

**PL 480 Food Aid**   Public Law 480, the U.S. Agricultural Trade Development and Assistance Act of 1954, provides for the distribution of surplus farm commodities to developing countries.

**Point Four**   The first major U.S. effort at postwar development assistance begun by President Truman in 1949.

**political economy**   A cultural pattern in which centralized political authority intervenes in the production and distribution of goods and services.

**privatization**   The use of commercial incentives and "free enterprise" as a development tool.

**public debt**   Amount owed by governments and paid off according to a specified scale and interest rate. External, or foreign, debt is payable to creditors outside the country.

**redistribution**   A form of exchange in which goods, such as foodstuff, are concentrated and then given out under the control of a central political authority.

**relations of production**   Karl Marx's term for the organization of labor.

**rent**   According to Adam Smith, production or labor provided to a landlord by his laborers in exchange for the use of his land.

**semiperiphery**   The intermediate area where labor was incorporated into the capitalist world system through sharecropping and serfdom rather than slavery.

**sexual division of labor**   The performance of separate economic activities, based on gender; for example, customarily, women gather plant food and men hunt. May also be referred to as gender division of labor.

**social class**   A group of people in a stratified society, such as elites and commoners, who share a similar level of access to resources, power, and privilege.

**social deficit**   Robert Textor's term for a country's failure to provide social equity and environmental quality, as distinguished from national monetary deficits.

**staple economy**   The state-controlled production, storage, and distribution of subsistence staples, such as potatoes and maize in the Inca case, to support non-food-producing specialist groups and for emergency aid.

**structure**   The social, economic, and political organization of a culture, which is shaped by the technological base, or infrastructure, according to Marvin Harris's cultural materialist theory.

**subsistence**   The production of basic survival resources such as food and shelter.

**subsistence economy**   Production and distribution carried on at the local community level, primarily for local consumption.

**surplus**   Subsistence production that exceeds the needs of the producer households and that is extracted by political leaders to support nonfood-producing specialists.

**specialists**   A full-time specialist is an individual who provides goods and services to elites in hierarchically organized societies. Such a specialist does not produce his or her own food but is supported from the surplus that is politically extracted by central authorities.

**target workers**   People who work only long enough to earn a specific amount of money, such as to pay taxes or buy certain basic necessities.

**Title XII**   The 1975 amendment to the Foreign Assistance Act of 1961 that created a partnership between AID and U.S. universities to transfer American agricultural technology to developing countries.

**tributary production**   A mode of production in which products are extracted as surplus from a self-supporting peasantry and used to support the state.

**U.N. Development Decade**   Ten-year periods beginning in 1961 for which the United Nations specifies development goals.

**unequal exchange**   Market-based exchanges in which one party is consistently able to accumulate a disproportionate share of the profit or wealth.

**unlimited good**   The belief in continuous economic growth often used to justify wealth inequality.

**use rights**   The right to use property, such as territory or ceremonies, owned by others.

**use value**   The value of goods produced for domestic consumption, usually within a kin-ordered mode of production.

**utilitarianism**   The use of economic profit, direct material advantage, or physical welfare such as food and shelter, as an explanation for cultural practices.

**vertical economy**   Village- and household-level subsistence production based on access to resources from different altitudinal zones.

**wages**   Cash or commodities advanced by the landlord to his laborers to provide for their maintenance in exchange for their labor.

**wealth economy**   The state-controlled production, storage, and distribution of wealth objects that support the status hierarchy.

**wealth-leveling device**    Any cultural means, such as ritual feasting, used to redistribute wealth within a community and thereby reduce inequality.

**world system**    An international hierarchy of diverse societies and cultures integrated into a single economic system based on unequal exchange that allows wealth to accumulate in the core.

# HUMAN BIOLOGY, PHYSICAL ANTHROPOLOGY

**archaic Homo sapiens**    The earliest, physically modern human, appearing perhaps 50,000–200,000 BP and showing little evidence of language and culture.

**australopithecine**    A bipedal, humanlike (hominid) ape, some of which made simple stone tools and were presumably human ancestors.

**biological explanation**    The use of evolutionary biology, physical type, or genetics to explain cultural variation.

**cohort**    A group of people of the same age, usually those born within the same 5-year period.

**demographic disruption**    Depopulation due to the impact of an uncontrolled frontier, followed by extinction or rapid growth due to disruption of prior fertility controls.

**demographic transition**    A change in a population from preindustrial high mortality, high fertility rates to low mortality, low fertility rates following industrialization.

**exponential growth**    The situation in which a population increases by an annual percentage rate and grows more and more rapidly in total size. This can be graphed as a steeply climbing curve and described by a mathematical function with an exponent.

**fertility rate**    Number of births per 1000 people per year, births per 1000 females, births per 1000 females of reproductive age, or as births per reproductive females of age-specific categories.

**founder effect**    The outcome that results when a small group of migrants who leave a larger population establishes a new population that contains only a portion of the parent population's genetic material.

**genocide**    The extermination of a human population.

**inclusive fitness**    A sociobiology concept referring to the degree to which individuals are successful in passing on a high proportion of their genes to succeeding generations.

**infant mortality**    Number of deaths of infants up to 1 year of age per 1000 live births.

**life expectancy**    Average years of life remaining for people of a given age, often expressed as average age at death, $E(0)$, for life expectancy at birth, or as $E(15)$ for an adult life expectancy, at age 15.

**mortality rate**    Number of deaths in a population per year per 1000 people.

**population explosion**    The sudden increase in rate of global population growth and the rapid rise in total population following the decline in mortality rates since 1950; related to improvements in public health.

**population pyramid**    A bar graph showing successive cohort survivorships, often divided by sex and 5-year age intervals.

**racism**    Attributes differences between cultures to physical differences in human populations and assumes that some peoples and cultures are inherently superior.

**reproductive success**    The differential increase of a given population in relation to another.

**sapienization**    The coevolution of human culture, language, and the human physical type that produced modern Homo sapiens, by at least 50,000 BP.

**selective female infanticide**    According to cultural materialist theory, a cultural pattern in which infant girls are selectively killed or neglected in favor of boys who will become hunters and warriors.

**shoveling**    A Sinodont characteristic found in many East Asian peoples, showing a ridge on the inside edge of the upper incisors.

**Sinodont**    A people thought to be the earliest modern human inhabitants of China, who were distinguished by unique dental patterns and derived from Sundadonts some 20,000 BP.

**social darwinism**    Assumes that only "superior" peoples and cultures are fit to survive.

**stationary population**    A no-growth population in which the annual fertility rate equals the annual mortality rate.

**Sundadont**    A human population with unique tooth forms originating in the Sunda region of Southeast Asia some 30,000 BP and thought to be the first settlers of China, where they became Sinodonts.

**Sundanoid**    The first peoples to occupy the Sunda region, which is now Island Southeast Asia, perhaps 60,000 BP; presumably included the ancestors of the first Australian settlers.

*trypanosomiasis*  Sleeping sickness, a disease caused by a parasitic protozoan in blood and spread by biting flies. Can be fatal to both humans and livestock.

*vital statistics*  Data on births, deaths, and marriages that relate to total size and rate of change of a population.

# KINSHIP AND SOCIAL ORGANIZATION

*achieved status*  Social position based on a person's demonstrated personal abilities apart from social status ascribed at birth.

*address*  A kinship term used by ego when speaking directly to a relative, such as "Hello, *father.*"

*affine*  A relative by marriage.

*age-class system*  A system in which individuals of similar age are placed in a named group and moved as a unit through the culturally defined stages of life. Specific rituals mark each change in age status.

*age grades*  A culturally defined stage of an age-class system such as childhood, adolescence, parenthood, and old age.

*age hierarchy*  A social system in which people are ranked by age.

*agnate*  Kin who is related through male links.

*alliance theory*  Assumes, from a male perspective, that particular marriage systems create interdependence between social groups that give and receive wives.

*ascribed status*  The social status that one is born into; includes gender, birth order, lineage, clan affiliation, and connection with elite ancestors.

*band*  A group of twenty-five to fifty people that camp and forage together.

*bilateral*  Groups either formed by tracing any line to a common ancestor or no descent groups present.

*bilocality*  Residence near either husband's or wife's kin, with no clear preference for either alternative; sometimes also called ambilocality.

*bride-service*  The cultural expectation that a newly married husband will perform certain tasks for his in-laws.

*bride-wealth*  Goods, often livestock, that are transferred from the family of the groom to the family of the bride in order to legitimize the marriage and the children of the couple.

*caste*  An endogamous, ranked, occupationally defined group, known as *jati* in India.

*clan*  A named group claiming descent from a common but often remote ancestor and sharing a joint estate.

*cognatic line*  A descent line traced to a common ancestor and that need not rely on exclusively male or female links.

*collateral relative*  A relative such as father's brother, who shares a common ancestor but is not a direct lineal ancestor.

*collaterality*  A component of meaning in kinship systems that sorts kin terms into two categories: those that distinguish between collateral and lineal relatives and those that do not. For example, a term placing father and father's brother in the same category does not distinguish between lineals and collaterals.

*consanguine*  A relative by a culturally recognized descent from a common ancestor; sometimes called a "blood" relative.

*cross-cousin*  A son or daughter of someone who is ego's mother's brother or father's sister.

*cross-cousin marriage*  A culturally defined preference for marriage with someone who is called cross-cousin.

*descent group*  A social group based on genealogical connections to a common ancestor.

*descriptive kinship*  Terms derived from combinations of the primary kin terms (F, M, B, Z, S, D). For example, an uncle might be called FB (father's brother).

*dialect tribe*  An intermarrying group of bands sharing a common language and culture and occupying a common territory.

*dreamtime ancestors*  Spiritual mythic beings who established aboriginal culture and founded specific descent groups.

*endogamy*  Marriage within a culturally defined group; the opposite of exogamy.

*ethnic group*  A dependent culturally distinct population that forms part of a larger state or empire and that was formally autonomous.

*exogamy*  Marriage outside a culturally defined group.

*extended family*  A joint household based on a parent family and one or more families of its married children.

*filiation*  A parent–child relationship link used as a basis for descent-group membership.

*genitor*  The biological father of a child.

*gerontocracy*  An age hierarchy that is controlled or dominated by the oldest age groups.

*harem*  From the Arabic word for "forbidden," refers to physically segregated domestic living space for women.

**household**   A social unit that shares domestic activities such as food production, cooking, eating, and sleeping, often under one roof, and usually based on the nuclear or extended family.

**hypergamy**   Marriage to someone of higher rank. For example, Hindu women may marry men of a higher sub-caste.

**hypogamy**   Marriage to someone of lower rank.

**incest taboo**   A prohibition on marriage or sexual relations between culturally specified categories of kin.

**Iroquois kinship**   A system of kinship terminology in which cross-cousins are distinguished from parallel cousins, who are sometimes called the same as siblings; often occurs together with cross-cousin marriage.

**joint family**   A large, Chinese extended family with several married sons.

**levirate**   A cultural pattern in which a woman marries a brother of her deceased husband.

**lineal relative**   A relative who is one of ego's direct lineal ancestors, such as father and father's father, or a direct lineal descendant, such as son and son's son.

**kinship terminology**   An ego-centered system of terms that specifies genealogical relationships of consanguinity and affinity in reference to a specific individual.

**lineage**   A descent group based on specific, known links to a common ancestor and sharing a joint estate; sometimes a subdivision of a clan.

**male supremacy complex**   A functionally interrelated series of presumably male-centered traits, including patrilocality, polygyny, inequitable sexual division of labor, male domination of headmanship and shamanism, and the ritual subordination of women.

**maloca**   Brazilian term for a communal house containing several families.

**matrilineage**   A lineage based on descent traced through a line of women to a common female ancestor and sharing a joint estate.

**matrilocality**   Residence near the wife's kin, normally near her parents.

**moiety**   One part of a two-part social division.

**neolocality**   Residence established independently of the kin of either husband or wife.

**nuclear family**   The primary family unit of mother, father, and their dependent children.

**Omaha**   A kinship terminological system in which the members of ego's mother's patrilineage are merged across generations and differentiated from the members of ego's father's patrilineage.

**parallel cousins**   A son or daughter of someone who is ego's mother's sister or father's brother.

**pater**   The culturally legitimate, or sociological, father of a child.

**patrilineage**   A lineage based on descent traced through a line of men to a common male ancestor and sharing a joint estate.

**patrilineal descent**   Descent traced through a line of men to a male ancestor.

**patrilocal residence**   A cultural preference for a newly married couple to live near the husband's parents or patrilineal relatives.

**polygyny**   A form of marriage in which a man may have more than one wife.

**primogeniture**   Preferential treatment to a couple's firstborn offspring or oldest surviving child; may be a basis for establishing social rank.

**purdah**   Hindi word for "veil" or "curtain," generalized to refer to physical separation of daily lives of men and women.

**rank**   Social position in a status hierarchy.

**reference**   A term that ego uses to refer to a relative when speaking about them indirectly, such as "He, that man over there, is my *father.*"

**relative age**   A distinction drawn between the younger and older of a pair of siblings.

**residence pattern**   The cultural preference specifying where a newly married couple should live in relation to the parents of each spouse.

**section system**   A social division into four (sections) or eight (subsections) intermarrying, named groups, which summarize social relationships; members of each group must marry only members of one other specific group.

**segmentary lineage system**   A system in which complementary opposition and genealogical principles of unilineal descent are used by residential groups as a basis for political mobilization in the absence of centralized political leadership.

**sibling-exchange marriage**   A cultural pattern in which a brother and sister marry another brother and sister.

**social class**   A group of people in a stratified society, such as elites and commoners, who share a similar level of access to resources, power, and privilege.

**social status**   A position that an individual occupies within a social system; defined by age, gender, kinship relationships, or other cultural criteria and involving specific behavioral expectations.

**social stratification**    A ranking of social statuses such that the individuals of a society belong to different groups having differential access to resources, power, and privilege.

**stem family**    A minimal extended Chinese family with one married son to carry on the patriline.

**structure**    The social, economic, and political organization of a culture, which is shaped by the technological base, or infrastructure, according to Harris's cultural materialist theory.

**Sudanese**    A highly "descriptive" kinship system, especially one that distinguishes four different types of cousins: FBS/D, FZS/D, MBS/D, MZS/D.

**unilineal descent group**    Membership based on descent traced through a line of ancestors of one gender to a common ancestor.

## LANGUAGES AND LINGUISTICS

**Afro-Asiatic language**    Includes the Near Eastern Semitic languages such as Egyptian, Arabic, and Hebrew, as well as the Cushitic languages of Ethiopia and Berber languages of North Africa.

**Altaic language**    A widespread group of Asian languages distributed from Turkey to Siberia and China, including Turkish, Mongolian, and Manchu.

**Amerind language**    Language family of all pre-Columbian indigenous peoples of South and Central America and most of North America.

**Austronesian language**    A group of several hundred related languages, also called Malayo-Polynesian, whose speakers are found in Southeast Asia, Taiwan, the Philippines, and Madagascar and throughout the Pacific.

**cognates**    Related words found in more than one language and that were derived from a common protolanguage.

**componential analysis**    A form of linguistic analysis that sorts kinship terms into categories according to the different components of meaning that each term distinguishes.

**core vocabulary**    A list of 100 or 200 words assumed to be universally present in all cultures and that are used by linguists to establish a glottochronology.

**dialect tribe**    An intermarrying group of bands sharing a common language and culture and occupying a common territory.

**glottochronology**    A method of estimating the relative date at which related languages separated from a common ancestral language, by calculating the percentage of cognates shared between the related languages.

**Indo-European language**    A very large language group with many major branches. Includes most modern European languages such as French, Spanish, Italian, and Portuguese, derived from Latin; Germanic languages such as English; Slavic languages such as Russian; and many languages in South Asia and Southwest Asia.

**lexicon**    A list of words.

**logographic**    A writing system in which the symbol represents a word.

**Nilo-Saharan language**    A very large phylum of related African-language families, whose speakers are spread throughout North and East Africa.

**Nilotic language**    A group of related Nilo-Saharan languages, whose speakers live in East Africa. Sometimes Nilotic refers to the very tall physical type of Nilotic speakers.

**Nostratic language**    The hypothetical language believed by some linguists to have been the Near Eastern ancestor to Indo-European, Afro-Asiatic, and Dravidian languages some 10,000 BP.

**phoneme**    Minimal unit of sound that carries meaning and is recognized as distinctive by the speakers of a given language.

**Polynesian language**    A group of closely related Austronesian languages spoken in Polynesia.

**Proto-Austronesian**    The parent language of all modern Austronesian languages, presumably present in Southeast Asia some 7000 BP.

**Proto-Polynesian**    The parent language of all modern Polynesian languages, presumably present in western Polynesia some 3500 BP.

**Sapir–Whorf hypothesis**    Suggests that one's view of the world is shaped by language, such that the speakers of different languages may live in different perceptual worlds.

**Sino-Tibetan language**    The language family that includes the major languages of China, Tibet, and Burma. By number of speakers, it is the world's second largest language group, after Indo-European.

## POLITICAL SYSTEMS

**acephalous**    A political system without central authority or permanent leaders.

**agromanagerial despotism**  Karl Wittfogel's explanation for the rise of the Mesopotamian state, arguing that the first rulers controlled irrigation and agriculture.

**anarchy**  The absence of centralized political authority and formal government institutions.

**aristocracy**  A political system in which a small, privileged elite rule.

**Arthasastra**  A text on statecraft from the classical period of Hindu civilization, detailing how the king could use political power to personal advantage.

**bigman**  A self-made leader in a small-scale culture. His position is temporary, depending on personal ability and consent of his followers.

**chiefdom**  A politically organized society with a permanent head, usually with one layer of control over more than one local community (see Chapter 6).

**circumscription**  Robert Carneiro's explanation for the development of political centralization. He argues that villagers may be forced to surrender their autonomy if they are unable to move away from authorities because of geographic barriers or neighboring societies.

**complementary opposition**  A situation in which people assume a group identity in political opposition to another group at the same level.

**cultural autonomy**  Self-determination by a cultural group.

**direct rule**  The use of European colonial administrators to control a native community at the local level.

**feud**  Chronic intergroup conflict that exists between communities in the absence of centralized political authority. May involve a cycle of revenge raids and killing that is difficult to break.

**gerontocracy**  An age hierarchy that is controlled or dominated by the oldest age groups.

**governing class**  The socioeconomic upper class that enjoys a disproportionate share of wealth and political and economic power in the country.

**Great Tradition**  The culture of the elite in a state-organized society with a written tradition that is not fully shared by nonliterate, village-level commoners.

**headman**  A political leader who coordinates group activities and is a village spokesman but serves only with the consent of the community and has no coercive power.

**indirect rule**  The situation in which European colonial administrators appointed local natives to serve as mediating officials, or "chiefs," to help them control local communities.

**integration**  The absorption of a formerly autonomous people into a dominant state society with the possible retention of ethnic identity.

**internal colony**  A territory within a state containing an indigenous population that is denied the right of self-determination.

**leopard-skin chief**  A respected Nuer religious practitioner who served as a conflict mediator. He was not a political leader and could use only ritual sanctions.

**liturgical government**  The use of ritually prescribed interpersonal relations and religious, moral authority as a primary means of social control in a state-level society.

**male supremacy complex**  A functionally interrelated series of presumably male-centered traits, including patrilocality, polygyny, inequitable sexual division of labor, male domination of headmanship and shamanism, and the ritual subordination of women.

**monumental architecture**  Large-scale permanent constructions, such as temples, palaces, or tombs, that require large labor forces and central planning.

**meritocracy**  Rule by those with demonstrated abilities. Chinese bureaucrats were selected through a highly competitive national examination system on Confucian literature.

**military–industrial complex**  The very large defense-related industries that emerged in the United States during World War II and that became a major force in economic and political affairs during the postwar period.

**national upper class**  The highest socioeconomic class in the United States, which also operates as a governing class.

**native problem**  The difficulty faced by colonial authorities who attempted to control and exploit very large and potentially rebellious native populations for the dispproportione advantage of a European minority.

**Parkinson's law**  Predicts the endless expansion of bureaucracy because, as work increases, individual bureaucrats will invariably add at least two new subordinates, whose presence will increase the work load.

**peace in the feud**  The divided loyalties of individuals in small-scale societies caused by overlapping networks of kinship and marriage that provide important incentives for ending feuds.

**political economy**  A cultural pattern in which centralized political authority intervenes in the production and distribution of goods and services.

**politicization**  The process of maintaining and expanding the power of central political authority, which becomes the dominant cultural process.

**power**   "The capacity of some persons to produce intended and foreseen effects on others" (Wrong 1979:2).

**power elite**   Members of the governing class and co-opted members of lower social classes, who are in controlling positions within leading national institutions.

**redistribution**   A form of exchange in which goods, such as foodstuff, are concentrated and then given out under the control of a central political authority.

**segmentary lineage system**   A system in which complementary opposition and genealogical principles of unilineal descent are used by residential groups as a basis for political mobilization in the absence of centralized political leadership.

**self-determination**   The right of any people to freely determine its own cultural, political, and economic future.

**small-nation alternative**   A proposal for restoring ecological balances and social equity by returning maximum autonomy and self-reliance to small-scale cultural communities within a framework of regional and global institutions.

**social class**   A group of people in a stratified society, such as elites and commoners, who share a similar level of access to resources, power, and privilege.

**social stratification**   A ranking of social statuses such that the individuals of a society belong to different groups having differential access to resources, power, and privilege.

**specialist**   A full-time specialist is an individual who provides goods and services to elites in hierarchichally organized societies. Such a specialist does not produce his or her own food but is supported from the surplus that is politically extracted by central authorities.

**split inheritance**   An Andean system of regulating succession to political office in which the principal son of a deceased ruler received political power and other heirs were given ritual power over the royal mummy.

**state**   A politically centralized society with at least two levels of authority above the local community.

**status rivalry**   Irving Goldman's explanation for the development of stratified Pacific chiefdoms from the intense political struggles between chiefs for greater personal power.

**theocracy**   State government based on religious authority or divine guidance. The Chinese emperor was the highest civil and religious leader.

**tribe, tribal**   A small-scale society or culture with no central political authority.

**trusteeship system**   U.N. supervision designed to convert former colonial territories into independent states.

# PREHISTORY

**absolute date**   Any date that can be expressed in a universal calender, such as BP (before present, before 1950) or BC (before Christ), and AD (*anno Domini,* year of our Lord) in the Christian calender.

**Andean cultural tradition**   Cultural patterns related to state organization in the Andean region, such as intensive agriculture, art styles, and religious patterns that have existed for some 3000 years.

**archaic**   Archaeologically recognized period of initial sedentism and subsistence intensification preceding domestication in North America.

**archaic Homo sapiens**   The earliest, physically modern human, appearing perhaps 50,000–200,000 BP and showing little evidence of language and culture.

**australopithecines**   A bipedal, humanlike (hominid) ape, some of which made simple stone tools and were presumably human ancestors.

**broad-spectrum subsistence revolution**   Kent Flannery's characterization of the postglacial intensification of subsistence activities that ultimately lead to domestication in the Near East.

**central place**   A settlement that serves as the focus of a regional communication network.

**Chinese co-tradition**   A distinctively Chinese archaeological culture that was in place some 5000 BP. *See* Proto-Chinese interaction sphere.

**domestication**   The process by which the reproduction of a wild plant or animal species is brought under human control in order to increase the supply (see Chapter 7).

**Fertile Crescent**   Near Eastern region including Mesopotamia and Egypt where some of the earliest civilizations arose.

**Harappa**   The archaeological site of an ancient city associated with Harappan civilization, located in the upper Indus Valley approximately 4000 BP.

**hilly flanks**   Foothills of the Zagros Mountains bordering Mesopotamia, believed by Braidwood to be the area where domestication first took place in the Near East.

**Holocene**   Geological period covering the 10,000 years since the end of the Pleistocene Epoch and the Ice Age up to the present.

**horizon style**   An archaeologically recognized cultural pattern that occurs over a wide area during the same period.

**incipient cultivation**   Early phase of the gradual process of domestication when it is difficult to distinguish between wild and domesticated forms but where settled village life, or sedentism, has begun.

*Lapita*   A distinctive pottery style that archaeologists use to trace the rapid spread of the early Austronesian settlers into Polynesia approximately 3000 BP.

*Lung-shan*   A regional Chinese culture, beginning approximately 5000 BP, that suggested the beginnings of social stratification and probable chiefdom organization and perhaps small states.

*megafauna*   Giant animals, such as mammoths and mastodons, most of which became extinct near the end of the last Ice Age.

*Mesolithic*   Archaeological Middle Stone Age stage of initial sedentism and subsistence intensification preceding domestication.

*microlithic tool*   A small, thin piece of sharp stone, often a fragment of a long blade, which may be mounted on a shaft.

*Mohenjo-Daro*   The archaeological site of an ancient city associated with Harappan civilization, located in the lower Indus Valley approximately 4000 BP.

*Neolithic*   Archaeological New Stone Age stage distinguished by ceramics, domestication, and settled village life.

*Neolithic revolution*   V. Gordon Childe's concept that emphasizes the dramatic cultural changes brought about by domestication and settled village life.

*overkill*   The theory that overhunting by human hunters contributed to the extinction of the Pleistocene megafauna.

*Paleolithic*   Archaeological Old Stone Age stage of mobile foraging.

*Pleistocene*   Geological epoch beginning approximately 2 million BP and ending about 10,000 BP.

*primary state*   A state that is assumed to have developed without direct influence from any other state.

*Proto-Chinese interaction sphere*   A region in the heartland of Chinese civilization where 5000 BP a common horizon style developed that emphasized religious elements that later became central features of the Chinese Great Tradition.

*relative chronology*   A sequence of events ordered relative to one another but that may not be reliably related to a universal calender.

*stylistic phase*   A relative archaeological time period based on distinctive design features or art styles expressed in material culture such as ceramics or textiles.

*sapienization*   The coevolution of human culture, language, and the human physical type that produced modern *Homo sapiens*, by at least 50,000 BP.

*Uruk period*   The archaeological time period when state organization first appeared in Mesopotamia.

# RELIGION, RITUAL, AND COSMOLOGY

*aniconic image*   A nonrepresentational image, whose symbolic meaning is entirely arbitrary.

*animatisim*   Once thought to be a stage in the development of religion involving a belief in *mana*.

*animism*   A belief in spirits, which occupy plants, animals, and people. Spirits are supernatural and normally invisible but may transform into different forms. Considered by cultural evolutionists to be the simplist and earliest form of religion.

*animistic thinking*   The soul concept used by tribal individuals as an intellectual explanation of life, death, and dream experiences, part of Edward Tylor's theory of animism as the origin of religion.

*collective representations*   Ideas, or thoughts, and emotions common to a society as a whole, especially in reference to the supernatural.

*complementary opposition*   A structural principle in which pairs of opposites, such as male and female, form a logical larger whole.

*correlative cosmology*   A belief system emphasizing the need to maintain proper time and space alignments between objects, people, events, and cosmic forces, to provide order and meaning to life.

*cosmogony*   An ideological system that seeks to explain the origin of everything: people, nature, and the universe.

*cosmology*   An ideological system that explains the order and meaning of the universe and people's places within it.

*dharma*   Hindu religious law, or duty, based on the sacred Vedic texts and classical myths.

*Dreaming*   An aboriginal English term referring to the mythic time and related objects and rituals that are the continuing bases of aboriginal culture, cosmogony, and cosmology.

*Dreaming paths*   Routes followed by Dreamtime ancestors during their mythic travels.

*Dreamtime ancestors*   Spiritual mythic beings who established aboriginal culture and founded specific descent groups.

**filial piety**   *Hsiao*, the ritual obligation of children to respect their ancestors, and especially the duty of sons to care for shrines of their patrilineal ancestors.

**five elements**   Metal, wood, water, fire, and earth, which played a prominent role in Chinese correlative cosmology.

**five pillars**   The basic requirements of Muslim religion, including a profession of faith in Allah and the Prophet Muhammad, daily prayer, alms giving, fasting, and pilgrimage.

**geomancy**   Divination based on alignments and topography, part of Chinese correlative cosmology.

**high shamanism**   The transformation of shamanistic spirit beliefs derived from small-scale cultures into a state religion supported by a stratified social hierarchy.

**icon**   A representational likeness, such as a painting or sculpture of an object.

**impurity**   Low ritual status attributed to association or contact with polluting biological events or products.

**Islam**   Surrender to the will of Allah.

**Jainism**   A religious system that arose together with Buddhism as a challenge to the basic teachings of Hinduism.

**karma**   The pattern of an individual's deeds in life and its impact on one's future existence.

**Keeper of the Game**   A spirit personality believed to control the supply of game animals and who punishes human behavior that shows disrespect for animals or threatens their viability.

**Koran**   The sacred text of Islam, based on God's message to the Prophet Muhammad.

**law of participation**   The assumption that a thing can participate in or be part of two or more things at once. Identified by Lucien Lévy-Bruhl as the principle underlying his concept of prelogical thought.

**law of sympathy**   Sir James Frazer's explanation for the logic underlying magic, sorcery, and shamanism. He thought that tribal peoples believed that anything ever connected with a person, such as hair or blood, could be manipulated to influence that person.

**leopard-skin chief**   A respected Nuer religious practitioner who served as a conflict mediator. He was not a political leader and could use only ritual sanctions.

**liminal phase**   An ambiguous phase of ritual transition in which one is on the threshold between two states.

**liturgical government**   The use of ritually prescribed interpersonal relations and religious, moral authority as a primary means of social control in a state level society.

**Little Tradition**   Ritual beliefs and practices followed by nonliterate commoners, especially rural villagers who are part of a larger state-level society.

**mana**   An impersonal supernatural force thought to reside in particular people and objects. In the Pacific, *mana* is the basis of chiefly power.

**mandate of heaven**   *T'ien-ming*, supernatural endorsement of the ruling Chinese emperor; in theory, dependent on performance.

**mentalist explanation**   Considers ideas, values, and symbols to be the primary force in cultural development.

**Muslim**   A believer in Islam.

**myth**   A narrative that recounts the activities of supernatural beings. Myths are often acted out in ritual and encapsulate a culture's cosmology and cosmogony and provide justification for culturally prescribed behavior.

**mythical thought**   Claude Lévi-Strauss's term for the thinking underlying myth and magic; logically similar to scientific thought but based on the science of the concrete and used for aesthetic purposes and to solve existential problems.

**natural symbols**   Inherent qualities of specific plants and animals used as signs or metaphors for issues that concern people.

**numinous**   The aesthetic or emotional experience of religion as an encounter with supernatural, holy, or divine power.

**peoples of the book**   Non-Islamic peoples such as Christians, Jews, and Hindus, who have their own sacred texts.

**polytheism**   A religious system based on belief in many gods or deities.

**prelogical thinking**   Lucien Lévy-Bruhl's characterization of the collective representations of tribal peoples, which he thought reflected concrete thought and a mystic reality unique to tribal cultures.

**purity**   Ritually superior status; a category in logical opposition to impurity.

**rite of passage**   A ritual marking a culturally significant change in individual's life cycle, such as birth, puberty, marriage, old age, and death.

**ritual pollution**   A dangerous spiritual condition caused by symbolically opposed categories becoming mixed or confused.

**sacred sites**   Specific locations and topographic features associated with important Dreaming events. May be centers for ritual activities.

*science of the concrete*    Thought based on perceptions and signs, images, and events, as opposed to formal science based on concepts.

*shaman*    A part-time religious specialist with special skills for dealing with the spirit world. May help his community by healing, by divination, and by directing supernatural powers against enemies.

*shamanic state of consciousness*    (SSC) An interpretation of the shamanic trance phenomenon that distinguishes it from the altered state of consciousness of schizophrenics. A shaman may enter and leave the SSC at will, remains aware of his surroundings, and uses the SSC for socially beneficial purposes.

*shari'a*    Islamic law; also the "path" or "road."

*Shi'ites*    A Muslim sect endorsing the line of imams most closely related to the Prophet Muhammad.

*Sunnites*    Muslims following the *Sunna*, or sayings of the Prophet Muhammad.

*superstructure*    The mental, ideological, or belief systems, as expressed in the religion, myth, and ritual of a culture. According to Marvin Harris's cultural materialist theory, superstructure is shaped by the structure.

*symbol*    Anything with a culturally defined meaning.

*tabu*    Actions that are forbidden under the sanction of supernatural punishment. *Tabus* may be imposed by chiefs and are supported by chiefly *mana*.

*Tantrism*    A Hindu and Buddhist cult that uses sensual pleasure as a form of ritual.

*theocracy*    State government based on religious authority or divine guidance. The Chinese emperor was the highest civil and religious leader.

*totem*    In Australia, specific animals, plants, natural phenomena, or other objects that originate in the Dreaming and are the spiritual progenitors of aboriginal descent groups. Elsewhere refers to any cultural association between specific natural objects and human social groups.

*tutelary deity*    A supernatural entity thought to be an ancestral founder and guardian over a specific descent group; sometimes associated with specific shrines or temples.

*Umma*    The Islamic community of believers.

*untouchable*    The most ritually impure caste group, whose members pollute higher-caste members by any form of contact.

*ziggurat*    A Mesopotamian temple-pyramid containing a shrine to the city's principal deity and serving as a ritual focus for the state religion.

# BIBLIOGRAPHY

AABY, PETER. 1977. "What Are We Fighting For?" 'Progress' or 'Cultural Autonomy'?" In *Cultural Imperialism and Cultural Identity*, edited by Carola Sandbacka, pp. 61–76. Transactions of the Finnish Anthropological Society, No. 2. Helsinki: Finnish Anthropological Society.

ADAMS, RICHARD N. 1985. "Population and Natural Selection in the Micro-Macro Perspective." In *Micro and Macro Levels of Analysis in Anthropology: Issues in Theory and Research*, edited by Billie DeWalt and Pertti Pelto, pp. 55–678. Boulder, Colo.: Westview.

ADAMS, ROBERT McC. 1981. *Heartland of Cities: Surveys of Ancient Settlement and Land Use on the Central Floodplain of the Euphrates*. Chicago and London: University of Chicago Press.

ADAMS, ROBERT McC. 1982. "Property Rights and Functional Tenure in Mesopotamian Rural Communities." In *Societies and Languages of the Ancient Near East: Studies in Honour of I. M. Diakonoff*, pp. 1–14. Warminster, Eng.: Aris & Phillips.

AHMED, LEILA. 1982. "Western Ethnocentrism and Perceptions of the Harem." *Feminist Studies* 8(3):521–534.

ALBERT, BRUCE. 1985. "Temps du Sang, Temps des Cendres. Representations de la Maladie, Systeme Rituel et Espace Politique chez les Yanomami du Sud-est (Amazonie Bresilienne)." Ph.D. dissertation, Universite de Paris X (Nanterre).

ALERS, J. OSCAR. 1971. "Well Being." In *Peasants, Power, and Applied Social Change: Vicos as a Model*, edited by Henry Dobyns, Paul Doughty, and Harold Lasswell, pp. 115–136. Beverly Hills, Calif. and London: Sage.

ALKIRE, WILLIAM H. 1965. *Lamotrek Atoll and Inter-Island Socioeconomic Ties*. Studies in Anthropology, no. 5 Urbana: University of Illinois Press.

ALLCHIN, BRIDGET, and ALLCHIN, F. RAYMOND. 1982. *The Rise of Civilization in India and Pakistan*. Cambridge, Eng.: Cambridge University Press.

ALLCHIN, F. RAYMOND. 1982. "The Legacy of the Indus Civilization." In *Harappan Civilization: A Contemporary Perspective*, edited by Gregory Possehl, pp. 325–333. New Dehli: Oxford and IBH Publishing.

ALVA, WALTER. 1990. "New Tomb of Royal Splendor." *National Geographic* 117(6):2–15.

*AMAZONIA INDIGENA*. 1981. "Pronunciamiento Sobre el Projecto Especial Pichis-Palcazu." *Amazonia Indigena* 1(3):3–5

AMBROSE, STANLEY H. 1984. "The Introduction of Pastoral Adaptations to the Highlands of East Africa." In *From Hunters to Farmers: The Causes and Consequences of Food Production in Africa*, edited by J. Desmond Clark and Steven Brandt, pp. 212–239. Berkeley: University of California Press.

AMERICAN PSYCHIATRIC ASSOCIATION (APA). 1980. *Diagnostic and Statistical Manual of Mental Disorders*, 3rd ed. Washington, D.C.: American Psychiatric Association.

AMERICAN SOCIOLOGICAL ASSOCIATION. 1986. *Directory of Members*. Washington, D.C.: American Sociological Association.

AMMERMAN, ALBERT J., and L. L. CAVALLI-SFORZA. 1984. *The Neolithic Transition and the Genetics of Populations in Europe*. Princeton, N.J.: Princeton University Press.

ANDERSON, RICHARD L. 1990. *Calliope's Sisters: A Comparative Study of Philosophies of Art*. New York: Prentice Hall.

ANTHROPOLOGICAL INSTITUTE OF GREAT BRITAIN AND IRELAND. 1903. "A Plea for the Scientific Study of the Native Laws and Customs of South Africa: A Memorial addressed by the Anthropological Institute and the Folklore Society to H.M. Secretary of State for the Colonies; and Subsequent Correspondence." *Man* 3(37):70–74.

*ANTI-SLAVERY REPORTER AND ABORIGINES' FRIEND*. 1917. "Conference upon the Future of German Colonies." *Anti-Slavery Reporter and Aborigines' Friend* 7(3):50–59.

ANZAAS (Australia and New Zealand Association for the Advancement of Science). 1914. "Welfare of Aborigines Committee." Report of the Fourteenth Meeting of the Australasian Association for the Advancement of Science 14:450–452.

ARENS, W. 1979. *The Man Eating Myth: Anthropology and Anthropophagy.* New York: Oxford University Press.

ARENSBERG, CONRAD M., and ARTHUR H. NIEHOFF. 1964. *Introducing Social Change: A Manual for Americans Overseas.* Chicago: Aldine.

ARGUELLES, JOSÉ. 1987. *The Maya Factor: Path Beyond Technology.* Santa Fe, N.M.: Bear.

ASCHER, MARCIA, and ROBERT A. ASCHER. 1981. *Code of the Quipu: Study in Media, Mathematics, and Culture.* Ann Arbor: University of Michigan Press.

ASHTON, T. S. 1969. *The Industrial Revolution 1760–1830.* London: Oxford University Press.

ASIMOV, ISAAC. 1971. "The End." *Penthouse* (January).

BAILEY, ROBERT C., G. HEAD, M. JENIKE, B. OWEN, R. RECHTMAN, and E. ZECHENTER. 1989. "Hunting and Gathering in Tropical Rain Forest: Is It Possible?" *American Anthropologist* 91(1):59–82.

BARNETT, HAROLD, and CHANDLER MORSE. 1963. *Scarcity and Growth: The Economics of Natural Resource Availability.* Baltimore: Johns Hopkins University Press.

BARNEY, GERALD O. (ed.). 1977–1980. *The Global 2000 Report to the President of the United States*, 3 vols. New York: Pergamon Press.

BASHAM, A. L. 1954. *The Wonder That Was India: A Survey of the Culture of the Indian Sub-Continent Before the Coming of the Muslims.* London: Sidgwick & Jackson.

BEAGLEHOLE, ERNEST. 1954. "Cultural Factors in Economic and Social Change." *International Labour Review* 69(5):415–432.

BEHRENS, CLIFFORD A. 1986. "Shipibo Food Categorization and Preference: Relationships Between Indigenous and Western Dietary Concepts." *American Anthropologist* 88(3):647–658.

BEIDELMAN, T. O. 1966. "The Ox and Nuer Sacrifice: Some Freudian Hypotheses About Nuer Symbolism." *Man* 1(4):453–467.

BEIDELMAN, T. O. (ed.). 1971. "Nuer Priests and Prophets: Charisma, Authority, and Power Among the Nuer." In *The Translation of Culture: Essays to E. E. Evans-Pritchard*, pp. 375–415. London: Tavistock.

BELAUNDE-TERRY, FERNANDO. 1965. *Peru's Own Conquest.* Lima, Peru: American Studies Press.

BELL, DIANE. 1987. "Aboriginal Women and the Religious Experience." In *Traditional Aboriginal Society: A Reader*, edited by W. H. Edwards, pp. 237–256. South Melbourne: Macmillan.

BELLWOOD, PETER S. 1980. "The Peopling of the Pacific." *Scientific American* 243(5):138–147.

BELLWOOD, PETER S. 1985. *Prehistory of the Indo-Malaysian Archipelago.* New York and Sydney: Academic Press.

BENEDICT, RUTH. 1934. *Patterns of Culture.* Boston: Houghton Mifflin.

BENNETT, JOHN W. 1976. *The Ecological Transition: Cultural Anthroplogy and Human Adaptation.* New York: Pergamon Press.

BERGESEN, ALBERT. 1990. "Turning World-System Theory on Its Head." *Theory, Culture and Society* 7:67–81.

BERGMAN, ROLAND W. 1974. "Shipibo Subsistence in the Upper Amazon Rainforest." Ph.D. dissertation, Department of Geography, University of Wisconsin-Madison. Ann Arbor, Mich.: University Microfilms.

BERLIN, BRENT. 1972. "Speculations on the Growth of Ethnobotanical Nomenclature." *Language in Society* 1:51–86.

BERLIN, BRENT, and ELOIS ANN BERLIN. 1983. "Adaptation and Ethnozoological Classification: Theoretical Implications of Animal Resources and Diet of the Aguaruna and Huambisa." In *Adaptive Responses of Native Amazonians*, edited by Raymond Hames and William Vickers, pp. 301–325. New York: Academic Press.

BERLIN, BRENT, DENNIS E. BREEDLOVE, and PETER H. RAVEN. 1973. "General Principles of Classification and Nomenclature in Folk Biology." *American Anthropologist* 75(1):214–242.

BERLIN, BRENT, and PAUL KAY. 1969. *Basic Color Terms: Their Universality and Evolution.* Berkeley and Los Angeles: University of California Press.

BERN, JOHN. 1979. "Ideology and Domination: Toward a Reconstruction of Australian Aboriginal Social Formation." *Oceania* 50(2):118–132.

BERNARDI, BERNARDO. 1985. *Age Class Systems: Social Institutions and Polities Based on Age.* Cambridge, Eng.: Cambridge University Press.

BERREMAN, GERALD D. 1979. *Caste and Other Inequities: Essays on Inequality.* Meerut, Uttar Pradesh, India: Ved Prakash Vatuk, Folklore Institute.

BERRY, J. W., and S. H. IRVINE. 1986. "Brocolage: Savages Do It Daily." In *Practical Intelligence: Nature and Origins of Competence in the Everyday World*, edited by Robert Sternberg and Richard Wagner, pp. 271–306. Cambridge, Eng.: Cambridge University Press.

BINFORD, LEWIS R. 1981. *Bones: Ancient Men and Modern Myths.* New York: Academic Press.

BINFORD, LEWIS R. 1984. *Faunal Remains from Klasies River Mouth.* New York: Academic Press.

BIRDSELL, JOSEPH B. 1957. "Some Population Problems Involving Pleistocene Man." *Cold Spring Harbor Symposium on Quantitative Biology* 22:47–70.

BIRDSELL, JOSEPH B. 1973. "A Basic Demographic Unit." *Current Anthropology* 14(4):337–350.

BOAS, FRANZ. 1911. *The Mind of Primitive Man.* New York: Macmillan.

BOAS, FRANZ. 1928. *Anthropology and Modern Life.* New York: Norton.

BOCQUET-APPEL, JEAN-PIERRE, and CLAUDE MASSET. 1981. "Farewell to Paleodemography." *Journal of Human Evolution* 11:321–333.

BODLEY, JOHN H. 1970. "Campa Socio-Economic Adaptation." Ph.D. dissertation, University of Oregon. Ann Arbor, Mich.: University Microfilms.

BODLEY, JOHN H. 1972a. "A Transformative Movement Among the Campa of Eastern Peru." *Anthropos* 67:220–228.

BODLEY, JOHN H. 1972b. *Tribal Survival in the Amazon: The Campa Case.* IWGIA (International Work Group for Indigenous Affairs) Document, no. 5. Copenhagen: IWGIA.

BODLEY, JOHN H. 1973. "Deferred Exchange Among the Campa Indians." *Anthropos* 68:589–596.

BODLEY, JOHN H. 1975. *Victims of Progress*. Menlo Park, Calif.: Cummings.

BODLEY, JOHN H. 1976. *Anthropology and Contemporary Human Problems*. Menlo Park, Calif.: Cummings.

BODLEY, JOHN H. 1981a. "Deferred Exchange Among the Campa: A Reconsideration." In *Networks of the Past: Regional Interaction in Archaeology*, edited by Peter Francis, F. J. Kense, and P. G. Duke, pp. 49–59. Calgary, Can.: University of Calgary Archaeological Association.

BODLEY, JOHN H. 1981b. "Inequality: An Energetic Approach." In *Social Inequality: Comparative and Developmental Approaches*, edited by Gerald Berreman, pp. 183–197. New York: Academic Press.

BODLEY, JOHN H. 1985. *Anthropology and Contemporary Human Problems*, 2nd ed. Mountain View, Calif.: Mayfield.

BODLEY, JOHN H. 1988. *Tribal Peoples and Development Issues: A Global Overview*. Mountain View, Calif.: Mayfield.

BODLEY, JOHN H. 1990. *Victims of Progress*, 3rd ed. Mountain View, Calif.: Mayfield.

BORGSTOM, GEORG. 1965. *The Hungry Planet*, 2nd ed. New York: Macmillan.

BOSERUP, ESTER. 1965. *The Conditions of Economic Growth*. Chicago: Aldine.

BOSERUP, ESTER. 1970. *Women's Role in Economic Development*. London: Allen & Unwin.

BOSTER, J. 1983. "A Comparison of the Diversity of Jivaroan Gardens with That of the Tropical Forest." *Human Ecology* 11(1):47–68.

BOURLIERE, FRANCOIS, and M. HADLEY. 1983. "Present-Day Savannas: An Overview." In *Ecosystems of the World 13: Tropical Savannas*, edited by Francois Bourliere, pp. 1–17. New York: Elsevier Scientific Publishing.

BOWDLER, S. 1977. "The Coastal Colonisation of Australia." In *Sunda and Sahul: Prehistoric Studies in Southeast Asia, Melanesia and Australia*, edited by J. Allen, J. Golson, and R. Jones, pp. 205–246. London: Academic Press.

BRAIDWOOD, ROBERT J., and BRUCE HOWE. 1960. *Prehistoric Investigations in Iraqi Kurdistan*. Studies in Ancient Oriental Civilization, no. 31. Chicago: University of Chicago Press.

BROWN, CECIL H. 1977. "Folk Botanical Life-Forms: Their Universality and Growth." *American Anthropologist* 79(2):317–342.

BROWN, CECIL H. 1979a. "Folk Zoological Life-Forms: Their Universality and Growth." *American Anthropologist* 81(4):791–817.

BROWN, CECIL H. 1979b. "Growth and Development of Folk Botanical Life Forms in the Mayan Language Family." *American Anthropologist* 6(2):366–385.

BROWN, HARRISON. 1956. "Technological Denudation." In *Man's Role in Changing the Face of the Earth*, edited by William Thomas, Jr., pp. 1023–1032. Chicago: University of Chicago Press.

BROWN, LESTER R. 1987. "Sustaining World Agriculture." In *State of the World 1987*, edited by Lester Brown et al., pp. 122–138. New York and London: Norton.

BROWN, LESTER R. 1989. "Reexamining the World Food Prospect." In *State of the World 1987*, edited by Lester Brown et al., pp. 41–58. New York and London: Norton.

BROWN, LESTER R., and SANDRA POSTEL. 1987. "Thresholds of Change." In *State of the World 1987*, edited by Lester Brown et al., pp. 3–19. New York and London: Norton.

BROWN, MICHAEL F. 1984. "The Role of Words in Aguaruna Hunting Magic." *American Ethnologist* 11(3):545–558.

BRUSH, STEPHEN B. 1976. "Man's Use of an Andean Ecosystem." *Human Ecology* 4(2):147–166.

BRUSH, STEPHEN B., and HEATH J. CARNEY, and ZOSIMO HUAMAN. 1981. "Dynamics of Andean Potato Agriculture." *Economic Botany* 35(1):70–88.

BUELL, RAYMOND L. 1928. *The Native Problem in Africa*, vol. 1. New York: Macmillan.

BUHLER, G. 1886. "The Laws of Manu." In *The Sacred Books of the East*, edited by F. M. Muller. Oxford, Eng.: Clarendon Press.

BURGER, RICHARD L., and NIKOLAAS J. VAN DER MERWE. 1990. "Maize and the Origins of Highland Chavin Civilization: An Isotopic Perspective." *American Anthropologist* 92(1):85–95.

BURNELL, ARTHUR COKE, and EDWARD W. HOPKINS (eds.). 1884. *The Ordinances of Manu*. London: Trubner.

BURTON, JOHN W. 1981. "Ethnicity on the Hoof: On the Economics of Nuer Identity." *Ethnology* 20(2):157–162.

CANNON, WALTER B. 1942. "'Voodoo' Death." *American Anthropologist* 44(2):169–181.

CARKNER, RICHARD W., WILLIAM E. REYNOLDS, and TYLER C. CLARK. 1983. *1983 Estimated Costs and Returns for a 25-Cow Beef Herd*. Farm Business Management Reports, Extension Bulletin 1042. Pullman: Cooperative Extension, College of Agriculture and Home Economics, Washington State University.

CARNEIRO, ROBERT L. 1960. "Slash-and-Burn Agriculture: A Closer Look at its Implications for Settlement Patterns." In *Men and Cultures: Selected Papers of the International Congress of Anthropological and Ethnological Sciences*, edited by A. Wallace, pp. 229–234. Philadelphia: University of Pennsylvania Press.

CARNEIRO, ROBERT. 1967. "On the Relationship Between Size of Population and Complexity." *Southwestern Journal of Anthropology* 23(3):234–243.

CARNEIRO, ROBERT L. 1970. "A Theory of the Origin of the State." *Science* 169(3947):733–738.

CARNEIRO, ROBERT. 1978. "The Knowledge and Use of Rain Forest Trees by the Kuikuru Indians of Central Brazil." In *The Nature and Status of Ethnobotany*. Anthropological Papers, no. 67, edited by R. Ford, pp. 210–216. Ann Arbor: Museum of Anthropology, University of Michigan.

CARNEIRO, ROBERT L. 1981. "The Chiefdom: Precursor of the State." In *The Transition to Statehood in the New World*, edited by Grant Jones and Robert Kautz, pp. 37–79. Cambridge, Eng.: Cambridge University Press.

CARNEIRO, ROBERT L. 1983. "The Cultivation of Manioc Among the Kuikuru of the Upper Xingu." In *Adaptive Responses of Native Amazonians*, edited by Raymond Hames and William Vickers, pp. 65–111. New York: Academic Press.

CARNEIRO, ROBERT L., and STEPHEN F. TOBIAS. 1963. "The Application of Scale Analysis to the Study of Cultural Evolution." *Transaction of the New York Academy of Sciences* (ser. 2) 26:196–207.

CAWTE, JOHN. 1974. *Medicine Is the Law: Studies in Psychiat-*

*ric Anthropology of Australian Tribal Societies*. Honolulu: University Press of Hawaii.

CAWTE, JOHN E. 1976. "Malgri: A Culture-Bound Syndrome." In *Culture-Bound Syndromes, Ethnopsychiatry, and Alternate Therapies*. Vol. 4 of *Mental Health Research in Asia and the Pacific*, edited by William Lebra. pp. 22–31. Honolulu: University Press of Hawaii.

CGIAR (CONSULTATIVE GROUP ON INTERNATIONAL AGRICULTURAL RESEARCH). 1980. *Consultative Group on International Development*. Washington, D.C.: CGIAR.

CHAGNON, NAPOLEON A. 1968a. *Yanomamo: The Fierce People*. New York: Holt, Rinehart & Winston.

CHAGNON, NAPOLEON A. 1968b. "Yanomamo Social Organization and Warfare." In *War: The Anthropology of Armed Conflict and Aggression*, edited by Morton Fried, Marvin Harris, and Robert Murphy, pp. 109–159. Garden City, N.Y.: Doubleday.

CHAGNON, NAPOLEON A. 1974. *Studying the Yanomamo*. New York: Holt, Rinehart & Winston.

CHAGNON, NAPOLEON A. 1977. *Yanomamo: The Fierce People*, 2nd ed. New York: Holt, Rinehart & Winston.

CHAGNON, NAPOLEON A. 1979. "Is Reproductive Success Equal in Egalitarian Societies?" In *Evolutionary Biology and Human Social Behavior: An Anthropological Perspective*, edited by Napoleon Chagnon and William Irons, pp. 374–401. North Scituate, Mass.: Duxbury Press.

CHAGNON, NAPOLEON A. 1983. *Yanomamo: The Fierce People*, 3rd ed. New York: Holt, Rinehard & Winston.

CHAGNON, NAPOLEON A. 1988. "Life Histories, Blood Revenge, and Warfare in a Tribal Population." *Science* (4843) 239:985–992.

CHAGNON, NAPOLEON. 1992. *The Yanomamo*, 4th ed. New York: Holt, Rinehart & Winston.

CHAI, CH'U, and WINBERG CHAI. 1967. "Introduction." In *Li Chi: Book of Rites*, vol. 1, translated by James Legge, pp. xxiii–lxxxiv. New Hyde Park, N.Y.: University Books.

CHANDLER, ROBERT F., JR. 1990. "Thoughts on the Global Issues of Food, Population, and the Environment." In *Sharing Innovation: Global Perspectives on Food, Agriculture, and Rural Development*, edited by Neil Kotler, pp. 169–185. Washington, D.C., and London: Smithsonian Institution Press.

CHANG, KWANG-CHIH. 1980. "Shang Civilization." New Haven, Conn., and London: Yale University Press.

CHANG, KWANG-CHIH. 1983. *Art, Myth, and Ritual: The Path to Political Authority in Ancient China*. Cambridge, Mass.: Harvard University Press.

CHANG, KWANG-CHIH. 1986. *The Archaeology of Ancient China*, 4th ed. New Haven, Conn.: Yale University Press.

CHANG, T. T. 1983. "The Origin and Early Culture of the Cereal Grains and Food Legumes." In *The Origins of Chinese Civilization*, edited by D. N. Keightley, pp. 65–94. Berkeley: University of California Press.

CHAO, KANG. 1986. *Man and Land in Chinese History: An Economic Analysis*. Stanford, Calif.: Stanford University Press.

CHILDE, V. GORDON. 1936. *Man Makes Himself*. London: Watts.

CHILDE, V. GORDON. 1950. "The Urban Revolution." *Town Planning Review* 21:3–17.

CIBA FOUNDATION. 1977. *Health and Disease in Tribal Socie-*

*ties*. CIBA Foundation Symposium 49, pp. 49–67. Amsterdam: Elsevier/Excerpta Medica/North-Holland.

CICERONE, RALPH J. 1989. "Methane in the Atmosphere." In *Global Climate Change: Human and Natural Influences*, edited by S. Fred Singer, pp. 91–112. New York: Paragon House.

CLAESSEN, HENRY J. M., and PETER SKALNIK (eds.). 1978. "The Early State: Theories and Hypotheses." In *The Early State*, pp. 3–29. The Hague, Paris, and New York: Mouton.

CLARK, GROVER. 1936. *The Balance Sheets of Imperialism: Facts and Figures on Colonies*. New York: Columbia University Press.

CLARK, J. DESMOND. 1984. "Prehistoric Cultural Continuity and Economic Change in the Central Sudan in the Early Holocene." In *From Hunters to Farmers: The Causes and Consequences of Food Production in Africa*, edited by J. Desmond Clark and Steven Brandt, pp. 113–126. Berkeley: University of California Press.

CLASTRES, PIERRE. 1977. *Society Against the State: The Leader as Servant and the Humane Uses of Power Among the Indians of the Americas*. New York: Urizen Books.

CLEAVE, T. L. 1974. *The Saccharine Disease*. Bristol, Eng.: John Wright.

CODRINGTON, R. H. 1891. *The Melanesians*. Oxford, Eng.: Clarendon Press.

COHEN, LEONARD A. 1987. "Diet and Cancer." *Scientific American* 257(5):42–48.

COHEN, YEHUDI (ed.). 1974. *Man in Adaptation*, 2nd ed. Chicago: Aldine.

COLCHESTER, MARCUS. 1984. "Rethinking Stone Age Economics: Some Speculations Concerning the Pre-Columbian Yanoama Economy." *Human Ecology* 12(3):291–314.

COLE, H. S. D. (ed.). 1973. *Models of Doom*. New York: Universe.

COLE, JOHN R. 1980. "Cult Archaeology and Unscientific Method and Theory." *Advances in Archaeological Method and Theory* 3:1–33.

COLLIER, JANE FISHBURNE. 1988. *Marriage and Inequality in Classless Societies*. Stanford, Calif.: Stanford University Press.

CONRAD, GEOFFREY W. 1981. "Cultural Materialism, Split Inheritance, and the Expansion of Ancient Peruvian Empires." *American Antiquity* 46:3–26.

CONRAD, GEOFFREY W., and ARTHUR A. DEMAREST. 1984. *Religion and Empire: The Dynamics of Aztec and Inca Expansionism*. Cambridge, Eng.: Cambridge University Press.

COOK, EARL. 1971. "The Flow of Energy in an Industrial Society." *Scientific American* 224(3):134–144.

CORRIS, PETER. 1968. *Aborigines and Europeans in Western Victoria*. Occasional Papers in Aboriginal Studies, no. 12, Ethnohistory Series, no. 1. Canberra: Australian Institute of Aboriginal Studies.

COTTERELL, ARTHUR, and DAVID MORGAN. 1975. *China's Civilization: A Survey of Its History, Arts, and Technology*. New York: Praeger.

COUGHENOUR, M. B., J. E. ELLIS, D. M. SWIFT, D. L. COPPOCK, K. GALVIN, J. T. McCABE, and T. C. HART. 1985. "Energy Extraction and Use in a Nomadic Pastoral Ecosystem." *Science* 230(4726):619–625.

COWLISHAW, GILLIAN. 1978. "Infanticide in Aboriginal Australia." *Oceania* 48(4):262–283.

CROSBY, ALFRED W. 1986. *Biological Imperialism: The Biological Expansion of Europe, 900–1900.* Cambridge, Eng.: Cambridge University Press.

CROSSON, PIERRE R., and NORMAN J. ROSENBERG. 1989. "Strategies for Agriculture." *Scientific American* 261(3): 128–135.

CUSACK, DAVID F. 1984. "Quinua: Grain of the Incas." *Ecologist* 14(1):21–31.

DAHL, GUDREN, and ANDERS HJORT. 1976. *Having Herds: Pastoral Herd Growth and Household Economy.* Stockholm Studies in Social Anthropology, no. 2. Stockholm: Department of Social Anthropology, University of Stockholm.

DALES, GEORGE F. 1964. "The Mythical Massacre at Mohenjo-Daro." *Expedition* 6(3):36–43.

DALES, GEORGE F. 1965. "Civilization and Floods in the Indus Valley." *Expedition* 7(4):10–19.

DALES, GEORGE F. 1966. "The Decline of the Harappans." *Scientific American* 214(5):92–100.

DALES, GEORGE F. 1982. "Mohenjodaro Miscellany: Some Unpublished, Forgotten, or Misinterpreted Features." In *Harappan Civilization: A Contemporary Perspective*, edited by Gregory Possehl, pp. 97–106. New Dehli: Oxford and IBH Publishing.

DALES, G. F., and R. L. RAIKES. 1968. "The Mohenjo-Daro Floods: A Rejoinder." *American Anthropologist* 70(5): 957–961.

D'ALTROY, TERENCE N., and TIMOTHY K. EARLE. 1985. "Staple Finance, Wealth Finance, and Storage in the Inka Political Economy." *Current Anthropology* 26(2):187–206.

DALY, HERMAN E. 1971. "Toward a Stationary-State Economy." In *The Patient Earth*, edited by John Harte and Robert Socolow, pp. 236–237. New York: Holt, Rinehart & Winston.

DANIKEN, ERICH VAN. 1970. *Chariots of the Gods?* New York: Putnam.

D'ANS, ANDRÉ-MARCEL. 1972. "Les Tribus Indigenes du Parc National du Manu." *Proceedings of the 39th International Americanists Congress.* 4:95–100.

D'ANS, ANDRÉ-MARCEL. 1981. "Encounter in Peru." In *Is God an American? An Anthropological Perspective on the Missionary Work of the Summer Institute of Linguistics*, edited by Søren Hvalkof and Peter Aaby, pp. 145–162. Copenhagen and London: IWGIA and Survival International.

DASMANN, RAYMOND. 1976. "Future Primitive: Ecosystem People Versus Biosphere People." *CoEvolution Quarterly* 11(Fall):26–31.

DAVIS, SHELTON H. 1976. "The Yanomamo: Ethnographic Images and Anthropological Responsibilities." In *The Geological Imperative: Anthropology and Development in the Amazaon Basin of South America*, edited by Shelton Davis and Robert Mathews, pp. 7–23. Cambridge, Mass.: Anthropology Resource Center.

DAVIS, SHELTON H. 1977. *Victims of the Miracle: Development and the Indians of Brazil.* Cambridge, Eng.: Cambridge University Press.

DEACON, JANETTE. 1984. *The Later Stone Age of Southernmost Africa.* Cambridge Monographs in African Archaeology 12, BAR International Series. Oxford, Eng.: BAR.

DENEVAN, WILLIAM. 1976. *The Native Population of the Americas in 1492.* Madison: University of Wisconsin Press.

DENNETT, GLENN, and JOHN CONNELL. 1988. "Acculturation and Health in the Highlands of Papua New Guinea." *Current Anthropology* 29(2):273–299.

DeWALT, BILLIE R. 1988. "The Cultural Ecology of Development: Ten Precepts for Survival." *Agriculture and Human Values* 5(1, 2):112–123.

DEWHURST, J. FREDERIC (ed.). 1947. *America's Needs and Resources: A Twentieth Century Fund Survey Which Includes Estimates for 1950 and 1969.* New York: Twentieth Century Fund.

DIAKONOV, IGOR M. (ed.) 1969. "The Rise of the Despotic State in Ancient Mesopotamia." In *Ancient Mesoptoamia, Socio-Economic History*, pp. 173–203. Moscow: Nauka Publishing House.

DIAMOND, STANLEY. 1968. "The Search for the Primitive." In *The Concept of the Primitive*, edited by Ashley Montagu, pp. 99–147. New York: Free Press.

DICKSON, F. P. 1981. *Australian Stone Hatchets: A Study in Design and Dynamics.* Sydney: Academic Press.

*DIRECTORY OF CORPORATE AFFILIATIONS 1991*, vol. 1. Wilmette, Ill.: National Register Publishing.

DIVALE, WILLIAM, and MARVIN HARRIS. 1976. "Population, Warfare and the Male Supremacist Complex." *American Anthropologist* 78(3):521–538.

DOBYNS, HENRY E., and PAUL L. DOUGHTY. 1976. *Peru: A Cultural History.* New York: Oxford University Press.

DOBYNS, HENRY F., PAUL. L. DOUGHTY, and HAROLD D. LASSWELL (eds.). 1971. *Peasants, Power, and Applied Social Change: Vicos as a Model.* Beverly Hills, Calif., and London: Sage.

DOLE, GERTRUDE. 1978. "The Use of Manioc Among the Kuikuru: Some Implications." In *The Nature and Status of Ethnobotany.* Anthropological Papers, no. 67, edited by R. Ford, pp. 217–247. Ann Arbor: Museum of Anthropology, University of Michigan.

DOMHOFF, G. WILLIAM. 1967. *Who Rules America?* Englewood Cliffs, N.J.: Prentice Hall.

DOMHOFF, G. WILLIAM. 1983. *Who Rules America Now? A View for the '80s.* Englewood Cliffs, N.J.: Prentice Hall.

DOUGLAS, MARY. 1966. *Purity and Danger: An Analysis of Concepts of Pollution and Taboo.* New York: Praeger.

DOW, JAMES. 1986. "Universal Aspects of Symbolic Healing: A Theoretical Synthesis." *American Anthropologist* 88(1): 56–69.

DULL, JACK L. 1990. "The Evolution of Government in China." In *Heritage of China: Contemporary Perspectives on Chinese Civilization*, edited by Paul Ropp, pp. 55–85. Berkeley: University of California Press.

DUMONT, LOUIS. 1970. *Homo Hierarchicus: An Essay on the Caste System.* Chicago: University of Chicago Press.

DUMONT, LOUIS. 1977. *From Mandeville to Marx: The Genesis and Triumph of Economic Ideology.* Chicago and London: University of Chicago Press.

DURKHEIM, ÉMILE. 1912. *The Elementary Forms of the Religious Life* (English translation 1915. London: Allen & Unwin).

DUSSEL, ENRIQUE. 1975. "Bartolome de Las Casas." *Encyclopaedia Britannica* 10:684–686.

DYER, IRWIN A. 1986. "Beef Cattle." In *Bioindustrial Ecosystems, Ecosystems of the World,* no. 21, edited by D. J. A. Cole and G. C. Brander, pp. 175–182. Amsterdam: Elsevier.

DYSON-HUDSON, RADA, and NEVILLE HUDSON. 1969. "Subsistence Herding in Uganda." *Scientific American* 220(2): 76–89.

EARLE, TIMOTHY. 1978. *Economic and Social Organization of a Complex Chiefdom: The Halelea District, Kaua'i, Hawaii.* Anthropological Papers, no. 63. Ann Arbor: Museum of Anthropology, University of Michigan.

EARLE, TIMOTHY. 1987. "Specialization and the Production of Wealth: Hawaiian Chiefdoms and the Inka Empire." In *Specialization, Exchange, and Complex Societies,* edited by Elizabeth Brumfiel and Timothy Earle, pp. 64–75. Cambridge, Eng.: Cambridge University Press.

EARLS, JOHN, and IRENE SILVERBLATT. 1978. "La Realidad Fisica y Social en la Cosmologia Andina." *Proceedings of the International Congress of Americanists* 42(4):299–325.

EASTMAN, LLOYD E. 1988. *Family, Fields, and Ancestors: Constancy and Change in China's Social and Economic History, 1550–1949.* New York: Oxford University Press.

EASTWELL, HARRY D. 1982. "Voodoo Death and the Mechanisms for Dispatch of the Dying in East Arnhem, Australia." *American Anthropologist* 84(1):5–18.

EBREY, PATRICIA. 1990. "Women, Marriage, and the Family in Chinese History." In *Heritage of China: Contemporary Perspectives on Chinese Civilization,* edited by Paul Ropp, pp. 197–223. Berkeley: University of California Press.

ECK, DIANA L. 1985. *Darsan: Seeing the Divine Image in India.* Chambersburg, Penn.: Anima Books.

EDGERTON, LYNNE T. 1991. *The Rising Tide: Global Warming and World Sea Levels.* Washington, D.C., and Covelo, Calif.: Island Press.

EISENBURG J., and R. THORINGTON, JR. 1973. "A Preliminary Analysis of a Neotropical Mammal Fauna." *Biotropica* 5(3):150–161.

EKELUND ROBERT B., JR., and ROBERT F. HEBERT. 1983. *A History of Economic Theory and Method,* 2nd ed. New York: McGraw-Hill.

ELKIN, A. P. 1933. "Wanted: A Positive Policy." *Sydney Morning Herald,* Oct. 13, p. 6.

ELKIN, A. P. 1934. "Anthropology and the Future of the Australian Aborigines." *Oceania* 5(1):1–18.

ERDOSY, GEORGE. 1988. "Urbanization in Early Historic India." BAR International Series 430. Oxford, Eng.: Oxford University Press.

EVANS-PRITCHARD, E. E. 1940. *The Nuer: A Description of the Modes of Livelihood and Political Institutions of a Nilotic People.* New York & Oxford, Eng.: Oxford University Press.

EVANS-PRITCHARD, E. E. 1951. *Kinship and Marriage Among the Nuer.* Oxford, Eng.: Oxford University Press.

EVANS-PRITCHARD, E. E. 1953. "The Nuer Conception of Spirit in Its Relation to the Social Order." *American Anthropologist* 55(2,pt.1):201–214.

FAIRSERVIS, WALTER A., JR. 1967. "The Origin, Character, and Decline of an Early Civilization." *American Museum Novitates* 2302:1–48.

FEDER, ERNEST. 1978. *Strawberry Imperialism: An Enquiry into the Mechanisms of Dependency in Mexican Agriculture.* The Hague: Institute of Social Studies.

FEHER, JOSEPH. 1969. *Hawaii: A Pictoral History.* Bernice P. Bishop Museum Special Publication, no. 58. Honolulu: Bishop Museum Press.

FEI, HSIAO-TUNG, and CHIH-I CHANG. 1945. *Earthbound China: A Study of Rural Economy in Yunnan.* Chicago: University of Chicago Press.

FELL, BARRY. 1976. *America B.C.: Ancient Settlers in the New World.* New York: Quadrangle.

FEUERWERKER, ALBERT. 1990. "Chinese Economic History in Comparative Perspective." In *Heritage of China: Contemporary Perspectives on Chinese Civilization,* edited by Paul Ropp, pp. 224–241. Berkeley: University of California Press.

FIELD, C. R. 1985. "The Importance to Rendille Subsistence Pastoralists of Sheep and Goats in Northern Kenya." In *Small Ruminants in African Ariculture,* edited by R. T. Wilson and D. Bourzat, pp. 188–197. Addis Ababa, Ethiopia: International Livestock Centre for Africa.

*FIFTH INTERNATIONAL DIRECTORY OF ANTHROPOLOGISTS.* 1975. Chicago and London: University of Chicago Press.

FIRTH, RAYMOND. [1936] 1957. *We the Tikopia: A Sociological Study of Kinship in Primitive Polynesia,* 2nd ed. New York: Barnes & Noble.

FIRTH, RAYMOND. [1940] 1967. "The Work of the Gods." In *Tikopia,* 2nd ed. London: Athlone Press.

FIRTH, RAYMOND. [1965] 1975. *Primitive Polynesian Economy.* New York: Norton.

FITTKAU, E., and H. KLINGE. 1973. "On Biomass and Trophic Structure of the Central Amazonian Rain Forest Ecosystem." *Biotropica* 5(1):2–14.

FLANNERY, KENT V. 1965. "The Ecology of Early Food Production in Mesopotamia." *Science* 147(3663):1247–1256.

FLANNERY, KENT V. 1972a. "The Cultural Evolution of Civilizations." *Annual Review of Ecology and Systematics* 3:399–426.

FLANNERY, KENT V. 1972b. "The Origins of the Village as a Settlement Type in Mesoamerica and the Near East: A Comparative Study." In *Man, Settlement and Urbanism,* edited by P. J. Ucko, R. Tringham, and G. W. Dimbleby, pp. 25–53. London: Duckworth.

FLOOD, JOSEPHINE. 1980. *The Moth Eaters.* Atlantic Highlands, N.J.: Humanities Press.

FLOOD, JOSEPHINE. 1983. *Archaeology of the Dreamtime.* Honolulu: University of Hawaii Press.

FLOWERS, NANCY M. 1983. "Seasonal Factors in Subsistence, Nutrition, and Child Growth in a Central Brazilian Indian Community." In *Adaptive Responses of Native Amazonians,* edited by Raymond Hames and William Vickers, pp. 357–390. New York: Academic Press.

FOSTER, GEORGE M. 1965. "Peasant Society and the Image of Limited Good." *American Anthropologist* 67(2):293–315.

FOSTER, GEORGE, M. 1969. *Applied Anthropology.* Boston: Little, Brown.

FRANK, ANDRÉ GUNDER. 1967. *Capitalism and Underdevelopment in Latin America.* New York: Monthly Review Press.

FRAZER, JAMES G. 1900. *The Golden Bough,* 3 vol. London: Macmillan.

FRAZER, SIR JAMES. 1905. "The Beginnings of Religion and Totemism Among the Australian Aborigines. Part II." *Fortnightly Review* 84:452–466.

FRAZER, SIR JAMES. 1910. *Totemism and Exogamy*, 4 vol. London: Macmillan.

FREED, STANLEY A., and RUTH S. FREED. 1981. "Sacred Cows and Water Buffalo in India: The Uses of Ethnography." *Current Anthropology* 22(5):483–490.

FREEDMAN, MAURICE. 1966. *Chinese Lineage and Society: Fukien and Kwangtung*. London School of Economics, Monographs on Social Anthropology, no. 33. London: Athlone Press.

FREEDMAN, MAURICE. 1979. *The Study of Chinese Society*. Stanford, Calif.: Stanford University Press.

FRERE, SIR H. BARTLE. 1881. "On the Laws Affecting the Relations Between Civilized and Savage Life, as Bearing on the Dealings of Colonists with Aborigines. *Journal of the Royal Anthropological Institute* 11:313–354.

FRIED, MORTON H. 1983. "Tribe to State or State to Tribe in Ancient China." In *The Origins of Chinese Civilization*, edited by D. N. Keightley, pp. 467–493. Berkeley: University of California Press.

FREUD, SIGMUND. 1913. *Totem and Taboo*. (In *Standard Edition of the Complete Psychological Works of Sigmund Freud* vol. 13, pp. ix–162. New York: Macmillan, 1959.)

GALATY, JOHN G. 1982. "Being 'Maasai'; Being 'People-of-Cattle': Ethnic Shifters in East Africa." *American Ethnologist* 9(1):1–20.

GEERTZ, CLIFFORD. 1963. *Agricultural Involution: The Process of Ecological Change in Indonesia*. Berkeley: University of California Press.

GELB, I. J. 1965. "The Ancient Mesopotamian Ration System." *Journal of Near Eastern Studies* 24(3):230–243.

GENNEP, ARNOLD L. VAN. 1909. *Les Rutes de Passage*. Paris: E. Nourry.

GENNEP, ARNOLD L. VAN. 1920. *L'Etat Actuel du Probleme Totemique*. Paris: E. Leroux.

GIBSON, McGUIRE. 1976. "By Stage and Cycle to Sumer." In *The Legacy of Sumer*. Vol. 4 of *Bibliotheca Mesopotamia*, edited by Denise Schmandt-Besserat, pp. 51–58. Malibu, Calif.: Undena Publications.

GLADWIN, THOMAS. 1970. *East is a Big Bird*. Cambridge, Mass.: Harvard University Press.

GLICKMAN, MAURICE. 1972. "The Nuer and the Dinka: A Further Note." *Man* 7(4):586–594.

GLUCKMAN, MAX. 1956. *Custom and Conflict in Africa*. New York: Barnes & Noble.

GODELIER, MAURICE. 1975. "Modes of Production, Kinship, and Demographic Structures." In *Marxist Analyses and Social Anthropology*, edited by Maurice Bloch pp. 3–27. New York: Wiley.

GOLDMAN, IRVING. 1970. *Ancient Polynesian Society*. Chicago and London: University of Chicago Press.

GOLDSMITH, EDWARD, ROBERT ALLEN, MICHAEL ALLABY, JOHN DAVOLL, and SAM LAWRENCE. 1972. *Blueprint for Survival*. Boston: Houghton Mifflin.

GOOD, KENNETH R. 1987. "Limiting Factors in Amazonian Ecology." In *Food and Evolution: Toward a Theory of Human Food Habits*, edited by Marvin Harris and Eric Ross, pp. 407–421. Philadelphia: Temple University Press.

GOODENOUGH, WARD HUNT. 1963. *Cooperation in Change: An Anthropological Approach to Community Development*. New York: Wiley.

GOODENOUGH, WARD H. 1965. "Yankee Kinship Terminology: A Problem in Componential Analysis." Part 2. *American Anthropologist* 67(5):259–287.

GOODLAND, ROBERT. 1982. *Tribal Peoples and Economic Development: Human Ecological Considerations*. Washington, D.C.: International Bank for Reconstruction and Development/World Bank.

GOODMAN, JEFFREY. 1981. *American Genesis: The American Indians and the Origins of Modern Man*. New York: Summit Books.

GOSH, A. 1982. "Deurbanization of the Harappan Civilization." In *Harappan Civilization: A Contemporary Perspective*, edited by George Possehl, pp. 321–324. New Dehli: Oxford and IBH Publishing.

GOULD, RICHARD A. 1969. "Subsistence Behavior Among the Western Desert Aborigines of Australia." *Oceania* 39(4):253–273.

GOULD, RICHARD A. 1970. *Spears and Spear-Throwers of the Western Desert Aborigines of Australia*. American Museum Novitates, no. 2403. New York: American Museum of Natural History.

GOULD, RICHARD A. 1980. *Living Archaeology*. Cambridge, Eng.: Cambridge University Press.

GOULD, RICHARD A. 1981. "Comparative Ecology of Food-Sharing in Australia and Northwest California." In *Omnivorous Primates: Gathering and Hunting in Human Evolution*, edited by Robert Harding and Geza Teleki pp. 422–454. New York: Columbia University Press.

GOULDING, MICHAEL. 1980. *The Fishes and the Forest: Explorations in Amazonian Natural History*. Berkeley: University of California Press.

GOULDING, MICHAEL. 1981. *Man and Fisheries on an Amazon Frontier*. The Hague: Dr. W. Junk.

GRAEDEL, THOMAS E., and PAUL J. CRUTZEN. 1989. "The Changing Atmosphere." *Scientific American* 261(3): 58–68.

GRAINGER, A. 1980. "The State of the World's Forests." *Ecologist* 10(1):6–54.

GRAY, ANDREW. 1987. "IWGIA Report on the ILO Meeting of Experts to Discuss the Revision of Convention 107 Geneva, 1–10 September, 1986." In *IWGIA Yearbook 1986: Indigenous Peoples and Human Rights*, pp. 73–92. Copenhagen: IWGIA.

GRAY, ANDREW. 1990. "The ILO Meeting at the UN, Geneva, June 1989: Report on International Labour Organisation Revision of Convention 107." In *IWGIA Yearbook 1989*, pp. 173–191. Copenhagen: IWGIA.

GREAT BRITAIN BOARD OF TRADE. 1909. *Statistical Abstracts for the Several British Colonies, Possessions, and Protectorates in Each Year from 1894 to 1908*, no. 46. London: His Majesty's Stationery Office.

GROSS, DANIEL R. 1975. "Protein Capture and Cultural Development in the Amazon Basin." *American Anthropologist* 77(3):526–549.

GUDSCHINSKY, SARAH C. 1956. "The ABC's of Lexicostatistics (Glottochronology)." *Word* 12:175–210.

HADINGHAM, EVAN. 1987. *Lines to the Mountain Gods: Nazca and the Mysteries of Peru*. New York: Random House.

HAILEY, WILLIAM MALCOLM. 1950. *Native Administration in the British African Territories. Part One, East Africa: Uganda,*

*Kenya, Tanganyika.* Colonial Office. London: His Majesty's Stationery Office.

HALLPIKE, C. R. 1979. *The Foundations of Primitive Thought.* Oxford, Eng.: Clarendon Press.

HALLPIKE, C. R. 1986. *The Principles of Social Evolution.* Oxford, Eng.: Clarendon Press.

HAMES, RAYMOND. 1987. "Game Conservation or Efficient Hunting?" In *The Question of the Commons: The Cultural Ecology of Communal Resources,* edited by Bonnie McCoy and James Acheson, pp. 92–107. Tucson: University of Arizona Press.

HAMILTON, ANNETTE. 1979. "A Comment on Arthur Hippler's Paper 'Culture and Personality Perspective of the Yolngu of Northeastern Arnhem Land: Part 1.'" *Mankind* 12(2):164–169.

HANDY, E. S. C., and E. G. HANDY. 1972. *The Native Planters in Old Hawaii: Their Life, Lore, and Environments,* Bernice P. Bishop Museum bull. 233. Honolulu: Bishop Museum Press.

HARNER, M. J. 1980. *The Way of the Shaman.* New York: Harper & Row.

HARRIS, MARVIN. 1965. "The Myth of the Sacred Cow." In *Man, Culture, and Animals,* edited by A. P. Vayda and A. Leeds, pp. 217–228. Washington, D.C.: American Association for the Advancement of Science.

HARRIS, MARVIN. 1966. "The Cultural Ecology of India's Sacred Cattle." *Current Anthropology* 7(1):51–59.

HARRIS, MARVIN. 1968. *The Rise of Anthropological Theory.* New York: Crowell.

HARRIS, MARVIN. 1971a. "A Comment on Heston: An Approach to the Sacred Cow of India." *Current Anthropology* 12(2):199–201.

HARRIS, MARVIN. 1971b. *Culture, Man, and Nature: An Introduction to General Anthropology.* New York: Crowell.

HARRIS, MARVIN. 1974. *Cows, Pigs, Wars, and Witches: The Riddles of Culture.* New York: Random House.

HARRIS, MARVIN. 1980. *Cultural Materialism: The Struggle for a Science of Culture.* New York: Random House/Vintage Books.

HARRIS, MARVIN. 1981. *America Now: The Anthropology of a Changing Culture.* New York: Simon & Schuster.

HARRIS, MARVIN. 1984. "A Cultural Materialist Theory of Band and Village Warfare: The Yanomamo Test." In *Warfare, Culture, and Environment,* edited by R. Brian Ferguson, pp. 111–140. New York: Academic Press.

HARRIS, MARVIN. 1985. *Good to Eat: Riddles of Food and Culture.* New York: Simon & Schuster.

HARRIS, MARVIN. 1988. *Culture, People, Nature: An Introduction to General Anthropology,* 5th ed. New York: Harper & Row.

HARTMANN, BETSY, and JAMES K. BOYCE. 1983. *A Quiet Violence: View from a Bangladesh Village.* San Francisco: Institute for Food and Development Policy.

HASLUCK, PAUL M. 1953. "The Future of the Australian Aborigine." 29th Meeting of the Australian and New Zealand Association for the Advancement of Science, Sydney. *Australian and New Zealand Association for the Advancement of Science* 29:155–165.

HASSAN, FEKRI A. 1981. *Demographic Archaeology.* New York: Academic Press.

HAWKES, JAMES F., and KRISTEN O'CONNELL. 1981. "Affluent Hunters? Some Comments in Light of the Alyawarra Case." *American Anthropologist* 83(3):622–626.

HAYDEN, BRIAN. 1977a. "Sticks and Stones and Ground Edge Axes: The Upper Palaeolithic in Southeast Asia?" In *Sunda and Sahul,* edited by J. Golson, J. Allen, and R. Jones, pp. 73–109. New York: Academic Press.

HAYDEN, BRIAN. 1977b. "Stone Tool Functions in the Western Desert." In *Stone Tools as Cultural Markers: Change, Evolution and Complexity.* Prehistory and Material Culture Series, no. 12, edited by R. V. S. Wright, pp. 178–188. Canberra: Australian Institute of Aboriginal Studies.

HAYDEN, BRIAN. 1979. *Palaeolithic Reflections: Lithic Technology and Ethnographic Excavation Among Australian Aborigines.* Canberra: Australian Institute of Aboriginal Studies.

HEADLAND, THOMAS N., KENNETH L. PIKE, and MARVIN HARRIS. 1990. *Emics and Etics: The Insider/Outsider Debate.* Newbury Park, Calif.: Sage.

HECKER, HOWARD M. 1982. "Domestication Revisited: Its Implications for Faunal Analysis." *Journal of Field Archaeology* 9:217–236.

HEILBRONER, ROBERT, and LESTER C. THUROW. 1987. *Economics Explained.* Englewood Cliffs, N.J.: Prentice Hall.

HEMMING, JOHN. 1978. *Red Gold: The Conquest of the Brazilian Indians.* Cambridge, Mass.: Harvard University Press.

HENRY, JULES. 1963. *Culture Against Man.* New York: Random House.

HERSKOVITS, MELVILLE J. 1926. "The Cattle Complex in East Africa." *American Anthropologist* 28(1):230–272, 28(2): 361–388, 28(3):494–528, 28(4):633–664.

HESTON, ALAN. 1971. "An Approach to the Sacred Cow of India." *Current Anthropology* 12(2):191–197.

HEYERDAHL, THOR. 1952. *American Indians in the Pacific: The Theory Behind the Kon-Tiki Expedition.* London: Allen & Unwin.

HIATT, L. R. 1984a. *Aboriginal Landowners: Contemporary Issues in the Determination of Traditional Aboriginal Land Ownership.* Oceania Monograph, no. 27. Sydney: University of Sydney.

HIATT, L. R. 1984b. "Your Mother-in-Law Is Poison." *Man* 19(2):183–198.

HIATT, L. R. 1987. "Aboriginal Political Life." In *Traditional Aboriginal Society,* edited by W. H. Edwards, pp. 174–188. South Melbourne: Macmillan.

HINMAN, HERBERT, WILLIAM MCREYNOLDS, RANDALL MILLS, ROLAND SCHIRMAN, and DAVID BRAGG. 1988. "Estimated Costs and Returns, 80-Cow Beef Enterprise, Southeastern Washington Grain Farms." Farm Business Management Reports, Extension Bulletin 1007. Pullman: Cooperative Extension, College of Agriculture and Home Economics, Washington State University.

HIPPLER, ARTHUR. 1977. "Cultural Evolution: Some Hypotheses Concerning the Significance of Cognitive and Affective Interpenetration During Latency." *Journal of Psychohistory* 4(4):419–460.

HIPPLER, ARTHUR. 1978. "Culture and Personality Perspective of the Yolngu of Northeastern Arnhem Land: Part 1. Early Socialization." *Journal of Psychological Anthropology* 1(2): 221–244.

HIPPLER, ARTHUR. 1979. "Comment on 'Development in the

non-Western world.'" *American Anthropologist* 8(2):348–349.

HIPPLER, ARTHUR. 1981. "The Yolngu and Cultural Relativism: A Response to Reser." *American Anthropologist* 83(2): 393–397.

HOBEN, ALLAN. 1982. "Anthropologists and Development." *Annual Review of Anthropology* 11:349–375.

HOEBEL, E. ADAMSON. 1968. *The Law of Primitive Man*. New York: Atheneum.

HOLMBERG, ALLAN R. 1971. "The Role of Power in Chanaging Values and Institutions of Vicos." In *Peasants, Power, and Applied Social Change: Vicos as a Model*, edited by Henry Dobyns, Paul Doughty, and Harold Lasswell, pp. 33–63. Beverly Hills, Calif., and London: Sage.

HOMEWOOD, K. M., and W. A. RODGERS. 1984. "Pastoralism and Conservation." *Human Ecology* 12(4):431–441.

HOPKINS, DIANE E. 1985. "The Peruvian Agrarian Reform: Dissent from Below." *Human Organization* 44(1): 18–32.

HOUSE OF COMMONS. 1837. *Report from the Select Committee on Aborigines (British Settlements)*. Imperial Blue Book, nr. 7, 425. British Parliamentary Papers.

HOWARD, ALAN. 1967 "Polynesian Origins and Migrations: A Review of Two Centuries of Speculation and Theory." In *Polynesian Culture History: Essays in Honor of Kenneth P. Emory*. Bernice P. Bishop Museum Special Publication, no. 56, edited by Genevieve Highland, Roland Force, Alan Howard, Marion Kelly, and Yosihiko Sinoto, pp. 45–101. Honolulu: Bishop Museum Press.

HSU, FRANCIS L. K. 1963. *Clan, Caste, and Club*. Princeton, N.J.: Van Nostrand.

HSU, FRANCIS L. K. (ed.). 1972. "American Core Value and National Character." In *Psychological Anthropology*, pp. 240–262. Cambridge, Mass.: Schenkman.

HSU, FRANCIS L. K. 1981. *Americans and Chinese: Passage to Difference*. Honolulu: University Press of Hawaii.

HUBERT, M. KING. 1969. "Energy Resources." In *Resources and Man*, edited by National Academy of Sciences, pp. 157–242. San Francisco: Freeman.

HUNN, EUGENE. 1985. "The Utilitarian Factor in Folk Biological Classification." In *Directions in Cognitive Anthropology*, edited by Janet Dougherty, pp. 117–140. Urbana and Chicago: University of Illinois Press.

HUTTON, J. H. 1963. *Caste in India: Its Nature, Function, and Origins*, 4th ed. London: Oxford University Press.

HYSLOP, JOHN. 1984. *The Inka Road System*. New York: Academic Press.

IDCA. See U.S. International Development Cooperation Agency.

II, JOHN PAPA. 1983. *Fragments of Hawaiian History*. Bernice P. Bishop Museum Special Publication, no. 70. Honolulu: Bishop Museum Press.

ILR (INTERNATIONAL LABOUR REVIEW). 1951. "Reports and Enquiries: First Session of ILO Committee of Experts on Indigenous Labour." *International Labour Review* 64(1): 61–84.

ILR (INTERNATIONAL LABOUR REVIEW). 1954. "Reports and Enquiries: The Second Session of the ILO Committee of Experts on Indigenous Labour." *International Labour Review* 70(5):418–441.

INTERNATIONAL DIRECTORY OF CORPORATE AFFILIATIONS 1990/91, vol. 1. Wilmette, Ill.: National Register Publishing.

IPCC (INTERGOVERNMENTAL PANEL ON CLIMATE CHANGE). 1991. *Climate Change: The IPCC Response Strategies*. Washington, D.C., and Covelo, Calif.: Island Press.

IRVINE, S. H., and J. W. BERRY. 1988. "The Abilities of Mankind: A Revaluation." In *Human Abilities in Cultural Context*, edited by S. H. Irvine and J. W. Berry, pp. 3–59. Cambridge, Eng.: Cambridge University Press.

ISBELL, WILLIAM H. 1978. "Environmental Perturbations and the Origin of the Andean State." In *Social Anthropology: Beyond Subsistence and Dating*, edited by Charles Redman, Mary Jane Berman, Edward Curtin, William Langhorne, Jr., Nina Versaggi, and Jeffery Wanser, pp. 303–313. New York: Academic Press.

JACOBSEN, THORKILD. 1976. *The Treasures of Darkness: A History of Mesopotamian Religion*. New Haven, Conn., and London: Yale University Press.

JACOBSEN, THORKILD, and ROBERT McC. ADAMS. 1958. "Salt and Silt in Ancient Mesopotamian Agriculture." *Science* 128 (3334):1251–1258.

JACOBSON, DORANNE. 1982. "Purdah and the Hindu Family in Central India." In *Separate Worlds: Studies of Purdah in South Asia*, edited by Hanna Papanek and Gail Minault, pp. 81–109. Dehli: Chanakya Publications.

JACOBSON, JODI L. 1989. "Abandoning Homelands." In *State of the World 1987*, edited by Lester Brown et al., pp. 59–76. New York and London: Norton.

JANSEN, EIRIK G. *Rural Bangladesh: Competition for Scarce Resources*. Oslo: Universitetsforlaget, Norwegian University Press.

JOHANNES, ROBERT E. 1981. *Words of the Lagoon: Fishing and Marine Lore in the Palau District of Micronesia*. Berkeley: University of California Press.

JOHNSON, ALLEN. 1975. "Time Allocation in a Machiguenga Community." *Ethnology* 14(3):301–310.

JOHNSON, ALLEN. 1983. "Machiguenga Gardens." In *Adaptive Responses of Native Amazonians*, edited by Raymond Hames and William Vickers, pp. 29–63. New York: Academic Press.

JOHNSON, ALLEN. 1985. "In Search of the Affluent Society." In *Anthropology: Contemporary Perspectives*, edited by David Hunter and Phillip Whitten, pp. 201–206. Boston: Little, Brown. (Reprinted from *Human Nature*, September 1978.)

JOHNSON, ALLEN, and CLIFFORD A. BEHRENS. 1982. "Nutritional Criteria in Machiguenga Food Production Decisions: A Linear-Programming Analysis." *Human Ecology* 10(2):167–189.

JOHNSON, GREGORY ALAN. 1973. *Local Exchange and Early State Development in Southwestern Iran*. Anthropological Papers, no. 51. Ann Arbor: Museum of Anthropology, University of Michigan.

JONES, P. D., T. M. L. WIGLEY, and P. B. WRIGHT. 1986. "Global Temperature Variations Between 1861 and 1984." *Nature* 322(6078):430–434.

JONES, RHYS, and BETTY MEEHAN. 1978. "Anbarra Concept of Colour." In *Australian Aboriginal Concepts*, edited by L. R. Hiatt, pp. 20–39. Canberra: Australian Institute of Aboriginal Studies.

JULIEN, CATHERINE J. 1982. "Inka Decimal Administration in

the Lake Titicaca Region." In *The Inca and Aztec States 1400–1800*, edited by George Collier, Renato Rosaldo, and John Wirth, pp. 119–151. New York: Academic Press.

KAPLAN, DAVID. 1960. "The Law of Cultural Dominance." In *Evolution and Culture*, edited by Marshall Sahlins and Elman Service, pp. 69–92. Ann Arbor: University of Michigan Press.

KATZ, SOLOMON H., and MARY M. VOIGT. 1986. "Bread and Beer: The Early Use of Cereals in the Human Diet." *Expedition* 28(2):23–34.

KAY, PAUL, and WILLETT KEMPTON. 1984. "What Is the Sapir-Whorf Hypothesis?" *American Anthropologist* 86(1): 65–79.

KEATINGE, RICHARD W. 1981. "The Nature and Role of Religious Diffusion in the Early Stages of State Formation: An Example from Peruvian Prehistory." In *The Transition to Statehood in the New World*, edited by Grant Jones and Robert Kautz, pp. 172–187. Cambridge, Eng.: Cambridge University Press.

KEATS, DAPHNE M., and JOHN A. KEATS. 1988. "Human Assessment in Australia." In *Human Abilities in Cultural Context*, edited by S. H. Irvine and J. W. Berry, pp. 283–298. Cambridge, Eng.: Cambridge University Press.

KEENLEYSIDE, H. L. 1950. "Critical Mineral Shortages." In *Proceedings of the United Nations Scientific Conference on the Conservation and Utilization of Resources*, pp. 38–46, August–September 1949, Lake Success, N.Y.: New York: United Nations.

KEIGHTLEY, DAVID N. 1990. "Early Civilization in China; Reflections on How It Became Chinese." In *Heritage of China: Contemporary Perspectives on Chinese Civilization*, edited by Paul Ropp, pp. 15–54. Berkeley: University of California Press.

KELLOGG, WILLIAM W. 1989. "Carbon Dioxide and Climate Changes: Implications for Mankind's Future." In *Global Climate Change: Human and Natural Influences*, edited by S. Fred Singer, pp. 37–65. New York: Paragon House.

KELLY, RAYMOND C. 1985. *The Nuer Conquest: The Structure and Development of an Expansionist System*. Ann Arbor: University of Michigan Press.

KENCHINGTON, RICHARD. 1985. "Coral-Reef Ecosystems: A Sustainable Resource." *Nature & Resources* 21(2):18–27.

KENNEDY, KENNETH A. R. 1982. "Skulls, Aryans and Flowing Drains: The Interface of Archaeology and Skeletal Biology in the Study of the Harappan Civilization." In *Harappan Civilization: A Contemporary Perspective*, edited by Gregory Possehl, pp. 289–295. New Dehli: Oxford and IBH Publishing.

KEYFITZ, NATHAN. 1989. "The Growing Human Population." *Scientific American* 261(3):119–126.

KING, F. H. 1911. *Farmers of Forty Centuries or Permanent Agriculture in China, Korea and Japan*. Madison, Wis.: Mrs. F. H. King.

KIRCH, PATRICK VINTON. 1985. *Feathered Gods and Fishhooks: An Introduction to Hawaiian Archaeology and Prehistory*. Honolulu: University of Hawaii Press.

KIRCH, PATRICK VINTON, and DOUGLAS E. YEN. 1982. *Tikopia: The Prehistory and Ecology of a Polynesian Outlier*. Bernice P. Bishop Museum, bull. 238. Honolulu: Bishop Museum Press.

KLICH, L. Z. 1988. "Aboriginal Cognition and Psychological

Nescience." In *Human Abilities in Cultural Context*, edited by S. H. Irvine and J. W. Berry, pp. 427–452. Cambridge, Eng.: Cambridge University Press.

KNUDSON, KENNETH E. 1970. "Resource Fluctuation, Productivity, and Social Organization on Micronesian Coral Islands." Ph.D. dissertation, University of Oregon.

KOHR, LEOPOLD. 1978. *The Breakdown of Nations*, reprint. New York: Dutton.

KRAMER, SAMUEL NOAH. 1963. *The Sumerians: Their History, Culture, and Character*. Chicago: University of Chicago Press.

KRANTZ, GROVER S. 1978. *Interproximal Attrition and Modern Dental Crowding*. Occasional Papers in Method and Theory in California Archaeology, no. 2, pp. 35–41. Society for California Archaeology.

KRANTZ, GROVER S. 1988. *Geographical Development of European Languages*. New York: Lang.

KROEBER, ALFRED. 1917. "The Superorganic." *American Anthropologist* 19(2):162–213.

KROEBER, A. L. 1948. *Anthropology*. New York: Harcourt, Brace & World.

KROEBER, ALFRED, and CLYDE KLUCKHOHN. 1952. *Culture, A Critical Review of Concepts and Definitions*. Papers of the Peabody Museum of American Archaeology and Ethnology, no. 1, Cambridge, Mass.: Harvard University.

KUPER, ADAM. 1982. "Lineage Theory: A Critical Retrospect." *Annual Review of Anthropology* 11:71–95.

LA LONE, DARRELL E. 1982. "The Inca as a Nonmarket Economy: Supply on Command Versus Supply and Demand." In *Contexts for Prehistoric Exchange*, edited by Jonathon Ericson and Timothy K. Earle, pp. 291–316. New York: Academic Press.

LAMBRICK, H. T. 1967. "The Indus Flood-Plain and the 'Indus' Civilization." *Geographical Journal* 133(4):483–495.

LANDSBERG, HANS H. 1964. *Natural Resources in America's Future: Patterns of Requirements and Availabilities 1960–2000*. Baltimore: Johns Hopkins University Press.

LANDSBERG, HELMUT E. 1989. "Where Do We Stand with the $CO_2$ Greenhouse Effect Problem?" In *Global Climate Change: Human and Natural Influences*, edited by S. Fred Singer, pp. 87–89. New York: Paragon House.

LANE-FOX PITT-RIVERS, A. H. 1872. "Address to the Department of Anthropology." *Report of the British Association for the Advancement of Science for 1871* 41:157–174.

LANE-FOX PITT-RIVERS, A. H. 1882. "Anniversary Address to the Anthropological Institute of Great Britain and Ireland." *Journal of the Royal Anthropological Institute* 11(4):488–509.

LANE-FOX PITT-RIVERS, A. H., DR. BEDDOE, MR. FRANKS, FRANCIS GALTON, E. W. BRABROOK, J. LUBBOCK, WALTER ELLIOT, CLEMENTS R. MARKHAM, and E. B. TYLOR. 1874. "Report of the Committee Appointed for the Purpose of Preparing and Publishing Brief Forms of Instructions for Travellers, Ethnologists, and other Anthropological Observers." *Report of the British Association for the Advancement of Science for 1873*, 43:482–488.

LANNING, EDWARD P. 1967. *Peru Before the Incas*. Englewood Cliffs, N. J. Prentice Hall.

LAPPE, FRANCIS MOORE, JOSEPH COLLINGS, and CARRY

FOWLER. 1979. *Food First: Beyond the Myth of Scarcity*. New York: Ballantine Books.

LAPPE, FRANCES MOORE, JOSEPH COLLINS, and DAVID KINLEY. 1981. *Aid as Obstacle: Twenty Questions About Our Foreign Aid and the Hungry*. San Francisco: Institute for Food and Development Policy.

LAPPE, FRANCES MOORE, RACHEL SCHURMAN, and KEVIN DANAHER. 1987. *Betraying the National Interest*. New York: Grove Press.

LARICK, ROY. 1986. "Age Grading and Ethnicity in the Style of Loikop (Samburu) Spears." *World Archaeology* 18(2): 269–283.

LARRICK, JAMES W., and JAMES A. YOST, JON KAPLAN, GARLAND KING, and JOHN MAYHALL. 1979. "Patterns of Health and Disease Among the Waorani Indians of Eastern Ecuador." *Medical Anthropology* 3(2):147–189.

LATHRAP, DONALD W. 1970. *The Upper Amazon*. New York: Praeger.

LATHRAP, DONALD W. 1977. "Our Father the Cayman, Our Mother the Gourd: Spinden Revisited, or a Unitary Model for the Emergence of Agriculture in the New World." In *Origins of Agriculture*, edited by C. A. Reed, pp. 713–751. The Hague: Mouton.

LEE, RICHARD B. 1981. "Is There a Foraging Mode of Production?" *Canadian Journal of Anthropology* 2(1):13–19.

LEE, RICHARD B., and IRVEN DEVORE (eds.) 1968. *Man the Hunter*. Chicago: Aldine.

LEE, RICHARD, and IRVEN DEVORE (eds.). 1968. "Problems in the Study of Hunters and Gatherers." In *Man the Hunter*, pp. 3–12. Chicago: Aldine.

LEFROY, ARCHDEACON. 1912. *The Future of Australian Aborigines*. Report of the Thirteenth Meeting of the Australasian Association for the Advancement of Science, Sydney, pp. 453–454.

LEGGE, JAMES. 1967. Li Chi: Book of Rites, 2 vols. New Hyde Park, N.Y.: University Books.

LEVINSON, DONALD. 1977. *A Guide to Social Theory: Worldwide Cross-Cultural Tests*, 5 vols. New Haven, Conn.: Human Relations Area Files.

LEVISON, M., R. G. WARD, and J. W. WEBB. 1973. *The Settlement of Polynesia: A Computer Simulation*. Minneapolis: University of Minnesota Press.

LÉVI-STRAUSS, CLAUDE. 1944. "The Social and Psychological Aspects of Chieftainship in a Primitive Tribe: The Nambikuara of Northwestern Matto Grosso." *Transactions of the New York Academy of Sciences* 7:16–32.

LÉVI-STRAUSS, CLAUDE. [1949] 1969. *The Elementary Structures of Kinship*. Boston: Beacon Press.

LÉVI-STRAUSS, CLAUDE. 1955. "The Structural Study of Myth." *Journal of American Folklore* 67:428–444.

LÉVI-STRAUSS, CLAUDE. 1963. *Totemism*. Boston: Beacon Press.

LÉVI-STRAUSS, CLAUDE. 1966. *The Savage Mind*. Chicago: University of Chicago Press.

LÉVI-STRAUSS, CLAUDE. 1969. *The Raw and the Cooked: Introduction to a Science of Mythology 1*. New York: Harper & Row.

LÉVI-STRAUSS, CLAUDE. 1973. *From Honey to Ashes: Introduction to a Science of Mythology 2*. New York: Harper & Row.

LÉVI-STRAUSS, CLAUDE. 1978. *The Origin of Table Manners: Introduction to a Science of Mythology 3*. New York: Harper & Row.

LEVY, REUBEN. 1962. *The Social Structure of Islam*. London: Cambridge University Press.

LÉVY-BRUHL, LUCIEN. [1922] 1923. *Primitive Mentality*. New York: Macmillan.

LÉVY-BRUHL, LUCIEN. 1926. *How Natives Think [Les Fonctions Mentales dans les Societes Inferieures]*. New York: Knopf.

LEWIS, BERNARD. 1960. *The Arabs in History*. New York: Harper Torchbooks.

LEWIS, D. 1976. "Observations on Route-Finding and Spatial Orientation Among the Aboriginal peoples of the Western Desert Region of Central Australia." *Oceania* 46(4): 249–282.

LEWIS, OSCAR. 1959. *Five Families: Mexican Case Studies in the Culture of Poverty*. New York: Basic Books.

LEWIS, OSCAR. 1961. *The Children of Sanchez*. New York: Random House.

LEWIS, OSCAR. 1966a. "The Culture of Poverty." *Scientific American* 215(4): 19–25.

LEWIS, OSCAR. 1966b. *La Vida: A Puerto Rican Family in the Culture of Poverty—San Juan and New York*. New York: Random House.

LEWIS, OSCAR. 1969. "The Possessions of the Poor." *Scientific American* 221(4): 114–124.

LEWIS-WILLIAMS, J. D., and T. A. DAWSON. 1988. "The Signs of all Times: Entopic Phenomenon in Upper Paleolithic Art." *Current Anthropology* 29(2): 201–245.

LINDENBAUM, SHIRLEY. 1987. "Loaves and Fishes in Bangladesh." In *Food and Evolution: Toward a Theory of Human Food Habits*, edited by Marvin Harris and Eric Ross, pp. 427–443. Philadelphia: Temple University Press.

LITTLE, MICHAEL A., and GEORGE E. B. MORREN, JR. 1976. *Ecology, Energetics, and Human Variability*. Dubuque, Iowa: Brown.

LIZOT, JACQUES. 1977. "Population, Resources and Warfare Among the Yanomami." *Man* 12(3/4): 497–517.

LIZOT, JACQUES. 1985. *Tales of the Yanamami: Daily Life in the Venezuelan Forest*. Cambridge, Eng.: Cambridge University Press.

LOBEL, PHIL S. 1978. "Gilbertese and Ellice Islander Names for Fishes and Other Organisms." *Micronesica* 14(2): 177–197.

LOUNSBURY, FLOYD G. 1964. "A Formal Account of the Crow- and Omaha-Type Kinship Terminologies." In *Explorations in Cultural Anthropology*, edited by Ward Goodenough, pp. 351–393. New York: McGraw-Hill.

LOURANDOS, HARRY. 1985. "Intensification and Australian Prehistory." In *Prehistoric Hunter-Gatherers: The Emergence of Cultural Complexity*, edited by Douglas Price and James A. Brown, pp. 385–423. New York: Academic Press.

LOURANDOS, HARRY. 1987. "Pleistocene Australia: Peopling a Continent." In *The Pleistocene Old World: Regional Perspectives*, edited by Olga Soffer, pp. 147–165. New York: Plenum Press.

LOZOFF, BETSY, and GARY M. BRITTENHAM. 1977. "Field Methods for the Assessment of Health and Disease in Pre-Agricultural Societies." In *Health and Disease in Tribal Societies*, CIBA Foundation Symposium, no. 49, pp. 49–67. Amsterdam: Elsevier/Excerpta Medica/North-Holland.

LUTEN, DANIEL B. 1974. "United States Requirements." In *Energy, the Environment, and Human Health,* edited by A. Finkel, pp. 17–33. Acton, Mass.: Publishing Sciences Group.

MALINOWSKI, BRONISLAW. 1929. "Practical Anthropology," *Africa,* 2(1): 22–38.

MALINOWSKI, BRONISLAW. 1944. *A Scientific Theory of Culture.* Chapel Hill: University of North Carolina Press.

MALINOWSKI, BRONISLAW. 1967. *A Diary in the Strict Sense of the Term.* New York: Harcourt, Brace & World.

MALO, DAVID. 1951. *Hawaiian Antiquities,* 2nd ed. Bernice P. Bishop Museum Special Publication, no. 2. Honolulu: Bernice P. Bishop Museum.

MALTHUS, THOMAS R. [1798, 1807] 1895. *An Essay on the Principle of Population.* New York: Macmillan.

MANNERS, ROBERT A. 1956. "Functionalism, Realpolitik, and Anthropology in Under-Developed Areas." *America Indigena* 16(1): 7–33.

MANNHEIM, BRUCE. 1991. *The Language of the Inka Since the European Invasion.* Austin: University of Texas Press.

MARSH, GEORGE PERKINS. 1864. *Man and Nature: Physical Geography as Modified by Human Action.* New York: Scribner.

MARTIN, P. S. 1967. "Prehistoric Overkill." In *Pleistocene Extinctions,* edited by P. S. Martin and H. E. Wright, Jr., pp. 75–120. New Haven, Conn.: Yale University Press.

MAYER, ADRIAN C. 1970. *Caste and Kinship in Central India: A Village and Its Region.* Berkeley and Los Angeles: University of California Press.

MCARTHUR, MARGARET. 1960. "Food Consumption and Dietary Levels of Groups of Aborigines Living on Naturally Occurring Foods." In *Records of the American-Australian Scientific Expedition to Arnhem Land.* Vol. 2 of *Anthropology and Nutrition,* edited by Charles Mountford, pp. 90–135. Melbourne: Melbourne University Press.

MCCARTHY, F. D., and MCARTHUR, MARGARET. 1960. "The Food Quest and Time Factor in Aboriginal Economic Life." In *Records of the American-Australian Scientific Expedition to Arnhem Land.* Vol. 2 of *Anthropology and Nutrition,* edited by Charles Mountford, pp. 145–194. Melbourne: Melbourne University Press.

MCCOY, JOHN. 1970. "Chinese Kin Terms of Reference and Address." In *Family and Kinship in Chinese Society,* edited by Maurice Freedman, pp. 209–226. Stanford, Calif.: Stanford University Press.

MCDONALD, DAVID. 1977. "Food Taboos: A Primitive Environmental Protection Agency (South America)." *Anthropos* 72: 734–748.

MCNEIL, WILLIAM H. 1987. *A History of the Human Community: Prehistory to the Present.* Englewood Cliffs, N.J.: Prentice Hall.

MEAD, MARGARET. 1942. *And Keep Your Powder Dry: An Anthropologist Looks at America.* New York: Morrow.

MEAD, MARGARET. 1961. *New Lives for Old.* New York: New American Library.

MEADOWS, DONELLA H., DENNIS L. MEADOWS, JORGEN RANDERS, and WILLIAM W. BEHRENS III. 1972. *The Limits to Growth.* New York: Universe.

MEEHAN, BETTY. 1977. "Hunters by the Seashore." *Journal of Human Evolution* 6: 363–370.

MEEHAN, BETTY. 1982. "Ten Fish for One Man: Some Anbarra Attitudes Towards Food and Health." In *Body, Land and Spirit: Health and Healing in Aboriginal Society,* edited by Janice Reid, pp. 96–120. St. Lucia: University of Queensland Press.

MEGGERS, BETTY J. 1954. "Environmental Limitation of the Development of Culture." *American Anthropologist* 56(5, pt. 1):801–824.

MEGGERS, BETTY J. 1971. *Amazonia: Man and Culture in a Counterfeit Paradise.* Arlington Heights, Ill.: AHM Publishing.

MEILLASSOUX, CLAUDE. 1981. *Maidens, Meal and Money: Capitalism and the Domestic Community.* Cambridge, Eng.: Cambridge University Press.

MELLAART, J. 1967. *Çatal Hüyük: A Neolithic Town in Anatolia.* London: Thames & Hudson.

MERRILEES, D. 1968. "Man the Destroyer: Late Quaternary Changes in the Australian Marsupial Fauna." *Journal of the Royal Society of Western Australia* 51:1–24.

MESAROVIC, MIHAJLO, and EDUARD PESTEL. 1974. *Mankind at the Turning Point: The Second Report of the Club of Rome.* New York: New American Library.

MICHAEL, FRANZ. 1964. "State and Society in Nineteenth-Century China." In *Modern China,* edited by Albert Feuerwerker, pp. 57–69. Englewood Cliffs, N.J.: Prentice Hall.

MIGLIAZZA, ERNEST C. 1982. "Linguistic Prehistory and the Refuge Model in Amazonia." In *Biological Diversification in the Tropics,* edited by Ghillean Prance, pp. 497–519. New York: Columbia University Press.

MILLER, DANIEL. 1985. "Ideology and the Harappan Civilization." *Journal of Anthropological Archaeology* 4:34–71.

MILLER, SOLOMON. 1967. "Hacienda to Plantation in Northern Peru: The Processes of Proletarianization of a Tenant Farmer Society." In *Contemporary Change in Traditional Societies.* Vol. 3, *Mexican and Peruvian Communities,* edited by Julian Steward, pp. 133–225. Urbana: University of Illinois Press.

MILLS, C. WRIGHT. 1956. *The Power Elite.* New York: Oxford University Press.

MINER, HORACE M. 1955. "Planning for the Acculturation of Isolated Tribes." *Proceedings of the 31st International Congress of Americanists,* 1: 441–446.

MINTZ, SIDNEY W. 1985. *Sweetness and Power: The Place of Sugar in Modern History.* New York: Viking/Penguin Books.

MINTZ, SIDNEY W., and ERIC R. WOLF. 1957. "Haciendas and Plantations in Middle America and the Antilles." *Social and Economic Studies* 6:380–412.

MOORE, ANDREW M. T. 1983. "The First Farmers in the Levant." In *The Hilly Flanks and Beyond: Essays on the Prehistory of Southwestern Asia.* Studies in Ancient Oriental Civilization, no. 36, pp. 91–111. Chicago: Oriental Institute, University of Chicago.

MORGAN, LEWIS HENRY. 1851. *League of the Ho-de-no-sau-nee, or Iroquois.* Rochester, N.Y.: Sage.

MORGAN, LEWIS HENRY. 1871. *Systems of Consanguinity and Affinity of the Human Family.* Washington, D.C.: Smithsonian Institution.

MORGAN, LEWIS HENRY. 1877. *Ancient Society.* New York: Holt.

MORRIS, CRAIG, and DONALD E. THOMPSON. 1985. *Huanaco*

*Pampa: An Inca City and Its Hinterland.* London: Thames & Hudson.

MOSELEY, MICHAEL EDWARD. 1975. *The Maritime Foundations of Andean Civilization.* Menlo Park, Calif.: Cummings.

MOSELEY, MICHAEL E., and K. C. DAY (eds.). 1980. *Chan Chan: The Desert City and Its Hinterland.* Albuquerque: University of New Mexico Press.

MOSELEY, MICHAEL E., and CAROL J. MACKEY. 1973. "Chan Chan, Peru's Ancient City of Kings." *National Geographic* 143(3):318–345.

MOUNTFORD, CHARLES P. 1965. *Ayers Rock: Its People, Their Beliefs, and Their Art.* Honolulu: East-West Center Press.

MUNN, NANCY D. 1969. "The Effectiveness of Symbols in Murngin Rite and Ritual." In *Forms of Symbolic Action: Proceedings of the 1969 Annual Spring Meeting of the American Ethnological Society,* edited by Robert Spencer, pp. 178–207. Seattle and London: American Ethnological Society.

MUNN, NANCY D. 1973. *Walbiri Iconography: Graphic Representation and Cultural Symbolism in a Central Australian Society.* Ithaca, N.Y., and London: Cornell University press.

MURAI, MARY, FLORENCE PEN, and CAREY D. MILLER. 1958. *Some Tropical South Pacific Island Foods: Description, History, Use, Composition, and Nutritive Value.* Hawaii Agricultural Experiment Station, bull. 110. Honolulu: University of Hawaii Press.

MURDOCK, GEORGE P. 1949. *Social Structure.* New York: MacMillan.

MURDOCK, GEORGE P. 1981. *Atlas of World Cultures.* Pittsburgh: University of Pittsburgh Press.

MURDOCK, GEORGE P., CLELLAN S. FORD, ALFRED E. HUDSON, RAYMOND KENNEDY, LEO W. SIMMONS, and JOHN W. M. WHITING. 1982. *Outline of Cultural Materials,* 5th ed., New Haven, Conn.: Human Relations Area Files.

MURRA, JOHN V. 1960. "Rite and Crop in the Inca State." In *Culture in History: Essays in Honor of Paul Radin,* edited by Stanley Diamond, pp. 393–407. New York: Columbia University Press.

MURRA, J. V. 1972. "'El Control Vertical' de un Maximo de Pisos Ecologicos en la Economia de las Sociedades Andinas." In *Vista de la Provincia de Leon de Huanuco (1562),* Vol. 2, edited by Inigo Ortiz de Zuniga, pp. 429–476. Huanuco, Peru: Universidad Hermillo Valdizan.

MYERS, FRED R. 1980. "The Cultural Basis of Politics in Pintupi Life." *Mankind* 12(3): 197–214.

NADER, LAURA. 1972. "Up the Anthropologist—Perspectives Gained from Studying Up." In *Reinventing Anthropology,* edited by Dell Hymes, pp. 284–311. New York: Pantheon Books/Random House.

*NATIONAL PROVISIONER.* 1990a. *National Provisioner* 202(2).

*NATIONAL PROVISIONER.* 1990b. *National Provisioner* 202(9).

NATIONAL RESEARCH COUNCIL, COMMITTEE ON MINERAL RESOURCES AND THE ENVIRONMENT. 1975. *Mineral Resources and the Environment.* Washington, D.C.: National Academy of Sciences.

NEEL, JAMES V. 1970. "Lessons from a 'Primitive' People." *Science* 170(3960):815–822.

NEWCOMER, PETER J. 1972. "The Nuer Are Dinka: An Essay on Origins and Environmental Determinism." *Man* 7(1): 5–11.

NIETSCHMANN, BERNARD. 1988. "Third World Colonial Expansion: Indonesia, Disguised Invasion of Indigenous Nations." In *Tribal Peoples and Development Issues: A Global Overview,* edited by John H. Bodley, pp. 191–207. Mountain View, Calif.: Mayfield.

NISSEN, HANS J. 1986. "The Archaic Texts from Uruk." *World Archaeology* 17(3):317–334.

NOLL, RICHARD. 1984. "The Context of Schizophrenia and Shamanism." *American Ethnologist* 11(1):191–192.

OBERG, KALVERO. 1955. "Types of Social Structure Among the Lowland Tribes of South and Central America." *American Anthropologist* 57(3, pt. 1):472–487.

OCHOLLA-AYAYO, A. B. C. 1979. "Marriage and Cattle Exchange Among the Nilotic Luo." *Paideuma* 25:173–193.

O'CONNELL, JAMES F., and KRISTEN HAWKES. 1981. "Alyawara Plant Use and Optimal Foraging Theory." In *Hunter-Gatherer Foraging Strategies,* edited by B. Winterhalder and E. A. Smith, pp. 99–125. Chicago: University of Chicago Press.

ODUM, HOWARD T. 1971. *Environment, Power, and Society.* New York: Wiley Inter-Science.

OLIVER, DOUGLAS L. 1989. *Oceania: The Native Cultures of Australia and the Pacific Islands,* 2 vols. Honolulu: University of Hawaii Press.

ONERN (OFICINA NACIONAL DE EVALUACIÓN DE RECURSOS NATURALES). 1968. *Inventario, Evaluación e Integración de los Recursos Naturales de la Zona del Rio Tambo-Gran Pajonal.* Lima, Peru: ONERN.

ORLOVE, BENJAMIN S. 1987. "Stability and Change in Highland Andean Dietary Patterns." In *Food and Evolution: Toward a Theory of Human Food Habits,* edited by Marvin Harris and Eric Ross, pp. 481–515. Philadelphia: Temple University Press.

PALMER, INGRID. 1972. *Science and Agricultural Production.* Geneva: U.N. Research Institute for Social Development.

PAPANEK, HANNA. 1982. "Purdah: Separate Worlds and Symbolic Shelter." In *Separate Worlds: Studies of Purdah in South Asia,* edited by Hanna Papanek and Gail Minault, pp. 3–53. Delhi: Chanakya Publications.

PARKINSON, C. NORTHCOTE. 1957. *Parkinson's Law and Other Studies in Administration.* Boston: Houghton Mifflin.

PARRY, JONATHAN P. 1979. *Caste and Kinship in Kangra.* London: Routledge & Kegan Paul.

PERRY, W. J. 1923. *The Children of the Sun.* London: Methuen.

PETERS, LARRY G., and DOUGLASS PRICE-WILLIAMS. 1980. "Towards an Experiential Analysis of Shamanism." *American Ethnologist* 7(3):397–418.

PETERSON, NICOLAS. 1986. *Australian Territorial Organization.* Oceania Monograph, no. 30. Sydney: University of Sydney.

PHILLIPSON, DAVID W. 1985. *African Archaeology.* Cambridge, Eng.: Cambridge University Press.

PIETRASZEK, GREG. 1990. "Cattlemen Face Future Competition with Confidence." *National Provisioner* 202(12):5–8.

PIKE, KENNETH L. 1954. *Language in Relation to a Unified Theory of the Structure of Human Behavior,* vol. 1. The Hague: Mouton.

POLANYI, KARL. 1957. *The Great Transformation: The Political and Economic Origins of Our Time.* Boston: Beacon Press.

POLANYI, KARL. 1977. *The Livelihood of Man.* New York: Academic Press.

POPENOE, PAUL. 1915. "One Phase of Man's Modern Evolution." *Proceedings of the 19th International Congress of Americanists* 19:617–620.

PORTEUS, S. D. 1917. "Mental Tests with Delinquents and Australian Aboriginal Children." *Psychological Review* 24(1): 32–42. (Reprinted in *The Psychology of Aboriginal Australians*, edited by G. E. Kearney, P. R. de Lacey, and G. R. Davidson, pp. 29–37. Sydney: Wiley, 1973.)

PORTEUS, S. D. 1931. *The Psychology of a Primitive People.* London: E. Arnold.

POSPISIL, LEOPOLD. 1972. *The Ethnology of Law.* Addison-Wesley Module in Anthropology, no. 12. Reading, Mass.: Addison-Wesley.

POSSEHL, GREGORY L. 1967. "The Mohenjo-Daro Floods: A Reply." *American Anthropologist* 69(1):32–40.

POSSEHL, GREGORY L. 1977. "The End of a State and Continuity of a Tradition: A Discussion of the Late Harappa." In *Realm and Region in Traditional India*. Program in Comparative Studies on Southern Asia, Duke University. Monograph and Occasional Papers Series, Monograph no. 14, edited by Richard Fox, pp. 234–254. Durham, N.C.

PRICE, A. G. 1950. *White Settlers and Native Peoples.* London: Cambridge University Press.

PRICE, T. DOUGLAS, and GARY M. FEINMAN. 1993. *Images of the Past.* Mountain View, Calif.: Mayfield.

PRICE, WESTON ANDREW. 1945. *Nutrition and Physical Degeneration: A Comparison of Primitive and Modern Diets and Their Effects.* Redlands, Calif.: Weston Price.

QUILTER, JEFFREY, and TERRY STOCKER. 1983. "Subsistence Economies and the Origins of Andean Complex Societies." *American Anthropologist* 85(3):545–562.

RADCLIFFE-BROWN, A. R. 1913. "Three Tribes of Western Australia." *Journal of the Royal Anthropological Institute* 43:143–195.

RADCLIFFE-BROWN, A. R. 1918. "Notes on the Social Organization of Australian Tribes." *Journal of the Royal Anthropological Institute* 48:222–253.

RADCLIFFE-BROWN, A. R. 1929. "The Sociological Theory of Totemism." Proceedings of the Fourth Pacific Science Congress. (Reprinted in *Structure and Function in Primitive Society*, edited by A. R. Radcliffe-Brown, pp. 117–132. New York: Free Press, 1965.)

RADCLIFFE-BROWN, A. R. 1930. Editorial. Oceania 1(1): 1–4.

RADCLIFFE-BROWN, A. R. 1941. "The Study of Kinship Systems." *Journal of the Royal Anthropological Institute.* (Reprinted in *Structure and Function in Primitive Society*, edited by A. R. Radcliffe-Brown, pp. 49–89. New York: Free Press, 1965.)

RADCLIFFE-BROWN, A. R. 1951. "The Comparative Method in Social Anthropology." *Journal of the Royal Anthropological Institute* 81:15–22.

RADCLIFFE-BROWN, A. R. 1958. Presidential Address to Section E. South African Association for the Advancement of Science, July 1928. (In *Method in Social Anthropology: Selected Essays by A.R. Radcliffe-Brown*, edited by M. N. Srinivas. Chicago: University of Chicago Press.)

RAIKES, ROBERT L. 1964. "The End of the Ancient Cities of the Indus." *American Anthropologist* 66(2):284–299.

RAIKES, ROBERT L. 1965. "The Mohenjo-Daro Floods." *Antiquity* 38(155):196–203.

RAMOS, ALCIDA R. 1987. "Reflecting on the Yanomami: Ethnographic Images and the Pursuit of the Exotic." *Cultural Anthropology* 2(3):284–304.

RANDALL, ROBERT A., and EUGENE S. HUNN. 1984. "Do Life-Forms Evolve or Do Uses for Life? Some Doubts About Brown's Universals Hypotheses." *American Ethnologist* 1(2): 329–349.

RAO, S. R. 1982. "New Light on the Post-Urban (Late Harappan) Phase of the Indus Civilization in India." In *Harappan Civilization: A Contemporary Perspective*, edited by Gregory Possehl, pp. 353–359. New Delhi: Oxford and IBH Publishing.

RAPPAPORT, ROY A. 1977a. "Maladaptation in Social Systems." In *The Evolution of Social Systems*, edited by J. Friedman and M. J. Rowlands, pp. 49–71. London: Duckworth.

RAPPAPORT, ROY A. 1977b. "Normative Models of Adaptive Processes: A Response to Anne Whyte." In *The Evolution of Social Systems*, edited by J. Friedman and M. J. Rowlands, pp. 79–87. London: Duckworth.

RAWSKI, EVELYN S. 1987. "Popular Culture in China." In *Tradition and Creativity: Essays on East Asian Civilization*, edited by Ching-I Tu, pp. 41–65. New Brunswick, N.J., and Oxford, Eng.: Transaction Books.

RAYMOND, J. SCOTT. 1981. "The Maritime Foundations of Andean Civilization: A Reconsideration of the Evidence." *American Antiquity* 46(4):806–821.

READ, C. H. 1897. "An Imperial Bureau of Ethnology." *British Association for the Advancement of Science, Report for 1896*, 66:928.

READ, C. H. 1901. "Presidential Address." *Journal of the Royal Anthropological Institute* 31:14–15.

REEVES, ROSSER. 1961. *Reality in Advertising.* New York: Knopf.

REDFIELD, ROBERT. 1941. *The Folk Culture of Yucatan.* Chicago: University of Chicago Press.

REDFIELD, ROBERT. 1947. "The Folk Society." *American Journal of Sociology* 52(4):295–298.

REDFIELD, ROBERT, RALPH LINTON, and MELVILLE J. HERSKOVITS. 1936. "Memorandum for the Study of Acculturation." *American Anthropologist* 38(1):149–152.

REDMAN, CHARLES L. 1978a. "Mesopotamian Urban Ecology: The Systemic Context of the Emergence of Urbanism." In *Social Archaeology: Beyond Subsistence and Dating*, edited by Charles Redman, Mary Jane Berman, Edward Curtin, William Langhorne, Jr., Nina Versaggi, and Jeffery Wanser, pp. 329–347. New York: Academic Press.

REDMAN, CHARLES L. 1978b. *The Rise of Civilization: From Early Farmers to Urban Society in the Ancient Near East.* San Francisco: Freeman.

REICHEL-DOLMATOFF, GERARDO. 1971. *Amazonian Cosmos: The Sexual and Religious Symbolism of the Tukano Indians.* Chicago: University of Chicago Press.

REICHEL-DOLMATOFF, GERARDO. 1976. "Cosmology as Ecological Analysis: A View from the Rain Forest." *Man* 11(3): 307–318.

REITZ, ELIZABETH J. 1988. "Faunal Remains from Paloma, an Archaic Site in Peru." *American Anthropologist* 90(2): 310–322.

RENFREW, COLIN. 1989. "The Origins of Indo-European Languages." *Scientific American* 261(4):106–114.

RESER, JOSEPH. 1981. "Australian Aboriginal Man's Inhumanity to Man: A Case of Cultural Distortion." *American Anthropologist* 83(2):387–393.

RIBEIRO, DARCY. 1957. *Culturas e Linguas Indigenas do Brasil.* Separata de Educação e Ciencias Soçais, no. 6. Rio de Janeiro: Centro Brasileiro de Pesquisas Educacionais.

RICHARDS, PAUL W. 1973. "The Tropical Rain Forest." *Scientific American* 229(6):58–67.

RIVIERE, PETER. 1969. *Marriage Among the Trio: A Principle of Social Organization.* Oxford, Eng.: Clarendon Press.

ROE, PETER G. 1982. *The Cosmic Zygote: Cosmology in the Amazon Basin.* New Brunswick, N.J.: Rutgers University Press.

ROSENBERG, NATHAN, and L. E. BIRDZELL, JR. 1990. "Science, Technology and the Western Miracle." *Scientific American* 263(5):42–54.

ROSS, JANE BENNETT. 1984. "Effects of Contact on Revenge Hostilities Among the Achuara Jivaro." In *Warfare, Culture, and Environment,* edited by R. Brian Ferguson, pp. 83–109. New York: Academic Press.

ROSS, W. McGREGOR. 1927. *Kenya from Within: A Short Political History.* London: Allen & Unwin.

ROWE, JOHN H. 1982. "Inca Policies and Institutions Relating to the Cultural Unification of the Empire." In *The Inca and Aztec States 1400–1800,* edited by George Collier, Renato Rosaldo, and John Wirth, pp. 93–118. New York: Academic Press.

ROWLAND, F. SHERWOOD. 1989. "Chlorofluorocarbons, Stratospheric Ozone, and the Antarctic 'Ozone Hole.'" In *Global Climate Change: Human and Natural Influences,* edited by S. Fred Singer, pp. 113–155. New York: Paragon House.

ROY, MANISHA. 1975. *Bengali Women.* Chicago and London: University of Chicago Press.

RUBINSTEIN, DON. 1978. "Native Place-Names and Geographic Systems of Fais, Caroline Islands." *Micronesica* 14(1):69–82.

RUHLEN, MERRITT. 1987. *A Guide to the World's Languages, Volume 1: Classification.* Stanford, Calif.: Stanford University Press.

SAHLINS, MARSHALL. 1958. *Social Stratification in Polynesia.* Seattle: University of Washington Press.

SAHLINS, MARSHALL. 1960. "Evolution: Specific and General." In *Evolution and Culture,* edited by Marshall Sahlins and Elman Service, pp. 12–44. Ann Arbor: University of Michigan Press.

SAHLINS, MARSHALL. 1961. "The Segmentary Lineage: An Organization of Predatory Expansion." *American Anthropologist* 63(2, pt.1):322–345.

SAHLINS, MARSHALL. 1963. "Poor Man, Rich Man, Big-Man, Chief: Political Types in Melanesia and Polynesia." *Comparative Studies in Society and History* 5:285–303.

SAHLINS, MARSHALL. 1965. "On the Ideology and Composition of Descent Groups." *Man* 65 (July/August), article 97, pp. 104–107.

SAHLINS, MARSHALL. 1968. "Notes on the Original Affluent Society." In *Man the Hunter,* edited by Richard Lee and Irven DeVore, pp. 85–89. Chicago: Aldine.

SAHLINS, MARSHALL. 1972. *Stone Age Economics.* Chicago: Aldine.

SAHLINS, MARSHALL. 1976a. "Colors and Cultures." *Semiotica* 16:1–22.

SAHLINS, MARSHALL. 1976b. *Culture and Practical Reason.* Chicago and London: University of Chicago Press.

SAHLINS, MARSHALL. 1976c. *The Use and Abuse of Biology: An Anthropological Critique of Sociobiology.* Ann Arbor: University of Michigan Press.

SAPIR, E. 1921. *Language.* New York: Harcourt Brace Jovanovich.

SCHATTENBURG, PATRICIA. 1976. "Food and Cultivar Preservation in Micronesian Voyaging." Miscellaneous Work Papers. *University of Hawaii Pacific Islands Program* 1:25–51.

SCHMANDT-BESSERAT, DENISE. 1982. "The Emergence of Recording." *American Anthropologist* 84(4):871–878.

SCHNEIDER, STEPHEN H. 1989. "The Changing Climate." *Scientific American* 261(3):70–79.

SCHUMACHER, E. F. 1973. *Small Is Beautiful: Economics as if People Mattered.* New York: Harper & Row.

SCHWARTZBERG, JOSEPH E. 1977. "The Evolution of Regional Power Configurations in the Indian Subcontinent." In *Realm and Region in Traditional India.* Monograph and Occasional Papers Series, Monograph no. 14, edited by Richard Fox, pp. 197–233. Durham, N.C.: Program in Comparative Studies on Southern Asia, Duke University.

SERVICE, ELMAN R. 1960. "The Law of Evolutionary Potential." In *Evolution and Culture,* edited by Marshall Sahlins and Elman Service, pp. 93–122. Ann Arbor: University of Michigan Press.

SERVICE, ELMAN. 1962. *Primitive Social Organization.* New York: Random House.

SERVICE, ELMAN R. 1975. *Origins of the State and Civilization: The Process of Cultural Evolution.* New York. Norton.

SHALER, NATHANIEL S. 1905. *Man and the Earth.* New York: Duffield.

SHAMASASTRY, R. (TRANS.). 1960. *Kautilya's Arthasastra.* Mysore, India: Mysore Printing and Publishing.

SHAPIRO, WARREN. 1981. *Miwuyt Marriage: The Cultural Anthropology of Affinity in Northeast Arnhem Land.* Philadelphia: Institute for the Study of Human Issues.

SHWEDER, RICHARD A. 1982. "On Savages and Other Children." *American Anthropologist* 84(2):354–366.

SHWEDER, RICHARD A. 1985. "Has Piaget Been Upstaged? A Reply to Hallpike." *American Anthropologist* 87:138–144.

SILLEN, ANDREW. 1986. "Dietary Reconstruction and Near Eastern Archaeology." *Expedition* 28(2):16–22.

SILVERMAN, JULIAN. 1967. "Shamans and Acute Schizophrenia." *American Anthropologist* 69(1):21–31.

SIMOONS, FREDERICK J. 1979. "Questions in the Sacred Cow Controversy." *Current Anthropology* 20(3):467–476.

SINDIGA, ISAAC. 1987. "Fertility Control and Population Growth Among the Maasai." *Human Ecology* 15(1):53–66.

SISKIND, JANET. 1973. *To Hunt in the Morning.* London: Oxford University Press.

SKINNER, G. WILLIAM. 1964. "Marketing and Social Structure in Rural China (Part 1)." *Journal of Asian Studies* 24(1):3–43.

SMITH, ADAM. 1776. *An Inquiry into the Nature and Causes of the Wealth of Nations,* Vol. 1. London: Strahan & Cadell.

SMITH, ANDREW B. 1984. "Origins of the Neolithic in the Sahara." In *From Hunters to Farmers: The Causes and Conse-*

*quences of Food Production in Africa*, edited by J. Desmond Clark and Steven Brandt, pp. 84–92. Berkeley: University of California Press.

SMITH, G. ELLIOT. 1928. *In the Beginning: The Origin of Civilization*. New York: Morrow.

SMITH, P. E. L., and T. C. YOUNG, JR. 1972. "The Evolution of Early Agriculture and Culture in Greater Mesopotamia: A Trial Model." In *Population Growth: Anthropological Implications*, edited by B. J. Spooner, pp. 1–59. Cambridge, Mass.: Massachusetts Institute of Technology.

SMITH, PHILIP E. L., and T. CUYLER YOUNG, JR. 1983. "The Force of Numbers: Population Pressure in the Central Western Zagros 12,000–4500 BC." In *The Hilly Flanks and Beyond: Essays on the Prehistory of Southwestern Asia*, pp. 141–162. Studies in Ancient Oriental Civilization, no. 36. Chicago: Oriental Institute, University of Chicago.

SMITH, RICHARD CHASE. 1977. *The Amuesha-Yanachaga Project, Peru: Ecology and Ethnicity in the Central Jungle of Peru*. Survival International Document 3. London: Survival International.

SMITH, WILBERFORCE. 1894. "The Teeth of Ten Sioux Indians." *Journal of the Royal Anthropological Institute* 24:109–116.

SOUTHALL, AIDAN. 1976. "Nuer and Dinka Are People: Ecology, Ethnicity and Logical Possibility." *Man* 11:463–491.

SPENCER, HERBERT. 1967. *The Evolution of Society: Selections from Herbert Spencer's Principles of Sociology*, edited by Robert Carneiro. Chicago: University of Chicago Press.

SPENCER, PAUL. 1988. *The Maasai of Matapato: A Study of Rituals of Rebellion*. Bloomington and Indianapolis: Indiana University Press.

SPENCER, ROBERT F., and ELDON JOHNSON. 1960. *Atlas for Anthropology*. Dubuque, Iowa: Brown.

*SPOKESMAN REVIEW*. 1991. "Biggest Beef Packer Put on Auction Block." *Spokesman Review*, February 29.

SRINIVAS, M. N. 1959. "The Dominant Caste in Rampura." *American Anthropologist* 61(1):1–16.

STEIN, GIL. 1986. "Herding Strategies at Neolithic Gritille: The Use of Animal Bone Remains to Reconstruct Ancient Economic Systems." *Expedtion* 28(2):35–42.

STEINHART, JOHN S., and CAROL E. STEINHART. 1974. "Energy Use in the U.S. Food System." *Science* 184 (4134): 307–316.

STEWARD, JULIAN H. 1936. "The Economic and Social Basis of Primitive Bands." In *Essays in Anthropology in Honor of Alfred Louis Kroeber*, pp. 331–350. Berkeley: University of California Press.

STEWARD, JULIAN H. 1949. "Cultural Causality and Law: A Trial Formulation of the Development of Early Civilization." *American Anthropologist* 51(1):1–27.

STEWARD, JULIAN H. 1955. *Theory of Culture Change*. Urbana: University of Illinois Press.

STOCKS, ANTHONY. 1983. "Cocamilla Fishing: Patch Modification and Environmental Buffering in the Amazon Varzea." In *Adaptive Responses of Native Amazonians*, edited by Raymond Hames and William Vickers, pp. 239–267. New York: Academic Press.

STOVER, LEON N., and TAKEKO KAWAI STOVER. 1976. *China: An Anthropological Perspective*. Pacific Palisades, Calif.: Goodyear.

SWANSON, G. E. 1960. *The Birth of the Gods*. Ann Arbor: University of Michigan Press.

SWENSON, SALLY, and JEREMY NARBY. 1986. "The Pichis–Palcazu Special Project in Peru—A Consortium of International Lenders." *Cultural Survival Quarterly* 10(1):19–24.

TAINTER, JOSEPH A. 1988. *The Collapse of Complex Societies*. Cambridge, Eng.: Cambridge University Press.

TAMBIAH, STANLEY JEYARAJA. 1985. *Culture, Thought, and Social Action: An Anthropological Perspective*. Cambridge, Mass., and London: Harvard University Press.

TAX, SOL. 1977. "Anthropology for the World of the Future: Thirteen Professions and Three Proposals." *Current Anthropology* 36(3):225–234.

TAYLOR, GRIFFITH. 1937. *Environment, Race, and Migration*. Chicago: University of Chicago Press.

TEXTOR, ROBERT. 1967. *A Cross-Cultural Summary*. New Haven, Conn.: HRAF Press.

TEXTOR, ROBERT B. 1991. "Toward Conceptualizing the 'Peace Dividend' Anthropologically." *Human Peace* 9(1–3): 1–6

THOMAS, NICHOLAS. 1989. "The Force of Ethnology." *Current Anthropology* 30(1):27–41.

THOMAS, VERL M. 1986. *Beef Cattle Production: An Integrated Approach*. Philadelphia: Lea & Febiger.

THOMSON, DONALD F. 1938. *Recommendations of Policy in Native Affairs in the Northern Territory of Australia*, no. 56.-F.2945. Canberra: Parliament of the Commonwealth of Australia.

TINDALE, NORMAN B. 1974. *Aboriginal Tribes of Australia: Their Terrain, Environmental Controls, Distribution, Limits, and Proper Names*. Berkeley: University of California Press.

TINDALE, NORMAN B. 1981. "Desert Aborigines and the Southern Coastal Peoples: Some Comparisons." In *Ecological Biogeography of Australia*, vol. 3, pt. 6, edited by Allen Keast, pp. 1853–1884. *Monographiae Biologicae*, vol. 41, The Hague: Dr. W. Junk.

TODD, IAN A. 1976. *Çatal Hüyük in Perspective*. Menlo Park, Calif.: Cummings.

TOYNBEE, ARNOLD J. 1934. *A Study of History*, 3 vols. London: Oxford University Press.

TURNER II, CHRISTY G. 1989. "Teeth and Prehistory in Asia." *Scientific American* 260(2):88–96.

TYLER, STEPHEN A. 1986. *India: An Anthropological Perspective*. Prospect Heights, Ill.: Waveland Press.

TYLOR, EDWARD B. 1871. *Primitive Culture*. London: Murray.

TYLOR, EDWARD B. 1889. "On a Method of Investigating the Development of Institutions: Applied to Laws of Marriage and Descent." *Journal of the Royal Anthropological Institute* 18:245–269.

UNITED NATIONS, DEPARTMENT OF SOCIAL AFFAIRS. 1952. *Preliminary Report on the World Situation: With Special Reference to Standards of Living*, E/CN.5/267/rev.1. New York: United Nations.

UNITED NATIONS. 1959. *International Labour Organisation Convention (No. 107) Concerning the Protection and Integration of Indigenous and Other Tribal and Semi-Tribal Populations in Independent Countries*. United Nations Treaty Series, no. 4738. New York: United Nations.

UNITED NATIONS, DEPARTMENT OF ECONOMIC AND SOCIAL AF-

FAIRS. 1963. *Report on the World Social Situation.* New York: United Nations.

UNITED NATIONS, DEPARTMENT OF ECONOMIC AND SOCIAL AFFAIRS. 1975. *1974 Report on the World Social Situation.* New York: United Nations.

UNITED STATES, AID (AGENCY FOR INTERNATIONAL DEVELOPMENT). 1985. *Blueprint for Development: The Strategic Plan of the Agency for International Development.* Washington, D.C.: Government Printing Office.

URTON, GARY. 1981. *At the Crossroads of the Earth and Sky: An Andean Cosmology.* Austin: University of Texas Press.

USDA (U.S. DEPARTMENT OF AGRICULTURE). 1978. *Palouse Cooperative River Basin Study.* Soil Conservation Service, Forest Service, Economics, Statistics, and Cooperatives Service. Washington, D.C.: Government Printing Office.

USDA (U.S. DEPARTMENT OF AGRICULTURE). 1987. *Agricultural Statistics.* Washington, D.C.: Government Printing Office.

U.S. DEPARTMENT OF COMMERCE. 1982. *U.S. Code, 1982 Edition.* Washington, D.C.: Government Printing Office.

U.S. DEPARTMENT OF COMMERCE, BUREAU OF THE CENSUS. 1987a. *Census of Manufacturers (1987). Industry Series, Meat Products.* Washington, D.C.: Government Printing Office.

U.S. DEPARTMENT OF COMMERCE, BUREAU OF THE CENSUS. 1987b. *Census of the Retail Trade (1987). Subject Series, Establishment and Firm Size.* Washington, D.C.: Government Printing Office.

U.S. DEPARTMENT OF COMMERCE, BUREAU OF THE CENSUS. 1989. *1987 Census of Agriculture,* vol. 1. Geographic Area Series, Part 47, Washington, State, and County Series. Washington, D.C.: Government Printing Office.

U.S. DEPARTMENT OF COMMERCE, BUREAU OF THE CENSUS. 1990. *Statistical Abstract of the United States: 1990,* 110th ed. Washington, D.C.: Government Printing Office.

U.S. INTERNATIONAL DEVELOPMENT COOPERATION AGENCY. 1987. *Development Issues: U.S. Actions Affecting Developing Countries. The 1987 Annual Report of the Chairman of the Development Coordination Committee.* Washington, D.C.: IDCA.

VALENTINE, CHARLES A. 1968. *Culture and Poverty: Critique and Counter-Proposals.* Chicago and London: University of Chicago Press.

VALENTINE, CHARLES A. 1971. "The 'Culture of Poverty': Its Scientific Significance and Its Implications for Action." In *The Culture of Poverty: A Critique,* edited by Eleanor Burke Leacock, pp. 193–225. New York: Simon & Schuster.

VALENTINE, CHARLES A., ET AL., 1969. "Culture and Poverty: Critique and Counterproposals." *Current Anthropology* 10(2/3):181–201.

VAN SCHENDEL, WILLEM. 1981. *Peasant Mobility: The Odds of Life in Rural Bangladesh.* Assen: Van Gorcum.

VARESE, STEFANO. 1972. "Inter-Ethnic Relations in the Selva of Peru." In *The Situation of the Indian in South America,* edited by W. Dostal, pp. 115–139. Geneva: World Council of Churches.

VATUK, SYLVIA. 1982. "Purdah Revisited: A Comparison of Hindu and Muslim Interpretations of the Cultural Meaning of Purdah in South Asia." In *Separate Worlds: Studies of Purdah in South Asia,* edited by Hanna Papanek and Gail Minault, pp. 54–78. Dehli: Chanakya Publications.

VAYDA, A. P. 1968. "Hypotheses About Functions of War." In *War: The Anthropology of Armed Conflict and Aggression,* edited by Morton Fried, Marvin Harris, and Robert Murphy, pp. 85–91. Garden City, N.Y.: Doubleday.

VERDON, MICHEL. 1982. "Where Have All Their Lineages Gone? Cattle and Descent Among the Nuer." *American Anthropologist* 84(3):566–579.

VICKERY, WILLIAM E. (ed.). 1988. *Internet 1988 Profiles of International Development Contractors and Grantees. Volume 1: United States.* Chapel Hill, N.C.: Network for International Technical Assistance.

VITOUSEK, PETER M., PAUL R. EHRLICH, ANNE H. EHRLICH, and PAMELA A. MATSON. 1986 "Human Appropriation of the Products of Photosynthesis." *BioScience* 36(6):368–373.

VOIGT, MARY. 1987. "Relative and Absolute Chronologies for Iran Between 6500 and 3500 BC." In *Chronologies in the Near East,* edited by O. Aurenche, J. Evin, and F. Hours, pp. 615–646. BAR International Series 379(ii). Oxford, Eng.: BAR.

WAKE, CHARLES STANILAND. 1872. "The Mental Conditions of Primitive Man as Exemplified by the Australian Aborigine." *Journal of the Royal Anthropological Institute* 1:78–84.

WALLERSTEIN, IMMANUEL. 1974. *The Modern World-System: Capitalist Agriculture and the Origins of the European World-Economy in the Sixteenth Century.* New York: Academic Press.

WALLERSTEIN, IMMANUEL. 1990. "Culture as the Ideological Battleground of the Modern World-System." *Theory, Culture & Society* 7:31–55.

WALSH, J., and R. GANNON. 1967. *Time Is Short and the Water Rises.* Camden, N.J.: Nelson.

WARNER, W. L. 1958. *A Black Civilization.* New York: Harper.

WARNER, W. LLOYD. 1959. *The Living and the Dead: A Study of the Symbolic Life of Americans.* Vol. 5 of *Yankee City Series.* New Haven, Conn.: Yale University Press.

WARNER, W. LLOYD, and J. O. LOW. 1947. *The Social System of the Modern Factory.* Vol. 4 of *Yankee City Series.* New Haven, Conn.: Yale University Press.

WARNER, W. LLOYD, and PAUL S. LUNT. 1941. *Social Life of a Modern Community.* Vol. 1 of *Yankee City Series.* New Haven, Conn.: Yale University Press.

WARNER, W. LLOYD, and PAUL S. LUNT. 1942. *The Status System of a Modern Community.* Vol. 2 of *Yankee City Series.* New Haven, Conn.: Yale University Press.

WARNER, W. LLOYD, and LEO SROLE. 1945. *The Social Systems of American Ethnic Groups.* Vol. 3 of *Yankee City Series.* New Haven, Conn.: Yale University Press.

WAUCHOPE, ROBERT. 1962. *Lost Tribes and Sunken Continents: Myth and Method in the Study of American Indians.* Chicago: University of Chicago Press.

WEAVER, THOMAS. 1985. "Anthropology as a Policy Science: Part II, Development and Training." *Human Organization* 44(3):197–205.

WEBER, MAX. [1904–1905] 1930. *The Protestant Ethic and the Spirit of Capitalism.* New York: Scribner.

WEBSTER, DAVID. 1981. "Late Pleistocene Extinction and Human Predation: A Critical Overview." In *Omnivorous Primates: Gathering and Hunting in Human Evolution,* edited by Robert Harding and Geza Teleki, pp. 556–595. New York: Columbia University Press.

WEI-MING, TU. 1990. "The Confucian Tradition in Chinese History." In *Heritage of China: Contemporary Perspectives on Chinese Civilization*, edited by Paul Ropp, pp. 112–137. Berkeley: University of California Press.

WEISS, GERALD. 1973. "A Scientific Concept of Culture." *American Anthropologist* 75(5):1376–1413.

WEISS, GERALD. 1975. *Campa Cosmology: The World of a Forest Tribe in South America*. Anthropological Papers, no. 52(5). New York: American Museum of Natural History.

WEISS, GERALD. 1988. "The Tragedy of Ethnocide: A reply to Hippler." In *Tribal Peoples and Development Issues*, edited by John H. Bodley, pp. 124–133. Mountain View, Calif.: Mayfield.

WEISS, KENNETH M. 1973. *Demographic Models for Anthropology*. Memoirs of the Society for American Archaeology, no. 27. Washington, D.C.: Society for American Archaeology.

WENDORF, FRED, and ROMUALD SCHILD. 1984. "The Emergence of Food Production in the Egyptian Sahara." In *From Hunters to Farmers: The Causes and Consequences of Food Production in Africa*, edited by J. Desmond Clark and Steven Brandt, pp. 93–101. Berkeley: University of California Press.

WERNER, DENNIS. 1983. "Why Do the Mekranoti Trek?" In *Adaptive Responses of Native Amazonians*, edited by Raymond Hames and William Vickers, pp. 225–238. New York: Academic Press.

WESTERN, DAVID, and VIRGINIA FINCH. 1986. "Cattle and Pastoralism: Survival and Production in Arid Lands." *Human Ecology* 14(1):77–94.

WHEATLEY, PAUL. 1971. *The Pivot of the Four Quarters: A Preliminary Enquiry into the Origins and Character of the Ancient Chinese City*. Chicago: Aldine.

WHEELER, JANE C. 1984. "On the Origin and Early Development of Camelid Pastoralism in the Andes." In *Animals and Archaeology*, vol. 3, edited by Juliet Clatton-Brock and Caroline Grigson, pp. 395–410. BAR International Series, no. 202. Oxford, Eng.: BAR.

WHITE, J. PETER, and JAMES F. O'CONNELL. 1982. *Prehistory of Australia, New Guinea and Sahul*. New York: Academic Press.

WHITE, LESLIE A. 1949. *The Science of Culture*. New York: Grove Press.

WHITE, LESLIE A. 1959. *The Evolution of Culture*. New York: McGraw-Hill.

WIENS, H. J. 1962. *Atoll Environment and Ecology*. New Haven, Conn.: Yale University Press.

WILLIAMS, STEPHEN. 1988. "Fantastic Archaeology: Fakes and Rogue Professors." Harvard University. *Symbols* (December):17–21.

WILSON, DAVID J. 1981. "Of Maize and Men: A Critique of the Maritime Hypothesis of State Origins on the Coast of Peru." *American Anthropologist* 83(1):93–120.

WILSON, EDWARD O. 1989. "Threats to Biodiversity." *Scientific American* 261(3):108–116.

WILSON, EDWARD O., and FRANCES M. PETER (eds.). 1988. *Biodiversity*. Washington, D.C.: National Academy Press.

WILSON, PETER J. 1988. *The Domestication of the Human Species*. New Haven, Conn., and London: Yale University Press.

WISE, MARY RUTH, EUGENE E. LOOS, and PATRICIA DAVIS. 1977.

"Filosofiá y Métodos del Instituto Linguistico de Verano." *Proceedings of the 42nd International Americanists Congress* 2:499–525.

WITTFOGEL, KARL A. 1957. *Oriental Despotism: A Study of Total Power*. New Haven, Conn.: Yale University Press.

WOLF, ARTHUR P. 1968. "Adopt a Daughter-in-Law, Marry A Sister: A Chinese Solution to the Problem of the Incest Taboo." *American Anthropologist* 70(5):864–874.

WOLF, ARTHUR P. (ed.). 1974. "Gods, Ghosts, and Ancestors." In *Religion and Ritual in Chinese Society*, pp. 131–182. Stanford, Calif.: Stanford University Press.

WOLF, ERIC R. 1955. "Types of Latin American Peasantry." *American Anthropologist* 57(3, pt.1):452–471.

WOLF, ERIC R. 1957. "Closed Corporate Peasant Communities in Mesoamerica and Central Java." *Southwestern Journal of Anthropology* 13(1):1–18.

WOLF, ERIC R. 1969a. "American Anthropologists and American Society." In *Concepts and Assumptions in Contemporary Anthropology*. Southern Anthropological Society Proceedings, no. 3, edited by Stephen Tyler, pp. 3–11. Athens, Ga.: Southern Anthropological Society.

WOLF, ERIC R. 1969b. *Peasant Wars of the Twentieth Century*. New York: Harper & Row.

WOLF, ERIC R. 1982. *Europe and the People Without History*. Berkeley: University of California Press.

WOODBURN, JAMES. 1982. "Egalitarian Societies." *Man* 17(3):431–451.

WOOD JONES, FREDERIC. 1928. "The Claims of the Australian Aborigine." *Report of the Eighteenth Australasian Association for the Advancement of Science* 18:497–519.

WOODRUFF, WILLIAM. 1966. *The Impact of Western Man*. London: Macmillan.

WOOLLEY, SIR LEONARD. 1982. *Ur "of the Chaldees."* London: Herbert Press.

WORLD BANK. 1983. *Annual Report*. Washington, D.C.: Author.

WORLD BANK. 1988–1991. *World Development Report*. Oxford, Eng., and New York: Oxford University Press.

WORTHAM, FRED, JR. 1990. "An Analysis of the Most Critical Issue . . . Public Lands." *Western Livestock Journal*, Section Two, Livestock Journal Plus, 40th Commercial Cattle Issue, pp. 7–8, 77.

WRIGHT, HENRY T. 1969. *The Administration of Rural Production in an Early Mesopotamian Town*. Anthropological Papers, no. 38. Ann Arbor: Museum of Anthropology, University of Michigan.

WRIGHT, HENRY T. 1984. "Prestate Political Formations." In *On the Evolution of Complex Societies: Essays in Honor of Harry Hoijer 1982*, edited by Timothy Earle, pp. 41–77. Malibu Calif.: Undena Publications.

WRIGHT, JOHN W. 1990. *The Universal Almanac*. Kansas City, Mo.: Andrews and McMeel.

WRONG, DENNIS. 1979. *Power: Its Forms, Bases, and Uses*. New York: Harper & Row.

WUERTHNER, GEORGE. 1989. "Public Lands Grazing: Who Benefits at What Costs?" *Western Wildlands: A Natural Resource Journal* 15(3):24–29.

YALMAN, NUR. 1963. "On the Purity of Women in the Castes of Ceylon and Malabar." *Journal of the Royal Anthropological Institute* 93:25–58.

YDE, JENS. 1965. *Material Culture of the Waiwai.* National-museets Skrifter. Ethnografisk Roekke 10. Copenhagen: National Museum.

YENGOYAN, ARAM A. 1981. "Infanticide and Birth Order: An Empirical Analysis of Preferential Female Infanticide Among Australian Aboriginal Populations." In *The Perception of Evolution: Essays Honoring Joseph B. Birdsell.* Anthropology UCLA, vol. 7, nos. 1 and 2, edited by Larry Mai, Eugenia Shanklin, and Robert Sussman, pp. 255–273. Los Angeles: Department of Anthropology, University of California.

YOFFEE, NORMAN. 1988a. "The Collapse of Ancient Mesopotamian States and Civilization." In *The Collapse of Ancient States and Civilizations,* edited by Norman Yoffee and George Cowgill, pp. 44–68. Tucson: University of Arizona Press.

YOFFEE, NORMAN. 1988b. "Orienting Collapse." In *The Collapse of Ancient States and Civilizations,* edited by Norman Yoffee and George Cowgill, pp. 1–19. Tucson: University of Arizona Press.

YOFFEE, NORMAN, and GEORGE L. COWGILL (eds.). 1988. *The Collapse of Ancient States and Civilizations.* Tucson: University of Arizona Press.

ZUIDEMA, R. TOM. 1990. *Inca Civilization in Cuzco.* Austin: University of Texas Press.

# Index

Page numbers in *italics* indicate figures.

## Photo Credits

**Chapter 1,** pg. 3, K. M. Bodley; pg. 10, The Granger Collection

**Chapter 2,** pg. 20, courtesy Barry S. Hewlett (top); pg. 20, © H. & J. Beste/Animals Animals (center); pg. 20, © Fritz Prenzel/Animals Animals (bottom); pg. 25, J.H. Bodley (top); pg. 25, coutesy Dept. of Library Services, American Museum of Natural History (bottom); pg. 27, © Irven DeVore/Anthro-Photo; pg. 29, courtesy Baldwin Spencer Collection, Museum of Victoria Council; pg. 34, courtesy Barry S. Hewlett; pg. 35, J. H. Bodley

**Chapter 3,** pg. 47, courtesy Rainforest Action Network, San Francisco; pg. 51, K. M. Bodley; pg. 63, courtesy Jesus Ignacio Cardoza; pg. 68, courtesy Jesus Ignacio Cardoza

**Chapter 4,** pg. 77, courtesy Rob Blumenschine; pg. 80, courtesy Elliot M. Fratkin; pg. 94, © J.F.E. Bloss/Anthro-Photo; pg. 103, © Smucker/Anthro-Photo

**Chapter 5,** pg. 108, © Margaret Thompson/Anthro-Photo; pg. 120, © Napoleon Chagnon/Anthro-Photo; pg. 123, © SEF/Art Resource, New York

**Chapter 6,** pg. 133, courtesy Barry S. Hewlett, pg. 139, Kenneth P. Emory/Bernice P. Bishop Museum, Hawaii; pg. 143, courtesy Barry S. Hewlett; pg. 149, © Pacific Stock; pg. 157, Bernice P. Bishop Museum, Hawaii

**Chapter 7,** pg. 170, drawings by Eliza McFadden from *Plato Prehistorian* by Mary Settegast, published by the Rotenberg Press, 1986. Permission to reprint courtesy the Rotenberg Press; pg. 172, courtesy Gregory Johnson, Hunter College of the City University of New York; pg. 175, © George Gerster/Comstock; pg. 176, The University Museum, University of Pennsylvania (Neg. # S8-139326); pg. 177, courtesy Denise Schmandt-Besserat, University of Texas at Austin/Deutsches Archaeologisches Institut, Abteilung, Baghdad; pg. 182, Neg.#330282, courtesy Department of Library Services, American Museum of Natural History; pg.185, Neg. #36787, Kay C. Lenskjold, American Museum of Natural History; pg. 188, from C. Morris and D. Thompson, 1985, *Huánco Pampa: An Inca City and its Hinterland,* London: Thames and Hudson, Reprinted with permission

**Chapter 8,** pg. 203, © Wally McNamee/Woodfin Camp & Associates; pg. 207, courtesy Peter J. Mehringer, Jr.; pg. 214, © Audrey Topping/Photo Researchers

**Chapter 9,** pg. 230, courtesy the Estate of George Dales and the Harappa Project, University of California at Berkeley; pg. 241, © S. Nagendra/Photo Researchers, Inc.; pg. 245, © Mimi Nichter/Anthro-Photo; pg. 249, © Rapho/Photo Researchers, Inc.

**Chapter 10,** pg. 257, courtesy Joy McBride; pg. 263, © Paolo Koon/Photo Researchers, Inc.; pg. 266, © John Phelan/D. Donne Bryant Stock Photo

**Chapter 11,** pg. 278, © Joel Gordon 1990; pg. 282, The Bettmann Archive; pg. 289, © Karl Lumholtz, 1902, *Among Cannibals,* New York: Charles Scribners; pg. 292, The Granger Collection

**Chapter 12,** pg. 308, courtesy Tim McCabe; pg. 318, The Bettmann Archive; pg. 325, © Lawrence Migdale/Photo Researchers, Inc.

**Chapter 13,** pg. 334, © Meiselas/Magnum Photos; pg. 347, © Betty Derig/Photo Researchers, Inc.; pg. 354, courtesy Christine Eber with appreciation to Maria Arias Pérez and Manuel Cura; pg. 355, © Bernard Pierre Wolff/Magnum Photos; pg. 359, courtesy Dr. Paul Doughty, University of Florida

**Chapter 14,** pg. 369, courtesy Photo Department, Peabody Essex Museum, Salem, Massachusettes; pg. 371, © Belinda Wright; pg. 375, K. M. Bodley; pg. 381, K. M. Bodley

**Chapter 15,** pg. 387, © Jeff Leone/Photo Researchers, Inc.; pg. 395, courtesy Rainforest Action Network, San Francisco; pg. 401, Archives Department, Biosphere 2, photo by Gill Kenny; pg. 406, © Franklin/Magnum Photos

**Chapter 16,** pg. 413, The Granger Collection; pg. 418, courtesy Phoebe Hearst Museum of Anthropology, University of California at Berkeley; pg. 419, courtesy Department of Anthropology, Columbia University; pg. 422, courtesy Maxine Margolis

## Text and Art Credits

**Pages 70, 72,** From *The Cosmic Zygote: Cosmology in the Amazon Basin* by Peter G. Roe. Copyright © 1982 by Rutgers, The State University.

**Page 87,** From "Marriage and Cattle Exchange Among the Nilotic Luo" by A. B. C. Ocholla-Ayayo in *Paideuma* 25: 173–193, 1979.

**Pages 92, 95, 97,** From "The Nuer and Neighbouring Peoples" in *The Nuer: A Description of the Modes of Livelihood and Political Institutions of a Nilotic People,* by E. E. Evans-Pritchard, 1940 Oxford University Press. Reprinted by permission of Oxford University Press.

**Page 96,** From "Being 'Maasai'; Being 'People-of-Cattle': Ethnic Shifters in East Africa" by John G. Galatay. *American Ethnologist,* 9: 1–20, 1982.

**Page 103,** From *The Maasai of Matapato: A Study of Rituals of Rebellion,* by Paul Spencer. Copyright © 1988 Indiana University Press. Reprinted by permission.

**Page 115,** From *Basic Color Terms: Their Universality and Evolution* by Brent Berlin and Paul Kay. Copyright © 1991 The Regents of the University of California.

**Page 132,** From *Southwest Pacific: A Geography of Australia, New Zealand, and Their Pacific Island Neighbors* by K. B. Cumberland. Copyright © 1968 by Praeger, an imprint of Greenwood Publishing Group, Inc., Westport, CT. Reprinted with permission.

**Page 140,** From *Oceania: The Native Cultures of Australia and the Pacific Islands* by Douglas L. Oliver. Copyright © 1989 by University of Hawaii Press. Reprinted with permission.

**Page 142,** From *Words of the Lagoon: Fishing and Marine Lore in the Palau District of Micronesia* by R. E. Johannes. Copyright © 1981 The Regents of the University of California.

**Page 154,** From *Hawaiian Antiquities* by David Malo. Bernice P. Bishop Museum, Special Publication 2, second edition. Honolulu: Bernice P. Bishop Museum.

**Page 161,** Reproduced, with permission, from the Annual Review of Ecology and Systematics, Volume 3. Copyright © 1972 by Annual Reviews Inc.

**Page 162,** From "The Application of Scale Analysis to the Study for Cultural Evolution" by Robert L. Carneiro & Stephen F. Tobias. *Transaction,* Series II, 26: 196–207.

**Page 179,** From *The Rise of Civilization* by Charles L. Redman. Copyright © 1978 by W. H. Freeman and Company. Reprinted with permission.

**Page 191,** From "La realidad fisica y social en la cosmologia Andina" by John Earls & Irene Silverblatt. International Congress of Americanists, Proceedings 42(4): 299–325.

**Pages 201–202,** From *Shang Civilization* by Kwang-chih Chang. Copyright © 1980 Yale University Press. Reprinted with permission.

**Page 219,** Derived from "A portion of the economic landscape in Szechwan . . ." in Marketing and Social Structure in Rural China (Part 1), *The Journal of Asian Studies* 24(1): 3–43.

**Page 253,** Adapted from *Purdah and the Hindu Family in Central India. In Separate Worlds: Studies of Purdah in South Asia* edited by Hanna Papanek & Gail Minault, 1982, Chanakya Publications.

**Page 265,** From "The Evolution of Regional Power Configurations in the Indian Subcontinent" by Joseph E. Schwartzberg, in *In Realm and Region in Traditional India* edited by Richard G. Fox, pp. 197–233. Duke University Program in Comparative Studies on Southern Asia, Monograph and Occasional Papers Series, Monograph 14.

**Page 267,** From *Religion and Empire: The Dynamics of Aztec and Inca Expansionism* by Geoffrey W. Conrad and Arthur A. Damarest. Copyright © 1984 by Cambridge University Press. Reprinted with permission.

**Page 306,** From *Environment, Power, and Society* by Howard T. Odum. Copyright © 1971 Howard T. Odum. Reprinted by permission of John Wiley & Sons, Inc.